CHILDREN'S LITERATURE

ENGAGING TEACHERS AND CHILDREN IN GOOD BOOKS

Daniel L. Darigan
West Chester University

Michael O. Tunnell
Brigham Young University

James S. Jacobs
Brigham Young University

Merrill
Prentice Hall

Upper Saddle River, New Jersey
Columbus, Ohio

Library of Congress Cataloging-in-Publication Data

Darigan, Daniel L.
    Children's literature: engaging teachers and children in good books / Daniel L.
Darigan, Michael O. Tunnell, James S. Jacobs.—1st ed.
      p. cm.
Includes bibliographical references.
ISBN 0-13-081355-9
    1. Children's literature. 2. Children—Books and reading. 3. Children's literature—Study
and teaching. I. Tunnell, Michael O. II. Jacobs, James S., 1945-III. Title.
PN1009.A1 D34 2002
809′.89282—dc21

                        2001030047

Vice President and Publisher: Jeffery W. Johnston
Editor: Linda Ashe Montgomery
Development Editor: Hope Madden
Production Editor: Mary M. Irvin
Design Coordinator: Diane C. Lorenzo
Text Design: Ceri Fitzgerald
Cover Design: Diane C. Lorenzo
Cover Art: David Wisniewski
Production Manager: Pamela D. Bennett
Photo Coordinator: Nancy Ritz
Director of Marketing: Kevin Flanagan
Marketing Manager: Krista Groshong
Marketing Coordinator: Barbara Koontz

This book was set in Galliard by Carlisle Communications, Ltd., and was printed and bound
by Courier Kendallville, Inc. The cover was printed by The Lehigh Press, Inc.

Photo Credits: Tony Freeman/PhotoEdit: 5; David Young-Wolff/PhotoEdit: 7;
Patricia Clark/PhotoDisc, Inc.: 13; Michael Newman/PhotoEdit: 33, 422, 498;
Murray Wilson/Omni-Photo Communications, Inc.: 40; Frank Stieman/PhotoEdit: 58, 438;
Jim Shannon: 84; Betsy Imershein: 93, 216; Dan Darigan: 95; Chris Soentpiet: 95; Roseanne
Soentpiet: 95; Houghton Mifflin: 100, 224; Rav St. Germain: 103; Lothrop, Lee & Shepard
Books: 119; Ann Egita: 134; Holiday House: 159; Penguin Putnam: 168, 214; Morrow: 170;
Andrew Brilliant: 238; Knopf: 241; Tim Keating: 247; Neil Sjoblom: 282; Fred Mertz: 279;
HarperCollins: 348; Charles Osgood/Chicago Tribune: 389; William Sacco: 343;
David Buffington/PhotoDisc, Inc.: 412; Scott Cunningham/Merrill: 417, 507;
Silver Burdett Ginn: 446; Pearson Learning: 465, 473; Richard Hutchings/PhotoEdit: 467;
Bob Daemmrich/The Image Works: 474; Russell D. Curtis/Photo Researchers, Inc.: 483;
Jacques Chenet/Woodfin Camp & Associates: 502.

Pearson Education Ltd., *London*
Pearson Education Australian Pty. Limited, *Sydney*
Pearson Education Singapore Pte. Ltd.
Pearson Education North Asia Ltd., *Hong Kong*
Pearson Education Canada, Ltd., *Toronto*
Pearson Educacion de Mexico, S.A. de C.V.
Pearson Education—Japan, *Tokyo*
Pearson Education Malaysia Pte. Ltd.
Pearson Education *Upper Saddle River, New Jersey*

10 9 8 7 6 5 4 3 2 1
ISBN 0-13-081355-9

To my three wonderful children, Kendra, Halley, and Luke—good readers all. And to my parents, Rush and Betty Darigan, who planted the seeds for my own love of reading and books—D.L.D.

To my students—M.O.T.

To Amy, Christian, Michael, Andrew, Elizabeth, Jonathan, Daniel, Matthew, and especially to their magnificent mother, Linda—J.S.J.

PREFACE

▼▼▼▼▼▼▼

Special Thanks

Welcome!

To Caldecott winner David Wisniewski, for the inspirational cover art he created specifically for this text. We have always loved his work and are so thrilled with his contribution! With crisp, clean lines, David has captured both the beauty and excitement we feel every time we open a good book.

We are also grateful to acclaimed children's book writer and illustrator Steven Kellogg for providing original art to accompany many of the text's features. Steven's paintings have graced over 100 books, and we are privileged to have all of his little critters and characters accent our text.

▼▼▼▼▼▼▼

What Makes This Book Different?

We believe a big key to successful reading instruction is bringing children and books so closely together that children respond in much the same way we adults do when we are lost in a great novel. All sense of space, place, and time dissolves and we become one with the book. We call this rarified state "engaged reading" and firmly believe that if we, as parents and teachers, help create the proper "fit" between reader and text, we will see real, purposeful reading like this take place.

Engaging Readers

In this book we describe that state of engaged reading in detail, discuss ways you can nurture it in your classroom, then offer you thousands of books across nine major genres ready to present to your students. Finally, we spend a great deal of time discussing how to teach most effectively using children's literature.

Visual Literacy

We believe the art involved in children's trade books is fascinating, often breathtaking, and well worth study. That's why the art contributed by David Wisniewski and Steven Kellogg means so much to us. That's also why we have included numerous full-color book covers and inside art throughout the text, including a special, in-depth look at picture book art in Chapter 2.

Highlighting Exceptional Literature

Because our purpose in writing this text is to engage our readers in the world of children's literature and to pass on our passion for this literature, we feature many trade book covers throughout the chapters. Booksellers and librarians tell us that the sure way to "sell" a book is to have it displayed on the shelf face out. So, we did the same on the pages of this book. We believe that by seeing books presented this way in this text, our readers will develop a real interest in seeking out the books we discuss. We also think we will make it easier for our readers to recognize these books in libraries, in bookstores, or on line.

In keeping with this philosophy, all the children's literature titles we discuss are highlighted in bold and italic for easy access. We think that it makes it easier on your eye as it moves down the page. At a glance you will be able to pick up titles you want to reference as you return to the text on subsequent readings. We have also painstakingly included as many up-to-date titles as possible without forsaking the classics.

Coverage of the best titles from multicultural and international literature is included, not just in its own chapter, but throughout the book. This reflects our belief that multicultural and international literature should not be segregated to its own study, but should be a constant part of a balanced literature program.

▼▼▼▼▼▼▼
Organization of This Book

Unit 1, Engaging Readers in Good Books, begins with a proactive approach to reading. We investigate first what books hold for us and what it means to become an *engaged* reader. We then look at criteria for judging a book, noting both the text and the pictures as major considerations.

Unit 2, The Good Books Themselves, deals with the specific genres in children's literature. Within each chapter we provide genre-specific criteria for evaluating books. We begin, as a new parent might, by discussing Picture Books and follow it with a chapter on Poetry. Next we look at Traditional Fantasy and its natural companion, Modern Fantasy. We then address the more "real" genres of Contemporary Realistic Fiction, Historical Fiction, and Multicultural and International Books. Finally we detail the important and kid-popular genres of Informational Books and Biography.

Unit 3, Using Good Books in the Classroom, turns our attention to the classroom. We focus first on how to motivate children to read. Then we address how to go about teaching reading using the wide variety of children's literature available to us today. Next we look at ways to assess and evaluate our teaching and the progress of our students. Finally, we concentrate on how we can teach across the curriculum using children's literature.

▼▼▼▼▼▼▼
Special Features

Text Sets

A text set, a group of interrelated titles perfect for read aloud and independent reading, begins each chapter. From this list of books, a student has chosen to read and respond to one title. That response, as well as an excerpt from the highlighted title, accompany the text set in the opening pages of each chapter. *Alternate Text Sets,* interspersed throughout the chapters, could also be used in either the college classroom setting or the elementary classroom with children.

Bookmark: Integrating Technology

This feature in every chapter encourages and guides Internet use to find author information, classroom activities, and resources for further research.

A Conversation With . . .

Appearing throughout the text are original interviews, which not only introduce readers to some of the most interesting personalities in children's literature, but also provide insight into the process, challenges, and goals of creating meaningful literature for young readers.

Featured authors and illustrators include: Lloyd Alexander, Joseph Bruchac, Karen Cushman, Cynthia DeFelice, Russell Freedman, James Cross Giblin, Susan Guevara, Lee Bennett Hopkins, James Howe, Steven Kellogg, Eric Kimmel, Lois Lowry, Bill Martin, Jr., Gary Paulsen, Allen Say, Alice Schertle, David M. Schwartz, Jerry and Eileen Spinelli, David Wiesner, and Paul O. Zelinski.

Teaching Ideas

These teaching examples and recommendations for covering chapter topics in K–8 classrooms help readers put children's literature into action.

Did You Know?

We include interesting facts about children's literature, the inside scoop on what is new and interesting in the field, and even a little gossip from time to time.

Margin Notes

- Integrate the use of the text's CD-ROM database of children's literature. This database includes over 14,000 children's titles and is searchable across eleven fields.
- Integrate our Companion Website, www.prenhall.com/darigan, referring readers to a wealth of additional resources, including meaningful links to the World Wide Web, self-assessment opportunities, and activities.

Book Lists

At the end of each chapter we include lists of books not mentioned within the body of the chapter, but which we believe are must-reads.

Fifteen More We Like annotates notable books we feel are important to the genre. *Others We Like* lists, other books we think everyone will want to read.

▼▼▼▼▼▼▼

Supplements

CD-ROM

Free with every copy of the text, this database of children's literature titles contains more than 14,000 titles searchable across eleven fields, including an exhaustive list of award winners.

Companion Website

This resource for students and professors, at www.prenhall.com/darigan, contains classroom cases, author interviews, activities, self-assessments, meaningful links, as well as a message board and chat facilities.

Instructor's Manual

This free supplement provides professors with chapter overviews, objectives, and a test bank.

Within the pages of any book is a promise: the promise of a good story—an evocative tale that may touch your heart or make you laugh. It may provide you with a fact or piece of data that you didn't know before. We hope this book is no exception. We'd love to think that you will enjoy reading this book now and return to it often. We also hope that this book will prompt you to delve deeper into the rich literature that is available to children. We hope you will see children's literature with new eyes and a fresh outlook as a consequence of reading these pages. We want you to become "engaged readers" so you can turn children across the nation and the world on to books.

▼▼▼▼▼▼▼
Acknowledgments

We are particularly indebted to our wonderful Development Editor, Hope Madden. Without her help, advice, level head, and devoted encouragement, this book would not have been so well organized, complete, and absolutely beautiful. Throughout the two years it took to complete this project she has always lived out her namesake, providing us with endless "hope." We would also like to thank Editor Linda Montgomery, Production Editor Mary Irvin, and Marketing Manager Krista Groshong for their dedicated and diligent work and the countless hours they put into the production of this text. So, too, we are indebted to our copy editor, Melissa Gruzs, who perfected this manuscript, making our conversational tone follow convention.

We are grateful to Deborah Thompson, College of New Jersey, for her knowledgeable treatment of Chapter 9—Multicultural and International Children's Books.

We are indebted to Ernest L. Bond, Salisbury State University, for the technological and children's literature know-how to provide the needed integration not only for our text, but also for the text's Companion Website.

Special thanks to Sam Sebasta, whose helpful comments and vast knowledge of the field guided us as we constructed this book. Special thanks, also, to the reviewers of this book for their comments and insights: Bonnie Armbruster, University of Illinois; Cyndi Georgis, University of Nevada–Las Vegas; Virginia Harris, Wayland Baptist University; Richard M. Kerper, Millersville University; Sam Sebasta, University of Washington; Joyce Thomas, Eastern Kentucky University; Maria Weimer, Madaille College; and Nillofur Zobairi, Southern Illinois University.

Our friends in the children's publishing world have been the lifeblood of this book. They have kept us up to date on all the books published every year. We would especially like to thank Bill Morris, Jeanne McDermott, Susan Hawk, Lori Benton, Marjorie Naughton, Jennifer Roberts, Lauren Wohl, Mimi Kaden, Terry Borzumato, Deborah Sloan, John Mason, Diane Foot, Elena Blanco, Lucy Del Priore, Jackie Harper, Kent Brown, Michael Eisenberg, Victoria Tisch, Catherine Balkin, Anne Irza-Leggat, Patricia Lee Gauch, Margaret McElderry, Beth Feldman, Debbie Hochman, Kathy Ward, Donna Bray, Kate and John Briggs, David Gale, Emily Easton, Karen Cardillo, Jazen Higgins, Alison Keehn, and Kathleen Rourke.

We also thank our students and helpers who did an enormous amount of legwork in research and offering clerical support: Anna DeRenzi, Eileen Lambert, J. B. Boff, Darlene Fatzinick, and Kendra Darigan from the West Chester University campus and Greg Bryan, Kristin Frey, Amy Johnson, Jori Robison, Ad Spofford, Kim Sylva, and Catharine Verhaaren from the Brigham Young University campus.

Discover the Companion Website Accompanying This Book

Children's Literature: Engaging Teachers and Children in Good Books
Companion Website: A Virtual Learning Environment

Technology is a constantly growing and changing aspect of our field that is creating a need for content and resources. To address this emerging need, Prentice Hall has developed an online learning environment for students and professors alike–Companion Websites–to support our textbooks.

In creating this Companion Website, our goal is to build on and enhance what *Children's Literature: Engaging Teachers and Children in Good Books* already offers. For this reason, the content for this user-friendly website provides the professor and student with a variety of meaningful resources.

▼▼▼▼▼▼▼

For the Professor

The Companion Website integrates **Syllabus Manager™**, an online syllabus creation and management utility.

- **Syllabus Manager™** provides you, the instructor, with an easy, step-by-step process to create and revise syllabi, with direct links into Companion Website and other online content without having to learn HTML.
- Students may logon to your syllabus during any study session. All they need to know is the web address for the Companion Website and the password you've assigned to your syllabus.
- After you have created a syllabus using **Syllabus Manager™,** students may enter the syllabus for their course section from any point in the Companion Website.
- Clicking on a date, the student is shown the list of activities for the assignment. The activities for each assignment are linked directly to actual content, saving time for students.
- Adding assignments consists of clicking on the desired due date, then filling in the details of the assignment—name of the assignment, instructions, and whether or not it is a one-time or repeating assignment.
- In addition, links to other activities can be created easily. If the activity is online, a URL can be entered in the space provided, and it will be linked automatically in the final syllabus.
- Your completed syllabus is hosted on our servers, allowing convenient updates from any computer on the Internet. Changes you make to your syllabus are immediately available to your students at their next logon.

▼▼▼▼▼▼▼

For the Student

Companion Website features for students include:

- **Interactive self-quizzes**—complete with automatic grading that provides immediate feedback for students.

  After students submit their answers for the interactive self-quizzes, the Companion Website **Results Reporter** computes a percentage grade, provides a graphic representation of how many questions were answered correctly and incorrectly, and gives a question by question analysis of the quiz. Students are given the option to send their quiz to up to four email addresses (professor, teaching assistant, study partner, etc.).

- **Activities**
  - *Web-based Activities* include Webquests, treasure hunts, subject samplers, thematic multimedia projects, and material on creating an educational website
  - *Communicating Activities* provide avenues and ideas for dialoguing with authors, students in other places, resource people, academic list serve, and online literature circles
  - *Writing and Publishing Activities* look at specific online opportunities, with book reviews, character sketch booktalks, lessons, projects, creative and collaborative writing
  - *Reading Activities* provide links to online literature, author/illustrator biographies, book reviews and supplemental information
  - *Research Activities* provide numerous links, ideas, and opportunities to do research online

- **Web Destinations**—links to www sites that relate to chapter content, including sites specifically chosen for their implications for Meeting the Needs of Every Student

- **Message Board**—serves as a virtual bulletin board to post—or respond to—questions or comments to/from a national audience

- **Chat**—real-time chat with anyone who is using the text anywhere in the country—ideal for discussion and study groups, class projects, etc.

To take advantage of the many available resources, please visit the *Children's Literature: Engaging Teachers and Children in Good Books* Companion Website at

www.prenhall.com/darigan

CONTENTS

• U N I T   2 •
The Good Books Themselves   71

▼▼▼▼▼▼▼▼
CHAPTER 3

PICTURE BOOKS   72

▼▼▼▼▼▼▼▼

CHAPTER 4

POETRY   114

▼▼▼▼▼▼▼

CHAPTER 5

▼▼▼▼▼▼▼

CHAPTER 6

▼▼▼▼▼▼▼
CHAPTER 7

CONTEMPORARY REALISTIC FICTION 234

CHAPTER 8

HISTORICAL FICTION   266

CHAPTER 9

MULTICULTURAL AND INTERNATIONAL CHILDREN'S BOOKS 290

CHAPTER 10

INFORMATIONAL BOOKS 324

▼▼▼▼▼▼▼
CHAPTER 11

BIOGRAPHY   368

• U N I T 3 •
Using Good Books in the Classroom 401

CHAPTER 12

MOTIVATING CHILDREN TO READ 402

CHAPTER 13

TEACHING READING USING CHILDREN'S LITERATURE 432

CHAPTER 14

EVALUATION AND ASSESSMENT   470

APPENDIX C

Publisher's Addresses 543

A Conversation With . . .

• U N I T 1 •

Engaging Readers in Good Books

WHY WE READ

1
CHAPTER
▼▼▼▼▼▼▼

If you want to cover

*Folktales From
Around the World*

Consider as a READ ALOUD

Fly, Eagle, Fly: An African Tale
by Christopher Gregorowski,
illustrated by Niki Daly and foreword
by Archbishop Desmond Tutu

Consider as a TEXT SET

*The First Strawberries:
A Cherokee Story*
by Joseph Bruchac,
illustrated by Anna Vojtech

Fire on the Mountain
by Jane Kurtz, illustrated by E. B. Lewis

Jaguarundi
by Virginia Hamilton,
illustrated by Floyd Cooper

The Tale of the Mandarin Duck
by Katherine Paterson,
illustrated by Leo and Diane Dillon

The Seven Chinese Brothers
by Margaret Mahy,
illustrated by Jean and Mou-sien Tseng

*Older Brother, Younger Brother:
A Korean Folktale*
by Nina Jaffe, illustrated by Wenhai Ma

THE SEVEN CHINESE BROTHERS
by Margaret Mahy; illus. by Jean and Mou-sien Tseng

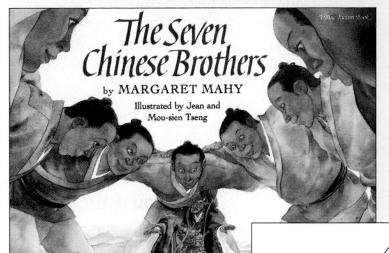

Seventh Brother's first tear swept one army north. His second tear swept the other army south.

Excerpt from *The Seven Chinese Brothers* by Margaret Mahy

Student Response

The book, The Seven Chinese Brothers, is about seven brothers who help each other when one of them gets in trouble. I liked the seventh brother. He had a power to cry hard. I drew a picture of him.

BY Alex, 8

Like most important questions, "Why read?" seems embarrassingly obvious. Reading simply *is* important. Period. We as teachers and parents know that, and we assume everyone else knows it as well. Even in today's climate of constant controversy and limitless lawsuits, where no one appears to agree with anyone on anything, reading receives unanimous support. An antireading position has no voice, claims no champion, and gets no press. The push is always toward more reading. So why is reading universally acclaimed?

To visit a classroom exploring the issues of Why We Read, please go to chapter 1 of our companion website at **www.prenhall.com/darigan**

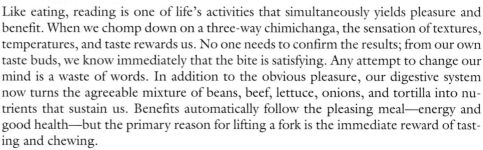

The Rewards of Reading

Like eating, reading is one of life's activities that simultaneously yields pleasure and benefit. When we chomp down on a three-way chimichanga, the sensation of textures, temperatures, and taste rewards us. No one needs to confirm the results; from our own taste buds, we know immediately that the bite is satisfying. Any attempt to change our mind is a waste of words. In addition to the obvious pleasure, our digestive system now turns the agreeable mixture of beans, beef, lettuce, onions, and tortilla into nutrients that sustain us. Benefits automatically follow the pleasing meal—energy and good health—but the primary reason for lifting a fork is the immediate reward of tasting and chewing.

Similarly, immediate reward is the one dependable criterion for determining why people choose to read—and you see them reading on the subway, waiting for a bus, in the mall. Beyond that, it is impossible to predict how a particular reader will be affected by print, as illustrated by the following actual incidents:

- Conventional wisdom says that a reader must comprehend a certain percentage of written material for reading to be successful, yet three-year-old Bobby Morgan, whose parents read to him regularly, got up early to spend time with *National Geographic,* which he preferred to picture books. His parents knew that he was comprehending only a fraction of the material, but he continued to spend hour after hour with the magazine.

- Common sense indicates that we seek comfortable surroundings when engaging in long activity like extended reading, yet Sean, a college student, drove to the bookstore on a snowy day to buy a new book and decided to spend a few minutes looking it over in his car before heading home. Time passed, and the sun set. To continue reading, Sean had to hold the book to the window so the lights from the parking lot would shine onto the page. Four hours later, he started his chilled car for the drive to his apartment.

- Educational practice says to match individual reading abilities with the difficulty of a text, yet Bill, a junior high student with second-grade reading skills, chose a book far beyond his tested level. A part of his school day was spent in intensified reading instruction in a lab setting, the last half hour devoted to uninterrupted individual reading. Educator Dan Fader watched Bill during his 30 minutes of reading time until the bell sounded. "Still absorbed in his reading, Bill closed the book, glanced at the cover, placed the book in his bag, and started for the door. Intrigued by this 13-year-old second-grade reader, I crossed his path at the door and walked with him as I asked, 'What are you reading?' '*Jaws.*' 'Is it good?' 'Yeah!' 'But isn't it hard?' 'Sure it's hard, but it's worth it!'" (Fader, 1976, p. 236).

Reading is Personally Satisfying

When we read words that have meaning for us, we know "it's worth it." No one needs to confirm the results. We, ourselves, have proven their value. Beyond the immediate satisfaction, a number of other benefits come our way: We gain an expanded vocabulary, increased word knowledge, improved reading skills, better communication skills, strengthened knowledge of language, new insights, power to compete in an information-driven age, and perhaps a certain amount of additional confidence. Engaging in the act of reading leads us down the sure path to becoming educated. But in the end, just like taking a bite of our favorite Mexican dish, the primary reason for turning pages is always the immediate reward.

Some novels provide that appeal from the first paragraph, as with *Speak* by Laurie Halse Anderson.

> It is my first morning of high school. I have seven new notebooks, a skirt I hate, and a stomachache.
>
> The school bus wheezes to my corner. The door opens and I step up. I am the first pick-up of the day. The driver pulls away from the curb while I stand in the aisle. Where to sit? I've never been a backseat wastecase. If I sit in the middle, a stranger could sit next to me. If I sit in the front, it will make me look like a little kid, but I figure it's the best chance I have to make eye contact with one of my friends, if any of them have decided to talk to me yet.

Nonfiction can have the same appeal. In *The Human Body: And How It Works* by Steve Parker, a double-page spread focuses on the skin. The first paragraph reads:

> On the outside, you are dead. Your hair and the surface of your skin are made of dead cells. But less than a millimeter away under the surface of your skin are some of the busiest cells in your body. They are continually dividing to make new layers of skin cells which harden and die, to replace the top layer of skin as it is worn away. Every day millions of dead skin cells rub off as you wash, dry yourself with a towel, get dressed and move about. Much of the "dust" in a house is dead skin which has rubbed off the bodies of people.

Two Benefits of Reading

Real reading, then, offers us two rewards. The first is immediate: The text pulls us into images and ideas at the very moment we travel through the words. Suddenly we realize that dust particles in a shaft of sunlight are bits of our own skin! We find ourselves delighted with this new thought.

The second reward of reading is long-term. The accumulated benefits—increased language and thinking skills plus additional knowledge, experience, and insight—add up to our becoming an educated person.

A Troubling Increase in Illiteracy

If we all agree that reading is so rewarding and beneficial, why don't more people spend more time at it? Why is our illiteracy rate so high? In 1992, the U.S. Office of Education commissioned an adult literacy survey with five levels of skills in the areas of prose, document, and quantitative proficiencies. Scores didn't follow an expected distribution according to percentiles. All could have ended up in the highest level if all were highly skilled. Yet 40 million to 50 million adults (20 to 23% of the population) scored in the lowest level (Kirsch, Jungeblut, Jenkins, & Kolstad, 1993, p. xiv).

To find out more about Eric Carle and other authors and illustrators on the World Wide Web, visit chapter 1 on the companion website at **www.prenhall.com/darigan**

BOOKMARK

INTEGRATING TECHNOLOGY: AUTHORS ON THE WORLD WIDE WEB

Numerous authors and illustrators now have well-designed websites providing readers with information about their lives, their literature, and the creative process. *Eric Carle,* author and illustrator of such well-known picture books as ***The Grouchy Ladybug*** and ***The Very Hungry Caterpillar,*** has constructed a site that provides not only the typical biography and information about his work, but also answers to frequently asked questions and a very useful bulletin board for exchanging teaching ideas.

The trend in the United States is not toward increased literacy. "The literacy proficiencies of young adults assessed in 1992 were somewhat lower, on average, than the proficiencies of young adults who participated in a 1985 literacy survey" (Kirsch et al. 1993, p. xvi). Scores on the verbal test of the Graduate Record Exam also show that college graduates' skills dropped 9% from 1965 to 1992 (Snyder & Hoffman, 1994, p. 310).

Why has reading declined among young adults during the last two decades (Zill & Winglee, 1988)? Why is the United States dead last among 26 industrialized nations in the number of new titles published annually per capita (UNESCO, 1990, Table 7.4)? Why does this powerful experience of being ravished by print seem to be limited to so few?

▼▼▼▼▼▼▼

Unengaged and Engaged Reading

Unengaged Reading

The reading we do tends to fall into two categories: unengaged and engaged reading. Unengaged reading is primarily the reading of necessity, the reading we do not choose but must do anyway. Usually this kind of reading is work or school related. Unengaged reading speaks to neither our heads nor our hearts. In the classroom, unengaged reading is frequently assigned reading, the reading of instructional materials, particularly those with questions at the end. These tend not to engage the reader.

Even novels can be misused by well-intentioned teachers who unwittingly prevent their students from experiencing the power of a book in a variety of ways. For example, teachers who supersede the story with a specific task can provide a barrier to finding meaning and excitement in print. In an effort to improve vocabulary, for example, teachers assign students to find the nine examples of onomatopoeia in the first chapter of Scott O'Dell's *Island of the Blue Dolphins*. Before asking students to read a chapter, teachers introduce the difficult vocabulary and ask students to locate the words, define them, and use them in sentences. When students know that a traditional book report (plot, setting, theme, characterization, style, point of view) is expected, they read books from a different and less personal perspective.

No immediate benefits and few lasting by-products can come from unengaged reading. If the reader is not involved with the text—not engaged in the information or the experience—the reading is empty and unproductive. It is even possible to read every word on a page and gain absolutely nothing from the activity. The deciding factor is always in the heart and mind of the reader.

One reason so few Americans read a book after leaving school is that they never have gone beyond assigned reading. Despite having completed the required reading that marks the path to high school graduation, a surprising number of supposedly educated graduates never have known the sustaining thrill of reading a book that speaks directly and personally to them. The reading they did was for someone else, according to someone else's rules and expectations, with the result that life never was breathed into the books they completed for their classes. Sad to say, the books never happened.

Many Unengaged Readers Become Aliterates

If the book and reader remain distant, literacy is at a dead end. Even the person with all the necessary skills to read well does not progress unless those skills are strengthened and polished by use. Without engaged reading, the person may be able to read but has become uninterested in doing so, or aliterate. The aliterate person has all the necessary know-how to unlock the meaning in print, but chooses not to pick up books. Cunningham and Allington (1999) report NAEP (National Assessment of Educational Progress) data that indicate 25% of fourth graders and 50% of eighth graders report reading *once a month or less* for their own interest (pp. 182–183)! As the sign over a small school library reminds us, "The person who can read and doesn't is no better off than the one who can't read."

It is only in personal reading that meaning making takes place, the kind of reading that sticks, and that is why we turn to print. Those who engage in personal reading find their reward in two areas: locating information and gaining experience.

Reading for Information

People who want certain information that is important to them will seek it out. We read for information when we check the sodium content in frozen dinners, plan the drive from Poughkeepsie to Pittsburgh, look in the dictionary for the meaning of *obfuscate,* check the newspaper ads for a furniture sale, follow the so-called directions for assembling a barbecue grill, or scan the note from Harold's teacher. No one makes us do those things. We choose to do them because the messages locked in those passages of print are interesting to us. Yet in each of these cases, someone else could read and summarize the content, and we would be satisfied. In her transactional theory of literature and reading, Louise Rosenblatt (1978) calls this reading for information "efferent" reading. We are motivated by getting the facts. Yet someone else could do the reading for us, supply us with the desired information, and we would be just as happy as if we had read the facts ourselves.

Engaged Reading

"Esthetic" reading, according to Rosenblatt (1978) is different from efferent because the goal is not the acquiring of information but participation in the experience. In esthetic reading, readers focus on what they are experiencing as their eyes pass over the words. This kind of reading cannot be summarized by another but must be done personally, because it is not centered on data. The facts are not the most important part; engagement with the experience is. Knowing the plot of Natalie Babbitt's *Tuck Everlasting* is not the same as experiencing with Winnie Foster her difficult choice between a natural life span and living forever as a young girl. Being told that Jeffrey in *Maniac Magee,* by Jerry Spinelli, topples the barriers between the black and white neighborhoods in Two Mills, Pennsylvania, comes nowhere close to being with him when he shakes up old prejudices. Reading for experience—esthetic reading—can no more be done by someone else and then reported to us than our eating can be

To find out more about The Doucette Index and other teaching ideas on the World Wide Web, visit chapter 1 of the companion website at **www.prenhall.com/darigan**

BOOKMARK

INTEGRATING TECHNOLOGY: ACTIVITIES USING THE WORLD WIDE WEB

The World Wide Web is an incredible resource both for locating classroom activities related to children's books and as a means of enhancing these activities. The *Doucette Index: K–12 Lesson Ideas for Literature,* created by the Faculty of Education at the University of Calgary, is a useful database that helps teachers by locating literature-related lesson plans on the Internet. Many of these lesson plans emphasize activities that utilize technology; some are quite detailed, and they are often tied to state and national standards. The database is searchable by author/illustrator and title. Even when these lessons do not fit your immediate context, they can spark ideas for connecting literature and technology to fit the needs of your students.

done by another. We don't want information on food flavors; we want those flavors to flow over our own taste buds. When we read for experience, we aren't satisfied simply by knowing where the book ends up. We want to make that journey to the final page ourselves. When we participate in the experience of a good book, our lives are never quite the same again.

Reading Must Be Personal

For reading to make a difference, it has to be personal. People do not turn to books because they want to study the author's use of vocabulary or have a desire to describe the major and minor characters any more than people attend movies to examine the cinematographer's use of the long shot or analyze the use of background music. We read fiction and go to the movies to get lost in the story, to see through eyes other than our own. Almost magically, participating in these vicarious experiences sheds light on our own lives. We compare, test, experience, and come away with new thoughts and visions, wondering how we would have responded in similar situations.

If someone, like the teacher forcing a focus on onomatopoeia in the first chapter of *Island of the Blue Dolphins,* forces us to shift our concentration from the experience to the externals, these elements—the form, the theme, the use of language—become the main reason for reading or viewing. As a result, reading the book or attending the movie may become no more than tedious labor. For instance, would our experience with a good movie be enhanced by having the manager of the theater pass out mandatory study guides to be completed while we watch the film? We would look over the questions, and our purpose for viewing the movie would shift from living the movie to ferreting out the correct responses. At the end, as the credits start to roll, we would realize we haven't seen the movie at all. We have witnessed a collection of facts we needed to identify and isolate. To enjoy the movie, we would likely choose to leave the theater and wait for the film to be released on videocassette.

Like viewing a movie, the act of reading can't serve two masters. We read either for ourselves or for some other purpose. When anything comes between the reader and the printed page, such as a teacher's expectation or an assignment, the reading tends to be unengaged and remains artificial—even if eyes continue to march across the rows of words. For example, how many of us have covered several pages of assigned reading in a textbook, only to discover that we have not registered one morsel of meaning? Yet we have also experienced being so consumed by a novel or biography that we do not notice when the chapters begin or end.

A reader can respond differently even to the same book. Lloyd Alexander, an author who attributes his success to childhood reading, discovered *Treasure Island* at home as a child and loved it—pure engaged reading. He lived with Jim, he pondered the story when he was away from the book, and he longed to return to the people and events of the tale. Years later, he was assigned the same novel in a high school English class. This time the reading did not produce the same involvement. Class discussion centered on elements he found uninteresting, assignments interfered with his experience, and he failed the final test "because I couldn't remember the construction of that damned blockhouse" (L. Alexander, personal communication, 1993). The teacher held "discussions" with the class but asked only factual questions, gave assignments that did not include Lloyd's focus, and graded success based on a test of specific and unimportant details. Instead of helping Lloyd get deeper into the story, the teacher's approach actually kept him from the book, turning an earlier engaged reading experience into an unengaged one.

Assigned, Engaged Reading

Does this mean that any book assigned in school automatically suffers the kiss of death? Of course not. An assigned book may begin as unengaged, uninteresting reading and yet become important, even invaluable, to the reader. For that to occur, however, it must receive the reader's personal stamp of approval. Somewhere between the covers, even with the full knowledge that the book is required reading, the reader must become personally interested in the book and engaged in the text. At that point, the book moves from assigned reading to personal reading. But if it never makes the switch, it never develops the power to influence or affect that one reader. (See Figure 1–1.)

We need to be aware of our own interaction with the text. Some readers have spent so much time reading for others that they have difficulty identifying their own responses to a book. Even some good students respond automatically to "What did you think about the book?" with thoughts such as, "What *should* I have thought about the book?" and "What *am* I supposed to think about the book?"

When we already have an interest in what we read, engaged reading comes naturally. No one wonders if the instructions to assemble a swing set for a much-loved but impatient 3-year-old will make good reading. The purpose is determined, and the reading engages immediately. Before the first word is read, we know the instructions are worth it. At a bookstore sale table, a Civil War buff picks up a book on Stonewall Jackson and is likely to buy it. A child with an interest in dinosaurs is drawn to a book on the subject. Even when a book is not particularly well written, the person who is interested in the topic becomes an engaged reader without persuasion or effort.

Classic unengaged reading often comes during traditional reading instruction time at school. There the focus is not on the text as a purveyor of meaning but on the text as underbrush, where the secret skills of reading hide out. The sentences and paragraphs serve as camouflage for initial consonant blends, prediction questions, comprehension checks, vocabulary words, and the objects of a multitude of other skills lessons.

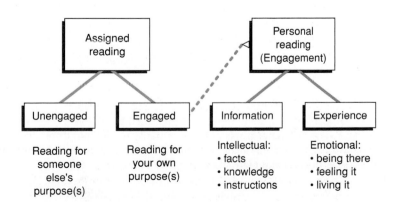

FIGURE 1–1
Unengaged and engaged reading.

This is not to say that the skills of reading are unimportant; the skills need to be learned, and students need the confidence that comes from understanding how language works and from knowing that they are skilled and competent readers. The problem comes when students are given a good story to read with the *primary goal* of identifying skill components in it. This emphasis is a bit like sitting down to Thanksgiving dinner and seeing only vitamins and minerals on your plate or, worse yet, being served a pile of pills instead of the steaming turkey and trimmings because, after all, those nutritional elements are what is important for fueling our bodily furnaces.

The Profile of an Engaged Reader

What makes readers engaged or unengaged? Engaged readers are not aware of the reading process. They may not even see words after the first sentence or two. In a story, they see scenes, people, action. In nonfiction, they test theories, think of applications, or chew on the facts. But in *neither* instance do they focus on the skills of reading. They are unaware of how many pages they have read or how long they have been at the book. They pace themselves accordingly, gulping down great whacking passages quickly or dawdling over a line that gives them particular delight. They never say, "Look at me. I have chosen the correct sound of *y* at the end of *happy*— long *e*. I didn't confuse it with the long *i* like at the end of *fly*. I know the meaning of these words. I can use each of them in a sentence. I am comprehending the meaning of this paragraph and can pick out the topic sentence with 80 percent accuracy." During engaged reading, there is no focus on skill, decoding, or vocabulary. When engaged readers come to a word they can't pronounce or define, they skip right over it without hesitation . . . or guilt. A real reader engaged in a book is no more aware of reading skills than a running back threading his way through the defensive team is aware of his ability to run. He is not saying, "Right foot, then left foot, now pivot 45 degrees on the next step"; his focus is on the game, and he simply uses his body to get where he wants to go. When something gets in the way, both the athlete and the reader improvise—self-correct—so the primary goal is still in sight and the pursuit continues.

So, why do we read? For personal and immediate reward. We read that which already interests us. And we learn new interests through reading a skillfully written account that takes us places we have never been before. We can experience the genuine pleasure of having assigned reading work its way under our skin and become part of us. Author Gary Paulsen, whose early years in Minnesota were spent largely in the library, suggested in a speech he gave to the Clarke Country Library Association that we should "read like a wolf eats" (1987): in great hulking bites, with vigor, as often and much as possible. In the middle of this enthusiastic sampling of print, we will find those things that personally are worth it, while allowing other materials to slough off naturally. All the while, we increase our range of reading skills and strengthen our education without being aware of either. The very real benefits come predictably and automatically.

Occasionally, we even stumble onto a benefit beyond expectation. For instance, the late actor Walter Matthau may have discovered the ultimate bonus of engaged reading. In response to the question "What book made the greatest difference in your life?" he wrote:

> The book that made the greatest difference in my life was *The Secret in the Daisy,* by Carol Grace, Random House, published 1955.
> The difference it made was enormous. It took me from a miserable, unhappy wretch to a joyful, glad-to-be-alive human. I fell so in love with the book that I searched out and married the girl who wrote it.
> Most sincerely,
> Walter Matthau (Sabine & Sabine, 1983, p. 29)

▼▼▼▼▼▼▼

Engaging Teachers in Reading

The Power of Example

Before we form any opinions about how reading instruction should proceed or even how children should respond to the reading they do, let's focus on you. . . the teacher. When it comes to teaching reading, teachers must *be* readers before they can help children become readers. That premise is the bedrock of successful reading education. In the educational quagmire of getting children to read—how to teach children to read, which assignments to give, what to do with class time, and how to evaluate their reading—nothing in the entire school has a greater impact on convincing children that books are worthwhile than teachers' reading habits (Perez 1986, p. 9). To witness and participate in real, engaged reading with an adult does more good than any educational program.

The United States Office of Education (USOE) underscores the importance of providing a model of a real reader. In an overview of reading instruction commissioned by the USOE, 10 principles and ideas were identified that would heighten literacy learning; one of the ten is teacher modeling (Sweet, 1993, p. 6).

Albert Schweitzer (1997) knew that nothing is more important than modeling in effecting change in people, including the students we teach. He noted that "example is not the main thing in influencing others. It is the only thing" (p. 388).

A Powerful Example of "Example"

An experiment with a preschool class demonstrated the power of example. As the teacher talked with the children who were seated on a rug, she walked to a table behind her and took a piece of candy from a bowl. Putting it in her mouth, she paused and then said to no one in particular, but in a voice loud enough the children could hear, "M-m-m-m. I like this candy. It tastes good to me." The morning discussion continued, but within a minute she took the candy from her mouth and put it on a napkin on the table behind her. After more conversation, she again went to the table, this time to a bowl holding different candy. Taking a piece, she put it in her mouth, made an unpleasant face, and said, "Oh. I don't like this candy. It doesn't taste good to me." But she kept it in her mouth until she'd eaten it. When the discussion was finished, she told the children they could go to one bowl or the other and take a piece of candy. Most of the children made a beeline for the second bowl, the one she said was not good but ate anyway (Larson, 1994). Her *actions* determined theirs; her words were empty.

A serious enemy of real learning is the kind of educational duplicity in the candy example. We adults influence children more by what we do than what we say, and teachers who speak one way but live another introduce an artificiality into education. They erroneously think children can be tricked into valuing what the teacher says instead of what the teacher believes and does. The insincerity of such teaching often results in student boredom and teacher burnout. Until teachers find a personal interest and excitement in what they teach, they never will teach it well.

People taught by excellent, energetic teachers who love their subjects know that the power felt in those classrooms came only in part from the accumulation of new knowledge. When students become excited about learning, the reason is not the subject matter but the teacher who breathes life into it.

▼▼▼▼▼▼▼

Benefits to Teachers Who Read

The miracle of education always has been the teacher: the human being who is first a learner and second a guide who enthusiastically leads others to learning. Teachers weak in their areas of instruction or not personally committed to a subject can make assignments and ask students to fill out work sheets, but those activities are not the kind that touch lives. Stimulation and enlightenment, which entice students to become involved in subject matter, come from people who are stimulated and enlightened. Teachers cannot successfully give away attitudes and ideas they do not own, particularly attitudes about books and reading.

Following are three benefits to teachers who read.

1. *Teachers who read gain new knowledge constantly.* Teachers who read keep growing intellectually, realizing anew how broad and interesting the world is and how little of it can be squeezed into the formal curriculum. From reading they learn how life began on Surtsey, the newest island in the world, coughed up from a volcano near Iceland; how thermometers work; how Columbus is viewed as both hero and villain or something in between.

Teachers who read also discover endless new ways to extend their subject areas. In science, they discover that air pressure can be revealed dramatically by boiling a spoonful of water in a soft drink can, then turning it quickly upside down and plunging it into an inch of water where it loudly and satisfyingly implodes. In social studies, they learn that Harriet Tubman's work to free slaves is even more heroic in light of the headaches and sleeping fits she suffered all her life. This was the result of having her skull broken when a storekeeper threw a fist-size scale weight at someone else and accidentally hit her.

2. *Teachers who read understand education better.* The range of information that comes to teachers who read broadly from trade books can help them develop and keep a wider view of what real learning is. Only interested learners can become interesting teachers. Teachers who read continue to challenge themselves in a broader arena than the school halls and curriculum. They have an easier time remembering the significance of their profession and keeping a true educational perspective, as pointed out by John W. Gardner (1981):

> The ultimate goal of the educational system is to shift to the individual the burden of pursuing his own education. This will not be a widely shared pursuit until we get over our odd conviction that education is what goes on in school buildings and nowhere else. Not only does education continue when schooling ends, but it is not confined to what may be studied in adult education courses. The world is an incomparable classroom, and life is a memorable teacher for those who aren't afraid of her. (pp. 11–12)

When our learning experiences are limited to only the school classroom, we have more difficulty remembering the "world" classroom. But reading books other than those traditionally associated with school helps us remember that life is a memorable teacher.

Teachers who know that life is a memorable teacher find it less difficult to take risks. Having learned not to be afraid of life, they can accept the inevitable difficulty and fumbling that accompany learning. Max Plank referred to this when he was awarded the Nobel Prize:

> Looking back. . . over the long and labyrinthine path which finally led to the discovery [of the quantum theory], I am vividly reminded of Goethe's saying that men will always be making mistakes as long as they are striving after something. (Beveridge, 1957, p. 60)

DID YOU KNOW?

Another more recent version of the Grimms' **The Sleeping Beauty** is found in Trina Schart Hyman's retelling. This book, also illustrated by Hyman, has many visual effects hidden in its pages. For example, notice the shape the thorny hedge takes when they open up for the King's son after 100 years of slumber. If you look closely, you'll notice the young queen's head with a pink rose at the tip of her nose.

Teachers who are continuing learners also can abandon more easily the false notion that they must be The Answer Person. When they see themselves in this new role as joint learners with their students, facing a question for which they have no answer loses much of its threat. For example, a teacher shared with her class the picture book ***Thorn Rose or the Sleeping Beauty,*** by the Grimm Brothers, where the story mentioned that not just the princess but also everything in the kingdom fell asleep for 100 years, including the flies in the kitchen. As the teacher showed the illustration of the prince entering Sleeping Beauty's bedchamber, a child spied spider webs attached to her hair and promptly asked, "If everything's asleep, where did the spider webs come from?" The teacher, a learner at heart, replied, "I don't know. How can *you* explain this?"

By gaining new knowledge and a better understanding of education, teachers are less apt to suffer burnout. Teachers who continually are learning new content and are aware of the processes of learning have more to draw on in teaching their students, are more enthusiastic, and are swayed less by the inevitable political winds that blow through the school district, the state, and the nation. Their vision tends to be broader, and they seem more able to cope with the unavoidable complexities, and even messiness, of education and life.

3. *Teachers who read influence students to become readers.* It is too simplistic to say that a teacher needs only to read in order to influence students to become true learners. Yet the effects of reading can help teachers become the kind of people who make a positive difference in the lives of students. By being readers, teachers offer students a living model of the positive results of spending time with books: natural enthusiasm for the printed page, ease in handling differing viewpoints, confidence in knowing how to find new information, and having ready knowledge at their fingertips, to name a few. Teaching and learning with a teacher who is a reader become much more than completing a set of work sheets or prepared learning activities. A teacher who is genuinely rewarded by personal reading, and who willingly shares this enthusiasm with students, will influence them in a host of unpredictable, positive ways. Teachers who are lifelong readers create students who are lifelong readers.

What kind of reading model do you currently offer students? Get out a piece of paper and a pen or pencil; it is time for a little self-assessment. The questionnaire in Figure 1–2 will help you take stock of your standing as a positive model of lifelong reading behaviors for the children you teach. Answer each question as fully and as honestly as you can. Don't skip to the end of the chapter to look at the scoring key or our analysis. When you have completed the survey, go to the end of the chapter (Figure 1–4) and score yourself.

▼▼▼▼▼▼▼

Practical Hints for Becoming a Better Reading Model

Students often come up to us after taking this self-assessment, students who have had us as teachers before, and they say, "I did better than I thought I would—I'm pretty proud of myself." Others don't fare so well. If you scored lower on the self-assessment form than you would have liked, all is not lost. It is never too late to adopt new reading practices and attitudes. Here are some helpful suggestions:

1. *Make reading easy in your life.* Imagine two people who sing the praises of reading, say they love books, and consider the time they spend with a good book absolutely delicious. Both are sincere, completely honest, and will stay up most of the night to finish a book that has captured them. . . or so they say. Yet, in reality, one of the people reads a good deal more than the other. Their response to item #7 under "Personal Model" often can distinguish the frequent reader from the infrequent one: "What are you going to read next?" Infrequent readers usually have difficulty coming up with a title. They stare at the ceiling for a while and do a fair amount of throat clearing before finally mentioning a book—if they name one at all. Most of the frequent readers, on the other hand, immediately identify a title. Frequent readers have made getting to the next book a natural, easy process in their lives; they usually have a stack

Personal Model

1. I read in a book for personal pleasure at least two different days per week.
   Yes   No
2. Two of my favorite authors for children are _____.
3. One of my favorite illustrators of children's books is _____.
4. The title of a picture book published during the past three years is
   _____.
5. The title of a children's chapter book published during the past three years is
   _____.
6. I have a personal library of more than 40 children's trade books.   Yes   No
7. The book I am going to read next is _____.
8. During the past 3 months, I found myself showing an interesting book to
   someone else or mentioning it in conversation. The title is _____.
9. My favorite genre or type of book is _____.
10. Two of my favorite authors for adults are _____.

Classroom Model

1. At least twice weekly I engage in personal reading where my students can see
   me with a book.   Yes   No
2. My students can identify at least one type of book I like or dislike.   Yes   No
3. I have a growing classroom library of trade books.   Yes   No
4. I introduce or "book talk" books with my students at least twice a week.
   Yes   No
5. I read aloud a picture book or from a chapter book to my class at least once
   every day.   Yes   No
6. I read aloud something other than books to my class daily.   Yes   No
7. Sustained Silent Reading (SSR) is a part of our daily schedule.   Yes   No
8. I always read in my own book during SSR.   Yes   No
9. I require my children to read regularly on their own outside of class.
   Yes   No
10. I run a regular book club program or encourage children to buy books and help
    make that possible.   Yes   No

FIGURE 1–2
How good a reading
model am I?

next to their beds, on a shelf, or in their nightstands, so when they finish their current book they slide into the next title without missing a beat. Every infrequent reader has to decide where the next book is coming from—book clubs, library visits, bookstore browsing, best-seller lists, or friends' recommendations—but frequent readers already have worked out a system for getting easily to that next new title.

2. *Model reader response.* Tell people about the books you read. Share your experiences with print. Talk with your students and others about your reading, reflecting the honest devotion, rejection, pleasure, frustration, analysis, or admiration that you feel for what you have read. Introduce your students to favorite books and characters. Copy from a book a passage or sentence that has meaning for you, and tack it up where others can see. Read aloud a section that has personal significance, and tell the class why. In short, show students how you feel about books, and encourage them to respond with the same honesty. Ask them for their feelings about what they are reading. And accept the feelings of the reader, regardless of your own.

3. *Remember to walk two reading paths simultaneously.* Every teacher should identify and feed personal reading interests. You ought to read books from favorite authors and subject areas, both for children and adults, with no thought to professional prepa-

To find out more about The Bulletin and other children's literature journals, visit chapter 1 on the companion website at **www.prenhall. com/darigan**

BOOKMARK

INTEGRATING TECHNOLOGY: ON-LINE JOURNALS KEEP YOU UP-TO-DATE

The CD-ROM that accompanies this text is an excellent source for locating books by a particular author or books with a related theme. It is also important to know some of the sources for reviews of current children's books both in print and on the Internet. Many journals related to children's literature now have an on-line component and are a readily accessible place to find reviews of the latest literature. *The Bulletin of the Centre for Children's Books,* for example, is a children's book review journal with a recently expanded website. Each month, the on-line portion of the journal gives starred reviews, a theme-based article, editorials, and a profile of an author or illustrator. The entire Bulletin is now on-line for subscribers.

---

ration. At the same time, you need to read children's books beyond the areas of your own personal interest to prepare for the variety of student interest that is in every class. These books do not have to be read with the same devotion, but your being familiar with titles outside your normal reading can make an enormous difference to your students. Recently, teachers have been reading and talking about all the Harry Potter books. Many are reading them not because fantasy is their first choice in genre but because they want to keep up with the students in their classes. And we have yet to find a teacher who doesn't like these books. That enthusiasm breeds such great rewards. The spring before the fourth book, *Harry Potter and the Goblet of Fire,* came out the schools were all abuzz with the knowledge that author J. K. Rowling had killed off one of the characters. Many times we heard teachers and children discuss this turn of events. "I sure hope she doesn't do away with Hagrid," teachers would cry. Students countered stoically, "She wouldn't kill him off; he is one of the main characters. It will have to be somebody not so important . . . "

4. *View books as shared experiences rather than as test fodder.* Children and adults experience the same emotions. Fear, joy, peace, jealousy, anger, and love—children and adult feel these in much the same way. When it comes to personal reading, which deals largely with emotions, children are our peers and not our clones. We should let children teach us as well. Sharing a book with children is much like visiting Disneyland with them: At the end of the day, the adult does not return to the motel to administer a quiz about the activities and rides. Participants relive the experience with each other.

A brief scene in an old black-and-white movie captures the essence of this chapter. The title of the film and names of actors have long been forgotten, but in it a couple returned from a date and the man was pressuring the woman for a kiss. (This was a *very* old movie.) She resisted. He persisted. She resisted. He *still* persisted. And so it went. In desperation, he finally said, "What if I simply steal a kiss and enjoy it without your permission?" Speaking slowly, she responded, "If *I* don't enjoy it, you *can't* enjoy it." The same is surely true for the classroom teacher who wishes to lead children to a love of books.

▼▼▼▼▼▼▼

What Constitutes a Good Book?

So let's go to "the kiss"! It is the book, the good book that can be enjoyed. When adults select books for children, we want to pick out good ones. The trouble is, we're not always sure what "good book" means. Left to our own choosing, we thumb through titles trying to find something that seems beneficial and desirable for young readers. We forge ahead, sometimes unaware of the criteria we use to determine what is "good."

We all have some preconceived ideas even though we may not be aware of exactly why we make our choices. Our first responsibility when selecting books, then, is to determine what our biases are. What *are* the criteria we respond to most? After years of polling our classes concerning this very question, here is some of what we have learned. Our students have regularly said:

1. We want books that teach lessons. We want children to learn the correct lessons about life. If a book teaches what we want taught, we call it a good book.
2. We want books with large, colorful illustrations. Young eyes need stimulation, and color provides it better than black and white. Also, the pictures need to be large enough for children to see clearly.
3. We want an absence of harshness. Children will run into difficulty soon enough; let them enjoy life now. Protect them from the tough side of living as long as possible.
4. We want an absence of scariness. We don't want to invite fears or nightmares.
5. We want an absence of swearing. We don't want books to model inappropriate language or behavior.
6. We want books that are short. And we want the reading to be easy.
7. We want books with simple vocabulary. We don't want to frustrate or overpower children.
8. We want books with familiar content. We think our child will respond to a book about zoos because we go to one often. If a book connects with a child's experience, it will be a better book.
9. We want books that are politically correct. We want the values and social views represented in the book to be what we consider appropriate.

You probably agreed with some of these ideas and were put off by others. But a problem with the reasons we just listed is that they are narrow and sometimes misguided; they focus on only a tree or two and miss the forest. If we want to help create lifelong readers—to choose books that appeal to the greatest range and number of children—we need to view the book as a whole instead of focusing on only a small element or two. And the most trustworthy standard for viewing the whole book is to look at the experience it offers. Titles of lasting value can almost be defined as experiences that re-create the very texture of life.

Problems can arise, however, in trying to convince others of the power of that experience. Generally, when we like a book—or don't like it—we assume the book deserves our response. When books please us, we think they are well written or have other measurable literary value. Works that leave us cold are somehow lacking in merit. It is largely human nature to think others will respond the way we do. The following two scenarios illustrate these extremes.

Case 1: "***The Wind in the Willows*** by Kenneth Grahame is a classic," he said. "It has received critical acclaim for almost 100 years, and I loved it. If you want a wonderful experience, take it now and read it." So she did. Her response, however, was different: It was one of total boredom. How do we explain that one person is thrilled by a book of accepted literary merit, recommends it to another, and the other person finds the supposedly wonderful book definitely ho-hum?

Case 2: The librarian held up a book between thumb and forefinger like a five-day-old fish. "The Goosebumps books lack quality and merit. This series is predictable and weak." Alvin, fifth grade, reads the beginning of R. L. Stine's ***Piano Lessons Can Be Murder*** and can't put it down until he finishes. A trained educator judges a title to be substandard literature, and yet Alvin considers it a good book. How can this be?

People often don't see eye-to-eye when it comes to judging whether a book is worthwhile because *good book* is a common phrase with two definitions, one is based on *quality* and the other on *taste*.

Quality

A good book is one created by a knowledgeable and skilled author where the elements of literature measure up under critical analysis. Quality is recognized by evaluating different elements of the book. Those elements may include the following: style and language, character, plot, setting, theme, tone, point of view, illustrations, mood, pacing, design and layout, and accuracy.

Style and Language

The words used to tell a story are at least as important as the story itself, and which words are chosen and how they are arranged is the style. The author's style can underscore or reflect an element of the story, as in **Maniac Magee,** where the short chapters and short sentences mirror the running and rapid movement of the main character. The arrangements of his words parallel the story itself, offering an additional element of unity.

> Maniac Magee was blind. Sort of.
>
> Oh, he could see objects all right. He could see a flying football or a John McNab fastball better than anybody.
>
> He could see Mars Bar's foot sticking out, trying to trip him up as he circled the bases for a home run.
>
> He could see Mars Bar charging from behind to tackle him, even when he didn't have the football.
>
> He could see Mars Bar's bike veering for a nearby puddle to splash water on him.
>
> He could see these things, but he couldn't see what they meant. He couldn't see that Mars Bar disliked him, maybe even hated him.
>
> When you think about it, it's amazing all the stuff he didn't see.

This skillful use of language not only draws readers into the writing but also is the foundation on which all the other elements of a book rest.

Character

Good books must have characters that are unique and believable. Those who live between the covers of a book must be as real as those who live across the street. It is impossible to identify with or have feelings for a person unless we know the individual, and it is the author's job to show us the character's personality so we can become involved with that life. Note how, in just a few paragraphs, Jack Gantos allows us to know his character Joey Pigza, a child suffering from Attention Deficit Hyperactive Disorder (ADHD) in **Joey Pigza Swallowed the Key**.

> At school they say I'm wired bad, or wired mad, or wired sad, or wired glad, depending on my mood and what teacher has ended up with me. But there is no doubt about it, I'm *wired*.
>
> This year was no different. When I started out all the days there looked about the same. In the morning I'd be okay and follow along in class. But after lunch, when my meds had worn down, it was nothing but trouble for me.
>
> One day, we were doing math drills in class and every time Mrs. Maxy asked a question, like "What's nine times nine?" I'd raise my hand because I'm really quick at math. But each time she called on me, even though I knew the answer, I'd just blurt out, "Can I get back to you on that?" Then I'd nearly fall out of my chair from laughing.

Plot

A good plot shows what happens to the people in the story in such a way that the reader cares about the outcome. Every plot must have a conflict, and how that conflict is resolved carries the book to its conclusion. Well-defined plots, according to author Pam Conrad (1991), introduce a question early on that can be answered *yes* or *no*. She calls this the "major dramatic question" and cautions that it is not asked outright. It is clear, however, that something is going to happen one way or another. Whether the answer is *yes* or *no,* and how the answer evolves, is the plot of the story. In Gary Paulsen's **Hatchet,** for instance, the question is, "Will Brian be rescued from the Canadian wilderness where he survived a plane crash?" In **Make Way for Ducklings**, by Robert McCloskey, the question is, "Will the ducks make the trip safely from the Charles River to the Public Garden?"

Setting

Where the book takes place is the setting, which can be as broad as a planet or as narrow as a room. When detailed and fleshed out, the physical surroundings add credibility and depth to the story—they place us in that time and situation. In Carol Fenner's powerful book **Randall's Wall,** we are introduced to Randall Lord and his forsaken family. Teachers and students can't seem to reach Randall because of the "wall" he has placed around himself. When the authorities attempt to intervene, we get a real sense of the horrendous conditions in which the Lord family is living.

> The stout woman from the Public Health Department knocked a second time at the door of the blighted old house. There was no doorknob, only a rag stuffed into the hole where the doorknob had been. A cold wind blew at her back. The snow, which had begun to fall thickly, whipped at her legs. Back in the driveway her car gave off a comforting mumble and her co-worker, a large bearded fellow, kept wiping the steamy passenger window so he could check on her. That was comforting, too.

Note how the simple reference to the rag in the doorknob gives us a far greater image of the rundown house than even a full-color picture could have. Fletcher (1993) reminds us that that "the bigger the issue, the smaller you write" (p. 49).

Illustrations

The art or photography in a book can strengthen and extend the content beyond the words. The marriage of illustration and text can yield an experience more powerful than either alone. Certainly Susan Guevara's East Los Angeles renderings in **Chato's Kitchen** and **Chato and the Party Animals** add a flavor that is *muy simpático* to Gary Soto's tales. The flair of the Mexican-American culture is detailed and made evident with Guevara's thick, boldly colored brush strokes. We feel as if we are entering a painting done on black velvet, a happy place where there is music and love and laughter.

Theme

The central idea of the story is the theme: friendship, coming of age, sibling rivalry, coping with the death of a pet, and adjusting to a new town, to name a few. Norton (1992) states that theme ties the plot, conflict, characters, and setting together. Beyond that it is also the statement that the author wants to convey about life or society (p. 214). It is the message the author is attempting to communicate. Kate DiCamillo aptly does that in her book **Because of Winn-Dixie** where her characters India Opal Buloni and her preacher father, despite great loss and sadness, learn to be thankful for what they have.

DID YOU KNOW?

It is said, "You can't judge a book by its cover." But the fact is that covers for books are very carefully designed. The hardcover is usually made to attract librarians who purchase these editions for their collections. Paperback covers are designed to attract the young readers themselves. If you dig through the bookstore, you may find a variety of covers for any one book. For example, Avi's **Wolf Rider** has gone through three permutations. The earlier covers were blood red and made to attract the mass market; more recent versions are toned down and not so violent.

Tone

The tone is the author's attitude toward the subject or audience in a particular book. Tone can reflect the wide range of human emotion from reverential to sarcastic, condescending to enthusiastic, to name just a few. Note how the first few lines of a book can set a remarkable tone:

My name is Francis Joseph Cassavant and I have just returned to Frenchtown in Monument and the war is over and I have no face. (from **Heroes** by Robert Cormier)

Just let me say right off the bat, it was a bike accident.
     It was about as "accidental" as you can get, too.

Illustrations by Susan Guevara, copyright © 2000 by Susan Guevara, from **Chato and the Party Animals** by Gary Soto, illustrated by Susan Guevara. Used by permission of G. P. Putnam's Sons, a division of Penguin Putnam, Inc.

Like Mick wasn't riding crazy. Or dodging in and out of traffic. And both of his hands were on the handlebars and all like that.

His tire just hit a rock. And he skidded into the back of a passing truck. And that was that. There wasn't a scratch on him. It was a head injury. Period. (from **Mick Harte Was Here** by Barbara Park)

The kitchen phone rang three times before Andy picked it up. "Hello?" he said.

A voice replied, "I just killed someone." (from **Wolf Rider: A Tale of Terror** by Avi)

The night I was born on Horse Creek, the sky rained fire. Dogs howled and growled. Arapaho warriors put on red war paint and did a death dance. (from **Adaline Falling Star** by Mary Pope Osbourne)

The first time Gayle slammed the bathroom door, her mother let it go. The second time, Mama's ears perked up, listening for familiar sounds. The third time Gayle ran into the bathroom, Mama was up the stairs and on Gayle's heels, witnessing what she already knew. Gayle, stooped over the toilet bowl, face flushed, body heaving, was pregnant. Again. (from **Like Sisters on the Homefront** by Rita Williams-Garcia)

Point of View

The point of view is the position taken by the narrator. Many stories are told in first person, where the main character "I" is telling the story. "Sometimes, when I stand back and take a good look, I think my parents are ambassadors from hell. Two of them, at least, the biological ones, the *big* ones" (from Chris Crutcher's "A Brief Moment in the Life of Angus Bethune" in **Athletic Shorts**). Or the story may be told from the perspective of the omniscient third person, where the narrator is looking in at the scene and telling us, the readers, what the main character, "he/she," is doing. "He heard it all, Charley did; heard the drums and songs and slogans and knew what everybody and his roost was crowing. There was going to be a shooting war" (from ***Soldier's Heart*** by Gary Paulsen).

Mood

The atmosphere evoked in the writing is the mood: spooky, hilarious, innocent, understated, exaggerated, and caustic are only a few. Here is Wil Weaver's startling beginning to his tragic story ***Striking Out***.

> "Billy's brother, Robert, would have been thirteen that summer.
> But here's how it happened.
> The accident.

On the lighter side, Barbara Robinson introduces the hilarious Herdmans in her ***The Best Christmas Pageant Ever***.

> The Herdmans were absolutely the worst kids in the history of the world. They lied and stole and smoked cigars (even the girls) and talked dirty and hit little kids and cussed their teachers and took the name of the Lord in vain and set fire to Fred Shoemaker's old broken-down toolhouse.

In both examples, the mood is set from the start. In a good book, this mood remains consistent or naturally becomes more positive and upbeat as characters, plot, and circumstances change.

Pacing

How quickly or slowly a story moves is pacing. Although most books tell their stories at a relatively constant rate, pacing can vary in volume according to the author's desire to linger over the content or move the story along. As we noted in ***Maniac Magee,*** the short, choppy sentences and the repetitive text quicken the pace. Later, when old Grayson, the man who took Maniac under his wing, who Maniac taught to read, lays dead behind the band shell, we see the shift from frenetic to pensive to thoughtful. Notice that in the first two paragraphs we have seven short sentences. "Grayson" is said three times. The third paragraph contains longer sentences, and the fourth, fifth, and sixth only two each—long, lyrical sentences so sad they break your heart.

> Maniac went over. "Grayson." He shook the old man. "Grayson?" He took the old man's hand. It was cold.
> "Grayson!"
> He didn't run to the Superintendent's office. He didn't run to the nearest house. He knew.
> He held the cold limp hand that had thrown the pitch that had struck out Willie Mays, that had betrayed the old man's stoic ways by giving him a squeeze. He began talking to the old man, about places he had been on the road, about places the two of them might have gone to, about everything.
> Then he began to read aloud. He read aloud all the books the old man had learned to read, and he finished with the old man's favorite, *Mike Mulligan's Steam Shovel.*
> When he looked out the window, it was night. He dragged his chest protectors alongside the old man's mat and lay down, and only then, when he closed his eyes, did he cry.

Design and Layout

Eye appeal of the cover, the colors, the choice of the font and its size, the margins, the spacing, the positions of page numbers—all of the visual elements of a book are a part of the design and layout. Something so simple as the movement from one double-page spread to the next is of utmost importance. Notice how, in Walter Dean Myers's ***Harlem,*** illustrator Christopher Myers adeptly angles the woman to face to the right—the direction we go when we read. Had he painted the woman facing left or directly at the reader, it would have halted the forward movement of the book.

They brought a call, a song
First heard in the villages of
Ghana/Mali/Senegal
Calls and songs and shouts
Heavy hearted tambourine rhythms
Loosed in the hard city
Like a scream torn from the throat
Of an ancient clarinet

A new sound, raucous and sassy
Cascading over the asphalt village
Breaking against the black sky over
1-2-5 Street.
Annnbouncing hallelujah
Riffing past resolution

From *Harlem: A Poem* by Walter Dean Myers, illustrated by Christopher Myers. © 1997 by Scholastic Press. Reprinted by permission.

Although the design and layout do not affect word order, they do affect where and how the words are placed on the page—particularly in picture books. The overall visual appeal of a book can determine if a potential reader will pick it up or march right on by.

Tension

Fiction without tension is bland. Tension makes the reader want to read on to see how the conflict is resolved and what happens to the people involved in the problem. Even in picture books, tension—a close relative of suspense—is what piques and sustains interest.

Accuracy

Whenever books deal with facts, whether centering on them in nonfiction or using them as background in fiction, they must be accurate. Writers need to do their homework in order to gain and keep readers' trust.

Believability

The key to creating a good book is to make everything believable. We know that fiction is the product of an imagination: The people never lived, the story is made up, and the setting is invented. So why do we care about these people who never were, doing things that never happened, in a place that may not exist? Because the emotional reality is absolutely true. Because their imagined lives reflect the realities of living, breathing people. Because we can get genuine experience through living side-by-side with fictional characters while they endure their trials and enjoy their successes. We participate, we enjoy, and we learn—all simultaneously. Yet if anything in the book reminds us that what we read is invented, the story loses its power. All the elements in a story must be logical, sensible, and consistent. In much the same way that the spell of a movie is broken when we notice a boom microphone hanging over the head of the police chief, authors are obligated to keep their facts and actions credible and their techniques out of sight when putting the book together.

Of the elements just listed, the first three—style and language, character, and plot—and the last—believability—provide the bulk of information when readers judge the quality of fiction. When a book reveals its story in powerful language, contains memorable characters, follows a compelling plot, and is believable, the fiction generally can be said to have "quality." To get a quick, thumbnail view of the potential power of the book, look at those four elements. But although these elements are important to a good book, their presence does not necessarily guarantee a positive reader response.

Taste

The second definition of a good book is simply "a book the reader likes," regardless of its quality. For instance, **The Wind in the Willows** is judged to be quality literature for children. This prototype of modern animal fantasy skillfully delineates the four main characters, contains satisfying action sequences, and is told in a rich and varied language. But some children do not find themselves engrossed in the story when they try to read it, nor do they particularly like to have it read aloud to them. The book has definite literary merit—it is critically a good book—yet for those who are not taken by the story, it has no appeal.

Conversely, the Goosebumps series, once the most popular series in print, wins no literary awards. Yet the books continue to be read by many who find pleasure in reading the tales of mystery and light horror. Children by the tens of thousands sail through the series and report that each Goosebumps story is a good book. Some adults may think that children who read such formulaic, shallow stories should at least feel shame for doing so, but so far no guilt has been detected in those who move quickly from one volume to the next.

So, when determining which books are good, an obvious problem surfaces: The positive feelings a reader has about a book are the same whether they come from a quality book or one of questionable merit. Readers call either book "good" as long as those feelings come during the time of turning pages. Were we able to correctly identify the sources of our positive responses, we would more accurately say, "I like this book because the author's skill took me places and showed me things I have not previously experienced." If the book is well crafted, is believable, and supplies all the elements needed for a rewarding new experience, the author should take a bow. What the writer of the book brought to the work creates this response. On the other hand, if we respond to a book because it serves as a link to something already a part of us, we would say something like "I liked this book because it connected with something I find appealing"—giving us a good scare, outwitting a bully, or reliving a personal memory. When our favorable response is triggered but not adequately developed by an author's writing, credit for the response goes to the reader. However, we generally don't examine our responses this closely. When we read and like the experience, that is good enough for us. Figure 1–3 depicts the roles and results of book quality and reader response.

Literary Merit of Book	Reader Response	Literary Merit of Book	Reader Response
1 +	+	+	− 2
3 −	+	−	− 4

FIGURE 1–3
Evaluating books:
Four possibilities.

▼▼▼▼▼▼▼

Evaluating Books: Four Possibilities

A book can be well written or poorly written, and a reader can respond positively or negatively to both strong and weak books. Quadrant 1 of Figure 1–3 shows that an author has written a book with literary merit, and the reader likes it. Take the extraordinarily popular book *Holes* by Louis Sachar. It won the Newbery Medal, has had a tremendous sales record, and has experienced great popularity with children and adult readers. We have no problem with a reader who responds positively to quality writing. A well-crafted book deserves no less.

Similarly, quadrant 4 presents no difficulty: The author shows little skill in producing a book of minimal merit, and the reader does not respond well to this flawed product. These two unshaded quadrants pose little problem for the teacher and student.

But problems may occur when a quality book is not well received. Quadrant 2 shows that an author has written a good book, but the reader doesn't care for it. Teachers who recognize quality may feel they are shirking their duty if they let a child believe that a book of high merit is of little value. Teachers who redouble their efforts to convince the unbeliever that something wonderful is being missed usually drive the unbelieving student further *from* the book.

In quadrant 3, the reader accepts a weak book with open arms. This scenario is often played out as a teacher tries to show the young reader just how poor the book really is. These sincere attempts are generally as successful as trying to dam the Mississippi River using a popsicle stick.

In both quadrants 2 and 3, the teacher needs to accept the honest feelings of the reader, misguided as they might be in the eyes of the adult, and continue to provide and introduce the better books. Doing so carries no guarantee that young readers will like them, but it does increase the chances that they will. Direct attacks on positive responses to poor quality books, however, almost guarantee that a rift will develop between teacher and student and, in the case of quadrant 2, between a student and a genuinely good book. So when children praise Goosebumps, introduce them to John Bellairs's *The House with the Clock in Its Walls* or to Barbara Brooks Wallace's *Peppermints in the Parlor*. They will see for themselves the compelling nature of these books and others like them.

Understanding that a positive response can be a result of either the author's skill or the reader's individual taste can help in solving some mysteries about how readers respond to books. For example, a British reviewer of children's books was surprised when her daughter, Alison, chose as her favorite book one that was far inferior to the many quality titles in their home. The story told of Peppermint, a pale kitten, who is last in a litter and alone after the others are matched with new families. Eventually, she is given to a girl who loves her, fusses over her, and prepares her so well for the cat show that Peppermint wins first prize. Alison's mother finally realized the appeal of Peppermint's story.

> Alison is an adopted child; her hair is pale straw, her eyes are blue; she was taken home, like Peppermint, to be loved and cared for and treasured. It was a matter of identification not just for the duration of the story but at a deep, warm, comforting and enduring level. . . . The artistically worthless book—hack-written and poorly illustrated—may, if the emotional content is sound, hold a message of supreme significance for a particular child. (Moss, 1977, pp. 141–142)

When a class of 30 college students read a not-very-good biography about Maria Tallchief, a Cherokee ballerina who captured the attention of the dancing world in the early 20th century, all but an enthusiastic handful of female students pronounced the book mediocre. Those five who loved the book couldn't understand why the others were not impressed by this story that had meant so much to them. During the short discussion, it was determined that each of the five students had taken and loved ballet as children. When they read about Maria Tallchief, they were reading their own stories.

For them, the book served as a link to an appealing personal experience. The others, without ballet backgrounds, did not find enough to interest them in the shallow way the author presented the story.

As adults working with children, we spend our time more productively in quadrants 1 and 2 in Figure 1–3 for two reasons. First, the more a book has to offer readers, the greater the chance the reader will respond. When Kevin Henkes identifies so precisely the reactions of an only child to the arrival of a new baby brother in *Julius, the Baby of the World,* the reader participates in the older daughter's jealousy and the turning point when a cousin's critical comments cause her to defend her new sibling. The author's range of emotion and humor is so broad that readers at a variety of levels are able to respond. The second reason we are more productive in quadrants 1 and 2 is the difficulty in matching readers with books that will connect with their lives in idiosyncratic ways. We have no way of knowing beforehand that Alison will find comfort in Peppermint or that five students will be linked to their ballet lessons by Maria Tallchief.

This whole evaluative process is somewhat like examining two new couches in Danish modern style. From a distance, they appear identical, but one reflects the true value of $1,800 and the other carries an honest price tag of $500. However, if allowed to inspect the couches at close range, even the nonprofessional should be able to determine which couch is of real quality and which is of lesser worth. We can determine the more expensive by examining the stitching, which should be close and even; the fabric, which should be tight and finely woven; the wood, which should be heavy, joined perfectly, well stained, and flawlessly finished. Once identified, however, the quality piece will not necessarily be welcomed into every living room. If Danish modern style does not appeal to me, it is of no importance that I now have the $1,800 couch. I can recognize its fine craftsmanship and can see that its shoddy counterpart is lacking in quality, but that does not make me want to own the fine couch if my taste runs counter to its appearance. Ultimately, the piece must please me before it gets my stamp of approval.

The late George Woods, longtime children's book critic for the *New York Times,* addressed the topic of evaluating children's books in a speech to an auditorium of college students. "How do we know a good book?" he asked his audience. Pens came to the ready for the scholar's definition. "We know a good book. . . (pause). . . because it hits us in the gut" (Woods, 1977).

The worth of a book is proved on the individual reader's nerve endings. Yet we know that some books simply are better constructed than others, offering a clearer understanding of the human experience and a deeper sense of pleasure. These quality books are the ones we need to introduce to children because they generally have more power to stir up interest where none is apparent and, over time, will catch more readers than will mediocre books. Yet we can't force these quality titles on children—we can only offer them. To become truly engaged readers, children must have the freedom to accept or reject a title. Just as we can't insist on a positive response to a book of quality, we can't erase a positive response to a poorly written book. Some young readers will respond with broad smiles and genuine affection to lower quality "good books." Attempting to change a convinced reader's mind that a book is not worthy of devotion is foolish and often counterproductive. All we can do, and should do, is continue to mention and offer different titles that may appeal to that reader. Allowing individual response is wisest in the long run. After all, if children read nothing, then our opportunity to broaden their taste and judgment about books is nonexistent.

In the end, the question of "good book" is one of respect: respect for the truly fine work of authors who pay their dues and create works of lasting value, and also respect for the response of individual readers who cast the deciding vote on a book's appeal. There is, after all, only one list of good books that is completely dependable. Not the winners of a certain award. Not titles that have proven themselves over time. Not the books with the current highest sales figures. The only list we can trust without reservation is our own.

Personal Model.

Each questions counts 2 points.

1. Yes = 2 points. If teachers aren't reading, they can't deliver an honest love of books to students.
2. 1 point for each author. Teachers who read children's books will respond more to some authors than others and need to recognize they have favorites.
3. 2 points for completion. Even die-hard upper elementary teachers need to be familiar with picture books.
4. 2 points for completion. If a teacher knows only old books, chances for reaching children are more limited.
5. 2 points for completion. See number 4.
6. One point for every 20 children's trade books you own (2 points maximum).
7. 2 points for completion. If you don't have an idea of what to read next, chances are you're not reading much.
8. 2 points for completion. If teachers never talk about the books they read, their influence will be limited.
9. 2 points for completion. Identifying a favorite type of book or genre is important self-knowledge.
10. 1 point for each author. Teachers who are readers generally will have a broader interest than just children's books.

Classroom Model.

Each "yes" response receives 2 points.

1. Yes = 2 points. Adults who are most successful in turning children into readers do not hide their own reading. This is as true at home as in the classroom. One of our graduate students read regularly, yet none of her four children valued books. Further conversation revealed she read only in the bathtub and in bed after the children were asleep. Because she never talked to them or in front of them about her reading, they had no idea at all that she liked books.
2. Yes = 2 points. If you emphasize personal reading with children, they need to learn about your personal reading, which includes the types of books you like and those that are not as appealing to you. Children deserve a teacher with identified favorites.
3. Yes = 2 points. We have a difficult time convincing children that books are worthwhile if none are at hand.
4. Yes = 2 points. Sharing titles consistently will give children needed and welcome reading options.
5. Yes = 2 points. Hearing books being read aloud is the most important classroom activity for turning children into readers.
6. Yes = 2 points. The more we immerse students in "real" reading, the better chance we have that they will become readers.
7. Yes = 2 points. SSR is the second most important classroom activity for turning children into readers.
8. Yes = 2 points. The key to a successful SSR program is seeing the teacher read.
9. Yes = 2 points. This is the most important out-of-class activity for turning children into readers.
10. Yes = 2 points. Book ownership is a mark of a truly literate person.

Each quiz has a maximum of 20 points. Scores and rating for each quiz, and the two combined, are as follows:

Personal or Classroom Score	Total Score	Rating
16–20	32–40	Stupendous. You're a fine model.
12–15	24–31	Very good. You're better than most.
8–11	16–23	Okay, but you need work.
4–7	8–15	Weak. Quick—get books into your life.
0–3	0–7	Don't have children or teach school just yet.

FIGURE 1–4   Scoring yourself as a reading model.

▼▼▼▼▼▼▼

Summary

In this chapter, we first answered the question, "Why read?" Clearly the advantages of reading are that it is personally rewarding, providing us with short- and long-term benefits. We made the distinction between unengaged and engaged reading, noting that fluent readers read for information and experience but that the important factor is that reading must be of personal significance. We looked at children who are engaged in reading and, further, at teachers' engaged reading. It is the powerful example of the teacher as reader that encourages children to pursue reading. Teachers who read gain new knowledge about the world around them and understand education better. We provided an instrument to determine how good a reader you are and then offered hints for becoming a better reading model. Next we looked at specific criteria we set up in determining what a good book is, noting quality and taste as two contributing factors in our evaluation. By concentrating on style and language, character, plot, setting, illustrations, theme, tone, point of view, mood, pacing, design and layout, tension, accuracy, and believability, we can make informed decisions on the quality of a book. Our taste in books is determined by their literary merit as well as by their appeal. In the end, it is the good teacher who can develop readers through modeling and solid instructional practices, introducing them to better quality literature.

▼▼▼▼▼▼▼

Children's Literature References

Anderson, Laurie Halse. (1999). *Speak*. New York: Farrar, Straus & Giroux.

Avi. (1986). *Wolf rider: A tale of terror*. New York: Collier.

Babbitt, Natalie. (1975). *Tuck everlasting*. New York: Farrar, Straus & Giroux.

Bellairs, John. (1973). *The house with the clock in its walls*. New York: Dial.

Bruchac, Joseph. (1993). *The first strawberries: A Cherokee story* (Anna Bojtech, Illus.). New York: Dial.

Cormier, Robert. (1998). *Heroes*. New York: Delacorte Press.

Crutcher, Chris. (1991). *Athletic shorts*. New York: Greenwillow.

DiCamillo, Kate. (2000). *Because of Winn-Dixie*. Cambridge, MA: Candlewick Press.

Fenner, Carol. (1991). *Randall's wall*. New York: McElderry.

Gantos, Jack. (1998). *Joey Pigza swallowed the key*. New York: Farrar, Straus & Giroux.

Grahame, Kenneth. (1908). *The wind in the willows*. New York: Scribner's.

Gregorowski, Christopher. (2000). *Fly, eagle, fly: An African tale* (Niki Daly, Illus.). New York: McElderry.

Grimm, Jacob, & Grimm, Wilhelm. (1975). *Thorn Rose* (Errol LeCain, Illus.). New York: Bradbury.

Hamilton, Virginia. (1995). *Jaguarundi* (Floyd Cooper, Illus.). New York: Scholastic.

Henkes, Kevin. (1990). *Julius, the baby of the world*. New York: Greenwillow.

Jaffe, Nina. (1995). *Older brother, younger brother: A Korean folktale* (Wenhai. Ma, Illus.). New York: Viking.

Kurtz, Jane. (1994). *Fire on the mountain* (E. B. Lewis, Illus.). New York: Simon.

Mahy, Margaret. (1990). *The seven Chinese brothers* (Jean Tseng & Mou-sien Tseng, Illus.). New York: Scholastic.

McCloskey, Robert. (1942). *Make way for ducklings*. New York: Viking.

Myers, Walter Dean. (1997). *Harlem*. New York: Scholastic.

O'Dell, Scott. (1960). *Island of the blue dolphins*. Boston: Houghton Mifflin.

Osbourne, Mary Pope. (2000). *Adaline falling star*. New York: Scholastic.

Park, Barbara. (1995). *Mick Harte was here*. New York: Knopf.

Parker, Steve. (1998). *The human body: And how it works* (Giovanni Caselli, Illus.). New York: Dorling Kindersley.

Paterson, Katherine. (1990). *The tale of the Mandarin ducks* (Leo Dillon & Diane Dillon, Illus.). New York: Dutton.

Paulsen, Gary. (1987). *Hatchet*. New York: Bradbury.

Paulsen, Gary. (1998). *Soldier's heart*. New York: Delacorte.

Robinson, Barbara. (1972). *The best Christmas pageant ever* (Judith Gwyn Brown, Illus.). New York: Harper & Row.

Rowling. J. K. (2000). *Harry Potter and the goblet of fire*. New York: Scholastic.

Sachar, Louis. (1998). *Holes*. New York: Farrar, Straus & Giroux.

Soto, Gary. (1995). *Chato's kitchen* (Susan Guevara, Illus.). New York: Putnam.

Soto, Gary. (2000). *Chato and the party animals* (Susan Guevara, Illus.). New York: Putnam.

Spinelli, Jerry. (1990). *Maniac Magee*. Boston: Little, Brown.

Stevenson, Robert Louis. (1883). *Treasure Island* (N. C. Wyeth, Illus.). New York: Scribner's. (Original work published in 1883)

Wallace, Barbara Brooks. (1980). *Peppermints in the parlor*. New York: Atheneum.

Weaver, Will. (1993). *Striking out*. New York: HarperCollins.

Williams-Garcia, Rita. (1995). *Like sisters on the homefront*. New York: Lodestar.

▼▼▼▼▼▼▼

Professional References

Beveridge, W. I. B. (1957). *The art of scientific investigation*. New York: Norton.

Conrad, P. (1991). Speech presented at the Chautauqua Writers Conference. Chautauqua, NY.

Cunningham, P. M., & Allington, R. L. (1999). *Classrooms that work: They can all read* (2nd ed.). New York: Longman.

Fader, D. (1976). *Hooked on books*. New York: Berkeley Books.

Fletcher, R. (1993). *What a writer needs*. Portsmouth, N H: Heinemann.

Gardner, J. W. (1981). *Self-renewal*. New York: Norton.

Kirsch, I., Jungeblut, A., Jenkins, L., & Kolstad, A. (1993). *Adult literacy in America: A first look at the results of the National Adult Literacy Survey*. Washington, DC: U.S. Office of Education and Educational Testing Service.

Larson, J. (1994). Personal interview in Provo, Utah. 9 September.

Moss, E. (1977). What is a good book? In M. Meek, A. Warlow, & G. Barton (Eds.), *The cool web* (pp. 140–142). London: Bodley Head.

Norton, D. E. (1992). *The impact of literature-based reading*. Upper Saddle River, NJ: Merrill/Prentice Hall.

Paulsen, G. (1987, January). *Books and early reading*. Speech given at Clarke County Library Association, Las Vegas, NV.

Perez, S. A. (1986). Children see, children do: Teachers as reading models. *The Reading Teacher, 40*, 8–11.

Rosenblatt, L. (1978). *The reader, the text, the poem*. Carbondale, IL: Southern Illinois University Press.

Sabine, G., & Sabine, P. (1983). *Books that made the difference*. Hamden, CT: Shoe String Press.

Schweitzer, A. (1997). In J. B. Simpson (Ed.), *Simpson's contemporary quotations* (p. 482). New York: HarperCollins.

Snyder, T. D., & Hoffman, C. M. (1994). *Digest of education statistics 1994*. Washington, DC: U.S. Department of Education.

Sweet, A. P. (1993). *Transforming ideas for teaching and learning to read*. Washington, DC: U.S. Department of Education.

UNESCO. (1990). *UNESCO statistical yearbook*. Paris: Author.

Woods, G. (1977, September). *Evaluating children's books*. Speech given at Brigham Young University.

Zill, N., & Winglee, M. (1988). *Who reads literature?* Washington, DC: Child Trends.

WHAT IS A GOOD BOOK?

2
CHAPTER
▼▼▼▼▼▼▼

If you want to cover
*Being a Bit
Different is Okay*

Consider as a READ ALOUD

Olivia by Ian Falconer

Consider as a TEXT SET

Somebody Loves You, Mr. Hatch
by Eileen Spinelli,
illustrated by Paul Yalowitz

Old Henry
by Joan Blos,
illustrated by Stephen Gammell

*John Patrick Norman McHennessy:
The Boy Who Was Always Late*
by John Burningham

The Painter Who Loved Chickens
by Olivier Dunrea

The Rooster's Gift
by Pam Conrad,
illustrated by Eric Beddows

Be Good to Eddie Lee
by Virginia Fleming,
illustrated by Floyd Cooper

THE PAINTER WHO LOVED CHICKENS
by Olivier Dunrea

The man worked as a painter. He painted pictures of people, poodles, and penguins. Many people bought these pictures. But what the man really wanted to paint was chickens. No one wanted pictures of chickens.

Excerpt from *The Painter Who Loved Chickens* by Olivier Dunrea

by Jared

Student Response

I drew the Barred Rock chicken because he looked cool. And because I thought he looked easy to draw. He wasn't easy to draw.

▼▼▼▼▼▼▼

The Words

"This book is well written." This statement is a common badge of praise often pinned on books of quality. But given our discussion in the first chapter concerning what makes a book "good," we would beg to ask now, "What, specifically, does *well written* mean?" Often it means nothing more than the speaker's way of saying the book is pleasing: If it pleases me, it must be well written. When used as evidence that we responded well to a book, the phrase "well written" has become a generalized catchall.

If a book is truly well written, that means the words between those covers have been arranged in magical patterns that stir deep emotional responses in readers. The words go far beyond relating the mere events of the story. The words make the book by defining character, moving the plot along, identifying the setting, isolating the theme, creating the tone, choosing the point of view, developing the mood, establishing the pace, making the story believable, and reporting information accurately.

Isolating each element from the others, however, does not give us a clear picture of exactly what makes a book so memorable. Certainly, for example, the plot must be well structured, but it cannot be separated from the major characters who are living the story. Conversely, well-defined characters lose their appeal if they are not involved in a compelling plot. The elements of writing are integrated and worked into a well-orchestrated whole by a talented writer.

Talented writers create works that are clear, believable, and interesting. Whatever the subject or literary element (or intended age group, for that matter), the writing must first of all be understandable (clear), then it must seem real (believable), and finally it must have appeal (interesting). A story is not good because it is about a particular topic or peopled with certain characters; it is good because of the way it is presented. A work of nonfiction is not good because of the subject matter; it is good because of the way it views and reveals the subject. Consider the two perspectives from which the following event can be viewed:

Case 1. The college football coach finished his 20th successful season and was honored at a banquet where his praises were sung loud and long. As dishes were cleared and tables taken down after the festivities, the coach talked with his friend, the college president. At one point, the coach paused and then asked, "President, I appreciate this evening more than you'll ever know. Yet sometimes I find a nagging question in my mind: Would all of you still love me if I lost football games instead of won them?"

"Sure, Coach, we'd love you just as much," the president said as he reached out his arm, pulled him in close, and looked him right in the eye. . . "And we'd miss you."

Case 2. A college student said to his classmate, "Did you hear that last night after the banquet honoring the football coach, the president said he'd be fired if he didn't keep up his winning record?"

In case 2, the reader gets all the pertinent information: the banquet in the coach's honor, the president and coach's conversation afterward, and the gist of their exchange. In the first example, the reader gets to participate in the event. A few details flesh out the scene, the coach shows some vulnerability, the president displays his administrative concern, and the reader has to figure out that the coach would be fired. The point is not revealed until the reader becomes a part of the story and draws that conclusion.

Human beings can't draw conclusions without information, and we gain information only through the five senses. If data can't enter through one of the holes in our heads (through sight, sound, taste, or smell) or through contact with some part of the body (through touch), they can't be processed. Good writers know readers need specific information—sensory detail—and take the trouble to provide it. Lesser writers generalize. The difference between providing sensory detail and generalizing is the difference between showing and telling. Where lesser writing *tells* by summarizing (as in

To visit a classroom exploring the issues of What Is a Good Book, please go to Chapter 2 of our companion website at **www.prenhall.com/darigan**

case 2), quality writing *shows* the reader what is going on by providing enough sensory detail to allow the reader to make personal discoveries and come to personal conclusions (as in case 1). Consider, for instance, the opening paragraph of Lloyd Alexander's **The Illyrian Adventure:**

> Miss Vesper Holly has the digestive talents of a goat and the mind of a chess master. She is familiar with half a dozen languages and can swear fluently in all of them. She understands the use of a slide rule but prefers doing calculations in her head. She does not hesitate to risk life and limb—mine as well as her own. No doubt she has other qualities as yet undiscovered. I hope not.

The reader is solidly introduced to Vesper Holly. Alexander reveals Vesper's particular personality by *showing* her skills, accomplishments, abilities, and interests. Had Alexander begun by *telling* us about Vesper, he might have summarized her character by saying, "Miss Vesper Holly is courageous, intelligent, daring, a skilled linguist, delightfully irreverent, and headstrong." We would then know what to expect of her, but we wouldn't know her as well.

The details the author provides give us real knowledge and understanding. If a friend who has been mostly a loner suddenly has a date and is excited, we share that excitement. We secure a promise from him or her to telephone us immediately after the event. The phone rings very late. "Remember how excited I was to go out tonight?" "Yes." "Remember how I had my hopes built up, maybe even a little too high?" "Yes." "Well, the evening was 10 times better than I had imagined. I'm tired now. Good night." Click.

As we sit holding the phone, we are unsatisfied. We want details, not because we are nosy (well, maybe a little bit) but because we can't understand without them. We can participate vicariously in the evening only when we have enough facts: Where did they go, what did they talk about, what did our friend think, whose hand brushed whose first? The phone call *told* us about the evening; what we wanted is to be *shown*.

The details we need from the printed page so we can participate in an experience come to us in various forms: precise vocabulary, figurative language, dialogue, music in language, understatement, and surprise observations. These terms do not constitute a comprehensive list but they are some examples of how words show detail in writing.

Precise Vocabulary

By age four, children have acquired most of the elements of adult language (Morrow, 1989). The only additional refinements take place in acquiring more complex structures and in semantics—learning new words and their meanings. Semantic development continues for the rest of their lives. With more than 800,000 words (300,000 being technical terms), English has the richest vocabulary of the 5,000-plus languages on the planet. One of the great pleasures of language is to find in this fertile and varied vocabulary precisely the right word to use in exactly the right place. Mark Twain described the difference between the right word and the almost right word as like the difference between lightning and the lightning bug. And the only way to learn the fine differences between words and to develop a broad personal vocabulary is to be surrounded by precise words that are used accurately. When Newbery-winning author Elaine Konigsburg writes for children, she tries "to expand the perimeter of their language, to set a wider limit to it, to give them a vocabulary for alternatives" (1970, pp. 731–732).

William Steig is a master of precise vocabulary and wider limits. In his **The Amazing Bone**, Pearl the pig, dressed in her flowered dress and sun bonnet, took her time coming home from school: "On Cobble Road she stopped at Maltby's barn and stood gawking as the old gaffers pitched their ringing horseshoes and spat tobacco juice." (If this sentence were written by someone afraid it is not accessible to the younger reader, it would come out something like: "She stopped at the barn and watched the old men play horseshoes.") Naming the road and the barn gives the story depth and credibility—the place seems to exist. "Gawking" identifies exactly the kind of looking she did—wide-eyed, unabashed staring. "Ringing horseshoes" provides a dimension of sound to the game, adding another layer to the picture. And "spat to-bacco juice" presents a side of the men and their activities that rounds them out. But the genius on this page is the selection of the word *gaffers*. English has a number of specific words for the phrase *old man: patriarch, ancient, graybeard, Nestor, grandfa-ther, gaffer, geezer, codger, dotard, Methuselah, antediluvian, preadamite, veteran, old-timer, old soldier, old stager, dean, doyen, senior, elder, oldest, first-born, seniority, pri-mogeniture* (Lewis, 1961). The only ones general enough to be considered for this setting are *codger, dotard, gaffer, geezer,* and *old-timer. The Oxford English Dictionary (Compact Edition* 1971) reports that each carries a specific view of old men:

> *Codger:* "A mean, stingy, or miserly (old) fellow; a testy or crusty (old) man" (p. 456)
> *Geezer:* "A term of derision applied to elderly persons" (p. 1125)
> *Gaffer:* "A term applied originally by country people to an elderly man or one whose position entitled him to respect" (p. 1103)
> *Dotard:* "One whose intellect is impaired by age; one whose dotage is in his second childhood" (p. 790)
> *Old-timer:* "[O]ne whose experience goes back to old times" (p. 1984)

Gaffer is the only term that is neither negative nor neutral. Its positive connotation com-plements the pleasant, unhurried scene while reflecting a strong image of the elderly.

The right words do not have to be fancy or obscure. Even ordinary words can be right. In Barbara Robinson's **Temporary Times, Temporary Places,** teenaged Mar-ilyn is stunned when she comes out of the church after an evening social to see her friend, Janet, walking away with the boy of their dreams, the one they have spent end-less hours discussing. He has never spoken to either of them, and here he is leaving with Janet. Carrying her sweater in her hand, Marilyn can only stare: "She was stand-ing on the steps of the church, mouth open, eyes wide, sweater dragging." With those six words—mouth open, eyes wide, sweater dragging—astonishment is *shown*. Robin-son has thought about what astonishment in this situation looks like and presented it precisely. The reader sees what Janet sees. A lesser writer, who tells instead of shows, would have written something like, "She was standing on the steps of the church, a look of astonishment on her face." This sentence tells readers they should feel aston-ishment, but it does not create the image or the experience. In Robinson's hands, the scene is more specific, more complete, and more believable.

Figurative Language

Simile, metaphor, personification, and imagery add layers of meaning and emotional power economically. In **Maniac Magee,** Jerry Spinelli describes March, the month leading winter into spring, as a brute: "During the night, March doubled back and grabbed April by the scruff of the neck and flung it another week or two down the road." Spinelli's personification of March reminds us vividly that this unpredictable month is given to sudden nastiness.

From Natalie Babbitt's **Tuck Everlasting** comes the lingering image of Mae Tuck, described as a "great potato of a woman." In five words, Babbitt creates a feel-ing for Mae's lumpy shape, her earthiness, her plainness, her lack of color, her solid-ness, her accessibility, and other earthy and dependable traits associated with a veg-etable that is not spectacular, fragile, or rare but is a nutritional staple.

Figurative language can add power and insight to whole paragraphs. It is one thing to say that Winnie Foster was made to do housework continually, but in **Tuck Everlasting,** the author underscores the seriousness of cleaning in Winnie's household by loading the description with images of war.

> Winnie had grown up with order. She was used to it. Under the pitiless double assaults of her mother and grandmother, the cottage where she lived was always squeaking clean, mopped and swept and scoured into limp submission. There was no room for carelessness, no putting things off until later. The Foster women had made a fortress

Cover from ***Tuck Everlasting,*** by Natalie Babbitt.
Copyright © 1975 by Farrar, Straus, Giroux.
Reprinted by permission of the publisher.

Cover from ***Maniac Magee,*** by Jerry Spinelli.
Copyright © 1990 by Little, Brown. Reprinted by
permission of the publisher.

out of duty. Within it, they were indomitable. And Winnie was in training.

When we read the paragraph, we get the solid impression that housecleaning in the Foster cottage is the focal point of life. Only when we go back and pick out the military terms Babbitt has chosen—double assaults, fortress, duty, in training—do we see the image of soldiers in battle that has helped persuade us of the Foster obsession with cleanliness.

Dialogue

Speech reveals character. When a person's mouth opens, truth emerges about personality, motives, desires, prejudices, and feelings. Bernard Waber has an ear for real speech that reveals the nuances, challenges, and bluffing responses of sibling conversation. In ***Ira Sleeps Over***, Ira has been invited to spend the night at a friend's house—his first sleepover. When his older sister learns of his plans, she asks:

"Are you taking your teddy bear along?"

DID YOU KNOW?

Our buddy Jim Trelease often reads aloud Bernard Waber's *Ira Sleeps Over* in his dynamic presentation. However, when he gets to just the best part—the part where we wonder what Ira will do—Trelease closes the book and puts it on the table in front of him. Calmly he says, "If you want to know what happens to Ira . . . go to your library and check out the book." An audible groan echoes across the audience, so badly do they want to know what happens.

"Taking my teddy bear along!" I said. "To my friend's house? Are you kidding? That's the silliest thing I ever heard! Of course, I'm not taking my teddy bear."

And then she said: "But you never slept without your teddy bear before. How will you feel, sleeping without your teddy bear for the very first time? Hmmmmmmm?"

In this brief exchange between brother and sister, Waber shows the older sister's need and ability to control her younger brother with what appears to be an innocent question: "Are you taking your teddy bear along?" What difference does it make to her if he takes it? None, but her job is to make his life miserable, and she performs it perfectly. His reply, a little too quick and laced with false bravado, shows his insecurity. And her final statement is a knockout punch that leaves him no chance to get to his feet, reminding him that he has never slept alone, asking how that would feel, and ending with that taunting "Hmmmmmmmm?"

If speech is not natural and not as individual as a particular personality, it shows the characters to be shallow and stiff, distracting from the story and consequently weakening it. Unnatural dialogue appears in Conalee Trepeck's *Fun at the Hospital* when Peter goes outside to see if he can get into the sandlot baseball game forming up near his house.

"Please let us play ball with you.
"We like to bat the ball and run,
"Playing baseball is so much fun."
It was Peter's turn to run around
When he slipped and fell down to the ground.

He ran into the house crying, "Mother!"
In back of him followed each brother.
"It hurts me, hurts me terribly, here!"
"Oh, let Mother look at it, dear."

Real boys and real mothers simply do not talk that way. This dialogue is written by someone who has forgotten what childhood is like, putting stilted words and formal sentences into the mouths of active boys. The author also seems out of touch with the way adults speak and react. This passage should show a screaming child and a frantic mother. Instead, we see cardboard people.

Music in Language

The sounds of words add to the appeal and strength of the story as they blend together, create emphasis, repeat tones, establish patterns, provide a cadence, and add variety. The rhythm in the refrain of Wanda Gág's *Millions of Cats* rings in our ears and burrows into our minds. She writes, "Cats here, cats there, cats and kittens everywhere. Hundreds of cats, thousands of cats, millions and billions and trillions of cats." The same is true of the rhyme in *Goodnight Moon* by Margaret Wise Brown: "Goodnight stars. Goodnight air. Goodnight noises everywhere."

Buford in *Buford the Little Bighorn,* by Bill Peet, is a small mountain sheep whose horns have grown enormously, way out of proportion to his body. They cause him balance problems, and he falls from craggy heights but is saved when his horns hook onto a small tree. From then on, his friends have to help him over the rough spots in their high, rocky world. To climb a steep ledge, two sheep from above grab his horns in their teeth and pull while one butts him skyward, giving "Buford a big boost from below." Those explosive *b*'s echo the heavy sounds and sudden movements of butting and boosting as well as link the phrase together by repeating the sound.

Because the eye does not reveal the fine points of language as accurately as the ear, it is common for authors to submit their writing to a final check by reading it aloud. In two versions of "Snow White," the queen questions the mirror in language that is subtly yet powerfully different. Submit the following two passages to the read-aloud test:

Mirror, mirror on the wall. Who is the fairest one of all? (Walt Disney Productions, 1973)

Mirror, mirror on the wall, Who is fairest of us all? (Grimm, 1972)

Uneven meter in the first example makes that passage more difficult to say aloud; the cadence is rougher and the sound choppier. The language in the second flows, falling smoothly and effortlessly from the mouth. The result is a more musical reading. The second also suggests an archaic form of speech that matches the "once upon a time" setting of the fairy tale.

Varied sentence length is another feature of language that appeals to the ear. In natural speech patterns, sentences are of differing length. These diverse sentences add variety to the language, creating balance, interest, and appeal. Read aloud the opening passages from the Disney and Grimm versions of "Snow White," paying attention to how they feel coming from the mouth and how they fall upon the ear.

Long ago there lived a princess named Snow White. She was a beautiful princess. And like all princesses she lived in a castle.
   Her stepmother, the queen, also lived in the castle. The queen had a magic mirror. Every day she looked into the mirror and asked the same thing.
   "Mirror, mirror on the wall. Who is the fairest one of all?"
   The mirror always gave her the same answer. "Oh, queen, YOU are the fairest one of all." (Walt Disney Productions, 1973)

Once it was the middle of winter, and the snowflakes fell from the sky like feathers. At a window with a frame of ebony a queen sat and sewed. And as she sewed and looked out at the snow, she pricked her finger with the needle, and three drops of blood fell in the snow. And in the white snow the red looked so beautiful that she thought to herself: "If only I had a child as white as snow, as red as blood, and as black as the wood in the window frame!" (Grimm, 1972)

For most readers, the many short sentences in the first example interrupt the flow of the story, creating a degree of choppiness. The varied sentence construction in the second helps produce a smooth and flowing narrative that reads with a musical quality. The first passage has 10 sentences; the second 4. The first has an average of 7.9 words per sentence; the second 23.5. More words per sentence are not necessarily an earmark of good writing, but in this case the longer sentences help weave stronger, more emotion-laden images.

Understatement

When facts and feelings are presented clearly in writing, readers draw their own conclusions without being told precisely what to think. Readers then participate in the experience instead of being led through it. Part of this participatory process is understatement, which presents minimal but carefully chosen facts and details without any explanatory comment. Understatement is simply very brief "showing." The opposites of understatement are sensationalism and overexplanation.

The power of understatement is evident in ***Tuck Everlasting***. Angus Tuck tries to convince young Winnie Foster, whom he has grown to love like his own child, not to drink from the same magical spring that has transformed the Tucks into people who cannot age or die. When the Tuck family is forced to move away, Angus is uncertain of what Winnie will do—let her life follow its natural course, as he counseled, or submit to the enticements of living forever. In the epilogue, Angus and Mae Tuck return to Winnie's town 60 years later and visit the cemetery. When he discovers her tombstone, Angus's throat closes and he briefly salutes the monument, saying, "Good girl." No long discourses with his wife about Winnie's wise decision. No fits of crying or sentimental remembrances. Just "good girl."

In ***A Summer to Die***, by Lois Lowry, the family is going through a period of mourning as it becomes clear that teenage Molly is going to die. On the way home from a particularly good hospital visit, the family sings childhood songs, capturing the comforting feelings of what life used to be like before Molly became so ill. After that scene, the next words are "Two weeks later, she was gone." There was no jarring phone call bringing news of the inevitable, no heap of details describing her last moments. We have lived through the disease, joined in the family's efforts to understand and draw together, and now the inescapable has arrived. That's all we need to know. Understatement gives power to writing because of what is not said and shows that an author trusts readers to make important, personal connections with the story.

Unexpected Insights

Like life, good stories contain occasional small surprises. We live with characters as they work their ways through problems but may be delighted suddenly by a small detour from the main story line or an eye-opening insight about the human experience. For instance, ***Maniac Magee*** wonders why the people in East End call themselves black. "He kept looking and looking, and the colors he found were gingersnap and light fudge and dark fudge and acorn and butter rum and cinnamon and burnt orange. But never licorice, which, to him, was real black." "That's absolutely right," we find ourselves saying.

Lloyd Alexander is famous for such insights. In his five-book series, The Prydain Chronicles, he offers readers sage advice. For example, in ***The High King***, Dwyvach Weaver-Woman presents a beautiful cloak to the girl Eilonwy. "Take this as a gift from a crone to a maiden," says Dwyvach, "and know there is not so much difference between the two. For even a tottering grandam keeps a portion of girlish heart, and the youngest maid a thread of old woman's wisdom." And to Taran in ***Taran Wanderer*** who is the main character on the hero's journey and wearied by his search, Hevydd the blacksmith counsels, "Life's a forge! . . . Yes, and hammer and anvil, too! You'll be roasted, smelted, and pounded, and you'll scarce know what's happening to you. But stand boldly to it! Metal's worthless till it's shaped and tempered!" Later when he is disappointed that he did not accomplish more while away on his quest, the enchanter Dallben points out in *The Book of Three*, "There are times when the seeking counts more than the finding."

Elements of Weak Writing

One simple way to define weak writing is to say it is the opposite of good writing—not clear but fuzzy, not believable but implausible, not interesting but dull. Beyond that, and particularly in children's books, some weak elements stand out: didacticism, condescension, and controlled vocabulary.

Didacticism

Didacticism is writing that pretends to be a story but is actually a thinly disguised lesson. Good books can and do provide lessons, but in good books, the lessons are secondary. They are secrets to be discovered rather than sermons to be suffered. The learning and insight arrive as additional gifts, by-products from rewarding experiences.

Didacticism was more evident in books from earlier times, in which small children or animals who were greedy or lazy, for instance, learned the error of their ways and became model citizens. Although some of that still exists, today's didacticism tends to lean more toward political correctness. Lessons about ecology, acceptable social behavior, and the rights of special interest groups overshadow the story in contemporary didactic books.

For example, *Hunting for Fur*, by Thierry Dedien, is clearly written with the protection of hunted fur-bearing animals set first and a story coming in a distant second. Koala and Panda find Wolf huddled in a blanket near a fire—thieves have stolen his fur. Banding together, the two unlikely animals go to the city, and at gunpoint steal back the furs worn by the "rabbit, mink, or wolf skin thie(ves)." They return skins the next day to all the rest of the naked animals, then head back to town saying, "it looks like our cousins in Africa need a helping hand." Look for the sequel. Now, we are certainly not against the ethical treatment of animals. Far from it. However, we *are* against didactic books that attempt to shove this issue down our throats.

Cover from *The Book of Three*, by Lloyd Alexander. Copyright © 1964 by Holt, Rinehart and Winston. Jacket art by Evaline Ness Bayard. Reprinted by permission of the publisher.

Condescension

Condescension may be slightly harder to pin down than didacticism. Evident mostly in books for very young readers, a condescending tone treats children as all too "precious" and overexplains things with a certain wide-eyed amazement that borders on phoniness. Condescension dilutes the power of language in nonfiction, such as labeling "esophagus" a "food tube." Adams (1990) warns that this type of writing can actually make passages more difficult to read because it dilutes the predictive context and forces the reader to overrely on the letter recognition network (p. 139).

In fiction, vacant cliches such as, "What fun! We like to share our toys with other boys and girls!" ring hollow in children's ears. The reality is that children can be selfish and certainly jealous of younger siblings infringing on their space. Better to read a book like Kevin Henkes's *Julius, the Baby of the World*, where young Lilly is struggling with her new brother's entrance into the family, unseating her as "the Queen." She spends "more than usual time in the uncooperative chair" and does her best to deny her brother's existence. Meanwhile, "her parents love him. They kissed his wet pink nose. They admired his small black eyes. And they stroked his sweet white fur."

Cover from *Julius, the Baby of the World* by Kevin Henkes. Copyright © 1990 by Greenwillow Books. Reprinted by permission of the publisher.

"Disgusting," said Lilly. Not until Lilly's mother plans a festive celebration honoring Julius does Lilly come to terms with her anger. Cousin Garland makes some nasty accusations about Julius—ones Lilly had echoed earlier—and Lilly comes to her senses and sticks up for her new little brother. In the end, the lived-through experiences make the message more convincing.

Controlled Vocabulary

Controlled vocabulary is a reading concept based on the idea that children learn to read certain easy words first, then graduate slowly to more difficult ones to avoid frustration. However, these so-called dumbed-down texts, which over-control vocabulary and arrange words in unnatural patterns ("I see the mat. The mat is tan. It is a tan mat."), often have proven to be more difficult for children to read and understand than text with interesting words and language patterns. The dumbed-down text does not correspond with what they have learned through the ear (Goodman, 1988).

Children can sometimes learn difficult words more easily than seemingly simple ones. If first graders are shown the words *surprise, was,* and *elephant,* the one they will learn to sight read first is *elephant.* Although it is longer and more difficult, it is also more specific. Try drawing a picture of a *surprise* or a *was.* The hardest of the three—the one that takes the most exposures to become included in children's sight vocabulary—is *was.*

In the 1980s, basal companies recognized the power of natural text and began to include excerpts from authentic literature as a part of their reading programs. However, in the 1990s, schools began buying and using sets of controlled-vocabulary paperback books instead of basal textbooks. Therefore, to meet demand, basal companies also began to include sets of controlled-vocabulary readers with their literature-based reading series. Today, teachers must choose wisely because, once again, reading materials available in the elementary schools may focus on a particular word pattern, largely ignoring the appeal of natural language and cohesive story.

In the final analysis, the idea of controlled vocabulary goes too far when the author's primary purpose is providing word practice instead of telling a good story. When an author focuses intently on simple words and language patterns, the writing likely will be artificial and colorless. Can't an author write a book with rigidly controlled vocabulary and an interesting story at the same time? It is unlikely, because a book can't serve two masters—the one more important to the author almost always takes over. Margaret Hillert's ***Why We Have Thanksgiving*** is a picture book designed as a controlled reader. The Thanksgiving story is filled with human pathos; it is a story of sacrifice and courage. But not so in Hillert's version, as this excerpt shows:

> Here we are on the boat. This is fun. Away we go. . . .What is this spot? Is it a good one? What will we do here? We have to work. We have to make a big house for boys and girls and mothers and fathers.

> See this come up, and this, and this. It is good to eat. And here is something to eat, too. Something little and red. Something good. We can get some for Mother and Father. Now, sit down. Sit down. It is good to have friends.

Never once does the word *Thanksgiving* appear or words like *corn* and *cranberry.* The text is so sparse, repetitive, and lacking in detail that a young reader can derive no sense of the human experience related to the first Thanksgiving. Not only does this book not show, but it doesn't even get as far as telling. It never answers the question implied in the title: Why do we have Thanksgiving?

Another title, Doreen Rappaport's *The Boston Coffee Party*, is also written for fledgling readers and recounts in a historical fiction format an actual event in American history. Certainly, as evident in the brief excerpt that follows, the vocabulary is gently controlled, but there is a natural rhythm to the text and an honest sense of story. The characters seem like real people, and there are not the gaping holes in the plot that make the Thanksgiving story incomprehensible.

"'See Spot. See Spot run. See Spot run and play...' What IS this garbage?"

> Just then the door opened. It was Aunt Harriet. She looked angry.
>
> "Do you know what Merchant Thomas has done," she cried. "He locked up forty barrels of coffee in his warehouse."
>
> "But why?" asked Mrs. Smith.
>
> "He is waiting until no one in Boston has coffee," said Aunt Harriet. "Then he will sell his coffee for a lot of money."
>
> "He is greedier than I thought," said Mrs. Homans.
>
> "We must teach him a lesson," said Aunt Harriet.
>
> "But what can we do?" asked Mrs. Smith.
>
> The room was quiet.
>
> "Let's have a party!" Sarah shouted suddenly.
>
> "Silly girl, this is no time for a party," said Mrs. Homans.
>
> "I mean a party like the men had when they threw English tea into the harbor," said Sarah.

In short, the standards for a well-written children's book are no different from the standards for any well-written book. The author treats the audience with respect and writes so that the text is honest and interesting. The literary devices employed to achieve that honesty and interest operate so smoothly they remain virtually invisible. The story in fictional works and the information in nonfiction are so compelling that the reader sails along, engrossed in the precise language and unaware of the talent and time necessary for making the final product appear so effortless.

BOOKMARK

INTEGRATING TECHNOLOGY: AUTHORS ON THE WORLD WIDE WEB

Numerous authors and illustrators of children's books have websites created by their publishers, by devoted fans, by scholars, or in some cases by the author him- or herself. Making connections with authors and illustrators can be a very effective way to motivate students and to emphasize the idea that literature is created by people. *Children's and Young Adults' Authors & Illustrators,* located on The Internet School Library Media Center's website, is an index of author and illustrator sites. On this site, there are links to pages that give author birthdays, print biographies of authors, pronunciation guides, author interviews, and a large collection of author and illustrator websites.

To find out more about authors and illustrators on the World Wide Web, visit Chapter 2 on the companion website at **www.prenhall.com.darigan**

▼▼▼▼▼▼▼

The Pictures

In this age of visual bombardment—daily overloads of images on computer screens, in magazines, on television, at the movies, and on the roadside—do children need even more images in picture books? The answer is a resounding "Yes!" The problem is not having *too much* to see but in their learning to be discriminating in *what* they see. We use the term *visual literacy* to describe this sort of discrimination. More than in any other generation, today's children need to develop discretion about what they view. Picture books are a perfect vehicle for opening a child's eyes to the beauty and power of art because they do not function like other books in which words alone tell a story or convey information.

Illustrations in the better picture books share the function of storytelling or concept teaching. In fact, in wordless picture books the illustrations do the whole job. So the pictures beg for active participation in their viewing, unlike so many of the random images that are flashed daily in front of each of us. Text and illustration weave together to communicate. To get the full measure of meaning and fulfillment from a good picture book, the reader must attend carefully to both (Kiefer, 1995).

Through the beautifully crafted picture books available today, young readers not only can become aware of the variety of artistic styles, media, and techniques that artists employ but also can develop a sense for judging quality.

Developing the Ability to "See"

Adults tend to sell children short when it comes to their abilities to perceive the world. Our university students, who are of course adults, say things such as, "This artwork is too sophisticated for children. Won't they OD on this?" Truth be known, children are generally more visually aware and alert than most adults (McDermott, 1974). The older we get, the more our visual awareness is likely to be dulled by overload or by the real or imagined expectations our educational systems have imposed on us that alter the way we view images. Over time, honest responses to art and other visual stimuli tend to be programmed out of most children. They begin to ignore their own reactions to the fascinating detail in the art in order to second-guess what they are "supposed to see," thus becoming basically less aware. This process is not much different from analyzing poetry with children until the beauty is beaten out of it. Watch closely as a young child feasts on the beautiful and detailed illustrations in a good book. Watch as their eyes dart all over the page. That unharnessed verve toward the visual features of a book is what we want to nurture.

As the three of us have read to our own children and to our elementary classes over the years, they have shown us detail in picture book illustrations that our supposedly sophisticated adult eyes overlooked. For example, we had read Arnold Lobel's **On Market Street** many times but had not noticed that the figure representing *T* for toys in this alphabet book had on her hands puppets of the immensely popular Frog and Toad characters. That is, we did not notice them until a child pointed them out. Frog and Toad were made famous in Newbery and Caldecott Honor books created by Arnold Lobel—husband of Anita Lobel, who illustrated in **On Market Street.** Children have shown us that the church tower clock in each illustration in Mitsumasa Anno's **Anno's Counting Book** always points to the hour that corresponds with the number being presented. And it was young Luke who pointed out during a readaloud session that there was a wolf in every spread of Ed Young's **Lon Po Po**. Notice how Young deftly blended the wolf's head into the landscape in the first double-page spread (illustration 1 in the montage starting on page 46).

Illustration in picture books is meant to delight, to capture attention, to tell a story or teach a concept, and to develop appreciation and awareness in children. Of course, appreciation is developed in part by consistent exposure to the wonderful varieties of art that are coupled with pleasing stories in today's picture books. Young children begin to sense something special in good art when they see lots of it. For example, Quincy had seen many fine picture books in his six short years. When he was listening to a new book, Margaret Mahy's *17 Kings and 42 Elephants*, which has jewel-like batik on silk paintings by Patricia McCarthy, he suddenly interrupted to say, "Dad, these pictures are marvelous!" "Marvelous" was a bit unexpected coming from such a little body, but more amazing was his evaluative response to the artwork. Quincy didn't have the understanding or the words to analyze McCarthy's work, but he simply knew it was good stuff. How did he know? Because he'd seen so many picture books that he'd developed a level of appreciation that governed his taste in illustrations. Taste and appreciation come by comparison. Taste is broadened and cultivated by exposure; it is narrowed or allowed to lie fallow by restricting experience, and the picture book is often neglected (Kiefer, 1995, p. 10). Indeed, if all that children see in the world of art are Saturday morning cartoons, then such will be the standard of art for them.

Functions of Illustrations in Picture Books

"The function of art is to clarify, intensify, or otherwise enlarge our experience of life" (Canady, 1980, p. 21). This statement is as true for picture book illustrations as it is for gallery paintings, but picture book artwork also must operate in a manner unique to its special format. Because picture books are made up of a series of illustrations that typically tell a story, the art may function in one or more of the following ways.

Establish Setting

Art is a natural for creating the setting in an illustrated book. Time periods in historical stories or far-flung cultural settings can be brought to life through illustrations in ways words cannot do. Look at Lloyd Alexander's *The Fortune-Tellers* as an example. This is a universal story that could have been set in any number of places and times, but Trina Schart Hyman's illustrations allow the story to spring suddenly into a certain place and time—the west African country of Cameroon in what Hyman calls "the fantastical present" (personal communication, January 27, 1995).

Define and Develop Characters

Artists can give characters an extra fleshing out through illustrations. Through the artwork in *Ira Sleeps Over*, for example, we learn much about Ira's parents that is not revealed in the text. We see his parents' interesting and somewhat untraditional lifestyle, especially for the time when the book was published. For instance, in one illustration, Ira's father is cooking dinner. *Frog Goes to Dinner*, a wordless picture book, relies completely on illustrations to define and develop the characters. Mercer Mayer is a marvel when it comes to using facial expressions to communicate what his characters are feeling. Note double-page illustration number 2, page 46, in the illustration montage, of the angry family driving home after they had been thrown out of Fancy Restaurant. Each family member harbors an individual response to the disaster.

Reinforce Text

The primary function of some picture book illustrations is to reinforce the text. Nonfiction picture books often fall into this category, with the illustrations and diagrams restating visually what the words say. However, illustrations in a picture storybook may function primarily to reinforce the story. Notice illustration number 3 on page 46 from Robert McCloskey's ever popular *Blueberries for Sal*, for example, where readers see what the text describes—the countryside in Maine as well as the characters who are out picking blueberries—but no major extensions to the text are evident.

DID YOU KNOW?

Illustrator Trina Schart Hyman often uses her family and neighbors as models for her paintings. You may be interested to know that in *The Fortune-Tellers,* the carpenter and main character of the book shown on pages 42 and 43 is her son-in-law Eugene, and she has cleverly placed her daughter Katrin and grandson Michou to the right near the table. Under the shade of the cabana, you'll see Trina herself along with her ex-husband Harris while Lloyd sits alone to the right. Those of us who know and love Lloyd are well aware of his penchant for being a bit of a worrier . . . hence Trina put the vultures on the roof above his head.

From ***The Fortune-Tellers*** by Lloyd Alexander, illustrated by Trina Schart Hyman, copyright © 1992 by Lloyd Alexander, text illustrations copyright © 1992 by Trina Schart Hyman. Used by permission of Dutton Children's Books, a division of Penguin Putnam, Inc.

Provide a Differing Viewpoint

One of the most enjoyable ways in which illustrations may function in a picture book is that of telling a story different from the text or even being in opposition to the words. In Colin McNaughton's ***Suddenly!***, the text says that "Preston was walking home from school one day when SUDDENLY! Preston remembered his mother had asked him to go to the store." However, notice, on page 46 of the montage, illustration 4 tells another tale: A wolf, never mentioned in the narrative, lurks near Preston and is somehow frustrated every time he pounces forward to make Preston his dinner.

Peter Spier's ***Oh, Were They Ever Happy*** is an example of words and text that are humorously in opposition to one another. Children, inadvertently left alone for the day (the baby-sitter has her days confused and doesn't show), decide to do something nice for their parents—paint the house. The words say "Neat job" and "Pretty color!" but the illustrations show what a horrible mess the kids are making. They paint the bricks and windowpanes; they finish one color of paint and take up another. Similarly, in Burningham's ***Come Away from the Water, Shirley***, the only words come from Shirley's parents, who nag her constantly to keep clean and stay safe during their day at the beach. In contrast, the illustrations show Shirley tuning out her parents' admonitions while her imagination takes her on a seaside adventure battling pirates.

Provide Interesting Asides

Sometimes picture book illustrations will be filled with interesting asides—subplots or details not necessarily related to the main story line. For example, many of Mitsumasa

"Better and better!" said the carpenter. "And shall we have a long life together?"

"The longest," replied the fortune-teller, again peering into the crystal ball. "Only one thing might cut it short: an early demise."

"Wonderful!" cried the carpenter. "Thank you, master seer, thank you."

With that, he left the fortune-teller and hurried homeward, impatient for all these good things to happen.

He had scarcely gone halfway when he thought of a dozen more questions he was burning to ask. So he turned around and ran back as fast as he could.

Anno's books employ this technique. In the wordless picture book ***Anno's Journey***, the main focus is a traveler whose journey takes him on horseback through the countryside, towns, and cities of historical Europe. A careful examination of the busy illustrations shows all sorts of wonderful surprises: fairy tale characters and famous historical figures blending into crowds of people, entertaining but brief human dramas such as a hotly contested foot race. You can even see his suggestion of Georges Seurat's *Sunday Afternoon on the Island of La Grande Jatte*. See for yourself in illustration number 5 on page 47.

Extend or Develop the Plot

The plot of a story may be advanced by illustrations. In wordless picture books, the whole plot is unfolded through pictures. Sometimes the plot is merely extended or rounded a little by the illustrations, as in Stephen Gammell's art in ***The Relatives Came***, seen in illustration number 6 on page 47. Gammell shows that one family's journey to a family reunion is a bit perilous because Dad isn't such a good driver. Although Cynthia Rylant's words say nothing about the driving, Dad levels the mailbox on the way out, loses suitcases, careens around mountain curves, and destroys their relatives' fence upon arrival.

Establish Mood

Illustrations are extremely effective in determining the mood of a picture storybook. ***The Polar Express***, by Chris Van Allsburg, is a Christmas story, and Christmas stories typically use a bright and cheery palette. The mood in Van Allsburg's story, however, is mysterious, and he uses dark colors to establish that mood. With muted reds and blues and even muted yellows along with plenty of black and brown, the artist creates an eerie feeling as a young boy watches a magical train steam its way into his front yard late Christmas Eve. The mood is maintained as the train whisks him and other children toward the North Pole, zipping past dark forests filled with wolves, as seen in illustration 7 on page 47.

Style and Media in Picture Book Illustrations

Artists are able to use a vast array of styles and media to create the illustrations in children's books today, partly because the technology of camera color separations makes reproducing sophisticated artwork feasible. In fact, some of the best and most varied artwork being done today appears in picture books. We know a professional artist who regularly checks the children's section at the public library to see what's new in picture books because he believes the best contemporary work is to be found there.

Styles in Art

Excellent artwork can, of course, be rendered in various styles, ranging from extremely realistic to abstract. Styles in children's artwork mirror many of the various art movements of the past and include realism, surrealism, expressionism, impressionism, naïve, and cartoon art.

Realism, or *representational,* style is a faithful reproduction of nature, people, and objects as they actually appear. The illustration in Paul O. Zelinsky's **Rapunzel** found on page 47 is representational.

Surrealism, simply stated, is realism skewed, often with unexpected details added. Take, for example, Anthony Browne's **Willy the Dreamer,** illustration number 9 on page 47. An easy chair with a stone base floating above an ocean teeming with bananas and a ship in a bottle on the horizon are all surrealistic qualities that make Browne's composition irresistible and beg us to look closer.

Expressionism, which is an attempt to give objective expression to inner experience, often makes use of bright colors and figures that are a bit disproportionate. This stylized form is evident in Vera B. Williams's **A Chair for My Mother,** as seen in illustration number 10 on page 48.

Another popular style is *impressionism,* which emphasizes light, movement, and usually color over detail. A fine example of impressionism is Emily Arnold McCully's Caldecott-winning **Mirette & Bellini Cross Niagara Falls,** seen in illustration number 11 on page 48 of the montage.

Naïve is a style that gives the appearance of being childish, perhaps lacking perspective or a sense of proportion. One of America's legendary naïve artists is Anna Mary Robertson Moses, better known as Grandma Moses. Her life, memoirs, and work are beautifully reviewed in W. Nikola-Lisa's simple book **The Year with Grandma Moses,** sampled in illustration number 12 on page 48.

There are, of course, other artistic styles, including *cartoon art,* as found in William Steig's **Pete's a Pizza.**

Use of Media

The various styles artists use to create their artwork may be rendered in a variety of artistic media. There are basically two categories of media: painterly and graphic.

Painterly media include the most common art materials, such as paint, pencil, and ink. In **Rapunzel,** Zelinsky used *oil paints,* an opaque layering of colors. Watercolors, which are translucent, were the medium for Wiesner's paintings in **Sector 7,** seen in illustration number 13 in the montage.

Chris Van Allsburg used *graphite,* or *pencil,* another painterly medium, in **The Widow's Broom,** seen in illustration number 14 on page 49.

For an enjoyable retrospective of different artistic styles over the years, you may want to introduce Anthony Browne's ***Willy's Pictures*** to your class. Browne adds surreal qualities to some of the greatest paintings of all time, maintaining the essence of the work with his characteristic twist. A pull-out section at the end of the book allows us to view the original artwork for comparison. You may also want to show and discuss Allen Say's ***The Sign Painter***. Both of these books present variations of Edward Hopper's *Early Sunday Morning* in unique ways.

Also in this category are *pen and ink,* which Rachel Isadora used in her classic ***Ben's Trumpet,*** seen in illustration number 15 on page 49 of the montage.

Other painterly media include the following: *colored pencils, pastels* (chalk), *charcoal, crayons, felt-tip markers, gouache* and *tempera* (opaque water-based paints), and *acrylics* (plastic paints).

Illustrator Floyd Cooper uses multiple media as he applies a thin wash of oil on illustration board. Then, using a common kneaded eraser, he rubs away the paint, thereby leaving the image. The softened effect that remains is then enhanced by Cooper with colored pencil, pastel, and inks to create stunning pictures with a grainy, ethereal flavor. As you look at illustration 16 of the montage, from Jane Yolen's ***Miz Berlin Walks,*** notice the skin of the girl on the right: The effect is created by the texture of the board showing through the oil wash. Note further that the flowers on her dress were applied after the oil had dried.

Artists apply their media directly to canvas, paper, or some other surface. Stefano Vitale works exclusively on wood, as shown in this cover of Angela Shelf Medearis's book ***Too Much Talk!*** in illustration number 17 of the montage.

But when artists use *graphic media,* they generally create the artwork elsewhere before applying it to the final surface. With *woodcuts,* for instance, the artist carves images in relief into a block of wood. Then inks or paints are applied to the wood and transferred to a surface such as paper. *Linoleum cuts* are similar in technique to woodcuts, but they produce a cleaner line, as in Mary Wormell's ***Hilda Hen's Scary Night,*** seen in illustration 18 on page 49.

Collage, another popular graphic technique, involves cutting and tearing shapes from paper or fabric and arranging them on the page, as in Ed Young's ***Seven Blind Mice*** in illustration 19. Collage may also include other objects that are attached to the surface, such as the breakfast cereal and wire hangers in David Diaz's illustrations for Eve Bunting's ***Smoky Night.*** David Wisniewski's dramatic illustrations in ***The Golem,*** created by overlaying intricate paper cutouts, are a sophisticated form of collage, seen in illustration number 20 on page 50 of the montage.

A graphic medium that looks a bit like pen and ink drawings is called *scratchboard.* A black ink coating is scratched away to show the white surface beneath; color may be added after the "drawing" is complete, as in ***Iron Horses*** by Verla Kay and illustrated by Michael McCurdy, sampled in illustration 21, page 50.

Even *photography* can be considered a graphic technique. Bruce McMillan's ***Mouse Views: What the Class Pet Saw*** uses color photography to give children a fresh look at their world. See for yourself in illustration 22 on page 50.

Artists will often mix media, using both graphic and painterly techniques together. A prime example is Molly Bang's ***The Paper Crane,*** seen in illustration 23 of the montage, which uses three-dimensional paper cutouts, traditional collage, and painterly techniques. Then each page was photographed to retain its three-dimensional quality.

The Pictures

The following illustrations accompany the discussion text and are meant to help you develop the ability to "see."

1. From *Lon Po Po,* by Ed Young

2. From *Frog Goes to Dinner,* by Mercer Mayer

The Purposes

Define and Develop Character

3. From *Blueberries for Sal* by Robert McCloskey

4. From *Suddenly!* by Colin McNaughton

Provide a Different Point of View

Provide Interesting Asides

5. From *Anno's Journey* by Mitsumasa Anno

Extend or Develop Text

6. From *The Relatives Came* by Cynthia Rylant, illustrated by Stephen Gammell

Establish Mood

7. From *The Polar Express* by Chris Van Allsburg

The Styles

Realism

8. From *Rapunzel* by Paul O. Zelinski

Surrealism

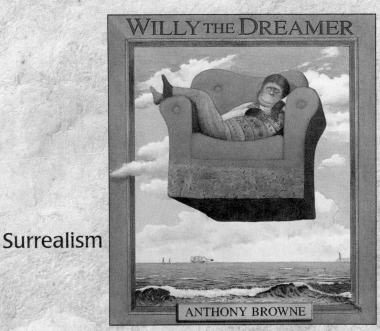

9. From *Willy the Dreamer* by Anthony Browne

Expressionism

10. From *A Chair for My Mother* by Vera B. Williams

Naïve

12. From *The Year with Grandma Moses* by W. Nikola-Lisa

Impressionism

11. From *Mirette & Bellini Cross Niagara Falls* by Emily Arnold McCully

The Media

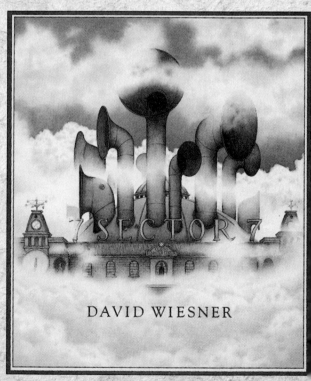

Watercolor

13. From *Sector 7* by David Wiesner

Multiple Media

Graphite

16. From *Miz Berlin Walks* by Jane Yolen, illustrated by Floyd Cooper

14. From *The Widow's Broom* by Chris Van Allsburg

Painterly Media on Wood

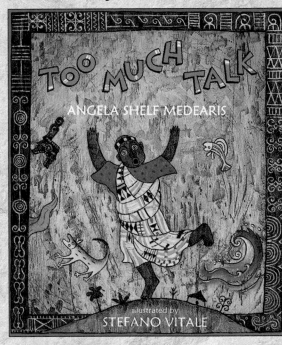

17. From *Too Much Talk!* by Angela Shelf Medearis, illustrated by Stefano Vitale

Pen and Ink

Linoleum Cuts

15. From *Ben's Trumpet* by Rachel Isadora

18. From *Hilda Hen's Scary Night* by Mary Wormell

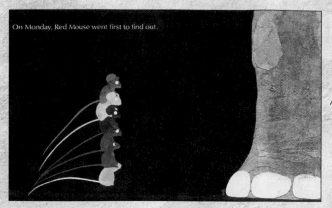

19. From *Seven Blind Mice* by Ed Young

Collage

20. From *Golem* by David Wisniewski

Scratchboard

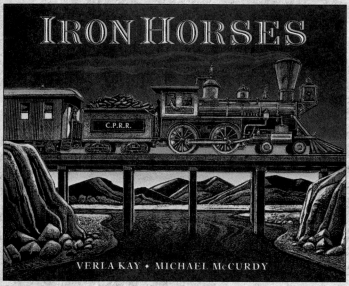

21. From *Iron Horses* by Verla Kay, illustrated by Michael McCurdy

Photography

Mixed Media

It happened just as the stranger had said. The owner had only to clap his hands and the paper crane became a living bird, flew down to the floor, and danced.

23. From *The Paper Crane* by Molly Bank

22. From *Mouse Views: What the Class Pet Saw* by Bruce McMillan

Line

24. From *Lost! A Story in String* by Paul Fleischman, illustrated by C. B. Mordan

25. From *Little Gold Star: A Spanish American Cinderella Tale* by Robert D. San Souci, illustrated by Sergio Martinez

Shape

26. From *Round Trip* by Ann Jonas

Color

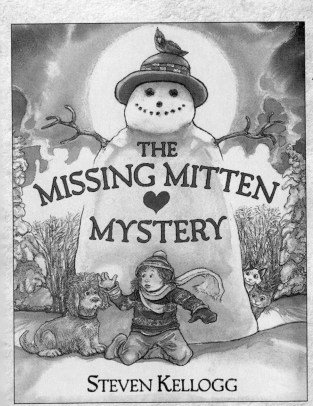

27. From *The Missing Mitten Mystery* by Steven Kellogg

28. From *St. George and the Dragon* by Margaret Hodges, illustrated by Trina Schart Hyman

51

29. From *Tuesday* by David Weisner

Composition

31. From *The Hunter* by Mary
Casanova, illustrated by Ed Young

Action and Detail

30. From *Deep in the Forest* by Brinton Turkle

32. From *The Secret of the Stones* by Robert D. San Souci, illustrated by James Ransome

33. From *Tops & Bottoms* by Janet Stevens

Book Design

34. From *Deep in the Forest* by Brinton Turkle

Visual Elements

Like all artists, picture book illustrators incorporate several visual elements into the creation of their pictures that subtly affect the way we respond to the art. These elements are line, shape, color, texture, and composition.

Line

Lines in illustrations are either curved or straight and may vary in thickness or length. They may run horizontally, diagonally, or vertically. They may be solid or broken. How line is used often plays an important role in what a picture communicates. For instance, notice in illustration 24 on page 51 how illustrator C. B. Mordan uses only line in his cover to **Lost! A Story in String,** by Paul Fleischman, to represent the trees, their shadows, the young girl, and her staff. The trees' shadows dissolve into a vanishing point placed somewhere off to the top right of the drawing, and the circular footsteps in the snow clearly indicate that this child is, indeed, lost. Further, the line of the trees' shadows, as well as the direction in which the girl is facing, all indicate movement to the right, beckoning us to open the book and begin reading.

Similarly, the dominant vertical lines of the trees in illustration 7 on p. 47, from Van Allsburg's **The Polar Express,** create a static look, as if this scene were a photograph capturing and arresting a moment in the flow of action. On the other hand, horizontal lines may suggest order or tranquillity.

Artists also use line to direct the viewer's eye. Sergio Martinez uses the line of the staircase to direct our eye back to the mansion of Don Miguel in **Little Gold Star: A Spanish American Cinderella Tale,** by Robert D. San Souci, as seen in illustration 25, page 51. Turning left at the top of the stairs, we are encouraged to enter the portals of the front door and back into the fiesta for feasting and dancing.

Shape

Shape is the two-dimensional form representing an object. Shapes may be simple or complex. The objects may be readily recognizable or so abstract that they are difficult to recognize. Curved shapes generally suggest things found in nature, and angular shapes depict objects built by humans. For example, illustration 26, page 51, from **Round Trip,** by Ann Jonas, shows from one perspective people sitting in a movie theater. Neither the theater nor the humans are clearly recognizable, only suggested by the shapes. The man-made items (seats, lights, screen) are angular forms, and the people are suggested by rounded forms representing heads.

Color

Color is a visual element with these traits: hue, value, and saturation. *Hue* is simply the color itself (red, blue, yellow), and is often categorized as either cool (blue, green, violet) or warm (red, yellow, orange). The cover of Steven Kellogg's **The Missing Mitten Mystery,** shown in illustration 27, page 51, uses a variety of shades of blue to create the crisp, cold feel of winter.

Value is the lightness or darkness of the color (dark blue, light green), achieved by adding black or white to the hue. As discussed earlier in this chapter, the mood of a picture may be manipulated by value, as in the mysterious mood achieved by the dark palette Van Allsburg used in **The Polar Express.** Finally, *saturation*, or *chroma*, is the brightness or dullness of a color. For example, the brightness of the colors in the picture from **The Fortune-Tellers,** illustrated by Trina Schart Hyman, creates a festive atmosphere, and the muted hues in Margaret Hodges's **Saint George and the Dragon,** shown in illustration 28 on page 51, add an appropriately ancient feeling to the story.

Illustrations also may be achromatic, rendered only in black, white, and the various shades of gray in between. See, for example, the illustrations from Mayer's **Frog Goes to Dinner** (p. 46) and Isadora's **Ben's Trumpet** (p. 49), where the illustrators rely on black and whites. On the other hand, monochromatic illustration, the use of only one hue such as the different values of brown, is represented in the previously mentioned **The Widow's Broom,** by Van Allsburg (p. 49).

Texture

Texture is a tactile sensation communicated by the artist: rough, smooth, hard, soft, and so on. Collage, as discussed earlier, is the most obvious way of creating texture in illustrations because of its three-dimensional qualities. The cutout crane in *The Paper Crane,* for instance, clearly has the sharp edges of a folded paper bird. However, illustrators most often create a sense of texture on a two-dimensional surface, as with the fabric of the automobile seats in *Frog Goes to Dinner.* Mercer Mayer used cross-hatching (the crossing of lines) to produce the coarse texture of the material in both the seats and the boy's suit.

Composition

Composition is the visual element that unifies all of the elements in an illustration.

> In arranging the elements on each page, including the printed type, the artist tries to obtain an effective balance between unity and variety and creates visual patterns that may be carried on from page to page. (Kiefer, 1995, p. 129)

For example, an artist may balance objects in an illustration by distributing them either evenly (symmetrically) or irregularly (asymmetrically). Another facet of composition concerns what is known as *object dominance:* Artists can ensure that certain shapes are dominant by making them larger or brighter in order to attract the eye. In illustration 29 from the montage from *Tuesday,* David Wiesner splits the picture evenly down the center from top to bottom. After the area's frogs have magically gained the ability to fly one Tuesday night, the remnant of their adventures is being investigated by the authorities as well as the press. The backgrounds of both sides of this illustration are balanced by the careful yet irregular placement of vehicles, people, and clouds. However, the police detective in the foreground is larger than any other individual and thus is the dominant figure. In this way, Wiesner directs the viewer's attention to the detective's actions. Because this book centers on these magical amphibians, take a second look at the clouds and see what you notice.

Further Evaluating Children's Book Illustration

According to Cianciolo (1976, p. 9), in quality picture book art "something of significance is said." In inferior picture books, the art all begins to look the same—flat line and color washes, as in books like the Sesame Street titles and most things from Disney (Hearne 1990). In other words, quality picture book art is individual and unique. Stereotypical artwork denies individuality, both in the artistic rendering and in the characters and settings represented. It is more difficult to relate to the human experience and to get involved with the story when the art depicts generic or stereotypical people and places. For example, Whitney Darrow's *I'm Glad I'm a Boy! I'm Glad I'm a Girl!* shows insipid girls and powerful boys who are devoid of other personality traits. The generic, flat line illustrations accompany text such as "Boys invent things. Girls use what boys invent." Together, illustrations and text go beyond the uninspiring to drop negative stereotyping to a new low.

Action and Detail

In better picture book illustrations, two basic elements tend to give individuality to the illustrations: action and detail. Action is important in picture storybooks in particular because the artwork moves the story along. Note illustration 30, page 52, from Brinton Turkle's *Deep in the Forest,* a role reversal version of "Goldilocks and the Three Bears." This scene freezes the action at the climax, but the illustration is by no means static. The tilt of the human forms as they barrel forward in pursuit and the wild-eyed little bear with fully stretched body and churning legs create for us a true sense of the chaotic, frenzied chase.

Sometimes action in illustrations is subtle but nevertheless suggests a great deal of activity. For example, in *Tuesday,* the police detective examines a lily pad suspended from a pencil, his quizzical look suggesting his mental activity. "Why and how?" he seems to ask himself, unable to fathom the hundreds of frogs who invaded the night-time sanctity of his town on flying lily pads. (See illustration 29 on p. 52.)

One of the ways picture book artists create tension in their work is by using illustrations to anticipate or foreshadow action. Look at the illustration we already noted from *Suddenly!* Preston is totally unaware of the wolf who is lurking just behind him and ready to pounce. We, as readers, are privy to this danger based only on his enormous shadow on the wall while the little pig happily trots along.

Certainly it is not difficult to see that details in illustrations tend to give the artwork depth and allow artists to assert their individuality. But even the power of a carefully placed line can make loosely drawn pictures say volumes. Consider illustration 31, page 52, from Mary Casanova's book *The Hunter,* illustrated by Caldecott Medal winner Ed Young. It is Young's spare use of line, the open mouth, and the wide-open, surprised eye that allow us to feel the hunter's surprise. A design feature that enhances this book is that the background is a matte finish while all the black lines and red highlights in the letters are glossy, accenting the lines even more.

Detail is evident in the use of perspective in many quality picture books. In illustration 32, page 52, Robert D. San Souci's *The Secret of the Stones,* the artist, James Ransome, shows a single scene from two very different perspectives. As they are walking home from the fields after a long day's work, John and Clara, a childless couple, come upon two white stones lying on the road. Thinking that she will use them to sharpen her knives, Clara puts them near the front door and forgets about them. But the next day, on return from the fields, they are surprised to find that all their chores have been mysteriously done. They learn that those two stones were really two children transformed by a powerful conjure man, and if they want to keep the children, they have to retrieve three things from him. Because his magic is so strong, John and Clara are both scared. Ransome first shows the couple from the back, looking in at the cabin, and the next scene shows the same view as if the conjure man was looking at them from his own front stoop.

This detail may seem a small thing, but the dual perspective provides a setting with depth and makes it a believable place. Obviously, Ransome envisioned this scene carefully and translated it into his illustrations, giving us a clear sense of being there.

Careful attention to detail often requires extensive research before an artist begins work on the illustrations. Depending on the book, illustrators may spend untold hours investigating the historical details of Ming Dynasty culture, the anatomy of wolves, or rain forest botany, for example. Trina Schart Hyman's illustrations for *Saint George and the Dragon* include drawings, primarily in borders surrounding the text, of plants and flowers indigenous to Britain during those magical times. In other illustrations in the book, you will note in the borders "white campion, one of the most ancient of wildflowers, introduced in Neolithic times. It is common in the fields and hedgerows of England" (Kiefer, 1995, p. 109).

In researching his book *Make Way for Ducklings,* Robert McCloskey filled notebooks with artistic studies of ducks—sketches of wing extensions and so on (Schmidt 1990). He even had ducks swimming in his bathtub and walking about his apartment to use as ready references. But, as Lee Bennett Hopkins states in his book *Pauses: Autobiographical Reflections of 101 Creators of Children's Books,* "The ducks never stood still. I had to slow them down somehow so I could make the sketches. The only thing that worked was red wine. They loved it and went into slow motion right away" (p. 128). In the videocassette *The Lively Art of Picture Books* (1965), McCloskey points out that even after he had spent the time to examine a tree from twig to branch to trunk to root, the examination may not be apparent to the viewer of the artistically rendered tree, but the tree was better for his having thought of it in such detail.

Indeed, detail is often subtle. In fact, most artistic devices are like cosmetics: They must not be too noticeable or they are not doing their job. Makeup, for instance, must enhance so that we say, "What a gorgeous face," not "What great eye shadow." A device that Maurice Sendak used in ***Where the Wild Things Are*** is so subtle that most readers don't notice they are being influenced by it. As Max's anger grows, so do the illustrations, getting larger and larger until they fill a full double-page spread. Then as Max's anger cools, the illustrations begin to shrink.

Book Design

Finally, the process of fine bookmaking gives us a few other evaluative considerations: The trim size and shape of books, choice of inside and cover fonts, and overall cover design are all scrupulously taken into account so that the match between the text, art, and design enhances the final product. For example, Janet Stevens has done some very interesting things in her Caldecott Honor book ***Tops & Bottoms***, as shown in illustration 33, page 53. Notice that the cover art appears to be situated sideways. In fact, the entire book is designed to be read "top to bottom." The story, a trickster tale with roots in European folktales as well as in slave stories from the American South, finds clever Hare tricking lazy Bear who wants to do no work—only reap the benefits of his bountiful land and crops. Mr. and Mrs. Hare concoct a plan that allows them to choose either the tops or bottoms of the plants in payment for doing all the weeding and harvesting. Notice how Stevens aptly sets the stage for this trickery on the full title page by using the gutter of the book as the separation point between top and bottom.

Other book design elements can set quality publications apart from the mundane. For example, the rainbow trail, a significant recurring design on Pueblo Native American pottery and other art forms, becomes a unifying factor as it leads the reader through ***Arrow to the Sun,*** by Gerald McDermott. Ann Jonas's ***Round Trip*** is designed to be read as a round trip: The illustrations are ingeniously created so that when we reach the end of the book, we flip it upside down and read it back to front. All the illustrations suddenly transform into new pictures, an optical illusion of sorts. At the same time, the round-trip theme is a part of the story—a trip into the city and home again.

Even small details like decorated endpapers enhance the visual appeal of a picture book. The endpapers inside the cover of a book actually bind the book to the cover and were traditionally white. However, not only are endpapers often brightly colored in many of today's books, but they often are illustrated, sometimes with original pieces not found inside. Good examples are the two original paintings by Jerry Pinkney in his ***Aesop's Fables***. The front endpapers show the tale of the "Tortoise and the Hare" and the back endpapers depict "Belling the Cat."

Other illustrative techniques extend art beyond the traditional designs. For example, Hyman's borders in ***Saint George and the Dragon*** give the look of observing the story through an old-fashioned window (see p. 51). Brinton Turkle's inclusion of art on the title and copyright pages is an important part of the storytelling process in ***Deep in the Forest,*** seen in illustration 34, page 53. These pages typically contain art only as embellishment or have none at all. Yet Turkle starts telling his story on the full title page, where the bear cub steps out of his safe environment to begin an adventure.

All these elements of picture book creation and production are what make the visual storytelling and concept teaching process so successful. Children have available to them some of the best of the current artistic endeavor. As teachers and parents, we have the opportunity to help our children become visually literate through fine picture books, to curb the numbing effects of mindless television viewing. Our charge is to offer our children the best in picture and in word, to give them an arsenal for making judgments and developing taste.

▼▼▼▼▼▼▼

Children's Books: History and Trends

Not until the 17th century did the notion of childhood dawn in the history of our Western world. The English philosopher John Locke influenced the prevailing attitudes

To find out more about Ezra Jack Keats and other authors and illustrators of classic children's books, visit Chapter 2 on the companion website at **www.prenhall.com/darigan**

BOOKMARK

INTEGRATING TECHNOLOGY: AUTHORS ON THE WORLD WIDE WEB

Among the many sites devoted to authors of classic children's books, one of the best conceived is the virtual exhibit of *Ezra Jack Keats.* The exhibit includes dummies, type-scripts, and original illustrations from seven of the "Peter" books (including ***The Snowy Day, Whistle for Willie,*** and ***Peter's Chair***) along with a biography of Keats. The site provides interesting historical information and, more importantly, it presents the process and ideas that go into the creation of a picture book. The section of the web-site entitled "The Making of a Keats Picture Book" presents a nice introduction to the book-making process and provides a context for the archival documents from the Peter books.

about children as much as anyone in his time. Locke's book *Some Thoughts Concerning Education,* published in 1693, suggested gentler ways of raising children. He even suggested that children's books be made available, books that were easy and pleasant to read. However, *childhood* was a concept held only among the affluent until well into the 20th century. As in the days before Locke, many children in both England and the United States continued to be treated as if they were small adults. Consider that child labor laws were not legislated until well into the 20th century in both countries. Kids dressed, worked, and lived like their adult counterparts, if that well. Therefore, within the general populace, the idea of special books for children was slow in coming.

Early Books for Children

As far back as the Middle Ages, books intended for young-sters existed in limited numbers in the form of handwritten texts available to only the extremely wealthy. However, be-cause literature aimed at young readers has reflected and al-ways will reflect society's attitudes about children, these early books were meant to indoctrinate. Most stories were available not in books but from the storytellers—fairy tales, myths, ballads, epics, and other stories from our oral tradi-tion. Of course, these stories were not meant for children, although they were allowed to listen. Over time, these mag-ical tales have become the property of childhood.

By the same token, books that were published in the early days of the printing press, books meant for adults, were also enjoyed and adopted by children. William Caxton, an English businessman and printer, produced several such books, including *Aesop's Fables,* which was decorated with woodcut illustrations. From that time forward, children have claimed many books meant for adult audiences, in-cluding such well-known titles as Daniel Defoe's *Robinson Crusoe,* Jonathan Swift's *Gulliver's Travels,* Johann Wyss's *The Swiss Family Robinson,* Walter Scott's *Ivanhoe,* and J. R. R. Tolkien's *The Hobbit.*

Literature intended specifically for children and pub-lished from the 15th through the 17th centuries still was de-signed to indoctrinate. The so-called hornbooks, or lesson paddles, existed as reading material for children for more than two centuries, beginning in the 1440s. Generally made of wood, these small paddles (about 3 by 5 inches) had pasted to them pieces of parchment on which were printed the alphabet, verses from the Bible, and the like. The term *hornbook* comes from the thin, transparent sheet of cow horn that covered and protected the parchment. Hornbooks were particularly popular among the Puritans in Colonial America, who believed children to be basically wicked, like adults, and therefore in need of saving. This pious attitude is clearly evident in the first book published for American children, John Cotton's catechism called *Spiritual Milk for Boston Babes in Either England, Drawn from the Breasts of Both Testaments for Their Souls' Nourishment.* First published in England in 1646, it was revised and published in America in 1656.

Despite the preachy, often unpleasant nature of children's literature in the early days of printing, one especially bright spot appeared in 1657: Johann Amos Comenius, a Moravian teacher and bishop, wrote *Orbis Pictus (The World in Pictures),* which is often called the first children's picture book. *Orbis Pictus* is filled with woodcut illustrations that work in harmony with the simple text to describe the wonders of the natural world.

In 1697, Charles Perrault, who had set about collecting the French fairy tales, published his enduring collection, *Tales of Mother Goose,* which included such old favorites as "The Sleeping Beauty" and "Cinderella." Here we find the first mention of Mother Goose, a figure popularized in many subsequent books and stories. Although Perrault's stories were popular with adults in the court of King Louis XIV, his fairy tale collection contains a frontispiece showing an old woman (presumably Mother Goose) telling stories to a group of children.

Even as early as the 16th century, a form of "underground" reading became popular. Called *chapbooks,* these crudely printed booklets were often sold by peddlers for pennies. Chapbooks became extremely popular in the 17th and 18th centuries and were the first real break from the oppressive, didactic, you-are-a-sinner books for children. Of course, the Puritans decried these tales of Robin Hood, King Arthur, and even an early rendition of "Froggie Went A-Courting." Yet, children and adults reveled in them, though often on the sly.

Chapbooks may have been indirectly responsible for what is perhaps the most important development in the history of children's literature—John Newbery's children's publishing house. Certainly Newbery was influenced by John Locke, who dared suggest that youngsters should enjoy reading, so it seems likely that he observed the popularity of chapbooks among children and decided that there was a market for true children's books. In any case, Newbery ushered in the age of children's books by beginning to publish exclusively for young readers. He released his first children's book in 1744. *A Pretty Little Pocket-Book* taught the alphabet not with catechism but with entertaining games, rhymes, and fables. Newbery published hundreds of titles (some of which he may have written himself), the most famous and enduring of which is *The History of Little Goody Two Shoes.* So great was Newbery's contribution to children's publishing that the oldest of the world's children's book prizes bears his name, America's John Newbery Medal. Nevertheless, the moralistic tale continued to dominate much of children's literature, even to a certain extent in Newbery's books.

Children's Books Come of Age

Folk and Fairy Tales

The beginning of the 19th century brought some of the most influential, honest, and lasting children's stories into print. Jacob and Wilhelm Grimm collected from oral sources the German variants of the folk and fairy tales and retold them in their *Household Tales,* which appeared in 1812 and included "Snow White" and "Rumpelstiltskin." Some of Hans Christian Andersen's original fairy tales were published in 1835 in a volume titled *Fairy Tales Told for Children.* The stories of this Danish author, such as "The Ugly Duckling" and "The Emperor's New Clothes," remain popular to this day.

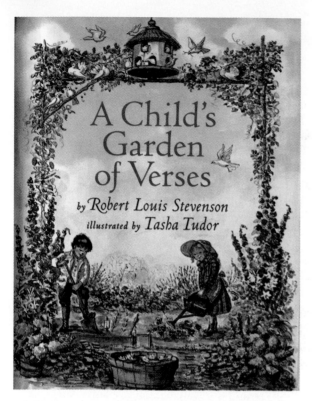

Reprinted with the permission of Simon & Schuster Books for Young Readers, an imprint of Simon & Schuster Children's Publishing Division from *A Child's Garden of Verses* by Robert Louis Stevenson, illustrated by Tasha Tudor. First Simon & Schuster books for Young Readers Edition, 1981. Revised format edition, 1999.

In Poetry

One of the century's greatest contributions to verse for children came from England. Edward Lear's **A Book of Nonsense,** a collection of outrageous limericks, became an immediate best-seller. Lear made the limerick famous, and it remains a favorite verse form among today's children. Robert Louis Stevenson's **A Child's Garden of Verses** is another poetry collection that children still love today.

Novels of the 19th Century

A number of noteworthy books surfaced during the second half of the 19th century. Fantasy novels emerged with the publication of such greats as *The Water Babies* by Charles Kingsley in 1884 and, of course, Lewis Carroll's (Charles Dodgson) **Alice's Adventures in Wonderland** in 1865. Other noteworthy titles include **At the Back of the North Wind** by George MacDonald, **The Adventures of Pinocchio** by Carlo Collodi, and the novels of Jules Verne, which mark the advent of the science fiction genre. Beginning with his **Journey to the Center of the Earth** in 1864, Verne created stories meant for adults but happily embraced by young readers.

Stories about contemporary life were especially preachy and pious until a monumental children's novel made its debut in 1868. **Little Women,** by Louisa May Alcott, was like a breath of fresh air, with its lively characters whose actions, words, and feelings reflected honest human experiences. The character of Jo March, for example, deviated radically from female characters of the past who were docile and certainly inferior to their male counterparts. In fact, Jo was something of a rebel, an early feminist, who railed constantly against what she considered the false set of standards dictated by the Victorian code of behavior.

Little Women set the course for many realistic novels that immediately followed its publication, including several more from Alcott herself. A few years later came Mark Twain's (Samuel Clemens) **The Adventures of Tom Sawyer** and Robert Louis Stevenson's **Treasure Island,** which was serialized in the magazine *Young Folks,* then published as a book in 1883. The last decade of the 19th century gave us Rudyard Kipling's masterpiece, **The Jungle Book.**

The Impact of Magazines

A number of magazines for children began publication during the 19th century. *St. Nicholas Magazine,* published in the United States starting in 1873, set standards of excellence in the world of children's literature. It was edited by Mary Mapes Dodge, author of **Hans Brinker, Or the Silver Skates.** The best-known children's authors and illustrators contributed to *St. Nicholas,* and several novels appeared first in the magazine in serialized form, including **Jo's Boys,** by Louisa May Alcott, **Sara Crewe,** by Frances Hodgson Burnett, and **The Jungle Book,** by Rudyard Kipling.

Book Illustration

Illustration of children's books also came of age during the 19th century. Illustrators gained status as printing techniques improved and color illustrations became more common. Publishers enticed well-known artists, such as George Cruikshank, who illustrated *Grimm's Fairy Tales* in 1823, to produce work for children's books. The artwork by the immortal Victorian-age illustrators in Great Britain, such as Randolph

To find out more about this and other historical collections on the WWW, visit Chapter 2 on the companion website at **www.prenhall.com/darigan**

BOOKMARK

INTEGRATING TECHNOLOGY: HISTORICAL COLLECTIONS ON THE WORLD WIDE WEB

Many libraries and organizations have used the World Wide Web quite effectively to make their historical collections accessible to the public. *Picturing Childhood,* an on-line version of the catalog produced to accompany an exhibition held at UCLA, is a wonderful introduction to the history of illustrated literature for children. Beautiful scanned images from Gustav Dore, Walter Crane, and many other figures of historical illustrated books accompany the text, making this a rich, informative site.

Caldecott, Kate Greenaway, and Walter Crane, rival the fine work being done today, in spite of comparatively primitive color printing methods. So influential were these artists that two major awards for children's book illustration today bear their names: the Randolph Caldecott Medal in the United States and the Kate Greenaway Medal in Britain. Randolph Caldecott is often noted as the first illustrator to show action in pictures, as evidenced in *The Diverting History of John Gilpin,* which has perhaps his best-remembered illustrations. In fact, the Caldecott Medal affixed to winning picture books is engraved with the most famous scene, John Gilpin's wild ride. American Howard Pyle also created stunning illustrations for classics like *The Merry Adventures of Robin Hood of Great Reknown,* which he also wrote.

20th-Century Children's Books

And so the domain of children's books, which began with groundbreaking books we still cherish today, was firmly established by the dawning of the 20th century. First was the birth of the modern picture storybook. Before Beatrix Potter wrote and illustrated her enduring story, **The Tale of Peter Rabbit,** illustrations in books for children, beautiful as they were, were primarily decorations. Potter incorporated colored illustration with text, page for page, thus using the pictures as well as the words to tell the story. Therefore, Beatrix Potter is considered the mother of the modern picture storybook, and *Peter Rabbit* is the firstborn.

Another first that occurred early in the 20th century was the publishing in 1900 of L. Frank Baum's **The Wonderful Wizard of Oz.** Modern fantasy had been primarily the domain of the Europeans, especially the British. **The Wonderful Wizard of Oz** was the first classic modern fantasy written by an American.

Many other enduring classics emerged in the first part of the century, such as J. M. Barrie's magical **Peter Pan in Kensington Gardens,** which was adapted in 1906 into a book from its original form as a play, and Lucy Maud Montgomery's 1908 Canadian classic, **Anne of Green Gables,** featuring the spunky, red-headed Anne Shirley. Also in 1908,

As a tribute to Frank Baum's seminal work, Peter Glassman has assembled a retrospective of various writers and artists who express their personal reactions in word and art in **Oz: The Hundredth Anniversary Celebration.** Thirty children's literature luminaries fill this book with illustrations and comments about how the book affected them. You could do the same in your own classroom by producing a book that contains children's similar contributions.

the granddaddy of animal fantasies appeared: Kenneth Grahame's ***The Wind in the Willows*** became the standard for all subsequent animal fantasy stories. Another trend-setting fantasy, A. A. Milne's gentle story of ***Winnie-the-Pooh***, was published in 1926.

Early-20th-Century Picture Books

While sterling illustrators like Arthur Rackham (*Mother Goose*) were at work in Britain, America produced its counterpart to Beatrix Potter—Wanda Gág. Her ***Millions of Cats*** is considered the first American picture storybook. Its descriptive pictures and rhythmic text have remained unforgettable: "Cats here, cats there, cats and kittens everywhere." Other landmark picture books from the first half of the 20th century include American favorites such as ***Goodnight Moon*** by Margaret Wise Brown, which is still a champion bedtime story, and ***Madeline***, Ludwig Bemelmans's 1939 story of the irrepressible little Parisian girl and her boarding school experiences. Dr. Seuss (Theodor Geisel), who became the most widely known of American children's book authors and illustrators, began his work in 1937 with ***To Think I Saw It on Mulberry Street***. Another immortal name in the history of children's picture books, Robert McCloskey, published ***Make Way for Ducklings***, which has become a modern classic, in 1941. This endearing tale of a spunky mother duck and her eight ducklings' dangerous trek through Boston to reach the Public Garden is loved by children today as much as ever.

Birth of the Children's Series Book

Along with the many noteworthy books, a number of popular but lesser quality books appeared during the first half of the 20th century. The books published by the Stratemeyer Syndicate created a publishing phenomenon that has extended into current times. Beginning in the late 19th century, Edward Stratemeyer saw the potential profit in publishing a quickly produced fiction series for young readers. Certainly series books had been published and done well before Stratemeyer, but he created a machine that pumped out thousands of titles over the years. Typically, Stratemeyer would outline plots and then turn the writing over to a host of ghost writers. He published his series books under various pseudonyms, which many children still believe belong to real authors. The Stratemeyer series titles include The Rover Boys, The Bobbsey Twins, Tom Swift, The Hardy Boys, and Nancy Drew. Despite their mediocre literary quality, series books today, such as the Animorphs and Goosebumps series, are the best-selling children's books by a wide margin (Chevannes, McEvoy, & Simson, 1997; Greenlee, Monson, & Taylor 1996; Saltman, 1997). The rage created by Harry Potter, written by J. K. Rowling, has raised the ante considerably. At the time of this writing, four books have been published in the series, yet children and adults alike on both sides of the Atlantic Ocean are anxiously awaiting the next installment. These books, however, have a much higher literary quality than any of the previously mentioned series and have outsold every children's book in the history of publishing.

The Second Half of the 20th Century

In the latter half of the 20th century, a revolution in the world of children's books occurred. The 1950s were a stable time for children's publishing: Books still had predictable plots and contained the basic decency and restrained good fun that most adults expected. Some enduring modern clas-

Harry Potter, characters, names, and all related indicia are trademarks of Warner Bros. © 2001.

sics were born during this decade, such as American E. B. White's **Charlotte's Web** and the British C. S. Lewis's **The Lion, the Witch and the Wardrobe.** In 1956, the major international award for children's writing, the Hans Christian Andersen Prize, was established by the International Board on Books for Young People.

The financial boom of the 1960s, which included large government grants to school libraries, helped make children's publishing big business. More books began to be published and sold, which is reflected by the rapid increase in the number of books chosen as Notables each year by the American Library Association: There were 19 Notable titles in 1956 and 62 Notables in 1964.

The Age of New Realism

Along with an increase in sales, the 1960s brought a revolution in writing and illustrating: the age of new realism. Long-standing taboos imposed on authors and illustrators began to break down as the social revolution of the 1960s began to boil. Few books before this time dealt with topics like death, divorce, alcoholism, and child abuse. In fact, books did not even show children and parents at odds with one another. And there were almost no quality books for children written by and about minorities. Then, in the early '60s, daring new books began to emerge. A picture book, Maurice Sendak's **Where the Wild Things Are,** and a novel, **Harriet the Spy,** by Louise Fitzhugh, are often credited with ushering in this age of new realism. Both were mildly controversial, partly because they showed children at odds with their parents. Max's mother in *Wild Things* loses her temper at his unruly behavior and sends him "to bed without eating anything." And Harriet's parents are aloof and too busy to be concerned with Harriet's day-to-day activities. Max's psychological fantasy, a vent for his frustration and for the anger he feels toward his mother, and Harriet's eventual need for psychotherapy were unsettling story elements for some adults.

The Snowy Day by Ezra Jack Keats, published in 1962, was the first picture book to show a black child as a protagonist. The book won the Caldecott Medal in 1963 and has remained a favorite.

Strong American high fantasy, rivaling the work of C. S. Lewis, also appeared in the 1960s, most notably the five books of The Prydain Chronicles by Lloyd Alexander, beginning with **The Book of Three.** Also, an American emphasis on both international books and on books written and illustrated by African-Americans was encouraged by the establishment of two awards in the 1960s: the Mildred L. Batchelder Award for translated books and the Coretta Scott King Award, both administered by the American Library Association.

Federal monies for school libraries in the United States dwindled in the 1970s, and the market for children's books shifted toward a consumer, or bookstore, market. This change in marketplace brought about a change in the books: In an effort to attract adult retail consumers of children's books, editors shifted some of their emphases to books for younger audiences and to books more lavishly illustrated. Thus, baby/board books, virtually indestructible little books for babies and toddlers, invaded bookstores. There was also a proliferation of so-called toy books—pop-up, scratch-and-sniff, texture books—which are typically too fragile for library and school markets. Toy books in the 1990s often emphasized the toy more than the book; a book might be packaged with a stuffed animal, an inflatable globe, or even a full-blown kit for building a pyramid or planting a terrarium.

Printing technologies also allowed for more affordable yet extremely sophisticated, full-color reproductions. Picture books became more colorful and the renderings increasingly showy, also a draw for bookstore patrons.

A Renewed Interest in the Series Book

Publishers further realized that the cheaper series books, published originally only in paperback, would sell quickly in bookstores, and so books like the Hardy Boys and a number of teenage romance series made a mammoth resurgence in the 1970s. The 1990s saw a proliferation of new paperback series titles—Goosebumps, Fear Street,

Animorphs, Saddle Club, American Girls, Bailey School Kids—as well as the repack-aging of older series such as the Boxcar Children and the Nancy Drew mysteries. Also, consumers began to find these books and other children's titles in stores not tradi-tionally connected with bookselling: Walmart, Target, T. J. Maxx, Sam's Club, Costco, and supermarket chains such as Stop & Shop (Rosen, 1997).

However, during the same decade, new realism spread its wings. Divorce seemed to be at least an underlying theme in nearly every contemporary realistic novel. In fact, shockingly realistic novels and picture books became the standard as authors addressed serious taboos. For example, the novels of Judy Blume, such as her controversial yet ex-tremely popular *Are You There God? It's Me, Margaret* and her even more explicit *Forever,* treated physical maturation and sex candidly. Authors of historical novels also dared to present young readers varied and often unpopular viewpoints about our past. Books such as James Lincoln Collier and Christopher Collier's *My Brother Sam Is Dead* began to look at the American Revolution from perspectives other than that of a righteous rebellion. Some regarded these efforts to represent history more accurately as unpatriotic. Embarrassing annals from American history also began to appear more frequently in books for young readers, such as Yoshiko Uchida's book *Journey to Topaz,* a fictionalized autobiographical account of life in the Japanese-American in-ternment camps during World War II.

It was also during the 1970s that African Americans won the Newbery and Caldecott Awards for the first time. In 1975, Virginia Hamilton received the Newbery Medal for *M. C. Higgins the Great,* and in 1976 Leo Dillon won the Caldecott Medal, along with his wife, Diane, for *Why Mosquitoes Buzz in People's Ears.*

The number of children's books published annually in the United States sky-rocketed from approximately 2,500 in 1970 to about 5,000 in the 1990s (Bogart, 1997, p. 506). A rise in institutional purchases of books was partly responsible for such growth. As teachers began to embrace literature-based reading philosophies and methodologies, schools began to purchase more and more trade books (books other than textbooks or reference books) for use in the classroom. Some school systems be-gan to allot a percentage of their textbook budget for the acquisition of children's books, and sales from school paperback book clubs (Trumpet Club, Scholastic, Troll, Weekly Reader) leaped into the hundreds of millions of dollars. At the same time, pub-lishers continued to do well in the retail market.

During the 1980s and '90s, colorful and skillfully illustrated picture books were the name of the game. Because children's publishers were doing well financially, the best illustrators were drawn to the field of picture book illustration. Both the money and the recognition were attractive. Even Wall Street had to pay attention when illus-trator Chris Van Allsburg negotiated an $800,000 advance for the book *Swan Lake,* by Mark Helprin. Of course, this sort of remuneration is an exception.

Big Business Reorganizations

The 1980s saw the formation of publishing conglomerates. Larger corporations, of-ten businesses having no relation to books, began purchasing publishing houses. Many long-standing American publishers became imprints of so-called umbrella com-panies or disappeared altogether. For example, the Macmillan Publishing Company purchased Atheneum and other publishing houses, until its children's book division comprised 11 imprints. Then Simon & Schuster bought Macmillan, and Paramount bought Simon & Schuster. Soon Viacom, the cable TV giant, snapped up Paramount. So children's book publishing became even bigger business.

In the mid-1990s, however, publishers began to experience the negative effects of growth. They had published more books than the demand required and were forced to downsize operations.

Minority Representation in Children's Literature

Although record numbers of books were being published, the number of books about minorities (diverse cultures) in America declined during the 1980s. Between the early

1970s and early '80s, the number of minority titles dropped by more than half, according to a list released by the New York Public Library (Rollock, 1989). However, in the 1990s, the number of books with characters representing diverse cultures started to rise (Micklos, 1996).

Growth in Nonfiction

Historical novels, which waned during the 1970s, began a comeback in the next decade, and nonfiction, informational books flourished. Although good informational books were available in earlier decades, an explosion of engaging, well-illustrated, and well-written nonfiction occurred. Informational books, which seldom appeared on Newbery Award lists, began to be honored more frequently. *Sugaring Time,* by Kathryn Lasky, *Commodore Perry in the Land of the Shogun,* by Rhoda Blumberg, *Volcano,* by Patricia Lauber, *The Wright Brothers* and *Eleanor Roosevelt: A Life of Discovery,* by Russell Freedman, and *The Great Fire,* by Jim Murphy, won Newbery Honors. *Lincoln: A Photobiography,* by Russell Freedman, published in 1987, was awarded the Newbery Medal.

One of the most exciting trends of the 1980s and '90s undoubtedly was the increased emphasis on quality nonfiction for all age levels. Indeed, informational books are better as a whole than they ever have been. The first national award strictly for nonfiction writing was established by the National Council of Teachers of English in 1990 and appropriately named the *Orbis Pictus* Award, in honor of the 17th-century picture book.

Beginning Reader Books Increase

Expanding the emphasis on books for the very young in the 1970s, an increased number of quality "I can read," or beginning reader picture books, appeared in the 1980s and '90s. The trendsetters in this area had emerged decades earlier with the 1957 publication of both *Little Bear*, by Else Minarik, and *The Cat in the Hat,* by Dr. Seuss. But the availability of large numbers of well-written books for fledgling readers occurred in the '80s. For example, HarperCollins publishes a series called "I Can Read Books," of which Minarik's *Little Bear* is a part. Fine authors who often have made a name by writing for older children have contributed to the series, which now offers parents, teachers, and children an exciting array of worthwhile beginning reader books.

20th-Century Poetry

Poetry also received more attention during the 1980s and '90s. Two books of poetry won Newbery Medals during this time: *A Visit to William Blake's Inn: Poems for Innocent and Experienced Travelers,* by Nancy Willard, and *Joyful Noise: Poems for Two Voices,* by Paul Fleischman. In 1977, the National Council of Teachers of English established the Excellence in Poetry for Children Award, a lifetime achievement award honoring poets who write for young readers.

Today, books for young readers are more varied and engaging than they ever have been. The advent of the Harry Potter books has taken children's publishing to a new high. At the time of this writing, Scholastic reports that over 40 million Harry Potter books have been published. Authors and illustrators of children's books continue to experiment with form and content. The rewards of this experimentation outweigh the obvious risks; many fine books are being published as a result. The 20th century is a testament to the legacy of John Newbery—a golden age in the history of children's literature.

▼▼▼▼▼▼▼

Summary

In this chapter, we looked at what constitutes a good book, citing both words and pictures as key points for evaluation. With regard to the words, we looked at how an author uses literary devices such as precise vocabulary, figurative language, compelling dialogue, appealing language, understatement, and unexpected insights to strengthen his or her story. Weak writing was discussed, including didacticism, condescension, and an overreliance on controlled vocabulary.

With regard to illustration in children's books, we noted the function they serve in picture books. Pictures establish the setting, define and develop characters, reinforce the text, provide a differing viewpoint, can add interesting asides, extend or develop the plot, and establish a mood. We discussed the various styles and media artists use in their craft and provided examples of specific children's book titles that exemplify each. Next we looked at the visual elements artists use such as line, shape, color, texture, and composition. We noted how action and detail are important in keeping the story moving forward to a satisfying conclusion.

We looked at the history of children's literature, beginning with stories that go back as far as Aesop's fables from the 15th century. We then looked at the evolution of children's books. Focusing more on works from the 20th century, we noted the effect the age of new realism has had on the art form, as well as important issues in the field such as minority representation in children's books, series books, the growth in nonfiction, beginning readers, and poetry.

▼▼▼▼▼▼▼▼

Children's Literature References

Aardema, Verna. (1975). *Why mosquitos buzz in people's ears* (Leo Dillon & Diane Dillon, Illus.). New York: Dial.

Alcott, Louisa May. (1968). *Little women* (Jessie Willcox Smith, Illus.). Boston: Little, Brown. (Original work published 1870)

Alcott, Louisa May. (1976). *Jo's boys.* New York: Grosset. (Original work published 1886)

Alexander, Lloyd. (1964). *The book of three.* New York: Holt.

Alexander, Lloyd. (1967). *Taran wanderer.* New York: Holt.

Alexander, Lloyd. (1968). *The high king.* New York: Holt.

Alexander, Lloyd. (1986). *The Illyrian adventure.* New York: Dutton.

Alexander, Lloyd. (1992). *The fortune-tellers* (Trina Schart Hyman, Illus.). New York: Dutton.

Andersen, Hans Christian. (1835). *Fairy tales told for children.*

Andersen, Hans Christian. (1999). *The ugly duckling.* New York: Morrow.

Anno, Mitsumasa. (1977). *Anno's counting book.* New York: Crowell.

Anno, Mitsumasa. (1978). *Anno's journey.* New York: Philomel.

Babbitt, Natalie. (1975). *Tuck everlasting.* New York: Farrar, Straus and Giroux.

Bang, Molly. (1985). *The paper crane.* New York: Greenwillow.

Barrie, James. (1982). *Peter Pan* (Trina Schart Hyman, Illus.) New York: Bantam. (Original work published 1906)

Baum, Frank. (1970). *The wonderful wizard of Oz* (W. W. Denslow, Illus.). New York: Macmillan. (Original work published 1900)

Bemelmans, Ludwig. (1939). *Madeline.* New York: Simon & Schuster.

Blos, Joan. W. (1990). *Old Henry* (Stephen Gammell, Illus.). New York Morrow.

Blumberg, Rhoda. (1985). *Commodore Perry in the land of the Shogun.* New York: Lothrop.

Blume, Judy. (1970). *Are you there God? It's me, Margaret.* New York: Bradbury.

Blume, Judy. (1975). *Forever.* New York: Bradbury.

Brown, Margaret Wise. (1947). *Goodnight Moon* (Clement Hurd, Illus.). New York: Harper & Row.

Browne, Anthony. (1998). *Willy the dreamer.* Cambridge, MA: Candlewick.

Browne, Anthony. (2000). *Willy's pictures.* Cambridge, MA: Candlewick.

Bunting, Eve. (1994). *Smoky night* (David Diaz, Illus.). New York: Harcourt.

Burnett, Frances Hodgson. (1963). *Sara Crewe* (revised as *The little princess*). New York: Harper. (Original work published 1888)

Burningham, John. (1977). *Come away from the water, Shirley.* New York: Harper.

Burningham, John. (1987). *John Patrick Norman McHennessy: The boy who was always late.* New York: Trumpet.

Caldecott, Randolph. (1878). *The diverting history of John Gilpin.* New York: Warne.

Carroll, Lewis. (1865). *Alice's adventures in Wonderland* (John Tenniel, Illus.). New York: Knopf.

Casanova, Mary. (2000). *The hunter* (Ed Young, Illus.). New York: Atheneum.

Caxton, William. 1484. *Aesop's fables.*

Collier, James Lincoln, & Collier, Christopher. (1974). *My brother Sam is dead.* New York: Four Winds.

Collodi, Carlo. (1881). *The adventures of Pinocchio* (Naiad Einsel, Illus.). New York: Macmillan.

Comenius, John Amos. (1970). *Orbis sensualiaum pictus.* Menston, England: Scolar. (Original work published 1656)

Conrad, Pam. (1996). *The rooster's gift* (Eric Beddows, Illus.). New York: Harper.

Darrow, Whitney. (1970). *I'm glad I'm a boy! I'm glad I'm a girl!* New York: Windmill/Simon & Schuster.

Dedien, Thierry. (1998). *Hunting for fur.* New York: Doubleday.

Defoe, Daniel. (1920). *Robinson Crusoe* (N. C. Wyeth, Illus.). New York: Scribner's. (Original work published 1719)

Dodge, Mary Mapes. (1975). *Hans Brinker; Or, the silver skates* (Hilda Van Stockum, Illus.). Philadelphia: Collins. (Original work published 1865)

Dunrea, Olivier. (1995). *The painter who loved chickens.* New York: Farrar, Straus & Giroux.

Falconer, Ian. (2000). *Olivia.* New York: Antheneum.

Fitzhugh, Louise. (1964). *Harriet the spy.* New York: Harper.

Fleischman, Paul. (1988). *Joyful noise: Poems for two voices.* New York: Harper.

Fleischman, Paul. (2000). *Lost! A story in string* (C. B. Mordan, Illus.). New York: Henry Holt.

Fleming, Virginia. (1993). *Be good to Eddie Lee.* (Floyd Cooper, Illus.). New York: Philomel.

Freedman, Russell. (1987). *Lincoln: A photobiography.* New York: Clarion.

Freedman, Russell. (1991). *The Wright brothers.* New York: Holiday House.

Freedman, Russell. (1993). *Eleanor Roosevelt: A life of discovery.* New York: Clarion.

Gág, Wanda. (1928). *Millions of cats.* New York: Coward McCann.

Glassman, Peter. (2000). *Oz: The hundredth anniversary celebration.* New York: Books of Wonder.

Grahame, Kenneth. (1908). *The wind in the willows* (Ernest H. Shepard, Illus.). New York: Scribner's.

Grimm, Jacob, & Grimm, Wilhelm. (1886). *Household tales* (Lucy Crane, Trans.; Walter Crane, Illus.). Dover. (Original work published 1812)

Grimm, Jacob, & Grimm, Wilhelm. (1972). *Snow-White and the seven dwarfs* (Randall Jarrell, Trans.; Nancy Eckholm Burkert, Illus.). New York: Farrar, Straus & Giroux.

Grimm, Jacob, & Grimm, Wilhelm. (1975). *Thorn Rose or the Sleeping Beauty* (Errol Le Cain, Illus.). New York: Bradbury.

Hamilton, Virginia. (1975). *M. C. Higgins the great.* New York: Macmillan.

Heins, Paul. (1974). *Snow White* (Trina Schart Hyman, Illus.). Boston: Little, Brown.

Helprin, Mark. (1989). *Swan Lake.* (Chris Van Allsburg, Illus.) Boston: Houghton Mifflin.

Henkes, Kevin. (1990). *Julius, the baby of the world.* New York: Greenwillow.

Hillert, Margaret. (1982). *Why we have Thanksgiving.* Chicago: Follett.

Hodges, Margaret. (1984). *Saint George and the dragon* (Trina Schart Hyman, Illus.). Boston: Little, Brown.

Hopkins, Lee Bennett. (1995). *Pauses: Autobiographical reflections of 101 creators of children's books.* New York: HarperCollins.

Isadora, Rachel. (1979). *Ben's trumpet.* New York: Greenwillow.

Jonas, Ann. (1983). *Round trip.* New York: Greenwillow.

Kay, Verla. (1999). *Iron horses* (Michael McCurdy, Illus.). New York: Putnam.

Keats, Ezra Jack. (1962). *The snowy day.* New York: Viking.

Kellogg, Steven. (2000). *The missing mitten mystery.* New York: Dial.

Kingsley, Charles. (1884). *The water babies.* Boston: Ginn.

Kipling, Rudyard. (1964). *The jungle book.* New York: Doubleday. (Original work published 1894)

Lasky, Kathryn. (1983). *Sugaring time* (Christopher Knight, Illus.). New York: Macmillan.

Lauber, Patricia. (1986). *Volcano.* New York: Bradbury.

Lear, Edward. (1946). *A book of nonsense.* New York: Dodd. (Original work published 1846)

Lewis, C. S. (1950). *The lion, the witch, and the wardrobe.* New York: HarperCollins.

Lobel, Arnold. (1981). *On Market Street* (Anita Lobel, Illus.). New York: Greenwillow.

Lowry, Lois. (1977). *A summer to die.* Boston: Houghton Mifflin.

MacDonald, George. (1871). *At the back of the north wind* (Arthur Hughes, Illus.). New York: Dutton.

Mahy, Margaret. (1987). *17 kings and 42 elephants* (Patricia McCarthy, Illus.). New York: Dial.

Martin, Jacqueline Briggs. (1998). *Snowflake Bentley* (Mary Azarian, Illus.). Boston: Houghton Mifflin.

Mayer, Mercer. (1974). *Frog goes to dinner.* New York: Dial.

McCloskey, Robert. (1942). *Make way for ducklings.* New York: Viking.

McCloskey, Robert. (1948). *Blueberries for Sal.* New York: Viking.

McCully, Emily Arnold. (2000). *Mirette & Bellini cross Niagara Falls.* New York: Putnam.

McDermott, Gerald. (1974). *Arrow to the sun.* New York: Viking.

McMillan, Bruce. (1993). *Mouse views: What the class pet saw.* New York: Holiday House.

McNaughton, Colin. (1995). *Suddenly!* San Diego: Harcourt.

Medearis, Angela Shelf. (1995). *Too much talk!* (Stefano Vitale, Illus.). Cambridge, MA: Candlewick Press.

Milne, A. A. (1926). *Winnie-the-Pooh* (Ernest H. Shepard, Illus.). New York: Scribner's.

Minarik, Else. (1957). *Little bear* (Maurice Sendak, Illus.). New York: Harper.

Montgomery, Lucy Maud. (1983). *Anne of Green Gables* (Jody Lee, Illus.). New York: Grosset. (Original work published 1908)

Murphy, Jim. (1995). *The great fire.* New York: Scholastic.

Newbery, John. (1765). *The history of little Goody Two-Shoes.* London: John Newbery.

Newbery, John. (1967). *A pretty little pocket-book.* San Diego: Harcourt. (Original work published 1744)

Peet, Bill. (1967). *Buford the little bighorn.* Boston: Houghton Mifflin.

Perrault, Charles. (1697). *Tales of Mother Goose.* Haverhill, MA: Peter Edes.

Pinkney, Jerry. (2000). *Aesop's fables.* New York: SeaStar.

Potter, Beatrix. (1902). *The tale of Peter Rabbit.* New York: Warne.

Pyle, Howard. (1968). *The merry adventures of Robin Hood of great reknown.* New York: Scribner's. (Original work published 1883)

Rappaport, Doreen. (1988). *The Boston coffee party* (Emily Arnold McCully, Illus.). New York: Harper & Row.

Nikola-Lisa, W. (2000). *The year with Grandma Moses.* New York: Henry Holt.

Rowling, J. K. (1997). *Harry Potter and the sorcerer's stone.* New York: Scholastic.

Rowling, J. K. (1998). *Harry Potter and the chamber of secrets.* New York: Scholastic.

Rowling, J. K. (1999). *Harry Potter and the prisoner of Azkaban.* New York: Scholastic.

Rowling, J. K. (2000). *Harry Potter and the goblet of fire* (Mary Grand Pré, Illus.). New York: Levine.

Rylant, Cynthia. (1985). *The relatives came* (Stephen Gammell, Illus.). New York: Bradbury.

San Souci, Robert D. (2000a). *Little Gold Star: A Spanish American Cinderella tale.* (Sergio Martinez, Illus.). New York: HarperCollins.

San Souci, Robert D. (2000b). *The secret of the stones.* (James Ransome, Illus.). New York: Phyllis Fogelman.

Say, Allen. (2000). *The sign painter.* Boston: Houghton.

Scott, Walter. (1998). *Ivanhoe.* New York: Oxford University Press. (Original work published 1820)

Sendak, Maurice. (1963). *Where the wild things are.* New York: Harper.

Seuss, Dr. (1975). *The cat in the hat.* New York: Random House.

Spier, Peter. (1978). *Oh, were they ever happy.* New York: Doubleday.

Spinelli, Eileen. (1991). *Somebody loves you, Mr. Hatch.* (Paul Yalowitz, Illus.). New York: Bradbury Press.

Spinelli, Jerry. (1990). *Maniac Magee.* Boston: Little, Brown.

Steig, William. (1976). *The amazing bone.* New York: Farrar, Straus & Giroux.

Steig, William. (1998). *Pete's a pizza.* New York: Harper.

Stevens, Janet. (1995). *Tops & bottoms.* San Diego: Harcourt.

Stevenson, Robert Louis. (1884). *A child's garden of verses* (Thea Kliros, Illus.). Longmans, Green.

Stevenson, Robert Louis. (1994). *Treasure Island* (N. C. Wyeth, Illus.). New York: Scribner's. (Original work published 1883)

Stevenson, Robert Lewis. (1999). *A Child's Garden of Verses* (Tasha Tudor, Illus.). New York: Simon & Schuster.

Swift, Jonathan. (1952). *Gulliver's travels* (Arthur Rackham, Illus.). New York: Dutton. (Original work published 1726)

Tolkien, J. R. R. (1977). *The hobbit.* New York: Random House. (Original work published 1937)

Trepeck, Conalee. (1964). *Fun at the hospital* (David L. McKay, Illus.). New York: Carlton Press.

Turkle, Brinton. (1976). *Deep in the forest.* New York: Dutton.

Twain, Mark (Samuel Clemens). (1994). *Tom Sawyer.* New York: Grosset. (Original work published 1876)

Uchida, Yoshiko. (1971). *Journey to Topaz.* New York: Scribner's.

Van Allsburg, Chris. (1985). *The polar express.* Boston: Houghton Mifflin.

Van Allsburg, Chris. (1992). *The widow's broom.* Boston: Houghton Mifflin.

Verne, Jules. (1986). *Journey to the center of the Earth.* New York: Penguin. (Original work published 1864)

Waber, Bernard. (1972). *Ira sleeps over.* Boston: Houghton Mifflin.

Walt Disney Productions. (1973). *Snow White and the seven dwarfs.* New York: Random House.

White, E. B. (1952). *Charlotte's web* (Garth Williams, Illus.). New York: HarperCollins.

Wiesner, David. (1991). *Tuesday.* New York: Clarion.

Wiesner, David. (1999). *Sector 7.* New York: Clarion.

Willard, Nancy. (1981). *A visit to William Blake's inn: Poems for innocent and experienced travelers* (Alice Provensen & Martin Provensen, Illus.). San Diego: Harcourt.

Williams, Vera B. (1982). *A chair for my mother.* New York: Greenwillow.

Wisniewski, David. (1996). *The golem.* New York: Clarion.

Wormell, Mary. (1996). *Hilda Hen's scary night.* New York: Harcourt.

Wyss, Johann. (1949). *Swiss family Robinson* (Lynd Ward, Illus.). New York: Grosset. (Original work published 1814)

Yolen, Jane. (1997). *Miz Berlin walks.* (Floyd Cooper, Illus.). New York: Philomel.

Young, Ed. (1989). *Lon Po Po: A Red-Riding Hood story from China.* New York: Philomel.

Young, Ed. (1992). *Seven blind mice.* New York: Philomel.

Zelinsky, Paul O. (1986). *Rumpelstiltskin.* New York: Dutton.

Zelinsky, Paul O. (1997). *Rapunzel.* New York: Dutton.

Zolotow, Charlotte. (1980). *Say it!* (James Stevenson, Illus.). New York: Greenwillow.

▼▼▼▼▼▼▼

Professional References

Adams, M. J. (1990). *Beginning to read: Thinking and learning about print.* Cambridge, MA: MIT Press.

Bogart, D. (Ed.). (1997). *The Bowker annual: Library and book trade almanac* (42nd ed.). New Providence, NJ: R. R. Bowker.

Canady, J. (1980). *What is art?* New York: Knopf.

Compact edition of the Oxford English Dictionary, The. (1971). New York: Oxford University Press.

Chevannes, I., McEvoy, D., & Simson, M. (1997). Big names top the charts. *Publishers Weekly, 244*(14), 58–64.

Cianciolo, P. (1976). *Illustrations in children's books.* Dubuque, IA: W. C. Brown.

Cotton, J. (1656). *Spiritual milk for Boston babes in either England, drawn from the breasts of both Testaments for their souls' nourishment.* Boston: S. G. for Hezekiah Usher. (Original work published 1846)

Goodman, K. (1988). Look what they've done to Judy Blume!: The basalization of children's literature. *The New Advocate, 1,* (1), 29–41.

Greenlee, A. A., Monson, D. L., & Taylor, B. M. (1996). The lure of series books: Does it affect appreciation for recommended literature? *The Reading Teacher, 50*(3), 216–225.

Hearne, B. (1990). *Choosing books for children: A commonsense guide.* New York: Delacorte.

Kiefer, B. Z. (1995). *The potential of picturebooks: From visual literacy to aesthetic understanding.* Upper Saddle River, NJ: Merrill/Prentice Hall.

Konigsburg, E. L. (1970). Double image. *Library Journal, 95,* 731–734.

Lewis, N. (1961). *The new Roget's thesaurus in dictionary form.* New York: Putnam.

Locke, J. (1989). *Some thoughts concerning education.* New York: Oxford University Press. (Original work published 1693)

McCloskey, R. (1965). In *The lively art of picture books.* Videocassette. Weston, CT: Weston Woods.

McDermott, G. (1974, September). *Image in Film and Picture Book.* Speech at The University of Georgia, Athens, GA.

Micklos, J., Jr. (1996). 30 years of minorities in children's books. *The Education Digest, 62*(1), 61–64.

Morrow, L. M. (1989). *Literacy development in the early years: helping children read and write.* Upper Saddle River, NJ: Merrill/Prentice Hall.

Robinson, B. (1972). *Temporary times, temporary places.* New York: Harper & Row.

Rollock, B. (1989). *Black experience in children's books.* New York: New York Public Library.

Rosen, J. (1997). They're everywhere you look. *Publishers Weekly, 244*(29), 120–123.

Saltman, J. (1997). Groaning under the weight of series books. *Emergency Librarian, 24,* (5), 23–25.

Schmidt, G. D. (1990). *Robert McCloskey.* Boston: Twayne.

•UNIT 2•

The Good Books Themselves

PICTURE BOOKS

3

CHAPTER
▼▼▼▼▼▼▼

If you want to cover

*Immigration Past and Present:
Coming to America*

Consider as a READ ALOUD

When Jessie Came Across the Sea,
by Amy Hest, illustrated by P. J. Lynch

American Too,
by Elisa Bartone, illustrated by Ted Lewin

Consider as a TEXT SET

***. . . If Your Name Was Changed at
Ellis Island,*** by Ellen Levine,
illustrated by Wayne Parmenter

***Coming to America: The Story of
Immigration,*** by Betsy Maestro,
illustrated by Susannah Ryan

Immigrant Kids, by Russell Freedman

The Memory Coat, by Elvira Woodruff,
illustrated by Michael Dooling

A Very Important Day, by Maggie Rugg
Herold, illustrated by Catherine Stock

The Lotus Seed, by Sherry Garland,
illustrated by Tatsuro Kiuchi

***Journey to Ellis Island: How My
Father Came to America,***
by Carol Bierman, illustrated by Laurie McGaw

WHEN JESSIE CAME ACROSS THE SEA
by Amy Hest, Illustrated by P. J. Lynch

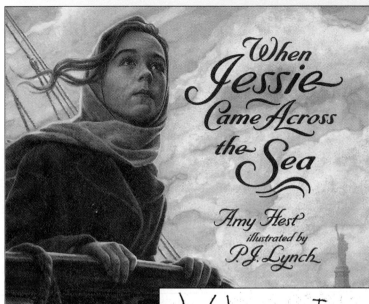

Dear Grandmother,
I miss you more than ever.
There's a library here with
rows of books. I want to read
them all. On Sundays I take
long walks on city streets and
don't get lost anymore. There
are flowers in the parks.
Love, Jessie

Excerpt from *When Jessie Came Across the Sea* by Amy Hest

Student Response

When Jessie came across The sea is a good book to read because I think it is inspiring. I like the character of Jessie because she never gives up. On a scale from one to ten I give it a twelve.

Cole 9

To visit a classroom exploring the issues of Picture Books, please go to Chapter 3 of our companion website at **www.prenhall.com/darigan**

Definition of the Picture Book

Picture books are defined by their format rather than by their content. Illustrations done in a wide range of media dominate each page and the running text is neatly placed on each page so that the book flows naturally from beginning to end. All of the major genres are represented in picture books, including poetry. The typical length of a picture book is 32 pages, and the trim size of the book is markedly larger than that of the average novel, to assure that both text and illustration fit comfortably on each double-page spread.

But what makes the picture book stand out most is the special collaboration that exists between the artist and the author. Barbara Cooney likened the picture book to a string of pearls, where the pearls represent the illustrations and the string represents the printed text. Neither can exist alone, which accents the *interdependence* between picture and text in this unique art object (Kiefer, 1995).

As we see throughout the pages of this chapter, a tremendous amount of work goes into creating a picture book, and major decisions need to be made throughout the process. Picture books are unique, because illustrations and text *share* the job of telling the story or detailing the content. No other type of literature works in the same manner.

Categories of Picture Books

In the past, picture books were often relegated to a status of bedtime stories or those "cute little books used to teach reading." But as we sample the wide range of picture books in this chapter, you will see that, indeed, there are numerous categories in this genre, and though they are excellent as the basis of a sound reading program, they are far more than "cute."

For the very young, there are baby/board books, counting books, concept books, a selected group of ABC books, and, with watchful supervision, engineered books.

ALTERNATE TEXT SET

Examples of Picture Book Categories

Read Aloud

My First Real Mother Goose/Board books

Text Sets

1 is One by Tasha Tudor/Counting books

The Everything Book by Denise Fleming/Concept books

My Little Red Toolbox by Stephen T. Johnson/Engineered books

Sector 7 by David Wiesner/Wordless Picture books

Is It Time? by Marilyn Janovitz/Predictable books

The Jungle ABC by Michael Roberts/ABC books

Poppleton Forever by Cynthia Rylant/Beginning Reader Picture books

Big Jabe by Jerdine Nolen/Picture Storybooks

To find out more about Harris Burdick stories and other activities on the World Wide Web, visit Chapter 3 on the companion website at **www.prenhall.com/darigan**

BOOKMARK

INTEGRATING TECHNOLOGY: ACTIVITIES USING THE WORLD WIDE WEB

The *Mysteries of Harris Burdick,* by Chris Van Allsburg, is an ideal book for motivating students to write. This book contains a series of beautiful but unrelated pictures, each with a title and a short caption. An introduction explains that these illustrations were left at a publishing house by a mysterious man who hopes the editor will be interested in his stories. After examining the illustrations, the excited editor wants to publish the stories, but for some reason Harris Burdick never returns. The context and the fascinating scenes depicted and the elements of the mysterious and the unusual have enticed many young writers to create stories using the illustrations as prompts. At this website, a fourth grade teacher, Mr. Salcedo, further motivates his students by having them publish their Harris Burdick stories.

Other groupings of picture books that are extremely beneficial in teaching emergent readers are wordless picture books, predictable books, and beginning reader picture books. These books, used in concert with an existing reading series or as the basis of an entire reading curriculum, are all tremendously useful to the primary teacher in bringing exciting, authentic stories to children.

Beyond the books used for pure reading instruction, there are highly sophisticated collaborations of art and word referred to as picture storybooks. These are suitable for the older, more fluent reader, or for the parent or teacher to read aloud to the less experienced, younger reader. Further, these picture storybooks offer students wonderful examples of clear, concise writing that model both the length and content we, as teachers, expect in their writing.

So, as in all but one of the books in our opening chapter text set, the picture book is often a creative collaboration between an author and a separate illustrator. But just as likely, a picture book can be written and illustrated by the same person, which is the case with virtually everything done by author/illustrators Patricia Polacco, Allen Say, Denise Fleming, Chris Van Allsburg, Emily Arnold McCully, and Tomie de Paola. A number of noted illustrators shift between writing and illustrating their own books and illustrating the work of others. Steven Kellogg, for example, (who created the icons used in the margins of this book) has a vast number of books he has done by himself but an impressively large number of collaborations with other authors as well.

Several basic picture book categories serve as a vehicle for discussing the wide variety available today. It is important to remember that these divisions are not mutually exclusive: A single book may fall into several of these categories.

Books for the Young

Baby/Board Books

Baby books, especially the board book variety, were firmly established as a distinct type of picture book in the early 1980s with the publication of Helen Oxenbury's books *Dressing, Family, Friends, Playing,* and *Working.* These comparatively armor-clad books are made from thick cardboard with clear plasticized coatings. They are meant to withstand the buffetings, dunkings, and suckings of babies and toddlers. Many of these baby books are wordless, and each page depicts a single object, such as a shoe or a spoon, that is common in a baby's environment. Sometimes single words or short phrases accompany illustrations.

Rosemary Wells's Max books are a bit more sophisticated. For example, in *Max's First Word*, big sister Ruby is trying to teach her little bunny brother how to talk, but

EVALUATING PICTURE BOOKS

- ▌ Categorization: Does this book fit into one of the basic categories of picture books?
- ▌ Quality: Is this book a good example of the category, perhaps a counting or picture story book, based on the set criteria?
- ▌ Plot: Does the plot adequately move the story forward?
- ▌ Style: Does the author use rich, descriptive language? Does the illustrator's work compliment or enhance the text?
- ▌ Character: Are the characters believable and well rounded?

Max's only word is "BANG!" No matter how she prompts him, "bang" is his only response—that is, until Ruby gives him an apple and says, "APPLE, Max. Say, APPLE." Max's final response: "Delicious."

Scholastic Books has recently begun producing a series of indestructible board books for the child who is a little older (over 3 years of age). In the "Finger Puppet Theater" stories illustrated by Peter Stevenson, they introduce classic folk tales such as *The Three Little Pigs*, and include small finger puppets of the main characters so children can act the story out as it is being read and later do it on their own.

A picture book trend evident in the last decade is the reissuing of regular format picture books in smaller, board book form.

Cover from *The Three Little Pigs*, illustrated by Peter Stevenson. Copyright © 1999 by Fernleigh Books. Reprinted by permission of Scholastic Inc.

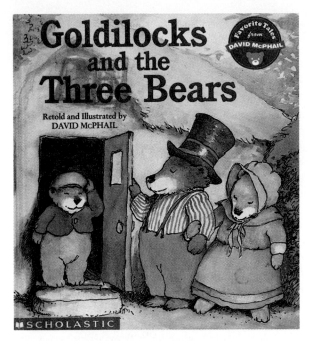

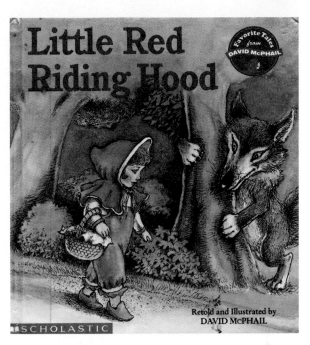

Cover from *Goldilocks and the Three Bears*, retold and illustrated by David McPhail. Copyright © 1995 by David McPhail. Reprinted with permission of Scholastic Inc.

Cover from *Little Red Riding Hood*, retold and illustrated by David McPhail. Copyright © 1995 by David McPhail. Reprinted with permission of Scholastic Inc.

ALTERNATE TEXT SET

Board Books Abound

Read Aloud

The Snowy Day, by Ezra Jack Keats

Text Set

Strega Nona, by Tomie de Paola

Freight Train, by Donald Crews

Grandfather Twilight, by Barbara Berger

One Red Sun: A Counting Book, by Ezra Jack Keats

Roll Over! A Counting Song, by Merle Peek

Wibbly Pig Can Make a Tent, by Mick Inkpen

Counting Books

Counting books were also one of the earlier types of picture books for children. Numbers and letters have always been considered the rudiments of early education. However, unlike ABC books, counting books usually do help children learn basic numbers and give them practice counting, typically from 1 to 10.

The simplest form of the counting book provides a printed Arabic number accompanied by the same number of like objects. John Burningham takes this format a bit further in the number section of his book *First Steps* by adding the cardinal number as well. For example, along with the picture of a single boy in a tree, he places both the Arabic number 1 and the word "one" in a box located in the top left-hand corner. In her brightly illustrated book *Count!*, Denise Fleming presents the Arabic number, an equal number of rectangular shapes, a word description of the animals shown on the page, and sparse text to accompany what those animals are doing. For instance, on the page for "four" it lists "four kangaroos" below the Arabic number and then states, "Bounce, kangaroos!"

More sophisticated counting books allow for personal discovery along with their beautiful illustrations. *Anno's Counting Book*, by Mitsumasa Anno, is a fine example. Anno begins with an important concept generally ignored in counting books: zero. Teachers who work with older elementary children can attest that many of them do not understand how zero works and therefore have problems with place value. So, Anno wisely introduces the idea of zero to children just beginning to learn numbers. The first double-page spread shows a barren snow-covered landscape. The Arabic number 0 is on the right side of the book, and an empty counting stick divided into 10 squares is on the left.

Each succeeding double-page spread shows the same scene, except the number of buildings, people, trees, animals, and other objects is increased as each number grows one larger. For example, on the spread for "seven," Anno has the Arabic numeral on the right and seven different-colored cubes stacked in front of the counting stick on the left. Also, the once-barren landscape now has sets of seven of a variety of objects: seven buildings, seven children, seven adults, seven evergreen trees, seven deciduous trees, seven colors in the rainbow, seven windows in one of the houses, seven pieces of laundry on the line, and so on. So much can be discovered in each scene that older children who mastered counting long ago still search the pictures to find all the sets of six, seven, or eight. Even the clock in the church tower always shows the hour for the number in question!

Besides the variety and opportunity for discovery, Anno also offers fledgling mathematicians one final boon: He does not stop at 10. Anno wisely chooses to go on to 11 and 12, two transitional numbers that do not conform to the usual pattern (one-teen and twoteen?). Anno also has applied the 12 numbers to other concepts. The seasons change throughout the scenes and correspond to the 12 months of the year. Twelve hours are, of course, on the face of the clock. As a whole package, *Anno's Counting Book* is a marvel: beautiful naive-style paintings, sound teaching processes, and pure entertainment.

A delightful book that goes beyond the number 10 is Alan Brooks's *Frogs Jump.* Illustrated by the effervescent Steven Kellogg, visual jokes abound as readers jump ahead and count back from 12. Another engaging counting book for children that has a fresh and interesting focus is *No Dodos: A Counting Book of Endangered Animals*, written and illustrated by Amanda Wallwork. Beginning with "1 whale" and continuing through 10, we are introduced to endangered animals ending with "zero . . . no dodos." Bruce Brooks has created a fascinating twist on the counting book, especially popular with young basketball enthusiasts, in his *NBA by the Numbers.* Using crisp action photographs we see "1 Alert Dribbler, 2 Tricky Passers, 3 Smart Layups," and so on. More detailed comments about how the game is played are included on each page, and will be enjoyed by the more sophisticated, fluent reader. Miriam Schlein looks at the different ways we can interpret "1" in her book *More Than One*, illustrated by Donald Crews. One can be one whale but one can also mean one pair, which is two. One can be one week, which is seven days, or one baseball team, which is nine players. Finally, *Crows: An Old Rhyme*, by Heidi Holder, takes an old rhyme, "One is for bad news, Two is for mirth, Three is a wedding, and Four is a birth . . . " and beautifully describes the progression in numbers through 12. A key at the back of the book discusses the symbols Holder uses in each plate and the significance for each. Finally, Keith Baker presents yet another old poem in his simple book *Big Fat Hen* with an additional verse that will delight the young child just learning to count.

ALTERNATE TEXT SET

Counting—In Traditional Verse

Read Aloud

Big Fat Hen by Keith Baker

Text Set

Cock-a-doodle-doo! by Emma Harding

Five Little Ducks by Ian Beck

Five Little Ducks: An Old Rhyme by Pamela Paparone

Five Little Pumpkins by Iris Van Rynbach

1, 2, Buckle My Shoe by Liz Loveless

There are a number of counting books that cross cultures and not only reinforce number concepts but also provide the reader with more information about other countries. *A Caribbean Counting Book*, by Faustin Charles and Roberta Arenson, is a collection of counting poems from across the islands of Jamaica, Barbados, Cuba, and Trinidad. *Uno, Dos, Tres; One, Two, Three*, by Pat Mora and illustrated by Barbara Lavallee, offers a charming rhyme with numbers in both Spanish and English. *Fiesta!*, by Ginger Foglesong Guy, finds three children (*tres niños*) shopping for a fiesta or party. Written in both Spanish and English, the text of each double-page spread simply asks "Que mas? What else?" which leads to the next number.

Finally, HarperCollins has put together a wonderful series of books known as *MathStart* which has been well received by children, teachers, and college educators alike. Author Stuart J. Murphy has been joined by some of the best illustrators in children's publishing to produce leveled books that provide developmentally appropriate math concepts for children in preschool through grade 2. Level One includes basic topics such as counting presented in a simple rhyming story. These books are a wonderful next step in using trade books to teach math concepts. For a more comprehensive list of topics and further information on MathStart, see chapter 10, "Informational Books."

Concept Books

Concept books introduce single, focused concepts to young children. They are essentially stepping stones into the informational books they will use as they get older. A typical topic is an investigation of colors, as in Mary Serfozo's *Who Said Red?*, Bruce McMillan's *Growing Colors*, and Ellen Stoll Walsh's *Mouse Paint*. Tana Hoban expands the concept of color in her wordless book *Colors Everywhere* by presenting a bright, bold photograph and, on the outer margins, bars of colors that are represented in that picture. The concept of opposites—open, closed; front, back; push, pull; near, far, coming, going, and tied, untied—is cleverly pictured in another of Hoban's books, *Exactly the Opposite.*

Geometric shapes are investigated in Rebecca Kai Dotlich's trio of rhymed books: *What is Round?*, *What is Square?*, and *What is a Triangle?* Colorful photographs by Maria Ferrari complement the text, making these perfect beginning books. Bright colors and dye-cut pages are used in Lois Ehlert's *Color Zoo* and *Color Farm*, the latter title being the first type of engineered book recognized by a Caldecott committee and receiving a Caldecott Honor Medal in 1990. Other notable examples of die-cut concept books are Ed Emberley's *Go Away, Big Green Monster!* and its sequel, *Glad Monster Sad Monster: A Book About Feelings*, by Ed Emberley and Anne Miranda.

Cover from **Color Farm**, written and illustrated by Lois Ehlert. Copyright © 1990 by Lois Ehlert. Used by permission of the HarperCollins Publishers.

Cover from **What Is Round?** by Rebecca Kai Dotlich. Illustrations Copyright © 1999 by Maria Ferrari. Used by permission of HarperCollins Publishers.

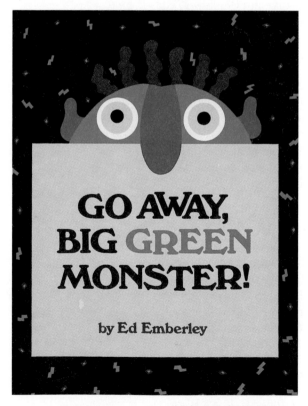

Cover from **Go Away, Big Green Monster!**, written and illustrated by Ed Emberly. Copyright © 1992 by Ed Emberly. Reprinted by permission of Little, Brown & Company.

So many wonderful concepts can be introduced and reinforced through the pages of this type of book. Margaret Miller, for example, investigates what it is like to get older in her book *Now I'm Big.* Using photographs, she compares, "When I was a baby I had a favorite stuffed animal and I played with blocks. Now I'm big! I take care of a real dog and I'm still playing with blocks but it's different."

A format that begs young "readers" to ponder a particular concept begins with a guess on one page and the solution on the next. For example, Tana Hoban has an entire series of "Look" books. Each book opens with a die-cut hole on the right-hand page revealing a photographed, colored shape. For example, in her book *Just Look*, all that is visible through the die-cut hole is a zigzagging of white and black.

Turning the page, we see a penguin's breast, wings, and head. The next page discloses over a dozen of the birds together on the beach, providing the reader with the whole context for the initial peek. In her *Look Book*, we see a curved shape against a green background. The next page reveals that it is the crooked neck of an ostrich standing in the grass.

Bruce McMillan uses a similar strategy in his books *Mouse Views: What the Class Pet Saw* and *Sense Suspense: A Guessing Game for the Five Senses.* In the first of these two books, the class mouse escapes from its cage. Each double-page spread poses a mystery: On the right-hand side, McMillan shows a close-up view of a familiar classroom object, and the young child is prompted to guess

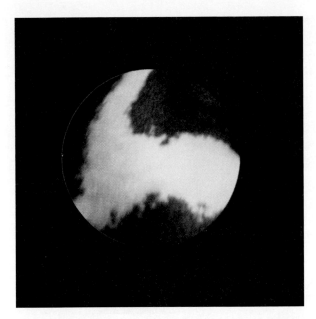

From ***Just Look*** by Tana Hoban. Copyright © 1996 by Tana Hoban. Used by permission of HarperCollins Publishers.

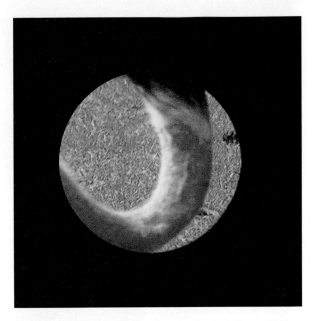

From ***Look Book*** by Tana Hoban. Copyright © 1997 by Tana Hoban. Used by permission of HarperCollins Publishers.

just what that might be. Turning the page shows the mouse sitting atop a stack of rulers and thus this mystery is solved. Other classroom objects such as building blocks, erasers, and scissors are investigated by this traveling rodent. ***Sense Suspense*** has the same format where familiar objects are presented, but this time the child must decide which of the five senses are necessary in determining what each of the objects might be.

Engineered Books

The category of engineered books is one of physical structure rather than of format or content. In fact, engineered books will always fall into at least one of the other categories we have mentioned in this chapter. But these books are particularly delightful to young children because of the way they fold out, flip up, and do some absolutely amazing things. Paul O. Zelinsky's book ***The Wheels on the Bus*** is an animated version of the familiar nursery song and uses a wide variety of manipulatives to match the text. For example, the bus doors swing open and a rider steps out, babies' mouths open and close as they cry, and true to the song, "The wipers on the bus go swish, swish, swish."

Zelinsky notes, "I did design the innards for some of the book. . . . I first made a really rough dummy with little written indications saying, 'I'd like the head to move.' 'I'd like the windshield wipers to go back and forth.' . . . I went out and bought some pop-up books, tore them apart, and looked inside. I made my own versions of four or five of the pages and some of those ended up being used. I didn't realize there were certain construction constraints such as not having a wire spring in a book because it might get eaten. . . . I laughingly thought they ought to make an aluminum version" (Darigan, 1997, pp. 60–67). Because of the vulnerability of these rather delicate books, we suggest that they be used with close supervision if they are to last.

Paper engineering involves the cutting, folding, riveting, or otherwise restructuring of the normal printed or illustrated page. Pop-up books are likely the best-known variety of the engineered book, and Robert Sabuda's ***The Wonderful Wizard of Oz*** is a very sophisticated example. Other simpler editions come from Jan Piénkowski, who has a long-standing reputation for unique pop-up books, such as ***Dinnertime, ABC Dinosaurs***, and ***Good Night: A Pop-Up Lullaby.*** Yet another engaging pop-up book is Keith Faulkner's ***The Wide-Mouthed Frog***, which will delight

From ***Wheels on the Bus***
by Paul O. Zelinsky,
copyright © 1990 by
Paul O. Zelinsky. Used by
permission of Dutton
Children's Books, a division
of Penguin Putnam, Inc.

Introducing:

TEACHING IDEAS

You can use a book to make a book. Barbara Valenta's pop-up book, ***Pop-O-Mania: How to Create Your Own Pop-Ups***, shows children how to enhance the books that they write by adding attractive pop-ups.

children with its exaggeration both in text and oversized engineered qualities. Robert Sabuda's pop-up books, ***The Christmas Alphabet*** and ***Cookie Count***, are noteworthy. His recent ***ABC Disney*** will delight the modern-day child because each letter of the alphabet pictures a pop-up of a favorite animated Disney character: *A* is for Ariel (from *The Little Mermaid*), *B* is for Bambi, and *C* is for Cinderella.

Often pop-ups include pull-tabs, cardboard wheels to be turned, and flaps to be lifted, thus allowing children to manipulate the pages. In Piénkowski's ***Haunted House***, for example, pull-tabs cause a skeleton to jump from a wardrobe and ducks in a wallpaper pattern to come to life and flap their wings.

Some engineered books rely completely on lifting flaps to reveal concept or story elements, as in Rod Campbell's ***Dear Zoo*** and ***Oh Dear!*** and Eric Hill's "Spot" books, such as ***Spot Bakes a Cake*** and ***Spot Goes to the Park.*** Another book of this type that provides a tactile experience is the classic ***Pat the Bunny***, by Dorothy Kunhardt, which allows children to pet a fuzzy little rabbit. A more recent contribution by Eric Hill, with his ***Spot's Big Touch and Feel Book***, has much of the "hands on" features of Kunhardt's book but is also designed as an indestructible board book.

Picture Books Used to Teach Emergent Readers

Bill Martin, Jr. is probably best known for the wonderful trade books he has written over the years that have helped launch emergent readers into fluent and joyful literacy. Books such as ***Brown Bear, Brown Bear, What Do You See?***, ***Polar Bear, Polar Bear, What Do You Hear?***, and ***Chicka Chicka Boom Boom*** are but a few of the titles that have become staple selections in primary classrooms all over the world. What many

teachers don't know is that Martin, who holds a Ph.D. from Northwestern University in Chicago, was a major influence in the literature-based curriculum we enjoy today. As the authors of *The Sounds of Language* series (1972a), Martin and Peggy Brogan set down some basic dimensions that would assure children's success in reading. Among them are the following:

1. Instilling children with the belief that they *can* read and that on the very first day of first grade, every child should have a book that he or she can joyfully read from cover to cover.
2. Cultivating joyous familiarity with a corps of language models and book experiences that serve as leavening to skill acquisition.
3. Incorporating sensitivities to text structure such as rhyme, rhythm, and phrase, sentence, and story patterns for the purpose of making meaning.
4. Capitalizing on familiar linguistic and cultural structures in launching children into reading.
5. Involving children aesthetically as well as intellectually in the printed page.
6. Holding "wholebook*success*" as a basic purpose of reading instruction. (p. 38)

BOOKMARK

INTEGRATING TECHNOLOGY: SOURCES ON THE WORLD WIDE WEB

The National Center for Children's Illustrated Literature (NCCIL), a nonprofit organization incorporated in February 1997, has a wonderful on-line component to its exhibits and educational programs, including ideas for using these books with children. They have highlighted some of today's finest artists, and their activities emphasize the art. See, for example, the activities related to the *David Wiesner* exhibit that extend students' understandings of his artwork and their own perceptions in imaginative ways.

To find out more about The National Center for Children's Illustrated Literature and other sources on the World Wide Web, visit Chapter 3 on the companion website at **www.prenhall.com/darigan**

A C O N V E R S A T I O N W I T H . . .

Bill Martin, Jr.

Right from the beginning, children love language. They love to hear their mother singing to them, to hear instruments being played, and it isn't long before they're picking out and using musical themes, words, and phrases that have color. Take, for example, the word "Cinderella." There is a melody to the way that word rolls off the tongue. In no time at all children express their favorite words, poems, and songs. We, as their family, listen to them and join in making their language more festive. It isn't long until the mother recognizes that a melody helps a child get over his crying spell and begins to use that melody in language to soothe her little one.

We can sing the song "Good night, sleep tight, don't let the bed bugs bite!" Now a child will not know why, but he or she will immediately recognize that this little song is humorous, that it is a part of language that he or she will eventually form into his or her own sentences.

The culture is filled with a wide range of linguistic melodies. Like . . . "Happy Birthday to you, Happy Birthday to you . . ." or "'Twas the night before Christmas, and all through the house, not a creature was stirring, not even a mouse" or "Here comes Peter Cotton Tail, Hoppin' down the bunny trail." These oral language events become the springboards into written text.

Of my most popular stories, I would hesitate to say that I really "wrote" them. It would be better to state that I "unwrapped" them. They just expressed themselves in poetic and melodic ways. The child uses the melody of language from the home to make meaning on the page. He or she reclaims the use of these poems and songs and rhythms. Take the old song (and I'm showing my age here) "School days, school days, good old golden rule days, reading and writing and 'rithmetic, taught to the tune of a hickory stick . . ." It could be the first time, or it could be the hundredth, when the child hears it and asks the parent, "What were school days like when you were young?" The child is reclaiming the phrase "school days" and innovating it in his or her own way. That is how language and speech and reading begin.

We just passed Thanksgiving, and the neighbor children here have been all abuzz with talk of turkey and their family trip to Houston.

It is a perfect example of how children absorb the linguistic structure not only of words, but of the sentences; not only of the sentences, but of the story. All we have to do is help the children anticipate the coming holiday and it can act as the impetus for their desire to read. How many children during the holiday season recognize and express a satisfaction, a pleasure for such language events? And it is this interweaving of these kinds of ideas, stories borrowed from other books, melodies from their mother's songs and other classroom play that provides them with the wherewithal to read and write.

To read more of this Conversation with Bill Martin, Jr., please visit Chapter 3 on our text's companion website at **www.prenhall.com/darigan**

Martin produced a series of what he referred to as "Instant Readers" that did exactly what we just mentioned. Take, for example, his poem ***When It Rains, It Rains***:

> When it rains, it rains.
> When it snows, it snows.
> When it fogs, it fogs.
> When it blows, it blows.
> When it's hot, it's hot.
> When it's cold, it's cold.
> When you're young, you're young.
> When you're old, you're old.
> When I'm merry, I'm merry.
> When I'm sad, I'm sad.
> When I'm good, I'm good.
> But when I'm bad . . .
> I'm perfectly horri . . . ble.

Children introduced to this short, predictable book are immediately successful when reading it because they are tapping what they already know about the way language works—the way the rhyme unfolds on the page, and the implicit knowledge they have about opposites. All of this knowledge predisposes the child to know what words will come next. Surely many will be chiming in and "reading" this book before the first read through is completed.

In the next section, we survey the wide variety of picture books that help serve the emergent reader in those early reading efforts.

Wordless Picture Books

Books without words may seem a contradiction in terms to some parents and teachers. "How can kids learn to read by just looking at pictures?" they ask. But, for young children, the wordless book can reinforce much of what they know about what books are and how they work. As they "read" by themselves or to their peers, they need to attend to such rudimentary concepts about print as how books move from front to back, or more sophisticated concepts such as the story's grammar, but always with the understanding that reading is for personal pleasure.

Further, teachers may find wordless picture books a suitable vehicle for practicing the language experience approach (Allen & Allen, 1968). In the Bill Martin, Jr. *Sounds of Language* series we mentioned earlier, there are various illustrations scattered throughout the book labeled simply "Here is a picture for storytelling." This allows the child, at his or her own level, to create a story based on the drawing at hand.

Children may want to create their own text for an action-packed wordless book such as **Clown**, by Quentin Blake, **Dylan's Day Out**, by Peter Catalanotto, and **Tuesday**, by David Wiesner. The teacher, aid, parent helper, or older student in the school can first record each student's dictated text in response to the wordless book. Then the children can read and reread their new, worded version of the picture book. Older children can try their hand at writing the words for a wordless picture book as a creative and meaningful writing experience. Take, for example, Andrew Jones's retelling of David Wiesner's *Free Fall* (1988). (See the Teaching Idea below.)

Above all, wordless picture books are meant to be enjoyed like any other book. They may tell stories, as in the ever enjoyable **Good Dog Carl** books, by Alexandra Day, or in the fantasy of **The Tooth Fairy**, by Peter Collington. Often these books teach concepts such as kindness, friendship, and the inevitability of loss, as shown in Raymond Briggs's classic **The Snowman** , or the futility of war and aggression, as in Nikolai Popov's **Why?**

Still other wordless books are stunning lessons in art. Mercer Mayer is credited with popularizing the wordless picture book, beginning in 1967 with the publication of **A Boy, a Dog, and a Frog.** Mayer's skill at telling a story and creating characters through illustrations is remarkable: Facial expressions speak with the power of words, visual actions foreshadow events, and the story line flows seamlessly. David Wiesner's work has been awarded the most prestigious U.S. prize for picture book art: a Caldecott Honor Medal in 1989 for *Free Fall* and the Caldecott Medal in 1992 for **Tuesday**. Indeed, wordless picture books have much to offer.

Introducing:

Have older students write the text line to their favorite wordless picture book. Shown here is a version of fifth grader Andrew Jones's book that was spinoff of David Wiesner's **Free Fall**.

"Sweet dreams, Johnny." That was the last thing Johnny remembered before falling asleep with his favorite book.

As he closed his eyes, Johnny pictured the land he saw outside the airplane window as he flew home from Grandma's that afternoon.

It was so familiar but somehow very different. He seemed to be floating . . . down . . . down . . . to the checkerboard ground.

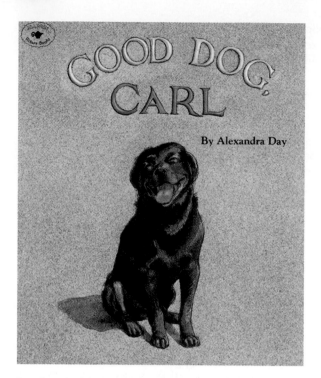

Reprinted with the permission of Simon & Schuster Books for Young Readers, an imprint of Simon & Schuster Children's Publishing Division from **Good Dog, Carl**, by Alexandra Day. Copyright © 1985 Alexandra Day.

Reprinted with the permission of Simon & Schuster Books for Young Readers, an imprint of Simon & Schuster Children's Publishing Division from **Carl's Birthday**, by Alexandra Day. Copyright 1995 Alexandra Day.

Predictable Books

As young children begin to read, predictable books, sometimes called pattern books, can often be their bridge into the world of independent reading. These picture books are characterized by repeated language patterns, story patterns, or other familiar sequences (Rhodes, 1981). When children become sensitive to these structures, the chances for making meaning is greatly increased. Take, for instance, Charles G. Shaw's classic, **It Looked Like Spilt Milk**, where a familiar "frame" is repeated over and over. Here are the first two double-page spreads.

> Sometimes it looked like Spilt Milk.
> But it wasn't Spilt Milk.
> Sometimes it looked like a Rabbit.
> But it wasn't a Rabbit.

You undoubtedly have recognized the frame or pattern . . .

> Sometimes it looked like _____.
> But it wasn't _____.

When children can get their arms around a pattern like this, it provides them with confidence as readers and teaches them an essential lesson about how print works: that there is predictability in what they read. Ken Goodman was driven by this notion in his early research and latched onto a concept coined by linguist Noam Chomsky, known as *tentative information processing*. By that he meant readers make tentative decisions as they strive to make sense of text, and they remain ready to modify their tentative decisions as they continue reading (Goodman, Goodman, & Bridges, 1990, p. 98). All a patterned text does is heighten the predictability.

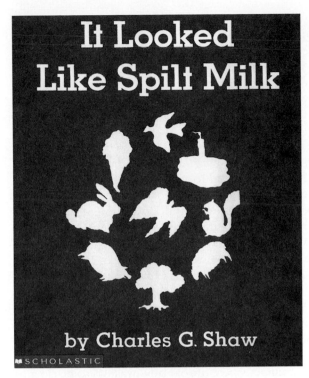

Cover from *It Looked Like Spilt Milk* by Charles G. Shaw. Copyright © 1947 by Charles G. Shaw, renewed 1975 by Ethan Allen. All rights reserved. Reprinted by permission of HarperCollins Publishers.

Cover from *Brown Bear, Brown Bear, What Do You See?* By Bill Martin, Jr., illustrated by Eric Carle. Copyright © 1967 by Bill Martin, Jr. Published by Henry Holt and Company. Reprinted by permission.

Now, you may ask, are the kids really reading? The answer is clearly that they are not . . . but they *are* launching into the reading-like behaviors Bill Martin describes at the beginning of this section.

The best of the predictable books are lively, use interesting words, and invite children to chime in. Martin's *Brown Bear, Brown Bear, What Do You See?* is a favorite in kindergartens all over the world:

> Brown Bear, Brown Bear, what do you see?
> I see a redbird looking at me.
> Redbird, redbird, what do you see?
> I see a yellow duck looking at me.
> Yellow duck . . .

Predictable books may use a *repeated story pattern*, often found in fairy and folktales, such as the troll's cry "Who's that tripping across my bridge?" from *Three Billy Goats Gruff* (Rounds, 1993) and the constant pleas for help from *The Little Red Hen* (Barton, 1993), "Who will help me . . . "

Other memorable books in this category are Pat Hutchins's *The Doorbell Rang*, where young Sam and Victoria are deciding how to split up a plate of cookies for tea that look and smell as good as Grandma's. However, the refrain states, " 'Nobody makes cookies like Grandma,' said Ma as the doorbell rang," which is repeated five more times to the book's conclusion. Mem Fox uses a similar technique in her beautiful book *Time for Bed.* The initial frame, "It's time for bed little mouse, little mouse, Darkness is falling all over the house," is repeated using different animals. "It's time for bed, little goose, little goose, The stars are out and on the loose." This pattern continues until the end of the book, which shows a little girl being put to bed by her mother: "The stars on high are shining bright—Sweet dreams, my darling, sleep well . . . good night!"

Cumulative tales provide even greater repetition, as is characterized by the traditional "The House That Jack Built." Mem Fox adds an inventive variation on this classic refrain when little Jessie gets a new pair of shoes in **Shoes From Grandpa.** Her sister says, "I'll get you a sweater when the weather gets wetter, to go with the blouse with ribbons and bows, to go with the skirt that won't show the dirt, to go with the socks from the local shops, to go with the shoes from Grandpa." Colin West has a very simple permutation on this type of tale in his *"I Don't Care!" Said the Bear.* As the bear is walking across the snowy landscape, he ignores the teeny-weeny mouse who admonishes him, "There's a moose on the loose and a bad-tempered goose and a pig who is big. . . " Predictably, every double-page spread ends with, "'I don't care,' said the bear, with his nose in the air" . . . that is, until he turns to see the mouse who he is definitely afraid of. "Then that great big old bear ran off back to his lair." Eric Carle uses an old song as the cumulative device in his delightful **Today Is Monday.** "Today is Monday, today is Monday, Monday, string beans, Tuesday, spaghetti, Wednesday, ZOOOOP . . . All you hungry children, come and eat it up!"

Often *songs or verses*, like the Eric Carle book we just mentioned, are predictable because of their familiarity as well as their repetitive language patterns. Books based on "There Was an Old Lady Who Swallowed a Fly" have appeared variously in picture book form for years. G. Brian Karas's *I Know an Old Lady* is a simple rendition of this book, and Simms Taback's version, **There Was an Old Lady Who Swallowed a Fly,** won the Caldecott Honor in 1999. A further variation on this theme is Alison Jackson's **I Know an Old Lady Who Swallowed a Pie**, illustrated by Judith Byron Schachner. In this latter text, the scene is set for Thanksgiving dinner where the old lady swallows some cider to moisten the pie "which was really too dry." As she eats, she swells and as she swells, she eventually rises up in the sky, ending up as a balloon in the Thanksgiving Day parade.

Familiar sequences such as numbers or days of the week can make for easily recognized patterns. Eric Carle's **The Very Hungry Caterpillar** follows an unconventional but voracious caterpillar through each day of the week as he eats one, then two, then three of certain foods not meant for caterpillar consumption. The familiarity of numbers and days helps children "read" this well-loved predictable picture book.

One major component in making a book predictable is the use of good ol' *rhythm and rhyme.* Take the text of Shirley Hughes's **Bathwater's Hot** as an example.

> Bathwater's hot, seawater's _____.
> Ginger's kittens are *very* young, but Buster's getting _____.

We can fill in the blanks because we know about opposites, rhythm, and rhyme. Other books with markedly solid characteristics like this are Kathleen Sullivan Carroll's **One Red Rooster** and Paul and Henrietta Stickland's **Dinosaur Roar!** Another delightful book written by Dorothy Butler is **Higgledy Piggledy Hobbledy Hoy**, where the words and rhymes simply roll off the tongue. A small boy and girl are marching along and singing:

> Higgledy piggledy hobbledy hoy,
> A good little girl and a bad little boy.
> Jiggery pokery rackety poo,
> It's a good little me and it's a bad little you.

Soon the tables are turned, however, and the girl becomes the "bad" one until they remember the picnic. "Abracadabra! Bring on the lunch! Cheesecake, cherry pie, munch, munch, munch! Ice cream, watermelon, lemonade plus—For good little, fast little, wonderful US!"

Martin and Brogan (1972a) describe an *interlocking text structure,* where one sentence is locked to the next by a repeated phrase. Once children become accustomed to the pattern, reading then becomes automatic. Like Martin's **Brown Bear**, Janet and Allan Ahlberg's classic **Each Peach Pear Plum** gives us the perfect example of such a text structure:

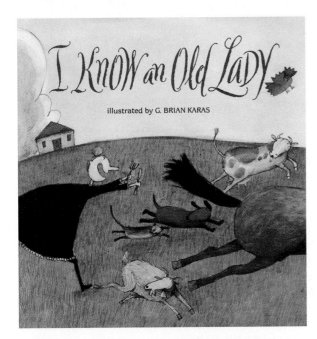

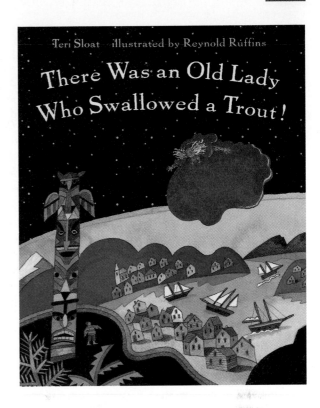

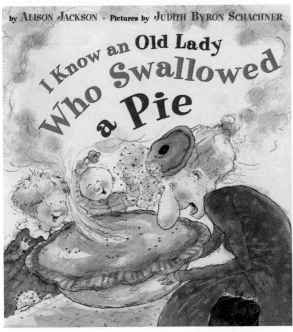

Cover from *I Know an Old Lady* by Rose Bonne and Alan Mills. Copyright © 1960 by Peer International (Canada) Limited. Copyright renewed. Illustrations copyright © 1994 by G. Brian Karas. All rights reserved. Published by Scholastic, Inc. Reprinted by permission.

Cover from *There Was an Old Lady Who Swallowed a Trout!* By Teri Sloat, illustrated by Reynold Ruffins. Text copyright © 1998 by Teri Sloat. Illustrations copyright © 1998 by Reynold Ruffins. All rights reserved. Published by Henry Holt and Company. Reprinted by permission.

Cover from *I Know an Old Lady Who Swallowed a Pie* by Alison Jackson, illustrated by Judith Byron Schachner, copyright © 1997 by Judith Byron Schachner. Reprinted by permission of Dutton Children's Books, a division of Penguin Putnam, Inc.

Each Peach Pear Plum
I spy Tom Thumb [*Here is where the interlocking structure becomes apparent.*]
Tom Thumb in the cupboard
I spy Mother Hubbard
Mother Hubbard down the cellar
I spy Cinderella. [*Can you figure out what the next two lines will be?*]
＿＿＿＿＿＿＿＿ on the stairs
＿＿ ＿＿＿＿ the Three ＿＿＿＿.

Note how each sentence locks to the next with the word repetition. Another more recent text such as this is Marilyn Janovitz's *Is It Time?* A wolf dad and his little cub are preparing for bed. The little one asks, "Is it time to run the tub?" Dad responds, "Yes, it's time to run the tub." "Is it time to rub-a-dub-dub?" "Yes, it's time to rub-a-dub-dub." Then the cumulative refrain kicks in with "Run the tub, rub-a-dub-dub."

One of our students showed us a clever way to extend the joy of **Chicka Chicka Boom Boom** by allowing the kids to actually "eat the alphabet": Cut out Jello Jigglers in the shape of the letters and arrange them on a plate. Or, being even more faithful to the book itself, copy the cut paper shapes of Lois Ehlert's cover on construction paper, laminate them, and let the children pick the their favorite letter right off the tree.

Returning to the interlocking text, the cub goes on: "Is it time to use the towel? . . . " and the call and response continue until it is "time to go to sleep and dream of sheep."

As we mentioned with Baby/Board books and the recent trend to reduce traditional and familiar titles into the smaller format, publishers are also providing teachers with enlarged versions of books known as "Big Books." The purpose of these larger books, as Holdaway (1979) states, is to imitate the lap reading that often goes on between parent and child. Teachers can use these books in a "shared reading" experience and point out various concepts about print, such as the way we track left to right, top to bottom, and front to back. However, a word of caution must be noted here: Many of these books are simply enlarged versions of the originals where the text may not be big enough for children to actually see it. Holdaway states that for the enlarged text to work, it must be easily visible at a distance of 10 meters. You may want to check the size of the type of a Big Book before you use it in class.

ABC Books

Alphabet books were one of the earliest varieties of illustrated books for children, and artists and authors continue to devise inventive ways of introducing the ABCs to children. In the 1986 Caldecott Honor Book *Alphabatics,* by Suse MacDonald, for example, we see each letter going through amazing acrobatic metamorphoses: *E* tips, turns, and mutates until it becomes the legs of an elephant; *F* begins falling forward as the two vertical stems become fins, and finally an evolved fish jumps out of its watery depths after a fly.

Certainly one of the most popular alphabet books ever written has to be Bill Martin, Jr.'s **Chicka Chicka Boom Boom.** The bright, graphic design of illustrator Lois Ehlert combined with the lilt and rhyme of the language in this book begs children to join in. One of the most difficult first grade classes we have ever seen chanted as one when given the opportunity to perform this delightful book for us. **A** told **B** and **B** told **C**, "I'll meet you at the top of the coconut tree." "Whee!" said **D** to **E F G**, "I'll beat you to the top of the coconut tree." However, the refrain warns, "Chicka chicka boom boom! Will there be enough room?" Well, "Chicka chicka, **Boom Boom!**" it turns out there isn't, and they all come tumbling down. The parents (capital letters, of course) come running to comfort their little miniscules "as the sun goes down on the coconut tree . . . "

Jim Aylesworth, with the help of illustrator Stephen Gammell, spins yet another poetic yarn in his **Old Black Fly.** By the way, when Aylesworth presents this in person, to children and teachers, he sings the entire text to a tune closely resembling "Mary Had a Little Lamb." You might want to give it a try; it goes:

> "Old black fly's been
> buzzin' around
> buzzin' around
> buzzin' around.
> Old black fly's been
> Buzzin' around,
> And he's had a very
> Busy bad day.
> He ate on the crust of the **Apple** pie.
> He bothered the **Baby** and made her cry.
> Shoo fly! Shoo fly! Shooo.

And so it goes. That feisty fly lands on something from the whole alphabet in turn until: "**SWAT!** Old black fly's done buzzin' around, and he won't be bad no more."

One of the most inventive ABC books in recent years is Cathi Hepworth's *Antics! An Alphabetical Ant*hology. Hepworth paints humanlike ants, whose personality traits represent words that begin with each letter of the alphabet and have the letters *a-n-t* embedded in them. For the letter *B*, Hepworth shows an Albert Einstein-type ant labeled "Brilliant," and for *I*, the illustration shows forlorn, turn-of-the-century "Immigrants" huddled nervously on the deck of a ship.

Other creative ways to use the alphabet as a text organizer are found in Lee Bennett Hopkins's *April Bubbles Chocolate: An ABC of Poetry* and Ashley Bryan's *ABC of African American Poetry.* Each letter features a short poem, or in the latter case, an excerpt of a poem. Chris Van Allsburg cleverly "stages" each letter in his book *The Z Was Zapped: A* appears with rocks tumbling all about it. On the back of the page, simply stated is, "Act 1: The *A* was in an Avalanche" and so on through the alphabet until Act 26, which ends with "The *Z* was finally zapped."

Two other books deserve note here, because like Suse MacDonald's *Alphabatics*, both *Alphabet City*, by Stephen T. Johnson, and *The Graphic Alphabet*, by David Pelletier, were recipients of Caldecott Honor Award, and both play with the letter forms in unique ways. Couching each letter in a city scene, Johnson photo-realistically paints the letters like the letter *A* shown on the cover of the book at the end of the barricade. Pelletier attempted to "retain the natural shape of the letter as well as represent the meaning of the word" as is shown with *Z* for zig-zag.

A very creative approach to the ABC book is found in two similar books for the alphabet audience. *Tomorrow's Alphabet,* by George Shannon and illustrated by Donald Crews, works this way: "*A* is for seed . . . tomorrow's apple. *B* is for eggs . . . tomorrow's birds." Mike Lester's book *A is for Salad* forces us to wonder, "A is for *salad*?" But look who is eating the salad. Ah yes, an alligator. Though "X" and "Y" are not as creatively presented, we still think this book will cause much thought and discussion.

The alphabet may also be used as a vehicle to introduce and categorize information or concepts for older children. For example, *Illuminations,* by Jonathan Hunt, is an ABC introduction to the Middle Ages: *A* is for Alchemist, *B* is for Black Death, and so on, and a brief description follows each term. The same format is followed in *Gone Forever!: An Alphabet of Extinct Animals,* by Sandra and William Markle and illustrated by Felipe Davalos, *An Alphabet of Dinosaurs*, by Peter Dodson and illustrated by Wayne D. Barlowe, Caldecott Medal winner *Ashanti to Zulu: African Traditions* by Margaret Musgrove and illustrated by Leo and Diane Dillon, *Turtle Island ABC,* by Gerald Hausman and illustrated by Cara and Barry Moser, and *Gathering the Sun: An Alphabet in Spanish and English* by Alma Flor Ada and illustrated by Simon Silva.

One word of caution about ABC books: Though creative, thought-provoking, and entertaining, most alphabet books are not very well suited for teaching the ABCs along with their phonic generalizations. Certainly these books can reinforce the child's notion of the alphabet, but that can just as easily be done by singing the traditional alphabet song (J. Thomas Gill, personal communication, 1999). In the main, ABC books are not intended to serve such a purpose. They are meant to introduce fascinating words and interesting concepts and most of all to entertain. However, if a teacher or parent insists on using an ABC book as a medium for teaching the alphabet and its

Chicka Chicka Boom Boom

by Bill Martin, Jr. and John Archambault

illustrated by Lois Ehlert

Reprinted with the permission of Simon & Schuster Books for Young Readers, an imprint of Simon & Schuster Children's Publishing Division from *Chicka Chicka Boom Boom* by Bill Martin, Jr., and John Archambault, illustrated by Lois Ehlert. Illustrations Copyright © 1989 by Lois Ehlert.

 Use the database to access over 100 other ABC books by simply using the descriptor "alphabet."

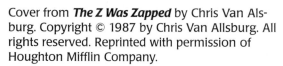

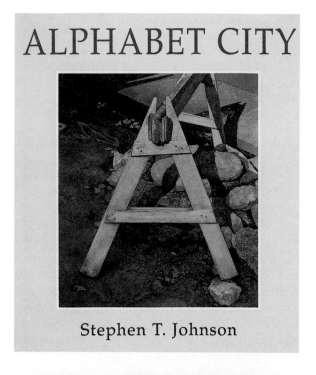

Stephen T. Johnson

Cover from ***The Z Was Zapped*** by Chris Van Allsburg. Copyright © 1987 by Chris Van Allsburg. All rights reserved. Reprinted with permission of Houghton Mifflin Company.

From ***Alphabet City*** by Stephen T. Johnson, copyright © 1995 by Stephen T. Johnson. Used by permission of Viking Kestrel, a division of Penguin Putnam, Inc.

Back cover from ***The Graphic Alphabet*** by David Pelletier. Copyright © 1996 by David Pelletier. Published by Orchard Books, an imprint of Scholastic Inc. Reprinted by permission.

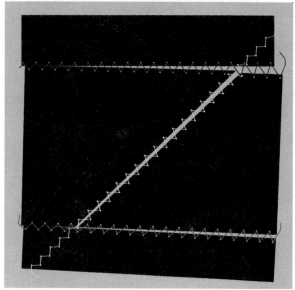

sounds, then care must be exercised to find some of the extremely rare books that conform to this task. Three criteria help to define this type of ABC book (Criscoe, 1988, p. 233).

1. Words used to represent each letter must begin with the common sound generally associated with that letter. In other words, blends, digraphs, and silent letters should be avoided. Our first example of Suse MacDonald's *Alphabatics* violates this principle in its use of *ark* for A, *elephant* for E, and *owl* for O.

2. Illustrations must represent each letter using only one or two objects that are easily identifiable by and meaningful to young children. Once again, *Alphabatics* often violates this rule. For instance, the word *insect* is used for the letter *I*, and the illustration shows an insect along with a large, bright yellow flower. A young child's attention may be drawn to the flower, and thus he or she may think "I" is for "flower."

A CONVERSATION WITH. . .

James Howe

Says Howe about his books, "The idea for the series was inspired by a young boy's question during one of my school visits. He asked, 'What is your favorite color?' 'Well, red is nice,' I told him. 'And yellow. I like bright colors.' I could see the answer didn't satisfy him, and when the assembly was over, I understood why. Looking down at what I was wearing that day, I saw a pink shirt and a pink-and-gray tie. I wondered, 'What do these kids think about a man who likes pink? Even though pink is not my favorite color,' I asked myself, 'Why wouldn't it be okay for a man's—or a boy's—favorite color to be pink?' Thus the character of Pinky was born.

"For the first time in my writing, I began to draw very directly on my own childhood. I was a lot like Pinky—nonathletic, academic, nurturing—and I collected stuffed animals. Throughout my elementary school years, one of my best friends was a girl named Bobbie. She was the inspiration for Rex, Pinky's neighbor and best friend. Like Rex, Bobbie was a tomboy and not a particularly good student.

"Although I intend the stories to be primarily about friendship and the trials and tribulations of being seven, I created the series as a way of countering some of the gender stereotyping that begins at a very young age. The messages are simple: It's okay for boys to like pink. It's okay for girls to like dinosaurs. It's okay for boys and girls to be friends. It's okay to be who you are."

---

3. Illustrations must represent objects that do not have several correct names, thus confusing young readers. *Alphabatics* uses *quail* for *Q*, which would certainly be identified as a bird by a child. Even the insect in the preceding example would likely be called a bee, a fly, or a bug.

To read more of this Conversation with James Howe, please visit Chapter 3 on our text's companion website at **www.prenhall. com/darigan**

Beginning Reader Picture Books

The beginning reader picture book is designed to give fledgling independent readers well-written yet easy-to-read materials. Both Dr. Seuss (Theodor Geisel) and Else Minarik put the beginning reader picture book on the map in 1957 with the publication of Seuss's *Cat in the Hat* and Minarik's *Little Bear.* Minarik's several Little Bear titles became part of Harper's I Can Read Book series, which continues to be one of the best collections of beginning reader picture books. The series represents all genres, including poetry, and often the books are written and illustrated by some of the best-known names in children's publishing, such as Arnold Lobel with his Frog and Toad books. In fact, *Frog and Toad Are Friends* was chosen as a Caldecott Honor Book in 1970, and *Frog and Toad Together* as a Newbery Honor Book in 1972. Harper also publishes the My First I Can Read Book series, with books that have few words yet tell strong stories. Usually the Harper I Can Read Books are divided into three to five short chapters to give young readers an early introduction to the format of longer books. However, each page is illustrated so that a picture book format is maintained.

Many other beginning reader series have been developed by other publishers in recent years: Dutton's Easy Reader, Random House's Stepping Stone, Simon & Schuster's Ready-to-Read, Dial's Easy-to-Read, Grosset & Dunlap's All Aboard Reading, Scholastic's Hello Reader!, Candlewick's Giggle Club, Dell's Yearling First Choice Chapter Book, the Holiday House Readers, Harcourt's Green Light Readers, and the Dino Easy Readers from Little, Brown.

Newbery winner Cynthia Rylant has created a series of easy-to-read picture books featuring Henry and his dog, Mudge, such as *Henry and Mudge and the Happy Cat, Henry and Mudge and the Best Day of All,* and *Henry and Mudge and the Sneaky Crackers,* as well as the easy reader series about Poppleton the pig and Mr. Putter and Tabby.

Likewise, James Howe has written a very engaging series of books featuring two friends, Pinky and Rex. The simple text is filled with many of the emotional traumas

PINKY and REX
and the
School Play
by James Howe
illustrated by Melissa Sweet

PINKY and REX
and the
New Neighbors
by James Howe
illustrated by Melissa Sweet

of growing up, such as dealing with jealousy, envy, friendships broken and friendships mended, and the usual family squabbles.

Not all beginning reader picture books are part of a series, of course, and excellent individual titles pop up on all of the publishers' lists. Adults often will choose any controlled vocabulary picture book for their children simply because the words are oversimplified and seem easy to read. However, many of these titles offer little more than vocabulary practice and are of limited interest to children.

Strong story and a fresh and lively writing style coupled with a wise control of vocabulary make for easier reading. Beginning reader picture books that are stilted and contrived, that follow the unnatural language patterns evident in the old-style Dick and Jane basal readers, are actually more difficult for young readers (Goodman, 1988).

Making a Picture Book

We seem to be peppered constantly by students and teachers, or their relatives—aunts, uncles, second cousins—who tell us they have "written a kiddie book" and are looking for an illustrator . . . "Do we have any ideas?" The first thing we tell them is that in virtually all cases, unless the author is also a proven illustrator, a manuscript is not submitted *with* illustrations. In fact, presenting such a thing probably irritates editors more than it helps.

To set the record straight on how this process works, and also to show how it can parallel what we do in our writing classrooms, we give you the general step-by-step

1. A manuscript arrives at the publishing house and is usually placed in what is known as a "slush pile." Assistant editors, trained to know what to look for, determine whether the text should be sent on to the senior editor or rejected.

2. The manuscript for **Coolies** gets to the desk of senior editor Patricia Lee Gauch at Philomel Books in New York City, where she decides that she will offer this author a contract for her book.

3. Author Yin takes advantage of another opportunity to make the text clear and concise.

4. Pages of the manuscript are edited with suggestions for changes.

5. The manuscript is sent to the copy editor, who makes sure spelling, punctuation, and grammar are correct.

6. Decisions are made to determine font size and style, and what the cover design will be. The book's text is set up just like it will appear in the final version. This is called the *galley*.

7. Gauch meets with art director Cecilia Yung, and together they decide that Chris Soentpiet would be the best choice to illustrate the book.

8. Chris prepares sketches, arriving at a final "dummy," where the entire book is laid out the way he thinks it should look in its final form.

9. Chris gets to work in his studio on the final paintings, which he does in full color.

10. Art director Yung and Gauch meet with Chris to make final changes in the illustrations.

11. Color proofs come back from the printer, and Patricia checks them against the originals, marking color corrections so the final book illustrations will remain as true to the art as possible.

12. All 32 pages of the book are printed front and back on a huge "press sheet." The book pages are so arranged that when the press sheet is folded and folded again until only one page is showing, all the pages are in the proper sequence.

13. Press sheets are cut, folded, gathered, sewn, trimmed, and bound into a hard cover.

14. The dust jacket is added and the book is ready for distribution.

15. The book is sent to stores across the country.

16. Yin and Chris Soentpiet appear at a local independent bookstore to autograph **Coolies**, their new book.

DID YOU KNOW?

Philomel Books took a big chance when they kept the name **Coolies** as the title of this stunning picture book. The connotation for this term has often been derogatory; however, Cecilia Yung, Hong Kong born and the Art Director of this book, assures us quite the opposite is true. Says Yung, "The direct translation of the honorable word *coolies* is actually 'bitter labor' and something all Chinese people are very proud of."

FIGURE 3–1   How a picture book is made.

process concerning how a picture book is made. We go from the time the author submits the manuscript until the time it arrives on the shelf in your bookstore. We think you will be quite surprised at the tremendous amount of decisions that need to be made and the sophistication involved in the making of a book. Finally, we take an in-depth look at *Coolies,* written by Yin and illustrated by Chris Soentpiet, to provide you with a behind-the-scenes view of how that particular book was made (Figure 3–1).

To find out more about Will Hillenbrand's site and other authors and illustrators on the World Wide Web, visit Chapter 3 on the companion website at **www.prenhall. com/darigan**

INTEGRATING TECHNOLOGY: AUTHORS ON THE WORLD WIDE WEB

Will Hillenbrand, illustrator and author of over 20 picture books, has created a detailed and extremely useful website. In addition to the biographical details and information about his books, Will has included a gallery of his work, teacher tips, and some wonderful downloadable material to help children (and adults) understand what goes into illustrating a children's book. The booklet "Starting from Sketch: Inside the Picture Book with Will Hillenbrand" is a terrific hands-on approach to teaching children about artistic process.

Picture Storybooks

Picture storybooks are written across all the genres and can address a wide range of themes and topics. We opened the chapter with a text set of books, "Immigration Past and Present: Coming to America," to show how numerous authors and illustrators have portrayed the way people from a wide range of countries immigrated to the United States over the years. But we could have just as easily focused on a topic of, say, "Friendship" or "Bears" and had an equally impressive assortment of books to choose from. Our point here is threefold: First, with the knowledge *you* already possess about books combined with the aid of your colleagues, your school and public librarians, your independent booksellers, and the database included with this text, you can create themes that will match your interests and the needs of your curriculum.

Second, the breadth of picture storybooks is tremendous; we could have written an entire book focusing on just the picture storybook. So, to give space to as many titles and topics as possible, we have embedded many of our suggestions for picture storybooks in other appropriate genre chapters. For example, we assembled a nice array of picture storybooks dealing with the prairie and westward expansion set in the latter half of the 19th century in the United States; though we could have listed those books here, we decided to place them in chapter 8, "Historical Fiction."

Finally, as we look at our groaning bookshelves stuffed with picture storybooks, we wonder how we can ever synthesize this rich subcategory of picture books into just a handful of "the greatest" or "the best" books; it would be virtually impossible. In fact, among even the three of us we would be hard put to arrive at a condensed list: After one book was mentioned five others would be remembered, and the conversation would go on and on.

What we do agree on, however, is that when we look at picture storybooks, we think three basic elements need to be kept in mind: plot, style, and character. Armed with those ideas, you, the reader (and subsequently the children in your classes), can judge whether a book would be on your "Pick-of-the-List" list. That being said, you will read through this next section and wonder, for example, *How could those guys have forgotten* **Chicken Sunday** *by Patricia Polacco? It's my favorite book! I cry every time I read it! And what about* **Pink and Say?** *My class last year thought it was great! And then here is her book* **The Keeping Quilt;** *you can't forget that . . .* Well, we certainly haven't meant to slight those books or any of the others you may cherish; they are probably all nestled in the database and waiting for you to rediscover them. We do mention notable examples of each of the elements to give you a feel for what we are talking about, and then we let you go out and discover what is wonderful by deciding for yourself.

DID YOU KNOW?

When we were recently in New York City visiting our friends at Penguin/Putnam, we were fortunate to see some of the original art for one of Patricia Polacco's newest books. Viewing the "real" art, we were struck by how much Polacco relies on wide-line felt-tip markers to make her pictures. Look at some of her books and see how she uses simple markers to create her wonderful illustrations.

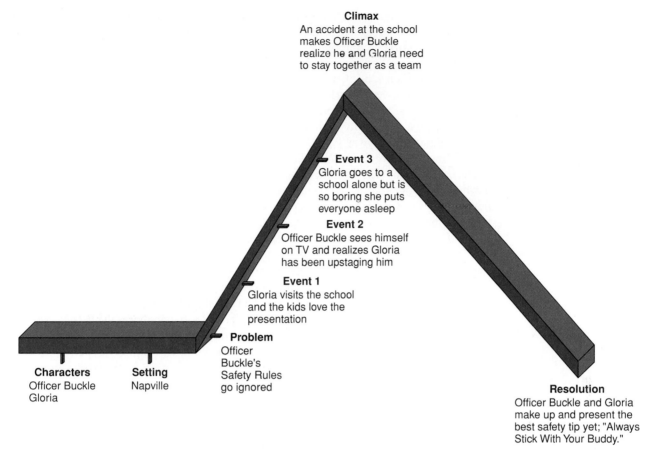

Climax
An accident at the school
makes Officer Buckle
realize he and Gloria need
to stay together as a team

Event 3
Gloria goes to a
school alone but is
so boring she puts
everyone asleep

Event 2
Officer Buckle sees himself
on TV and realizes Gloria
has been upstaging him

Event 1
Gloria visits the school
and the kids love the
presentation

Problem
Officer
Buckle's
Safety Rules
go ignored

Characters
Officer Buckle
Gloria

Setting
Napville

Resolution
Officer Buckle and Gloria
make up and present the
best safety tip yet; "Always
Stick With Your Buddy."

FIGURE 3–2   Graphic design of the Story Mountain organizer for *Officer Buckle and Gloria.*

Using the graphic organizer we refer to as a Story Mountain (see Figure 3–2), you can demonstrate the story's setting, rising action, and resolution, giving your students a greater understanding of the structure of the story and deepening their appreciation of the plot.

Introducing:

TEACHING IDEAS

▼▼▼▼▼▼▼

Components of a Good Picture Storybook

If you concentrate on the elements of plot, style, and character, you will be able to make well-informed choices in the books you want to share with the children in your classes.

Plot

As we have already discussed and will mention again and again throughout this book, story is essential to engaged reading. Without it, there is little reason for the child to read on, and *plot* is the key to a good, well-paced story. Let's look at Peggy Rathman's Caldecott Medal winner *Officer Buckle and Gloria.* Officer Buckle, of the Napville Police Department, is in charge of safety. He knows *all* the rules, but when he presents safety tips to kids, nobody listens—that is, until the department buys a police dog named Gloria. When she accompanies Officer Buckle, she sits behind him, but unbeknownst to him, she upstages him by mimicking the rules as he reads them. As a consequence of Gloria's tomfoolery, the two are a big hit, and the next day they receive an enormous envelope of fan mail. After that, everybody wants to invite Officer Buckle and Gloria to their school, and the two successfully present all over Napville.

One day, however, a television news team tapes their presentation, and that night Officer Buckle sees what Gloria has been doing behind his back. He becomes upset, and when Mrs. Toppel invites him for their safety speech he refuses, grumbling, "Nobody looks at me, anyway!"

Mrs. Toppel replies, "Well! How about Gloria? Could she come?" Gloria is sent to the school, but without Officer Buckle she is boring and puts everyone asleep. That is when the school suffers its biggest accident ever, which begins with a puddle of banana pudding. A landslide of kids ends up running into Mrs. Toppel, who lets loose her hammer, which bops little Claire on the head (fortunately, she was exercising Safety Tip #7 at the time, "Always Wear a Crash Helmet . . .").

The next day, Officer Buckle gets a stack of letters from all the kids in the school detailing the accident. Realizing that he and Gloria were a great team, Officer Buckle accepts his mistake and adheres to the best safety tip of all (#101, in case you've forgotten): "Always Stick With Your Buddy." This delightful story is perfectly paced, has a rising series of events that reaches a climax, and is satisfyingly resolved.

Let's look at the way Rathman plotted this story. Showing kids how a story is constructed helps them more accurately predict what is going to happen from one event to the next. Further, it aids them when they are reading future stories independently, because knowing the basic story framework, children make better sense of what they read, and the closer a story matches the organization of a particular story, the greater the comprehension is likely to be (Vacca, Vacca, & Gove, 2000).

We would like to show you a story scheme, or graphic organizer, that demonstrates our point. We call this a "Story Mountain," and find it very useful as an aid in thinking about the way a story is constructed (see Figure 3–2).

If we were to note one author who has consistently presented us with great story over the years, it would certainly have to be Bill Peet. Beginning with an illustrious career at the Walt Disney Studios, Peet made many memorable movies such as *The 101 Dalmatians, Dumbo,* and *The Sword in the Stone* and created unforgettable characters such as Gus, Jaq, and Lucifer in movie version of *Cinderella.* After 27 years, he left Disney and concentrated on being an author and illustrator of books for children. Since then, Peet has produced dozens of books that are timeless and engaging and all of which are *still* in print! His love of animals is best exemplified with books like **Farewell to Shady Glade, The Whingdingdilly,** and **Chester the Worldly Pig.** His passion for trains and the railroad came out in **Smokey** and **The Caboose Who Got Loose.** Further, Peet has always had a special place in his heart for the circus, and that is represented in books such as **Pamela Camel, Ella,** and **Randy's Dandy Lions.**

Peet was superb at spinning an enjoyable yarn, and often it was done in rhyme. In his **Kermit the Hermit,** he begins:

DID YOU KNOW?

According to Bill Peet himself, he was one of the people closest to the great, but often difficult, Walt Disney. Peet discusses their rocky, roller-coaster relationship in his autobiography and provides lots of interesting anecdotes about his years at the Disney Studios. For more inside information, look at his Caldecott Honor book **Bill Peet: An Autobiography.**

> In Monterey Bay there's a jumble of rock
> Stacked up like a castle across from the dock.
> The king of this castle, an old crab called Kermit,
> Lived all by himself in a cave like a hermit.

Kermit, a greedy and grumpy crabby old crab, collects all sorts of junk like "a broken jackknife, a pair of old shoes, things that a crab couldn't possibly use" and squirrels it away in his little cave. One day, a dog captures the curmudgeonly crustacean on one of his sojourns across the sand. In the nick of time, a young boy saves his life and returns him to his castle of rocks. Kermit searches for a way to return the boy's kindness and is whisked into a series of deep-sea adventures.

Cover from *Pamela Camel* by Bill Peet. Copyright © 1984 by Bill Peet. Reprinted by permission of Houghton Mifflin Company. All rights reserved.

Cover from *Kermit the Hermit*, written and illustrated by Bill Peet. Copyright © 1965 by Bill Peet. Reprinted by permission of Houghton Mifflin Company. All rights reserved.

Though Bill Peet's career as an author and illustrator has ended, books like *Kermit the Hermit* will live on for thousands of children in future generations as representative of what great story and pictures can do.

When thinking of plot as one of the overarching elements in picture storybooks, we must also consider theme as an important factor in this mix. *Theme,* or the overall message the author/illustrator is trying to impart—the message that tells us something enduring about life—is worthy of special attention. Allen Say's *Grandfather's Journey* is the preeminent example of a worthy theme. It investigates the notion of belonging and home in a personal and touching way. Children's literature expert Barbara Kiefer (1995) has told us that this is clearly one of the most perfect picture books ever produced.

Style

Author *style* is the second element we consider to be worthy of consideration when judging a picture storybook. When children develop a sensitivity to words and sentence structure, they begin to become aware of how these images reflect the mood of the story, how they increase tension, or how the world can be visualized in new and different ways (Norton, 1992). Take, for instance, this great series of sentences from *Dove Isabeau* by Jane Yolen. Young Isabeau had "hair [that] was the color of the tops of waves when the sun lights them from above, and her eyes were as dark blue as the sea." Her mother took sick and "died at last, when winter had a hold on both the land and their hearts." Her father, Lord Darnton, remarried "all too hastily, because he needed to believe in life again." Now, given what we know about traditional folktales, the stage is set for the entrance of a wicked stepmother, and Yolen doesn't let us down one bit. The way she describes her, though, is absolutely masterful—"The woman he wed had eyes the green of May but a heart as bleak as February." Wow! That simile sums up just how deceptive and dastardly this woman really is.

A CONVERSATION WITH. . .

Allen Say

I didn't realize that I was a storyteller till I was about 50. Here I had studied visual arts, all my background is in visual arts, and I'm good at them—photography, cartooning, painting. I was a full-fledged advertising photographer for 20 years of my adult life. But, at age 50—when I sent away my drawings for the ***Boy of the Three-Year Nap***—I began to have the sneaking suspicion that maybe I should write my own stories! But, along with that came the cold realization that I was terrified of writing in English.

I was 16 when I came here, and the only English course that I have ever taken actually was the dumbbell English, and I flunked it so fast that I didn't know what hit me. I mean, I was writing in the Japanese style—sort of a formless, stream-of-consciousness writing.

My stories are essentially autobiographical but I didn't do this intentionally; I can say this in hindsight. I look back and it probably makes perfect sense, because I think every artistic work is essentially autobiographical. I mean, you can't invent something that you don't understand or know about. So my book ***The Sign Painter*** is, in a way, a biography of the heart. I was a sign painter. It's a portrayal of a budding artist, meaning me, and a budding artist lives completely in the world of art. He views the world through art. And in this case, here's this Asian boy viewing America through American art. That's my justification.

About my three books ***Tree of Cranes***, ***Grandfather's Journey***, and ***Tea With Milk***—they go to-

gether. They form a sort of strange trilogy, and again it was totally unintentional. I hate the sequel things that go in sequence; had I done it intentionally, of course, the sequence would have been different: ***Grandfather's Journey*** would have come first, then ***Tea With Milk***, and finally ***Tree of Cranes***.

When I make a book, I start out with a very nebulous idea, or several ideas, and I paint the first picture. By the time I'm through with it, the next picture is pretty much conceptualized. This process, by the way, drives my editor, Walter Lorraine, crazy. But . . . I keep going, and frequently by the time I'm finished with the story it is completely different from what I had initially imagined it to be.

By the way, common sense is the worst thing you can have as an artist. Preconceptions are never any good. I am firmly of the opinion that any artistic work that is made with full consciousness is never worth a nickel.

I think my work explores an area that hasn't been done by others. The contribution that I think I've made is that I'm the guy who introduced the Asian child into mainstream American life. I call this a very subversive act. And I succeeded doing it, and I'm proud of it.

To read more of this Conversation with Allen Say, please visit Chapter 3 on our text's companion website at **www.prenhall.com/darigan**

When we read this story aloud to elementary students, middle school children, or to our college students, we find that it pays great returns to make note of those rich phrases: It plants the seeds for students to find favorite examples figurative of language themselves. Further, it prompts them to add these kinds of literary images to their own writing.

Another example of rich language comes from Pam Conrad's book ***Blue Willow.*** This beautifully illustrated book is a lasting legacy to the wonderful picture books and novels Ms. Conrad wrote for children of all ages. In it, Kung Shi Fair lives with her father, a rich merchant, on River Wen. Note how Conrad uses just the right similes to describe this beautiful young daughter: "Kung Shi Fair was a beautiful girl with hands as small as starfish, feet as swift as sandpipers, and hair as black as the ink on her father's scrolls." Because her mother was dead, her father doted on the girl, and anything Kung Shi Fair wanted, he gave her. When she asked for a "moon pavilion of (her) very own," he "built one . . . surrounded by peonies that filled the air with sweetness, and bamboo that sounded like wings beating in the wind."

Kung Shi Fair meets Chang the Good at the river's edge. "He was a young fisherman who counted his wealth in nets and cormorants and the slant of the wind across the river's surface." He was strong and steady and well loved. The two retreat to the moon pavilion, and here Conrad foreshadows the tragedy that hangs like a dark veil over the rest of this book: "but the people of the village have told this story ever since. This was the beginning of the story, the good, the happy part." The language, the use of similes, the foreshadowing, and the visual images as well as the paintings in this book are both painfully and breathtakingly beautiful. The entire story is, predictably, pictured on the Blue Willow plate pattern for all to see and remember.

A Closer Look at the Style of Two Consummate Author/Illustrators

Let's take a look at the structure two authors used in their books as it applies to style. Written 54 years apart, there would be nothing that these two books would seem to have in common other than that they are picture storybooks, yet a closer examination shows a remarkable similarity in construction. *Blueberries for Sal,* winner of the Caldecott Honor by Robert McCloskey, opens in a time long gone by. Looking at the endpapers, we see a cozy kitchen with an old-fashioned woodburning stove, pots steaming on the back. We see a mother and her daughter at a round leaf table canning blueberries using the old rubber rings and glass jars with metal-clasp tops.

The book begins with Little Sal and her Mother going to pick blueberries on Blueberry Hill. Mother reminds Sal that they will take the berries they pick home to can for the winter. Instead, Sal eats the berries she picks while her mother begins to fill her tin pail. Sal, with an empty pail, struggles along in an effort to keep up with her mother. When she catches up and reaches into her mother's pail, the bottom has by now been covered; Mother reminds her that she "wants to take her berries home and can them for next winter." Sal plunks herself down in the middle of some blueberry bushes and happily eats away as her mother moves on up the hill. On the other side of Blueberry Hill, Little Bear and his mother come along. His mother tells him to "eat lots of berries and grow big and fat. We must store up food for the long, cold winter." Little Bear also has trouble keeping up with his mother, so he sits in a clump of bushes and merrily eats away while his mother moves on up the hill.

Notice how both characters, Little Sal and Little Bear, are easily wearied and end up eating blueberries? What happens to Sal happens to Little Bear and vice versa throughout the remainder of the book. This structure makes the text predictable for children, presents the perfect conflict, and then gently resolves it in the end.

Kevin Henkes, in similar fashion, uses a parallel style in his book *Chester's Way.* He begins, "Chester had his own way of doing things . . . " In a dialogue bubble, Chester states, "Hello, my name is Chester. I like croquet and peanut butter and making my bed." The obvious inference we, as readers, make is that *this* kid is different (although maybe a little concrete sequential around the edges?). For example, he always cuts his sandwiches diagonally, double-knots his shoes, and carries "a miniature first-aid kit in his back pocket. Just in case."

Chester's friend Wilson is the same way. In fact, they do everything together. They play baseball (but they never swing on the first pitch), ride bikes (and always use their hand signals), and eat at the same time (but rarely between meals). As they both sit in a comfortable stuffed chair reading "Advanced Croquet Tips," Wilson's parents remark that they can hardly "tell those two apart." The following refrain appears and is repeated periodically throughout the rest of the text, "Chester and Wilson. Wilson and Chester. That's the way it was."

Then, "Lilly moved into the neighborhood. LILLY had <u>her</u> own way of doing things . . . " In a dialogue bubble, Lilly states, "I'm Lilly! I am the Queen! I like EVERYTHING!" Lilly, unlike Chester and Wilson, wears band-aids all over her arms and legs, never leaves the house without one of her nifty disguises, and carries "a loaded squirt gun in her back pocket. Just in case."

"She definitely has a mind of her own," observes Chester to Wilson. The two proceed to ignore and rebuff Lilly. But that cannot last for long. Lilly works her way into the two boys' lives and then it becomes, "Chester and Wilson and Lilly, Lilly and Wilson and Chester. That's the way it was."

Illustrations by Susan Guevara, copyright © 2000 by Susan Guevara, from **Chato and the Party Animals** by Gary Soto, illustrated by Susan Guevara. Used by permission of G. P. Putnam's Sons, a division of Penguin Putnam, Inc.

Juxtapose this with McCloskey's "Little Bear and Little Sal's mother and Little Sal and Little Bear's mother were all mixed up with each other among the blueberries on Blueberry Hill," and you can see how these two books are similar. Like Robert McCloskey, Kevin Henkes has used this structure of parallel construction to build a story that is predictable, is highly entertaining, and furthers the story line in a delightful way.

Kiefer (1995, p. 118) takes the notion of style one step further by connecting it to art.

Character

Another element we think necessary in studying and evaluating picture storybooks is *character.* Central to any story are characters who seem real, who develop as the story progresses, and who, ultimately, change in some way from beginning to end.

Susan Guevara, illustrator of Gary Soto's **Chato's Kitchen** and the sequel **Chato and the Party Animals,** has created a strong sense of character with her stylized scratchboard paintings of this inner-city Latino cat and his friends.

Well-rounded characters seem to jump off the page and into our lives. Through their actions and dialogue, we see them change significantly. Take another book by Kevin Henkes, *Julius, the Baby of the World,* as an example. Our old friend Lilly is having a bit of trouble with her new baby brother. He is certainly getting a lot of attention, and we must remember Lilly is "the queen." Again, we see the parallel construction in this new refrain about how Lilly and her parents feel about Julius:

> Her parents loved him.
> They kissed his wet pink nose.
> They admired his small black eyes.
> And they stroked his sweet white fur.
> Lilly thought his wet pink nose was slimy.
> She thought his small black eyes were beady.
> And she thought his sweet white fur was not so sweet . . .
> "Julius is the baby of the world," chimed Lilly's parents.
> "Disgusting," said Lilly.

As you might guess, with all of the spunk of a young mouse like Lilly, she gets into quite a bit of hot water over the way she treats Julius. She makes noise while he is sleeping, when she is supposed to tell him "how beautiful he is and how we love him . . . Lilly has her own idea." In the dialogue bubbles she chants, "I hate you. You're ugly." She even tries to scare baby Julius with her nifty disguises. Here Henkes is at his best, for he simply states, "Lilly spent more time than usual in the uncooperative chair."

After an altercation with her cousin Garland, Lilly realizes where her heart really lies and changes drastically during the course of the book. Moreover, the theme of this story seems to be played out in houses all over the country, to one extent or another, where sibling rivalry becomes an issue after the birth of a new baby. Young children (and we've even presented this book to kids into the intermediate grades) can see and appreciate the way the Lilly's character develops and changes. With this dash of humor,

Susan Guevara

I steal. I steal as much as I can. I really just take as much information as I can from all places that I can to stick it in the big bowl of my head and stir it all up and see what comes out.

Generally, I'll read a manuscript and I'll get a feel for its world. And in the same way that the author has used style and voice and dialogue and vocabulary and all the writer's tools that he or she has to create this world, I have at my disposal every possible tool to do the same visually. So I can use whatever medium I need to create a technique that reflects that world.

For **Chato's Kitchen** I just started scrounging around for material. I figured a short, low-riding dog would be a wiener dog, right? But then I found out that there are wire-haired wiener dogs, and they have incredible attitudes with big bushy eyebrows and beards. I went to a breeder's house and took a lot of photos of her dogs.

And then I had discovered Gronk, who is a Mexican-American muralist. He was at the Mexican museum at the time I was working on **Chato's Kitchen** and he had these gigantic wall paintings. It wasn't until that time, and how many years have I been out of art school?—that I realized that you can't have bright color just by slapping lots of bright color down. You have to put a lot of muted color around it and then the bright color will really pop. A really in-tense blue that really pops off the page because of all these muted colors around it.

I also had this vision of black velvet paintings. They have this incredible depth and richness to them and they're so di-mensional. They're so in-credibly tacky and beauti-ful at the same time. Then I stumbled across scratchboard. It had a nice sort of semimatte quality. It was like this highly saturated look with just one layer of paint because the black was com-ing through.

On a personal level, I thought about my family. My grandma, the smell of her house and the way she made her enchiladas and the things that I remember from her and my grandpa. And, of course, my own dad. He really is thankful to be alive. Family is every-thing to him, and as long as his girls—my mom, my sister, and I—are happy and healthy, he's a con-tented man. He just, you know, wakes up in the morn-ing and says, "God, I'm so happy to be alive. What's for breakfast?" You know, and this to me seems very Chato-esque.

And so that was a good starting place.

Henkes lets us see how upsetting a new arrival can be to a family, yet how eventually all can be worked out. Noting this change as we read the book aloud to our classes helps them to notice how it occurs in the subsequent books they read themselves.

For the older reader, there is no better example of how a character changes than in Cynthia Rylant's book *An Angel for Solomon Singer,* illustrated by Peter Catalan-otto. Solomon Singer lives alone in New York City. He dreams of things he doesn't have such as a balcony, a fireplace, a porch swing, a cat, a purple wall. He wanders the streets listening to the voices of all who pass, and wishes, instead, for the conversations of crickets. He is a lonely, unhappy man.

One evening, he stops at a restaurant called the Westway Café. Skimming the menu, he reads the words: "The Westway Café—where all your dreams come true." The waiter greets him with one of the finest sentences ever written for children. Rylant intones, "A voice quiet like Indiana pines in November said, 'Good evening, sir,' and Solomon Singer looked up into a pair of brown eyes that were lined at the corners from a life of smiling." Singer orders his food along with one of his wishes—a balcony (but he didn't say the balcony out loud). The next night he returns and, with his food, he orders an-other of his wishes—a fireplace (but he didn't say the fireplace out loud). Night after night he returns and slowly, over time, he becomes transformed. His wanderings become much like the days when he lived back home in Indiana. Now the voices of all who pass sound like the conversations of friendly crickets. The waiter's name, as it turns out, is An-gel and "Solomon Singer has found a place he loves and he doesn't feel lonely anymore."

To read more of this Conversation with Susan Guevara, please visit Chapter 3 on our text's companion website at **www.prenhall.com/darigan**

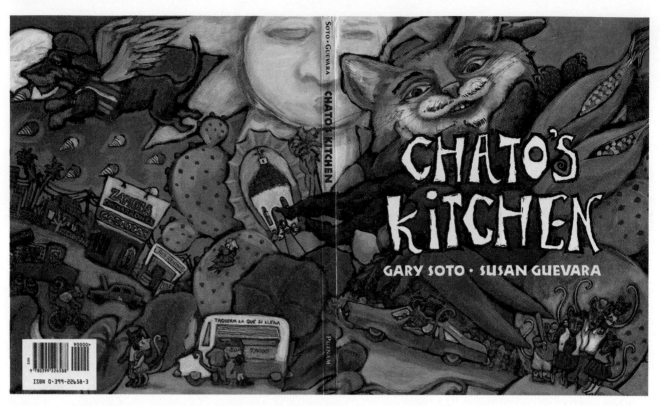

From ***Chato's Kitchen*** by Gary Soto, illustrated by Susan Guevara, copyright © 1995 by Susan Guevara, illustrations. Used by permission of G. P. Putnam's Sons, a division of Penguin Putnam, Inc.

Illustrator Peter Catalanotto's interpretation of this text is expressive and vibrant, and it shows the subtle changes that occur in Singer's character in a dramatic, creative way. Not until page 9 do we get a clear view of Solomon's face. All perspectives up to this point are either heavily shadowed or merely reflections, such as the ones seen in his teapot or in the window in his room. But the painting on pages 9 and 10 is very important: In it, we see a photo-realistic portrayal of the hectic evening streets of Manhattan, Singer with the collar up on his full-length coat, hands clutching it tightly closed. He looks terribly unhappy, almost fearful. On the next page, Catalanotto shows only Singer's feet at the top of the page and the rest of the illustration is merely his reflection in a large puddle.

When Darigan read this book to his fifth-grade class, they were totally absorbed in this one illustration. They wanted him to turn it upside down so they could get a better view of Singer. The kids were so touched by the sadness of this man.

Then one little girl raised her hand and said, "You know, you don't need to worry, Dr. D. Things will get better. See the rainbow at the edge of the puddle?" Sure enough, we looked and there *was* a rainbow.

Later that year, when we saw Catalanotto, we mentioned that child's observation and he said that, yes, he had placed that rainbow there and it was for that very reason. That little girl was the first he'd heard of who had noticed it, and he was thrilled.

After that, Darigan's class was totally "into" both the story and the accompanying pictures. It took almost 45 minutes to read this book through the first time because of all the conversation that went on.

Two double-page spreads later, when the class met the "smiling-eyed waiter," another child noticed yet another rainbow on the clock behind his head. "He is going to be the one to help him, I bet," noted the child. A child sitting on the floor right at Darigan's feet noticed the reflection of Solomon Singer in the spoon he is holding up. Another child said, "I've seen his reflection a lot of times already." So the class backtracked,

For many, many nights Solomon Singer made his way west, carrying a dream in his head, each night ordering it up with his supper. When he reached the end of his list of dreams (the end was a purple wall), he simply started all over again and ordered up a balcony (but he didn't say the balcony out loud).

From ***An Angel for Solomon Singer*** by Cynthia Rylant, illustrated by Peter Catalanotto. Text copyright © 1992 by Cynthia Rylant. Illustrations copyright © 1992 by Peter Catalanotto. Published by Orchard Books, an imprint of Scholastic, Inc. Reprinted by permission.

looking at each spread for Solomon's reflection. This was a good lesson in not letting the story itself dictate the lesson. Darigan's first reaction was to keep reading ahead, yet the class had a great desire to discuss and dissect these marvelous illustrations.

The class was most interested in how Catalanotto depicted the passage of time. Night after night, Singer orders up his supper and a dream. Beginning with only a crescent moon in the upper left-hand corner of the double-page spread shown here, the illustrator allows the image of the moon to bleed down the page and into each of the dreams—the balcony, the fireplace, the swing, and so on. Eventually, as the moon continues its steady descent and the waxing of the lunar body increases, it eventually becomes Singer's plate. The way Catalanotto slips from the abstract on the left-hand side of the spread to the realistic view of Angel and Solomon was a favorite of the kids.

On the next spread, the transformed Singer is seen walking the streets, head up and with a self-assured smile on his face, his coat open. It is worth backtracking to page 9 again to see the tremendous contrast to when Solomon earlier felt so fearful and suspicious.

He went to the Westway Café every night for dinner that first year and still goes there. Each night, when he orders his dinner, he keeps his dreams in his head. One of his dreams, in fact, has come true. He sneaked a cat into his hotel room. On the dedication and publisher's page, which in this case is the very last page of the book, we see Solomon's reflection once again in the cracked bathroom mirror, gently holding his cat. When children can see how character becomes well-rounded and changed, they go an entire step deeper in their appreciation of the books they have read.

Picture books are an abundant resource for initiating children into the worlds of literacy and image. Never before have we had such choices. Today's books are some of the finest ever made available for young readers. This genre of book can get kids started on the road to literacy, teach them all the necessary aspects of learning to read, and can help enrich their lives through good story, for it is the best books that make the most profound impressions on young minds.

▼▼▼▼▼▼▼

Summary

In this chapter, we began by providing a definition of the picture book and discussing the various categories they fall into: baby/board books, counting books, concept books, ABC books, engineered books, wordless picture books, predictable books, beginning reader picture books, and picture story books. We discussed how a picture book is made and what the basic criteria are for judging a picture book, noting plot, style, and development of character as key considerations.

▼▼▼▼▼▼▼

Fifteen More of Our Favorites

Alexander, Lloyd. (1992). *The fortune-tellers* (Trina Schart Hyman, Illus.). Dutton. (Picture story.) A carpenter goes to a fortune-teller and finds the predictions about his future come true in an unusual way.

Burton, Virginia Lee. (1939). *Mike Mulligan and his steam shovel*. Houghton Mifflin. (Picture story.) Mike Mulligan and his steam shovel Mary Anne prove that they can dig as much in one day as 100 men can dig in a week.

Crews, Donald. (1978). *Freight train*. Greenwillow. (Concept.) Colors and the names of the cars on a freight train are introduced with sparse but rhythmic text and brilliantly colored illustrations. A Caldecott Honor Book.

Henkes, Kevin. (1988). *Chester's way*. Greenwillow. (Picture story.) Best friends Chester and Wilson meet their match when Lilly comes into the neighborhood.

Martin, Bill Jr., & Archambault, John. (1985). *The ghost-eye tree* (Ted Rand, Illus.). Holt. (Picture story.) Walking down a dark lonely road on an errand one night, a brother and sister argue over who is afraid of the dread Ghost-Eye tree.

McCloskey, Robert. (1941). *Make way for ducklings*. Viking. (Picture story.) A city park in Boston eventually provides a safe home for ducklings and their Mallard parents. Winner of the Caldecott Medal

Mollel, Tololwa. (1990). *The orphan boy* (Paul Morin, Illus.). Clarion. (Picture story.) In Africa, an old man who tends cattle is surprised by the sudden appearance of a boy with mysterious powers who helps with the chores and brings prosperity.

Rogasky, Barbara. (1986). *The water of life* (Trina Schart Hyman, Illus.). Holiday House. (Picture story.) Adaptation of a Grimm tale: a prince searching for the Water of Life to cure his dying father finds an enchanted castle, a lovely princess, and treachery from his older brothers.

San Souci, Robert D. (1989). *The talking eggs* (Jerry Pinkney, Illus.). Dial. A Southern folktale in which kind Blanche, following the instruction of an old witch, gains riches, while her greedy sister makes fun of the old woman and is duly rewarded. A Caldecott Honor and Coretta Scott King Honor.

Sendak, Maurice. (1963). *Where the wild things are*. Harper. (Picture story.) A naughty little boy, sent to bed without his supper, sails to the land of the Wild Things, where he becomes their king. Winner of the Caldecott Medal.

Steig, William. (1982). *Doctor DeSoto*. Farrar. (Picture story.) A clever mouse dentist outwits his wicked fox patient. A Newbery Honor Book.

Turkle, Brinton. (1976). *Deep in the forest*. Dutton. (Wordless.) A variation of "Goldilocks and the Three Bears" which finds the little bear intruding.

Van Allsburg, Chris. (1981). *Jumanji*. Houghton Mifflin. (Picture story.) Left on their own for an afternoon, two bored and restless children find more excitement than they bargain for in a mysterious and mystical jungle adventure board game. Winner of the Caldecott Medal.

Waber, Bernard. (1972). *Ira sleeps over*. Houghton Mifflin. (Picture story.) A little boy is excited at the prospect of spending the night at his friend's house but worries about how he'll get along without his teddy bear.

Wood, Audrey. (1984). *The napping house* (Don Wood, Illus.). Harcourt. (Predictable.) In this cumulative tale, a wakeful flea atop a number of sleeping creatures causes a commotion, with just one bite.

▼▼▼▼▼▼▼

Others We Like

ABC

Aylesworth, Jim. (1992). *Old black fly* (Stephen Gammell, Illus.). Holt.

Cleary, Beverly. (1998). *The hullabaloo ABC* (Ted Rand, Illus.). Morrow.

Ehlert, Lois. (1989). *Eating the alphabet*. Harcourt.

Falls, C. B. (1998). *ABC book*. Morrow.

Garten, Jan. (1994). *Alphabet tale* (Muriel Batherman, Illus.). Greenwillow.

Grimes, Nikki. (1995). *C is for city* (Pat Cummings, Illus.). New York: Lothrop.

Johnson, Stephen T. (1995). *Alphabet city*. Viking.

Jonas, Ann. (1990). *Aardvarks, disembark!* Greenwillow.

Kitchen, Bert. (1984). *Animal alphabet*. Dial.

Lobel, Anita. (1990). *Allison's zinnia*. Greenwillow.

Lobel, Arnold. (1981). *On Market Street* (Anita Lobel, Illus.). Greenwillow.

MacDonald, Suse. (1986). *Alphabatics*. Bradbury.

Martin, Bill, Jr., & Archambault, John. (1989). *Chicka chicka boom boom* (Lois Ehlert, Illus.). Holt.

Miranda, Anne. (1996). *Pignic: An alphabet book in rhyme* (Rosekrans Hoffman, Illus.). Boyds Mills.

Shannon, George. (1996). *Tomorrow's alphabet* (Donald Crews, Illus.). Greenwillow.

Tapahonso, Luci, & Schick, Eleanor. (1995). *Navajo ABC: A Diné alphabet book* (Eleanor Schick, Illus.) New York: Simon & Schuster.

Van Allsburg, Chris. (1987). *The Z Was Zapped: A Play in Twenty-Six Acts*. Houghton Mifflin.

Counting

Carlstrom, Nancy White. (1996). *Let's count it out, Jesse Bear* (Bruce Degen, Illus.). Simon & Schuster.

Ehlert, Lois. (1990). *Fish eyes*. Harcourt.

Fleming, Denise. (1992). *Count!* Holt.

Geisert, Arthur. (1992). *Pigs from 1 to 10*. Boston: Houghton Mifflin.

Giganti, Paul, Jr. (1992). *Each orange had 8 slices: A counting book* (Donald Crews, Illus.). Greenwillow.

Hague, Kathleen. (1999). *Ten little bears: A counting rhyme* (Michael Hague, Illus.). Morrow.

Johnson, Stephen T. (1998). *City by numbers*. Viking.

Marzollo, Jean. (1994). *Ten cats have hats: A counting book* (David McPhail, Illus.). Scholastic.

Merriam, Eve. (1993). *12 ways to get to 11* (Bernie Karlin, Illus.). Simon & Schuster.

Pinczes, Elinor J. (1993). *One hundred hungry ants* (Bonnie Mackain, Illus.). Houghton Mifflin.

Pinczes, Elinor J. (1995). *A reminder of one* (Bonnie Mackain, Illus.). Houghton Mifflin.

Rankin, Laura. (1998). *The handmade counting book*. Dial.

Sloat, Teri. (1991). *From one to one hundred*. Dutton.

Walsh, Ellen Stoll. (1991). *Mouse count*. Harcourt.

Concept

Barton, Byron. (1986). *Trains*. Crowell.

Davis, Lee. (1994). *The lifesize animal opposites book*. Dorling Kindersley.

Ehlert, Lois. (1989). *Color zoo*. Lippincott.

Jonas, Ann. (1989). *Color dance*. Greenwillow.

Hoban, Tana. (1990). *Exactly the opposite*. Greenwillow.

Hoban, Tana. (1998). *So many circles, so many squares*. Greenwillow.

Koch, Michelle. (1991). *Hoot, howl, hiss*. Greenwillow.

McMillan, Bruce. (1991). *Eating fractions*. Scholastic.

Micklethwait, Lucy. (1993). *A child's book of art: Great pictures, first words*. Dorling Kindersley.

Micklethwait, Lucy. (1995). *Spot a dog*. Dorling Kindersley.

Scieszka, Jon. (1995). *Math curse* (Lane Smith, Illus.). Viking.

Serfozo, Mary. (1988). *Who said red?* (Keiko Narahashi, Illus.). McElderry.

Walsh, Ellen Stoll. (1989). *Mouse paint*. Harcourt.

Participation

Anno, Mitsumasa. (1983). *Anno's U.S.A.* Philomel.

Burton, Marilee Robin. (1988). *Tail toes eyes ears nose*. Harper.

Carlstrom, Nancy. (1986). *Jesse Bear, what will you wear?* Macmillan.

Gág, Wanda. (1928). *Millions of cats*. Putnam.

Handford, Martin. (1987). *Where's Waldo?* Little, Brown.

Hill, Eric. (1980). *Where's Spot?* Putnam.

Martin, Bill, Jr. (1993). *Old devil wind* (Barry Root, Illus.). Harcourt.

Marzollo, Jean. (1997). *I spy super challenger: A book of picture riddles* (Walter Wick, Photog.). Scholastic.

Rosen, Michael. (1989). *We're going on a bear hunt* (Helen Oxenbury, Illus.). McElderry.

Yoshi. (1987). *Who's hiding here?* Picture Book Studio.

Wordless

Baker, Jeannie. (1991). *Window*. Greenwillow.

Briggs, Raymond. (1978). *The snowman*. Random House.

Collington, Peter. (1987). *The angel and the soldier boy*. Knopf.

Day, Alexandra. (1985). *Good dog, Carl*. Green Tiger.

Geisert, Arthur. (1991). *Oink*. Knopf.

Goodall, John. (1988). *Little Red Riding Hood*. McElderry.

Goodall, John. (1998). *Creep castle*. McElderry.

Jenkins, Steve. (1995). *Looking down*. Houghton.

Martin, Rafe. (1989). *Will's mammoth* (Stephen Gammell, Illus.). Putnam.

Schories, Pat. (1991). *Mouse around*. Farrar, Straus & Giroux.

Spier, Peter. (1982). *Rain*. Doubleday.

Rohmann, Eric. (1994). *Time flies*. Crown.

Wiesner, David. (1988). *Free fall*. Lothrop.

Wiesner, David. (1991). *Tuesday*. Clarion.

Wouters, Anne. (1992). *This book is too small*. Dutton.

Predictable

REPEATED PATTERNS

Berry, Holly. (1994). *Busy Lizzie*. North-South.

Brown, Ruth. (1981). *A dark dark tale*. Dial.

Carlstrom, Nancy White. (1986). *Jesse Bear, what will you wear?* (Bruce Degen, Illus.). Macmillan.

Carle, Eric. (1969). *The very hungry caterpillar*. Philomel.

Carle, Eric. (1990). *The very quiet cricket*. Philomel.

Fox, Mem. (1988). *Hattie and the fox* (Patricia Mullins, Illus.). Bradbury.

Gravois, Jeanne M. (1993). *Quickly, Quigley*. Tambourine.

Marzollo, Jean. (1994). *Ten cats have hats: A counting book*. Scholastic.

Slobodkina, Esphyr. (1947). *Caps for sale*. Addison-Wesley.

Waddell, Martin. (1992). *Farmer Duck* (Helen Oxenbury, Illus.). Candlewick.

Wood, Audrey. (1985). *King Bidgood's in the bathtub* (Don Wood, Illus.). Harcourt.

Ziefert, Harriet. (1995). *Oh, what a noisy farm!* Tambourine.

CUMULATIVE TALES

Emberley, Barbara. (1967). *Drummer Hoff* (Ed Emberley, Illus.). Simon & Schuster.

Hayes, Sarah. (1990). *The grumpalump*. Clarion.

Melmed, Laura Krauss. (1996). *The marvelous market on Mermaid*. Lothrop.

Neitzel, Shirley. (1995). *The bag I'm taking to Grandma's*. Greenwillow.

Neitzel, Shirley. (1997). *We're making breakfast for Mother*. Greenwillow.

FAMILIAR SONGS OR VERSES

Beck, Ian. (1992). *Five little ducks*. Henry Holt.

Morley, Carol. (1994). *Farmyard song*. Simon & Schuster.

Sendak, Maurice. (1962). *Chicken soup with rice*. Harper.

Sweet, Melissa. (1992). *Fiddle-i-fee: A farmyard song for the very young*. Little, Brown.

Voce, Louise. (1994). *Over in the meadow: A traditional counting rhyme*. Candlewick.

Watson, Wendy. (1994). *Fox went out on a chilly night*. Lothrop.

PREDICTABLE RHYTHM AND RHYME

Brink, Carol Ryrie. (1994). *Goody O'Grumpity* (Ashley Wolff, Illus.). North-South.

Brown, Margaret Wise. (1947). *Goodnight Moon*. Harper.

Degen, Bruce. (1983). *Jamberry*. Harper.

Gilman, Phoebe. (1985). *Jillian Jiggs*. Scholastic.

Hayes, Sarah. (1986). *This is the bear*. Candlewick.

Hayes, Sarah. (1995). *This is the bear and the bad little girl*. Candlewick.

Yolen, Jane. (2000). *Off we go!* (Laurel Molk, Illus.). Little, Brown.

INTERLOCKING TEXT

Ahlberg, Janet, & Ahlberg, Allan. (1979). *Each peach pear plum*. Viking.

Cohen, Caron Lee. (1996). *Where's the fly?* Greenwillow.

Janovitz, Marilyn. (1994). *Look out, bird!* North-South.

Janovitz, Marilyn. (1996). *Can I help?* North-South.

Numeroff, Laura. (1985). *If you give a mouse a cookie* (Felicia Bond, Illus.). HarperCollins.

Numeroff, Laura. (1991). *If you give a moose a muffin* (Felicia Bond, Illus.). HarperCollins.

Numeroff, Laura. (1998). *If you give a pig a pancake* (Felicia Bond, Illus.). HarperCollins.

Beginning Reader

Baker, Barbara. (1988). *Digby and Kate* (Marsha Winborn, Illus.). Dutton.

Bulla, Clyde Robert. (1987). *The chalk box kid* (Thomas B. Allen, Illus.). Random House.

Byars, Betsy. (1990). *Hooray for the Golly Sisters!* (Sue Truesdell, Illus.). Harper.

Cohen, Miriam. (1990). *First grade takes a test* (Lillian Hoban, Illus.). Greenwillow.

Lobel, Arnold. (1970). *Frog and Toad are friends.* Harper.

Lobel, Arnold. (1981). *Uncle Elephant.* Harper.

Minarik, Else. (1957). *Little bear* (Maurice Sendak, Illus.). Harper.

Rylant, Cynthia. (1990). *Henry and Mudge and the happy cat* (Sucie Stevenson, Illus.). Bradbury.

Rylant, Cynthia. (1997). *Poppleton* (Mark Teague, Illus.). Blue Sky (Scholastic).

Sharmat, Marjorie Weinman. (1992). *Nate the great and the stolen base* (Marc Simont, Illus.). Coward.

Seuss, Dr. (1957). *The cat in the hat.* Houghton Mifflin.

Van Leeuwen, Jean. (1990). *Oliver pig at school* (Ann Schweninger, Illus.). Dial.

Picture Story

Ackerman, Karen. (1988). *Song and dance man* (Stephen Gammell, Illus.). Knopf.

Allard, Harry. (1977). *Miss Nelson is missing* (James Marshall, Illus.). Houghton Mifflin.

Bemelmans, Ludwig. (1939). *Madeline.* Viking.

Bunting, Eve. (1989). *The Wednesday surprise* (Donald Carrick, Illus.). Clarion.

Burningham, John. (1985). *Grandpa.* Crown.

Cooney, Barbara. (1982). *Miss Rumphius.* Viking.

Hall, Donald. (1979). *Ox-cart man.* (Barbara Cooney, Illus.). Viking.

Crowe, Robert. (1976). *Clyde Monster* (Kay Chorao, Illus.). Dutton.

Day, Alexandra. (1990). *Frank and Ernest play ball.* Scholastic.

Demi. (1997). *One grain of rice: A mathematical folktale.* Scholastic.

dePaola, Tomie. (1975). *Strega Nona.* Prentice Hall.

Fox, Mem. (1990). *Possum magic.* (Julie Vivas, Illus.). Harcourt.

Hamilton, Virginia. (2000). *The girl who spun gold* (Leo Dillon & Diane Dillon, Illus.). Scholastic.

Hoban, Russell. (1964). *Bread and jam for Frances* (Lillian Hoban, Illus.). Harper.

Keats, Ezra Jack. (1971). *Apt. 3.* Macmillan.

Kellogg, Steven. (1979). *Pinkerton, behave!* Dial.

Lionni, Leo. (1967). *Frederick.* Knopf.

Mayer, Mercer. (1968). *There's a nightmare in my closet.* Dial.

McKissack, Patricia C. (1988). *Mirandy and Brother Wind.* (Jerry Pinkney, Illus.). Knopf.

McCloskey, Robert. (1948). *Blueberries for Sal.* Viking.

Meddaugh, Susan. (1994). *Martha calling.* Houghton Mifflin.

Pattison, Darcy. (1991). *The river dragon* (Jean Tseng & Mou-sien Tseng, Illus.). Lothrop.

Peet, Bill. (1983). *Buford the little bighorn.* Houghton Mifflin.

Rathmann, Peggy. (1995). *Officer Buckle and Gloria.* Putnam.

Rylant, Cynthia. (1985). *The relatives came* (Stephen Gammell, Illus.). Bradbury.

Schwartz, Amy. (1988). *Anabelle Swift, kindergartner.* Orchard.

Scieszka, Jon. (1989). *The true story of the three little pigs!* (Lane Smith, Illus.). Viking.

Seuss, Dr. (Theodore Geisel). (1938). *The 500 hats of Bartholomew Cubbins.* Vanguard.

Small, David. (1985). *Imogene's antlers.* Crown.

Stevens, Janet. (1995). *Tops & bottoms.* Harcourt.

Stevenson, James. (1977). *Could be worse!* Greenwillow.

Tunnell, Michael O. (1997). *Mailing May* (Ted Rand, Illus.). Tambourine/Greenwillow.

Van Allsburg, Chris. (1992). *The widow's broom.* Houghton Mifflin.

Viorst, Judith. (1972). *Alexander and the terrible, horrible, no good, very bad day* (Ray Cruz, Illus.). Atheneum.

Wood, Audrey. (1987). *Heckedy Peg* (Don Wood, Illus.). Harcourt.

Yolen, Jane. (1987). *Owl moon* (John Schoenherr, Illus.). Putnam.

Yolen, Jane. (1998). *Raising Yoder's barn* (Bernie Fuchs, Illus.). Little, Brown.

Engineered

Ahlberg, Janet, & Ahlberg, Allan. (1986). *The jolly postman or other people's letters.* Little, Brown.

Carle, Eric. (1986). *My very first book of sounds.* Crowell.

Carter, Noelle, Carter, David. (1990). *I'm a little mouse: A touch & feel book.* Holt.

Ehlert, Lois. (1990). *Color farm.* Lippincott.

Goodall, John. (1988). *Little Red Riding Hood.* McElderry.

Hill, Eric. (1991). *Spot goes to the park.* Putnam.

Milne, A. A. (1987). *Pooh and some bees (Pooh carousel book)* (Ernest H. Shepard, Illus.; paper engineering by Paulette Petrovsky.). Dutton.

Monfried, Lucia. (1989). *Dishes all done* (Jon Agee, Illus.). Dutton.

Pieńkowski, Jan. (1979). *Haunted house.* (Paper engineering by Tor Lokvig.) Dutton.

Pieńkowski, Jan. (1993). *ABC dinosaurs.* (Paper engineering by Rodger Smith & Helen Balmer.) Dutton.

Sabuda, Robert. (1994). *The Christmas alphabet.* Orchard.

Sabuda, Robert. (1997). *Cookie count.* Little Simon.

Zelinsky, Paul O. (1990). *The wheels on the bus.* (Paper engineering by Rodger Smith.) Dutton.

Baby/Board

Bohdal, Susi. (1986). *Bobby the bear*. North-South Books.

Boynton, Sandra. (1995). *Blue hat, green hat*. Little Simon.

Dickens, Lucy. (1991). *At the beach*. Viking.

Duke, Kate. (1986). *What bounces?* Dutton.

Hill, Eric. (1985). *Spot at play*. Putnam.

Hoban, Tana. (1985). *What is it?* Greenwillow.

Oxenbury, Helen. (1981). *Dressing*. Simon & Schuster.

Oxenbury, Helen. (1982). *Mother's helper*. Dial.

Oxenbury, Helen. (1986). *I can*. Random House.

Pfister, Martin. (1996) (1992). *The rainbow fish*. North-South Books.

Tafuri, Nancy. (1987). *My friends*. Greenwillow.

▼▼▼▼▼▼▼

Children's Literature References

Ada, Alma Flor. (1997). *Gathering the sun: An alphabet in Spanish and English* (Simon Silva, Illus., Rosa Zubizarreta, Trans.). New York: Lothrop.

Ahlberg, Janet, & Alhberg, Allan. (1979). *Each peach pear plum*. New York: Viking.

Anno, Mitsumasa. (1982). *Anno's counting book*. New York: Philomel.

Aylesworth, Jim. (1992). *Old black fly* (Stephen Gammell, Illus.). New York: Holt.

Baker, Keith. (1994). *Big fat hen*. San Diego: Harcourt.

Barton, Byron. (1993). *The little red hen*. New York: HarperCollins.

Bartone, Elisa. (1996). *American too* (Ted Lewin, Illus.). New York: Lothrop.

Beck, Ian. (1992). *Five little ducks*. New York: Holt.

Berger, Barbara. (1981). *Grandfather twilight*. New York: Philomel.

Bierman, Carol. (1998). *Journey to Ellis Island: How my father came to America* (Laurie McGaw, Illus.). New York: Hyperion.

Blake, Quentin. (1995). *Clown*. New York: Holt.

Briggs, Raymond. (1978). *The snowman*. New York: Trumpet.

Brooks, Alan. (1996). *Frogs jump* (Steven Kellogg, Illus.). New York: Scholastic.

Brooks, Bruce. (1997). *NBA by the numbers*. New York: Scholastic.

Bryan, Ashley. (1997). *Ashley Bryan's ABC of African American poetry*. New York: Atheneum.

Burningham, John. (1994). *First steps: Letters, numbers, colors, opposites*. Cambridge, MA: Candlewick.

Butler, Dorothy. (1991). *Higgledy piggledy hobbledy hoy* (Lyn Kriegler, Illus.). New York: Greenwillow.

Campbell, Rod. (1982). *Dear zoo*. New York: Four Winds.

Campbell, Rod. (1983). *Oh dear!* New York: Four Winds.

Carle, Eric. (1969). *The very hungry caterpillar*. New York: Philomel.

Carle, Eric. (1993). *Today is Monday*. New York: Philomel.

Carroll, Kathleen Sullivan. (1992). *One red rooster* (Suzette Barbier, Illus.). Boston: Houghton Mifflin.

Carter, Anne. (1981). *Dinner time*. Los Angeles: Price Stern Sloan.

Catalanotto, Peter. (1989). *Dylan's day out*. New York: Orchard.

Charles, Faustin, & Arenson, Roberta. (1996). *A Caribbean counting book*. Boston: Houghton Mifflin.

Collington, Peter. (1995). *The tooth fairy*. New York: Knopf.

Conrad, Pam. (1999). *Blue willow* (S. Saelig Gallagher, Illus.). New York: Philomel.

Crews, Donald. (1978). *Freight train*. New York: Greenwillow.

dePaola, Tomie. (1975). *Strega Nona*. Upper Saddle River, NJ: Merrill/Prentice Hall.

Day, Alexandra. (1985). *Good dog, Carl*. New York: Green Tiger.

Day, Alexandra. (1995). *Carl's birthday*. New York: Farrar, Straus & Giroux.

Dodson, Peter. (1995). *An alphabet of dinosaurs* (Wayne D. Barlowe, Illus.). New York: Scholastic.

Dotlich, Rebecca Kai. (1999a.). *What is round?* (Maria Ferrari, Illus.). New York: HarperCollins.

Dotlich, Rebecca Kai. (1999b.). *What is square?* (Maria Ferrari, Illus.). New York: HarperCollins.

Dotlich, Rebecca Kai. (2000). *What is a triangle?* (Maria Ferrari, Illus.). New York: HarperCollins.

Ehlert, Lois. (1989). *Color zoo*. New York: Lippincott.

Ehlert, Lois. (1990). *Color farm*. New York: Lippincott.

Emberley, Ed. (1992). *Go away, big green monster!* Boston: Little, Brown.

Emberley, Ed, & Miranda, Anne. (1997). *Glad monster, sad monster: A book about feelings*. Boston: Little, Brown.

Faulkner, Keith. (1996). *The wide-mouthed frog* (Jonathan Lambert, Illus.). New York: Dial.

Fleming, Denise. (1992). *Count!* New York: Holt.

Fleming, Denise. (2000). *The everything book*. New York: Holt.

Fox, Mem. (1989). *Shoes from Grandpa* (Patricia Mullins, Illus.). New York: Orchard.

Fox, Mem. (1993). *Time for bed* (Jane Dyer, Illus.). San Diego: Harcourt.

Freedman, Russell. (1980). *Immigrant kids*. New York: Scholastic.

Garland, Sherry. (1993). *The lotus seed* (Tatsuro Kiuchi, Illus.). San Diego: Harcourt.

Guy, Ginger Foglesong. (1996). *Fiesta!* (Rene King Moreno, Illus.). New York: William Morrow.

Harding, Emma. (1993). *Cock-a-doodle-doo!* New York: Holt.

Hausman, Gerald. (1994). *Turtle Island ABC* (Cara Moser & Barry Moser, Illus.). New York: HarperCollins.

Henkes, Kevin. (1988). *Chester's way*. New York: Greenwillow.

Henkes, Kevin. (1990). *Julius, the baby of the world*. New York: Greenwillow.

Hepworth, Cathy. (1992). *Antics! An alphabetical anthology*. New York: Putnam.

Herold, Maggie Rugg. (1995). *A very important day* (Catherine Stock, Illus.). New York: Morrow.

Hest, Amy. (1997). *When Jessie came across the sea* (P. J. Lynch, Illus.). Cambridge, MA: Candlewick Press.

Hill, Eric. (1991). *Spot goes to the park*. New York: Putnam.

Hill, Eric. (1994). *Spot bakes a cake*. New York: Putnam.

Hill, Eric. (2000). *Spot's big touch and feel book*. New York: Putnam.

Hoban, Tana. (1990). *Exactly the opposite*. New York: Greenwillow.

Hoban, Tana. (1995). *Colors everywhere*. New York: Greenwillow.

Hoban, Tana. (1996). *Just look*. New York: Greenwillow.

Hoban, Tana. (1997). *Look book*. New York: Greenwillow.

Holder, Heidi. (1987). *Crows: An old rhyme*. New York: Farrar, Straus & Giroux.

Hopkins, Lee Bennett. (1994). *April bubbles chocolate: An ABC of poetry* (Barry Root, Illus.). New York: Simon.

Howe, James. (1997). *Pinky and Rex and the new neighbors*. New York: Aladdin.

Howe, James. (1998). *Pinky and Rex and the school play*. New York: Atheneum.

Hughes, Shirley. (1985). *Bathwater's hot*. New York: Lothrop.

Hunt, Jonathan. (1989). *Illuminations*. New York: Bradbury.

Hutchins, Pat. (1986). *The doorbell rang*. New York: Greenwillow.

Inkpen, Mick. (1995). *Wibbly Pig can make a tent*. New York: Viking.

Jackson, Alison. (1997). *I know an old lady who swallowed a pie* (Judith Byron Schachner, Illus.). New York: Dutton.

Janovitz, Marilyn. (1994). *Is it time?* New York: North-South Books.

Johnson, Stephen, T. (1995). *Alphabet city*. New York: Viking.

Johnson, Stephen T. (2000). *My little red toolbox*. San Diego: Harcourt.

Karas, G. Brian. (1960). *I know an old lady*. New York: Scholastic.

Keats, Ezra Jack. (1962). *The snowy day*. New York: Viking.

Keats, Ezra Jack. (1968). *One red sun: A counting book*. New York: Viking.

Kunhardt, Dorothy. (1940). *Pat the bunny*. Racine, WI: Western.

Lester, Mike. (2000). *A is for salad*. New York: Putnam.

Levine, Ellen. (1993). *. . . If your name was changed at Ellis Island* (Wayne Parmenter, Illus.). New York: Scholastic.

Lobel, Arnold. (1970). *Frog and Toad are friends*. New York: Harper & Row.

Lobel, Arnold. (1972). *Frog and Toad together*. New York: Harper & Row.

Loveless, Liz. (1993). *1, 2, buckle my shoe*. New York: Hyperion.

MacDonald, Suse. (1986). *Alphabatics*. New York: Bradbury.

Maestro, Betsy. (1996). *Coming to America* (Susannah Ryan, Illus.). New York: Scholastic.

Markle, Sandra, & Markle, William. (1998). *Gone forever! An alphabet of extinct animals* (Felipe Davalos, Illus.). New York: Atheneum.

Martin, Bill, Jr. (1967). *Brown Bear, Brown Bear, what do you see?* (Eric Carle, Illus.). New York: Holt.

Martin, Bill. Jr., (1991). *Polar Bear, Polar Bear, what do you hear?* (Eric Carle, Illus.). New York: Holt.

Martin, Bill, Jr., & Archambault, John. (1989). *Chicka chicka boom boom* (Lois Ehlert, Illus.). New York: Simon & Schuster.

Mayer, Mercer. (1967). *A boy, a dog, and a frog*. New York: Dial.

Mayer, Mercer. (1974). *Frog goes to dinner*. New York: Dial.

McCloskey, Robert. (1948). *Blueberries for Sal*. New York: Viking.

McMillan, Bruce. (1988). *Growing colors*. New York: Mulberry.

McMillan, Bruce. (1993). *Mouse views: What the class pet saw*. New York: Holiday.

McMillan, Bruce. (1994). *Sense suspense: A guessing game for the five senses*. New York: Scholastic.

Miller, Margaret. (1996). *Now I'm big*. New York: Greenwillow.

Minarik, Else. (1957). *Little Bear*. New York: Harper & Row.

Mora, Pat. (1996). *Uno, dos, tres; One, two, three* (Barbara Lavallee, Illus.). New York: Clarion.

Musgrove, Margaret. (1976). *Ashanti to Zulu: African traditions* (Leo Dillon & Diane Dillon, Illus.). New York: Dial.

My first real Mother Goose. (2000). New York: Scholastic.

Nolen, Jerdine. (2000) *Big Jabe* (Kadir Nelson, Illus.). New York: Lothrop.

Oxenbury, Helen. (1981a). *Dressing*. New York: Wanderer Books.

Oxenbury, Helen. (1981b). *Family*. New York: Wanderer Books.

Oxenbury, Helen. (1981c). *Friends*. New York: Wanderer Books.

Oxenbury, Helen. (1981d). *Playing*. New York: Wanderer Books.

Oxenbury, Helen. (1981e). *Working*. New York: Wanderer Books.

Paparone, Pamela. (1995). *Five little ducks: An old rhyme*. New York: North-South Books.

Peek, Merle. (1969). *Roll over! A counting song*. New York: Clarion.

Peet, Bill. (1962). *Smokey*. Boston: Houghton Mifflin.

Peet, Bill. (1965). *Kermit the hermit*. Boston: Houghton Mifflin.

Peet, Bill. (1966). *Farewell to Shady Glade*. Boston: Houghton Mifflin.

Peet, Bill. (1970). *The whingdingdilly*. Boston: Houghton Mifflin.

Peet, Bill. (1971). *The caboose who got loose*. Boston: Houghton Mifflin.

Peet, Bill. (1978). *Ella*. Boston: Houghton Mifflin.

Peet, Bill. (1980a). *Chester the worldly pig*. Boston: Houghton Mifflin.

Peet, Bill. (1980b). *Randy's dandy lions*. Boston: Houghton Mifflin.

Peet, Bill. (1984). *Pamela camel*. Boston: Houghton Mifflin.

Peet, Bill. (1989). *Bill Peet: An autobiography*. Boston: Houghton Mifflin.

Pelletier, David. (1996). *The graphic alphabet*. New York: Orchard.

Pieńkowski, Jan. (1979). *Haunted house*. New York: Dutton.

Pieńkowski, Jan. (1993). *ABC dinosaurs*. New York: Dutton.

Pieńkowski, Jan. (1999). *Goodnight*. (Paper engineering by Helen Balmer & Martin Taylor.) Cambridge, MA: Candlewick.

Pieńkowski, Jan, & Carter, Anne. (1981). *Dinner time*. (Paper engineering by Marcin Stajewski & James Roger Diaz.) New York: Gallery Five/Fenn.

Polacco, Patricia. (1988). *The keeping quilt*. New York: Simon & Schuster.

Polacco, Patricia. (1992). *Chicken Sunday*. New York: Philomel.

Polacco, Patricia. (1994). *Pink and Say*. New York: Philomel.

Popov, Nikolai. (1996). *Why?* New York: North-South Books.

Potter, Beatrix. (1902). *The tale of Peter Rabbit*. New York: Warne.

Rathmann, Peggy. (1995). *Officer Buckle and Gloria*. New York: Putnam.

Roberts, Michael. (1998). *The jungle ABC*. New York: Hyperion.

Rounds, Glen. (1993). *Three Billy Goats Gruff*. New York: Holiday House.

Rylant, Cynthia. (1990). *Henry and Mudge and the happy cat* (Susie Stevenson, Illus.). New York: Bradbury.

Rylant, Cynthia. (1992). *An angel for Solomon Singer* (Peter Catalanotto, Illus.). New York: Orchard.

Rylant, Cynthia. (1995). *Henry and Mudge and the best day of all*. New York: Bradbury.

Rylant, Cynthia. (1998a). *Henry and Mudge and the sneaky crackers*. New York: Simon & Schuster.

Rylant, Cynthia. (1998b). *Poppleton forever* (Mark Teague, Illus.). New York: Blue Sky Press.

Sabuda, Robert. (1994). *The Christmas alphabet*. New York: Orchard.

Sabuda, Robert. (1997). *Cookie count*. New York: Little Simon.

Sabuda, Robert. (1998). *ABC Disney*. New York: Disney.

Sabuda, Robert. (2000). *The wonderful wizard of Oz: A commemorative pop-up*. New York: Simon & Schuster.

Say, Allen. (1991). *Tree of cranes*. Boston: Houghton Mifflin.

Say, Allen. (1993). *Grandfather's journey*. Boston: Houghton Mifflin.

Say, Allen. (1999). *Tea with milk*. Boston: Houghton Mifflin.

Say, Allen. (2000). *The sign painter*. Boston: Houghton Mifflin.

Schlein, Miriam. (1996). *More than one* (Donald Crews, Illus.). New York: Greenwillow.

Serfozo, Mary. (1988). *Who said red?* (Keiko Narahashi, Illus.). McElderry.

Seuss, Dr. (1957). *The cat in the hat*. New York: Random House.

Shannon, George. (1996). *Tomorrow's alphabet* (Donald Crews, Illus.). New York: Greenwillow.

Shaw, Charles, G. (1947). *It looked like spilt milk*. New York: Scholastic.

Snyder, Dianne. (1988). *The boy of the three-year nap* (Allen Say, Illus.). Boston: Houghton Mifflin.

Soto, Gary. (1995). *Chato's kitchen* (Susan Guevara, Illus.). New York: Putnam.

Soto, Gary. (2000). *Chato and the party animals* (Susan Guevara, Illus.). New York: Putnam.

Stevenson, Peter. (1999). *The three little pigs*. New York: Scholastic.

Stickland, Paul, & Stickland, Henrietta. (1994). *Dinosaur roar!* New York: Dutton.

Taback, Simms. (1997). *There was an old lady who swallowed a fly*. New York: Viking.

Tudor, Tasha. (2000). *1 is one*. New York: Simon & Schuster. (Original work published 1956)

Valenta, Barbara. (1997). *Pop-o-mania: How to create your own pop-ups*. New York: Dial.

Van Allsburg, Chris. (1987). *The Z was zapped*. Boston: Houghton Mifflin.

Van Rynbach, Iris. (1995). *Five little pumpkins*. Honesdale, PA: Boyds Mills Press.

Wallwork, Amanda. (1993). *No dodos: A counting book of endangered animals*. New York: Scholastic.

Walsh, Ellen Stoll. (1989). *Mouse paint*. San Diego: Harcourt.

West, Colin. (1996). *"I don't care!" said the bear*. Cambridge, MA: Candlewick.

Wiesner, David. (1988). *Free fall*. New York: Lothrop.

Wiesner, David. (1992). *Tuesday*. New York: Clarion.

Wiesner, David. (1999). *Sector 7*. New York: Clarion.

Woodruff, Elvira. (1999). *The memory coat* (Michael Dooling, Illus.). New York: Scholastic.

Yin. (2001). *Coolies* (Chris Soentpiet, Illus.). New York: Philomel.

Yolen, Jane. (1989). *Dove Isabeau* (Dennis Nolan, Illus.). San Diego: Harcourt.

Zelinsky, Paul O. (1990). *The wheels on the bus*. New York: Dutton.

▼▼▼▼▼▼▼

Professional References

Allen, R. V., & Allen, C. (1968). *Language experience in reading.* Chicago: Encyclopaedia Britannica.

Criscoe, B. (1988). A pleasant reminder: There is an established criteria for writing alphabet books. *Reading Horizons, 28*(4), 232–234.

Darigan, D. L. (1997). A breakfast with the authors: Bruce Coville and Paul O. Zelinsky. *Journal of Children's Literature, 23*(2), 60–67.

Goodman, K. (1988). Look what they've done to Judy Blume!: The basalization of children's literature. *The New Advocate, 1*(1), 29–41.

Goodman, Y., Goodman, K., & Bridges, L. (1990). *The whole language catalogue.* Glencoe, IL: McGraw-Hill.

Holdaway, D. (1979). *The foundations of literacy.* Portsmouth, NH: Heinemann.

Kiefer, B. Z. (1995). *The potential of picturebooks: From visual literacy to aesthetic understanding.* Upper Saddle River, NJ: Merrill/Prentice Hall.

Martin, B., & Brogan, P. (1972a). *The sounds of language.* Instant Reader Teacher's Guide, Level 1. New York: Holt, Rinehart and Winston.

Martin, B., & Brogan, P. (1972b). *Sounds of a young hunter.* Teacher's Edition. New York: Holt, Rinehart and Winston.

Norton, D. E. (1992). *The impact of literature-based reading.* Columbus, OH: Merrill.

Rhodes, L. K. (1981). I can read! Predictable books as resources for reading and writing instruction. *Reading Teacher, 34*(5), 511–517.

Vacca, R., Vacca, J., & Gove, A. (2000). *Reading and learning to read.* New York: Longman.

POETRY

4

CHAPTER

If you want to cover

A Passel of Poetry

Consider as a READ ALOUD

The Random House Book of Poetry for Children, selected by Jack Prelutsky, illustrated by Arnold Lobel

Consider as a TEXT SET

Arroz con leche: Popular Songs and Rhymes from Latin America, by Lulu Delacre

Brown Angels: An Album of Pictures and Verse, by Walter Dean Myers

Brown Honey in Broomwheat Tea, by Joyce Carol Thomas, illustrated by Floyd Cooper

Chinese Mother Goose Rhymes, by Robert Wyndham, illustrated by Ed Young

How Now, Brown Cow, by Alice Schertle, illustrated by Amanda Schaffer

Meet Danitra Brown, by Nikki Grimes, illustrated by Floyd Cooper

Sing to the Sun, by Ashley Bryan

BROWN ANGELS
by Walter Dean Myers

Prayer

Shout my name to the angels

Sing my song to the skies

Anoint my ears with wisdom

Let beauty fill my eyes

Excerpt from *Brown Angels*
by Walter Dean Myers

Student Response

My favorite poem from "<u>Brown Angels</u>" was "<u>Prayer</u>". It was really beautiful. It made me think about how the first thing you want the baby to experience is love. You want it to hear music, see beauty, and you always want to make sure it never sees, hears, or feels anything else. You want to give it the world.

Eva   age 11

Karen Lammey has been teaching school for only five years but she knows, unquestionably, the important place poetry holds in her classroom. She uses poetry with her first graders every single day, many times a day. Her mornings begin with a poem. She and the class welcome in the seasons and holidays with an abundance of poetry. Units of study in all the curricular areas, such as science, math, health, and especially, social studies, have poetry naturally embedded into them. And because Ms. Lammey knows how highly predictable poetry can be, it becomes the major vehicle in her reading program.

Children are able to read "instantly" when good poetry is placed before them. Take, for example, the traditional Mother Goose rhyme:

> Hey diddle, diddle,
> The cat and the fiddle,
> The cow jumped over the moon;
> The little dog laughed
> To see such sport
> And the dish ran away
> With the spoon.

To visit a classroom exploring the issues of Poetry, please go to Chapter 4 of our companion website at **www.renhall.com/darigan**

"The children immediately pick up on the rhythm and rhyme of poetry," she says. "Many of the selections are already known to them, but more importantly they begin making connections between what their ears hear and what they see in front of them on the poetry chart. That is the beginning of reading."

And this can be done with any and all of Mother Goose. "To market, to market, to buy a fat pig . . . " "Humpty Dumpty sat on a wall . . . " "Little Jack Horner sat in a corner . . . " "Mary, Mary, quite contrary . . . " The possibilities are enormous. And when you have exhausted Mother Goose, you can go on to other authors, work like Jack Prelutsky's wonderful pair of books, *Ride a Purple Pelican* and *Beneath a Blue Umbrella,* or Lee Bennett Hopkins's "I Can Read Books," *Questions, Surprises,* and *Weather.*

Lest you think all this exposure dulls the children's delight and desire for poetry, that they would rather read picture books and "real" materials, consider the way second grader Jonathon explained it to his teacher: "Ms. Lammey, a story just talks but a poem sings."

Unfortunately, poetry does not receive the same attention in our elementary and secondary schools as other literary forms. For several years, we have taken informal polls in our undergraduate preservice elementary classrooms and they continue to confirm that a large percentage of these students enter teacher training with an ambivalence toward, or even a distinct dislike for, poetry. From one to two thirds of each class admits such negative attitudes. Is the alarming frequency of these attitudes due to teaching practices that alienate children from poetry? Could it be the poetry that we, as teachers, are introducing to children? Is it that teachers, themselves, don't particularly care for poetry? Or could it be, simply, the absence of poetry in the curriculum? Whatever the reason, the fact remains that if many of our young teachers enter the field with an indifference toward poetry—or worse—then it is likely that a similar feeling will be passed to our children.

There is far more to poetry than meets the eye, and the best way to discover its secrets and its treasures is to read plenty of it. In the chapter's opening text set, we have given you what we consider a sound beginning list of poetry. You may want to start there. Next you could investigate in more depth a poet you are particularly attracted to. It may be that you are drawn to some of the tried and true poets such as Mary O'Neill, Rachel Field, and Ogden Nash from *The Random House Book of Poetry for Children* or to more contemporary poets such as Nikki Grimes and Alice Schertle.

Next, we provide you with a brief overview of the basic forms of poetry and additional poets and titles to explore. Looking at these suggestions will give you more depth

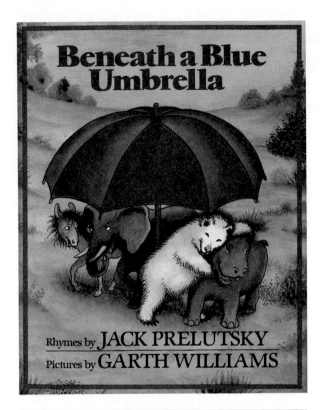

Cover from *Beneath a Blue Umbrella,* by Jack Prelutsky, pictures by Garth Williams. Copyright © 1990 by Jack Prelutsky. Pictures copyright © 1990 by Garth Williams. Published by Greenwillow Books. Reprinted by permission.

Cover from *Questions,* by Lee Bennett Hopkins, illustrated by Carolyn Croll. Copyright © 1992 by Lee Bennett Hopkins, illustration © 1992 by Carolyn Croll. Published by HarperCollins. Reprinted by permission.

Cover from *Surprises,* selected by Lee Bennett Hopkins, illustrated by Megan Lloyd. Copyright © 1984 by Harper & Row. Published by Harper & Row. All rights reserved. Reprinted by permission.

To find out more about *Serious Play* and other sources on the World Wide Web, visit Chapter 4 on the companion website at **www.prenhall.com/darigan**

BOOKMARK

INTEGRATING TECHNOLOGY: SOURCES ON THE WORLD WIDE WEB

Serious Play: Reading Poetry with Children: This exhibit created by the Academy of American poets "is intended to offer some ideas on how to help your children to join that community: check out the following links for ideas on teaching poetry to children, links to interesting sites, information on appropriate poets, and dozens of great poems for younger children." The website is an amazing resource that includes biographies of over 200 poets, over 600 poems on-line (many of them in audio as well as text), discussion forums, and a calendar of poetry-related events. People who register can create notebooks with their favorite poems and other information, links to numerous poetry-related sites, and multiple search engines.

across the genre. Finally, we dedicate the remaining part of the chapter to giving you ideas about how you can share poetry with your students. We think that this will be the stimulus for you and your students to embrace poetry and include it into your daily program.

Forms of Poetry

Poetry is distinguishable from prose primarily because of its utterly concise use of language and, even more important, its distinct patterns or forms. This variety of patterns also distinguishes one form of poetry from another. Here are a few of the forms teachers commonly use in elementary school.

Narrative Poems

DID YOU KNOW?

Ted Rand ran into an interesting situation with his illustrations for Longfellow's poem *Paul Revere's Ride.* An astronomer whose wife happened to be a teacher contacted him and stated that his research for an article he had done for a professional journal in his field showed that though the moon was visible on the night of Revere's famous ride, the one Rand painted was not correct. Calculations showed that on that particular night, the moon would have been in a gibbous stage, looking more like a flat tire. Though the astronomer was most interested in authenticity, he had to agree Rand's beautiful full moon was far more artistic and was a good choice.

Narrative poems, simply stated, tell stories. Children usually enjoy narrative poetry because they are naturally attuned to story and this makes it is easy for them to understand. Shel Silverstein and Jack Prelutsky lead the way in light verse and poetry that could be placed at the beginning of this category. Perennial favorites are Silverstein's poems such as "Smart" and "Sarah Cynthia Sylvia Stout," both which are found in his collection *Where the Sidewalk Ends.* Prelutsky's holiday books, among so many others, render some wonderful poems such as "If Turkeys Thought" from *It's Thanksgiving* and "The Ghoul" from *Nightmares: Poems to Trouble Your Sleep* for the older reader.

Probably the best-loved narrative poem in the United States is Clement Moore's *The Night Before Christmas.* Yet another classic example is Henry Wadsworth Longfellow's *Paul Revere's Ride,* which is available in a picture book version handsomely illustrated by Ted Rand.

Other superb examples of this narrative form are Nikki Grimes's *Meet Danitra Brown,* David L. Harrison's *Somebody Catch My Homework,* and Jeff Moss's pair of books, *The Butterfly Jar* and *The Other Side of the Door.* For the older reader, Mel Glenn writes gripping epics, as seen from the perspective of a variety of characters in his *Who Killed Mr. Chippendale?: A Mystery in Poems, The Taking of Room 114: A Hostage Drama in Poems,* and *Jump Ball,* to mention only a few.

A CONVERSATION WITH. . .

Alice Schertle

First, when you are writing a poem, you have a picture you want to paint or a tale you want to tell. You are fortunate when it becomes kind of second nature to incorporate poetic elements such as enjambment and rhythm into your lines. It never happens the first time. At least, it doesn't for me. I go back and rewrite and polish. A poem often happens right on the page. It is often as much of a surprise to me as I hope it is to a reader. I will begin writing and let the poem take me where it wants to go. The sounds of words often lead me where I want to go, in odd directions. And I kind of let that happen and see what kind of poem it wants to be.

I started out writing fiction, writing picture books. Later, I moved into poetry, but I have always loved poetry. That really is where my heart is. I think I was, in a sense, a little bit afraid to tackle poetry. I had such a profound respect for it and loved wonderful poetry myself. It took me a little while to get up the nerve to actually try it, but I am glad I did.

One thing I love about poetry is that you have never finished reading it. You can read it over and over again. I don't feel quite that way about prose, although there are many wonderful books, many novels that I have certainly read more than once. But not the way I read a poem, where I will go back again and again because there always seems to be another layer to uncover—another way to appreciate the poem.

Real poetry asks you to participate. It doesn't just spoon feed you the way verse does. You can read a wonderful verse and enjoy it, but you read it once

and that seems to be enough. Sure, you enjoy it. It tastes good and it is done. But you are never quite finished with real poetry. You can go back to it again and again and savor something new in it. It is one of the reasons I love it so much.

Poetry gives something to the mind and to the heart and to the ear. It gives you something to think about; that is the gift for the mind. And it gives something to the heart in that it makes you feel. Poetry can make you feel sad or happy, or it might even express menace or danger or often mystery, but there is emotion in poetry. Then, of course, there is a feast for the ear as well. I think it reverberates. It resonates in your mind and it asks you back. And then, it doesn't speak to you quite the same way twice. You uncover new things each time you read.

You know, there is a wonderful paradox about poetry, I always think, which is that poetry shows you the world in a new way. It can be a startling way. It takes even familiar things and makes you feel as if you have never really seen them before. At the same time, a good poem is so right on, that it makes you feel as if you knew that all the time, which is kind of the wonderful paradox of poetry. At the same time it is giving something new and fresh, it feels so right that you almost think, "Yes, I knew that, I just didn't realize that I knew it. I just didn't realize that I knew it until I read this poem."

Ballads are a subcategory of narrative poems that have been adapted for singing or are used to create a musical effect, such as the popular American ballads "On Top of Old Smoky," "Casey Jones," and "The Ballad of John Henry."

Lyric Poems

Lyric poetry is melodic or songlike—as if it were being accompanied by a lyre. Generally, it is descriptive, focusing on personal moments, feelings, or image-laden scenes, and it is lyric poetry that most children end up reading. Robert Louis Stevenson's *A Child's Garden of Verses*, which includes many notable poems such as "The Swing," "My Shadow," and "The Wind," has been beautifully illustrated by Tasha Tudor and more recently by Diane Goode. Dorothy Kennedy's collection *I Thought I'd Take My Rat to School Today: Poems for September to June* offers many thoughtful and humorous lyric examples for school-age children (and their teachers). Her collaboration with husband, X. J. Kennedy, in *Talking Like the Rain: A First Book of Poems* provides great lyric poems for the younger child.

To read more of this Conversation with Alice Schertle, please visit Chapter 4 on our text's companion website at **www.prenhall.com/darigan**

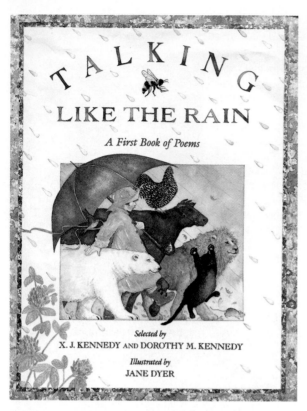

Cover from **Talking Like the Rain: A First Book of Poems** selected by X. J. Kennedy and Dorothy M. Kennedy, illustrated by Jane Dyer. Text copyright © 1992 by X. J. and Dorothy M. Kennedy Ltd. Illustrations copyright © 1992 by Jane Dyer. Published by Little, Brown & Company. Reprinted by permission of Little, Brown & Co.

Haiku

Haiku poetry is traditionally made up of 17 syllables. The first line contains five syllables, the second seven syllables, and the third the final five syllables. In the section "Why Children May Learn to Dislike Poetry," we point out a general caution regarding the use of haiku poetry in your classroom, but this is not to say you should keep haiku out of your classroom. You should read these lovely poems to your class and offer opportunities for children to try their hand at writing them. However, haiku is not for everybody and is not as easy as it appears. Superb collections of this art form are J. Patrick Lewis's **Black Swan White Crow** and Myra Cohn Livingston's **Cricket Never Does: A Collection of Haiku and Tanka.**

Limericks

Limericks are humorous poems that were popularized in 1846 with the publication of Edward Lear's **Book of Nonsense.** Most children are familiar with the rhyming scheme and verse patterns of limericks, where the first, second, and fifth lines rhyme:

A thrifty young fellow of Shoreham
Made brown paper trousers and woreham;
   He looked nice and neat
   Till he bent in the street
To pick up a pin; then he toreham.
Anonymous

Limericks are great fun for children in the intermediate and middle school grades, and collections that shouldn't be missed are John Ciardi's **The Hopeful Trout and Other Limericks,** Myra Cohn Livingston's **A Lollygag of Limericks** and **Lots of Limericks,** and X. J. Kennedy's **Uncle Switch: Looney Limericks.**

Concrete Poems

A concrete poem is written or printed on the page in a shape representing the poem's subject. It is a form of poetry that is meant to be seen even more than heard and often does not have a rhyming scheme or a particular rhythm. Of note in this form are a number of concrete poems found in Michael Spooner's **A Moon in Your Lunchbox,** as well as most of the wonderful poems in Joan Bransfield Graham's **Splish Splash.**

J. Patrick Lewis

Reprinted with permission of Atheneum Books for Young Readers, an imprint of Simon & Schuster Children's Publishing Division from *Black Swan White Crow* by J. Patrick Lewis, illustrated by Chris Manson. Jacket illustrations copyright © 1995 Chris Manson.

Reprinted with the permission of Margaret K. McElderry Books, an imprint of Simon & Schuster Children's Publishing Division from *Cricket Never Does* by Myra Cohn Livingston, illustrated by Kees de Klefte. Jacket illustration copyright © 1997 Kees de Klefte.

Free Verse

Free verse, though relying on rhythm and cadence for its poetic form, is mostly un-rhymed and lacks a consistent rhythm. Its topics are typically quite philosophical or abstract—but intriguing. The poem presented in this chapter by Valerie Worth ("Cow," p. 122) is an example of free verse. Arnold Adoff, in particular, has mastered this form and often examines the everyday as in his "food" books, *Chocolate Dreams: Poems* and *Eats.* In his book *Black Is Brown Is Tan,* he describes a happy interracial family where the mother is black and the father white.

▼▼▼▼▼▼▼

Elements of Poetry

Looking beyond the forms used in poetry, another distinguishing feature of the so-phistication in genre is the use of a wide variety of poetic devices. Poets apply figura-tive language, personification, rhythm, rhyme and repetition, alliteration and asso-nance, and imagery, to name just a few. (A number of the poems presented in upcoming pages are NCTE Poetry Award winners, taken from Bernice Cullinan's *A Jar of Tiny Stars: Poems by NCTE Award-Winning Poets.*)

Cover from **all the small poems and fourteen more**
by Valerie Worth, illustrated by Natalie Babbitt. Text
copyright © 1994 by Valerie Worth, illustrations
copyright © 1994 by Natalie Babbitt. Published by
Farrar, Straus and Giroux. Reprinted by permission
of the publisher.

Figurative Language

Comparing two unlike objects often provides us, as readers, with a new way of understanding the object or concept being described. This is especially true when that something is beyond our realm of experience. For example, not too many of us are intimately acquainted with cows, yet Valerie Worth, winner of the NCTE Poetry Award in 1991, helps us build a better picture of these big bovines in her poem "Cow," from her book *all the small poems and fourteen more.*

COW

The cow
Coming
Across the grass
Moves
Like a mountain
Toward us;
Her hipbones
Jut
Like sharp
Peaks
Of stone,
Her hoofs
Thump
Like dropped
Rocks:
Almost
Too late
She stops.

By comparing the cow's physique to a mountain, Worth more clearly introduces us to the cow's pointed hips and large, lumbering size.

Personification

Key to the word *personification* is *person.* When a poet uses this device, he or she is giving an inanimate object human qualities. Notice how Barbara Esbensen, winner of the NCTE Poetry Award in 1994, does just this in her poem "Pencils."

EVALUATING   POETRY

- Form: Does the poetry you are reading have a discernible form such as narrative, lyric, limerick, haiku, concrete, and free verse?
- Elements of poetry: Does the poetry you are reading tastefully use figures of speech such as simile, metaphor, and personification?
- Sounds of language: Does the poetry read with rhythm, rhyme, and repetition?
- Sounds of words: Does the poetry include alliteration and assonance, making the words sing?
- Content: Are the poems enjoyable, and do they make you think or look at the world in a different way?

PENCILS

The rooms in a pencil
are narrow
but elephants   castles and watermelons
fit in
In a pencil
noisy words yell for attention
and quiet words wait their turn
How did they slip
into such a tight place?
Who
gives them their
lunch?
From a broken pencil
an unbroken poem will come!
There is a long story living
in the shortest pencil
Every word in your
pencil
is fearless   ready to walk
the blue tightrope lines
Ready
to teeter and smile
down   Ready to come right out
and show you
thinking!

Pencils can no more yell than eat lunch, but Esbensen offers us a fresh look at these everyday objects by her personification of them.

Lilian Moore, winner of the NCTE Poetry Award in 1985, breathes life into the city in her poem "Foghorns," found in *The Random House Book of Poetry.*

FOGHORNS

The foghorns moaned
        in the bay last night
    so sad
    so deep
I thought I heard the city
        crying in its sleep.

Rhythm, Rhyme, and Repetition

Oftentimes a poet will use the sound of language to help impress on us the image being described. Rhythm, rhyme, and repetition all work to create a cadence that is pleasing to the ear yet brings more meaning to the poem. Take, for instance, the poem "Song of the Train" written by David McCord, winner of the NCTE Poetry Award in 1977.

SONG OF THE TRAIN

Clickety-clack,
Wheels on the track,
This is the way
They begin the attack:
Click-ety-clack,
Click-ety-clack,
Click-ety, *clack*-ety,
Click-ety
Clack.

Clickety-clack,
Over the crack,
Faster and faster
The song of the track:
Clickety-clack,
Clickety, clack
Clickety, clackety,
Clackety
Clack.
Riding in front,
Riding in back,
Everyone hears
The song of the track:
Clickety-clack,
Clickety-clack,
Clickety, *clickety,*
Clackety
Clack.

In a style similar to that of his popular poem "Pickety Fence," McCord uses rhythm to help build up a head of steam as we see this poetic train begin rumbling down the line. His repetition of the word "Click-ety-clack" and all of its variations makes us feel the movement of the train. Finally, his predictable rhyme patterns with the word "clack"—"track," "attack," "crack," and "back"—are never forced but add naturally to the cadence of the poem.

Repetition can be something as simple as repeating one word at the beginning of a line yet so effective. Take, for example, the winner of the 1980 NCTE Poetry Award, Myra Cohn Livingston's poem "My Box."

MY BOX

Nobody knows what's there but me,
Knows where I keep my silver key
and my baseball cards
and my water gun
and my wind-up car that doesn't run,
and a stone I found with a hole clear through
and a blue-jay feather that's *mostly* blue,
and a note that I wrote to the guy next door
and never gave him—and lots, lots more
of important things that I'll never show
to anyone, *anyone* else I know.

Livingston's repetition of the word "and" propels the poem forward and acts as a comfort at the beginning of each line.

Aileen Fisher, winner of the NCTE Poetry Award in 1978, uses the same technique in the poem "Fall," from **The Coffee-Pot Face,** by beginning the first three stanzas of the poem with the same line. Notice, though, how she breaks the pattern in the fourth, foreshadowing the poem's end.

FALL

The last of October
We lock the garden gate.
(The flowers have all withered
That used to stand straight.)
The last of October
We put the swings away
And the porch looks deserted
Where we liked to play.

The last of October
The birds have all flown,
The screens are in the attic,
The sandpile's alone:

Everything is put away
Before it starts to snow—
I wonder if the ladybugs
Have any place to go!

Alliteration and Assonance

Alliteration is the repetition of an initial sound in a word, and *assonance* is an internal vowel sound that provides a partial rhyme. Notice how Arnold Adoff, winner of the NCTE Poetry Award in 1988, uses both in his poem "My Forehead ON Cold Glass Of Window," from *Touch the Poem.*

My Forehead ON Cold Glass Of Window

My	Nose	On Cold Glass Of Window.			
My	Lips	Kiss	Perfect	Mouth	On
					This
					Frost
					Face
				Of Window,	
We	Shine	Together	In Dark	Night.	

Adoff uses the long *o* sound in "Nose" and "Cold" and the short *i* in "Window," "Lips," and "Kiss" to provide us with a soothing interior sound. Try reading this poem out loud in a slow, measured way and you'll see what we mean. Also note the alliteration in his sentence: "My Lips Kiss Perfect Mouth On This Frost Face Of Window."

Poet X. J. Kennedy, winner of the NCTE Poetry Award in 2000, applies these same techniques when describing two bobsledding elephants in his book *Elympics.*

BOBSLED

Swift as the wind, Eileen and Trish,
Two tusky girls in goggles,
Take a bobsled ride down a slippery slide
All bumps and wiggle-woggles.

Cover from *Touch the Poem* by Arnold Adoff, illustrations by Lisa Desimini. Illustrations copyright © 2000 by Lisa Desimini. Reprinted by permission of The Blue Sky Press, an imprint of Scholastic Inc.

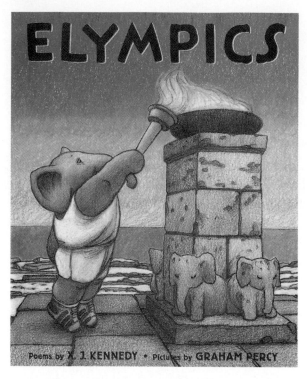

Cover from *Elympics* by X. J. Kennedy, illustrated by Graham Percy. Text copyright © 1999 by X. J. Kennedy, illustrations copyright © 1999 by Graham Percy. Used by permission of Philomel Books, a division of Penguin Putnam, Inc.

They lean to the left, they lean to the right—
While jetting down, they're getting
Their balance right—girls, don't wipe out!
That might be too upsetting.

They round a bend. They near the end.
Officials wave a checkered
Flag to tell all the world they've won!
They've set a new speed record!

Why are they champs? They've practiced hard
In frosty winter weather,
And now they're like twin sister birds
Who've learned to sing together.

Imagery

Using the senses of sight, sound, touch, smell, and taste, a poet can create a mood, setting, or experience. Take, for example, NCTE Poetry Winner for 1982 John Ciardi's classic poem, "Mummy Slept Late and Daddy Fixed Breakfast," which comes from *The Random House Book of Poetry.* This sensory feast alludes to all the senses and includes everything a good poem should have—except Daddy's waffle.

MUMMY SLEPT LATE AND DADDY FIXED BREAKFAST

Daddy fixed the breakfast.
He made us each a waffle.
It looked like gravel pudding.
It tasted something awful.

"Ha, ha," he said, "I'll try again.
This time I'll get it right."
But what *I* got was in between
Bituminous and anthracite,

"A little too well done? Oh well,
I'll have to start all over."
That time what landed on my plate
Looked like a manhole cover.

I tried it with a fork:
The fork gave off a spark.
I tried it with a knife and twisted it
Into a question mark.

I tried it with a hack-saw.
I tried it with a torch.
It didn't even make a dent.
It didn't even scorch.

The next time Dad gets breakfast
When Mummy's sleeping late,
I think I'll skip the waffles.
I'd sooner eat the plate!

Ciardi has us chuckling because he makes use of so many visual references as these poetic children are attempting to consume these aborted breakfast attempts.

Eve Merriam, winner of the NCTE Poetry Award in 1981, offers a more subtle interpretation in this poem bursting with fresh sights.

FRESH PAINT

It glistens on this wall
that turns
whatever color I conjure
when I close my eyes:

green for the moss of
memories on a stone

blue for ice caves in August

scarlet for the banners of maple leaves
triumphant in the fall

yellow for the lights
of a homebound car in the fog

white for the drift of
cherry blossoms

orange for tiger flames
leaping in the bonfire

violet for daybreak
and violet for dusk

black for the warmth of darkness

and look
how the word *don't* is painted out
so the sign reads

touch.

Cover from *Fresh Paint: New Poems,* by Eve Merriam, woodcuts by David Frampton. Text copyright © 1986 by Eve Merriam, woodcuts copyright © 1986 by David Frampton. Published by Macmillan. Reprinted by permission.

▼▼▼▼▼▼▼

Poetry's Power

Thus far, we have discussed the forms and elements of poetry. But what makes poetry "sing," as young Jonathon states at the beginning of this chapter, is not just the way the poem was written or the devices used. In the end, to be successful, the poem must touch our heart, tickle our funny bone, or prompt us to look at something in a different way. Poet and educator Georgia Heard states that all her poems start with a strong feeling she has about something (1989, p. 10). Form and the devices the poet uses can follow, but first the content must be there. For example, when Darigan and his fifth-grade class were studying a text set of books based on families in distress, young Karen was prompted to write a poem in response to the sadness of homeless people. Form was certainly present and she used none of the aforementioned devices, but the poem's power hits us squarely between the eyes in the last line.

HOMELESS

The homeless make me sad
just to see them out there starving
Digging through the garbage cans
   just to find food to eat.
They don't know anything
all they know is that they are homeless
And they want to be like "You!"
By Karen Blachly

Yet another powerful example of poetry describing the powerful events in our lives comes from Eloise Greenfield, winner of the NCTE Poetry Award in 1997.

KEEPSAKE

Before Mrs. Williams died
She told Mr. Williams
When he gets home
To get a nickel out of her
Navy blue pocketbook
And give it to her
Sweet little gingerbread girl
That's me

I ain't never going to spend it.

Notice how the last line ties the poem together and gives it its tremendous power. Poetry mirrors, explains, and interprets life. It is concise, bounded by form, and rich in language; ultimately, good poetry "sings."

▼▼▼▼▼▼▼

Why Children May Learn to Dislike Poetry

The crazy part about all of this is that children have a natural affinity for poetry. It is exhibited well before they enter school by their love for nursery rhymes, jingles, childhood songs, and finger games. As we mentioned in the introduction, children relish Mother Goose from the time before they can talk, and that fondness *can* carry on throughout the grades. However, it must be nurtured and supported by the wise teacher. Poetry must be abundantly displayed and joyfully read in every classroom, every day. Children should have the opportunity to write their own original poems or spin-offs on ones they love. For example, in their *The Lore and Language of School-children* (1959), Iona and Peter Opie note the following humorous couplets based on "Mary had a little lamb," which allow older children the opportunity to parody the very rhymes they so dearly loved when they were young.

Mary had a little lamb,
You've heard this tale before,
But did you know she passed her plate
And had a little more?

Mary had a little lamb,
She fed it castor oil,
And everywhere the lamb would go
It fertilized the soil.

Mary had a little lamb
It was a little glutton
She fed it ice cream all day long
And now it's frozen mutton. (p. 90)

However, it seems that at some time during the course of their schooling, a great number of children seem to change their minds about the appeal of poetry. And indeed, some of our teaching practices may be responsible. When asked what sorts of poetry-related school activities they found distasteful, our undergraduate students invariably listed these: memorizing and reciting, writing poetry, and the heavy-duty analysis of a poem's structure and meaning. Many students reported a distaste for playing the "I know the true meaning of this poem; it's your job to discover it" game with their teachers. Poet and anthologist Lee Bennett Hopkins refers to this kind of teaching as the "DAM approach—Dissecting, Analyzing, and *meaninglessly* Memorizing poetry to death" (1998, p. 14).

Teacher as Purveyor of Poetry

In reality, we as teachers may not be as enthusiastic about poetry as some of the other genres in children's literature. We all know that a blasé attitude about any topic translates directly to the children in our classes and determines, in large part, whether they will embrace or reject that subject. Poetry is just as susceptible. Surely if we ignore poetry in our daily routine, relegating it to that special unit we have to teach each year, we send a clear message about how we feel about the genre. Further, if we ask children to write poems only in certain forms and about specific topics, or if we force them to memorize and recite poems during that same unit, we set them and ourselves up for failure.

You first may want to think about using poetry in a different way altogether. Traditionally, however, poetry is most often dealt with by teaching a few forms and providing children with the opportunity to practice writing poems following the form as a template. Haiku, a very sophisticated and revered Japanese poetry form, is commonly the structure most often selected for this assignment because it is seemingly so simple. Nothing could be further from the truth. Sure, haiku is three lines with a five-seven-five syllable pattern and often expresses something about nature. For example, look at this haiku written by David McCord (from **One at a Time**):

> Take the butterfly:
> Nature works to produce him.
> Why doesn't he last?

Haiku may be short, but it is *anything* but simple. Poet and scholar X. J. Kennedy (1986) relates that because of its brevity, haiku cannot really delve deeply into any one topic but, because it is so highly compressed, it must *imply* a great deal. As we already mentioned, this form often has to do with nature, so a blossom could indicate spring; a crow on a branch, autumn; snow, winter (p. 76). Because it is a rather abstract, sophisticated form, children actually require a great deal of experience and maturity to understand and appreciate haiku. Thus, as the studies of children's poetry preferences indicate, generations of children have been taught to despise haiku (Fisher & Natarella, 1982; Kutiper & Wilson, 1993; Terry, 1974). With proper instructional techniques, however, children can and do learn to appreciate this elegant verse form.

Obviously, teachers who dislike poetry may have negative effects on the poetry attitudes of their children. However, the overzealous teacher who dearly loves poetry may cause problems, too, by rushing headlong into poems too sophisticated for the elementary audience. Children can become overwhelmed by the complicated structures, intense imagery, and figurative language rendered by the traditional poets. When pushed at an early age to analyze and discover deeply couched meanings, their excitement about poetry wanes rapidly.

Look at Children's Poetry Preferences

Studies of children's poetry preferences reveal children's common dislikes about poetry. The results of several of the best-known studies were summarized by Kutiper and Wilson (1993, p. 29):

1. The narrative form of poetry [and limericks] was popular with readers of all ages, whereas free verse and haiku were the most disliked forms.

To find out more about Poetry Web Books and other activities on the World Wide Web, visit Chapter 4 on the companion website at **www.prenhall.com/darigan**

BOOKMARK

INTEGRATING TECHNOLOGY: ACTIVITIES USING THE WORLD WIDE WEB

Poetry Pals The K–12 Student Poetry Publishing Project is a wonderful collaborative project that classrooms may join as partners. The project incorporates the reading and writing of poetry and provides students the opportunity to publish their own poetry on-line. The website provides related lesson plans, samples of different types of poetry, resources for teachers, and links to numerous other poetry sites. From 1997 to 2000, students participated not only from around the U.S. but also from over 25 countries around the world!

Introducing:

TEACHING IDEAS

For the older, hard-core poetry haters, music is often the road to recovery. Students tend not to associate the lyrics of songs they know and love with poetry. However, teachers of older children have changed students' negative attitudes toward this genre by duplicating the lyrics of popular tunes and distributing them as (go figure!) poems. Songs by popular artists of the day offer beautiful messages, are poetic, and can act as the potential jump-start into the genre.

2. Students preferred poems that contain rhyme, rhythm, and sound.
3. Children most enjoyed poetry that contained humor, familiar experiences, and animals. They disliked poems about nature.
4. Younger students (elementary and middle school/junior high age) preferred contemporary poems.
5. Students disliked poems that contained visual imagery or figurative language.

So, armed with this knowledge, let's take this information about what children like and dislike and use it to inform our teaching. Bernard Lonsdale and Helen Mackintosh best express how we should approach poetry in the elementary schools:

> Experiences with poetry should be pleasurable and should never be associated with work. Teachers defeat their own purpose if they attempt to analyze the structure or form of the poem other than to show whether it rhymes; what the verse pattern is; and whether it is a ballad, a limerick, a lyric poem, or perhaps haiku. Children in elementary schools should be asked questions of preference and of feeling rather than of knowing. (1973, p. 213)

Children have less opportunity for preference and feeling when the teacher makes all the decisions about poetry and its use in the classroom. If the teacher selects one poem for the entire class to memorize, far fewer children will respond positively than if each is allowed to choose a favorite poem to commit to memory. If the teacher presents one form of poetry, then insists afterward that everyone write a poem in that style, the overall response is less enthusiastic than waiting until two or three forms have been introduced and permitting students to select the type they wish to write. Finally, the insightful teacher can help students see that their poems may be free of form yet extremely personal and powerful. The principle of allowing children to make choices, whenever possible, is closely associated with success in presenting poetry in the elementary classroom.

PEANUTS® by Charles M. Schultz

▼▼▼▼▼▼▼

Building Appreciation for Poetry

Children who have learned a dislike for poetry can be lured back by teachers who capitalize on the winning power of light, humorous verse, and no collection of light verse and poetry has done more to attract children to this genre than Shel Silverstein's *Where the Sidewalk Ends.* Young readers hungrily latch onto Silverstein's light-hearted, sometimes irreverent, poems about contemporary childhood. Jim Trelease (1995) states that teachers and librarians insist it is the most frequently stolen book from their schools and libraries—a pretty powerful endorsement, indeed.

Another well-known poet, Jack Prelutsky, writes poems that are similar to Silverstein's, but he has many more collections from which to choose and presents a more varied array of themes throughout his body of work. In fact, Prelutsky's collection *The New Kid on the Block* actually edged out *Where the Sidewalk Ends* as the most circulated poetry book in the libraries of schools selected for a poetry preference study (Kutiper & Wilson, 1993). Here is the poem that opens the collection:

THE NEW KID ON THE BLOCK

There's a new kid on the block,
and boy, that kid is tough,
that new kid punches hard,
that new kid plays real rough,
that new kid's big and strong,
with muscles everywhere,
that new kid tweaked my arm,
that new kid pulled my hair.

That new kid likes to fight,
and picks on all the guys,
that new kid scares me some,
(that new kid's twice my size),
that new kid stomped my toes,
that new kid swiped my ball,
that new kid's really bad,
I don't care for her at all.

But as Kutiper and Wilson point out, the light verse that children tend to prefer must not remain their only poetry diet. Just as we wouldn't feed kids only cookies and cupcakes, the wise teacher slips in a nutritious side dish here and a healthy main course there. Pretty soon our bodies crave *more* than just the snacks—in fact, we find them to be just too "lite" and desire something more substantive. Snacks are to food what light verse is to an appreciation of real poetry. We can use rhythmic, humorous verse to build

Cover from *The New Kid on the Block* by Jack Prelutsky, illustrated by James Stevenson. Text copyright © 1984 by Jack Prelutsky, illustrations copyright © 1984 by James Stevenson. Published by Greenwillow Books. Reprinted by permission.

Cover from ***Where the Sidewalk Ends: The Poems and Drawings of Shel Silverstein.*** Copyright © 1974 by Shel Silverstein. Published by Harper & Row. Reprinted by permission of the publisher.

Cover from ***A Light in the Attic,*** written and illustrated by Shel Silverstein. Copyright © 1981 by Shel Silverstein. Published by Harper & Row. Reprinted by permission.

the taste for poetry in general. Then, using contemporary and traditional poetry in ever-increasing portions, we can bridge children's interests so they develop the palate for more sophisticated forms of poetry.

The Teacher Makes the Difference

But it is the *teacher* who must point out and direct that process. Surely, children will always gravitate to the humorous and irreverent poems in Shel Silverstein's book ***A Light in the Attic,*** yet it is the wise teacher who will also point out the beautifully touching poems in that collection, such as this one:

THE LITTLE BOY AND THE OLD MAN

Said the little boy, "Sometimes I drop my spoon."
Said the little old man, "I do that too."
The little boy whispered, "I wet my pants."
"I do that too," laughed the little old man.
Said the little boy, "I often cry."
The old man nodded, "So do I."
"But worst of all," said the boy, "it seems
Grown-ups don't pay attention to me."
And he felt the warmth of a wrinkled old hand.
"I know what you mean," said the little old man.

After reading this poem, you will first want to ask the children what they think. Certainly reactions will be varied, ranging from how different this poem is from the rest in the book to personal connections children might make to older relatives and neighbors. The wise teacher allows those initial responses to emerge before looking at the poetic elements the text represents.

Next, you will want to point out what a remarkable poem this is, sharing some insights you have about it. We noticed what a perfectly balanced, serious poem this is and that it pits humor against sadness with a form far more sophisticated than many of the others in the book. Like the bulk of the poems Silverstein wrote, the first four lines set up a light, almost whimsical, tone (poking fun at clumsiness and incontinence) that is continued into the fifth line beginning with, "Said the little boy . . ." But then, in the exact middle of the poem, when the child states he often cries, we are hit right between the eyes for the first time with the fact that this is going to be a very serious commentary. By poem's end, we are left with such an overwhelming sadness—the neglected segments of our society, our children and elders, have been portrayed so succinctly and with such power—and in only 84 words.

Let's take a brief look at what Silverstein does technically. He begins with "Said the little boy . . ." Not the way we talk day to day, is it? He could just as easily have accented a strong alliteration and started the poem, "The little boy <u>s</u>aid, "<u>S</u>ometimes I drop my <u>s</u>poon." That wouldn't have been too bad, but wisely, he does otherwise. He says that phrase ("said the little boy" or "said the little old man") five times throughout the poem—that means it appears in half the lines.

Again, as we've noted, he uses the exact middle of the poem to change the tone with the words "I often cry." In that line, it is like we have just crested a hill and are starting on the downward course. To further build up steam, Silverstein does something very clever: Notice that he uses a period at the end of the first six lines. Those periods halt our reading just enough, to give us that singsong rhythm he is so well known for. Yet at the end of the seventh line, he eliminates the period and, if you read the line without stopping, which is exactly what he intended, it hurtles you downward toward the tragic ending: "But worst of all," said the boy, "it seems grown-ups don't pay attention to me." *Pause.* "And he felt the warmth of a wrinkled old hand . . . I know what you mean, said the little old man."

We warn you: This is not going to be the children's natural favorite in this book! In fact, a child who has finished the entire text during Silent Sustained Reading will probably not even remember he or she read it at all. But, the good teacher is the one who builds on kids' natural enthusiasm for Shel Silverstein's poetry as a whole, points out this gem, and paves the way for other more sophisticated poetry.

Now, you may be wondering if we have not dissected and analyzed "The Little Boy and the Old Man" too much. We think not. Looking more deeply into a poem is a wonderful experience and a duty we have as teachers! How else will you and children learn more about the finer points of the genre? But the teacher who delves headlong into this kind of analysis *first* runs the risk of overkill that we mentioned concerning the overzealous teacher. Let the children first enjoy the poem for its story, its humor, its images, its emotion—then go on to notice the finer points of the poem.

Poetry Every Day

As a first step, teachers can simply share poems daily, with no ulterior motive other than to build appreciation. This helps create students (and maybe future teachers) who will have a lifelong interest in poetry. In Darigan's fifth-grade classroom, he placed a hand-lettered, poster-sized poem on the outside door leading to the veranda. That way, whenever the children lined up to go trekking off to lunch or the playground for recess, they would read the poem together. Darigan found that rather than carp at the kids for not getting quiet enough—quickly enough—the choral reading focused the class and prepared them to joyfully head out.

The class generally started the morning off with a poem—usually a poem for two voices (we describe that later in the chapter in great detail) and again found that it was the perfect way to set the tone for learning and literacy. One teacher we know simply wrote a new poem on the chalkboard each day without reading or referring to it. Soon students were commenting on the poem, and some began writing down the ones they liked. All of these ideas are great starting points for getting the kids enthused about poetry.

A CONVERSATION WITH . . .

Lee Bennett Hopkins

I don't think there is any such thing as writers; there are only rewriters. To me, whatever I am writing is a draft. It takes me sometimes a week or month to perfect one poem. You write and then you rewrite, and you sculpt like a sculptor would take a piece of clay. You take the words and make them important. And you chop and you add, and go back and relook at things. The rewriting is an important part of the writing process. Poetry in particular has to be sculpted.

I don't believe in having children write poetry in 45 minutes. No poet can do it. I can't do it. You don't teach long division in 15 minutes. You don't write haiku in 20 minutes. Writing, to me, is a very sacred form. You perfect it. It is like playing baseball: You don't teach children to do a home run. They practice on becoming a good batter, and you practice on being a good writer.

The thing is to read a lot or have them read it if they can, depending on the grade level. Get them to know it, get them to know these poets. I want them to get into the true emotions of life, and only poetry can do that. There are poems I still read and get goose bumps, real goose bumps.

Take poems and combine them with curriculum and they work like magic. My philosophy is that poetry should be used every single day. I have used it with everything. I have used Langston Hughes's "Hold Fast to Dreams" with *The Giver;* it is what Jonas is talking about at the end of the book. When I am doing something nonfiction on dinosaurs, I use a dinosaur poem.

There is a difference between light verse and poetry. Light verse is usually humorous. There is nothing wrong with that, but I want children to reach above that and learn that there are poems about everything under the sun, from fireflies to fire hydrants. I want them to feed on Frost, to savor Sandburg. I want them to heartbreak with Langston Hughes. You want to get them beyond the cutsie and the funny and get them into true poetry. It's like going to McDonald's or a gourmet restaurant. You want to help them reach up. You don't want to give them hamburgers and French fries for the rest of their life.

To read more of this Conversation with Lee Bennett Hopkins, please visit Chapter 4 on our text's companion website at **www.prenhall. com/darigan**

ALTERNATE TEXT SET

Poetry and Anthologies of Lee Bennett Hopkins

Read Aloud

School Supplies

Text Set

Been to Yesterdays: Poems of a Life

Ragged Shadows: Poems of Halloween Night

Through Our Eyes: Poems and Pictures about Growing Up

Good Rhymes, Good Times

Good Books, Good Times!

Spectacular Science

Marvelous Math

My America: A Poetry Atlas of the United States

Poetry Across the Curriculum

We have also found that poetry fits nicely into, say, a social studies or science unit. What better way to discuss American History, for example, than to select poems from Lee Bennett Hopkins's ***Hand in Hand: An American History Through Poetry***?

In Darigan's fifth-grade class, he was working through the unit in their Social Studies text that covered the American Revolutionary War. He thought it would be appropriate to read Henry Wadsworth Longfellow's "Paul Revere's Ride" to the class, because he had loved that poem so much as a child. In fact, he was certain that his enthusiasm would be infectious and the children would come away reciting many of the lines themselves.

Well, one thing about teaching—you can always count on a surprise around every corner. He hauled out his old copy of *The Arbuthnot Anthology of Children's Literature,* which was the only source he had readily available, and began chanting, "Listen, my children, and you shall hear of the midnight ride of Paul Revere . . . " About halfway through the second stanza, he noted a general uneasiness among the children. By the third stanza, there was definite unrest, and by the fourth—outright rebellion. So much for teaching about war! Clearly they weren't getting anything out of this poem. Many a

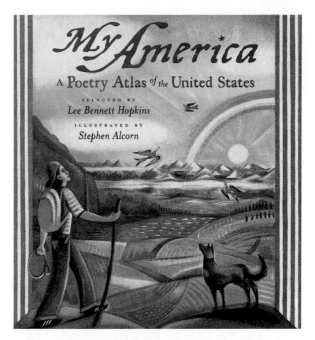

Reprinted with the permission of Simon & Schuster Books for Young Readers, an imprint of Simon & Schuster Children's Publishing from *My America: A Poetry Atlas of the United States.* Selected by Lee Bennett Hopkins, illustrated by Stephen Alcorn. Illustrations copyright © 2000 by Stephen Alcorn.

Cover from ***Hand in Hand: An American History Through Poetry.*** Selected by Lee Bennett Hopkins, illustrated by Peter M. Fiore. Illustrations copyright © 1994 by Peter M. Fiore. Published by Simon & Schuster. All rights reserved. Reprinted by permission.

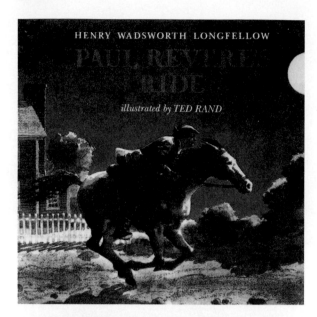

HENRY WADSWORTH LONGFELLOW

illustrated by TED RAND

From **Paul Revere's Ride** by Henry Wadsworth Longfellow, illustrated by Ted Rand, copyright © 1990 by Ted Rand, illustrations. Copyright © 1990 by Dutton Children's Books. Used by permission of Dutton Children's Books, a division of Penguin Putnam, Inc.

teacher would have trudged on through the next seven stanzas, dragging those poor babies along and thinking, *I'm doing this because it is good for you!* Well, he chose to halt (by the Old North Church, by the way) and assess what was going on. "Kinda boring, Dr. D," they seemed to all agree. "At least there could be some pictures."

The next morning, he came in armed with Ted Rand's illustrated picture book version of *Paul Revere's Ride.* He held up the book, allowing them all to see the gorgeous illustrations—like he always did—and throughout the entire 11 verses of the poem, you could have heard a pin drop. There was rapt attention, and it was clearly all due to the masterful paintings by this wonderful illustrator.

"What about science?" you might ask. You might want to read the wry and witty poems of Alice Schertle in her book **Advice for a Frog,** illustrated by Norman Green, which presents 14 poems about animals, many of whom are endangered or on the brink of extinction. Or for the younger children, you may want to share **Antarctic Antics: A Book of Penguin Poems,** by Judy Sierra and illustrated by Jose Aruego and Ariane Dewey.

The fact of the matter is that poetry fits into any area of the curriculum. In language arts, for example, Ruth Heller has written and beautifully illustrated a number of books in poetry that present the parts of speech.

You could give us virtually any unit of study and we could spit out poetry to enhance that unit. With the use of the database included with this book, you can easily access poetry by "retaining" books related to your theme or topic and then "trimming" the list by entering the genre of "poetry" and the titles will automatically pop up, ready to print.

Another wonderful resource for themed studies is the collection of 572 poems we mentioned at the beginning of the chapter in **The Random House Book of Poetry for Children,** by Jack Prelutsky. There is a comprehensive subject index in the back of the book to help you choose poems particularly fitting for your area of the curriculum.

The key to getting children excited about poetry is consistent, unfettered exposure to good poems by the enthusiastic teacher who begins mixing light verse and more artistic poetry. Because poetry is really meant to be *heard* more than read silently, the avenue to poetry appreciation for many students is the oral highway. Therefore, teachers should read poems aloud—fresh selections as well as old favorites—on a regular, daily basis. And with *feeling,* for goodness sake!

Memorizing Poems

We have always invited students to commit poems to memory and then share them with the class—both at the university and in the elementary classroom. We think that the process of memorizing is beneficial, but there is a point at which we, as teachers, cannot force the issue for fear of inhibiting enthusiasm. If we mandate a poem from each child—worse yet, the *same* poem from each child—then we limit our chances for success.

There are some students who are hesitant about getting up in front of their peers, whereas others will actually be blasé about the whole affair. Darigan had one student who wasn't the least bit timid but lacked a commensurate emotion with the poem she recited. She jumped up ready to recite Robert Frost's famous "Stopping By Woods on a Snowy Evening." Her head bobbed back and forth, sideways, as she droned: w*hose woodstheseareIthinkIknowhishouseisinthevillagethoughhewillnotseemestoppingheretowatchhis*

woodsfillupwithsnow. Breath! *mylittlehorse . . .* When she finished, a gush of air exited from her lungs and she flopped back down in her seat, content at having completed the assignment.

She received credit for knowing all the words to this poem—not tripping up on a single one. But, Darigan posed, "Where was the feeling? Maybe you could try it this way." He began, for he, too had this poem committed to memory. Slowly, slowly, he said, "Whose woods these are (*and he paused briefly, with a bit of uplifting lilt to the word "are" to indicate that he really did wonder whose woods these are*) I think I know. (*period—stop for second—pause!*) His house is in the village, though; (*a little longer pause for the semicolon*) He will not see me stopping here to watch his woods fill up with snow." (*No pause at the end of the line after the word "here."*) There was no sing-song cadence but a true outpouring of feeling at the word—the content of this wonderful poem. The next class she got up and re-recited that same poem and because she had obviously practiced, it was spectacular. Poetry can, and should, be dynamic.

Choral Poetry

Choral speaking is another oral/aural method for sharing poetry. Through choral speaking, children get the opportunity to play with words and their sounds—to both hear and manipulate the language. Remember when we mentioned May Hill Arbuthnot's *Anthology of Children's Literature* earlier? In that text, she endorsed her own variation on this idea with what she referred to as a "verse choir." Dividing higher and lower voices, just as a music director would consider altos and sopranos, the students recited poems that were rewritten or adapted for performance purposes. Though her directions are quite lengthy and detailed (14 pages in all), they are well worth reading. We offer yet another example here that worked in Darigan's fifth-grade classroom; one he refers to as "Choral Poetry—for Two or More Voices."

When Darigan went back to teaching fifth grade after completing his doctoral work, he was mightily influenced by his professors, the books he had read, and most certainly the wisdom of Bill Martin, Jr. His determined efforts to keep poetry alive in homes and classrooms had a tremendous effect on Darigan, who was bound to keep a heavy emphasis on poetry in his own classroom. That was, until he met his class.

A wonderful teacher hint, especially for the younger kids, is to display each of the poems you read on enlarged charts. Many teachers, like Ms. Lammey, keep spiral-bound chart packs of poetry and present them from an easel while they have the children gathered around them on the floor. But you can also simply print the poems out on plain butcher paper (which is cheaper), laminate them, and then display them around the room by clamping them onto skirt hangers. You can then easily hang the poems from the ceiling using small metal or plastic plant hangers available at any hardware store. You essentially have poetry banners hanging all over the room—what a great endorsement for poetry.

Prompted by a friend, teacher Joanne Johnson, Darigan decided to open the year using poetry from Paul Fleischman's Newbery-winning *Joyful Noise.* Joanne said her multi-aged third- and fourth-grade class loved these poems and would beg to do them over and over. These marvelous poems, written for two voices, are about insects such as fireflies, grasshoppers, cicadas, and crickets, to mention only a few.

This is how they work: The poem is formatted on the page in two columns, and the two readers recite the parts much like a "musical duet." Often the parts are read alternately in a call and response mode, but just as often the parts are read simultaneously (it may be exactly the same words or, occasionally, a different text).

Here is a snippet of Fleischman's poem "House Crickets."

We don't live in meadows cricket or in groves	cricket
	We're house crickets living beneath this gas stove
cricket Others may worry cricket about fall	cricket cricket
	We're scarcely aware of the seasons at all
cricket	cricket

The poem continues through each of the seasons, discussing the advantages of being a domesticated cricket, so to speak.

Darigan would never forget the reaction of the class after that first reading of this poem. He had divided the class in half and placed the poem on an overhead transparency for the entire group to see. They read through it the first time, and Darigan was the director; they seemed a bit tentative . . . but it was only their first time. Here is the very end:

For while others are ruled by the sun in the heavens, we live in a world of fixed Fahrenheit cricket our unchanging steadfast and stable bright blue pilot light.	For while others are ruled whose varying height brings the seasons' procession, we live in a world cricket thanks to *our* sun: reliable bright blue pilot light.

There was a long pause when the class finished. Darigan proudly stood there like Sir George Solti in front of the Chicago Symphony Orchestra and waited for the applause.

Deafening silence!

"Dr. D," one of the students timidly said, "I didn't like that too much."

"Yeah, me either," chimed in another.

"Actually, I hate poetry!" said a third. Then the avalanche poured down—echoing that same sentiment over and over again.

He was devastated. He felt like saying (in his snootiest voice), "You know, this won the Newbery Medal in 1989—where is your taste? And by the way, Mrs. Johnson's *third and fourth graders* over at Goshen Elementary *loved* this poem. Get a life!" Of course, he didn't say any of that . . . but he certainly thought it! And he stewed over that a good part of the rest of the day.

But Darigan was committed to making poetry a part of his curriculum that year, and he finally figured out that the kids weren't to blame for not liking this poem or poetry, in general. After all, they had never really had it as part of their curriculum—except for what they had been taught from the basal reader. He believed that this notion of poems in two voices had distinct possibilities. He just needed to adapt it for the students, instead of making *them* adapt to *his* notion of what should be.

A Poetic Intervention

It wasn't until later that week, while reading through Lynn Joseph's book, *Coconut Kind of Day: Island Poems,* that Darigan bumped into an idea that might work.

Cover from *Joyful Noise: Poems for Two Voices* by Paul Fleischman, illustrated by Eric Beddows. Text copyright © 1988 by Paul Fleischman, illustrations copyright © 1988 by Eric Beddows. Published by Harper & Row. Reprinted by permission.

Her poem "Splash" is a brief narrative poem about two girls who, along with many others in the community, go down to the shore of their little island late in the afternoon to help the fishermen pull in the day's catch. He saw some great possibilities, indeed. First, it had a real rhythm that the kids ought to like. Next, it was written in the Caribbean vernacular; notice the line "grab de nets like we big and strong."

It didn't take Darigan long to figure out—two columns, two voices—that he could adapt this poem to Fleischman's format. He divided the class in half, one side reading the left, the other reading the right as a call and response.

Splash!	Afternoon tide rollin'.
Heave!	Fishermen pullin' seine.
Come on!	Jasmine pulls me along.
Grab!	de nets like we big and strong.
Sink!	our feet deep down in de sand.
Hold!	on tight with both we hands.
Pull!	and tug and pull some more.
Show!	de fish who go win this war.
Crash!	We fall and de fish laughin'
Grunt!	We up and pullin' again.
Wet!	and sandy through and through.
Oh no!	I wonder what Mama go do.
Look!	A big wave rollin' in.
Hurray!	Is now we bound to win!

Darigan introduced the poem, providing the class with a little bit of background and then proceeded to read through it for the first time. "Now you try it." They read it together . . . still a bit tentative, they were. But . . . they asked, "Could we, maybe, try that again?"

"Well . . . " he said slowly, "we do have a lot to do today . . . but, okay." Inside, he was shouting, "YES! Yes, yes, yes!" They really liked it!

From then on, they started the day with this poem or one like it that Darigan adapted for two voices. They read and performed poems by Shel Silverstein, N. M. Bodecker, Sharon Bell Mathis, e. e. cummings, and, of course, Bill Martin, Jr.

Preparing a Choral Poem for the Classroom

Darigan adapted a poem that Arnold Adoff, one of the recipients of the prestigious NCTE Poetry Award, wrote and that can be found in his collection **Sports Pages.** This example shows you how he broke up poems so that you can do the same thing with favorite poems in your class.

First, Darigan relied on call and response a majority of the time, because the students seemed to really enjoy volleying a line back and forth. Then, to accent points, he had both sides of the class read an important line simultaneously. Sometimes he would offset the lines so that half of the students read one line, which was repeated by the other half of the class in the next line.

Here is Darigan's adaptation of Adoff's poem:

You bring the ball down the court. The pick is set. the ball is faster the defensive hands and heads. and you get free! into the big girl at the key. and shoots The crowd roars.	the pick is set. The movement of the ball is faster than all the defensive hands and heads. get free! You pass into the big girl at the key. She turns and scores. The crowd roars.

Notice the offset lines that began "The movement of the ball *is faster* . . . " The left side of the class repeated "the ball" while the right side rolled ahead with "is faster than all the hands and heads . . . " This juxtaposition of lines added a rolling rhythm across the classroom—much like a wave beating down toward a shoreline. Also, notice how the lines that are read simultaneously add a real punch to the meaning of the poem, like is found in the finale. Bouncing the lines back and forth builds excitement just like a loose ball in the free-throw lane in heavy traffic. Darigan wrote, "she turns [spoken on the right side], and shoots [spoken on the left side], and scores [back to the right side]" then finished with the class chiming in unison: "the crowd roars!" Darigan's students grew to love this form of poem, which led them to a far greater appreciation of the genre in general and of more sophisticated poems as well.

Teachers Are the Key to Success

Teachers do much to convince children of the worth of poetry when they share what is personally delightful. When Darigan was a seventh grader, his principal introduced one of the monthly school assemblies with, "Here is Mr. Schwartz. He is an expert on poetry. I am sure you will all love his presentation and *pay him his due respect*" (i.e., you are dead meat if any of you clowns in the back start goofing off!).

Well, this fireplug-of-a-man swaggered to the middle of the stage, looked at the 300 kids looking straight back at him, crouched down, and began:

> The outlook wasn't brilliant for the Mudville Nine that day;
> The score stood four to two, with but one inning yet to play;
> And so when Cooney died at first, and Burrows did the same,
> A sickly silence fell upon the patrons of the game . . .

Yes, he was reciting Ernest Thayer's famous poem, "Casey at the Bat." He certainly had Darigan's interest as well as that of every single boy-who-hated-poetry in the gym. By the time Casey had two strikes on him and the fans note "The sneer is gone from Casey's lip, his teeth are clenched in hate/ He pounds with cruel violence his bat upon

the plate," this guy had gone crazy on stage. He mimed every movement, pounding the plate with his make-believe bat, face red with fury and frustration. At the climax of the poem: "And now the pitcher holds the ball, and now he lets it go/And now the air is shattered by the force of Casey's blow," Darigan was jolted back in his seat at the impact. After what seemed to be interminable minutes, he began again . . .

Oh, somewhere in this favored land the sun is shining bright,
The band is playing somewhere, and somewhere hearts are light;
And somewhere men are laughing, and somewhere children shout,
But there is no joy in Mudville—mighty Casey has struck out.

This man was actually crying on stage—so wrapped up was he in this poem. He followed that with Robert W. Service's spellbinding poem set in the frozen Yukon, "The Cremation of Sam McGee." From that point on, Darigan was hooked on poetry *forever*. Years later, as a young teacher, he committed these same poems to memory (his first ever) and recited them, he hopes, with the same enthusiasm as Mr. Schwartz.

What we can learn from all of this is that poems are always more successful when they are ones *you* honestly like. Start compiling a folder that is readily accessible containing *your* favorite poems. Many years ago when we visited Bill Martin's apartment in New York City, we were certainly impressed with his 23rd-floor view of Manhattan. But what most caught our fancy was the presence of the six 5-drawer filing cabinets Bill had behind his desk. "These are filled with *some* of the poems I like the best," he said. Imagine—six cabinets. We *all* have our work cut out for us, don't we?

Further, we suggest that you begin a special bookshelf in your classroom to hold favorite poetry volumes. Keep it stocked with your books, ones the kids have brought in from home, and, of course, ones you borrow from your school and public libraries.

If you as a teacher do not have a collection of personal favorites, it is only because you have not read enough poetry. Your librarian, colleagues, and certainly the database included in this text will help lead you to poems you enjoy and will subsequently share with your class. In "Building a Poetry Collection" (p. 143), we give you some specific ideas about enlarging that file.

Knowing the strong connection between reading and writing, the pleasure of writing poetry should also be modeled in a similar way. We recall a sixth-grade teacher who genuinely enjoyed writing limericks for his students, and whose students soon became so enamored with limericks that they chose to stay in during recess to write poems! In the last section of this chapter, we address how to include students' writing of poetry into your program.

▼▼▼▼▼▼▼▼

The NCTE Poetry Award

To encourage the sharing of poetry with children and to raise the awareness of teachers about the quality of the poetry available, the National Council of Teachers of English established an award to recognize a living poet whose body of work for children ages 3 to 13 is deemed exceptional. The NCTE Award for Excellence in Poetry for Children was presented annually from 1977 until 1982, after which the council began awarding it every 3 years.

The works of the poets who have won the NCTE Poetry Award are certainly not as well known among children as those of Silverstein and Prelutsky. However, they provide teachers a reservoir of fine poetry that is both very accessible to children and of better artistic quality than the popular lighter verse. *A Jar of Tiny Stars: Poems by NCTE Award-Winning Poets,* edited by Bernice E. Cullinan, includes all the winners through Barbara Esbensen. Because we see these poets and their work as exceptional exemplars of poetry, we have included their poems throughout the chapter.

▼▼▼▼▼▼▼

Building a Poetry Collection

As we have stressed throughout this chapter, your first concern in building a suitable poetry collection for your classroom is the selection of poems that you like and that will meet the needs of children who are in the process of *developing* an appreciation of poetry. This means including a variety of poems that will match the differing tastes and levels of sophistication you will meet every fall. To "hook 'em in," make sure to include plenty of light and humorous verse. Begin with the best: Jack Prelutsky and his *A Pizza the Size of the Sun* and *It's Raining Pigs and Noodles* are great books to start with. Shel Silverstein is the favorite with his perennially popular *Where the Sidewalk Ends* and *A Light in the Attic.* Brod Bagert's shorter collections that include his *Chicken Socks* and *Elephant Games* will further prompt children to take a second look at this genre. The poetry of James Stevenson and his "corn" series, *Sweet Corn, Popcorn,* and *Candy Corn,* as well as Douglas Florian with his *Laugh-eteria,* add to this collection of popular favorites. From there you can move to story poems, then to selections that create vivid images or that express our hard-to-communicate feelings and to poetry that plays with the sounds of language.

Cover from *A Jar of Tiny Stars: Poems by NCTE Award-Winning Poets.* Edited by Bernice E. Cullinan, illustrated by Andi MacLeod. Portraits by Marc Nadel. Copyright © 1996. Published by Wordsong, Boyds Mills Press, distributed by St. Martin's Press. All rights reserved. Reprinted by permission of the publisher.

Poetry in Our Textbooks

Clearly you cannot rely on textbooks to supply poetry for your classroom. For one thing, basal readers simply do not have enough poetry. In an informal count of the various readers and "literary anthologies" we have laying around our office and in the university curriculum collection, we saw an average of only a *dozen* poems in each volume, hardly enough to constitute a solid background in poetry.

Also, you ought to know this tidbit of information: Poems, as well as other literary works, are protected by copyright laws that run throughout the author's lifetime—*plus* 50 years. Textbook companies and other anthologizers find it less expensive to choose poems that are in what is known as the "public domain." In other words, many of the poems you read in those collections are by poets who have been dead a long time. This means that the editor doesn't have to pay a permission fee to reprint the poems. As a result, basals and anthologies may be heavily weighted on the side of older poetry. Now, don't get us wrong: Some of the old poems in these collections appeal to modern children. However, contemporary poetry—found largely in single, thin volumes or specific collections—generally has a stronger draw for today's reader.

Works by a Single Poet

As we have been saying all along, the world of children's books offers teachers, parents, and caregivers an almost endless supply of poetry. The reading list at the end of this chapter is representative of the excellent collections available in your libraries and bookstores that provide a broad range of poetry to meet every need. Many books of poetry are collections of a single poet's work. For example, each of the winners of the

To find out more about Janet Wong's site and other poets on the World Wide Web, visit Chapter 4 on the companion website at **www.prenhall.com/darigan**

BOOKMARK

INTEGRATING TECHNOLOGY: AUTHORS ON THE WORLD WIDE WEB

Much poetry is meant to be read orally, and *Janet Wong,* author of **A Suitcase of Seaweed, Buzz, Behind the Wheel** and numerous other books, has created a beautiful website that takes this into account. Her site not only gives the inside scoop on her books, poems and stories, but also provides real audio readings from seven of them. Janet founded the UCLA Immigrant Children's Art Project, a program focused on teaching refugee children to express themselves through art, and she is a recipient of the International Reading Association's Celebrate Literacy Award. The information revealed about her books and her life add tremendously to her literature.

NCTE Poetry Award has numerous collections that contain only their work. Books such as Lilian Moore's *Poems Have Roots,* John Ciardi's *You Read to Me, I'll Read to You,* and Barbara Esbensen's *Dance With Me* are representative examples of those collections.

Anthologies

However, we have listed some fine general anthologies as well. We mentioned earlier the collection of poems in *The Random House Book of Poetry,* selected by Jack Prelutsky, but also of great note is *Sing a Song of Popcorn,* compiled by Beatrice Schenk de Regniers et al. Both books have themed sections, such as a collection of weather poems and animal poems, and both provide a balance of modern and traditional poets. The former contains 572 poems and the latter 128—a sizable body of poetry to draw on, indeed. What makes *Sing a Song of Popcorn* so very inviting is that each section is illustrated by one of nine Caldecott-winning artists. Among this prestigious list are Trina Schart Hyman, Maurice Sendak, Leo and Diane Dillon, Richard Egielski, and Arnold Lobel. A grouping of classic poems about the United States is found in Neil Philip's *Singing America: Poems that Define a Nation,* illustrated on black-and-white scratchboard by Michael McCurdy and including classic poets such as Walt Whitman, Langston Hughes, Emily Dickinson, Henry Wadsworth Longfellow, and Edna St. Vincent Millay.

A number of specialized anthologies appear in the reading list as well. These collections contain poems about a particular topic and are by a variety of poets in one book. Myra Cohn Livingston, an NCTE Poetry Award winner, is also known for the many specialized collections she has published, such as *Cat Poems, Poems for Mothers, Birthday Poems, Halloween Poems, Valentine Poems,* and *Poems for Jewish Holidays.* Both Lee Bennett Hopkins and Jack Prelutsky have collected an enormous body of poetry with anthology topics ranging from sports to laughter to school. In the database that accompanies this text, the two have over 50 titles listed. Yet another book in this section of short, specialized anthologies must include Mary Ann Hoberman's *My Song Is Beautiful: Poems and Pictures in Many Voices,* also with a host of prestigious poets and illustrators.

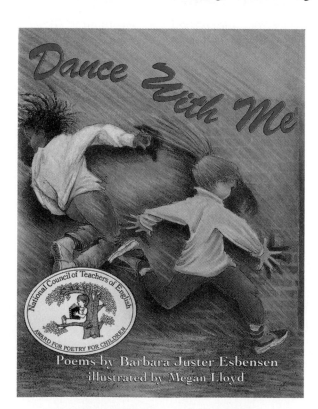

Cover from **Dance with Me** by Barbara Juster Esbensen, illustrated by Megan Lloyd. Text copyright © 1995 by Barbara Juster Esbensen, illustrations copyright © 1995 by Megan Lloyd. Published by HarperCollins Publisher. Reprinted by permission.

Make your students anthologists. As they read poetry every day, have them record their favorites, just as an anthologist would. After a while, patterns in their preferences will form, and that will become the seed of an idea for their anthology. They can illustrate their book and, of course, include a few original poems they have written themselves. After all, the word *anthology* comes from *anthologos,* "gathering flowers"—an apropos image for a collection of poetry, don't you think?

Single-Poem Picture Books

The single-poem picture book is another variety of poetry book that is particularly useful for giving children a taste of the more traditional and sometimes more sophisticated poet. For example, Susan Jeffers has illustrated a stunning picture book version of *Stopping by Woods on a Snowy Evening* by Robert Frost (1978), and Ed Young has hauntingly illustrated Frost's *Birches,* both of which will attract the most reluctant poetry reader.

▼▼▼▼▼▼▼

Include a Writing Component in Your Poetry Program

With all of the research regarding the connection between reading and writing, it would seem irresponsible for us, as educators, not to include writing as a natural component. But a word of caution! If you wish to introduce the writing of poetry along with the kids' own wide reading of poetry, we would strongly suggest that before you proceed you refer to the research of Kutiper and Wilson (1993) that we mentioned earlier in the chapter.

The first thing to remember is this: Do NOT start by having children write haiku or diamante or cinquain—or any other "form" of poetry, for that matter. They "hate" it, remember? It was *number one* on the researchers' list. In fact, diamante and cinquain are simply NOT poetry. Diamante, for instance, is merely a seven-line language template. Carole Cox (1999) wisely refers to it as just a "pat-

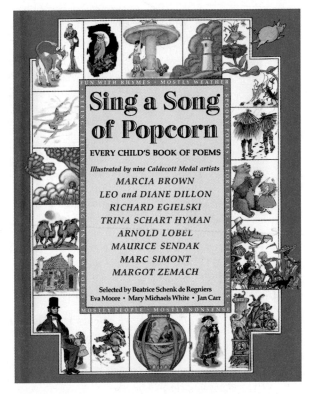

Cover from *Sing a Song of Popcorn: Every Child's Book of Poems.* Selected by Beatrice de Regniers, et al., © by Scholastic Inc. Reprinted by permission of Scholastic Inc.

tern" where the first line contains a noun, the second two describing adjectives, the third three participles, the fourth four describing nouns, the fifth three more participles, the sixth two adjectives, and the seventh a noun. Cinquain, predictably, is a five-line pattern where the first line is the title, the second line a description, the third an action, the fourth a feeling, and the fifth a reference to the title. Let's make a point here: When was the last time you saw an introspective diamante poem written by Robert Frost? How about a cinquain by Elizabeth Barrett Browning? No luck? Perhaps Emily Brontë? One of the major reasons they didn't write poetry in that form is for one simple reason: It isn't poetry!

Lee Bennett Hopkins told us that the form of diamante was invented only recently and for one reason alone: as a classroom language exercise. And to be quite honest, kids smell this kind of thing out instantly. So, a word to the wise: If you are going to have students write poetry, start off immediately by having them write *real* poetry. That means having them write poems that address their feelings, their senses, their critical observations about life and the world around them—then and only then will you see some incredible work.

▼▼▼▼▼▼▼

Summary

In this chapter, we first looked at the basic forms of poetry. We discussed narrative poems, lyric poems, limericks, haiku, concrete poetry, and free verse. Next we investigated elements of poetry, noting the application of figurative language; personification; rhythm, rhyme, and repetition; alliteration and assonance; and imagery. Given this rich background of language available in poetry, we examined why children may nonetheless learn to dislike poetry. We looked at how teachers can build an appreciation for poetry and reawaken children's natural interest in the genre.

Teachers who do not know the rich and vibrant world of children's poetry have a responsibility not only to discover the bounty that awaits them but also to use it to help stem the tide of ambivalence toward poetry among their students. A well-rounded classroom and school library poetry collection can have something for everyone. By sharing and enjoying poetry frequently, teachers and children together will build a lifelong appreciation, as the following poem by Eloise Greenfield (from *I Love and Other Poems*) expresses:

THINGS

Went to the corner
Walked in the store
Bought me some candy
Ain't got it no more
Ain't got it no more

Went to the beach
Played on the shore
Built me a sandhouse
Ain't got it no more
Ain't got it no more

Went to the kitchen
Lay down on the floor
Made me a poem
Still got it
Still got it

Further, by attending to the various forms of poetry, the elements poets use, and subjects that touch and entertain, teachers can build in children a solid appreciation for the genre and develop lifelong poetry lovers.

▼▼▼▼▼▼▼

Fifteen More of Our Favorites

Adoff, Arnold. (1973). *Black is brown is tan* (Emily Arnold McCully, Illus.). Harper. Describes in verse the life of brown-skinned mama, white-skinned daddy, their children, and assorted relatives.

Edens, Cooper. (1998). *The glorious Mother Goose*. Athenenum. A collection of 42 Mother Goose poems illustrated by classic artists such as Kate Greenaway and Jessie Wilcox Smith.

Esbensen, Barbara. (1992). *Who shrank my grandmother's house?* (Eric Beddows, Illus.). Harper. A collection of poems about childhood discoveries concerning everyday objects and things.

Fleischman, Paul. (1988). *Joyful noise: Poems for two voices* (Eric Beddows, Illus.). Harper. A collection of poems (divided into two columns to be read together by two people) describing the characteristics and activities of a variety of insects. Winner of the Newbery Medal.

Goldstein, Bobbye S. (1992). *Inner chimes: Poems on poetry*. Boyds Mills. A lovely collection of poems about poetry.

Hopkins, Lee Bennett. (1998). *Climb into my lap: First poems to read together* (Kathryn Brown, Illus.). Simon & Schuster. A collection of delightful poems meant to be read aloud.

Merriam, Eve. (1987). *Halloween ABC* (Lane Smith, Illus.). Macmillan. Each letter of the alphabet introduces a different, spooky aspect of Halloween.

O'Neill, Mary. (1989). *Hailstones and halibut bones* (John Wallner, Illus.). Doubleday. A striking collection of poems about color that was originally published in 1961.

Opie, Iona, & Opie, Peter. (1992). *I saw Esau: The schoolchild's pocket book* (Maurice Sendak, Illus.). Candlewick. A small pocket edition of tongue-in-cheek school poems wryly illustrated by Sendak.

Prelutsky, Jack, (Ed.). (1983). *The Random House book of poetry for children* (Arnold Lobel, Illus.). Random House. More than 550 poems by American, English, and anonymous authors.

Prelutsky, Jack. (1984). *The new kid on the block* (James Stevenson, Illus.). Greenwillow.

Humorous poems about such strange creatures and people as Baloney Belly Billy and the Gloopy Gloopers.

Rogasky, Barbara. (1994). *Winter poems* (Trina Schart Hyman, Illus.). Scholastic. A delightful collection of winter poems set in illustrator Hyman's own home and the local countryside.

Schwartz, Alvin. (1992). *And the green grass grew all around: Folk poetry from everyone* (Susan Truesdell, Illus.). HarperCollins. A rollicking collection of poems, chants, and songs.

Silverstein, Shel. (1974). *Where the sidewalk ends.* Harper. An extremely popular collection of humorous, somewhat irreverent poems written for children.

Yolen, Jane. (1987). *The three bears rhyme book* (Jane Dyer, Illus.). Harcourt. A collection of Yolen's original poems that center around "Goldilocks and the Three Bears." We particularly like her poem "Read to Me."

▼▼▼▼▼▼▼

Others We Like

Florian, Douglas. (1994). *Beast feast.* Harcourt.

George, Kristine O'Connell. (1997). *The great frog race and other poems* (Kate Kiesler, Illus.). Clarion.

Janeczko, Paul B. (1998). *That sweet diamond* (Carole Katchen, Illus.). Atheneum.

Kennedy, Dorothy M. (1998). *Make things fly* (Sasah Meret, Illus.). McElderry.

Kennedy, X. J. (1986). *Brats* (James Watt, Illus.). Atheneum.

Lansky, Bruce (Ed.). (1991). *Kids pick the funniest poems* (Stephen Carpenter, Illus.). Meadowbrook.

Larrick, Nancy (Ed.). (1968). *Piping down the valleys wild* (Ellen Raskin, Illus.). Delacorte.

Lewis, J. Patrick. (1990). *A Hippopotamusn't* (Victoria Chess, Illus.). Dial.

Lewis, J. Patrick. (1996). *Riddle-icious* (Debbie Tilley, Illus.). Knopf.

McNaughton, Colin. (1994). *Making friends with Frankenstein: A book of monstrous poems and pictures.* Candlewick.

Mathis, Sharon Bell. (1991). *Red dog blue fly: Football poems* (Jan Spivey Gilchrist, Illus.). Viking.

Morrison, Lillian. (1992). *At the crack of the bat* (Steve Cieslawski, Illus.). Hyperion.

Philip, Neil. (1995). *Singing America* (Michael McCurdy, Illus.). Viking.

Prelutsky, Jack. (1976). *Nightmares: Poems to trouble your sleep* (Arnold Lobel, Illus.). Greenwillow.

Prelutsky, Jack. (1993). *The dragons are singing tonight* (Peter Sís, Illus.). Greenwillow.

Rosen, Michael. (1998). *Classic poetry: An illustrated collection* (Paul Howard, Illus.). Candlewick.

Shaw, Alison. (1995). *Until I saw the sea: A collection of seashore poems.* Henry Holt.

Shields, Carol Diggory. (1995). *Lunch money and other poems about school* (Paul Meisel, Illus.). Dutton.

Sierra, Judy. (1998). *Antarctic antics: A book of penguin poems* (Jose Aruego & Ariane Dewey, Illus.). Harcourt.

Spinelli, Eileen. (1999). *Tea party today: Poems to sip and savor* (Karen Dugan, Illus.). Boyds Mills.

Volavkova, H. (Ed.). (1994). *. . . I never saw another butterfly: Children's drawings and poems from Terezin Concentration Camp, 1942–1944.* Random House.

Picture Books

Baylor, Byrd. (1986). *I'm in charge of celebrations* (Peter Parnall, Illus.). Scribner's.

Frost, Robert. (1978). *Stopping by woods on a snowy evening* (Susan Jeffers, Illus.). Dutton.

Hoberman, Mary Ann. (1978). *A house is a house for me* (Betty Fraser, Illus.). Viking.

Longfellow, Henry Wadsworth. (1983). *Song of Hiawatha* (Susan Jeffers, Illus.). Dial.

McNaughton, Colin. (1995). *Here come the aliens!* Candlewick.

Noyes, Alfred. (1981). *The highwayman* (Charles Keeping, Illus.). Oxford University Press.

Service, Robert W. (1987). *The cremation of Sam McGee* (Ted Harrison, Illus.). Greenwillow.

Siebert, Diane. (1989). *Heartland* (Wendell Minor, Illus.). Crowell.

Thayer, Lawrence Ernest. (2000). *Casey at the bat: A ballad of the republic sung in the year 1888* (Christopher Bing, Illus.). Handprint.

Easy to Read

Brown, Marc (Ed.). (1987). *Play rhymes.* Dutton.

Hopkins, Lee Bennett (Ed.). (1987). *More surprises* (Megan Lloyd, Illus.). Harper.

Hopkins, Lee Bennett (Ed.). (1994). *Weather: Poems for all seasons* (Melanie Hall, Illus.). Harper.

Hopkins, Lee Bennett. (1995). *Small talk: A book of short poems* (Susan Gaber, Illus.). Harcourt.

James, Simon. (2000). *Days like this.* Candlewick.

Kuskin, Karla. (1992). *Soap soup and other verses.* Harper.

Livingston, Myra Cohn (Ed.). (1989). *Dilly dilly piccalilli: Poems for the very young* (Eileen Christelow, Illus.). McElderry.

Moore, Lilian. (1995). *I never did that before* (Lilian Hoban, Illus.). Atheneum.

Opie, Iona (Ed.). (1996). *My very first Mother Goose* (Rosemary Wells, Illus.). Candlewick.

Prelutsky, Jack. (1980). *Rolling Harvey down the hill* (Victoria Chess, Illus.). Greenwillow.

Prelutsky, Jack. (1983). *It's Valentine's Day* (Yossi Abolafia, Illus.). Greenwillow.

▼▼▼▼▼▼▼

Children's Literature References

Adoff, Arnold. (1973). *Black is brown is tan* (Emily Arnold McCully, Illus.). New York: Harper.

Adoff, Arnold. (1979). *Eats* (Susan Russo, Illus.). New York: Lothrop.

Adoff, Arnold. (1986). *Sports pages* (Steve Kuzma, Illus.). New York: Lippincott.

Adoff, Arnold. (1989). *Chocolate dreams: Poems* (Turi MacCombie, Illus.). New York: Lothrop.

Adoff, Arnold. (2000). *Touch the poem* (Lisa Desimini, Illus.). New York: Scholastic.

Arbuthnot, May Hill. (1961). *The Arbuthnot anthology of children's literature.* Glenview, IL: Scott, Foresman.

Bagert, Brod. (1993). *Chicken socks* (Tim Ellis, Illus.). Honesdale, PA: Boyds Mills Press.

Bagert, Brod. (1995). *Elephant games and other playful poems to perform* (Tim Ellis, Illus.). Honesdale, PA: Boyds Mills Press.

Bing, Christopher. (2000). *Ernest L. Thayer's Casey at the bat: A ballad of the republic sung in the year 1888.* Brooklyn, NY: Handprint Books.

Bryan, Ashley. (1992). *Sing to the sun.* New York: HarperCollins.

Ciardi, John. (1962). *You read to me, I'll read to you* (Edward Gorey, Illus.). New York: Lippincott.

Ciardi, John. (1989). *The hopeful trout and other limericks* (Susan Meddaugh, Illus.). New York: Houghton Mifflin.

Cullinan, Bernice E. (Ed.). (1996). *A jar of tiny stars: Poems by NCTE award-winning poets.* Honesdale, PA: Wordsong/Boyds Mills.

DeFelice, Cynthia. (1996). *Casey in the bath* (Chris Demarest, Illus.). New York: Farrar, Straus & Giroux.

Delacre, Lulu. (1989). *Arroz con leche: Popular songs and rhymes from Latin America.* New York: Scholastic.

de Regniers, Beatrice Schenk, Moore, Eva, White, Mary Michaels, & Carr, Jean. (Comps.). (1988). *Sing a song of popcorn.* New York: Scholastic.

Esbensen, Barbara Juster. (1995). *Dance with me.* New York: HarperCollins.

Fisher, Aileen L. (1933). *The coffee-pot face.* New York: Robert M. McBride.

Fleischman, Paul. (1988). *Joyful noise* (Eric Beddows, Illus.). New York: HarperCollins.

Florian, Douglas. (1999). *Laugh-eteria.* San Diego: Harcourt Brace.

Frost, Robert. (1978). *Stopping by woods on a snowy evening* (Susan Jeffers, Illus.). New York: Dutton.

Frost, Robert. (1988). *Birches* (Ed Young, Illus.). New York: Henry Holt.

Glenn, Mel. (1996). *Who killed Mr. Chippendale? A mystery in poems.* New York: Dutton.

Glenn, Mel. (1997). *The taking of room 114.* New York: Dutton.

Glenn, Mel. (1997). *Jump ball: A basketball season in poems.* New York: Dutton.

Graham, Joan Bransfield. (1994). *Splish splash* (Steve Scott, Illus.). New York: Ticknor & Fields.

Greenfield, Eloise. (1978). *Honey, I love and other poems* (Leo Dillon & Diane Dillon, Illus.). New York: HarperCollins.

Grimes, Nikki. (1994). *Meet Danitra Brown* (Floyd Cooper, Illus.). New York: Lothrop.

Harrison, David L. (1993). *Somebody catch my homework* (Betsy Lewin, Illus.). Honesdale, PA: Boyds Mills Press.

Heller, Ruth. (1987). *A cache of jewels and other collective nouns.* New York: Scholastic.

Heller, Ruth. (1988). *Kites sail high: A book about verbs.* New York: Scholastic.

Heller, Ruth. (1989). *Many luscious lollipops: A book about adjectives*. New York: Grosset & Dunlap.

Heller, Ruth. (1990). *Merry-go-round: A book about nouns*. New York: Scholastic.

Heller, Ruth. (1991). *Up, up and away: A book about adverbs*. New York: Grosset & Dunlap.

Heller, Ruth. (1995). *Behind the mask: A book about prepositions*. New York: Grosset & Dunlap.

Heller, Ruth. (1997). *Mine, all mine: A book about pronouns*. New York: Grosset & Dunlap.

Heller, Ruth. (1998). *Fantastic! Wow! And unreal! A book about interjections and conjunctions*. New York: Grosset & Dunlap.

Hoberman, Mary Ann. (1994). *My song is beautiful: Poems and pictures in many voices*. Boston: Little, Brown.

Hopkins, Lee Bennett. (1984). *Surprises* (Megan Lloyd, Illus.). New York: Harper & Row.

Hopkins, Lee Bennett. (1990). *Good books, good times!* (Harvey Stevenson, Illus.). New York: HarperCollins.

Hopkins, Lee Bennett. (1992a). *Questions* (Carolyn Croll, Illus.). New York: HarperCollins.

Hopkins, Lee Bennett. (1992b). *Through our eyes: Poems and pictures about growing up* (Jeffrey Dunn, Photog.). Boston: Little, Brown.

Hopkins, Lee Bennett. (1993). *Ragged shadows: Poems of Halloween night* (Giles Laroche, Illus.). Boston: Little, Brown.

Hopkins, Lee Bennett. (1994a). *Hand in hand: An American history through poetry* (Peter M. Fiore, Illus.). New York: Simon & Schuster.

Hopkins, Lee Bennett. (1994b). *Weather* (Melanie Hall, Illus.). New York: HarperCollins.

Hopkins, Lee Bennett. (1995a). *Been to yesterdays: Poems of a life*. Honesdale, PA: Boyds Mills.

Hopkins, Lee Bennett. (1995b). *Good rhymes, good times* (Frané Lessac, Illus.). New York: HarperCollins.

Hopkins, Lee Bennett. (1996). *School supplies* (Renée Flowers, Illus.). New York: Simon & Schuster.

Hopkins, Lee Bennett. (1999a). *Marvelous math* (Karen Barbour, Illus.). New York: Simon & Schuster.

Hopkins, Lee Bennett. (1999b). *Spectacular science* (Virginia Halstead, Illus.). New York: Simon & Schuster.

Joseph, Lynn. (1990). *Coconut kind of day: Island poems* (Sandra Speidel, Illus.). New York: Lothrop.

Kennedy, Dorothy M. (1993). *I thought I'd take my rat to school: Poems for September to June* (Abby Carter, Illus.). Boston: Little, Brown.

Kennedy, X. J. (1997). *Uncle Switch: Looney limericks* (John O'Brien, Illus.). New York: McElderry.

Kennedy, X. J. (1999). *Elympics* (Graham Percy, Illus.). New York: Philomel.

Kennedy, X. J., & Kennedy, Dorothy M. (1992). *Talking like the rain: A first book of poems* (Jane Dyer, Illus.). Boston: Little, Brown.

Lear, Edward. (1946). *The complete nonsense book*. New York: Dodd. (Original work published 1846)

Lewis, J. Patrick. (1995). *Black swan white crow* (Chris Manson, Illus.). New York: Atheneum.

Livingston, Myra Cohn. (1974). *The way things are and other poems*. New York: McElderry.

Livingston, Myra Cohn. (1978). *A lollygag of limericks* (Joseph Low, Illus.). New York: McElderry.

Livingston, Myra Cohn. (Ed.). (1986). *Poems for Jewish holidays* (Lloyd Bloom, Illus.). New York: Holiday House.

Livingston, Myra Cohn. (Ed.). (1987a). *Cat poems* (Trina Schart Hyman, Illus.). New York: Holiday House.

Livingston, Myra Cohn. (1987b). *Valentine poems*. New York: Holiday House.

Livingston, Myra Cohn. (Ed.). (1988). *Poems for mothers* (Deborah Kogan Ray, Illus.). New York: Holiday House.

Livingston, Myra Cohn. (1989a). *Birthday poems*. New York: Holiday House.

Livingston, Myra Cohn. (1989b). *Halloween poems* (Stephen Gammell, Illus.). New York: Holiday House.

Livingston, Myra Cohn. (1991). *Lots of limericks* (Rebecca Perry, Illus.). New York: McElderry.

Livingston, Myra Cohn. (1997). *Cricket never does: A collection of haiku and tanka* (Kees de Kiefte, Illus.). New York: McElderry.

Longfellow, Henry Wadsworth. (1990). *Paul Revere's ride* (Ted Rand, Illus.). New York: Dutton.

McCord, David. (1970). *One at a time*. Boston: Little, Brown.

Merriam, Eve. (1986). *Fresh paint* (Woodcuts by David Frampton.) New York: Macmillan.

Moore, Lilian. (1997). *Poems have roots* (Tad Hills, Illus.). New York: Atheneum.

Moss, Jeff. (1989). *The butterfly jar* (Chris Demarest, Illus.). New York: Bantam.

Moss, Jeff. (1991). *The other side of the door* (Chris Demarest, Illus.). New York: Bantam.

Myers, Walter Dean. (1993). *Brown angels: An album of pictures and verse*. New York: HarperCollins.

Opie, Iona. (1996). *My very first Mother Goose* (Rosemary Wells, Illus.). Cambridge, MA: Candlewick.

Opie, Iona. (1999). *Here comes Mother Goose* (Rosemary Wells, Illus.). Cambridge, MA: Candlewick.

Philip, Neil. (1995). *Singing America: Poems that define a nation* (Michael McCurdy, Illus.). New York: Viking.

Polacco, Patricia. (1988). *Casey at the bat: A ballad of the republic sung in the year 1888*. New York: Putnam.

Prelutsky, Jack. (1976). *Nightmares: Poems to trouble your sleep* (Arnold Lobel, Illus.). New York: Greenwillow.

Prelutsky, Jack. (1982). *It's Thanksgiving* (Marylin Hafner, Illus.). New York: Greenwillow.

Prelutsky, Jack. (1984). *The new kid on the block* (James Stevenson, Illus.). New York: Greenwillow.

Prelutsky, Jack. (1986). *Ride a purple pelican* (Garth Williams, Illus.). New York: Greenwillow.

Prelutsky, Jack. (1990). *Beneath a blue umbrella* (Garth Williams, Illus.). New York: Greenwillow.

Prelutsky, Jack. (1996). *A pizza the size of the sun* (James Stevenson, Illus.). New York: Greenwillow.

Prelutsky, Jack. (2000a). *It's raining pigs & noodles* (James Stevenson, Illus.). New York: Greenwillow.

Prelutsky, Jack. (Ed.). (2000b). *The Random House book of poetry* (Arnold Lobel, Illus.). New York: Random House.

Schertle, Alice. (1994). *How now, brown cow?* (Amanda Schaffer, Illus.). San Diego: Harcourt Brace.

Schertle, Alice. (1995). *Advice for a frog* (Norman Green, Illus.). New York: Lothrop.

Schertle, Alice. (1996). *Keepers* (Ted Rand, Illus.). New York: Lothrop.

Schertle, Alice. (1999a). *A lucky thing* (Windell Minor, Illus.). San Diego: Harcourt Brace.

Schertle, Alice. (1999b). *I am the cat* (Mark Buehner, Illus.). New York: Lothrop.

Sierra, Judy. (1998). *Antarctic antics: A book of penguin poems.* San Diego: Harcourt Brace.

Silverstein, Shel. (1974). *Where the sidewalk ends.* New York: Harper & Row.

Silverstein, Shel. (1981). *A light in the attic.* New York: Harper & Row.

Spooner, Michael. (1993). *A moon in your lunch box* (Ib Ohlsson, Illus.). New York: Henry Holt.

Stevenson, James. (1995). *Sweet corn.* New York: Greenwillow.

Stevenson, James. (1998). *Popcorn.* New York: Greenwillow.

Stevenson, James. (1999). *Candy corn.* New York: Greenwillow.

Stevenson, Robert Louis. (1947). *A child's garden of verses* (Tasha Tudor, Illus.). New York: Oxford University Press.

Stevenson, Robert Louis. (1998). *A child's garden of verses* (Diane Goode, Illus.). New York: William Morrow.

Thomas, Joyce Carol. (1993). *Brown honey in broomwheat tea* (Floyd Cooper, Illus.). New York: HarperCollins.

Worth, Valerie. (1994). *all the small poems and fourteen more* (Natalie Babbitt, Illus.). New York: Farrar, Straus & Giroux.

Wyndham, Robert. (1968). *Chinese Mother Goose rhymes* (Ed Young, Illus.). New York: Philomel.

▼▼▼▼▼▼▼▼

Professional References

Arbuthnot, M. H. (1961). *The Arbuthnot anthology of children's literature.* Glenview, IL: Scott, Foresman.

Cox, C. (1999). *Teaching language arts: A student- and response-centered classroom.* Boston: Allyn & Bacon.

Fisher, C. J., & Natarella, M. A. (1982). Young children's preferences in poetry: A national survey of first, second and third graders. *Research in the Teaching of English, 16*(4), 339–354.

Heard, G. (1989). *For the good of the earth and sun.* Portsmouth, NH: Heinemann.

Hopkins, L. B. (1998). *Pass the poetry, please!* New York: HarperCollins.

Kennedy, X. J. (1986). *An introduction to poetry.* Glenview, IL: Scott, Foresman.

Kutiper, K., & Wilson, P. (1993). Updating poetry preferences: A look at the poetry children really like. *The Reading Teacher, 47*(1), 28–35.

Lonsdale, B. J., & Mackintosh, H. K. (1973). *Children experience literature.* New York: Random House.

Opie, I., & Opie, P. (1959). *The lore and language of schoolchildren.* Oxford: Oxford University Press.

Terry, A. C. (1974). *Children's poetry preferences.* Urbana, IL: NCTE Research Report No. 16.

TRADITIONAL FANTASY

5

CHAPTER

▼▼▼▼▼▼

If you want to cover

Variants of the Cinderella Theme Across the Cultures

Consider as a READ ALOUD

Raisel's Riddle,
by Erica Silverman,
illustrated by Susan Gaber

Consider as a TEXT SET

Chinye: A West African Folk Tale,
by Obi Onyefulu,
illustrated by Evie Safarewicz

Cinderella,
by Amy Ehrlich,
illustrated by Susan Jeffers

The Egyptian Cinderella,
by Shirley Climo, illustrated by Ruth Heller

The Korean Cinderella,
by Shirley Climo, illustrated by Ruth Heller

Moss Gown, by William H. Hooks,
illustrated by Donald Carrick

The Rough-Face Girl,
by Rafe Martin, illustrated by David Shannon

*Yeh Shen: A Cinderella Story from
China,* by Ai-Ling Louie,
illustrated by Ed Young

THE EGYPTIAN CINDERELLA
by Shirley Climo, illustrated by Ruth Heller

THE EGYPTIAN CINDERELLA

by Shirley Climo • illustrated by Ruth Heller

"Behold!" cried Amasis. "In all this land there is none so fit to be queen!"

"But Rhodopis is a slave!" protested one of the servant girls.

Kipa sniffed. "She is not even Egyptian."

"She is the most Egyptian of all," the Pharaoh declared. "For her eyes are as green as the Nile, her hair as feathery as papyrus, and her skin the pink of a lotus flower."

Excerpt from *The Egyptian Cinderella* by Shirley Climo

Student Response

To visit a classroom exploring the issues of Traditional Fantasy, please go to Chapter 5 of our companion website at **www.prenhall. com/darigan**

Traditional tales had their beginnings around the hearthside and campfire. The stories were almost always fantastic in nature, involving magic, trickery, and deception, with characters ranging from talking animals to heroes to fools. Originally, these tales provided entertainment for adults, who freely altered details as they were told and re-told. As adults shared these stories with one another, children surely lounged about the fringes and listened. In modern times, many of the tales have shifted from their origin with an adult audience to being identified with children.

Because these stories were born of the oral tradition, no one really knows who first told each tale or where a particular version originated. In the end, it's not really as important to know the "where" or "when" as it is to know that as teachers and parents, we are enormously fortunate to have such a varied and rich selection of traditional fantasy at our fingertips.

▼▼▼▼▼▼▼

Traditional Fantasy Defined

Simply stated, traditional fantasy is the literature that originated orally and has no identifiable author. Now keep in mind that we often associate many of these tales with a particular collector or reteller such as the Brothers Grimm, who are probably most commonly known. Though Jacob and Wilhelm Grimm never wrote any original stories themselves, they collected, retold, and recorded in print the European variants of some of the best-known traditional tales in Western culture in their *Kinder-und Haus-mauchen* or, translated into English, *Household Stories*. Such stories as "Cinderella," "Sleeping Beauty," and "Little Red Riding Hood" are but a few of the tales credited to this twosome.

Another collector is Charles Perrault, who actually preceded the Brothers Grimm in collecting many of the European tales in his *Contes de ma Mère L'Oye*. He filed away the hard edges of many of the tales so that they would be more acceptable to the genteel folk of the French court of Louis XIV. Among the stories included in his collection of eight tales were "Cinderella," "Little Red Riding Hood," and "Puss in Boots."

Other collectors who are not as well known by the general masses provide us with many of the tales we still tell today. In his *English Fairy Tales,* Joseph Jacobs collected the British tales loved by young children, such as "The Three Little Pigs," "Jack and the Beanstalk," "Henny-Penny," and "The Little Red Hen." Peter Asbjørnsen and Jorgen Moe gathered the Scandinavian tales into a volume titled *East o' the Sun and West o' the Moon* which, in addition to the title selection, contained "The Three Billy Goats Gruff," "The Husband Who Was to Mind the House," and "Boots and His Brothers."

Tales from the oral tradition are part of the fabric of every culture. *The Arabian Nights,* often referred to as *The Thousand and One Nights,* were recorded and translated into English during the 18th century. Included in this group of tales are "Aladdin," "Ali Baba and the Forty Thieves," and "The Seven Voyages of Sinbad the Sailor."

The stories in *The Arabian Nights* were a result of the horrible revenge King Riar exacted against all the young women in his country of Persia. Learning that his wife had been untrue, he had her put to death. Then, in his anger, he married a new woman every day and had her, too, put to death the next day. Only after Riar's grand vizier's daughter, Scheherazade, stepped forward with a plan was the curse broken. The very morning after their wedding, she began telling the king a fascinating story but was unable to finish before the call to prayers. Because the king so badly wanted to hear the ending of the tale, he let her live another day. This same pattern continued for many days, and when Scheherazade came to the end of a story, she deftly wove it into the beginning of a new story, and so over the course of one thousand and one nights Scheherazade lived. Finally (and men can be SO dense, sometimes), the king realized he would be a fool to kill someone he loved so dearly, so he renounced his evil plan, and was once more a good and kind king.

ALTERNATE TEXT SET

The Arabian Nights

Read Aloud

The Tale of Aladdin and the Wonderful Lamp, by Eric A. Kimmel,
illustrated by Ju-Hong Chen

Text Set

The Tale of Ali Baba and the Forty Thieves, by Eric A. Kimmel, illustrated
by Will Hillenbrand

Aladdin and Other Tales from the Arabian Nights, by Rosalind Kerven,
illustrated by Nilesh Mistry

Arabian Nights: Three Tales, by Deborah Nourse Lattimore

The Seven Voyages of Sinbad the Sailor, by John Yeoman, illustrated by
Quentin Blake

The Rose's Smile: Farizad of the Arabian Nights, by Kavid Kherdian,
illustrated by Stefano Vitale

Tales From Across Cultures

Other collections of traditional tales from the Middle East include the Hodja stories
from Turkey that tell of the wisdom of Nasredden Hodja, and the Jataka stories from
India that are centered on the lives of Buddah.

The masterful storytelling of Nobel Prize–winner Isaac Bashevis Singer has preserved much of the folklore of Jewish tradition. His stories "Zlateh the Goat," "Mazel
and Schlimazel," "The Fools of Chelm and the Stupid Carp," and "The Golem" capture the rich folk heritage of the Jewish people.

Tales from the Asian-, African-, and Native-American traditions abound and are
available to children, most often in stunning picture book versions. These are extremely important additions to the body of traditional literature, which we discuss in
detail in chapter 9, "Multicultural and International Children's Books."

To find additional
titles in traditional
fantasy, search
the database on
the CD that accompanies this
book.

What Isn't Traditional Fantasy

Quite often, stories are written by modern authors but are patterned after traditional
tales. Works by the gifted 19th century Danish author Hans Christian Andersen, for
example, are often lumped into this category by many of our students. Andersen's
"The Little Match Girl," "The Steadfast Tin Soldier," and "The Princess and the Pea"
are but a few examples of this great man's work that are often mislabeled as traditional
fantasy. Rudyard Kipling's collection of *Just-So Stories* is also often confused with this
genre. Recent examples include books such as Katherine Paterson's **The King's Equal**
and Natalie Babbitt's **Bub or the Very Best Thing.** However, these are all better characterized as "literary folk and fairy tales" and are considered modern fantasy stories.
They originated in written form, though they keep similar plot structure, characterization, and setting. These and an abundance of other tales are discussed at length in
chapter 6, "Modern Fantasy."

- Characterization: Are the characters believable and well rounded?
- Plot: Is the plot believable, and does it move forward?
- Theme: Is there any discernable theme or message the author seems to be imparting?
- Setting: Is the setting consistent with the genre in that it occurs in the distant past?
- Categorization: Does the tale basically fit into one of the categories of the genre? For example, is it a folktale, tall tale, fable, myth, epic or legend, or religious story?
- Type of Folktale: If it is a folktale, does it fall into a discernible category such as a pourquoi tale, noodlehead tale, or fairy tale?

▼▼▼▼▼▼▼

Characteristics of Traditional Fantasy

Characterization

Traditional stories differ in various ways from more modern writings and, therefore, are held to a different critical standard. For example, characters must be well developed in modern stories, whereas character development in traditional tales is generally lean and spare. Think of Cinderella, for example. How rounded is her character? We are actually given to know very little about her. How does she feel about her ill treatment? about her change in fortune? What are her interests? We don't even know much about her physical appearance. If listeners and readers are told about her personality or thoughts, it is only in general terms. For instance, we read, "She wept at her mother's grave." The reader must then infer information about Cinderella, but rarely are we told outright what is going on in her mind.

The fact is that characters in traditional stories are generally archetypes; they are meant to be symbolic of certain basic human traits, such as good and evil. So, instead of the gradations of character we see in modern stories, where a character may reveal the mix of good and bad present in all of us, in traditional tales we tend to find single-faceted characters who typically do not change during the course of the story.

Take, for example, the tale of "Rumpelstiltskin." The miller's daughter is duped into having to spin straw into gold. When she is unable to accomplish such a task, a tiny little man comes into the room and, for a small price, spins the straw into gold. The greedy king realizes what a gold mine he has—literally—and demands her to spin more straw into gold in a much larger room. As the amount of straw escalates so, too, does the price the little man asks. When she arrives in the third and final room, she has given him all her worldly possessions and there is nothing left for the miller's daughter to bestow but her first-born son; her only recourse. One year later, after the miller's daughter and the king marry and their first son is born, the little man returns for his payment, the child. Touched by her tears, he gives the new queen a second chance to keep the baby: If she can guess his name within the next 3 days, the child will remain hers. Of course, she *does* luckily guess the man's name but to very the end, the girl remains helpless, the king self-centered and greedy, and Rumpelstiltskin ruthless.

Traditional tales, then, are stories of the human experience told in primary colors, the nuances of life stripped away to reveal the basic components: love, fear, greed, jealousy, mercy, and so on. Therefore, traditional stories from around the world are basically alike because fundamental human characteristics and motivations are universal.

Using simple props found around the house, you can add to a story's impact. We read *Boots and His Brothers* by first showing a miniature plastic shovel and ax, along with a walnut in a shell. When each is introduced in the story, the reaction is "aha" and the experience is deepened.

Plot

Plots are also simple and direct in traditional fantasy. And because the tales generally were told by and among the common folk, they are often success stories that show the underdog making good—the youngest son or daughter, the little tailor, unwanted children, the fool, and so on. And success is often obtained against overwhelming odds, such as accomplishing impossible tasks.

Eric Kimmel's retelling of the Norwegian tale of *Boots and His Brothers* is just such a book. Three brothers, Peter, Paul, and Boots, are off to the king's palace to accomplish three tasks: They first need to cut down a huge oak that blocks all the sunlight coming through the windows; second, they need to dig a well in the iron mountainside; and finally, they must fill that well with pure, sweet water. Boots's brothers were said to be "rough and rude" so, on their journey, when they meet an old woman on the road who offers friendly advice, the two put her off and trek on down the trail. Boots, who is kind and thoughtful, listens to the old granny's advice and, of course, is ultimately able to achieve the three tasks while the king's dogs drive off the two older brothers. Young Boots is rewarded for his deeds with his weight in gold and half the kingdom, too.

DID YOU KNOW?

Typical to Eric Kimmel's style in retelling folk tales, he has softened many of the stories without affecting the content. For example, in his *Old Woman and Her Pig,* he removed the hanging of the butcher and the killing of the ox. In his version of *Boots and His Brothers,* rather than having Boots's brothers Peter and Paul beheaded, they are simply chased off by the king's dogs. His feeling is that these retellings aren't meant to "replace the original, but rather to provide a lighter alternative" (from the author's note found in *The Old Women and Her Pig*).

Cover from *Boots and His Brothers: A Norwegian Tale,* retold by Eric A. Kimmel, illustrated by Kimberly Bulcken Root. Copyright © 1992 Eric A. Kimmel (text); copyright © 1992 Kimberley Bulcken Root (Illustrations). Published by Holiday House. Reprinted by permission of the publisher.

ALTERNATE TEXT SET

Tales by Eric Kimmel

Read Aloud

Three Sacks of Truth, illustrated by Robert Rayevsky

Text Set

Anansi and the Talking Melon, illustrated by Janet Stevens

Hershel and the Hanukkah Goblins, illustrated by Trina Schart Hyman

Bearhead, illustrated by Charles Mikolaycak

Iron John, illustrated by Trina Schart Hyman

Gershon's Monster, illustrated by Jon J Muth

The Jar of Fools, illustrated by Mordicai Gerstein

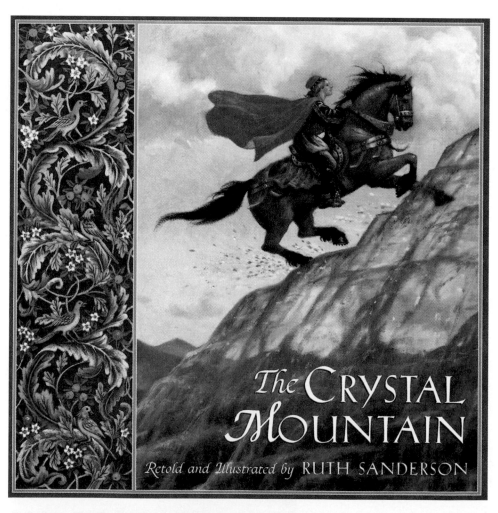

Cover from **The Crystal Mountain,** retold and illustrated by Ruth Sanderson. Copyright © 1999 by Ruth Sanderson. Published by Little, Brown & Company. Reprinted by permission of Little, Brown & Company.

A CONVERSATION WITH. . .

Eric A. Kimmel

I have always loved fairy tales. It goes way, way back to when I was a young kid. My grandma lived in our house from the time I was born until she died when I was 18. She was really an old country grandma. She grew up in a little town in Austria-Hungary. Her father was a baker and had a little farm on the outskirts of town. She grew up with the peasant kids, never going to school and running barefoot in the fields in the summer and swimming in the river. She never went to school, but she was very literate with a wealth of oral tales. She would sit and tell me all kinds of stories. So I grew up with tales about witches, little creepy things in the forest, ghosts, and spirits.

I also remember my Uncle Abe, who went to an American Legion sale and showed up at our house one Sunday with all these books that he thought I might like. They were fairly cheap and he knew I liked to read. One book was an edition of Hans Christian Andersen's tales and one was an edition of Grimm that was absolutely wonderful. The third was two enormous volumes of the King James Old Testament. They were huge and I still have them today, but they are in fragments because I literally read them to pieces.

As I was growing up, "long ago and far away" seemed far more interesting than the "here and now," which was the Eisenhower era. Everything then was crew cuts and button-down shirts, keep your mouth shut and do as you were told. I also had two wonderful teachers—first grade was Mrs. McGroarty and third grade was Mrs. Miles. They loved reading and books and, to me, it was all marvelous and exciting.

What I try to do in many of my books is to convey to the reader that same love and joy and sense of excitement that I got as a child. One of my most recent books, *Seven At One Blow,* is one I read when I was 7 years old. It was contained in the collection my Uncle Abe got me. *Iron John* is another great example of one I grew up with. So I don't need to hunt through ancient stories for material. I write stories I have known my whole life. They are truly a labor of love.

What I do in my writing is to combine, mix, and change. I like taking the pieces, scattering them around, and putting them back together in new combinations to see what comes out. Hershel, for example, from *Hershel and the Hanukkah Goblins,* is a traditional Jewish figure from eastern European folklore. I took a piece from a Russian story called *Ivanko the Bear's Son,* where there was a goblin who lived in a lake, I multiplied it by eight, and used Hershel as the hero. Because I liked that story so much, I then transformed it into the book *Bearhead.*

So I do change the story around. But every teller who ever told a story changes the story, and that directly affects the way I approach books and the way I understand them. You cannot tell the same story twice; it always changes because with each telling *you* are different, and the *audience* is different. You get new ideas and try them out, you even forget things; so because the story is always changing, I don't feel any qualms about changing it when I write the story as a picture book. I don't feel shackled to the original text. I know that the so-called original text is simply one version of the story, set down at one particular moment in time. I like to think that I write as if I am addressing a bunch of kids around a campfire. I ask myself what is going to make them pay attention. What is going to make them laugh? With that in mind, I craft a tale that I hope they will like.

Theme

Story lines in traditional fantasy are accompanied by typical themes, such as the rewards of mercy, kindness, and perseverance. Notice that books like *East o' the Sun and West o' the Moon, The Water of Life,* and *The Crystal Mountain* all characterize the younger kind brother who, against great odds, persists and eventually attains his just reward. Justice, particularly the punishment of evil, is typical, and the power of love conquers all. Another version of Ruth Sanderson's book *The Crystal Mountain* is found in Robert D. San Souci's *The Enchanted Tapestry,* illustrated by László Gál.

To read more of this Conversation with Eric A. Kimmel, please visit Chapter 5 on our text's companion website at **www.prenhall.com/darigan**

Setting

Settings are quickly established and always in the distant past. Rarely do we meet up with a tale that doesn't start "Once upon a time . . ." or contain some such variant.

ALTERNATE TEXT SET

Run, Run, Run After the "Gingerbread Man"

Read Aloud

The Gingerbread Man, by Jim Aylesworth, illustrated by Barbara McClintock

Text Set

The Gingerbread Man, by Barbara Baumgartner, illustrated by Norman Messenger

The Gingerbread Boy, by Richard Egielski

The Gingerbread Man, by Eric A. Kimmel, illustrated by Megan Lloyd

The Gingerbread Man: An Old English Folktale, by John A. Rowe

The Gingerbread Baby, by Jan Brett

The Runaway Tortilla, by Eric A. Kimmel, illustrated by Randy Cecil

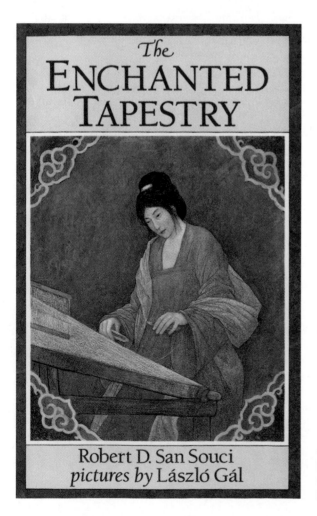

Time always seems to pass quickly. Rip Van Winkle sleeps 20 years in the blink of an eye, and Sleeping Beauty slumbers 100 years with equal brevity. Beauty resides with the Beast for days, weeks, even months before returning to the bedside of her sick father in "Beauty and the Beast." Spring arrives all too soon in "Snow White and Rose Red," for that means the friendly bear, who has stretched out on their hearth every night during the long cold winter, must stay in the forest to protect his treasure.

Repeated Elements

Another hallmark of traditional stories is repeated patterns or elements. The magical number three appears frequently in tales: Rumpelstiltskin's three evenings of spinning straw into gold, Cinderella's three visits to the ball, Jack's three trips up the beanstalk. Often a refrain is repeated throughout the story: "Fee, fi, fo, fum. I smell the blood of an Englishman" from "Jack and the Beanstalk," or "Run, run, run, as fast as you can, you can't catch me, I'm the Gingerbread Man!"

Cover from ***The Enchanted Tapestry: A Chinese Folktale,*** retold by Robert D. San Souci, pictures by László Gál. Copyright © 1987 László Gál, illustrations. Used by permission of Dial Books for Young Readers, a division of Penguin Putnam, Inc.

BOOKMARK

INTEGRATING TECHNOLOGY: AUTHORS/ILLUSTRATORS ON THE WORLD WIDE WEB

Many authors of contemporary realistic fiction have websites that discuss their books and their life. Sometimes the author will provide other materials of interest to readers. Author and illustrator *Jan Brett,* many of whose stories are marvelous retellings of folktales, such as *The Mitten* and *Town Mouse, Country Mouse,* has created one of the most engaging children's literature sites on the World Wide Web. The array of colorful and thought-provoking material on her website makes it useful and attractive to children and teachers alike. In addition to games, postcards, and masks (which can be printed for dramatizations), for each of her books she has written an illustrated letter that includes information concerning their creation. One can discover, for example, how she used her husband as the model for Berlioz the Bear.

To find out more about Jan Brett's site and other authors/illustrators of traditional fantasy, visit Chapter 5 on the companion website at **www.prenhall.com/darigan**

▼▼▼▼▼▼▼

Types of Traditional Fantasy

Categories of any genre of literature are never cast in concrete. In fact, authorities will forever disagree on a universal system that adequately categorizes traditional fantasy. Even if we were fortunate enough to have consensus on solid, distinct classifications of folktales, there would still be arguments on which tale fits into which category. You might read Tololwa Mollel's *The Orphan Boy*, for example, and decide that it is the perfect pourquoi tale. Your grade partner across the hall may read the same book and remain steadfast that though there *are* aspects of pourquoi in the story, it is clearly a fairy or wonder tale. This isn't a reason to start World War III. What actually ensues is something very wonderful. You *could* just simply have a friendly discussion and debate about it. No fights or grudges necessary.

We present our view of what constitutes traditional stories in hopes of your keeping in mind that this list is merely a tool for introducing you to the stories themselves.

DID YOU KNOW?

As beautiful as the illustrations by Paul Morin were for Mollel's **The Orphan Boy,** he could not have won the Caldecott Medal. Why not? Morin is from Canada, and the Caldecott is limited to citizens of the United States only. He could, however, have won the prestigious Kate Greenaway Medal (see Appendix B for more details).

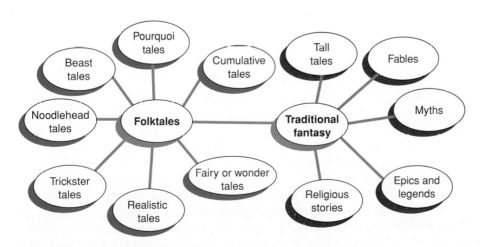

FIGURE 5–1 A web of traditional fantasy.

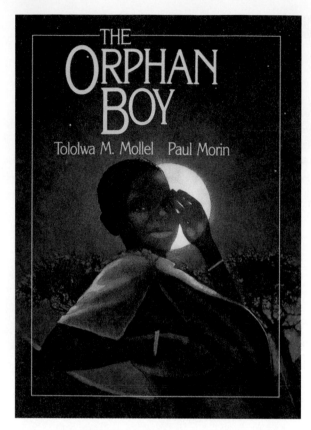

Cover from **The Orphan Boy**, by Tolowa M. Mollel, illustrated by Paul Morin. Cover illustration copyright © 1990 by Paul Morin. Reprinted by permission of Clarion Books/Houghton Mifflin Company. All rights reserved.

Folktales

Quite rightly, all traditional stories could be called folktales or stories of the people. In fact, Bosma (1992) uses folktales as the umbrella term under which all traditional fantasy falls. For classroom purposes, and because we simply like this organizational framework, we use this heading to encompass the most common kinds of folktales, including cumulative tales, pourquoi tales, beast tales, noodlehead tales, trickster tales, realistic tales, and, of course, the fairy or wonder tales.

Cumulative Tales

These stories are "added upon" as the telling unfolds. Typically, the story is told up to a certain point, then begun again from near the beginning. Probably the best-known example is "The House That Jack Built." It begins:

This is the house that Jack built.
This is the malt that lay in the house that Jack built.
This is the rat that ate the malt that lay in the house that Jack built.
This is the cat that ate the rat that ate the malt that lay in the house that Jack built.

With each new addition, the teller starts again, each time adding a new wrinkle to the story, expanding the chain of events or the list of participants.

Another common example of this form is "I Know an Old Lady Who Swallowed a Fly." We remember this simple folk poem like this—sing along if you like:

I know an old lady who swallowed a fly. I don't know why she swallowed a fly. Perhaps she'll die.

I know an old lady who swallowed a spider that wiggled and tickled and jiggled inside her. She swallowed the spider to catch the fly. I don't know why she swallowed a fly. Perhaps she'll die.

Simms Taback won the Caldecott Honor for his rendition of this lively story which he titled **There Was an Old Lady Who Swallowed a Fly.** Bold illustrations using mixed media are enhanced by the use of die-cut holes in the old lady's stomach showing each animal she consumes. Inserted throughout the book are an abundance of visual jokes that will beg revisiting this book long after the story is memorized.

Across cultures, there are some very interesting cumulative tales. Take, for example, Katya Arnold's Russian version of "The Mitten" she entitled **Knock, Knock, Teremok.** Of African origin are two wonderful examples in this same classification. **Bringing the Rain to Kapiti Plain: A Nandi Tale,** written by Verna Aardema and illustrated by Beatrice Vidal, is a classic in most elementary schools, appearing in both paperback and big book versions. Yet another cumulative tale is embedded in the collection by the same author in her book **Misoso: Once Upon a Time Tales from Africa,** now also available in paperback. "Goso the Teacher" is a Swahili narrative poem that rings with rhythm and rhyme and will delight children of all ages. (Included in the collection are numerous other tales and fables from across the African continent.)

Our friend Bill Martin, Jr. (personal communications) has been telling the story of "The Old Woman and Her Pig" for decades. This story is cumulative but also takes the form of what Martin refers to as an "interlocking" tale. It is a text structure well worth mentioning because it occurs often; once children have grasped the concept, it will help them read with far greater fluency because it adds to the predictability of what they are reading. As Martin describes it, an interlocking text is one where the sentences do not simply repeat or add on; they actually interlock one to another. Here is how it works:

> An old woman found a sixpence, so she went to town and bought a pig. On her way home, she came to a stile and she said, "Pig, pig, jump over the stile or I shall not get home tonight."
> But the pig said, "No, I will not jump over the stile."
> So the old woman walked along and walked along until she came to a dog. She said, "Dog, dog, nip pig. Pig will not jump over the stile and I shall not get home tonight."
> But Dog said, "No, I will not nip pig."
> So the old woman walked along and walked along until she came to stick. She said, "Stick, stick, beat Dog. Dog will not nip pig, pig will not jump over the stile, and I shall not get home tonight."
> But the stick said, "No, I will not beat Dog."

Notice how each piece interlocks with the next, creating a chain of events that link together. Two notable examples of the retelling of this tale are Eric A. Kimmel's version illustrated by Giora Carmi and Rosanne Litzinger's version, both titled *The Old Woman and Her Pig.*

Pourquoi Tales

Pourquoi means "why" in French. These charming folktales generally answer questions or give explanations for the way things are, particularly in nature. Probably the most notable example of a book in this classification is the Caldecott Medal winner for 1976, retold by Verna Aardema and illustrated by Leo and Diane Dillon, titled *Why Mosquitoes Buzz in People's Ears.* These tales are often linked with a subcategory known as "creation" tales, or stories telling how the world was created and came to be as it is known today. Examples of "creation" tales are found in Eric Meddern's *The Fire Children: A West African Creation Tale,* illustrated by Frané Lessac, and in Margaret Mayo's *When the World Was Young: Creation and Pourquoi Tales,* illustrated by Louise Brierley.

Other tales that can be designated and are deserving note in the pourquoi category are *Why the Sky Is Far Away,* by Mary-Joan Gerson, *How the Ostrich Got Its Long Neck,* by Verna Aardema, and *Why the Sea Is Salt,* by Vivian French. All of these stories provide the reader with explanations as to how these natural phenomena came to be.

Beast Tales

Beast tales, simply stated, are stories with animals as the principal players. The animals typically represent humans and are therefore anthropomorphized. Typical to this category are stories such as "The Three Little Pigs," "The Three Billy Goats Gruff," and "The Bremen Town Musicians."

A set of books to note from this classification that are perfect for comparison are the variations on the story of the mouse parents who want to find the perfect mate for their daughter. After a long search where they interview the sun, the clouds, the wind, and the wall, they discover that the perfect mate is the common field mouse who is right in their own backyard. Ed Young's *Mouse Match,* which is a uniquely designed book using an accordion, paper-folded format, is illustrated in collage. The form, which is reminiscent of his *Seven Blind Mice,* is a beautiful edition that has the entire text written in Chinese on the reverse side of the illustration. Eric A. Kimmel's *The Greatest of All* is the Japanese version of the same story that finds a father mouse scouring the countryside for a suitable husband for his mouse daughter who he considers to be the "greatest of all." There are two versions of this tale set in modern times, which draw directly from the traditional roots of the story and make wonderful comparisons to the Young and Kimmel editions: Joy Cowley's *The Mouse Bride* and Joel Cook's *The Rat's Daughter* set the story in contemporary times but remain true to the original.

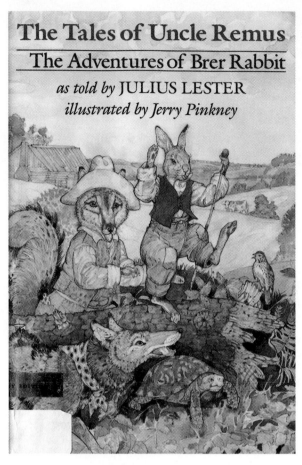

Cover by Julius Lester, illustrated by Jerry Pinkney, from ***The Tales of Uncle Remus*** by Julius Lester, illustrated by Jerry Pinkney, copyright © 1987 by Jerry Pinkney, illustrations. Used by permission of Dial Books for Young Readers, a division of Penguin Putnam, Inc.

From ***The Last Tales of Uncle Remus*** by Julius Lester, illustrated by Jerry Pinkney, copyright © 1994 by Jerry Pinkney, illustrations. Used by permission of Dial Books for Young Readers, a division of Penguin Putnam, Inc.

Trickster Tales

Often listed as a subcategory of the beast tale, the trickster tale features a wily character who outsmarts everyone else in the story. Sometimes the trickster is sly and mischievous like Brer Rabbit from the Uncle Remus stories. In other stories, the trickster is wise and helpful, as in some of the Anansi the Spider Man folktales from Africa. For example, in Gail Haley's Caldecott Medal–winning book *A Story, a Story,* we find Anansi the Spider Man outwitting three formidable opponents as payment for the purchase of the Sky God's stories for his people.

Children will enjoy reading the many variants of Anansi and comparing and contrasting them. Among the most notable stories considering the pesky side of this trickster spider is the series written by Eric A. Kimmel and illustrated by Janet Stevens: *Anansi and the Moss-Covered Rock, Anansi Goes Fishing,* and *Anansi and the Talking Melon. Ananse's Feast* by Tololwa M. Mollel portrays yet another tale about this trickster but in this book, Akye the Turtle deals back a trick or two himself from the Ashanti tradition.

The better side of Anansi can be seen in Verna Aardema's *Anansi Does the Impossible,* which is a variation of *A Story, a Story.* The major difference between the two is that in Aardema's text, Anansi enlists the aid of his wife to obtain the stories from the Sky God. You will also want to read "Anansi and the Phantom Food," another of Aardema's stories from a collection previously mentioned, *Misoso: Once Upon a Time Tales from Africa.*

ALTERNATE TEXT SET

Tricksters in Many Cultures

Read Aloud

Brother Rabbit, by Minfong Ho & Sapahan Ros (Cambodia)

Text Set

Sungura and Leopard, by Barbara Knutson (African Swahili)

Papagayo, by Gerald McDermott (Amazon Rain Forest)

Raven, by Gerald McDermott (Pacific Northwest)

Zomo the Rabbit, by Gerald McDermott (West Africa)

Jackal's Flying Lesson, by Verna Aardema (Khoikhoi—Southern Africa)

Ma'ii and Cousin Horned Toad, by Shonto Begay (Navajo)

Doctor Bird, by Gerald Hausman (Jamaica)

The Tale of Rabbit and Coyote, by Tony Johnston (Mexico)

Coyote, by Gerald McDermott (American Southwest)

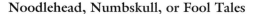

You can create a graphic organizer with your class comparing the two "personalities" of Anansi.

Noodlehead, Numbskull, or Fool Tales

These humorous stories center on the escapades of characters who are . . . well, not too bright. Many of our students are shocked at this entire story type. But consider that we all have had times in our lives when we felt pretty stupid. Haven't you done some things you'd just as soon forget about that were done out of total ignorance? All these stories do is to chuckle goodheartedly at some of the numbskull things we humans do.

Sometimes the characters really make a mess of things with their incredibly stupid mistakes; other times, circumstances seem to get beyond their control and providence rewards them. A significant set of stories from the Jewish tradition deals with the foolish people who live in the Polish town of Chelm. Nobel Prize winner Isaac Bashevis Singer has a wonderful collection of these tales in his *Stories for Children* in which "The Fools of Chelm and the Stupid Carp" appears. David Adler and Eric A. Kimmel deal with Chanukuh and the fools of Chelm in their books *Chanukah in Chelm* and *The Chanukkah Tree* respectively. Steve Sandfield pokes further fun at the residents of Chelm in his book *Strudel, Strudel, Strudel,* which explains why teachers there cannot live on top of a hill, own a trunk with wheels, or eat apple strudel.

Another set of books that deals with noodleheads is the versions of the "The Fool and His Flying Ship," most notably represented by the Caldecott-winning book *The Fool of the World and the Flying Ship,* written by Arthur Ransome and illustrated by Uri Shulevitz. Other distinguished versions of this book include the Christopher Denise variation of the same title and Dennis McDermott's beautifully illustrated version of the Andrew Lang retelling of *The Flying Ship.*

A last set of books is yet another twist on the fool story. Wanda Gág wrote a book that-our-editor-doesn't-want-us-to-mention-because-it-is-out-of-print-but-we-love-it-so-so-much-we-can't-NOT-include-it. Go to your library and borrow this one! ***Gone is Gone*** is the story of a peasant who thinks his wife does very little at home all day while he slaves away in the fields. Therefore, he switches roles and, man, does he get his comeuppance! Everything goes wrong, and when his wife returns at the end of the day (and, for her part, survives it quite admirably), she consoles him that he will do better the next. "Nay, nay!" cried Fritzl. "What's gone is gone, and so is my housework from this day on . . . let me go back to my work in the fields, and never more will I say that my work is harder than yours." Two new editions of this story that *are* still in print are ***Easy Work! An Old Tale,*** retold by Eric A. Kimmel, and ***The Day Hans Got His Way,*** by David Lewis Atwell.

Realistic Tales

Realistic tales often are rooted in an actual historical event and can feature a real figure from history, or they may simply be based on something that could have happened. They are included here because of their oral origins but, in any case, these folktales have few, if any, elements of fantasy. "Dick Whittington and His Cat," a story with a main character who is supposed to have later become the mayor of London, is one example. From the colonial American tradition comes the story of "Johnny Appleseed" based on the real character of John Chapman, who cleared land throughout the untamed "West" and planted apple seeds in Pennsylvania, Ohio, and northern Indiana.

Yet another example of a realistic tale is the engaging story of "Stone Soup," in which an unfriendly town refuses to feed incoming soldiers. In a classic example of this story by Marcia Baum, one particularly clever soldier uses a "magic stone" to dupe a reluctant old woman into feeding him what he calls stone soup. Dianne Snyder's 1988 book ***The Boy of the Three-Year Nap,*** illustrated by Allen Say (who won the Caldecott

ALTERNATE TEXT SET

Johnny Appleseed

The True Tale of Johnny Appleseed by Margaret Hodges, illustrated by Kimberly Bulcken Root

Johnny Appleseed by Reeve Lindbergh, illustrated by Kathy Jakobsen

Johnny Appleseed by Steven Kellogg

BOOKMARK

To find out more about Tales of Wonder and other sources of traditional fantasy on the Internet, visit Chapter 5 on the companion website at **www.prenhall.com/darigan**

INTEGRATING TECHNOLOGY: FOLKLORE ON THE WORLD WIDE WEB

For much of the history of the world, oral literature has been the most widely used form of literature, and in some cultures it still is. Many stories and folktales from around the world have been made into picture books and collections for children. Versions of these tales are copyrighted by the author retelling them but the tales themselves belong to the public domain. Many of these stories are collected on the World Wide Web. *Tales of Wonder: Folk and Fairy Tales from Around the World* has an extensive collection of folktales organized by country or region of origin. Tales of Wonder is a site specifically designed with child readers in mind, so the versions of folktales are appropriate for students in elementary school and up.

Honor that year), is a wonderful example of the realistic tale where a mother's wit, and not the use of magic, forces a lazy boy into action.

A final favorite where just a smidgen of magic helps move the story forward is Aaron Shepard's ***The Gifts of Wali Dad: A Tale of India and Pakistan.*** Wali Dad is a simple grass cutter. Having few needs, he finds he has saved a sizable amount of money with which he purchases a golden bracelet. He gives it to the noblest lady in all the world, the young queen of Khaistan. This starts a hilarious chain of events based on too much good luck and unrelenting giving. Extravagance and exaggeration pile one on top of the other until eventually his problem is solved. Wali Dad is able to return to his simple life and is never bothered with too much good fortune again.

Fairy or Wonder Tales

Of all the folktales, the fairy tale, more appropriately known as the wonder tale, is the most magical. In these we see enchantments that go beyond talking animals to fairy godmothers, wicked witches, giants, and ogres. Magical objects such as mirrors, cloaks, swords, cauldrons, and rings are scattered through these tales, providing us, as readers, with mystic fascination. In reality, there are relatively few of these tales that actually contain fairies, yet the term endures.

Fairy tales are extremely popular with young listeners and readers. "Snow White," "Cinderella," "Sleeping Beauty," "Beauty and the Beast," and "Aladdin and His Wonderful Lamp" are but a few well-known examples of fairy tales. As children grow older, they are fascinated by the different versions and variants of these oft-told tales. Consider the text set of Cinderella stories that opens the chapter. The wide range of variation in story, character, and setting makes these kinds of tales perfect for the middle grade reader to enjoy and study.

Read A Conversation with Paul O. Zelinsky on p. 168 and visit Chapter 5 on our text's companion website at **www.prenhall.com/darigan**

ALTERNATE TEXT SET

Fairy Tales by Paul O. Zelinsky

Rumpelstiltskin   *Swamp Angel*

Hansel and Gretel   *Rapunzel*

Introducing:

Using versions and variants of different folk and fairy tales, you can have your class create comparison charts.

Tall Tales

Exaggeration is the major stylistic element in tall tales. Many of the tall tales from the United States grew out of the push to open the North American continent to settlement. Tall-tale characters, such as Paul Bunyan, Pecos Bill, Johnny Appleseed, John Henry, and Old Stormalong, were based either on actual people or on a composite of rough-and-tumble lumberjacks, sailors, or cowboys.

More recent additions to this genre include titles portraying women as the major protagonist. ***Cut From the Same Cloth: American Women of Myth, Legend and Tall Tale,*** by Robert D. San Souci, offers a wonderful collection of these stories. *Sally*

You can search the CD-ROM accompanying this book for "Snow White," "Beauty and the Beast," "Sleeping Beauty," or "Cinderella."

A CONVERSATION WITH . . .

Paul O. Zelinsky

I was born and raised in suburban Chicago and never consciously thought about becoming an illustrator and author of children's books until my years at Yale University. Under the influence of Maurice Sendak, I became convinced that turning my art major into a career of making picture books would be something I could really accomplish. Now, years later, I work in my own studio, which is halfway between our house and the school in which my wife teaches and my youngest daughter, Rachel, attends.

The process I go through in making a picture book begins with a lot of research, after which I make a very rough layout. In the case of *Rapunzel*, the early stage was writing the text. Research for the illustrations was next, which was followed by making up a very rough dummy; I needed to figure out how to fit the story into 40 pages, and it helped to determine what fell where to make the story move well.

I used models for this project, so I made rough sketches of what I wanted first, set the models in those positions, and photographed them. In general, I find that I need to have a real person in front of me because, sometimes, I realize that my initial sketches are anatomically impossible. For example, the shape of the way an arm goes into the body or the way the outline looks may not work, so I am able to easily make adjustments before I get started. Next, I make more refined sketches to determine how the colors will go and then, and only then, do I start the actual paintings.

Now that my daughters, Anna and Rachel, are getting older I have been able to use them in various ways in my books. Rather than going back and getting a model to pose again because I see that I have an arm wrong, I'll just ask Anna to come over and sit with her arm just so. I have put the girls in my books, as well. For instance, in my book *The Wheels on the Bus* they are represented in a more impressionistic way: The little girl with a ponytail carrying a notebook looks to me like Anna, and the little blond baby with a straight line for a mouth really does look like Rachel did at that age.

I have illustrated a number of retellings of the classic fairy tales: *Rumpelstiltskin, Hansel and Gretel,* and most recently *Rapunzel.* But it was with *Rapunzel* that I really came up against the limitations of my knowledge and technique. As an interloper in the august tradition of Italian Renaissance painting, I have been humbled by my own attempts to achieve effects that any Renaissance painter's apprentice could have tossed off as though it were nothing: billowing drapery or the glint from a finger-nail or light falling on tree leaves.

By the way, the tower in my version is not a place where Rapunzel was brutally tortured. I wasn't looking at the sorceress as a personification of evil at all. In the French retelling of this fairy tale, from which my version is heavily influenced, the setting is a silver tower in the middle of the forest with only one window but many, many extremely elegant and luxurious rooms. The girl, Rapunzel, who is actually named after parsley, has every new fashion that comes around, and though she is isolated, she is very well off.

To get a better idea of it, I also grew the real plant "rapunzel." I managed to get the seeds through a catalog in England and grew them in pots on my roof. We ate it in salads and it was really quite good— a little biting but remarkably like watercress. There is supposed to be a crunchy, edible root as well, though when we pulled ours up, the root had not really thickened. Rapunzel actually comes from the bellflower family, genus *campanula,* which is another reason I chose to use the more elegant belltower, or *campanile.* I liked the distinct similarity between the two words and it made me believe I was on the right track.

As a side note, Steve Johnson, who won the Caldecott Honor for his book *Alphabet City,* is my neighbor. We know each other well, and when he was illustrating the cover of Donna Jo Napoli's novelized retelling of the Rapunzel story *Zel,* he borrowed my pictures of the rapunzel plant when he was painting. You can see what it looks like right on the cover. I also offered him the phone number of my model for the prince, which would have been the funniest thing if he had used him. As it turned out he didn't, *but* the Rapunzel on that same cover is an old friend of my daughter Anna.

As a last point of interest, I placed our cat in the book. I'm not sure what my motivation really was in doing so except that it thrilled the heck out of my daughters. We got this cat about one and one-half years ago, and there he is up in the tower with Rapunzel. If you look closely, you get a real sense of the passage of time as you read the book; he gets larger and fills out as the book progresses. In the end, the cat follows the reunited couple out of the wilderness and back to the prince's kingdom—where he, too, lives a long life, happy and contented.

From ***Rapunzel,*** by Paul O. Zelinsky, copyright © 1997 by Paul O. Zelinsky. Used by permission of Dutton Children's Books, a division of Penguin Putnam, Inc.

Ann Thunder Ann Whirlwind Crockett, by Steven Kellogg, and ***Swamp Angel,*** by Anne Isaacs, are two other notable picture book examples, the latter winning the Caldecott Honor with illustrations by Paul O. Zelinsky.

Tall tales, of course, exist beyond the American culture. For instance, Margaret Mahy retold an old Chinese tale in her ***The Seven Chinese Brothers,*** which is beautifully illustrated by the husband-and-wife team of Jean and Mou-sien Tseng and tells of seven brothers who use their amazing talents, such as the ability to swallow an entire sea, to ward off the conquests of the evil emperor. An African variant of this tale can be found in Gerald McDermott's ***Anansi the Spider: A Tale from the Ashanti,*** which tells of the time that Anansi fell into trouble. His amazing six sons, who all had special powers like the Chinese Brothers, locate and save him. The tale ends with a pourquoi flare, telling how the moon came to be in the sky as a bonus to this delightful tale. Further, the Brothers Grimm recorded their own variant that can be found with extremely dark and foreboding illustrations by Sergei Goloshapov in ***The Six Servants.***

Cover from ***Anansi the Spider: A Tale from the Ashanti,*** adapted and illustrated by Gerald McDermott. Copyright © 1972 by Gerald McDermott. Published by Henry Holt and Company, Inc. Reprinted by permission of the publisher.

Fables

Fables are generally extremely brief stories expressly meant to teach a lesson, and they usually conclude with a moral. Many time-honored morals are part of our everyday speech; old adages such as "Time solves many problems," "Necessity is the mother of invention," "A bird in the hand is worth two in the bush," and "Haste makes waste" are but a few examples.

A CONVERSATION WITH . . .

Steven Kellogg

I initially came into contact with American tall tales during a unit on mythology and folklore when I was in the fourth grade. I was immediately fascinated with the cast of characters that ran the gamut from the oversized, but benign, Paul Bunyan to the scrappy and boisterous riverman, Mike Fink. As a class, we traced the roots of each of these larger-than-life characters through their various geographic regions and occupations. I was intrigued by the outrageous exaggeration and preposterous humor that characterized the recountings of the adventures of these heroes as they surmounted the formidable challenges that confronted them.

   Though the visual accompaniment that I had imagined for these stories was vibrant, colorful, and exuberant, when I went to the library to find books that echoed the imagery that I was spinning in my head, I found the fare to be disappointingly Spartan. I was delighted, some 30 years later, when David Reuther, then editor-in-chief at Morrow Junior Books, expressed an interest in having me retell and illustrate a new version of my favorite tall tale character, **Paul Bunyan.** I decided to place a strong emphasis on Bunyan's American-ness and have his story unfold on a journey across the country ending in the vast, primeval wilderness of Alaska, emphasizing this extraordinary hero's timeless quality and the fact that he is being reborn for every person who experiences his legend.

   For my next project in the series, I turned to the world's greatest cowboy, **Pecos Bill,** who is to cattle ranching what Paul Bunyan is to logging. His legend sprang from the plains and canyons of the Southwest. As part of my research, I visited the region and experienced its wonderful landscape and its astonishing light, which I tried to capture in the illustrations. This tale naturally led to the retelling of **Mike Fink,** the tale of a Keelboatman, a daring and rugged breed of navigator who carried cargo thousands of

miles from remote wilderness outposts to the port of New Orleans. In my version, Mike overcomes early defeats by wrestling grizzlies in order to successfully challenge the reigning King of the Keelboatmen. Only after years of triumph does Mike meet his match, which coincides with the arrival of the mighty Mississippi steamboat that takes over the river trade.

   My next foray into the genre came in a character with whom I had always been intrigued. **Sally Ann Thunder Ann Whirlwind Crockett** played a prominent role in the Davy Crockett almanacs, and my research led me to fashion a book about this resourceful and spunky wife of the greatest woodsman in America. She proved to be just as capable in dealing with hardships and dangers of frontier life as the menfolk. In the end, she gets the upper hand on Mike Fink himself, flattening and flinging him five miles upriver.

   I Was Born About 10,000 Years Ago was inspired by the 19th-century song of the same title, which had been sung around campfires for decades and popularized by performers such as Pete Seeger, Odetta, and Elvis Presley. It continues in the tall tale tradition by spinning a good-natured yarn where the narrator boldly injects himself into various biblical and historical settings with improbable and humorous results.

   I love all of these tall tale characters for the boundless energy that was necessary for them to meet the challenges of frontier life, and, despite the hostility of their environment, all flourished as rugged individuals. This tall tale mythology is part of our national heritage and encourages us in our struggles toward self-actualization while generously enriching our lives.

To read more of this Conversation with Steven Kellogg, please visit Chapter 5 on our text's companion website at **www.prenhall. com/darigan**

ALTERNATE TEXT SET

Tall Tales by Steven Kellogg

Johnny Appleseed

Sally Ann Thunder Ann Whirlwind Crockett

Paul Bunyan

Mike Fink

Pecos Bill

I Was Born About 10,000 Years Ago

Besides the well-known collection of Aesop's fables from Greece, there are the Bidpai fables of East India collected in the *Panchatantra*. Further, there are the Jataka stories, also from India, that are about Gautama Buddha and tell of his progressive reincarnations as animals and are good talking beast tales (Arbuthnot, 1961, p. 231). Finally, a collection of fables by the Frenchman Jean de La Fontaine must be noted. Drawing from both Aesop and Bidpai, Jean de La Fontaine, a contemporary of Charles Perrault, placed many of his fables in verse in his *One Hundred Fables.*

More recently, many of these fables have been retold in an expanded form with a far more detailed plot line and more full-color illustrations as picture books. For example, no fewer than three illustrators have expanded the few original paragraphs of Aesop's fable "Town Mouse, Country Mouse," and Jan Brett, Helen Craig, and Carol Jones have all made it into a full-fledged picture book. Jones has also authored and illustrated two other fables, **The Lion and the Mouse** and **The Hare and the Tortoise.** Using die-cut "peepholes," she provides the reader with a snippet of the next page and encourages the reader to predict what will happen next.

Caldecott Medal winner Ed Young retold and illustrated the traditional fable entitled **Donkey Trouble.** A poor but simple man and his equally simple grandson are on their way to the market to sell their last possession, a donkey. At seemingly every hill in the desert, they are given unsolicited advice on how to proceed and they dutifully follow each suggestion. In the end, they lose their donkey but learn that "to prosper, they must follow their own hearts."

Two other fables come from less common cultural sources. **The Cat and the Cook and Other Fables of Krylov**, retold by Ethel Heins and illustrated by Anita Lobel, contains wise and witty Russian fables that have no written moral at the end. Gisela Dürr has rewritten and illustrated in beautiful pencil renderings **Aesop's Fables,** also without the moral. The absence of moral in these stories makes it incumbent on the reader to fill in that part and would make a very nice assignment for the child who has had ample experience with fables.

From Mexico comes Shirley Climo's retelling of **The Little Red Ant and the Great Big Crumb,** where a small ant in the colony discovers a crumb of cake but feels herself too weak to carry it back to the anthill. She searches for someone to help her and finds that one person seems to always be stronger than the next. Lizard (*el lagarto*) wasn't as strong as the sun (*el sol*) who wasn't as strong as spider (*la araña*) and so on. In the end she discovers that *she* was strong enough all the while, whereupon she carries the tasty morsel back and feasts on it all winter. Though this is a fable, it is a very nice companion to some books we noted earlier in the chapter.

Myths

Myths grew out of early people's need to understand and explain the world around them and their own existence, and therefore they recount the creation and tell of the gods and goddesses who control the fate of humans. Many myths are creation tales or similar to pourquoi folktales because they attempt to explain nature. For example, the Greek myth of Apollo explains how and why the sun travels across the sky each day. Jane Yolen's retelling of **Sky Dogs** explains how horses came to one tribe of Native Americans, and George Crespo's retelling of **How the Sea Began** clarifies how the oceans came to be.

Every culture has its myths, although the Greek myths are perhaps the best known in the Western world. Numerous collections noting myths around the world are readily available and are a welcome addition to any classroom or school library. The international flavor of mythology is evident in Virginia Hamilton's collection of creation myths, **In the Beginning: Creation Stories from Around the World,** and Geraldine McCaughrean's volumes **The Golden Hoard** and **The Bronze Cauldron.** To better understand these stories, a handy companion is Neil Philip's **The Illustrated Book of Myths,** which not only presents retellings of many favorite myths but also includes sidebar information and photographs that further explain settings and artifacts.

Other collections focus on the myths of a particular culture. For instance, Lulu Delacre's ***Golden Tales: Myths, Legends and Folktales from Latin America*** is a breathtaking volume of stories from the early Americas. ***The Random House Book of Greek Myths,*** by Joan D. Vinge, contains many of the familiar tales from that tradition, and Mary Pope Osborne's ***Favorite Norse Myths*** refers to stories with Viking influence.

Numerous picture books are available that describe the rich mythology of humankind and make these stories particularly enjoyable for children. Recalling the first time we read, for example, ***D'Aulaires' Book of Greek Myths*** to our own children, it became quite clear how much background knowledge was necessary before the "enjoyment" part kicked in. Just following the huge number of characters with strange names appeared at the outset to be such a daunting task for such young minds. For instance, here is a short paragraph, which is less dense than text from ***D'Aulaires,*** from ***The Random House Book of Greek Myths*** dealing with Hermes: "Hermes' mother was Maia, a Titan's daughter. She lived in a cave hidden so deep inside Mother Earth that Hera never knew Maia had married Zeus. As a result Maia was able to give birth to Hermes without any trouble from Hera." Certainly a 9- or 10-year-old would need quite a bit of background to absorb this. Our own children all grew up loving the classic myths, but much of that was buffered and supported by good picture books we read to them that told the basic stories but also provided the necessary context for their understanding.

Three such stories describe the character Atalanta, a Greek princess, who refuses to marry any man unless he can beat her in a footrace. Shirley Climo's ***Atalanta's Race: A Greek Myth,*** illustrated by Alexander Koshkin, is a wonderful companion to Claire Martin's version, ***The Race of the Golden Apples,*** illustrated by Leo and Diane Dillon. Jane Yolen includes her own version, "Atalanta the Huntress," in her short story collection ***Not One Damsel in Distress: World Folktales for Strong Girls,*** illustrated by Susan Guevara.

The Greek superhero Hercules is well portrayed in Kathryn Lasky's ***Hercules: The Man, the Myth, the Hero;*** the story is written in the first person, adding a very personal view to his exciting life. In Robert Burleigh's version, ***Hercules,*** illustrated by Raul Colón, provides a simpler selection concentrating on the final and most difficult of Hercules's 12 labors: He must travel to the Underworld and bring back Cerberus, the three-headed dog.

Another pair of books that work together well are those concerning the winged horse, Pegasus. In Jane Yolen's adaptation, ***Pegasus, the Flying Horse,*** accompanied by Li Ming's spacious paintings, and Marianna Mayer's ***Pegasus,*** illustrated by K. Y. Craft's detailed oil over watercolor renderings, we are introduced to Bellerophon, who obtains the help of the winged equine in order to battle the monstrous Chimaera.

Another wonderful effort by K. Y. Craft comes with her paintings in ***Cupid and Psyche,*** authored by Marie Charlotte Craft. This book beautifully details one of the greatest love stories of all time between Psyche, the most beautiful woman in the world, and the Greek god Cupid.

Noting myths that cross cultures, we must include Gerald McDermott's ***Musicians of the Sun.*** In this retelling of an Aztec tale, the Lord of the Night sees that the

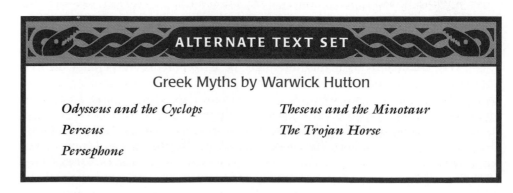

ALTERNATE TEXT SET

Greek Myths by Warwick Hutton

Odysseus and the Cyclops   *Theseus and the Minotaur*

Perseus   *The Trojan Horse*

Persephone

Earth is a sad place, and so he sends the Wind to release the four musicians that the Sun is holding prisoner. With the aid of Turtle Woman, Fish Woman, and Alligator Woman, the Wind is able to cross the sea, where he confronts and defeats the Sun. Returning the musicians, the Earth becomes a happier and more joyful place, where even the Sun blesses them with his light.

From the ancient Egyptian culture comes Leonard Everett Fisher's ***The Gods and Goddesses of Ancient Egypt.*** Fisher gives thumbnail biographies of each of the major gods and goddesses and uses a flat illustration style that compliments the period.

One variety of myth focuses on the heroic quest rather than on the mysteries of planet Earth. The hero myth, such as the story "Jason and the Argonauts," is a grand adventure that usually involves the intervention of heavenly beings. A picture book version of this story can be found in Leonard Everett Fisher's ***Jason and the Golden Fleece,*** and the classic novel on the quest is found in ***The Golden Fleece and the Heroes that Lived Before Achilles,*** by Padraic Colum. This hero myth is related to the epic, which we discuss in the next section.

Epics and Legends

The line separating epics and legends tends to blur. The unifying feature is the hero tale, which includes the hero myth, but epics and legends also have their own distinguishing qualities.

Epics, or hero tales, tend to be lengthy stories or even a series of tales that focus on a particular hero. Examples are the tales of the Trojan War included in *The Iliad,* and the return of Odysseus (Ulysses) from Troy to his home in Ithaca in *The Odyssey.* Both of these epics are also steeped in the mythology of ancient Greece. *Beowulf,* the most famous piece of Old English literature, is another well-known epic. Retellings of these classics that are accessible to young children and can be found in the simplified comic-book style version of Marcia Williams's ***The Iliad and the Odyssey.*** For the older, middle-grade reader, Rosemary Sutcliff's ***Black Ships Before Troy: The Story of* The Iliad** and ***The Wanderings of Odysseus: The Story of* The Odyssey** are well written and are graced with the beautiful illustrations of Alan Lee.

For the older reader, we suggest Paul Fleischman's very creative book ***Dateline: Troy*** as a timely companion to the Sutcliff volumes. Providing a succinct retelling of the Trojan War, Fleischman places on the opposing page cogent news clippings of a similar or related event in recent history. For example, when Agamemnon is attempting to set sail for Troy, his fleet is buffeted by turbulent seas, causing him to sail south of his destination. Finding out that he has upset the goddess Artemis with his willful boasting and that she is the cause of these wild seas, his only solution is to humble himself to her. Tragically, this means he must sacrifice his cherished daughter, Iphigenia, who gladly allows the priest to sever her head with his heavy knife. On the opposite page of this brief part of the tale is a news clipping dated October, 1967, reading: "War Protester Burns Herself to Death Here: Immolation of Viet Peace Advocate Takes Place in Front of Federal Building."

The heroes in legends are rooted a bit more firmly in history than they are in the epic. This means that *The Iliad could* be considered an epic or a legend. But because of its historical content, King Arthur might be more appropriately placed on the legend side of this duality. There are certainly many mythic stories of Arthur, but those are balanced by historical accounts that would indicate he indeed existed and that he unified the British tribes around 500 A.D. There are quite a few wonderful books describing Arthur and his Round Table. Longer works with detailed story lines for the older reader include Michael Morpurgo's ***Arthur: High King of Britain,*** illustrated by Michael Foreman, Robin Lister's ***The Legend of King Arthur,*** illustrated by Alan Baker, and Molly Perham's ***King Arthur and the Legends of Camelot,*** illustrated by Julek Heller. Shorter picture books on the subject are represented by Hudson Talbott's ***Excalibur*** and ***King Arthur: The Sword in the Stone.***

Using the database on the CD included with this textbook, you can search across 11 fields, including grade level, topic, and description.

Robin Hood, probably more thief than hero, is a character from ballad and legend, and is well represented in the short novel ***Robin's Country,*** by Monica Furlong. Also, in one of the companion texts to Michael Morpurgo's book dealing with King Arthur comes his ***Robin of Sherwood.*** Finally, there is a wonderful picture book to be noted that is written by Barbara Cohen and beautifully illustrated by David Ray, entitled ***Robin Hood and Little John.***

Of course, legendary characters also appear in the tall tales of North America, as we have mentioned; Mike Fink, Davy Crockett, Johnny Appleseed, John Henry, and Casey Jones are at the top of the list of characters whose personas became bigger than life.

Religious Stories

Classifying religious stories as traditional fantasy or as myths may bother many people, but *myth* in this sense can be broadly defined as the quest to discover and share truth concerning the spiritual aspects of existence. Stories derived from the sacred writings of Buddhism, Christianity, Hinduism, Islam, and other religions of the world contribute to this arena of traditional literature.

Books and stories in this category include parables and Old Testament stories. Figuring in this category are any number of legends or apocryphal tales with religious connections, such as Ruth Robbins's ***Baboushka and the Three Kings*** and Tomie dePaola's ***The Legend of Old Befana.*** Both of these books are variants of a Christmas story about an old woman too busy to follow the Three Wise Men.

Another example of a common religious story is based on the event of the great flood that wipes out virtually all of humankind, allowing a fresh beginning. We see this from the Judeo-Christian tradition in two versions of the story of Noah's ark in Ann Jonas's ***Aardvarks, Disembark!*** and Patricia Lee Gauch's ***Noah.*** Emery and Durga Bernhard describe a great flood in their book ***The Tree That Rains,*** taken from the Huichol Indians of Mexico. Finally, the Navajo have a similar myth that is noted in Gerald Hausman's story "The Great Flood," which can be found in ***Coyote Walks on Two Legs: A Book of Navajo Myths and Legends,*** illustrated by Floyd Cooper.

Outside the Christian tradition are other examples that include ***Iblis,*** by Shulamith Levey Oppenheim, which presents an Islamic version of the Old Testament story of Adam and Eve and the fall from Paradise. In addition, we have ***Buddha Stories,*** also known as the Jataka tales, retold by Demi, and the novel ***Rama: A Legend,*** by Jamake Highwater, both based on a Hindu epic.

▼▼▼▼▼▼▼

The Universal Nature of Traditional Fantasy

Although tales certainly vary from culture to culture, it is amazing how alike in form they are, and how the basic sorts of literary elements are similar in Chinese stories, in stories from the Native-American tribes, and in stories from Europe (Frye, 1964). Because traditional tales deal with such basic human experiences, stories like "Cinderella" surface in nearly every part of the world. We opened this chapter by listing a basic collection of "Cinderella" variants. Though certainly different in setting and detail, there is a fascinating similarity among all of them. Listed in the text set that follows are other Cinderella-like stories to show you the ranges of their origins.

For a listing of more than two dozen variants of Cinderella, consult the CD-ROM that accompanies this text.

Another example of the pervasiveness of traditional stories appears in modern literature as well as in our day-to-day conversations: It is not uncommon to see the allusions to traditional literature used in both. Often we speak and write using a sort of old-tale shorthand; in fact, it is a part of the cultural cement that binds us together. We nod knowingly when someone says or writes "Misery loves company," "One good turn deserves another," "Don't count your chickens before they're hatched," or "You're judged by the company you keep." These maxims come from Aesop, who some scholars think collected most of his fables from more ancient oral sources.

ALTERNATE TEXT SET

"Cinderella" Variants From Around the World

Read Aloud

Mufaro's Beautiful Daughters, by John Steptoe (Zimbabwe; African)

Text Set

Fair, Brown & Trembling, by Jude Daly (Ireland)

The Irish Cinderlad, by Shirley Climo (Ireland)

Kongi and Potgi, by Oki S. Han (Korea)

Smoky Mountain Rose, by Alan Schroeder (United States; Appalachian)

Sootface, by Robert D. San Souci (Native American; Ojibwa)

The Turkey Girl, by Penny Pollock (Native American; Zuni)

Further, we have absorbed many words into our language that have direct roots to the ancient myths. For example, the word *volcano* comes from *Vulcan,* the Roman god of fire. We eat *cereal,* a word that is a derived from *Ceres,* goddess of agriculture. We get *furious,* which comes from the *Furies,* three snakes in Greek and Roman myth who punish unavenged crimes. We have the nine Muses from Greek myth, who preside over literature and the arts, to thank for the word *music*—though these days, and from our perspective, what echoes from open car windows and jolts the ground is more akin to "volcano," but perhaps that is only *sour grapes.* But, then again, that's Aesop.

The Greek and Roman myths as well as European fairy tale variants are alluded to continually in novels written by Western authors. Note the distinct part "Little Red Riding Hood" plays in Lois Lowry's Newbery-winning historical novel, ***Number the Stars,*** which takes place during World War II. Anna, the main character, makes her way through the woods with a basket of food containing a hidden packet of chemical designed to disarm the wolf's, or rather the guard dogs', ability to smell the Danish escapees. She suddenly feels as if she's walked this way before.

> The handle of the straw basket scratched her arm through her sweater. She shifted it and tried to run.
>
> She thought of a story she had often told to Kirsti as they cuddled in bed at night.
>
> "Once upon a time there was a little girl," she told herself silently, "who had a beautiful red cloak . . ."

Perhaps one of the clearest examples of how an old tale is evident in our everyday lives is this political cartoon shown in Figure 5–2. It was published in *The Chicago Tribune* after a number of day care centers in the Chicago area were charged with child abuse and molestation. Because "Hansel and Gretel" is basic to our literary culture, the cartoon needs no caption.

Finally, certainly one of the most important elements traditional fantasy has to offer children is that it provides a rich sense of culture. Nowhere does the bounty of a people come more alive than in story. Further, we see that this is doubly important for our youngsters because not only are they able to see themselves and their culture in tales but they are afforded the rare opportunity to view endless other cultures as well. In so doing they are discovering both the unique and universal each people has to offer (Darigan, 1996).

A way to examine this notion is to look at a basic motif in all cultures: the creation tale. Even the earliest humans wondered how the world got to be here, how humankind came to be. Four North American Native American versions of creation are Ellen Jackson's ***The Precious Gift: A Navaho Creation Myth,*** Nina Jaffe's ***The Golden Flower: A Taino Myth from Puerto Rico,*** Jaime Olieiero's ***The Day the Sun Was Stolen,*** and John Bierhorst's ***The Woman Who Fell From the Sky: The Iroquois Story of Creation.*** Mary-Joan Gerson offers a Mayan version of the creation story in her ***People of Corn: A Mayan Story.*** One of our favorites is Eric Maddern's ***The Fire Children: A West African Creation Tale,*** where Nyame, the sky god, visits earth and the spirit people Aso Yaa and Kwaku Ananse. The two attempt to hide the children they have created from clay and are in the process of firing them when Nyame arrives; how long the children are in the fire determines what their skin color will be. Through reading excellent books such as the ones mentioned here, children see how each cultural group attempts to define itself and see furthermore the similarities in each.

▼▼▼▼▼▼▼▼

The Value of Fantasy Stories

However simple and straightforward traditional fantasy may seem, it is the mother of all literature. There are literally no character types, basic plots, or themes that have not been explored in the oral tradition. Indeed, noted child psychologist Bruno Bettelheim (1977) believes that no other literature better prepares children to meet the complexities of adult life. As we have already noted, it is the nature of the traditional tale to be spare in characterization and clear and concise in setting, plot, and theme. These well-defined elements provide the child with the necessary guidelines for life that neither preach nor dictate. The reader, alone, is left to decide the good and right way and then apply it to his or her own life experiences.

Benefits to the Child Reader

In the story of "Rapunzel," for example, we see a true balance between good and evil, right and wrong. Rapunzel's birth mother, who is pregnant with her, is lured by her desire for the rampion (another name for the plant rapunzel) that she sees growing in the sorceress's garden next door. Her health begins to deteriorate to the point that when she is at death's door, the husband must climb the forbidden wall to the witch's garden, steal into the enclosure, and pull up a goodly amount of the green, which his wife makes into a salad and eats greedily. Her health returns but, so too, does her desire for more rampion.

Once again the husband goes back to the garden, only to be caught this time. After he explains his dire situation, the sorceress allows him to take all of the vegetable he wants under the condition that she get the child when it is born. She goes on to assure the husband that she will take good care of the girl and keep her away from the harsh ways of the world. With seemingly no other alternative, for his wife needs the rampion to live, he acquiesces.

At this point, our shocked students almost always object—vociferously—to the ruthlessness of the sorceress and the unfairness of the request. But let's consider this: The husband, to save his own life and that of his wife and child, has broken the law by stealing. That is crime number one. He *could* have sacrificed himself, but selfishly, he *gives away* their only child for the greater good of the couple. During the climax of our class discussion, someone always picks up on that detail. Neither the husband nor later the wife seems to be any too concerned about their baby, and they willingly give it up. In the end, it is the metaphorical trade of rampion for rampion (Bettelheim, 1977, p. 17).

Now you, too, may be a bit disgruntled by this turn of events. Admittedly, trading a kid for a bit of antipasto doesn't seem to be fair. But let's look at how this idea effects the child, as reader. Bettelheim (1977) notes that as a result of many rereadings of this tale, one of his 5-year-old patients was *reassured* by this story's message. His grandmother, who took care of him during the day while his single mother worked, had to go to the hospital, which naturally upset his entire existence. He repeatedly asked for this story to be read to him and found *security* at the mention of the substitute mother (his grandmother) who is represented in the story by the sorceress. So what normally could be viewed as a representation of negative, selfish behavior was capable of having a most reassuring meaning under this boy's special circumstances (Bettelheim, 1977, p. 17).

Later in the story, Rapunzel uses her fantastically long hair to allow both the sorceress *and* the prince into her tower. Rapunzel uses her own body, her own resources, to solve her problem; to grow and mature. Bettelheim again discusses how that same 5-year-old boy reacted: "More important, Rapunzel found the means of escaping her predicament in her own body—the tresses on which the prince climbed up to her room in the tower. That one's body can provide a lifeline reassured him that, if necessary, he would similarly find in his own body the source of his security" (p. 17). Finally, at the end of the story when the blinded prince has been wandering through the wilderness in search of his lost Rapunzel, it is her tears that fall into his eyes and clear his sight. Again, she has used her own body to improve her situation.

As a last note to this wonderful tale, we see Rapunzel growing up and coming of age. She moves from the dependence on the sorceress to independence in making her own choices, to eventually marrying the prince and beginning a family of her own.

As we can see, good versus evil, mighty versus meek, and deceitful versus sincere are starkly portrayed in traditional fantasy. Bettelheim admits that the fairy tale simplifies all situations (p. 8), but it is precisely this explicit delineation of polar opposites that contributes to the child's seeing the advantages of moral behavior. Good and evil are equally present in these stories, but it is not that the "bad guy gets it" in the end that teaches right versus wrong. Rather, it is that the child reader identifies with the hero during the struggle, and when victory is won, the child also wins. As adults, we are often brutally aware of how "real life" presents myriad difficult situations and gray areas that tend to make our decisions quite difficult and complex.

This is where the folk and fairy tale is essential in the child's diet of good books: It feeds both the soul and mind, providing an uncluttered, nonpreachy story that defines the consequences of certain behaviors. It affords the child the opportunity to face problems in their most fundamental form. This simplicity of character and story is the key element for which decisions are to be made.

Bettelheim states that "it is important to provide today's modern child with images of heroes who have to go out into the world all by themselves and who, although originally ignorant of the ultimate things, find secure places in the world by following their right way with deep inner confidence" (1977, p. 11). Traditional fantasy, then, is a wonderful metaphor for human existence, and because of its rich imagery and dreamlike quality, it speaks to us deeply.

Rich Language

Beyond the social and emotional advantages of the genre, unless these stories have been "dumbed down" for printing in educational reading materials or oversimplified picture books you find on grocery store racks, traditional tales are a blueprint for rich, masterful language. We mentioned in chapter 2 the difference between the Disney version of *Snow-White and the Seven Dwarfs* and the version that Randall Jarrell translated of the Brothers Grimm. This sophisticated language sings like the melody strings of a sitar, whereas the mundane versions simply drone as a consequence of the resonance of the strings from above. Take, for instance, this excerpt from Sir George Webbe Dasent's translation of **East o' the Sun and West o' the Moon.** After we are introduced to a poor farmer and his pretty children, the story begins. "Well, one day, 'twas on a Thursday evening late and at the fall of the year, the weather was so wild and rough outside that the walls of the cottage shook. It was cruelly dark, and rain fell and wind blew. There they all sat around the fire, busy with this thing and that when, all at once, something gave three taps on the windowpane." Or consider Howard Pyles's turn-of-the-century description in his **King Stork** of the young drummer who has just met the king of all storks and been given a little bone whistle to blow whenever he was in need of help. "The drummer trudged on the way he was going, as merry as a cricket, for it is not everybody who cracks his shins against such luck as he had stumbled over, I can tell you." Note the rich language and conversational tone used in both examples, making them a feast for the ears and begging to be read aloud.

Besides giving us modern readers a common ground for communicating, traditional fantasy—in fact, fantasy literature in general—offers us certain benefits that realistic fiction cannot do with quite the same power. Lloyd Alexander (1968), who had drawn liberally from the well of ancient stories to write his modern high-fantasy books, encapsulates these benefits into four notable points.

> First, on the very surface of it, the sheer delight of "let's pretend" and the eager suspension of disbelief; excitement, wonder, astonishment. There is an exuberance in good fantasy quite unlike the most exalted moments of realistic fiction. Both forms have similar goals; but realism walks where fantasy dances. . . .
>
> [Second, fantasy has the] ability to work on our emotions with the same vividness as a dream. The fantasy adventure seems always on a larger scale, the deeds bolder, the people brighter. Reading a fantasy, we never get disinterested bystanders. To get the most from it, we have to, in the best sense of the phrase, "lose our cool." . . .
>
> Another value of fantasy [is its ability to develop a capacity for belief]. . . . In dealing with delinquency—I do not mean the delinquency that poverty breeds, but the kind of cold-hearted emptiness and apathy of "well-to-do," solid middle-class delinquents—one of the heart-breaking problems is interesting these young people in something. In anything. They value nothing because they have never had the experience of valuing anything. They have developed no *capacity* for believing anything to be really worthwhile.
>
> I emphasize the word *capacity* because, in a sense, the capacity to value, to believe, is separate from the values or beliefs themselves. Our values and beliefs can change. The capacity remains.
>
> Whether the object of value is Santa Claus or Sunday school, the Prophet Elijah or Arthur, the Once and Future King, does not make too much difference. Having once believed wholeheartedly in something, we seldom lose the ability to believe. . . .
>
> Perhaps, finally, the ability to hope is more important than the ability to believe. . . . Hope is one of the most precious human values fantasy can offer us—and

offer us in abundance. Whatever the hardships of the journey, the days of despair, fantasy implicitly promises to lead us through them. Hope is an essential thread in the fabric of all fantasies, an Ariadne's thread to guide us out of the labyrinth, the last treasure in Pandora's box.

Reprinted with permission of Lloyd Alexander from "Wishful Thinking—or Hopeful Dreaming." *The Horn Book 44* (August 1968), 387–390.

▼▼▼▼▼▼▼▼

In Defense of Traditional Fantasy

> About once every hundred years some wiseacre gets up and tries to banish the fairy tale. Perhaps I had better say a few words in its defence, as reading for children. (Lewis 1980, p. 213)

These words by C. S. Lewis, known for his enduring fantasy series, the Chronicles of Narnia, were written as part of his defense of traditional tales in 1952. Yet, it seems we don't need to wait 100 years: "Wiseacres" are always attempting to censor traditional stories. We have already discussed the importance of fairy and folktales, but now we wish to provide some responses to the major complaints against traditional literature. Tunnell (1994) notes four categories of objection: It presents children with unwarranted psychological fantasy, it is too violent, it frightens young children, and it is a waste of time. These concerns have been voiced for many decades, but a more recent trend deals with issues relating traditional fantasy to sexism, racism, and problems with retellings from authors outside the their own culture.

Psychological Fantasy

Some adults fear that fantasy stories will lead children to be somehow out of touch with reality, to suffer from fantasy in the clinical, psychological sense of the word. However, psychological fantasy, the inability of the mind to distinguish what is real, does not result from reading literary fantasy. In fact, children who read stories that contain "unrealistic" elements—animals that talk, magical events, time travel—are actually less at risk of losing touch with the realities of daily life. Bruno Bettelheim (1977) confirmed this position when he said that fairy stories not only are safe for children but also necessary, and that children deprived of a rich fantasy life (which traditional tales provide) are more likely to seek a psychological escape through avenues such as black magic, drugs, and astrology. Through fairy and folktales, children may vicariously vent the frustrations of being a child controlled by an adult world, for they subconsciously identify with the heroes of the stories who are often the youngest, smallest, least powerful characters (Hansel and Gretel, Cinderella, Aladdin). They also are given a sense of hope about their ultimate abilities to succeed in the world.

C. S. Lewis goes a step further, believing that certain realistic stories are far more likely to cause problems than good fantasy. He points to adult reading as an example:

> The dangerous fantasy is always superficially realistic. The real victim of wishful reverie . . . prefers stories about millionaires, irresistible beauties, posh hotels, palm beaches, and bedroom scenes—things that really might happen, that ought to happen, that would have happened if the reader had had a fair chance. . . . [T]here are two kinds of longing. The one is an askesis, a spiritual exercise, and the other is a disease. (1980, p. 215)

Violence

Critics suggest that violent acts in some traditional tales will breed violence in young children. The work of psychologist Ephraim Biblow (1973) proves how

To find out more about The
Little Red Riding Hood Project
and other possible activities
for integrating folklore and
technology, visit Chapter 5 on
the companion website at
www.prenhall.com/darigan

INTEGRATING TECHNOLOGY: ACTIVITIES USING THE WORLD WIDE WEB

One of the most interesting activities to use when working with folktales is the comparison of alternate versions. Contemporary versions of "Little Red Riding Hood" are plentiful, but it can also be quite interesting to compare these books to earlier versions. At the University of Southern Mississippi, researchers have put together an extensive collection of texts and illustrations from retellings of the story in *The Little Red Riding Hood Project*. Students can create a display of scenes from early and contemporary versions and discover the commonalities and distinctions. Then they might discuss why these differences exist, or they might use what they now know about the folktale to write their own version.

wrong-minded this sort of thinking is. In his experimental study, Biblow showed that children with rich fantasy lives responded to aggressive films with a significant decrease in aggressive behavior, whereas "low-fantasy" children exhibited a tendency toward increased aggression.

The low-fantasy child, as observed during play, presented himself as more motorically oriented, revealed much action and little thought in play activities. The high-fantasy child, in contrast, was more highly structured and creative and tended to be verbally rather than physically aggressive (Biblow, 1973, p. 128).

Much of the violence in fairy and folktales involves the punishment of truly evil villains. Children are concerned from an early age with the ramifications of good and bad behavior, which is represented in fundamental, archetypal ways in traditional stories. Research psychologist Lawrence Kohlberg's stages of moral development describe the young child (up to about age 8) as being in the "premoral stage," which basically means that "the child believes that evil behavior is likely to be punished and good behavior is based on obedience or avoidance of evil implicit in disobedience" (Lefrancois, 1986, p. 446). According to Bettelheim (1977), the evil person in fairy tales who meets a well-deserved fate satisfies a child's deep need for justice to prevail. Sometimes this requires destroying the evil.

Violence in movies and many books cannot be equated with the violence in fairy and folktales. Even in the Grimm version of "Cinderella," one of the bloodiest of fairy stories, the violent acts are surprisingly understated. Both truly wicked stepsisters mutilate themselves (a trimmed heel and a cut-off toe) to make the slipper fit and are revealed by the blood. Later, birds peck out their eyes as punishment for their treachery. Yet, the tale simply, compactly states the fact of each violent act. We don't read of viscous fluid streaming down faces or blood spurting on walls and floors; that's the stuff of slasher horror movies, sensationalism designed to shock or titillate, but not a careful comment on justice.

Risks to Young Children

Many adults worry that some traditional tales will frighten children, causing nightmares and other sorts of distress. However, because dangerous story elements, such as wicked witches or dragons, are far removed in both time and place from the lives of children, they prove much less frightening than realistic stories of danger that focus on real-life fears (Smith 1989). Lewis (1980) feels that insulating a child completely from fear is a disservice. "Since it is so likely they will meet cruel enemies, let them at least have heard of brave knights and heroic courage. Otherwise you are making their destiny not bright but darker" (p. 216).

Fairy and folktales provide children a message of hope. No matter how bleak the outlook or how dark the path, these stories promise children that it is possible to make it through and come out on top. In fact, children who recoil from strong images of danger in fairy tales have the most to gain from the exposure (Smith, 1989).

> Stop for a minute and remind yourself how long the fairy tale has been with us— in every nation and civilization. Surely there must be something important here, an insight so important as to transcend time and geography and cultures to arrive in the twentieth century still intact. There are, for example, nearly seven hundred different versions of *Cinderella* from hundreds of cultures. Nevertheless, they all tell the same story—a truly universal story.
>
> What distinguishes the fairy tale is that it speaks to the very heart and soul of the child. It admits to the child what so many parents and teachers spend hours trying to cover up or avoid. The fairy tale confirms what the child has been thinking all along—that it is a cold, cruel world out there and it's waiting to eat them alive.
>
> Now, if that were *all* the fairy tale said, it would have died out long ago. But it goes one step further. It addresses itself to the child's sense of courage and adventure. The tale advises the child: Take your courage in hand and go out to meet that world head-on. According to Bruno Bettelheim, the fairy tale offers this promise: If you have courage and if you persist, you can achieve your heart's desire. . . .
>
> By recognizing the child's daily fears, by appealing to his courage and confidence, and by offering him hope, the fairy tale presents the child with a means by which he can understand his world and himself. (Trelease, 1995, p. 77)

Some adults feel they can circumvent the problem of frightening children by choosing softened versions of fairy and folktales. This approach may have the opposite effect, however, causing children to become more distressed. Trousdale (1989) tells the story of a mother who used only the softened version of "The Three Little Pigs" with her young daughter. In this version, the pigs are not eaten, and the wolf is not killed in boiling water. Instead, he comes down the chimney, burns his derriere, rockets up the chimney, and disappears into the sunset, never to been seen again. The little girl said, "He's gonna come back," and began to have nightmares. Trousdale (1989, p. 77) advised the child's mother to read the Joseph Jacobs version, in which the wolf dies; Trousdale soon received a letter that said, "Well, we put the Big Bad Wolf to rest." The evil was destroyed and thus the threat eliminated. The nightmares stopped.

But All of This is Surely a Waste of Time

Perhaps the most insidious complaint is that traditional fantasy is a waste of time. Adults simply do not select fairy or folktales to use with children in favor of more substantial stories and books about the real world. However, no genre of literature better fosters creativity than fantasy (both traditional and modern). Recall that Biblow's study showed high-fantasy children to be "more highly structured and creative" (1973, p. 128). Russian poet Kornei Chukovsky (1968) feels that fantasy is "the most valuable attribute of the human mind and should be diligently nurtured from the earliest age" (p. 17). He even points out that great scientists have acknowledged this fact and quotes eminent British physicist John Tindale on the subject:

> Without the participation of fantasy . . . all our knowledge about nature would have been limited merely to the classification of obvious facts. The relation between cause and effect and their interaction would have gone unnoticed, thus stemming the progress of science itself, because it is the main function of science to establish the link between the different manifestations of nature, since creative fantasy is the ability to perceive more and more such links. (Chukovsky, 1968, p. 124)

As the story goes, a woman with a mathematically gifted son asked Albert Einstein how she should best foster his talent. After a moment of thought, Einstein answered,

"Read him the great myths of the past—stretch his imagination" (Huck, 1982, p. 316). Teachers bemoan the lack of creative and critical thinking in today's students. How, then, can we not promote the very books and stories that cultivate imaginative thought?

Issues of Racism, Sexism, and Authenticity

Great debates are being waged over traditional fantasy and how racist and sexist stereotypes are propagated and promoted through the use of such titles in classrooms and homes. We take a look at the issues and provide you with food for thought in making book selection decisions.

Racism

You may remember from your childhood the story of **The Five Chinese Brothers**—in fact, this book is still in print both in hardcover and paperback. For years this book has been attacked for portraying a stereotypic view of Chinese people. The only color, beyond the black lines in this early picture book for children, is yellow, the hue of a school bus, making these five identical brothers hideously offensive to many.

Similarly, Keith Baker has been faulted for inaccuracies in his paintings of the Japanese culture in his book **The Magic Fan.** When discussing the book during a doctoral seminar a number of years ago, Darigan asked one of the members of his cohort, who was Japanese, about his opinions of the book. He chuckled at the Chinese-style bridge in the little Japanese town, he was amused at the kimono the carpenter wore that would have been worn only in the temple, but he was thoroughly engaged by the story and not offended by the errors.

What is offensive to one in a culture may be innocuous to another. When Darigan read aloud Ed Young's **Seven Blind Mice** to a group of teachers in Dallas, Texas a number of years ago, the subsequent discussion proved interesting indeed. His objective in reading the book was to cement the notion that, as reading teachers, we need to focus on the whole first and not teach discrete skills in isolation.

In the book, seven blind mice discover a strange "something" by their pond (it happens to be an elephant). Each mouse in turn strikes out on a different day of the

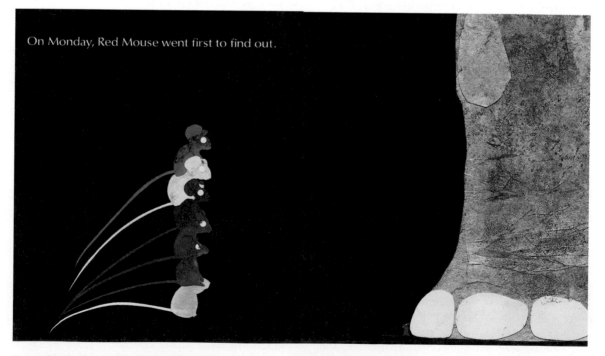

On Monday, Red Mouse went first to find out.

From **Seven Blind Mice** by Ed Young, copyright © 1992 by Ed Young. Used by permission of Philomel Books, a division of Penguin Putnam, Inc.

week to determine what it might be. On Monday, Red Mouse ventures out and, because he investigates only the Something's leg, returns to say it is a pillar. On Tuesday, Green Mouse gives it a try, but investigating only its trunk, he determines it must be a snake. Each day finds a mouse of another color setting out to conclude the real nature of this Something. Finally on Sunday, White Mouse goes forth and, unlike the others, she makes a thorough examination of the Something and agrees that what each mouse before her said was indeed true. It is "sturdy as a pillar, supple as a snake," etc., "but altogether the Something is an elephant." An African-American teacher in the front row loved this book so much that she almost yanked it out of Darigan's hand wanting to get the citation so she could purchase it herself. Teachers across the entire room seemed to agree: This was a wonderful book and worthy of reading to children as well as to colleagues. However, one teacher near the back raised her hand and said she was very hurt by the book. When she heard that the mouse to discover the identity of the elephant was a White Mouse she said it was like someone had stuck a knife in her stomach and twisted it. Her objection was that, as so often seen in literature throughout the years, the White man comes to the rescue. A lively discussion ensued and, as it turned out, both perspectives were validated. But it points out the fact that within any one culture many opinions can exist.

Sexism

Concerns over sexist portrayals of characters in traditional fantasy are common. For example, the story of "Cinderella" is consistently attacked for portraying stepmothers negatively and for allowing only a narrow view of women to be seen, basing a high value on beauty and on marriage as the ultimate goal in life. In *Mirror, Mirror: Forty Folktales for Mothers and Daughters to Share,* Jane Yolen spoke eloquently on this very subject, putting it into perspective: "What a bum rap [Cinderella] has gotten over the years, specifically since the 1950s when Walt Disney got hold of her. She is a much more able young woman than Disney would have us believe. She dissembles, works magic, tends her mother's grave, offers assistance to her godmother, is a capable seamstress, hairdresser and cook. And in the case of the Grimm's version, she even directs the birds to help her."

Moving Beyond Political Correctness

Author and editor Hazel Rochman, a white South African woman, writes extensively on this subject in her book *Against Borders: Promoting Books for a Multicultural World* (1993) and addresses political correctness *and* the resultant backlash it has created as the primary culprit in this argument. Looking at these issues as well as a multitude of others, her plea is for balance and her thesis is to resist extremes (p. 18). What both sides seem unable to do "is allow for ambiguity. One of the their constant mistakes is to take what the narrator says, or what one character says, as the voice of the author . . . If you judge every character to be the author, then you can never allow debate in a book, never have a protagonist who has an ugly or erroneous thought, never have a narrator who's less than perfect—perfect, that is according to the current fashion" (p. 18). In the end, no one book "can do it all." Multiple perspectives always need to be present.

That is not to say that we should not be ever vigilant to note inaccuracies in the books we read and present to children. Educator and scholar Junko Yokota, a Japanese woman herself, reviews books written for children and has related many incidents to us about inaccuracies she has discovered. Among the most glaring she has uncovered are illustrations of kimonos worn in a style reserved only for those on their way to the crematorium. One book portrayed an open, public display of physical affection between a father and daughter, something that would never occur in the Japanese culture. In that same book, made-up names for characters that only "sound" Japanese were used.

One of the positive aspects of the movement toward political correctness is that publishers have become extremely careful as they produce books to meet the high standards necessary for our children. Virtually every publishing house now sends their books out before production to experts, like Yokota, for cultural verification.

Advice for Teachers

Of course, the problem becomes, "How can we as teachers, who may not be a part of the particular culture about which we are reading, ever know what is authentic and what is not?" Our answer is first to be aware of the fact that inaccuracies may occur. Despite the most rigorous measures authors, illustrators, editors, and art directors take, mistakes can slip through in the making of a book. Secondly, as Rochman (1993) relates, we should not expect one book to carry the whole ethnic group experience, nor should we expect one writer to be representative of a whole ethnic group (p. 21).

Finally, we would suggest that rather than throw out tales that might be considered racist or sexist by today's standards, teachers should extend those books with others that show positive, accurate ethnic experiences and characters. When considering racial stereotypes, you may want include Margaret Mahy's *The Seven Chinese Brothers,* illustrated by Jean and Mou-sien Tseng, along *with* the version of *The Five Chinese Brothers.* The Tsengs' illustrations deftly portray and add depth to these characters. With your guidance, children will readily be able to draw conclusions about what they like about each book and, in the process, keep the discussions open rather than closing them with strident rhetoric.

Sexism can be viewed with a different lens by introducing children books with divergent perspectives. For example, Selina Hastings's book *Sir Gawain and the Loathly Lady,* stunningly illustrated by Juan Wijngaard, has been questioned by feminists for its answer to the question, "What is it that women want most?" Hastings's response is simply that women want "to have their own way" (p. 16). A nicely matched companion to this is Ethyl Johnston Phelps's retelling of the same story in her collection *The Maid of the North,* where she says much the same thing but in a way that sounds far more proactive and assertive. Phelps states the answer is that what a woman "desires above all is the power of sovereignty—the right to exercise her own will" (p. 40). Further, you will want to introduce children to books like Jane Yolen's *Not One Damsel in Distress: World Folktales for Strong Girls,* illustrated by Susan Guevara, and *The Serpent Slayer,* by Katrin Tchana and illustrated by Trina Schart Hyman. These books offer tales about strong female characters that have too long been discounted and kept out of print.

Writing Outside One's Own Experience

Hazel Rochman (1993) addresses this issue with yet another dose of common sense. *Can* a person write outside his or her own experience? Rochman states that assuredly the "good writer" can. If that were not the case, then how could Lloyd Alexander write about the Chinese tradition as he did in his book *The Remarkable Journey of Prince Jen,* which was awarded as winner of *Booklist*'s Top of the List for fiction in 1991? How could Suzanne Fisher Staples, a white American journalist and author of *Shabanu, Daughter of the Wind,* write about the experiences of a young Pakistani girl's betrothal to an older wealthy man and win a Newbery Honor and have the book honored as an American Library Association Notable Children's Book? How could Avi, a man, write about a girl's experience, as he did in his book, *The True Confessions of Charlotte Doyle,* and be awarded a Newbery Honor? How could Kimberly Willis Holt, a woman, write about a boy's experience, as she did in *When Zachary Beaver Came to Town* and win the National Book Award? Taking the argument a step further, how could Christopher Paul Curtis write about a young African-American boy during the Depression as he did in *Bud, Not Buddy,* when he was born decades after the fact? Similarly, how could Jane Yolen write about the Holocaust *and* time travel, as she did in *The Devil's Arithmetic,* when she experienced neither?

Rochman's theory continues: If an author were to write only about his or her own experience, this mentality would mean that an African American could write only about African American experiences, and a Japanese person could write only about Japanese experiences. What about an Irish Jew like Patricia Polacco, who grew up in the mixed neighborhood of Oakland, California and had more African American friends than not? What could she write about?

Further, would this mean that ultimately "blacks should read only about blacks, Latinos about Latinos, locking us into smaller and tighter boxes" (p. 22)? In the end, if an author could write *only* about his or her own experience, we would be relegated to one author, one book. Period. In Rochman's mind, this mentality echoes to "the mad drumbeat of apartheidspeak" (p. 22), of which she knows quite a bit.

In the end, she states, "Anybody can write about anything—if they're good enough. There will always be inauthentic or inaccurate books, and defining authenticity on some exclusionary basis or other won't change a thing. The only way to combat inaccuracy is with accuracy—not with pedigrees" (p. 23).

▼▼▼▼▼▼▼

Summary

In this chapter, we defined what is and is not traditional fantasy, using oral roots with no identifiable author as its distinguishing trademark. We analyzed the common characteristics of traditional fantasy, emphasizing characterization, plot, theme, setting, and repeated story elements. We then looked at the different types of traditional fantasy. Under the category of folktales, we described cumulative tales, pourquoi tales, beast tales, trickster tales, Noodlehead tales, realistic tales, and fairy tales. Next we investigated tall tales, fables, myths, epics and legends, and religious stories. We noted the values of traditional fantasy and the benefits it provides children. Finally, we looked at a number of controversial issues related to traditional fantasy. Though some people object to traditional fantasy because they claim it potentially leads children away from reality, is too violent and frightening, is simply a waste of time, and promotes sexual and racial stereotypes, we attempted to dispel any of these notions by accenting all the positive effects this genre has on our youth.

▼▼▼▼▼▼▼

Fifteen More of Our Favorites

Collections and Chapter Books

Davol, Marguerite W. (1995). *Papa Alonzo Leatherby: A collection of tall tales from the best storyteller in Carroll County.* Simon & Schuster. When Papa Alonzo Leatherby's tall tales about New England freeze solid one extra cold winter, they have to be thawed out and preserved in ingenious ways.

Hamilton, Virginia. (2000). *The people could fly: American Black folktales* (Leo and Diane Dillon, Illus.). Knopf. Retold African American folktales of animals, fantasy, the supernatural, and desire for freedom, born of the sorrow of the slaves, but passed on in hope. (Original work published 1985)

Martin, Rafe. (1996). *Mysterious tales of Japan* (Tatsuro Kiuchi, Illus.). Putnam. Collection of translated Japanese folk tales, including "Urashima Taro," "Kogi," "The Crane Maiden," and "The Boy Who Drew Cats."

Osborne, Mary Pope. (1998). *Favorite medieval tales* (Troy Howell, Illus.). Scholastic. A collection of well-known tales from medieval Europe, including "Beowulf," "The Sword in the Stone," "The Song of Roland," and "Gudren and the Island of the Lost Children."

Philip, Neil. (1996). *American fairy tales: From Rip Van Winkle to the Rootabaga stories* (Michael McCurdy, Illus.). Hyperion. Includes works and discussion of Washington Irving, Nathaniel Hawthorne, Howard Pyle, Louisa May Alcott, L. Frank Baum, Ruth Plumly Thompson, and Carl Sandburg.

Schwartz, Howard, & Rush, Barbara. (1996). *The wonder child & other Jewish fairy tales* (Stephen Fieser, Illus.). HarperCollins. An illustrated collection of Jewish fairy tales from various countries.

Sutcliff, Rosemary. (1981). *The sword and the circle.* Dutton. (See the other books in the King Arthur trilogy: *Light beyond the forest: The quest for the Holy Grail* and *The road to Camlann.*) Retells the adventures of King Arthur, Queen Guenevere, Sir Lancelot, and other knights of the Round Table.

Picture Books

Beneduce, Ann Keay. (1999). *Jack and the beanstalk* (Gennady Spirin, Illus.). Philomel. Retelling of the story of Jack, who climbs to the top of a giant beanstalk, where he uses his quick wits to outsmart an ogre and make his and his mother's fortune.

Bodkin, Odds. (1998). *The crane wife* (Gennady Spirin, Illus.). Harcourt. A retelling of the traditional Japanese tale about a poor sail maker who gains a beautiful but mysterious wife skilled at weaving magical sails.

Choi, Yangsook. (1997). *The sun girl and the moon boy: A Korean tale*. Knopf. A hungry tiger tries to trick a brother and sister into opening their door by pretending to be their absent mother.

Greene, Ellin. 1994. *Billy Beg and his bull* (Kimberly Bulcken Root, Illus.). Holiday House. With magical gifts from the bull his mother had given

him, the son of an Irish king manages to prove his bravery and win a princess as his wife.

Kimmel, Eric A. (1993). *Three sacks of truth* (Robert Rayevsky, Illus.). Holiday House. With the aid of a perfect peach, a silver fife, and his own resources, Petit Jean outwits a dishonest king and wins the hand of a princess.

McDermott, Gerald. (1975). *The stonecutter: A Japanese folk tale*. Penguin. Not even the mightiest mountain is immune to a determined stonecutter.

Shepard, Aaron. (1998). *The crystal heart: A Vietnamese legend* (Joseph Daniel Fiedler, Illus.). Atheneum. The sheltered and privileged daughter of a mandarin comes to understand the consequences of her naïve, yet cruel, words to a fisherman.

Steptoe, John. (1987). *Mufaro's beautiful daughters: An African tale*. Lothrop. Mufaro's two beautiful daughters, one bad-tempered, one kind and sweet, go before the king who is choosing a wife. An African variant of Cinderella. A Caldecott Honor Book.

▼▼▼▼▼▼▼

Others We Like

Chapter Books and Collections

Evslin, Bernard. (1984). *Hercules* (Joseph A. Smith, Illus.). Morrow.

Doherty, Berlie. (1998). *Tales of wonder and magic* (Juan Wijingaard, Illus.). Candlewick.

Hamilton, Virginia. (1995). *Her stories* (Leo Dillon & Diane Dillon, Illus.). Scholastic (Blue Sky).

Hayes, Sarah. (1993). *The Candlewick book of fairy tales* (P. J. Lynch, Illus.). Candlewick.

Heaney, Marie. (2000). *The names upon the harp* (P. J. Lynch, Illus.). Arthur A. Levine/Scholastic.

Low, Alice. (1985). *The Macmillan book of Greek gods and heroes* (Arvis Stewart, Illus.). Macmillan.

Osborne, Mary Pope. (1991). *American tall tales* (Michael McCurdy, Illus.). Knopf.

Osborne, Mary Pope. (1993). *Mermaid tales from around the world* (Troy Howell, Illus.). Scholastic.

Philip, Neil. (1999). *Celtic fairy tales* (Isabelle Brent, Illus.). Viking.

Pinkney, Jerry. (2000). *Aesop's fables*. SeaStar Books.

Sierra, Judy. (1996). *Nursery tales around the world* (Stefano Vitale, Illus.). Clarion.

Sutcliff, Rosemary. (1996). *The wanderings of Odysseus* (Alan Lee, Illus.). Delacorte.

Walker, Paul Robert. (1997). *Little folk: Stories from around the world* (James Bernardin, Illus.). Harcourt.

Yolen, Jane. (1986). *Favorite folktales from around the world*. Pantheon.

Picture Books

Aardema, Verna. (1975). *Why mosquitoes buzz in people's ears* (Leo Dillon & Diane Dillon, Illus.). Dial.

Byrd, Robert. (1999). *Finn MacCoul and his fearless wife*. Dutton.

Craft, K. Y. (2000). *Cinderella*. SeaStar Books.

Demi. (1994). *The firebird*. Holt.

Fisher, Leonard. (1990). *Jason and the golden fleece*. Holiday House.

Goble, Paul. (1985). *The girl who loved wild horses*. Bradbury.

Haley, Gail. (1970). *A story, a story*. Atheneum.

Hunter, Mollie. (1994). *Gilly Martin the fox* (Dennis McDermott, Illus.). Hyperion.

Lester, Julius. (1994). *John Henry* (Jerry Pinkney, Illus.). Dial.

Lester, Julius. (1999). *Uncle Remus: The complete tales* (Jerry Pinkney, Illus.). Phyllis Fogelman Books.

Martin, Rafe. (1993). *The boy who lived with the seals* (David Shannon, Illus.). Philomel.

Martin, Rafe. (2000). *The language of birds* (Susan Gaber, Illus.). Putnam.

Mayer, Marianna. (1978). *Beauty and the beast* (Mercer Mayer, Illus.). Four Winds.

Mayer, Mercer. (1978). *East of the sun and west of the moon*. Four Winds.

McDermott, Gerald. (1974). *Arrow to the sun.* Viking.

Perrault, Charles (1990) *Puss in boots* (Fred Marcellino, Illus., Malcolm Arthur, Trans.). Farrar, Straus & Giroux.

San Souci, Robert D. (1989). *The talking eggs* (Jerry Pinkney, Illus.). Dial.

San Souci, Robert D. (1992). *Sukey and the mermaid* (Brian Pinkney, Illus.). Four Winds.

Seth, Vikram. (1994). *Arion and the dolphin* (Jane Ray, Illus.). Dutton.

Stevens, Janet. (1995). *Tops & bottoms.* Harcourt.

Wisniewski, David. (1996). *Golem.* Clarion.

Yolen, Jane. (1997). *The sea man* (Christopher Denise, Illus.). Philomel.

Young, Ed. (1989). *Lon Po Po: A Red Riding Hood story from China.* Philomel.

▼▼▼▼▼▼▼

Children's Literature References

Aardema, Verna. (1975). *Why mosquitoes buzz in people's ears* (Leo Dillon & Diane Dillon, Illus.). New York: Dial.

Aardema, Verna. (1981). *Bringing the rain to Kapiti Plain: A Nandi tale* (Beatriz Vidal, Illus.). New York: Dial.

Aardema, Verna. (1994a). *How the ostrich got its long neck* (Marcia Brown, Illus.). New York: Scholastic.

Aardema, Verna. (1994b). *Misoso: Once upon a time tales from Africa* (Reynold Ruffins, Illus.). New York: Knopf.

Aardema, Verna. (1995). *Jackal's flying lesson: A Khoikhoi tale* (Dale Gottlieb, Illus.). New York: Knopf.

Aardema, Verna. (1997). *Anansi does the impossible! An Ashanti tale* (Lisa Desimini, Illus.). New York: Atheneum.

Adler, David A. (1997). *Chanukah in Chelm* (Kevin O'Malley, Illus.). New York: Lothrop.

Alexander, Lloyd. (1991). *The remarkable journey of Prince Jen.* New York: Dutton.

Arnold, Katya. (1994). *Knock, knock, Teremok! A traditional Russian tale.* New York: North-South Books.

Asbjørnsen, Peter, & Moe, Jorgen. (1957). *East o' the sun and west o' the moon.* Garden City, NY: Junior Deluxe Editions.

Atwell, David Lewis. (1992). *The day Hans got his way: A Norwegian folktale* (Debby Atwell, Illus.). Boston: Houghton Mifflin.

Avi. (1990). *The true confessions of Charlotte Doyle.* New York: Orchard.

Aylesworth, Jim. (1998). *The gingerbread man* (Barbara McClintock, Illus.). New York: Scholastic.

Babbitt, Natalie. (1994). *Bub or the very best thing.* New York: HarperCollins.

Baker, Keith. (1989). *The magic fan.* San Diego: Harcourt Brace.

Baumgartner, Barbara. (1998). *The gingerbread man* (Norman Messenger, Illus.). New York: DK Publishing.

Begay, Shonto. (1992). *Ma'ii and Cousin Horned Toad: A traditional Navajo story.* New York: Scholastic.

Bernhard, Emily. (1994). *The tree that rains: The flood myth of the Huichol Indians of Mexico* (Durga Bernhard, Illus.). New York: Holiday House.

Bierhorst, John. (1993). *The woman who fell from the sky: The Iroquois story of creation* (Robert Andrew Parker, Illus.). New York: Morrow.

Bishop, Claire Huchet. (1938). *The five Chinese brothers* (Kurt Wiese, Illus.). New York: Coward-McCann.

Brett, Jan. (1994). *Town mouse, country mouse.* New York: Putnam.

Brett, Jan. (1999). *Gingerbread baby.* New York: Putnam.

Brown, Marcia. (1947). *Stone soup.* New York: Scribner's.

Burleigh, Robert. (1999). *Hercules* (Raul Colón, Illus.). San Diego: Harcourt.

Climo, Shirley. (1989). *The Egyptian Cinderella* (Ruth Heller, Illus.). New York: HarperCollins.

Climo, Shirley. (1993). *The Korean Cinderella* (Ruth Heller, Illus.). New York: HarperCollins.

Climo, Shirley. (1995a). *Atalanta's race: A Greek myth* (Alexander Koshkin, Illus.). New York: Clarion.

Climo, Shirley. (1995b). *The little red ant and the great big crumb* (Francisco X. Mora, Illus.). New York: Clarion.

Climo, Shirley. (1996). *The Irish Cinderlad* (Loretta Krupinski, Illus.). New York: HarperCollins.

Cohen, Barbara. (1995). *Robin Hood and Little John* (David Ray, Illus.). New York: Philomel.

Colum, Padraic. (1921). *The golden fleece and the heroes who lived before Achilles.* New York: Macmillan.

Cook, Joel. (1993). *The rat's daughter.* Honesdale, PA: Boyds Mills Press.

Cowley, Joy. (1995). *The mouse bride* (David Christiana, Illus.). New York: Scholastic.

Craft, M. Charlotte. (1996). *Cupid and Psyche* (K. Y. Craft, Illus.). New York: Morrow.

Craig, Helen. (1992). *The town mouse and the country mouse.* Cambridge, MA: Candlewick Press.

Crespo, George. (1993). *How the sea began: A Taino myth.* New York: Clarion.

Curtis, Christopher Paul. (1999). *Bud, not Buddy.* New York: Delacorte.

Dasent, George Webbe. (1992). *East o' the sun and west o' the moon* (P. J. Lynch, Illus.). Cambridge, MA: Candlewick Press.

Daly, Jude. (2000). *Fair, brown & trembling.* New York: Farrar, Straus & Giroux.

D'Aulaire, Ingri, & D'Aulaire, Edgar. (1962). *D'Aulaires' book of Greek myths.* New York: Doubleday.

Delacre, Lulu. (1996). *Golden tales: Myths, legends and folktales from Latin America.* New York: Scholastic.

Demi. (1997). *Buddha stories.* New York: Holt.

Denise, Christopher. (1994). *The fool of the world and the flying ship*. New York: Philomel.

dePaola, Tomie. (1980). *The legend of old Befana*. San Diego: Harcourt.

Dürr, Gisela. (1994). *Aesop's fables*. New York: North-South Books.

Egielski, Richard. (1997). *The gingerbread boy*. New York: Laura Geringer.

Ehrlich, Amy. (1985). *Cinderella* (Susan Jeffers, Illus.). New York: Dial.

Fisher, Leonard Everett. (1990). *Jason and the golden fleece*. New York: Holiday House.

Fisher, Leonard Everett. (1997). *The gods and goddesses of ancient Egypt*. New York: Holiday House.

Fleischman, Paul. (1996). *Dateline: Troy*. Cambridge, MA: Candlewick Press.

French, Vivian. (1993). *Why the sea is salt* (Patrice Aggs, Illus.). Cambridge, MA: Candlewick Press.

Furlong, Monica. (1995). *Robin's country*. New York: Knopf.

Gág, Wanda. (1935). *Gone is gone*. New York: Coward.

Gauch, Patricia Lee. (1994). *Noah* (Jonathan Green, Illus.). New York: Philomel.

Gerson, Mary-Joan. (1992). *Why the sky is far away: A Nigerian folktale* (Carla Golembe, Illus.). Boston: Little, Brown.

Gerson, Mary-Joan. (1995). *People of corn: A Mayan story* (Carla Golembe, Illus.). Boston: Little, Brown.

Grimm, Jacob, & Grimm, Wilhelm. (1882). *Household stories*. London: Macmillan.

Grimm, Jacob, & Grimm, Wilhelm. (1996). *The six servants* (Sergei Goloshapov, Illus.). New York: North-South.

Haley, Gail. (1970). *A story, a story*. New York: Atheneum.

Hamilton, Virginia. (1988). *In the beginning: Creation stories from around the world*. San Diego: Harcourt.

Han, Oki S. (1996). *Kongi and potgi: A Cinderella story from Korea*. New York: Dial.

Hastings, Selina. (1985). *Sir Gawain and the loathly lady* (Juan Wijngaard, Illus.). New York: Mulberry.

Hausman, Gerald. (1995). *Coyote walks on two legs: A book of Navajo myths and legends* (Floyd Cooper, Illus.). New York: Philomel.

Hausman, Gerald. (1998). *Doctor Bird: Three lookin' up tales from Jamaica* (Ashley Wolff, Illus.). New York: Philomel.

Heins, Ethel. (1995). *The cat and the cook and other fables of Krylov* (Anita Lobel, Illus.). New York: Greenwillow.

Highwater, Jamake. (1994). *Rama: A legend*. New York: Henry Holt.

Holt, Kimberly Willis. (1999). *When Zachary Beaver came to town*. New York: Henry Holt.

Ho, Minfong, & Ros, Saphan. (1997). *Brother Rabbit: A Cambodian tale* (Jennifer Hewitson, Illus.). New York: Lothrop.

Hodges, Margaret. (1997). *The true tale of Johnny Appleseed* (Kimberly Bulcken Root, Illus.). New York: Holiday.

Hooks, William H. (1987). *Moss gown* (Donald Carrick, Illus.). New York: Clarion.

Hutton, Warwick. (1989). *Theseus and the Minotaur*. New York: McElderry.

Hutton, Warwick. (1992). *The Trojan horse*. New York: McElderry.

Hutton, Warwick. (1993). *Perseus*. New York: McElderry.

Hutton, Warwick. (1994). *Persephone*. New York: McElderry.

Hutton, Warwick. (1995). *Odysseus and the Cyclops*. New York: McElderry.

Isaacs, Anne. (1994). *Swamp angel* (Paul O. Zelinsky, Illus.). New York: Dutton.

Jackson, Ellen. (1996). *The precious gift: A Navajo creation myth* (Woodleigh Hubbard, Illus.). New York: Simon & Schuster.

Jacobs, Joseph. (1932). *English fairy tales* (John D. Batten, Illus.). New York: Grosset & Dunlap.

Jaffe, Nina. (1996). *The golden flower: A Taino myth from Puerto Rico* (Enrique O. Sánchez, Illus.). New York: Simon & Schuster.

Jarrell, Randall. (1972). *Snow White and the seven dwarfs* (Nancy Ekholm Burkert, Illus.). New York: Farrar, Straus & Giroux.

Johnson, Steven T. (1995). *Alphabet city*. New York: Viking.

Johnston, Tony. (1994). *The tale of Rabbit and Coyote* (Tomie dePaola, Illus.). New York: Putnam.

Jonas, Ann. (1990). *Aardvarks, disembark!* New York: Greenwillow.

Jones, Carol. (1995). *Town mouse, country mouse*. Boston: Houghton Mifflin.

Jones, Carol. (1996). *The hare and the tortoise*. Boston: Houghton Mifflin.

Jones, Carol. (1997). *The lion and the mouse*. Boston: Houghton Mifflin.

Kellogg, Steven. (1984). *Paul Bunyan*. New York: Morrow.

Kellogg, Steven. (1986). *Pecos Bill*. New York: Morrow.

Kellogg, Steven. (1988). *Johnny Appleseed*. New York: Morrow.

Kellogg, Steven. (1992). *Mike Fink*. New York: Morrow.

Kellogg, Steven. (1995). *Sally Ann Thunder Ann Whirlwind Crockett*. New York: Morrow.

Kellogg, Steven. (1996). *I was born about 10,000 years ago*. New York: Morrow.

Kerven, Rosalind. (1998). *Aladdin and other tales from the Arabian nights* (Nilesh Mistry, Illus.). New York: DK Publishing.

Kherdian, David. (1997). *The rose's smile: Farizad of the Arabian nights* (Stefano Vitale, Illus.). New York: Henry Holt.

Kimmel, Eric A. (1988a). *Anansi and the moss covered rock* (Janet Stevens, Illus.). New York: Scholastic.

Kimmel, Eric A. (1988b). *The Chanukah tree* (Giora Carmi, Illus.). New York: Holiday House.

Kimmel, Eric A. (1989). *Hershel and the Hanukkah goblins* (Trina Schart Hyman, Illus.). New York: Holiday House.

Kimmel, Eric A. (1991a). *Bearhead: A Russian folktale* (Charles Mikolaycak, Illus.). New York: Holiday House.

Kimmel, Eric A. (1991b). *The greatest of all: A Japanese folktale* (Giora Carmi, Illus.). New York: Holiday House.

Kimmel, Eric A. (1992a). *Anansi goes fishing* (Janet Stevens, Illus.). New York: Holiday House.

Kimmel, Eric A. (1992b). *Boots and his brothers* (Kimberly Bulcken Root, Illus.). New York: Holiday House.

Kimmel, Eric A. (1992c). *The old woman and her pig* (Giora Carmi, Illus.). New York: Holiday House.

Kimmel, Eric A. (1992d). *The tale of Aladdin and the wonderful lamp* (Ju-Hong Chen, Illus.). New York: Holiday House.

Kimmel, Eric A. (1993a). *The gingerbread man* (Megan Lloyd, Illus.). New York: Holiday House.

Kimmel, Eric A. (1993b). *Three sacks of truth: A story from France* (Robert Rayevsky, Illus.). New York: Holiday House.

Kimmel, Eric A. (1994a). *Anansi and the talking melon* (Janet Stevens, Illus.). New York: Holiday House.

Kimmel, Eric A. (1994b). *Iron John* (Trina Schart Hyman, Illus.). New York: Holiday House.

Kimmel, Eric A. (1996). *The tale of Ali Baba and the forty thieves* (Will Hillenbrand, Illus.). New York: Holiday House.

Kimmel, Eric A. (1998a). *Easy work! An old tale* (Andrew Glass, Illus.). New York: Holiday House.

Kimmel, Eric A. (1998b). *Seven at one blow* (Megan Lloyd, Illus.). New York: Holiday House.

Kimmel, Eric A. (2000a). *Gershon's monster* (Jon J Muth, Illus.). New York: Scholastic.

Kimmel, Eric A. (2000b). *The jar of fools: Eight Hanukkah stories from Chelm* (Mordicai Gerstein, Illus.). New York: Holiday House.

Kimmel, Eric A. (2000c). *The runaway tortilla* (Randy Cecil, Illus.). Delray Beach, FL: Winslow.

Kipling, Rudyard. (1982). *Just so stories* (Victor Ambrus, Illus.). New York: Rand. (Original work published 1902)

Knutson, Barbara. (1993). *Sungura and Leopard: A Swahili trickster tale*. Boston: Little, Brown.

La Fontaine, Jean de. (1906). *One hundred fables*. Boston: Ginn.

Lang, Andrew. (1996). *The flying ship* (Dennis McDermott, Illus.). New York: Morrow.

Lasky, Kathryn. (1997). *Hercules: The man, the myth, the hero* (Mark Hess, Illus.). New York: Hyperion.

Lattimore, Deborah Nourse. (1995). *Arabian nights: Three tales*. New York: Joanna Cotler Books.

Lindbergh, Reeve. (1990). *Johnny Appleseed* (Kathy Jakobsen, Illus.). Boston: Little, Brown.

Lister, Robin. (1988). *The legend of King Arthur* (Alan Baker, Illus.). New York: Doubleday.

Litzinger, Rosanne. (1993). *The old woman and her pig: An old English tale*. San Diego: Harcourt.

Louie, Ai-Ling. (1990). *Yeh-Shen* (Ed Young, Illus.). New York: Philomel.

Lowry, Lois. (1989). *Number the stars*. Boston: Houghton Mifflin.

Lynch, P. J. (1992). *East o' the sun and west o' the moon*. Cambridge, MA: Candlewick.

Maddern, Eric. (1993). *The fire children: A west African creation tale* (Frané Lessac, Illus.). New York: Dial.

Mahy, Margaret. (1990). *The seven Chinese brothers* (Jean Tseng & Mou-sien Tseng, Illus.). New York: Scholastic.

Martin, Claire. (1991). *The race of the golden apples* (Leo Dillon & Diane Dillon, Illus.). New York: Dial.

Martin, Rafe. (1992). *The rough-face girl*. New York: Putnam.

Mayer, Marianna. (1998). *Pegasus* (K. Y. Craft, Illus.). New York: Morrow.

Mayo, Margaret. (1996). *When the world was young: Creation and pourquoi tales* (Louise Brierley, Illus.). New York: Simon & Schuster.

McCaughrean, Geraldine. (1995). *The golden hoard: Myths and legends of the world* (Bee Willey, Illus.). New York: McElderry.

McCaughrean, Geraldine. (1996). *The silver treasure* (Bee Willey, Illus.). New York: McElderry.

McCaughrean, Geraldine. (1997). *The bronze cauldron: Myths and legends of the world* (Bee Willey, Illus.). New York: McElderry.

McCaughrean, Geraldine. (1998). *The crystal pool: Myths and legends of the world* (Bee Willey, Illus.). New York: McElderry.

McDermott, Gerald. (1972). *Anansi the Spider: A tale from the Ashanti*. New York: Henry Holt.

McDermott, Gerald. (1992). *Papagayo: The mischief maker*. San Diego: Harcourt.

McDermott, Gerald. (1993a). *Coyote: A trickster tale from the American Southwest*. San Diego: Harcourt.

McDermott, Gerald. (1993b). *Raven: A trickster tale from the Pacific Northwest*. San Diego: Harcourt.

McDermott, Gerald. (1993c). *Zomo the rabbit: A trickster tale from West Africa*. San Diego: Harcourt.

McDermott, Gerald. (1997). *Musicians of the sun*. New York: Simon & Schuster.

Melmed, Laura Krauss. (1994). *Prince Nautilus* (Henri Sorensen, Illus.). New York: Lothrop.

Mollel, Tololwa. (1990). *The orphan boy* (Paul Morin, Illus.). New York: Clarion.

Mollel, Tololwa. (1997). *Ananse's feast: An Ashanti tale* (Andrew Glass, Illus.). New York: Clarion.

Morpurgo, Michael. (1994). *Arthur: High king of Britain* (Michael Foreman, Illus.). San Diego: Harcourt Brace.

Morpurgo, Michael. (1996). *Robin of Sherwood* (Michael Foreman, Illus.). San Diego: Harcourt Brace.

Napoli, Donna Jo. (1996). *Zel*. New York: Dutton.

Olieiero, Jaime. (1995). *The day the sun was stolen* (Sharon Hitchcock, Illus.). New York: Hyperion.

Onyefulu, Obi. (1994). *Chinye: A West African folk tale* (Evie Safarewicz, Illus.). New York: Viking.

Oppenheim, Shulamith Levey. (1994). *Iblis* (Ed Young, Illus.). San Diego: Harcourt Brace.

Osborne, Mary Pope. (1996). *Favorite Norse Myths* (Troy Howell, Illus.). New York: Scholastic.

Paterson, Katherine. (1992). *The King's equal* (Vladimir Vagin, Illus.). New York: HarperCollins.

Perham, Molly. (1993). *King Arthur and the legends of Camelot* (Julek Heller, Illus.). New York: Viking.

Perrault, Charles. (1697). *Contes de ma Mère L'Oye*.

Phelps, Ethyl Johnston. (1987). *The maid of the north: Feminist folk tales from around the world* (Lloyd Bloom, Illus.). New York: Henry Holt.

Philip, Neil. (1995). *The illustrated book of myths: Tales & legends of the world* (Nilesh Mistry, Illus.). New York: Dorling Kindersley.

Pollock, Penny. (1996). *The turkey girl* (Ed Young, Illus.). Boston: Little, Brown.

Pyle, Howard. (1973). *King stork* (Trina Schart Hyman, Illus.). Boston: Little, Brown.

Ransome, Arthur. (1968). *The fool of the world and the flying ship* (Uri Shulevitz, Illus.). New York: Farrar, Straus & Giroux.

Robbins, Ruth. (1960). *Baboushka and the three kings.* New York: Parnassus.

Rogasky, Barbara. (1986). *The water of life* (Trina Schart Hyman, Illus.). New York: Holiday House.

Rowe, John A. (1996). *The gingerbread man: An old English folktale.* New York: North-South Books.

San Souci, Robert D. (1987). *The enchanted tapestry* (László Gál, Illus.). New York: Dial.

San Souci, Robert D. (1993). *Cut from the same cloth: American women of myth, legend and tall tale* (Brian Pinkney, Illus.). New York: Philomel.

San Souci, Robert D. (1994). *Sootface: An Ojibwa Cinderella story* (Daniel San Souci, Illus.). New York: Doubleday.

Sanderson, Ruth. (1999). *The crystal mountain.* Boston: Little, Brown.

Sanfield, Steve. (1995). *Strudel, strudel, strudel* (Emily Lisker, Illus.). New York: Orchard.

Schroeder, Alan. (1997). *Smoky mountain Rose: An Appalachian Cinderella* (Brad Sneed, Illus.). New York: Dial.

Shepard, Aaron. (1995). *The gifts of Wali Dad: A tale of India and Pakistan* (Daniel San Souci, Illus.). New York: Atheneum.

Silverman, Erica. (1999). *Raisel's riddle* (Susan Gaber, Illus.). New York: Farrar, Straus & Giroux.

Singer, Isaac Bashevis. (1984). *Stories for children.* New York: Farrar, Straus & Giroux.

Snyder, Dianne. (1988). *The boy of the three-year nap* (Allen Say, Illus.). Boston: Houghton Mifflin.

Staples, Suzanne Fisher. (1989). *Shabanu, daughter of the wind.* New York: Knopf.

Steptoe, John. (1987). *Mufaro's beautiful daughters* New York: Lothrop.

Sutcliff, Rosemary. (1993). *Black ships before Troy: The story of the Iliad* (Alan Lee, Illus.). New York: Frances Lincoln.

Sutcliff, Rosemary. (1995). *The wanderings of Odysseus: The story of the Odyssey* (Alan Lee, Illus.). New York: Delacorte Press.

Taback, Simms. (1997). *There was an old lady who swallowed a fly.* New York: Viking.

Talbott, Hudson. (1991). *King Arthur: The sword in the stone.* New York: Morrow.

Talbott, Hudson. (1996). *Excalibur.* New York: Morrow.

Tchana, Katrin. (2000). *The serpent slayer: And other stories of strong women* (Trina Schart Hyman, Illus.). Boston: Little, Brown.

Vinge, Joan D. (1999). *The Random House book of Greek myths* (Oren Sherman, Illus.). New York: Random House.

Williams, Marcia. (1996). *The Iliad and the Odyssey.* Cambridge, MA: Candlewick Press.

Yeoman, John. (1996). *The seven voyages of Sinbad the sailor* (Quentin Blake, Illus.). New York: McElderry.

Yolen, Jane. (1990). *Sky dogs* (Barry Moser, Illus.). San Diego: Harcourt.

Yolen, Jane. (1998a). *The Devil's arithmetic.* New York: Viking.

Yolen, Jane. (1998b). *Pegasus, the flying horse* (Li Ming, Illus.). New York: Dutton.

Yolen, Jane. (2000). *Not one damsel in distress: World folktales for strong girls* (Susan Guevara, Illus.). San Diego: Harcourt.

Yolen, Jane, & Stemple, Heidi. (2000). *Mirror, mirror: Forty folktales for mothers and daughters to share.* New York: Viking.

Young, Ed. (1992). *Seven blind mice.* New York: Philomel.

Young, Ed. (1995). *Donkey trouble.* New York: Atheneum.

Young, Ed. (1997). *Mouse match: A Chinese folktale.* San Diego: Harcourt.

Zelinsky, Paul O. (1984). *Hansel and Gretel.* New York: Dutton.

Zelinsky, Paul O. (1986). *Rumpelstilkstin.* New York: Dutton.

Zelinsky, Paul O. (1990). *The wheels on the bus.* New York: Dutton.

Zelinsky, Paul O. (1997). *Rapunzel.* New York: Dutton.

▼▼▼▼▼▼▼

Professional References

Alexander, L. (1968). Wishful thinking—or hopeful dreaming. *The Horn Book, 44,* 382–390.

Arbuthnot, M. H. (1961). *The Arbuthnot anthology of children's literature.* Glenview, IL: Scott, Foresman.

Bettelheim, B. (1977). *The uses of enchantment: The meaning and importance of fairy tales.* New York: Vintage.

Biblow, E. (1973). Imaginative play and the control of aggressive behavior. In J. L. Singer (Ed.), *The child's world of make-believe* (pp. 104–128). New York: Academic Press.

Bosma, B. (1992). *Fairy tales, fables, legends, and myths: Using folk literature in your classroom.* New York: Teachers College Press.

Chukovsky, K. (1968). *From two to five.* Los Angeles: University of California Press.

Darigan, D. (1996). *Multicultural literature: Discovering the unique and the universal.* Paper presented at the Penn State University Children's Literature Matters Conference, State College, PA.

Frye, N. (1964). *The educated imagination.* Bloomington, IN: University of Indiana Press.

Huck, C. (1982). I give you the end of a golden string. *Theory Into Practice, 12*(4), 315–325.

Lefrancois, G. R. (1986). *Of children*. Belmont, CA: Wadsworth.

Lewis, C. S. (1980). On three ways of writing for children. In S. Egoff, G. T. Stubbs, & L. F. Ashley (Eds.), *Only connect* (pp. 207–220). New York: Oxford University Press.

Rochman, H. (1993). *Against borders: Promoting books for a multicultural world*. Chicago: ALA Book/Booklist Publications.

Smith, C. A. (1989). *From wonder to wisdom*. New York: New American Library.

Trelease, J. (1995). *The read-aloud handbook* (4th ed.). New York: Penguin.

Trousdale, A. (1989). Who's afraid of the big bad wolf. *Children's Literature in Education, 20*(2), 68–79.

Tunnell, M. O. (1994). The double-edged sword: Fantasy and censorship. *Language Arts, 71*(8), 606–612.

Wartenberg, A. (1995, June/July). Using fairy tales with older children. *Reading Today*, p. 26. Newark, DE: International Reading Association.

MODERN FANTASY

6

CHAPTER

▼▼▼▼▼▼▼

If you want to cover
Dealing With Dragons

Consider as a READ ALOUD

Dove Isabeau,
by Jane Yolen, illustrated by Dennis Nolan

The Dragon's Pearl,
by Julie Lawson, illustrated by Paul Morin

***Everyone Knows What a Dragon
Looks Like,*** by Jay Williams,
illustrated by Mercer Mayer

The Dragon's Boy,
by Jane Yolen

Consider as a TEXT SET

Dealing With Dragons,
by Patricia C. Wrede

Dragon of the Lost Sea,
by Laurence Yep

Dragon's Blood, by Jane Yolen

Dragon's Milk, by Susan Fletcher

Jeremy Thatcher, Dragon Hatcher,
by Bruce Coville

Searching for Dragons,
by Patricia C. Wrede

THE DRAGON'S BOY
by Jane Yolen

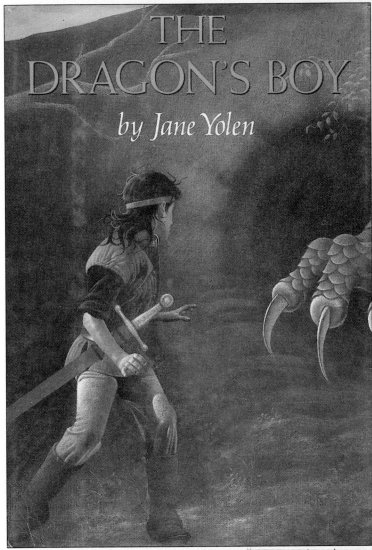

"Excellent," the dragon repeated. *"And I've been needing a boy just your age for some time."*

Not to eat! *Artos thought wildly.* Perhaps I'd better point out how small I am, how thin.

But the dragon went on as if it had no idea of the terror it had just instilled in Artos. "A boy to pass my wisdom on to. So listen well, young Artos of Sir Ector's castle."

Excerpt from *The Dragon's Boy* by Jane Yolen

Student Response

The book, The Dragon's Boy is about a boy who stumbles in on a dragon's cave. The dragon asks the boy if he wants gold, jewels or wisdom. The boy picks wisdom. The dragon gives the boy wisdom day-by-day. He once gave the boy a gem and the boy bought a sword with it. The boy forgot about going to the dragon's cave and made friends with some older boys. The boy remembers the dragon and goes to his cave. The boy finds out that the dragon was really a person in a costume.

Andy age 12

To visit a classroom exploring the issues of Modern Fantasy, please go to Chapter 6 of our companion website at **www.prenhall.com/darigan**

The modern fantasy of **Harry Potter and the Sorcerer's Stone,** by J. K. Rowling, as well as the other books in that series, has swooped down on the world's readership as fast and furious as a rousing game of "Quidditch." In the past few years, these books have drawn in an entirely new audience of both children and adults who would probably never have contemplated the genre of modern fantasy before.

What has this renewed interest in modern fantasy meant to booksellers? Bookstore owner Hannah Schwartz (personal communication) states that with the advent of Harry Potter "people suddenly became aware of children's books as literature. It jumped from being simply being a kid's book to a *real* book, and we found that adults were avidly reading children's books. Beyond that we, as a society, are excited about an author like we traditionally have been about athletes and movie stars. It has elevated the entire industry to a different level, making it cool to read."

Modern fantasy, great modern fantasy, was alive and well long before Harry Potter whisked onto the scene. Let's take a close look at what this rich and wonderful genre has to offer.

▼▼▼▼▼▼▼

Definition of Modern Fantasy

As with traditional fantasy, modern fantasy can be differentiated from the other genres by the simple fact that the reader is presented with story elements that run counter to the natural and physical laws of our known world. Events akin to magic spring forth from the page, and if the book is written well we, as readers, believe it. Characters are transformed, animals talk, magical forests spring up at our feet, and we join in the adventure as if it were as simple and common as going to the mall.

"So," we hear you say, "that is awfully reminiscent of what you told us about traditional fantasy back in chapter 5."

"Aha!" we counter. "You *are* learning . . . and you are making important connections. And you're 100 percent right!" The principal difference between the two is that stories in traditional fantasy were handed down from the oral tradition; modern fantasy was not. Further, modern fantasy stories have known authors—in fact, most of them are still living. Of course, they may still have many of the same trappings as a good old Grimm fairy tale, but upon close examination, you'll see a difference.

Cover from **The Swan's Gift,** Text © 1995 by Brenda Seabrooke; Illustrations © 1995 by Wenhai Ma. Reproduced by permission of the publisher Candlewick Press Inc., Cambridge, MA.

As you read through this chapter and further through the genre, you will note over and again how much modern and traditional fantasy are alike. In fact, at times you will be so convinced of the traditional nature of many of these tales that you'll wonder if they are modern or simply some of the traditional stories you missed as a child. The treatment the author, illustrator, and book designer give the book may have much to contribute to this confusion. On initially looking at Brenda Seabrooke's **The Swan's Gift,** for example, you might be convinced that this is the retelling of a traditional tale. A poor farmer, whose crops have failed, goes out on a winter's day to shoot game for his starving family. He comes upon a swan floating in the middle of a pond whose "stark white feathers gleamed against the dark water." But he cannot bring himself to shoot it. He is rewarded for his goodness when the swan flies up overhead for, as the drops of water are shed from his wing feathers, they hit the snow and freeze into diamonds. He, of course, collects them and is then able to save his family. The story, the accompanying warm watercolor illustrations, and the overall design of the book duplicate the traditional feel of a story handed down orally, but Seabrooke's story is an original, modern story.

By this chapter's end you, too, will be able to identify the basic motifs of modern fantasy and make an intelligent approximation as to which category this tale, or any other tale for that matter, fits.

▼▼▼▼▼▼▼
The Truth in Fantasy—A Metaphor for Life

Before we go any further, we want to add one more point regarding fantasy that is of particular importance in understanding and appreciating the genre: The psychological power of fantasy has been well documented by Bettelheim (1976), as we noted in Chapter 5 on traditional fantasy. Human development specialist Charles A. Smith goes on to support the significance of story, quite often fantasy, and, in his book *From Wonder to Wisdom* (1989), he provides concrete examples of hundreds of books that help build character concepts such as courage, kindness, and coming to terms with grief. In the end, we agree with Susan Cooper (1981) when she states that "fantasy is the metaphor through which we discover ourselves" (p. 16). So, first, let's investigate the nature of metaphor and how that fits into the fantasy picture.

Webster defines *metaphor* as "a figure of speech containing an implied comparison." At its most basic level, all language is the mere representation of "the stuff of our lives"—the objects we possess (or want to possess), our actions, our emotions, and the like. Taken quite globally, though, all language can be viewed as metaphor, can't it? We give a real object a name, which is essentially a metaphor. In your hands, for instance, you hold this book. But the label we, in the English-speaking world, have attached to "book" is only our metaphorical representation for the object. Each culture, of course, attaches its own verbal, and often, written representations for all of these things in our lives.

Now, if we take the concept of metaphor up a notch in sophistication, then we come to the kind of metaphors and similes we studied in our high school English classes. (You remember . . . a metaphor is the comparison of two unlike objects, and a simile does the same thing using "like" or "as.") Every day, we use metaphorical expressions such as "The project went *smooth as silk*" and "The small fifth-grader was *as strong as an ox.*" Though a bit bland and clichéd, these are the kind of metaphors (actually *similes* in this case) we are talking about. Take, for example, the refreshing metaphor Laurence Yep uses in his ***Dragon of the Lost Sea,*** which is one of the text set novels we list in the chapter opener. Yep begins the third chapter with "The moon rose bright and clear that night, slipping through the barred window and *spilling across the floor in a long, striped rectangle almost like a tiger's pelt.*" Using this vivid figure of speech makes that image jump into life, doesn't it? Here is another description, this time of a pit dragon named Blood Brother, in Jane Yolen's book ***Dragon's Blood.*** She states, "his color was strong, and *his scales, when clean, had the sheen and polish of hundreds of small rainbow mirrors.*" When we read this, it conjured up the iridescent colors illustrator Trina Schart Hyman gives to her own dragon as it rears back, fiery-breathed and poised, ready to strike in Margaret Hodges's ***St. George and the Dragon.***

These kinds of expressions, Mr. Webster continues, are comparisons "in which a word or phrase ordinarily and primarily used of one thing is applied to another." Used like this, metaphors and similes clarify and cement images in the reader's mind far more substantially than mere descriptions.

Now, this notion raises us to yet another plane when thinking about metaphor that relates specifically to fantasy. Sad to say, some adults, in fact many adults, categorically dismiss all fantasy point blank, whether it be traditional fantasy, modern fantasy, or science fiction. These naysayers would say fantasy is nothing more than peripheral fluff. "It's simply too whimsical," they interject; "we want our young people's reading to be grounded firmly in reality." However, these adults miss the point totally. Good fantasy actually tells the truth about life. It clarifies the human condition and

Illustration from ***Saint George and the Dragon,*** by Margaret Hodges. Illustration copyright © 1984 by Trina Schart Hyman. By permission of Little, Brown and Company.

captures the essence of our deepest emotions, dreams, hopes, and fears. And, quite frankly, if fantasy, both traditional and modern, does not do these things, it fails.

Fantasy casts light on the realities of life in much the same way a metaphor illustrates truth in our language. On the evening news and in daily papers, the language of fantasy in the form of metaphor is commonplace. Consider the following: "County medics *see light at the end of the tunnel.*" "Lawmakers *torpedo* peace plan." "During the inquiry, the congressman *played his cards close to his vest.*" How can news writers get away with such wild statements when no tunnel was anywhere near the county medics, the lawmakers did not use a torpedo on the peace plan, and no cards were evident at the congressional inquiry? The answer is that metaphor is an acceptable way of enhancing communication. In its broad definition, metaphor is figurative language that strengthens writing in at least three ways:

1. *Metaphor speeds understanding.* Metaphor makes the abstract become concrete by introducing an image, resulting in quicker comprehension of a situation. "County medics are confident their current troubles will be resolved in the near future" describes the situation adequately, but using the metaphor of the tunnel introduces the idea more quickly and with more power.

2. *Metaphor creates interest.* No one misunderstands "Lawmakers vote against peace plan," but "Lawmakers torpedo peace plan" is more precise, richer, and consequently more interesting. The image of "torpedo" makes the action more deliberate and more vigorous.

3. *Metaphor adds emotional appeal.* With the additional layer of meaning introduced by metaphor, the message goes beyond the intellect to act upon the emotions. Without the metaphor, we know the congressman involved in the inquiry was secretive and careful in his responses. The metaphor stirs the emotions with suggestions of "game playing," "calculating," and "intense personal interest."

Yet metaphor is more than the sum of these parts. Simply stated, it involves the reader more readily with the story or message, allowing for quicker learning, more precise understanding, and longer retention because of the images used. And fantasy, which is a large, worked-out metaphor, illuminates the truths about life in the same way. Children can read directly in other genres about friendship, sacrifice, selfishness, the fear of death, and death itself, but the insight is somehow more meaningful when shown metaphorically.

Take the quintessential animal fantasy **Charlotte's Web,** written by E. B. White. Every single one of those characteristics is portrayed clearly, concisely, and convincingly through the lives of Wilbur the pig, Templeton the rat, and Charlotte the spider. Because Charlotte is a spider, she can embody all selflessness without losing credibility. On the other hand, if a character in realistic fiction were dedicated completely to doing good and had no flaw or foible, he or she would not be believable.

Straightforward informational writing or realistic fiction often cannot do nearly as adequate a job in dealing with a wide range of serious and sensitive topics as can fantasy. Take, for instance, the obsession humans seem to have over youthful appearance and their great desire to want to live forever. Certainly the tremendous profits seen in the fashion, beauty, and plastic surgery industries are proof positive that we, as a people, are doing everything in our power to waylay our inevitable demise. Although the argument certainly can be made that living forever would be favorable to the alternative, the fact is that "to every thing there is a season." The earth would dangerously overpopulate if death were to cease. Further, living forever holds many unforeseen difficulties but these issues are hard to explore, even in realistic fiction. No one can honestly present the alternate view because all people from this world, including those in realistic fiction, are destined to die.

Yet the fantasy world created by Natalie Babbitt in **Tuck Everlasting** allows young Winnie Foster and the Tuck family to probe this difficult and complex concept with perfect aplomb. When readers listen vicariously to a family who has lost the ability to age or die, which is what has happened to the Tucks, new light is shed on the appropriateness of eventual death. Understanding the place of death, one of real life's greatest fears and challenges, is seen most clearly in the metaphor of fantasy.

▼▼▼▼▼▼▼

Evaluating Modern Fantasy

Besides looking for the overarching metaphor, it is important to keep an eye out for the following specific elements that help determine the quality of modern fantasy.

Rooted in Reality

Keep in mind that good modern fantasy takes the best from those original forms and gives them a fresh face using truly authentic elements. In the end, for the fantasy to work it must be, as Natalie Babbitt (1986) states, "deeply rooted in reality" (p. 2). Lloyd Alexander (1981) continues, "Storytellers, in realism or fantasy, create illusions, not clinical studies. The test of the latter is how accurately they convey specific facts. The test of illusion is how thoroughly it convinces us of its reality; how strongly it resonates in our emotions; how deeply it moves us to new feelings and new insights" (p. 4).

Author Jane Yolen related a wonderful anecdote that accents this point at the Penn State University "Children's Literature Matters" conference a number of years ago. She was working on the description of the hatching of dragon eggs for her book **Heart's Blood** and was reading it to her friend and neighbor, noted author Patricia MacLachlan. In the text, young Pit Master Jakkin and his dragon, Heart's Blood, view the hatching of a new generation of dragon.

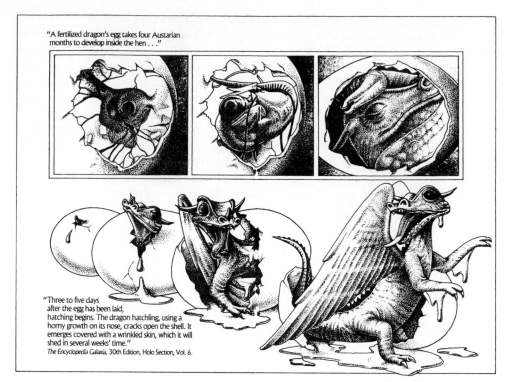

"A fertilized dragon's egg takes four Austarian months to develop inside the hen . . ."

"Three to five days after the egg has been laid, hatching begins. The dragon hatchling, using a horny growth on its nose, cracks open the shell. It emerges covered with a wrinkled skin, which it will shed in several weeks' time."
The Encyclopedia Galaxia, 30th Edition, Holo Section, Vol. 6.

From **Heart's Blood,** by Jane Yolen. Drawings by Tom McKeveny. Copyright © 1984 by Jane Yolen. Published by Dell Publishing, a division of Bantam Doubleday Dell Publishing Group, Inc. Reprinted by permission.

Jane Yolen writes books across all genres. For a listing of her work in modern fantasy, consult the database on the CD that accompanies this text.

A slight crack appeared in the egg. It jetted across the rounded side, leaving a scar-like trail that looked like an old river and its tributaries.

Heart's Blood tapped the egg once more. This time there was an unmistakable tap in return, and the egg split open into uneven halves. In the larger half lay a curled form: tiny wrinkled, the color of custard scum and covered with the remains of green-yellow birth fluids. Slowly it lifted its heavy head, and Jakkin saw a horny bump on its nose.

The dragonling stretched one front foot and then the other, then heaved itself to its feet. The eggshell rocked, and the little dragon tumbled out, landing on its nose.

When she finished reading the passage, Yolen noted the long silence at the other end of the line. MacLachlan, caught up with the description said, "Jane, I never knew dragons hatched from eggs." Jane, who was expecting a response to her writing and not necessarily the content responded, "Patty, dragons never existed." Yolen's description was so real it WAS to be believed. Such is the magic of modern fantasy.

Internal Consistency

Though the miraculous elements we see in modern fantasy may vary greatly, the quality fantasy story does not employ fantastic elements casually. In fact, fantasy is probably the most difficult genre to write because an author must create a new set of physical laws and then conform unerringly to them. Even the tiniest slip can destroy the credibility of the story. Again, Alexander (1965) recognizes the need for this sort of specialized internal consistency:

Once committed to his imaginary kingdom, the writer is not a monarch but a subject. Characters must appear plausible in their own setting, and the writer must go along with the inner logic. Happenings should have logical implications. Details should be tested for consistency. Shall animals speak? If so, do *all* animals speak? If not, then which—and how? Is it essential to the story, or lamely cute? Are there enchantments? How powerful? If an enchanter can perform such-and-such, can he not also do so-and-so? (pp. 143–144)

BOOKMARK

INTEGRATING TECHNOLOGY: ACTIVITIES USING THE WORLD WIDE WEB

There are many sites on the World Wide Web devoted to Harry Potter and author J. K. Rowling, and most of them are created and maintained by young fans. Many of these sites include interactive elements, chatrooms and message boards, creative writing, and artwork by readers. At some of these sites, students can submit their own Harry Potter–related work, which in itself is strong motivation for fans of the series to read and write. Kathleen T. Horning of the Cooperative Children's Book Center has selected and annotated some of the best of these web pages at *Harry Potter: Selected Links on the World Wide Web,* an excellent site for those who just cannot get enough of Harry Potter, and for those who want to find interesting, interactive ways to motivate students to write and dialogue in response to literature.

To find out more about using Harry Potter sites in the classroom and other activities related to the genre of fantasy on the World Wide Web, visit Chapter 6 on the companion website at **www.prenhall. com/darigan**

Modern fantasy stories are not merely a matter of make-believe, and though that suspension of disbelief must be ever present, we must hold this genre to the same basic standards that we do all the others.

Characterization

We have already noted the strong link between modern fantasy and traditional fantasy that is evidenced in the way characters are portrayed. In chapter 5, we pointed out that characters in traditional fantasy tend to be flat, actually representing archetypes symbolic of basic human traits. We find the same to be true with modern fantasy. Yet with more modern perspectives in mind, authors have the advantage of being able to add another richer, deeper dimension to their characters.

For instance, in Alma Flor Ada's **The Malachite Palace,** illustrated by Leonid Gore, we find a princess living alone and unhappily with no friends to call her own save her lady-in-waiting, her governess, and the queen. However, she can hear the laughter and shouting of the town's children outside the ornate gates of her malachite palace and, much to the disgruntlement of her elders, wishes to be with them. With the aid of a lovely yellow songbird, she finds her own inner strength, defies her caregivers, and scampers into the fields beyond the palace to be with the other children. A character *this* feisty doesn't usually occur in traditional fantasy and is more a function of our contemporary mores and values. Other such examples in modern fantasy are seen in Marcia Vaughan's **Whistling Dixie** and Ellen Jackson's **Cinder Edna.** The former finds young Dixie wheedling her mother any way she can to keep all the preposterous pets she finds in the Hokey Pokey Swamp, and the latter describes the straight-thinking, practical Edna, neighbor to Cinderella who prospers by being thrifty and working hard.

In the fantasy novel, however, we find quite round characters who must operate, as we said earlier, within the boundaries of their own fantastic world but who do so with complete believability. Readers won't easily put up with a wand to magically change or enlighten the character; they crave the adventure and journey the main character must take and will believe the character only if he or she develops logically over time. Consider the trials and tribulations young Harry must endure as he winds his way through the Hogwarts School of Witchcraft and Wizardry in J. K. Rowling's **Harry Potter and the Sorcerer's Stone.** Nothing happens easily in this or any of the subsequent books in the series. We get to know and love Harry, Hermione, and Hagrid as much as we get to know and dislike Uncle Vernon, Aunt Petunia, and Dudley. But it is the way Rowling develops these characters that makes us believe them.

- Metaphor: Does this book act as a metaphor for life and illustrate its truths more clearly?
- Rooted in reality: Does the reality of the book ring true? Is it believable?
- Internal consistency: Are the settings and events throughout the book consistent and believable?
- Characterization: In a picture book, does the character represent a universal value? Does he or she go beyond being simply flat and one-dimensional? In a novel, is the character well developed and believable?
- Examination of universal truths: Are certain universal truths alluded to in this book? Does the book make you consider life or world issues in a new way?

Modern Fantasy Examines the Universal Truths

Often we find the underlying theme in modern fantasy to be an examination of the basic issues of the human condition. Certainly Robert O'Brien, in his classic ***Mrs. Frisby and the Rats of NIMH,*** and daughter, Jane Leslie Conly, in her sequel ***Rasco and the Rats of NIMH,*** address societal issues, not the least of which are protecting the environment, taking care of your fellow human, and the necessity to interact peacefully.

Avi levels a similar indictment on society in his series called the Tales from Dimwood Forest. Beginning with his first book, ***Poppy,*** a young deer mouse finds she must deal with the big bully Mr. Ocax, the owl, who has proclaimed himself king of Dimwood Forest. Under the guise that he is protecting one and all from the horrible porcupines, Mr. Ocax lords power over all the animals. It is not until Poppy meets up with Ereth, the curmudgeonly old porcupine, that she discovers what is real and true. This novelized fable acts as an allegory to our own predicament in the real world.

ALTERNATE TEXT SET

Tales from Dimwood Forest by Avi

Poppy	*Ragweed*
Poppy and Rye	*Ereth's Birthday*

▼▼▼▼▼▼▼

Six Basic Fantasy Motifs

Let's now take a look at the essence of modern fantasy. Even though these stories all contain one or more magical elements, some stories have a higher "fantasy quotient" than others. For example, Judi and Ron Barrett's modern classic ***Cloudy With a Chance of Meatballs*** contains one basic magical element in its setting having its own *peculiar situation:* You see, it just so happens that in the land of Chewandswallow, by most standards, everything was pretty normal—except for the fact that at breakfast, lunch, and dinner everything the people ate came down from the sky. Foods like hamburgers, mashed potatoes, pancakes, and hot dogs all rained down on the grateful residents. That is, until the weather "took a turn for the worse." One day, it poured nothing but Gorgonzola cheese and then the next, broccoli—overcooked. When the exaggeration used in this book reaches its climax, the people of Chewandswallow are forced to sail to another friendly town and set up life anew. The inclusion of this one magical element makes this enjoyable book a prime example of a simple modern fantasy.

For a book at the other end of the spectrum where multiple magical elements are involved, we should consider Hans Christian Andersen's classic, *The Snow Queen.* One of our favorite editions of this modern tale is the translation by Naomi Lewis that is hauntingly illustrated by Angela Barrett and quite handsomely produced by Candlewick Press of Cambridge, Massachusetts. In this complex story, we find that young Kay is missing from the village but his best friend, Gerta, is going in search of him. After days, months, and finally years, and with the assistance of a variety of animals and humans, Gerta finally locates him in the Ice Palace in Lapland, where everything is cold and empty and loveless. The Snow Queen has left for the warm lands and Kay is alone. However, before she departs, the queen kisses "away his shivering" and leaves him with a heart that is "little more than a lump of ice." It is Gerta's outpouring of human emotion and the hot tears she weeps that warm and eventually melt Kay's ice heart. The two are then able to escape the clutches of the Snow Queen and return home to "summer, warm delightful summer." In this tale, magic abounds—animals and inanimate objects talk, we are transported to the imaginary world of the Ice Palace, we get a heavy dose of that ongoing fight between good and evil, and we follow Gerta on a classic hero journey. As opposed to *Cloudy With a Chance of Meatballs,* this tale calculates at the top of the scale.

Reprinted with the permission of Atheneum Books for Young Readers, an imprint of Simon & Schuster Children's Publishing Division from *Cloudy With a Chance of Meatballs,* by Judi Barrett, illustrated by Ron Barrett. Drawings copyright © 1978 Ron Barrett.

Now, there are some very basic reasons why these and other tales are considered fantasy. Any guesses?

Well, obviously the biggest consideration in what makes fantasy . . . well, *fantasy* is the fact that *magic* is at work. Magic is the key. But more specifically, as you read further in this genre and begin to scrutinize its distinct characteristics, you should begin to see patterns emerge. For instance, you will note that events and objects seem to cluster themselves in groups of three. Further, you will see unworldly transformations begin to take place—animals can take human form and humans, somehow, can take the shape of animals. You will also begin to notice that specific character types begin to pop up over and over again—character types like wicked stepmothers, trolls, the lazy (or wise) younger brothers, and fairy godmothers.

In the jargon of folk literature, these "patterns" are known as *motifs.* Folklorists are at odds on their view of motifs, at least in regard to what they are and how many there are. At one end of the spectrum there is Stith Thompson, who published his *Motif-index of Folk Literature* (1932), listing hundreds of motifs basic to all folk and fairy tales. For example, motif number R221 is listed as the "flight from the ball." We think there is no better reference for the scholar of folklore, but for classroom use, we like to defer to Linda Lee Madsen (1976) who, in her thesis work, determined that there are six basic fantasy motifs to be considered (pp. 76–77):

1. magic
2. other worlds

3. good versus evil
4. heroism and the hero's quest
5. special character types
6. fantastic objects

So if we look at that fantasy quotient we noted earlier, tales with only one or two of these fantasy motifs can been labeled "low fantasy" (Woolsey, 1989, p. 112) or "fanciful tales" (Arbuthnot, 1952, p. 250). We, however, like to think of them as "light fantasy," which is our own mediation between the pejorative "low" and whimsical implied in "fanciful." Those stories steeped in *all* six motifs would be considered examples of modern high fantasy.

Next we look at each of these motifs more closely, describing each in greater detail, and then give you some specific examples of literary folk and fairy tales, fantasy novels, and science fiction for each. This will help you understand the genre better, which, of course, will transfer to the kids in your class. A better understanding of the motifs will aid you in choosing books appropriate for your curricular needs, and finally, and probably most importantly, will help you and your students enjoy and appreciate the finer points of this incredible genre.

Magic

Broadly viewed, magic is the most common and basic of elements in fantasy literature. In fact, each of the other five motifs are tinged by magic to one degree or another. Magic is often a part of the setting, thus explaining otherwise unexplainable events. For example, in one of the text set books we recommend at the beginning of the chapter, Patricia Wrede's *Searching for Dragons,* the setting of the Enchanted Forest is replete with magic. King Mendanbar is monarch over this realm and, in his own words states, "Magic makes things much simpler." Well, at least to a point. This particular forest had quite a few peculiar rules of its own and, worse yet, things were always shifting. For instance, Mendanbar found that "if he drank from the wrong stream and got turned into a rabbit . . . he would have just as much trouble getting back to normal as anyone else." He recollected getting rid of donkey ears when he was 8 years old just for eating the wrong salad and remembered what a royal pain that had been. But the magic, of course, had certain advantages as well. When Mendanbar had to go anywhere quickly or when things went awry, all he had to do was reach out and gather a "handful of magic" from an invisible network that crisscrossed the forest. Wrede describes:

> It felt a lot like taking hold of a handful of thin cords, except that the cords were invisible, floating in the air, and made his palms tingle when he touched them. And, of course, each cord was actually a piece of solid magic that he could use to cast a spell if he wanted. In fact, he had to concentrate hard to *keep* from casting a spell or two with all that magic crammed together in his hands.

But beyond setting, magic is just as easily bestowed on people, animals, and objects. When Mendanbar attempts to adjust things after discovering a newly devastated portion of the forest destroyed by a dragon, he wipes his hands on his shirt and the sweat from his brow and hears:

> "Are you quite finished?" said a voice from a tree above his head.
> Mendanbar looked up and saw a fat gray squirrel sitting on a branch, staring down at him with disapproval.
> "I think so," Mendanbar said. "For the time being, anyway."
> "For the time being?" the squirrel said indignantly. "What kind of an answer is that? Not useful, that's what I call it, not useful at all . . . "

Where else but in fantasy can a self-respecting squirrel chew out his sovereign? But poor Mendanbar gets it from every angle. Willin, his elderly elf steward, is forever keeping him on his toes with lists as long as the elf is tall reminding him of protocol and imperial formalities. Even the carved wooden gargoyle in his castle study offers curmudgeonly advice. That, of course, is nothing compared to his meeting the headstrong Princess Cimorene, whom we meet in the first book in the series, *Dealing with Dragons.*

Patricia C. Wrede's Enchanted Forest Chronicles are unique, contemporary, old and other-worldly all in one breath. We, as readers, are kept on our toes at every turn, never quite sure whether we are in medieval times or contemporary times—with a medieval edge. But no matter; we are so completely and thoroughly immersed in the saga the difference becomes inconsequential.

In contrast to the abundance of magic in the Wrede quartet, we return to the classic *Charlotte's Web,* which is equally part of the genre, but where the only hint of magic is the ability the barnyard animals have to think, speak, and act like humans. In fact, this is the only one of the six motifs that appears in the book.

DID YOU KNOW?

The books in the Enchanted Forest Chronicles are arranged in order as we show them here, and it is best to read them that way. However, each can be read as a stand-alone book and enjoyed that way, too. In fact, Wrede wrote book number four, *Talking to Dragons,* first and then at the advice of her editor, Jane Yolen, wrote the other three books as prequels.

Other Worlds or Secondary Worlds

In much of fantasy, a special geography or universe is established, a place wherein magic can freely operate. Sometimes these worlds are simply long, long ago. Others are sophisticated societies where maps are necessary for reference—don't you just love the maps? Many years ago, Jim and Mike heard that Dan had neglected his major fantasy responsibility and not read the entire series of Lloyd Alexander's Prydain Chronicles. Dan whined, "Hey, I read the first two years ago in my Children's Lit class—but I had so many other books to read I really couldn't think about it. . . ."

"Well, Danny Boy, if you want to be part of this book, you HAD BETTER read all five!" was their pointed response. Well, over the course of the next two weeks, he joyfully read the entire series from stem to stern. It was an experience that absolutely and categorically cemented his love for Lloyd and his writing in particular and for high fantasy in general . . . forever. He learned so much about life from Taran—maxims that he still sets as life's standards.

But, as they were talking about the series, he said, "I wish there was some sort of map for Prydain. I have to admit, at times I got kinda lost."

"Maps?" these two Alexander scholars shouted in unison. "There's a map at the beginning of each book—what, are you blind?" Well, unfortunately, we discovered that in the Dell Yearling paperback version of these marvelous tales, the editorial decision had been made to eliminate the maps, thereby robbing the child and adult reader of that resource. The solution to this problem? We suggest you march right over to Mr. Xerox and, with a hardcover edition in hand—for it does still have the map in the front of each of the five books—copy and distribute it to your classes! It's legal. We've checked!

The worlds created by fantasy authors, exactly like Alexander does in Prydain, are just the sorts of other worlds we're talking about—they are *almost* recognizable as the one we know but operate with a different set of governing rules. Other well-known fantasy worlds you may be familiar with include the land of Oz that L. Frank Baum created in

Introducing:

If everybody in the class is going to read one or all of the Alexander books, you may want to make a bulletin-board-sized map of the Land of Prydain for all the kids to refer to. First, make a photocopy of the map of the Land of Prydain (found in the front of the hardcover edition only) then turn it into an overhead transparency. By projecting that image onto a wall covered with white butcher paper, you can have a few children in your class use wide-lined magic markers to "draw the map," placing it in gigantic proportions. We're reasonably certain Evaline Ness, who did the originals, would approve.

TEACHING IDEAS

To find out more about The Mythopoeic Society and other sources of information about fantasy on the World Wide Web, visit Chapter 6 on the companion website at **www.prenhall.com/darigan**

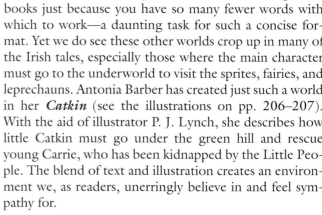

BOOKMARK

INTEGRATING TECHNOLOGY: PUBLISHERS ON THE WORLD WIDE WEB

The Mythopoeic Society is a nonprofit international literary and educational organization for the study, discussion, and enjoyment of fantasy and mythic literature, especially the works of J. R. R. Tolkien, C. S. Lewis, and Charles Williams. The site includes information on annual Mythopoeic Conferences, Discussion Groups, the Mythopoeic Awards, three periodical publications, and a Links page for the fields of science fiction and fantasy literature, mythic studies, and folklore. A great resource for those interested in Tolkien, C. S. Lewis, Arthurian studies, and fantasy in general.

The Wonderful Wizard of Oz. Further, there is Middle Earth, which J. R. R. Tolkien constructed in *The Hobbit,* Narnia, the setting for *The Lion, the Witch, and the Wardrobe,* by C. S. Lewis, and Neverland, where *Peter Pan,* by J. M. Barrie, lives.

A more recent world created by story spinner Sid Hite is found in his *Answer My Prayer.* Hite's nation of Korasan, just to the north and west of the Brillian Sea, is the setting for a marvelous yarn that even reaches into the heavens for one of its characters. Lydia Swain, a young girl who seeks aid from the angels, is assigned the lazy sleepyhead, Ebol, to answer her prayer. The love story turns into a political and potentially ecological fracas as the local politicos attempt to clear the land of the beautiful jeefwood forests. To the end, we believe in this land and though contemporary, it maintains an old-world feel of a more simple time gone by.

Other-world settings are a bit hard to do in picture books just because you have so many fewer words with which to work—a daunting task for such a concise format. Yet we do see these other worlds crop up in many of the Irish tales, especially those where the main character must go to the underworld to visit the sprites, fairies, and leprechauns. Antonia Barber has created just such a world in her *Catkin* (see the illustrations on pp. 206–207). With the aid of illustrator P. J. Lynch, she describes how little Catkin must go under the green hill and rescue young Carrie, who has been kidnapped by the Little People. The blend of text and illustration creates an environment we, as readers, unerringly believe in and feel sympathy for.

Good Versus Evil

The ancient, archetypal theme of good versus evil is what myth is all about, and modern fantasy stories often have a strong mythological base. "Fantasies are concerned with how good and evil manifest themselves in individuals" (Madsen 1976, p. 49). This basic theme, of course, gives rise to the conflict in a story, and, once again, without conflict there is no story. Fantasy readers usually have no trouble aligning characters on the sides of light and dark, because fantasy characters typically are not fence sitters. Such is the case in Audrey Wood's *Heckedy Peg.* "Down the dusty road

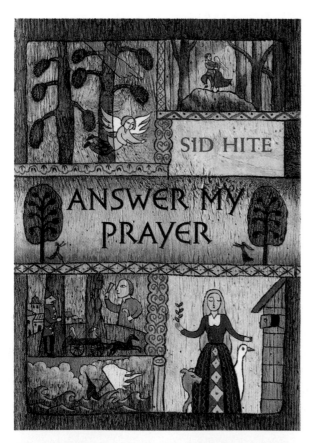

Cover from **Answer My Prayer,** by Sid Hite, jacket illustration by Stefano Vitale. Text copyright © 1995 by Sid Hite; jacket illustration copyright © 1995 by Stefano Vitale. Published by Henry Holt and Company, Inc. Reprinted by permission of the publisher.

and far away, a poor mother once lived with her seven children, Monday, Tuesday, Wednesday, Thursday, Friday, Saturday, and Sunday"—as you would expect, these are the "good guys." The mom leaves for the market but sternly admonishes, "don't let a stranger in and don't touch fire."

As you will notice in the cover illustration (see p. 208), the witch, Heckedy Peg, rumbles across the bridge (see her in the window?) and pays a visit on the unsuspecting, fun-loving children. The obvious foreshadowing noted earlier finds the witch entering the house, capturing the children, and turning them into food. Interrupting her feast at just the right moment, however, the mother returns and, with the aid of a friendly little bird and her own ingenuity, is able to confound the witch, return her children to normal, and chase off the witch once and for all. Don Wood's luscious oil paintings create a dark, foreboding mood that makes this book a perfect example of good versus evil in picture book fantasy form.

Now, hang onto that notion of good versus evil and let us explain something very important about fantasy: As we have said many times before, where narrative is concerned there has to be conflict, and this is particularly true in fantasy. Without conflict there would be no story. But, don't be fooled into thinking that you can equate "good and bad" as being the same as the fantasy motif of "good versus evil."

Here is an example of a book that is not modern fantasy but clearly portrays the classic struggle of good and bad as it relates to children. In Steven Kellogg's picture storybook **Best Friends,** we see that Kathy, the main character, is at odds with her best friend, Louise Jenkins. Louise has gone away to summer camp and has the *audacity* to have a wonderful time and make all sorts of new friends. Kathy is crestfallen. In anger and frustration, she wishes "a volcanic eruption would blow [the camp at] Pine Cone Peak into pebbles." Her mother tells her not to be jealous. But when her new neighbor's dog, Sarah, has puppies, Kathy says she will "keep all of them" so her *ex*-friend, Louise, can't have any. Her entire attitude and behavior could be characterized as "bad," but that is a far cry from "evil."

But within the context of fantasy, and here we are usually referring to high fantasy, the ultimate personification of "bad" is evil. It is said that somewhere inside us we all possess a dark side, the part of us that often remains hidden and dormant. Ursula LeGuin (1979) refers to it as "the shadow [that] is on the other side of our psyche, the dark brother of the conscious mind . . . we meet it in our dreams, as sister, brother, friend, beast, monster, enemy, guide. It is all we don't want to, can't, admit into our conscious self, all the qualities and tendencies within us which have been repressed, denied, or not used" (pp. 53–54). It is to this side, which we all hate to admit we possess, that fantasy speaks. The beauty of this genre is that generally by book's end (or series's end), the dark is overcome and defeated.

Certainly Susan Cooper's **The Dark Is Rising** and the books in the series that surround it are prime examples of this battle between good and evil. In this, the second book, we find that young Will Stanton is the last of the Old Ones, an immortal whose task it is to stave off the forces of evil or, as Cooper refers to it, the Dark. Will must find the six Signs of Life to fend off evil. It is not until the final book in the series, **Silver on the Tree,** that Will and the Welsh boy, Bran, vanquish the Dark for good. Here are the five books in the series, and the order in which they appeared:

1. *Over Sea, Under Stone* (1965)
2. *The Dark Is Rising* (1973)
3. *Greenwitch* (1974)
4. *The Grey King* (1975)
5. *Silver on the Tree* (1977)

Other noteworthy books that embody this motif of good versus evil are Philip Pullman's haunting **Clockwork: Or All Wound Up,** Jane Yolen's **Wizard's Hall** and, of course, J. K. Rowling's series beginning with **Harry Potter and the Sorcerer's Stone.**

DID YOU KNOW?

You may be interested to know that Don Wood always uses live models for the characters he paints. In fact, when a book is ready to be illustrated, he and his wife, Audrey, usually have a party, invite all their friends, and then set up each scene with all the settings and costumes provided. They ran into a bit of trouble, though, when attempting to find the right woman to play the part for the witch, Heckedy Peg. Audrey was the model for the mother. But, naturally, no other woman wanted to pose for this witch's heinous role . . . and rightly so. She is, indeed, a nasty character. Guess who ended up as Heckedy Peg? You can look on the back dust jacket and find the answer—only with a beard. It turned out to be Don, himself.

Heroism and the Hero's Quest

Natalie Babbitt (1987), drawing upon the writings of mythologist Joseph Campbell (1968) in his book *The Hero With a Thousand Faces,* explains that the hero's quest will always follow an age-old pattern that has become the backbone of many of today's fantasy stories. This "hero's round" is a circular journey, ending where it began. It is a time-honored template for various types of stories, though the hero's quest originated in traditional fantasy. The following six elements are drawn from Babbitt's interpretation of the most common structure of the hero's quest.

    1. *The hero is called to adventure by some sort of herald.* In Lloyd Alexander's first book in the Prydain Chronicles, **The Book of Three,** Taran is lured to adventure by Hen Wen, a magical pig whom he follows on a wild chase, much the same way Alice follows the white rabbit in Lewis Carroll's **Alice's Adventures in Wonderland.** Heralds from other stories include Gandalf in J. R. R. Tolkien's **The Hobbit,** the little dog, Toto, in L. Frank Baum's **The Wonderful Wizard of Oz,** and Mr. Tumnus in C. S. Lewis's **The Lion, the Witch, and the Wardrobe.**

    2. *The hero crosses the threshold into the other world or into a place that is no longer safe and secure.* The hero leaves a place of relative safety and enters a world of danger.

Sometimes he or she will pass from the familiar modern world into a forbidding secondary world, as do the children in ***The Lion, the Witch, and the Wardrobe,*** who pass through the magical wardrobe into the land of Narnia, and Dorothy in ***The Wonderful Wizard of Oz.*** In some stories, however, the hero already lives in an imaginary kingdom, as does Bilbo Baggins in ***The Hobbit,*** and he is compelled to leave his hearth and home to undertake a perilous journey.

   3. *The hero must survive various trials in the new environment.* Heroes often face both physical hardship and emotional setbacks. They may suffer the pain of long treks through bitter winter weather or the pain of having dear friends relinquish their lives for a noble cause. They likely will be driven to examine their own hearts. The quest becomes the hero's refining fire. The smith, Hevydd, tells Taran in ***Taran Wanderer,*** "Life's a forge! . . . Yes, and hammer and anvil, too! You'll be roasted, smelted, and pounded and you'll scarce know what's happening to you. But stand boldly to it! Metal's worthless till it's shaped and tempered!"

   4. *The hero is assisted by a protective figure.* Protective figures provide a sense of security in a tension-filled world. Older, wiser, and sometimes more powerful, the protective figure may serve as the hero's mentor. Readers will identify Dallben in The Prydain Chronicles, Gandalf in ***The Hobbit,*** Glinda, the Good Witch of the North, in ***The***

Cover from **Heckedy Peg,** by Audrey Wood, illustrated by Don Wood. Text copyright © 1987 by Audrey Wood. Jacket illustration copyright © 1987 by Don Wood. Published by Harcourt Brace & Company. Reprinted by permission.

Wonderful Wizard of Oz, and Aslan in **The Lion, the Witch, and the Wardrobe** as protective figures.

5. *The hero matures, becoming a "whole person."* Did Edmund change in **The Lion, the Witch, and the Wardrobe**? How about Dorothy in **The Wonderful Wizard of Oz**? Both of these characters matured significantly during the course of their quests. Taran from the Prydain books grows from a foolish boy to a man worthy of ascending to the High Kingship of Prydain. The hero motif involves the age-old rites-of-passage theme, wherein the young are initiated into the ranks of adulthood.

6. *The hero returns home.* This step completes the hero's round. In each Prydain book, Taran returns to his home on Dallben's farm, and then symbolically finds "home" when he discovers his true destiny in the final book, **The High King.** In all of the high fantasy novels we discuss in this section, every young hero returns home as his or her quest draws to an end.

Special Character Types

Fantasies may include characters who come either from our legendary past or from an author's vivid imagination. These characters are rarely typical human beings. Characters from our legendary past often hail from traditional tales and include fairies, pixies, giants, wicked witches, ogres, vampires, wizards, dwarfs, and elves.

Legendary Celtic characters are often portrayed as seals and merfolk. Seals who shed their skins when they come on land and take human form are known as *selkies.* Mermen and mermaids are also peppered throughout traditional Irish and Scottish tales. Modern picture book fantasy, original tales based on these special character types, are ripe for comparison and worthy of spending time making comparison charts. Here is a beginning list of these tales:

ALTERNATE TEXT SET

"Selkie Books"

Read Aloud

"Mrs. Fitzgerald the Merrow" in *A Treasury of Mermaids,* by Shirley Climo

Text Set

The Seal Prince, by Sheila MacGill-Callahan, illustrated by Kris Waldherr

Selkie, written and illustrated by Gillian McClure

Nicholas Pipe, by Robert D. San Souci, illustrated by David Shannon

Greyling, by Jane Yolen, illustrated by David Ray

The Seal Mother, written and illustrated by Mordicai Gerstein

Some special character types created in recent years by fantasy authors have become quite well known, such as Tolkien's hobbits, who appear in the Lord of the Rings trilogy. Another character type not so well known but nonetheless interesting has been created by multitalented author Avi. Montmers, as he calls them, are small, rabbit-like animals who have long, jackrabbit-like ears, plump bodies covered with short, rough, and curly hair, large flat feet, and skinny legs and appear in his book *Perloo the Bold.* Perloo, a mild-mannered scholarly type of Montmer, becomes the chosen one to succeed Jolaine the Good as leader against the conniving of her heir-apparent and son, Berwig the Big. Clear descriptions of these creatures, as well as a deep sense of who they are and why they act as they do, are hallmarks in this high-action book of good versus evil.

One final character type that creeps up in fantasy and one we alluded to earlier in the book *Catkin* is that of the dislocated changeling—a wee babe or child who is taken from its own home and often transformed. Remember how Carrie was kidnapped by the Little Folk and taken to their world below? Well, in Eloise McGraw's *The Moorchild,* we meet Saaski, as she is called by her mortal "parents," and though she is the product of both humans and the Folk, she has been rejected from the Mound and placed in the care of humans. Though a difficult child growing up, she attempts to make her way among those of the village who are unlike her and who scorn and taunt her. This captivating story presents a clear image of this character type and, acting as a potential metaphor for those children who feel much the same way, will lead to rich discussions about being "different." A gentle way to introduce this book, by the way, would be to read aloud Jane Yolen's *Child of Faerie, Child of Earth,* illustrated by Jane Dyer. Here, in lovely rhymed meter, Yolen describes a faerie and a mortal who meet but realize their two worlds are much too different for either to join the other. In the end, they remain fast friends and visit from time to time while staying in their respective worlds.

Reprinted with the permission of Margaret K. McElderry Books, an imprint of Simon & Schuster Children's Publishing Division from *The Moorchild,* by Eloise McGraw. Jacket illustration copyright © 1996 Eloise McGraw.

Fantastic Objects

Characters in fantasy stories often employ magical props to accomplish their heroic or evil deeds. These objects, such as magic cloaks, swords, staffs, cauldrons, and mirrors, are imbued with power. Some well-known props are Dorothy's pearl slippers in *The Wonderful Wizard of Oz,* the White Witch's wand in *The Lion, the Witch, and the Wardrobe,* and the dreadful ring that falls into Bilbo Baggin's hands in *The Hobbit.* More recently, Philip Pullman has introduced a mysterious and rare, compass-like scientific instrument known as an "Alethiometer," which can be used to answer any question in his stunning fantasy novel *The Golden Compass (His Dark Materials).*

On a far lighter note, Hagrid, the gentle giant and friend in *Harry Potter and the Sorcerer's Stone,* takes the young first-year student at Hogwart's School of Witchcraft and Wizardry shopping for necessary supplies, a few of which are, indeed, fantastic. They include: one wand, one cauldron (pewter, standard size 2)—of course—along with "an owl OR a cat OR a toad." Of course, parents are reminded "THAT FIRST YEARS ARE NOT ALLOWED THEIR OWN BROOMSTICKS." These magic objects only set the stage for the rest of the books, and the whole broomstick issue becomes extraordinarily important later in the book when Harry becomes a master at flying and the star of the Hogwart's Quidditch team.

Front and back cover from ***Child of Faerie, Child of Earth*** by Jane Yolen, illustrated by Jane Dyer. Text copyright © 1997 by Jane Yolen; illustrations copyright © 1997 by Jane Dyer. Published by Little, Brown and Company. Reprinted by permission of the publisher.

Don't think that magical and fantastic objects are limited to novels; picture books, too, hold some interesting gems. Take, for example, the original tale by Teresa Bateman entitled ***The Ring of Truth,*** which has been deftly illustrated in the Celtic fashion by Omar Rayyan. Patrick O'Kelley is certainly full o' the blarney, so much so that when a contest is announced in County Donegal, it seems to one and all that Patrick would be the likely winner. However, the king of the leprechauns thinks differently about this upstart boaster. He tricks Patrick into wearing an emerald ring that compels him to tell only the truth. However, the truth is that when Patrick divulges what really happened to him, it sounds to the judges more outrageous than his usual blarney and he wins the contest anyway.

Another interesting object of magic is found in Laura Krauss Melmed's ***Prince Nautilus.*** When Fiona, daydreaming on the seashore, finds a "perfect milk-white spiral" seashell and holds it up to her ear, she is surprised to hear the voice of a prince cry out. Telling his story of how an evil wizard reduced him to the size of a minnow and trapped him inside the shell, he begs her to follow his directions so as to break the spell. In this variant on the Cinderella theme, Fiona's lazy sister, Columbine, whose heart was "as cold as kelp," acts in selfish ways and, of course, loses the chance to marry the prince. By the way, one of the side benefits of the modern tale is that when Nautilus finally is released from his curse and asks Fiona for her hand in marriage, she *turns him down*! You don't see that happening in a traditional tale, now, do you? Fiona honestly states, "Prince Nautilus, I cannot marry you now. For years I have longed to see the wide world and its wonders. After this taste of adventure, I am hungry for more." The next morning they set sail, Fiona, Nautilus, and Fiona's father, for bold adventure "and what they found would quite astound—but that's another tale!" How refreshing!

In summary, some books operate strongly in only one of these six motifs, such as ***The Wind in the Willows,*** by Kenneth Grahame, and ***Charlotte's Web,*** where talking animals qualify as the only "magic." Then there is ***Tuck Everlasting,*** by Natalie Babbit, which arguably incorporates four of the six motifs: magic, good vs. evil, the hero's round, and fantastic objects. On the other hand, L. Frank Baum's ***The Wonderful Wizard of Oz*** and J. K. Rowling's ***Harry Potter and the Sorcerer's Stone*** operate in all six

of the motifs and thus can be classified as a high fantasy. So you see why we like the definition Madsen puts forward: It makes it very simple to determine where a book might be placed on the low/high fantasy spectrum.

▼▼▼▼▼▼▼
Categories of Modern Fantasy

As with most of the literary genres in children's literature, you may find it hard to peg a book as belonging in one single category. By now you've undoubtedly noticed the caution we throw out in virtually every chapter about how a book may, at first, seem to fit into one category, only to turn out later that certain features and considerations make it seem to fit into another. Such is decidedly the case with modern fantasy. So, with that bit of information, we are going to begin by dividing the genre into three main categories: literary folk and fairy tales, fantasy novels, and science fiction. We first give you a brief overview of each of these categories. Next we introduce and describe the major motifs that appear in modern fantasy. At the end of this section, we focus on specific ways these motifs are employed in this genre. By knowing these ideas, you can begin to make some informed choices about the books you may want to use in this genre and how you can fit them into your classroom curriculum.

Literary Folk and Fairy Tales

The category of *literary folk and fairy tales* is the one we give to the picture books in this genre that have the feel of traditional fantasy and use many of the same conventions and motifs, but that are modern with respect to their authorship. Remember we said at the beginning of the chapter that the main difference between traditional fantasy and modern fantasy is simply that the stories in traditional fantasy were handed down from the oral tradition? Modern fantasy includes original tales written with the same flavor as their antecedents but penned in modern times by authors such as Hans Christian Andersen, Jane Yolen, Bill Peet, Susan Meddaugh, David Small, and William Steig.

In the "Dealing With Dragons" text set that opens this chapter, we noted Jane Yolen's picture book ***Dove Isabeau.*** This is what we consider the perfect example of a literary folk and fairy tale. Set "once upon a time," the story introduces us to the lovely Isabeau and her admirer, Kemp Owain. Here is a snippet of the poetic beginning: "On the cold northern shores of Craig's Cove, where the trees bear leaves only three months of the year, there stood a great stone castle with three towers. In the central tower lived a girl named Isabeau, and she was fair."

As in many of the traditional folk tales we know, we immediately have the dynamic setup of "girl meets boy," except in this case there is a subtle but noticeable difference: Yolen tells us of Isabeau's beauty, but then goes on to explain, "No one loved her more than the king's son, Kemp Owain. He had been sent beyond the sea for several years to get learning and to study the great magicks. All his boyhood he had loved Dove Isabeau; he had always looked beyond her face and gentle form, loving her for her spirit and for the fire that lay beneath the skin." Notice the shift of affection? Yolen doesn't have this character, Kemp Owain, fall in love with her beauty, so common in the traditional tales we survey in chapter 5; Kemp Owain loves her "for her spirit and for the fire that lay beneath the skin."

As in "Snow White," Isabeau's mother dies unexpectedly and Lord Darnton, her father, marries again "all too hastily." The relationship between Dove and her stepmother, who unbeknownst to all was a witch, becomes the central story arc in the book. In it, we find the witch casting a spell on the unsuspecting Isabeau who is transformed into a dragon, a mighty wyrm. Next Yolen tricks us, for she has Kemp Owain ride into the picture at just the right moment and, in a predictable fashion, sacrifices himself for Dove's sake: By allowing the wyrm to kiss him thrice, he is turned completely to stone.

Returning to her human form, Isabeau once again climbs the stairs to her stepmother's tower room where she learns that only the blood of the innocent young girl she once was will save Kemp Owain. After young Dove vanquishes the witch, who falls to the rocks below from the open tower window, Yolen cleverly solves the mystery and restores Kemp Owain as well to his human form. Owain, who delighted in Isabeau's spirit and fire "which he had always known was hidden beneath her gentle form, called her his fierce guardian, his mighty warrior, and his glorious dragon queen for all the long, happy years they ruled the kingdom together." Note how gently, yet compellingly, Yolen places her female protagonist in such a positive and powerful light. She has broken the mold of the male-dominated, traditional story, yet maintained the essence of the story form itself. Such are the possibilities in the literary folk and fairy tale.

DID YOU KNOW?

There are a number of pourquoi stories written as modern fantasy. You may be most acquainted with ones penned by Rudyard Kipling in his ***Just So Stories,*** where he attempts to explain natural phenomena such as why the elephant got his long nose, the leopard his spots, and the camel his hump. Don't miss the delicious rendition of Kipling's *Just So Stories* read by actor Jack Nicholson with music provided by the wonderful voice of Bobby McFerrin. See the Companion Website for more information.

Fantasy Novels

Within the genre of modern fantasy, the category of *fantasy novel* is of our own making and really has no parallel in traditional fantasy. Let's look at why this is so. First, we must go back *again* to the basic difference between traditional fantasy and modern fantasy. Traditional fantasy comprises those stories that were handed down from the oral tradition. But that is only part of fantasy novel's distinction; length is just as much a guiding indicator here. Certainly, if we look at some of the older authors that we still consider to be part of modern fantasy, such as Hans Christian Andersen, Howard Pyle, and Oscar Wilde, we note a story length far greater than the standard 32-page picture book length we are used to today. However, these tales would still fall into the previously mentioned category we described as the literary folk and fairy tale.

What we are now examining are books that are of novel length but that still contain motifs and attributes of their more traditional relative, the folk and fairy tale. Many authors come to mind when thinking about excellent books that have been written in this category but for us, the most consistent and most engaging storyteller this category

BOOKMARK

INTEGRATING TECHNOLOGY: AUTHORS ON THE WORLD WIDE WEB

Perhaps because of the imaginative quality of the genre, fantasy books and their authors are among the most likely to have an elaborate and active web presence. *T. A. Barron,* author of *The Lost Years of Merlin,* has created a wonderful site that includes information about all of his books, maps of his fantasy lands, a discussion of the writing process, and answers to frequently asked questions. You can register for "Merlin's Newsletter," and upon request Barron will send a gift package of posters and maps. He even encourages readers to e-mail him with questions.

To find out more about T. A. Barron and other authors and illustrators on the World Wide Web, visit Chapter 6 on the companion website at **www.prenhall.com/darigan**

has ever seen is Lloyd Alexander. Alexander includes all of the major motifs that we list later in the chapter but moreover, and for us most important, each of his books contains a compelling story with believable characters that beg us to read on—book after book after book. Consider just a small sampling of his work. Of his five books in the Chronicles of Prydain, he was justly awarded the Newbery Honor for *The Black Cauldron* and the Newbery Medal for *The High King.* More recent titles, such as *The Remarkable Journey of Prince Jen* and *The Arkadians,* all represent novel-length books with many of the standard motifs such as magic, other worlds, special characters, and good versus evil. In his most recent modern fantasy, *The Iron Ring,* we see great storytelling with an epic high adventure flair. Tamar, the young king of Sundari, sets out on the journey of his life in search of a way to make good his debt due to a fouled wager. With the aid of an odd assortment of talking animals and, of course, the love of his life, he upholds his belief in honor and duty as he braves all sorts of ordeals and catastrophes. The fantasy novel, then, retains the motifs of modern fantasy but it is sustained at the novel length.

Science Fiction

The category of science fiction generally appears in chapters about modern fantasy. However, it differs from all of the stories described up until this point. Sylvia Louise Engdahl (1971) states, "Science fiction differs from fantasy not in subject matter but in aim, and its unique aim is to suggest real hypotheses about mankind's future or about the nature of the universe" (p. 450). However, there is a brand of science fiction that would be better labeled science fantasy.

What we thought to be impossible only yesterday is now coming true today. Consider that Jules Verne's *Twenty Thousand Leagues Under the Sea* was deemed preposterous when it was first published back in 1869. Yet the idea of submarines and such is as commonplace today as zip-lock bags and microwave ovens—inventions the three of us had no notion of when we were children ourselves. In fact, when we were in grade school, the notions of instant electronic mail, organ transplants, and even space travel were beyond our imaginings. Today, they are, of course reality. Such is the "stuff" of science fiction. Though we define and describe science fiction in greater detail later, we must note here that with the incredible technological advances we've seen even in only the past decade, the science fiction of today is fast becoming the reality of tomorrow.

What the science fiction author does that sets this writing apart from the fantasy novel is use scientific fact and theory to speculate on what, within reason, could happen in the future. The catch here, echoing back to what we quoted Lloyd Alexander as saying earlier, is that we must be convinced of this "reality" for it to work. Take, for example, Richard Peck's pair of books, *Lost in Cyberspace* and *The Great Interactive Dream Machine.* Josh Lewis's best friend, Aaron Zimmer, has been able to program his computer to zap the boys back and forth in time in the former title, and in the latter he turns his

If you want to find more books of science fiction, search the database that accompanies this text—you will be able to choose from well over 100 more titles.

A CONVERSATION WITH. . .

Lloyd Alexander

Janine, my wife, was cleaning the attic, an activity in which I was taking no part. I wanted nothing to do with it. She found a big mess of papers, bags spilling stuff all over; I said, "Just throw it away. It's archeology." I think she unearthed my filing system from 1940. And out of that mess—this is a staggering true story—came a brown envelope. Very ratty, ragged looking—envelope with something in it. I didn't know what was in there. So, I opened it up and there was the text of *The Fortune-Tellers.* And I looked and thought, hmm, when did I do that? I recognized it as my own. My fingerprints were all over it and it was mine, but I don't remember doing that. Isn't that strange?

It was my first draft because it was all marked up. As I read, it started coming back to me. I had the weird idea that I wanted to do a collection of short stories, more like, at one time, fables. I wanted to do a collection of them, and I even had the insane idea that maybe I would try to illustrate them. I remember that I had written this and I had put it aside. I liked what I had written but I figured I couldn't do pictures, so I put it aside and, somehow in the course of 25 years, it had been taken up in the attic and it stayed there forever. And there it was. Now isn't that something?

I really had forgotten all about it. It had gone completely out of my mind and it cracked me up! I thought, I've got to have some fun with this. I will send this to my editor and tell her exactly what happened.

What a joke. Look what I found! When you're through, toss it out because I'm cleaning out the attic. Well, she phoned me a couple of days later, saying, "Are you crazy? I'm not going to throw this out. This is a picture book and furthermore, Trina Hyman wants to illustrate it."

Gee, that's great. Isn't that terrific? So Trina had only one question. She could do one of two things. She could do it as the nonexistent medieval fairy tale place, whatever that may be. Or, and this sounds pretty wild, she suggested setting it in Cameroon, where her daughter Katrin was serving in the Peace Corps. In the end, I think I changed only three or four words. I changed "forest" to "savanah"; I changed "bear" to "lion"; I changed "cheese monger" to maybe "cloth merchant." Something like that.

Later, Trina told me that her son-in-law, Eugene, read the story and said, you know that sounds like a Cameroonian folk tale. The only other thing that Trina told me is that indeed all those people are real. That was partly her family. And her son-in-law's family. It's his aunt, his parents, and Mishu, who was Trina's only grandson at the time.

So indeed, that's how it came about.

To read more of this Conversation with Lloyd Alexander, please visit Chapter 6 on our text's companion website at **www.prenhall.com/darigan**

computer into a wish-granting machine—though the catch is they can't seem to control its idiosyncratic whims. Therein lies the story. Peck has taken the commonplace computer and realized it in a different way to the delight of all intermediate, upper-grade readers.

Katherine Lasky leaps ahead in time over a thousand years in her book *Star Split,* where she introduces us to 13-year-old Darci Murlowe, who is only beginning to see the ill effects of genetic engineering. As she uncovers an underground movement waged to quell the predictable life of a genetic profile, the problem in the story is that, according to the Bio Union, Darci herself was illegally cloned as an infant and is both evidence of and criminal in their society's most shocking capital crime. Using what we already know about the scientific concepts of cloning and genetic engineering, Lasky very adeptly introduces the reader to the heretofore make-believe world of DNA alteration. In the end, Darci discovers more about her own culture and its limitations, but most of all she discovers her own soul. Science fiction, then, introduces us to life that could be, based on what we know now.

Science Fantasy

Science fantasy stories play loosely with scientific fact, and the plots are often mixed with magical occurrences. In **Mrs. Frisby and the Rats of NIMH,** scientists have created a race of super intelligent rats—they can read medicine bottles and signs on walls, and, most important to them, open their cages. After their escape, they establish a secret community complete with electricity and other technological devices. When Mrs. Frisby, a normal field mouse, has her home and family placed into grave danger by the farmer's plow, she goes to the rats of NIMH for assistance. The *fantasy* element is represented by these animals talking to one another.

The Animorphs, a popular paperback series that we discussed in chapter 2, is another example of science fantasy. Several young people are endowed by a dying, benevolent alien with the power to "morph" into various animals in order to fight against an invasion of evil alien beings. Thus the motif of *special character types* is addressed, but more important is the alien's use of magic to confer to the human children the ability to morph.

When we think about magic in fantasy, we realize that it is unexplainable; it is just there, without source or reason. On the other hand, the magic of true *science fiction* is rooted firmly in scientific fact. Take, for example, the magic used in "Cinderella" is fantasy. The fairy godmother simply has the power to turn the pumpkin into a coach, the mice into coachmen. If it were science fiction, she would zap the pumpkin with a molecular rearranger (Alexander, 1973).

Science fiction also concerns itself with the way scientific possibilities might affect human societies, as in Robert C. O'Brien's **Z for Zachariah,** which describes the aftermath of a nuclear holocaust. Karen Hesse's chilling commentary on the ills of nuclear power is the focus in her **Phoenix Rising,** and the demise of the entire planet Earth and the subsequent move humans need to make to the planet Shine are accented in Jill Paton Walsh's **The Green Book.** Science fiction also looks at future worlds, future societies, and the way they have evolved; such is the case in Lois Lowry's **The Giver** and its companion, **Gathering Blue.** In both, we are introduced to future worlds, the first very sophisticated, the second comparatively primitive, but in both, we see how the children negotiate the rules and mores of their individual societies.

Futuristic Fiction

Science fiction is also concerned with the way in which scientific possibilities might affect societies of human or alien beings, or both. Therefore, it is sometimes called *futuristic fiction*. This combination of scientific fact and scientific possibility is evident in such works as Nancy Farmer's **The Ear, the Eye, and the Arm.** Farmer starts with facts about the devastation of nuclear accidents and goes on to offer a view of how a society thus affected might look in the 22nd century. Then she extrapolates the scientific facts about the unusual effects radiation might have on human beings by creating three characters whose mutations have given them abnormal capabilities.

▼▼▼▼▼▼▼

Specific Ways Fantasy Motifs Are Employed

Within the three previously mentioned categories of modern fantasy, we have noted literary folk and fairy tales, fantasy novels, and science fiction. We have described the six major motifs—magic, other worlds, good versus evil, heroism and the hero's quest, special character types, and fantastic objects—that we often find are employed in modern fantasy. However, modern fantasy stories are most often categorized by the type of fantastic story element that is used:

- animal fantasy
- toys and objects imbued with life
- tiny humans
- peculiar characters and situations
- imaginary worlds
- magical powers
- supernatural tales
- time travel fantasies
- high fantasy
- variants, lampoons, and sequels
- books wedged between fantasy and fiction

James Howe
The *Bunnicula* books

After many years of projecting my own conversations—intelligent or otherwise—on my pets, it seemed entirely natural and right to tell the story of Bunnicula from the point of view of a dog. In retrospect, I suspect I was influenced not only by *Charlotte's Web* and my own imaginative relationship with my pets, but also by Charles M. Schulz's Peanuts comic strip and the Marx Brothers. All of these have one thing in common: They merge the worlds of the adult and the child. In the Peanuts strip, children act and talk like adults while remaining firmly rooted in the world of childhood. The Marx Brothers behave like children while existing in the world of adults. And animals—those in my Bunnicula series, as well as *Charlotte's Web* and other animal fantasies—are often a combination of the adult and the child. Writing from the point of view of the child/adult, I was freed from the

constrictions of either world and able to take potshots at both.

For most people—myself included—the books "written by" Harold are thought of as "The Bunnicula books." But Bunnicula, for me, is the least interesting aspect of the series, and he doesn't even appear in all the books. He is the mystery around whom three of the books turn. But Harold and Chester—and, in the later books, Howie—are the most interesting characters and the most fun to write. Harold and Chester are Watson and Holmes. And Howie, well, Howie is me as a little kid, forever running around pantingly seeking approval of his elders (in my case, three older brothers) with his bad jokes and boundless enthusiasm.

To read more of this Conversation with James Howe, please visit Chapter 6 on our text's companion website at **www.prenhall. com/darigan**

Animal Fantasy

Animal fantasy, for example, is the tag often given to stories that depart from reality exclusively because of talking animals. Such is the case with E. B. White's immortal *Charlotte's Web,* A. A. Milne's *Winnie-the-Pooh,* Roald Dahl's *James and the Giant Peach,* and the now-classic tale of the vampire rabbit, *Bunnicula: A Rabbit-Tale of Mystery.*

More recent modern animal fantasy titles include Brian Jacques's ever popular *Redwall* and the many books in that series. Here we see high fantasy at its best with swashbuckling, swaggering, sword-swinging mice, under the revered champion Martin the Warrior, and their adventures in Mossflower country in the Redwall Abbey. Peggy Christian has added a new twist to animal fantasy with *The Bookstore Mouse.* In this book, we meet a very literate rodent who, living in an antiquarian bookstore, delights not only in eating the delicious words he finds in the many volumes sitting on the shelf but also in throwing harsh and sharp words at his enemies. When, by accident, he falls into a real story, he is confronted with the adventure of his life where he must attempt to defeat the dragon Censor. Finally, Lois Lowry's *Stay! Keeper's Story* represents a very sophisticated text with humor equally as witty and smart as that found in Milne's *Winnie-the-Pooh* series. In this first-person story, we follow Keeper around his "hood" as he deals with his various masters and adventures that come in and out of his life, but we are always aware of his commitment to finding his long lost sister.

Toys and Objects Imbued With Life

First of all, let's clarify a point: *Pinocchio,* by Carlo Collodi, more recently adapted in a "theatrical" setting by Ed Young, was neither written nor created by Walt Disney Studios—that also goes for "The Little Mermaid," "Beauty and the Beast," and "The Jungle Book." These all are modern tales that were adapted by Walt Disney as full-length animated features. As for "Pinocchio," the timeless story of this mischievous little puppet who comes to life and suffers the consequence of his own poor choices is the perfect example of this element of fantasy where toys or objects magically spring to life.

In Virginia Lee Burton's classic ***Choo Choo: the Runaway Engine***, we find, other than that this engine has a name, nothing remarkable or fantastic until we are almost one third of the way through the book. That is when Choo Choo makes up her mind to strike out on her own. She says to herself, "I am tired of pulling all these heavy coaches. I could go much faster and easier by myself, then all the people would stop and look at me, just me, and they would say, 'What a smart little engine! What a fast little engine! What a beautiful little engine! Just watch her go by herself!' "

Look at the marvelous design work that went into the making of this book. As in all of Burton's books, she made every effort to blend the text and the illustration, the words becoming a mere continuation of the drawings. See how the tracks spread apart on this page? They are approaching us from the vanishing point in the center but so, too, does the text continue the design.

On yet another double-page spread, you can see how Burton merges text and drawing into the basic shapes of diamonds and circles. We read down the left-hand side of the page and, following the train at the bottom of the page, our eye is naturally directed to the right. Then, starting at the top, you can first note how the smoke and shape of the train fade back into the distance, providing a clear sense of the speed and movement. The train comes chugging around the bend while the text acts as the transition to the lower half of the spread, neatly curving into the lower illustration, much like the shape of a figure eight. As the train prepares to go through the crossing, Burton wisely chooses to direct it to the right, which spills us on to the next double-page spread.

DID YOU KNOW?

In one of our classes, a huge "discussion" ensued about who authored the story of "The Little Mermaid." One of our students was ready to come to blows, adamant that the sea princess who wanted to become human was indeed named Ariel and that the whole tale was written by none other than—you got it— Walt Disney, himself. There was no convincing her—and, we might add, quite a few others in the class—that Hans Christian Andersen was the actual author. Only after we pulled out a copy of the original and showed her the publisher's page was she finally convinced. This experience did make us think seriously about the impact Disney has had, in general, on children's literature and, in particular, on folk and fairy tales.

Illustration from ***Choo Choo: The Runaway Engine*** by Virginia Lee Burton. Copyright 1937 by Virginia Lee Burton; copyright renewed © 1965 by Virginia Lee Demetrios. Reprinted by permission of Houghton Mifflin Company. All rights reserved.

Karen Radler Greenfield has taken the age-old theme of the couple unable to have children and given it new life in her book **The Teardrop Baby.** An old wizard woman transforms the couple's tears into a child of their own. Of course, the wizard woman intends, after 7 years, to return and take the baby back—or so the future is foretold in a fortune inserted in a freshly baked loaf of bread. In the end, the young teardrop boy outsmarts the ragged woman with a fortune of his own.

Yet another permutation of this theme is seen in Laura Krauss Melmed's **Little Oh,** illustrated by Jim LaMarche. In this tale ostensibly set in Japan, a lonely woman folds an origami doll that magically comes to life. Not satisfied with her simple, solitary life, the doll becomes restless and is tilted out into the world to follow a "Tom Thumb" type of an adventure until she comes upon a white crane who is mourning the loss of her dear husband. Little Oh, as she is called, sings songs her mother taught her, comforts the crane, and is rewarded as the bird flies her back home. This touching story comes to a satisfying conclusion when Little Oh is returned to her family and is transformed into a live little girl.

Full-length novels that also continue the theme of toys and inanimate objects coming to life include Sylvia Waugh's series, beginning with **The Mennyms** and Lynn Reid Banks's quartet, beginning with the **Indian in the Cupboard.** These books investigate the joys and troubles inherent in this magical transformation.

Tiny Humans

The Wee Folk, or leprechauns, are a common character type in Celtic tales. Mortals continually attempt to trick them into giving up their gold, which is supposedly hidden underground. A few notable examples of these Irish tales are shown in the Selkie Alternate Text Set we mention in the section on special character traits. These books would be great fun around St. Patrick's Day or as the motivation and introduction to a cultural studies unit you might be doing in your classroom.

One of the most beautiful and engaging picture books from recent years in this or any genre is Laura Krauss Melmed's **The Rainbabies,** illustrated by Jim LaMarche. When an old couple is unable to have children they are blessed one night with a magical occurrence. Note the rich language Melmed uses to set the scene:

> One spring night . . . when a broad ribbon of white light slid across the old woman's pillow. Her eyes flew open as she sat bolt upright. Though she could hear the steady tattoo of rainfall on the rooftop, her gaze met the white face of the full moon, peering round-mouthed through her window.
>
> The old woman shook her husband. "Wake up, old man, I've heard the moonshower brings good fortune to everyone it touches!"

As you might expect, their wish is granted and they discover "nestled among the wet blades of grass and wildflowers . . . a dozen shimmering drops of water, each holding a tiny baby no larger than [the old woman's] her big toe!"

The next three episodes of the story deal with various attempts on the rainbabies' safety, but always the old couple endures. However, one evening, they are visited by the mysterious and beautiful Mother Moonshower, who has another surprise for them. The magic expressed in both word and illustration makes this one of the classics for all times.

Probably the most recognized classic in this category is **The Borrowers,** by Mary Norton, which tells of a family of tiny people who live under a grandfather clock and "borrow" the extras from the human "beans" who live above. More recently, **The Minpins,** by Roald Dahl, is a nice addition to this grouping of books and an excellent read aloud for younger children.

The Alternate Text Set that follows presents "A Little Fantasy" for intermediate readers where the main characters in each of the books are "Tiny Folks."

ALTERNATE TEXT SET

A "Little" Fantasy

Read Aloud

The Indian in the Cupboard, by Lynne Reid Banks

Text Set

The Castle in the Attic, by Elizabeth Winthrop

A Cricket in Times Square, by George Selden

The Afternoon of the Elves, by Janet Taylor Lisle

The Fairy Rebel, by Lynne Reid Banks

The Littles, by John Peterson

Peculiar Characters and Situations

Both traditional and modern fantasy are filled with characters that are strange and different. Take, for instance, Patricia Rae Wolff's *The Toll-Bridge Troll,* where young Trigg meets a troll on the way to school who will not let him pass over his bridge unless he pays a penny toll. Trigg, however, is able to trick the not-so-bright imp three times running with his clever riddles. In the end, the mother troll sends her little one off to school with Trigg so he can get smarter himself. Readers, both young and old alike, will enjoy this tale written with a Rebus-like text where thumbnail illustrations are interspersed throughout, featuring line drawing by Kimberly Buclken Root. Further, Root's distinctive, full color paintings on opposing pages of text hint at the old-world flavor of the tale while maintaining the contemporary characters and situation.

Marcia Vaughan has introduced a couple of new character type to the standard "unusual character" list, going beyond your run-of-the-mill sprites, witches, and goblins. In her delightful book with a Southern flair, *Whistling Dixie,* illustrated by Barry Moser, young Dixie Lee comes home with a little bitty gator, a slithery snake, and a hoot owl, but her mother is dubious about where she should keep them. Dixie Lee figures that she should put them in places meant to turn away nasty creatures like the "churn turners," "bogeymen," and "mist sisters," all coming out of the Hokey Pokey Swamp—such as down the well, in Grandpappy's gomper jar (where he keeps his false teeth), and up the chimney. Unfortunately, when Grandpappy does come home, he gets a real surprise with all those varmints around. That night, those very nasty creatures oozed out of the swamp, and as the sun trades places with the moon, everyone realizes "what good critters Dixie Lee had brought home after all."

Lloyd Alexander uses a man's desire for good luck as the basis of the conflict in his *The House Gobbaleen,* illustrated by Diane Goode. Tooley longed for good luck but seemed to get only the opposite: His potatoes grew small, his roof leaked, and his pig broke out of her sty and rooted up his cabbages. When a strange fellow, Hooks by name, enters the picture, Tooley is sure and certain he is one of the "Friendly Folk" who has been sent to give him luck. Tooley's cat Gladsake assures him otherwise, but it is too late—Hooks enters their house and the only luck he distributes is bad luck. After Gladsake aids in ridding of the pesky imp, Tooley never complains about his luck again.

Fantasy novels that have unusual characters include, of course, P. L. Travers's classic *Mary Poppins,* also made popular by Mr. Disney, and more recently William Mayne's *Hob and the Goblins* and the others in that series. Of particular note is Susan Cooper's *The Boggart,* which finds the Volnik family of Toronto, Canada being haunted by an ancient and mischievous spirit who hails from a castle in Scotland, having been accidentally locked into a roll-top desk and shipped to Canada.

Yet another wonderful character is introduced in David Almond's ***Skellig.*** This neatly crafted, well-written text deftly feeds out the line of the story, the nature of this odd character, and allows us, as readers, to slowly imagine what this Skellig might be. Having moved into a new house and troubled by his sister's serious illness, Michael retreats to a dilapidated garage and comes upon an angel-like figure. Hauntingly written and graphically picturesque, this book is a page-turner that will keep reader's interest until the very end.

Imaginary Worlds

DID YOU KNOW?

You might be interested to know that the 1964 version of ***Charlie and the Chocolate Factory*** was, of needs, revised in 1973 when pressure was placed on Dahl by his publisher. Given the context of the early sixties and the lack of sensitivity to Civil Rights, Dahl naively portrayed the Oompa-Loompas, the diligent factory workers he imported from abroad, as stereotypes of simple, happy-go-lucky Black Africans. In the original edition, he goes so far as to refer to them as "pygmies . . . imported right from Africa." The 1973 revision said the Oompa-Loompas came from a make-believe country called Loompaland. Fortunately, the derogatory reference to "pygmies" was dropped, but despite the obvious changes he made, there is still much left to be desired in this particular part of the text. Note that we don't suggest you throw this book out wholesale for this one flaw, however. We would hope that you keep this book in your curriculum but point out to your children the nature of the problems with this section. You could explain that this is a consequence of the times and of cultural ignorance than being mean-spirited and racist. Once you have discussed this, you can proceed to relish the rest of this delightful book.

Lewis Carroll created an imaginary world in his classic ***Alice's Adventures in Wonderland,*** wherein we follow Alice as she plunges down the rabbit hole into a dreamlike world of mad hatters, double-talk, and word play. In 1964, Roald Dahl similarly created a fantastic environment when he wrote his extremely popular ***Charlie and the Chocolate Factory.*** In this story further popularized by the movie version (but not nearly as good as the book), young Charlie Bucket, a poor child living with his parents and both sets of grandparents, is one of five children who has won an opportunity to tour Willie Wonka's famous chocolate factory. There they will learn all of Wonka's secrets of candy making, as well as receive a lifetime supply of chocolate. Once inside the factory, we are introduced to a miraculous world only children (and lunatic chocolate-loving adults like us) would appreciate. In the Chocolate Room, for example, Wonka emphatically states that he would settle for nothing less than a beautiful environment for his candy making and so he created a verdant valley right in the middle of the factory, complete with a flowing chocolate river. A sophisticated system of glass pipes supplies hot melted chocolate to all the other special candy-making rooms throughout the factory. It even has a chocolate waterfall.

Dahl also created a very believable environment in one of his other popular novels, ***James and the Giant Peach.*** We feel as if we are crawling in the enormous peach ourselves with his graphic descriptions: "The tunnel was damp and murky, and all around him there was the curious bittersweet smell of fresh peaches. The floor was soggy under his knees, the walls wet and sticky, and peach juice dripped from the ceiling. James opened his mouth and caught some of it on his tongue. It tasted delicious."

One of the great advantages of modern fantasy is our ability, at the turn of the page, to enter a world literally beyond our imaginings. For instance, Janet Taylor Lisle created an arboreal wonderland in her book ***Forest,*** and Avi did the same on the ground in his book ***Poppy.*** And speaking of woodlands, Patricia Wrede sustained yet another similar setting in her four-book Enchanted Forest series, beginning with ***Dealing With Dragons,*** which we list in the chapter's opening text set. As we mentioned earlier, by creating these imaginary worlds, the author can then manipulate events based on the particular rules for that setting. Again, only when and if that world is "real" can the reader make the all-important leap of faith into the fantastic.

Magical Powers

Specific to the presence of magic in modern fantasy, we often find characters who are given magical powers that can turn out to be either for good or for ill. Because of his overwhelming desire for gold, the king gets his wish in "King Midas and the Golden Touch" with disastrous results. Lynne Reid Banks took this notion one step further with a full, novelized version of this tale in her epic ***The Adventures of King Midas.*** For the younger readers or ones not so proficient, Patrick Catling presents a variant on that theme in his book *The Chocolate Touch.* Young Patrick is so crazy about chocolate that he, too, is given a magical power: He can make anything he likes turn to chocolate by a single touch. All too soon, he discovers the shortsightedness in his decision but must go through quite a bit of misery before the magic is countered.

In the preceding books, we see magical powers used for personal gain. In David Small's *Paper John,* we find that the opposite occurs. A gangly young John comes waltzing into town and because he is so adept at making things from folded paper— from his own house to boats to sail for the children on the pond—he holds a tremendous fascination with the populace. But, then, when a dark and devilish character slithers into town and starts wreaking havoc on the citizens, it is John who uses his magic to quell the little man and send him on his way.

In Barbara Helen Berger's *The Jewel Heart,* Pavelle, a young stringless marionette, has Gemino play violin to accompany her dances. But Gemino, who has a jewel for a heart, is missing, and Pavelle finally finds him injured, torn to tatters, and without his heart—the work of a nasty woodrat. She sews him new clothes and gives him a heart that was only one brown seed. Saddened that she has nothing better, she weeps and the tears magically allow the seed to bud and turn into a beautiful flower "finer than any jewel." The soft and subtle airbrushed illustrations that are classic Berger add depth to this simple story of love and magic.

Supernatural Tales

Tales of ghosts and other-worldly encounters abound in children's literature. Books such as Tony Johnston's *The Ghost of Nicholas Greebe* and Margaret Hodges's *Molly Limbo* offer chilling examples of what can be done in this short format. Two books that are aimed at the early reader and that come in a short novel form are Sharon Creech's *Pleasing the Ghost* and Catherine Dexter's *A is for Apple, W is for Witch.* In the former, Creech introduces us to young Dennis, who is being visited by many ghostly spirits, but when his recently passed uncle Arvie inhabits his room, he is haunted by the many puzzles that are thrown in his path and that have to do with this recent tragedy. In the latter, we meet Apple Olsen, who is pretty irked with Barnaby Thompson for accusing her mother of being a witch. In an effort at retaliation, Apple takes magic into her own hands too early and gets herself into a bushel of trouble.

 On the CD that accompanies this book, if you search for the simple descriptor "ghost," you will get almost 200 books from which to choose.

ALTERNATE TEXT SET

Ghosts and Spirits

Read Aloud

Stonewords, by Pam Conrad

Text Set

Wait Till Helen Comes, by Mary Downing Hahn

The Darkling, by Charles Butler

Great Ghost Stories, by Barry Moser

School Spirits, by Michael O. Tunnell

Haunted Waters, by Mary Pope Osborne

The Vampire's Beautiful Daughter, by S. P. Somtow

Have your students choose a time (either in the past or in the future) that they would like to visit. Further, have them pick a place and a reason for the visit, and they have the makings of a time travel story of their own.

Time Travel Fantasies

Darigan and Woodcock (1999) state that traveling through time, whether into the past or the future, has long been a dream of children and adults alike. Certainly we have all pondered, while standing at a historic site, what it would have been like to have been there when that "history" was happening, or what it would be like to be whisked ahead in time to know how the upcoming big decisions in our lives or our society will affect us and how it will all turn out. The time travel book allows us to live out those time switches vicariously.

Nowhere is fantasy tested more than in the time travel novel. The modern-day child is thrown back in time and if we, as readers, are to believe this unlikely phenomenon, the reality of the past must be as crystal clear as that of our present. Take, for example, Caroline B. Cooney's Time Travel Trilogy, where the meticulously researched, detailed descriptions of 100 years ago draw us, unerringly, into the time and place.

A wide body of time travel books exists for children and young adults, layered and plotted with all sorts of different twists and turns. In some, there is a desire by the protagonist to alter personal or family history, as in Pam Conrad's **Stonewords.** In others, attempts are made to help avert a major disaster, as in David Wiseman's **Jeremy Visick.** In most cases, the main character is thrown back in time, whereas in others, such as Jane Resh Thomas's **The Princess in the Pigpen,** a child from a previous period is catapulted into the all too fast-paced and modern 20th century. Sometimes the time travel seems to occur for no apparent reason, as in Jackie French's **Somewhere Around the Corner,** and in other novels, the character "needs to" return to the past and so is swept away. In all cases, the main character, as well as the reader, learns something valuable, not only about history and the conditions of the times, but more important, about him- or herself as well, and so too, has grown.

High Fantasy

As we mentioned earlier, high fantasy is actually easy to distinguish if you use Madsen's guidelines. If a book contains all the major six fantasy motifs, then it can be considered under the category of high fantasy. Certainly all of the Prydain Series, including Lloyd Alexander's **The High King,** C. S. Lewis's **The Lion, the Witch, and the Wardrobe,** and Brian Jacques's **Redwall,** as well as the others in the series, should be considered in this list. Also to be noted as high fantasy at its finest is Susan Cooper's The Dark Is Rising series (see p. 205) which most notably pits good against evil, has a variety of very creative magical objects, and is replete with magic.

Variants, Lampoons, and Sequels

Since the appearance of Jon Scieszka's landmark **The True Story of the Three Little Pigs,** illustrated by Lane Smith, which retells "The Three Little Pigs" from the wolf's perspective, we have seen an enormous number of books published that poke fun at or that continue a fairy tale already in progress. Scieszka himself has done that in his **The Frog Prince, Continued,** which acts as the sequel to the traditional "Frog Prince," and then in a variety of tales in his rollicking **The Stinky Cheese Man and Other Fairly Stupid Tales.** For instance, instead of Andersen's "The Princess and the Pea," we have "The Princess and the Bowling Ball"; for "Little Red Riding Hood," we chortle at his

After reading widely through as many variants, lampoons, and sequels as students can find, have them attempt a "Fractured" tale of their own. The more they understand how the stories work as a consequence of their reading, the more enjoyment they will receive poking fun at the original tale.

lampoon "Little Red Running Shorts"; and for the "Gingerbread Man," who could forget "The Stinky Cheese Man"? Quotes the main character, "Run, run, run, as fast as you can. You can't catch me I'm the Stinky Cheese Man." Each is written with a contemporary, humorous slant. And because there is a lively banter between Jack of "Jack and the Beanstalk" fame and the chicken from "The Little Red Hen," we have a continuity across all the stories, though selected favorites can still be shared during what should prove to be a hilarious read-aloud session.

And speaking of Jack, in this list of fairy tale sequels we must include Raymond Briggs's *Jim and the Beanstalk,* which finds Jim, son of Jack, climbing the vine once again, only to find the giant old and decrepit. Rather than be eaten, Jack fixes up the giant with new eyeglasses, false teeth, and a wig for his balding skull. For his kindness, he receives a huge gold coin, and in the end runs away from the rejuvenated giant, avoiding his fate of becoming the main ingredient in a "boy sandwich." With any sequel, having knowledge of the original tale adds to the enjoyment, and Briggs's story is no exception.

Books that offer a different perspective AND are written from another perspective would have to include Susan Meddaugh's *Cinderella's Rat,* which tells the story from the eyes of the rat who was turned into a coachman (well, coach boy) on Cinderella's big night out at the ball. Enjoying his new form, he recognizes his sister (still a rat) and takes her to a local wizard for a changeover. But the wizard has a bad charm day because he turns her first into a cat, then a girl who meows, and then a girl who barks. Rather than make it any worse, he tells them to return the next day. But as the clock strikes midnight, the boy turns back into a rat, and the sister . . . well, she was pretty useful to have around. She barks and keeps away all the cats.

Gail Carson Levine has presented a twist to the Cinderella story in her Newbery Honor book, *Ella Enchanted.* In this book, Cinderella has been given the spell of always being obedient. This eventually proves to act as a curse to the young girl and explains her actions based on the traditional fairy tale.

Yet another hilarious sequel/lampoon is found in *Cinder Edna,* by Ellen Jackson, which introduces us to Cinderella's neighbor, Edna. Both are under the influence of a wicked stepmother and stepsisters. But whereas Ella lounges around bemoaning her fate, Edna takes charge of her life: She mows lawns and cleans birdcages for extra spending money and even knows how to make tuna casserole 16 ways. At the ball, Ella predictably ends up with the handsome prince, Randolph, but Edna meets and falls in love with his brother, Rupert, who runs a recycling plant back behind the castle. The contemporary twist to this delightful tale makes for a wonderful addition to the "Cinderella" stories.

While we're on the subject of Cinderella, we must also note recent versions of the tale that add a new twist to the same theme. In Helen Ketteman's *Bubba the Cowboy Prince: A Fractured Texas Tale* and Caralyn Buehner's *Fanny's Dream,* we get versions of the tale with a true flavor of Americana, with the first written as a tale from the wild, wild west, and the latter written from the down-home farm perspective. Other books that lampoon or poke fun at their original roots are *Sleepless Beauty,* by Frances Minters, a hip-hop cosmopolitan version of "Sleeping Beauty," *The Three Little Javelinas,* by Susan Lowell, which retells the "Three Little Pigs" from the perspective of three collared peccaries (New World relatives of swine but not true pigs), and *Whuppity Stoorie,* by Carolyn White, which is a version of "Rumpelstiltskin."

A CONVERSATION WITH. . .

David Wiesner

I can trace my book, **The Three Pigs,** back to one of those eye-opening experiences as a kid watching Bugs Bunny. Elmer Fudd chases Bugs Bunny, and then they go spinning around on an endless chase. All of a sudden, in the middle of a scene, they go running off the edge of the film. You can see the frame and where the sprockets would be. Then, suddenly, out of this blank white space, they stop and look and go "ahh" and turn around and run back onto the filmstrip. I can distinctly remember the first time I ever saw it, the whole idea of them running out of one reality into this other place. It was just so cool.

I started thinking about the most basic fairy tales or kids' stories. Things like "Goldilocks and the Three Bears," and the "Three Little Pigs." Some of the stuff about the Three Pigs caused the light bulbs to start to go on. Each time it gets read, the pigs get eaten up. They must get pretty darn tired of that.

They all have their own personalities. The pig who builds brick houses, he is sort of like the smart one of the bunch. He is the leader and the strong pig. The straw pig is always leaping about; he is always kind of tripping over things and knocking stuff over. He is the one who knocks over the panels, and the whole format of the book just collapses. The panels are lying on the ground and we are in this big open white space that was behind the pictures. And once I began to find out about the pigs and who they were and their motivation and things, the story pretty quickly took shape and went to a nice place.

They had a desire to look for a home sort of, where they can belong. In fact, they can go in and out of other stories—Hey Diddle Diddle—each of these stories has a different look to it. They go into a pen-and-ink old fairy tale folk tale world where they find a dragon about to be slain by a knight, and they take him out of the story with them. The cat and the fiddle have left their story, too. Now there is this growing band of characters looking for a better life. They think that they will go back and re-create their own world the way they want it. They pick up all the pieces and reassemble the format of the book. Then they reenter the story. The story all of a sudden picks up where it left off. The wolf is knocking on the door of the brick house. The door pops open and out comes this giant dragon. The dragon is so large he knocks the text on top of the page and letters go flying everywhere. The characters pick up the letters and at the end they rewrite and redraft and they are all sitting and having soup in front of the house. The cat's playing the fiddle, and they are cooking a big meal. On the one hand it is very simple, but it also has multiple levels and things going on. It all came together really nicely.

To read more of this Conversation with David Wiesner, please visit Chapter 6 on our text's companion website at **www.prenhall.com/darigan**

Margie Palatini's effervescent and hilarious *Piggie Pie!* has a number of fantasy elements at work yet clearly is a modern tale. The main character, Gritch the Witch, is hungry and has a great desire, naturally, for Piggie Pie; don't we all. After consulting her *Old Hag Cookbook* and checking her pantry shelves, she realizes she has all the standard ingredients—"one eye of a fly, two shakes of a rattlesnake's rattle, and three belly hairs of a possum." What she really needs is "eight plump piggies." She checks the Yellow Pages and finds just what she needs. She could simply call "EI-EI-O," but being proactive, Gritch decides to go "over the river and through the woods" to find her eight little porkers. Zooming in on "Old MacDonald's Farm" with her magic broom, she leaves a vapor trail warning, "Surrender Piggies." The startled swine, who also happen to be pretty smart, dress up as various other farm animals and dupe poor Gritch. In the end, she encounters a beleaguered wolf who has been "chasing three pigs for days." He warns her away from these crafty critters, and the two return to Gritch's house, smacking their lips and thinking "lunch." This delightful tale draws its charm from the more traditional sources but retains a bright feel in its modern trappings.

Finally, there have been a number of wonderful attempts by contemporary authors to write original fables maintaining the essence of the form. Valiska Gregory has written an original pair of fables based on the themes of peace and environmental sensitivity in her *When Stories Fell Like Shooting Stars.* The illustrations, done in oil on

Cover from *Piggie Pie!,* by Margie Palatini, illustrated by Howard Fine. Cover illustration copyright © 1995 by Howard Fine. Published by Clarion Books-Houghton Mifflin Company. All rights reserved. Reprinted by permission.

wooden boards by Stefano Vatale, give this book a strong Native American feel yet really never state a cultural influence. Avi, no newcomer to taking a chance with style and form, has written an original picture book fable in his *The Bird, the Frog, and the Light.* He has gone on to write novelized fables we mentioned earlier, including *Poppy* and *Poppy and Rye.*

Lastly, a couple of authors have stepped "over the line" with outrageous fables based on contemporary events and characters. Among them are Paul Rosenthal's *Yo, Aesop! Get a Load of These Fables* and Jon Scieszka's *Squids Will Be Squids: Fresh Morals for Modern Fables.* These fractured fables are set with contemporary flare, yet knowledge of the original Aesop is helpful for the child to totally appreciate the sophisticated humor both volumes bring to the reader. Jon recently shared with one of our university audiences that while he was a classroom teacher, he called one of his kids' parents but, instead, got the child. He honestly told Scieszka that his mother wasn't home—she was having her mustache removed. So, years later, Jon wrote the fable about Little Walrus who receives a call for his mother from Whale. Little Walrus replies, "She's out having the hair taken off her lip."

Moral: You should always tell the truth. But if your mom is out having the hair taken off her lip, you might want to forget a few of the details.

Quite a number of fantasy novels have followed this same pattern that either expanded a traditional folk tale, extended the story as a sequel, or were written from the perspective of an unexpected character. For example, Donna Jo Napoli has done all three of these things in her book *The Magic Circle.* She has taken the traditional tale of "Hansel and Gretel" and not only has rewritten it as a full-length novel, but also has related it from the perspective of the witch, and takes it beyond where the traditional tale ends. She has done the same thing in a number of her other books, such as *Zel,* which is the novelized retelling of "Rapunzel," and *Spinners,* which retells the story of "Sleeping Beauty."

Many older middle-grade or young adult readers will want to investigate one or more of the following expanded versions of a traditional folk tale written as a novel.

ALTERNATE TEXT SET

Going Beyond the Original Tale

Read Aloud

The Magic Circle, by Donna Jo Napoli

Text Set

The Adventures of King Midas, by Lynne Reid Banks

In a Dark Wood, by Michael Cadnum

Ella Enchanted, by Gail Carson Levine

The Princess Test, by Gail Carson Levine

Rose Daughter, by Robin McKinley

Zel, by Donna Jo Napoli

Spinners, by Donna Jo Napoli

John Morressy has written a stunning novel that parallels a Faustian theme in his book *The Juggler.* Beran, a peasant in a medieval village, makes a pact with the devil so he can become the greatest juggler of all time. Only after the disastrous results of his decision does he attempt to rectify the situation but, in the end, it may be too late. In Susan Fletcher's novel *Shadow Spinner,* we are presented with the story of "Scheherazade and the One Thousand and One Nights" but from the viewpoint of a young crippled girl who has been brought into the harem because of her unusual talent for telling stories.

Books Wedged Between Fantasy and Fiction

There are a number of books that just simply defy categorization, yet they still maintain that feel of fantasy. For example, Avi's *Midnight Magic* certainly has all the trappings of original modern fantasy, yet in the end there is no magic present, no other worlds, etc. Other books that fall into this category include William Manes's unique book *An Almost Perfect Game,* where young Jake and his brother begin to wonder if their baseball scorecard is actually controlling the destiny of the players and the outcome of the game they are attending.

Other books in this category include the controversial *The War of Jenkins' Ear,* by Michael Morpurgo, *Afternoon of the Elves,* by Janet Taylor Lisle, Ellen Kindt McKinsey's *Under the Bridge,* and another of Lisle's books, *The Lost Flower Children.* In all of these books, magic seems to hover yet never alight on any of these books. Finally, we have argued and fretted for years about where to actually place Lloyd Alexander's *Westmark* as well as the two other books in the trilogy, *The Kestrel* and *The Beggar Queen.*

▼▼▼▼▼▼▼▼

A Final Word About Modern Fantasy

The power of fantasy is reflected in the fact that many of the classic children's stories, those that have withstood the test of time, are fantasies: *Peter Pan, Winnie-the-Pooh,*

The Wonderful Wizard of Oz, The Wind in the Willows, and *Mary Poppins.* Certainly, good fantasy stories speak clearly and convincingly about real life, as author Lloyd Alexander (1968) observed: "I suppose you might define realism as fantasy pretending to be true; and fantasy as reality pretending to be a dream" (p. 386).

> And so they lived many happy years, and the promised tasks were accomplished. Yet long afterward, when all had passed away into distant memory, there were many who wondered whether King Taran, Queen Eilonwy, and their companions had indeed walked the earth, or whether they had been no more than dreams in a tale set down to beguile children. And, in time, only the bards knew the truth of it. (*The High King,* p. 285)

Lloyd Alexander's epic five-book fantasy series called The Prydain Chronicles ends with these words in *The High King.* Those who have lived vicariously in the imaginary kingdom of Prydain and survived its trials with Taran and Eilonwy yearn to hold on to those golden, mythical times as surely as they reach out longingly to hold onto a pleasant dream. This is the legacy traditional fantasy gives to modern fantasy— a sense of the magical that extends back to our ancient roots. "Magic had its feet under the earth and its hair above the clouds. . . . [In] the beginning, Magic was everywhere and nowhere" (Colwell, 1968, p. 178).

▼▼▼▼▼▼▼

Summary

In this chapter, we have looked at modern fantasy; how its basic elements defy natural and physical laws of our known world but how it is often compared to traditional fantasy. Modern fantasy maintains many of the trappings of the old, oral tales but is most distinguished from them by the fact that these tales were written by contemporary authors and often concern themselves with more current issues and predicaments. We discussed the importance metaphor plays in the success and believability of fantasy. Next we provided guidelines for the reader to evaluate modern fantasy, paying careful attention to its roots in reality, internal consistency, characterization, and its ability to examine universal truths. We identified six basic fantasy motifs of this genre: magic, other worlds, good versus evil, heroism and the hero's quest, special character types, and fantastic objects. We then looked at the categories of modern fantasy, which include literary folk and fairy tales, fantasy novels, and science fiction. Finally, we looked at ways fantasy motifs are employed, such as stories that include animal fantasy, imaginary worlds, time travel, and tiny humans. Fantasy, and modern fantasy in particular, offers us the ability to see outside our own world while also providing us with the lens to look back at our world with greater clarity.

▼▼▼▼▼▼▼

Fifteen More of Our Favorites

Avi. (1988). *Something upstairs.* Avon. Kenny discovers that his new Rhode Island home is haunted by the spirit of a black slave boy who asks Kenny to go to the early 19th century to prevent his murder by slave traders.

Bond, Nancy. (1976). *A string in the harp.* McElderry. Relates what happens to three American children, unwillingly transplanted to Wales for 1 year, when one of them finds an ancient harp tuning key that takes him back to the time of the great 6th-century bard of Taliesin.

Coville, Bruce. (1994). *Oddly enough.* Harcourt. A collection of nine short stories featuring an angel, unicorn, vampire, werewolf, and other unusual creatures.

Dahl, Roald. (1982). *The BFG.* Knopf. Kidsnatched from her orphanage by a Big Friendly Giant who spends his life blowing dreams to children, Sophie concocts with him a plan to save the world from man-gobbling giants.

Fleischman, Sid. (1972). *McBroom's wonderful one-acre farm* (Quentin Blake, Illus.). Greenwillow. Three humorous tall-tale adventures on McBroom's wonderful one-acre prairie farm.

Fleischman, Sid. (1995). *The 13th floor: A ghost story*. Greenwillow. When his older sister disappears, 12-year-old Buddy Stebbins follows her back in time and finds himself aboard a 17th-century pirate ship captained by a distant relative.

Hurmence, Belinda. (1982). *A girl called Boy*. Clarion. A pampered young black girl who has been mysteriously transported back to the days of slavery struggles to escape her bondage.

Irving, Washington. (2000). *Rip Van Winkle* (Arthur Rackham, Illus.). SeaStar. A man who sleeps for 20 years in the Catskill Mountains awakes to a much-changed world. (Original work published 1905)

McKinley, Robin. (1978). *Beauty: A retelling of the story of beauty and the beast*. Harper & Row. Kind Beauty grows to love the Beast, at whose castle she is compelled to stay. Through her love, she releases him from the spell that had turned him from a handsome prince into an ugly creature.

Nesbit, E. (2000). *The magic city*. SeaStar. An extremely unhappy 10-year-old magically escapes into a city he has built out of books, chessmen, candlesticks, and other household items. (Original work published 1910)

Pinkwater, Daniel. (1999). *The Hoboken chicken emergency*. Atheneum. Arthur goes to pick up the turkey for Thanksgiving dinner but comes back with a 260-pound chicken.

Pullman, Philip. (1998). *Clockwork*. Scholastic. Long ago in Germany, a storyteller's story and an apprentice clockwork-maker's nightmare meet in a menacing, lifelike figure created by the strange Dr. Kalmenius.

Stearns, Michael. (1993). *A wizard's dozen: Stories of the fantastic*. Harcourt Brace. Twelve short stories by popular and award-winning authors Bruce Coville, Patricia C. Wrede, Will Shetterly, Charles de Lint, Betty Levin, and Jane Yolen.

Vande Velde, Vivian. (1985). *A hidden magic* (Trina Schart Hyman, Illus.). Harcourt. Lost in a magic forest and separated from her prince, Princess Jennifer seeks help from a kindly young sorcerer in battling an evil witch.

Voigt, Cynthia. (1984). *Building blocks*. Scholastic. A time-warp experience helps a boy understand his father.

▼▼▼▼▼▼▼

Others We Like

Barron, T. A. (1996). *The lost years of Merlin*. Philomel. (See the others in The Lost Years of Merlin epic.)

Bellairs, John. (1973). *The house with a clock in its walls*. Dial. (See the other in the Lewis Barnavelt series.)

Billingsley, Franny. (1999). *The folk keeper*. Atheneum.

Dahl, Roald. (1988). *Matilda*. Viking Kestrel.

Dickinson, Peter. (1989). *Eva*. Delacorte.

Duncan, Lois. (1976). *Summer of fear*. Little, Brown.

Griffin, Peni R. (1993). *Switching well*. McElderry.

Haddix, Margaret Peterson. (2000). *Turnabout*. Simon & Schuster.

Hanley, Victoria. (2000). *The seer and the sword*. Holiday House.

Hite, Sid. (1992). *Dither farm*. Henry Holt.

Jansson, Tove. (1994). *Moominpappa's memoirs*. Farrar, Straus & Giroux.

Jones, Diana Wynne. (1995). *Cart and cwidder*. Greenwillow. (See the other books in the Dalemark Quartet.)

Lawrence, Louise. (1996). *Dream-weaver*. Clarion.

Le Guin, Ursula K. (1968). *A wizard of Earthsea*. Parnassus. (See the other books in the Earthsea trilogy.)

L'Engle, Madeleine. (1962). *A wrinkle in time*. Farrar, Straus & Giroux. (See other books in the Time series.)

Levy, Robert. (1995). *The misfit apprentice*. Houghton Mifflin.

Morris, Gerald. (1998). *The squire's tale*. Houghton Mifflin.

Paulsen, Gary. (1998). *The Transall saga*. Delacorte.

Pearce, Philippa. (1958). *Tom's midnight garden*. Lippincott.

Prince, Maggie. (1996). *The house on Hound Hill*. Houghton Mifflin.

Pullman, Philip. (1999). *The firework-maker's daughter*. Scholastic/Arthur A. Levine.

Regan, Dian Curtis. (1995). *Princess Nevermore*. Scholastic.

Smith, Sherwood. (1990). *Wren to the rescue*. Harcourt Brace. (See the other books in the Wren series.)

Easier to Read

Brown, Jeff. (1964). *Flat Stanley* (Tomi Ungerer, Illus.). Harper & Row.

Cleary, Beverly. (1965). *The mouse and the motorcycle.* Morrow.

Cuyler, Majorie. (1995). *Invisible in the third grade* (Mirko Gabler, Illus.). Henry Holt.

Griffin, Adele. (2001). *Witch twins.* Hyperion.

Key, Alexander. (1965). *The forgotten door.* Scholastic.

King-Smith, Dick. (1985). *Babe: The gallant pig.* Crown.

Napoli, Donna Jo. (1992). *The prince of the pond* (Judith Byron Schachner, Illus.). Dutton.

Scieszka, Jon. (1991). *Knights of the kitchen table* (Lane Smith, Illus.). Viking. (See other books in the Time Warp Trio series.)

Smith, Robert Kimmel. (1972). *Chocolate fever* (Gioria Fiammenghi, Illus.). Coward.

Wright, Betty Ren. (1994). *The ghost comes calling.* Scholastic.

Picture Books

DeFelice, Cynthia. (2000). *Cold feet* (Robert Andrew Parker, Illus.). DK Ink.

Henkes, Kevin. (1996). *Lilly's purple plastic purse.* Greenwillow.

Kellogg, Steven. (1977). *The mysterious tadpole.* Dial.

Meddaugh, Susan. (1992). *Martha speaks.* Houghton Mifflin. (See other books in the Martha series.)

Peet, Bill. (1971). *How Droofus the dragon lost his head.* Houghton Mifflin.

Pyle, Howard. (1997). *Bearskin* (Trina Schart Hyman, Illus.). Morrow Junior.

Rosenberg, Liz. (1993). *Monster Mama* (Stephen Gammell, Illus.). Putnam.

Small, David. (1986). *Imogene's antlers.* Crown.

Small, David. (1987). *Paper John.* Farrar, Straus & Giroux.

Steig, William. (1969). *Sylvester and the magic pebble.* Farrar, Straus & Giroux.

Steig, William. (1982). *Dr. De Soto.* Farrar, Straus & Giroux.

Van Allsburg, Chris. (1979). *The garden of Abdul Gasazi.* Houghton Mifflin.

Williams, Suzanne. (1997). *Library Lil* (Steven Kellogg, Illus.). Dial.

Wood, Audrey. (1996). *The Bunyans* (David Shannon, Illus.). Blue Sky Press/Scholastic.

▼▼▼▼▼▼▼▼

Children's Literature References

Ada, Alma Flor. (1998). *The malachite palace* (Leonid Gore, Illus.). New York: Atheneum.

Alexander, Lloyd. (1964). *The book of three.* New York: Holt.

Alexander, Lloyd. (1965). *The black cauldron.* New York: Holt.

Alexander, Lloyd. (1967). *Taran wanderer.* New York: Holt.

Alexander, Lloyd. (1968). *The high king.* New York: Holt.

Alexander, Lloyd. (1981). *Westmark.* New York: Random House.

Alexander, Lloyd. (1982). *The kestrel.* New York: Dutton.

Alexander, Lloyd. (1984). *The beggar queen.* New York: Dutton.

Alexander, Lloyd. (1991). *The remarkable journey of Prince Jen.* New York: Dutton.

Alexander, Lloyd. (1995a). *The Arkadians.* New York: Dutton.

Alexander, Lloyd. (1995b). *The house gobbaleen* (Diane Goode, Illus.). New York: Dutton.

Alexander, Lloyd. (1997). *The iron ring.* New York: Dutton.

Almond, David. (1999). *Skellig.* New York: Delacorte.

Andersen, Hans Christian. (1993). *The snow queen* (Naomi Lewis, Trans., Angela Barrett, Illus.). Cambridge, MA: Candlewick Press.

Avi. (1994). *The bird, the frog, and the light: A fable* (Matthew Henry, Illus.). New York: Orchard.

Avi. (1995). *Poppy* (Brian Floca, Illus.). New York: Orchard.

Avi. (1998a). *Perloo the bold* (Marcie Reed, Illus.). New York: Scholastic.

Avi. (1998b). *Poppy and Rye* (Brian Floca, Illus.). New York: Avon.

Avi. (1999a). *Midnight magic.* New York: Scholastic.

Avi. (1999b). *Ragweed* (Brian Floca, Illus.). New York: Avon.

Avi. (2000). *Ereth's birthday* (Brian Floca, Illus.). New York: HarperCollins.

Babbitt, Natalie. (1975). *Tuck everlasting.* New York: Farrar, Straus & Giroux.

Banks, Lynne Reid. (1989). *The fairy rebel.* New York: Camelot.

Banks, Lynne Reid. (1990). *The Indian in the cupboard* (Brock Cole, Illus.). New York: Avon.

Banks, Lynne Reid. (1992). *The adventures of King Midas* (Jos A. Smith, Illus.). New York: Morrow.

Barber, Antonia. (1994). *Catkin: Mouse hunter, closer than friend, wind dancer at the bough's end* (P. J. Lynch, Illus.). Cambridge, MA: Candlewick Press.

Barrett, Judi. (1978). *Cloudy with a chance of meatballs* (Ron Barrett, Illus.). New York: Aladdin.

Barrie, J. M. (1906). *Peter Pan.* New York: Scribner's.

Bateman, Teresa. (1997). *The ring of truth* (Omar Rayyan, Illus.). New York: Holiday House.

Baum, L. Frank. (1900). *The wonderful wizard of Oz.* New York: G. M. Hill.

Berger, Barbara Helen. (1994). *The jewel heart.* New York: Philomel.

Briggs, Raymond. (1970). *Jim and the beanstalk.* New York: Coward-McCann.

Buehner, Caralyn. (1996). *Fanny's dream* (Mark Buehner, Illus.). New York: Dial.

Burton, Virginia Lee. (1937). *Choo Choo: The runaway engine.* New York: Scholastic.

Butler, Charles. (1998). *The darkling.* New York: McElderry.

Cadnum, Michael. (1998). *In a dark wood.* New York: Orchard.

Carroll, Lewis. (1865). *Alice's adventures in Wonderland.* London: Macmillan.

Catling, Patrick. (1979). *The chocolate touch.* New York: William Morrow.

Christian, Peggy. (1995). *The bookstore mouse* (Gary Lippincott, Illus.). San Diego: Harcourt Brace.

Climo, Shirley. (1997). *A treasury of mermaids: Mermaid tales from around the world* (Jean Tseng & Mou-sien Tseng, Illus.). New York: HarperCollins.

Collodi, Carlo. (1904). *Pinocchio.* Boston: Ginn.

Conly, Jane Leslie. (1986). *Rasco and the rats of NIMH* (Leonard Lubin, Illus.). New York: HarperCollins.

Conrad, Pam. (1990). *Stonewords.* New York: HarperCollins.

Cooney, Caroline B. (1995). *Both sides of time.* New York: Bantam Doubleday Dell.

Cooney, Caroline B. (1996). *Out of time.* New York: Bantam Doubleday Dell.

Cooney, Caroline B. (1998). *Prisoner of time.* New York: Bantam Doubleday Dell.

Cooper, Susan. (1965). *Over sea, under stone* (Margery Gill, Illus.). San Diego: Harcourt Brace.

Cooper, Susan. (1973). *The dark is rising.* New York: Collier.

Cooper, Susan. (1974). *Greenwitch.* New York: Scholastic.

Cooper, Susan. (1975). *The grey king.* New York: Scholastic.

Cooper, Susan. (1977). *Silver on the tree.* New York: Scholastic.

Cooper, Susan. (1993). *The boggart.* New York: McElderry.

Coville, Bruce. (1991). *Jeremy Thatcher, dragon hatcher* (Gary A. Lippincott, Illus.). New York: Pocket Books.

Creech, Sharon. (1996). *Pleasing the ghost.* New York: HarperCollins.

Dahl, Roald. (1961). *James and the giant peach* (Nancy Ekholm Burkert, Illus.). New York: Knopf.

Dahl, Roald. (1964). *Charlie and the chocolate factory* (Joseph Schindelman, Illus.). New York: Bantam.

Dahl, Roald. (1991). *The minpins.* New York: Viking.

Dexter, Catherine. (1996). *A is for apple, W is for witch* (Capucine Mazille, Illus.). Cambridge, MA: Candlewick Press.

Farmer, Nancy. (1994). *The ear, the eye, and the arm.* New York: Orchard.

Fletcher, Susan. (1989). *Dragon's milk.* New York: Aladdin.

Fletcher, Susan. (1998). *Shadow spinner.* New York: Atheneum.

French, Jackie. (1995). *Somewhere around the corner.* New York: Henry Holt.

Gerstein, Mordicai. (1986). *The seal mother.* New York: Dial.

Grahame, Kenneth. (1908). *The wind in the willows.* London: Methuen.

Greenfield, Karen Radler. (1994). *The teardrop baby* (Sharleen Collicott, Illus.). New York: HarperCollins.

Gregory, Valiska. (1996). *When stories fell like shooting stars* (Stefano Vitale, Illus.). New York: Simon & Schuster.

Hahn, Mary Downing. (1985). *Wait till Helen comes: A ghost story.* New York: Houghton Mifflin.

Hesse, Karen. (1994). *Phoenix rising.* New York: Henry Holt.

Hite, Sid. (1995). *Answer my prayer.* New York: Henry Holt.

Hodges, Margaret. (1984). *St. George and the dragon* (Trina Schart Hyman, Illus.). Boston: Little, Brown.

Hodges, Margaret. (1996). *Molly Limbo* (Elizabeth Miles, Illus.). New York: Atheneum.

Howe, Deborah, & Howe, James. (1979). *Bunnicula: A rabbit-tale of mystery* (Alan Daniel, Illus.). New York: Atheneum.

Jackson, Ellen. (1994). *Cinder Edna* (Kevin O'Malley, Illus.). New York: Mulberry.

Jacques, Brian. (1987). *Redwall.* New York: Philomel.

Johnston, Tony. (1996). *The ghost of Nicholas Greebe* (S. D. Schindler, Illus.). New York: Dial.

Kellogg, Steven. (1986). *Best friends.* New York: Puffin Pied Piper.

Ketteman, Helen. (1997). *Bubba the cowboy prince: A fractured Texas tale* (James Warhola, Illus.). New York: Scholastic.

Kipling, Rudyard. (1982). *Just so stories* (Victor G. Ambrus, Illus.). New York: Rand. (Original work published 1902)

Kipling, Rudyard. (1987). *Just so stories* (Jack Nicholson, Narr.). New York: Rabbit Ears/Simon & Schuster.

Lasky, Kathryn. (1999). *Star split.* New York: Hyperion.

Lawson, Julie. (1993). *The dragon's pearl* (Paul Morin, Illus.). New York: Clarion.

Levine, Gail Carson. (1997). *Ella enchanted.* New York: HarperCollins.

Levine, Gail Carson. (1999a). *The fairy's mistake* (Mark Elliott, Illus.). New York: HarperCollins.

Levine, Gail Carson. (1999b). *The princess test* (Mark Elliott, Illus.). New York: HarperCollins.

Lewis, C. S. (1950). *The lion, the witch, and the wardrobe.* New York: Macmillan.

Lisle, Janet Taylor. (1989). *Afternoon of the elves.* New York: Watts.

Lisle, Janet Taylor. (1993). *Forest.* New York: Orchard.

Lisle, Janet Taylor. (1999). *The lost flower children.* New York: Philomel.

Lowell, Susan. (1992). *The three little javelinas.* Flagstaff, AZ: Northland.

Lowry, Lois. (1993). *The giver.* Boston: Houghton Mifflin.

Lowry, Lois. (1997). *Stay! Keeper's story.* Boston: Houghton Mifflin.

Lowry, Lois. (2000). *Gathering blue.* Boston: Houghton Mifflin.

MacGill-Callahan, Sheila. (1995). *The seal prince* (Kris Waldherr, Illus.). New York: Dial.

Manes, Stephen. (1995). *An almost perfect game.* New York: Scholastic.

Martin, Bill, Jr. (1983). *Brown bear, brown bear, what do you see?* (Eric Carle, Illus.). New York: Henry Holt.

Martin, Bill, Jr., & John Archambault (1989). *Chicka chicka boom boom* (Lois Ehlert, Illus.). New York: Simon & Schuster.

Mayne, William. (1994). *Hob and the goblins.* Boston: Houghton Mifflin.

McClure, Gillian. (1999). *Selkie.* New York: Farrar, Straus & Giroux.

McGraw, Eloise. (1996). *The moorchild.* New York: McElderry.

McKenzie, Ellen Kindt. (1994). *Under the bridge.* New York: Henry Holt.

McKinley, Robin. (1997). *Rose daughter.* New York: Greenwillow.

Meddaugh, Susan. (1997). *Cinderella's rat.* Boston: Houghton Mifflin.

Melmed, Laura Krauss. (1992). *The rainbabies* (Jim LaMarche, Illus.). New York: Lothrop.

Melmed, Laura Krauss. (1994). *Prince Nautilus* (Henri Sorenson, Illus.). New York: Lothrop.

Melmed, Laura Krauss. (1997). *Little Oh* (Jim LaMarche, Illus.). New York: Lothrop.

Milne, A. A. (1926). *Winnie-the-Pooh.* New York: Dutton.

Minters, Frances. (1996). *Sleepless beauty.* New York: Viking.

Morpurgo, Michael. (1995). *The war of Jenkins' ear.* New York: Philomel.

Morressy, John. (1996). *The juggler.* New York: Henry Holt.

Moser, Barry. *Great ghost stories.* New York: Morrow.

Napoli, Donna Jo. (1992). *The magic circle.* New York: Dutton.

Napoli, Donna Jo. (1996). *Zel.* New York: Dutton.

Napoli, Donna Jo. (1999). *Spinners.* New York: Dutton.

Norton, Mary. (1953). *The borrowers.* New York: Harcourt Brace.

O'Brien, Robert C. (1971). *Mrs. Frisby and the rats of NIMH* (Zena Bernstein, Illus.). New York: Scholastic.

O'Brien, Robert C. (1975). *Z for Zachariah.* New York: Atheneum.

Osborne, Mary Pope. (1994). *Haunted waters.* Cambridge, MA: Candlewick Press.

Palatini, Margie. (1995). *Piggie pie!* (Howard Fine, Illus.). New York: Clarion.

Peck, Richard. (1995). *Lost in cyberspace.* New York: Dial.

Peck, Richard. (1996). *The great interactive dream machine.* New York: Dial.

Peterson, John. (1970). *The littles* (Roberta Carter Clark, Illus.). New York: Scholastic.

Pullman, Philip. (1996). *The golden compass.* New York: Knopf.

Pullman, Philip. (1998). *Clockwork: Or all wound up.* New York: Scholastic.

Rosenthal, Paul. (1998). *Yo, Aesop!: Get a load of these fables* (Marc Rosenthal, Illus.). New York: Simon & Schuster.

Rowling, J. K. (1998). *Harry Potter and the sorcerer's stone.* New York: Scholastic.

San Souci, Robert D. (1997). *Nicholas Pipe* (David Shannon, Illus.). New York: Dial.

Scieszka, Jon. (1989). *The true story of the three little pigs!* (Lane Smith, Illus.). New York: Viking.

Scieszka, Jon. (1991a). *The frog prince, continued* (Steve Johnson, Illus.). New York: Viking.

Scieszka, Jon. (1991b). *The stinky cheese man and other fairly stupid tales* (Lane Smith, Illus.). New York: Viking.

Scieszka, Jon. (1998). *Squids will be squids* (Lane Smith, Illus.). New York: Viking.

Seabrooke, Brenda. (1995). *The swan's gift* (Wenhai Ma, Illus.). New York: Candlewick Press.

Selden, George. (1960). *A cricket in Times Square* (Garth Williams, Illus.). New York: Farrar, Straus & Giroux.

Small, David. (1987). *Paper John.* New York: Farrar, Straus & Giroux.

Somtow, S. P. (1997). *The vampire's beautiful daughter.* New York: Atheneum.

Thomas, Jane Resh. (1989). *The princess in the pigpen.* New York: Clarion.

Tolkien, J. R. R. (1937). *The hobbit.* London: G. Allen and Unwin.

Travers, P. L. (1934). *Mary Poppins.* London: G. Howe.

Tunnell, Michael O. (1997). *School spirits.* New York: Holiday House.

Vaughan, Marcia. (1995). *Whistling Dixie* (Barry Moser, Illus.). New York: HarperCollins.

Verne, Jules. (1869). *Twenty thousand leagues under the sea.* New York: Barnes & Noble.

Walsh, Jill Paton. (1982). *The green book.* New York: Farrar, Straus & Giroux.

Waugh, Sylvia. (1994). *The Mennyms.* New York: Greenwillow.

White, Carolyn. (1997). *Whuppity Stoorie* (S. D. Schindler, Illus.). New York: Putnam.

White, E. B. (1952). *Charlotte's web* (Garth Williams, Illus.). New York: HarperCollins.

Williams, Jay. (1988). *Everyone knows what a dragon looks like* (Mercer Mayer, Illus.). New York: Aladdin.

Winthrop, Elizabeth. (1990). *The castle in the attic.* New York: Bantam Doubleday Dell.

Wiseman, David. (1981). *Jeremy Visick.* Boston: Houghton Mifflin.

Wolff, Patricia Rae. (1995). *The toll-bridge troll* (Kimberly Bulcken Root, Illus.). San Diego: Harcourt Brace.

Wood, Audrey. (1987). *Heckedy Peg* (Don Wood, Illus.). San Diego: Harcourt Brace.

Wrede, Patricia C. (1985). *Talking to dragons.* New York: Scholastic.

Wrede, Patricia C. (1990). *Dealing with dragons.* New York: Scholastic.

Wrede, Patricia C. (1991). *Searching for dragons.* New York: Scholastic.

Yep, Laurence. (1982). *Dragon of the Lost Sea.* New York: Harper & Row.

Yolen, Jane. (1982). *Dragon's blood.* San Diego: Harcourt Brace.

Yolen, Jane. (1984). *Heart's blood*. New York: Delacorte Press.

Yolen, Jane. (1989). *Dove Isabeau* (Dennis Nolan, Illus.). San Diego: Harcourt Brace.

Yolen, Jane. (1990). *The dragon's boy*. New York: HarperCollins.

Yolen, Jane. (1991a). *Greyling* (David Ray, Illus.). New York: Philomel.

Yolen, Jane. (1991b). *Wizard's hall*. San Diego: Harcourt Brace.

Yolen, Jane. (1997). *Child of faerie, child of earth* (Jane Dyer, Illus.). New York: Little, Brown.

▼▼▼▼▼▼▼

Professional References

Alexander, L. (1965). The flat-heeled muse. *The Horn Book, 41,* 141–146.

Alexander, L. (1968). Wishful thinking—or hopeful dreaming. *The Horn Book, 44,* 382–390.

Alexander, L. (1973). Letter to Shelton L. Root, Jr. 20 February.

Alexander, L. (1981). The grammar of story. In B. Hearne & M. Kaye (Eds.), *Celebrating children's books* (pp. 3–13). New York: Lothrop.

Arbuthnot, M. H. (1952). *Time for fairy tales: Old and new*. Glenview, IL: Scott, Foresman.

Babbitt, N. (1986). The roots of fantasy. *The Bulletin, 12* (2), 2–4.

Babbitt, N. (1987). Fantasy and the classic hero. *School Library Journal, 34,* 25–29.

Bettelheim, B. (1976). *The uses of enchantment*. New York: Vintage.

Campbell, J. (1968). *The hero with a thousand faces* (2nd ed.). Princeton, NJ: Princeton University Press.

Colwell, E. (1968). An oral tradition and an oral art: Folk literature. *Top of the News, 24,* 174–180.

Cooper, S. (1981). Escaping into ourselves. In B. Hearne & M. Kaye (Eds.), *Celebrating children's books* (pp. 14–23). New York: Lothrop.

Darigan, D., & Woodcock, M. L. (1999). Time travel. *Book links*. Chicago: American Library Association.

Engdahl. S. L. (1971). The changing role of science fiction in children's literature. *The Horn Book, 47,* 449–455.

LeGuin, U. (1979). *The language of the night: Essays on fantasy and science fiction*. New York: Putnam.

Madsen. L. L. (1976). *Fantasy in children's literature: A generic study*. Master's thesis, Utah State University.

Neufeldt, V. E. (1988). *Webster's new world dictionary, third college edition*. New York: Simon & Schuster.

Smith, C. A. (1990). *From wonder to wisdom: Using stories to help children grow*. New York: Plume.

Thompson, S. (1932). *Motif-index of folk-literature*. Bloomington: Indiana University Press.

Woolsey, D. (1989). Dreams and wishes: Fantasy literature for children. In J. Hickman & B. Cullinan (Eds.), *Children's literature in the classroom: Weaving Charlotte's web* (pp. 109–120). Needham Heights, MA: Christopher Gordon.

CONTEMPORARY REALISTIC FICTION

7

CHAPTER
▼▼▼▼▼▼▼

If you want to cover
Books by Jerry Spinelli

Consider as a READ ALOUD

Maniac Magee

Consider as a TEXT SET

Crash
Wringer
Dump Days
Space Station Seventh Grade
The Library Card

CRASH
by Jerry Spinelli

KNOPF

Jerry Sp

Student Response

I turned his chocolate pudding upside down on his tray.

He did the same to mine.

By now the whole place was in an uproar. Mike and I had started out laughing. We weren't anymore. There was no way I was going to stop. I've never been No. 2 in my life. I can't stand to lose. More than that, I just won't. Like one of my T-shirts says: REFOOZE TO LOOZE.

Excerpt from *Crash* by Jerry Spinelli

I read through *CRASH* and I especially liked the detail. At the dance, ~~Clash~~ Crash asked Dawn to dance and it gives a great picture of what she looked like. It gave good detail of what people were doing. I could tell everything that was happening. The book had great similies. For example: Abby glued the pieces of bark on the tree like a jigsaw puzzle. I also thought it was funny. Some of the situations were stuff that sounded like something that would happen to me or my friends. I know my temper can get the best of me and so that reminded me of Crash.

Michael, 12

To visit a classroom exploring the issues of Contemporary Realistic Fiction, please go to Chapter 7 of our companion website at **www.prenhall. com/darigan**

For a complete listing of Lowry's Anastasia Krupnik books and Byars's Bingo Brown series, consult the database on the CD that accompanies this text.

Contemporary realistic fiction tells of a story that never happened but that *could* have happened. The events and the characters in contemporary realistic fiction flow from the author's imagination, just as they do in fantasy. However, unlike fantasy, which includes at least one element not found in this world, everything in contemporary realistic fiction is possible on planet Earth.

Contemporary realistic fiction deals with the condition of human life as we know it. Readers come face to face with kids much like themselves dealing with many of the same kinds of problems and situations they are presented with in their own daily lives. For example, many children would find it difficult not to identify with the crazy shenanigans of a character like Lois Lowry's Anastasia in *Anastasia Krupnik* and the rest of the books in that series or the ever-ebullient Bingo in Betsy Byars's hilarious series beginning with *The Burning Questions of Bingo Brown*. In books such as these, children can be seen fighting with their parents and siblings over mundane and monumental issues. They can be found falling in and out of love, getting into scrapes with their friends and neighbors, and doing myriad "kid" kinds of things.

▼▼▼▼▼▼▼▼

Elements of Contemporary Realistic Fiction

The incidents that appear during the course of the story may have actually happened to the author, as was the case with all of the events in Gary Paulsen's *Hatchet*. They could be based on events that were related to the author by another person, as was the case in John Reynolds Gardiner's *Stone Fox*. More often than not, however, the seed of the idea for the book comes from an event or series of events the author has experienced or viewed and then embellished with his or her own imagination. Lois Duncan, author of *I Know What You Did Last Summer,* states, "Writing becomes a combination of personal experience and imagination. I take a kernel of reality to give the story a realistic feel and expand it and move to the next step by asking, 'What if?'" (personal communication, July, 1999).

But, just as important to children, contemporary realistic fiction deals with unusual problems or situations that may be foreign to the children's own experiences and that exist in other places and cultures that have, heretofore, remained unknown to them. Where else but within the pages of a book can a child safely experience the horrors of terrorism, racism, and religious persecution, or the pain of dealing with physical, mental, or emotional constraints and limitations? Further, the reader of this genre comes to grips with situations dealing with many of the basic conditions of humanity, such as death, developing sexuality, mental illness, aging, and alcoholism.

One element specific to contemporary realistic fiction is that all events are set in the present or near present. As we see in this chapter, the genre also spans an enormously broad range of contemporary content and issues. Examples swing from Jerry Spinelli's books *Maniac Magee, Crash,* and *Wringer*, all three of which deal with peer pressure and the pain and struggle of growing up in a sometimes cruel and heartless society, to John Marsden's book *Tomorrow, When the War Began,* which chronicles a group of young adults who are unknowingly faced with the aftermath of an invasion of their country that occurred while they were on a camping trip in the outback of Australia. M. E. Kerr's *Deliver Us From Evie* very boldly addresses the clash of values that occurs when a young Iowa farm girl falls into a lesbian relationship with the daughter of the town's most powerful and influential family.

Importance of Story

W. Somerset Maugham disclosed the secret of writing an appealing book: "There are three rules for writing a good novel. Unfortunately, no one knows what they are" (Stephens, 1990, p. 543). The exact recipe for solid writing does not exist, for if it did, anyone privy to the "formula" could predictably crank out one award winner after an-

To find out more about *The End of the Rainbow* and other on-line literature on the World Wide Web, visit Chapter 7 on the Companion Website at **www.prenhall.com/darigan**

BOOKMARK

INTEGRATING TECHNOLOGY: ACTIVITIES USING THE WORLD WIDE WEB

More and more stories and books are being published on the Internet; many are self-published and of questionable quality, but some high-quality contemporary literature is also appearing as both e-books and on websites. A full-text electronic version of Bjarne Reuter's **The End of the Rainbow** is available on the Penguin Putnam publisher's website. This is the final book in a trilogy about Buster Oregon Mortensen, the first book of which won the Mildred Batchelder Award for the best children's book published in translation. Unfortunately, translated books often do not sell in large quantity in the United States. The publishers felt so strongly that they wanted to make the book available to American audiences that they ended up publishing the entire translation on the World Wide Web.

other. All readers recognize one unfailing earmark of a good novel: It must tell a satisfying story. Every memorable work of fiction presents a conflict or problem that affects human beings. How this obstacle is overcome *is* the story. Writers of contemporary realistic fiction draw on their own backgrounds or observe life around them to tell their stories. Take, for example, the seed of the idea that was to become Rita Williams-Garcia's third novel. In describing one of her troubled main characters, she states,

> [My] character, Gayle, in *Like Sisters on the Homefront,* is completely fiction. The only thing real about her is that when I was 18 years old and getting ready to go off to college I saw this girl I knew standing in the doorway of her house. She had her baby brother on her hip and I was so excited to see the baby. I had not known her mother had had a baby. I said, "Oh, I didn't know your mom had a baby."
>
> That twelve-year-old girl looked at me with such an attitude and simply said, "That's my baby." She was so blasé about it and a little more than annoyed with me. It was like "what was wrong with me." That incident from 1975 stayed with me. I always knew I was going to write not so much about her, that particular girl, but just simply that matter-of-factness about trading off one's girlhood, stunting one's own growth, and just that whole notion of breeding life and death. (Darigan, 1999, pp. 80–89).

Identifying With Contemporary Realistic Fiction

Of all the genres in children's literature, contemporary realistic fiction is, understandably, the most popular (Monson & Sebesta, 1991). People are naturally interested in their own lives, and this genre is specifically about "my life." This is "my" world. This is how "I" live. This story is about a girl or boy like me. Because the characters in contemporary realistic fiction are similar to people in our own community, town, or neighborhood, the reader gets to know them quickly and feel as if he or she has known them a long time. The main character, in particular, can become a kindred spirit. The character experiences the same disappointments and hopes, rejections, and joys as the reader, who is amazed and thrilled to find someone who sees the world through a similar lens. Certainly, readers can connect with the lives of those from the past as well as with fantasy characters, but something about the "here and now" packs an additional emotional punch.

A friend recently spoke to us about S. E. Hinton's **The Outsiders,** the story of the violently explosive enmity waged between the "society kids" and the "greasers." Because our friend grew up part of the latter group, this book spoke to her in a very personal way while she was going through the rocky traumas of her own teen years. "My group of friends and I were, indeed, living in Ponyboy's world. My best girlfriend

A CONVERSATION WITH. . .

Lois Lowry

I will start by saying that when I was a kid, realistic fiction was what I liked best. The books I loved most were, first of all, realistic fiction, badly done. And into that category I will put things like **The Bobbsey Twins** and **Nancy Drew**. And then, as I became a little older and a little more discriminating, I gravitated toward realistic fiction, well done. And into that category I would put the two books that introduced me to literature of that level, **The Yearling** and **A Tree Grows in Brooklyn.** Both of them were realistic, although their realism was very different from the realism of my own life. But I recognized them as realistic. And they were the first books that gave me the sense of entering into another person's life, and participating in that life in a realistic way through fiction.

Those were the books I liked best. Books that felt real to me, whose people felt real, whose people I wanted to know and even live next door to. So it's probably not surprising that when I began to write for kids, it was in that genre. My very first one, **A Summer to Die,** although it was fiction, did grow out of my own real life and my family's experience with the death of my sister. So I've always, in those books, tried to create a main character surrounded by a family and an extended circle of neighbors, friends, and acquaintances who seem quite real and with whom one would enjoy spending, if not a life next door, certainly a period of time in a book.

Anastasia, in her first book, lives with her family in Cambridge, Massachusetts about four blocks away from where I'm currently sitting at my desk looking out into my yard. And in the second book they move, but only to a suburb of Boston. And I know Boston well.

The first Anastasia book was published in 1979, which means that it was written in 1978. At that time, Jimmy Carter was president and his daughter, Amy, would have been about 10 years old. I really got a kick out of Amy Carter because she was such a realistic kid, as opposed to previous presidential daughters who seemed so perfect. My father had been dentist to the Nixon girls, and he always came home and reported how well groomed and polite they were so that I always wanted to throw up when I was a teenager. At any rate, Amy Carter was misbehaved and had straggly hair and braces on her teeth, I think, and untied shoes—and so I found her kind of appealing, and she was there in my subconscious.

And Sam spun off along the way because of kids who wrote and asked for a book about Sam. And after its publication, it was very well received by kids who, it turned out, did enjoy reading about somebody much younger than they because the book is written on a somewhat sophisticated level so that they're able, I think, to laugh at their own earlier selves and look back on their own earlier childhood with a degree of affectionate humor. And teachers enjoyed the books, the Sam books, because they use them as read-alouds for second/third grade with great success. And so they're always eager for another Sam book. So I suppose I'll continue to do both.

To read more of this Conversation with Lois Lowry, please visit Chapter 7 on our text's companion website at **www.prenhall.com/darigan**

and I checked the book out of the library and, because we both wanted to read it so badly, decided to read it together, side by side, page after page. When we reached the end and it said, 'When I stepped out into the bright sunlight from the darkness of the movie house, I had only two things on my mind: Paul Newman and a ride home . . .' we turned to the first page and began to read it all over again. This was so much the way we were growing up."

Books that deal with specific cultures, nationalities, minorities, and subgroups also provide a connection between each of those communities and the rest of the world. They act as a vehicle to accent the diversity of our lives while, at the same time, detailing the universality of our existence. All readers like to find at least an occasional title that reflects their lives, and it is the lack of books dealing with other cultures that can draw protest from members of a group who desire to read about something accurate and close to home. Because realistic fiction helps confirm our own membership in the human race, children's publishers and authors continue to represent the spectrum of minorities present in the United States—racial groups, different religions, stories from specific regions of the country—but not all bases have yet been covered. For in-

ALTERNATE TEXT SET

Deafness

Read Aloud

Dovey Cove, by Frances O'Roark Dowell

Text Set

A Dance To Still Music, by Barbara Corcoran

The Truth Trap, by Frances A. Miller

The Gift of the Girl Who Couldn't Hear, by Susan Shreve

Raging Quiet, by Sherryl Jordan

Can You Feel the Thunder?, by Lynn McElfresh

stance, the half-million people in the United States who are Deaf (capitalized to indicate they belong to the Deaf culture, not just that they do not hear). At the time of this writing, they are represented by only a small handful of picture storybooks and novels currently in print in America. A few informational picture books are also available, detailing facts about sign language and what life is like for the nonhearing, but being represented by only this small number of books leaves the Deaf without the confirmation of their lives and enrichment provided in a story about "someone like me." And, as important, the lack of such books also means that others have less opportunity to get to know and understand the Deaf.

The importance of identifying with one's own life is the main reason children's books have children as the protagonists. A general guideline is that the age of the main character be approximately the age of the reader. For this reason, *Rescue, Josh McGuire,* a captivating survival tale written by Ben Mikaelsen, was published as a children's book even though Mikaelsen had written the book with an adult audience in mind. Because the main character is a young boy, its market and audience are the same—young readers. The rule of thumb is that children will read about characters who are slightly older than they are but are hesitant about reading books with characters who are younger.

Familiarity helps explain why many children who have not yet discovered the pleasures books can bring often find their first successful reading experiences with contemporary realistic fiction. Trying out a new book is a big risk for the reader, and those not steeped in personal reading experiences are less likely to take chances. Contemporary realistic fiction offers less of a gamble because the book contains familiar elements. The reader meets a familiar character who lives in a familiar world and who faces similar situations. A detailed introduction is less important, for much of the groundwork already exists for a relationship, or even a friendship, to develop between reader and character. Youngsters are consistently drawn in to a book with a beginning such as this one by Avi in his book *Windcatcher.*

> "Dad," Tony Souza said, "what's money *for* if you can't spend it?" It was a Saturday, the first day of summer vacation, but to Tony his vacation already felt like a disaster.

A child bickering with his father about money? On the very first day of summer vacation? A summer vacation that has been devastated from the start? Now, that is the beginning that grabs the reluctant reader and refuses to let go until the very last page.

EVALUATING   CONTEMPORARY REALISTIC FICTION

- **Story:** Is the story compelling and well written?
- **Character:** Are the characters believable and well developed? Do they change?
- **Setting:** Is the setting well described, giving a true sense of place?
- **Conflict:** Is there a noticeable type of conflict, such as a person against some inner or outside force? (Person against Person, Person against Nature, etc.)
- **Didacticism:** Is the book overpreachy, with too blatant a message?
- **Controversy:** Is the book potentially controversial based on its theme, characters, or topic?

Conflict

We know that conflict, the way it is presented as well as the way it is resolved, makes the story compelling and begs us to read on. Something in the story must happen. Something must go wrong. When it doesn't, we, as readers, are sorely disappointed. Take John Coy's ***Night Driving*** as an example. Though this is a sentimental picture book about a boy and his father traveling west in their car through the night, we are met in every double-page spread with an expectation that something will happen, but we are constantly left wanting. "Goodness," we say to ourselves, "when will something *happen?*"

In the book, Dad says, "Many animals come out at night," and we think *maybe they will hit a deer.* "Kaflump, kaflump . . ." They experience a flat tire instead. We surmise that some mishap may ensue. But, with spare tire on, Dad lets down the car and off they go. He further says, "That moon is so bright we could drive without headlights." So he slows down, turns off the lights, and courses the road with only the moonlight to guide them. Will something happen *now?* Unfortunately, it never does. The book becomes nothing more than a listing of night driving experiences and, though charming, leaves us with a sense of incompleteness. Nothing has happened.

Conflict sets up the natural "tension" in a book, and how that tension builds, how it is dealt with, and, consequently, how it is relieved becomes the story. Typically, when teaching reading, or writing for that matter, we ask children to pay particular heed to conflict and the various forms it takes. By specifically noting these, we provide an overriding organizational framework for which meaning can be made. Because conflict tends to be separated into four categories—Person Against Self, Person Against Person, Person Against Nature, and Person Against Society (Fletcher, 1993; Norton, 1992)—and because it is such a natural teaching tool, we will use these categories as our guideposts in organizing contemporary realistic fiction.

Person Against Person

When looking at contemporary realistic fiction using these four categories as organizers, it became immediately clear to us that the most frequently used of the four is "Person Against Person." Indeed, this particular focus on conflict describes the day-to-day issues most children face. It is the everyday story of our lives: Friends get angry with each other, parents bicker with their children (and vice versa), boys love and hate girls (and vice versa), and brothers can *never* seem to get along with their sisters (and vice versa).

Jerry Spinelli, who won the Newbery Medal for his book ***Maniac Magee,*** has a special knack for capturing the voice and the very essence of children's conflicts. In ***Crash***, we meet our main character head-on in the first lines of the book: "My real name is John. John Coogan. But everybody calls me Crash, even my parents." The seventh-grade football star, who has two overextended parents and an activist sister, colludes with his friend Mike Deluca in terrorizing a young Quaker boy, Penn Webb, who lives just up the street. When Crash's grandfather suffers a stroke and must come live with the family, the stage is set for change, acceptance, and understanding to take place.

Jerry and Eileen Spinelli

Jerry Spinelli

There's not a formula for the approach to each book. They can be different. In one case, one book began by a literal visitation from the muse. *They say Maniac Magee was born in the dump.* That sentence came out of the thin air. **Fourth Grade Rats** began simply. *First Grade Baby; Second Grade Cats; Third Grade Angels, Fourth Grade Rats*—I just remembered that schoolyard chant. Fourth Grade Rats—there's a perfect title for a kid's book. There's got to be a book behind that title. So I just wrote down the title at the top of the first page and then sat down for a few days trying to cook up a story that would fit that title.

As for **Crash,** I guess I just thought it would be interesting to write a story from the point of view of a kid that—I don't even think I thought of him as a bully. It just became the tag that was put on him. I thought he was an interesting kind of a kid to take a look at, to see if I could start him out kind of rotten and maybe turn him around and juxtapose him against an interesting character I had in mind by the name of Penn Webb. And it wasn't much more than that.

As far as **Wringer** is concerned, that came right out of a newspaper. The *Philadelphia Inquirer* always carried, once a year, a story about the pigeon shoot at a town not too far away, and I knew there was a story there, I just didn't know how to get into it. So I mulled it over for years, kept it on the back burner. Then one day it occurred to me that the way into this story was by way of one of these kids whose job it was to gather the bodies of the dead and dying pigeons from the shooting fields. The ones that were not already dead, to wring their necks. And what would happen if such a kid came of age in such a town but did not want to become a wringer, in a town where all the boys were expected to. Bam! There's the story.

See, almost every book has a different kind of methodology to it, a different kind of beginning. So you just follow that trail wherever it leads.

Eileen Spinelli

Well, I guess **Mr. Hatch** came from different neighbors that I've known over the years. I think we all know those people who are shy, or a little standoffish or downright grumpy. Just not someone you would go out of your way to know, and yet if somehow you're put in a position to know them, you change your mind about them, and you see that actually a lot of them are quite lovable. I also think that everybody really responds to being loved. No matter how hard-hearted the person, I think if they feel loved, then they respond.

The root of **Night Shift Daddy** is the fact that my father, when I was about 6, worked night shift. And I just remember when he would leave for work—especially in the wintertime. My memory is of a winter night, looking out the window, and he didn't have a car at the time so he would walk up to the bus stop. Just seeing him walking through the cold snow, and he'd have one of those old-fashioned black lunchkits. I would just watch him until he disappeared into the darkness of the bus stop. And then, **When Momma Comes Home Tonight**—I look at my daughters-in-law and my daughter who worked and I am amazed and struck by what wonderful mothers they are and how they have the energy. That is a little homage to young working mothers that I know. They do it all and do it well.

The dynamics of peer strife are extended even further in his book **Wringer.** In this story based on a real yearly event that, to this day, still takes place in Pennsylvania, young Palmer LaRue dreads the coming of his 10th birthday: That is when he will become a "wringer." As the capstone event to the town's Family Fest, a pigeon shoot is held where these young boys, known as "wringers," either retrieve dead birds or snap the necks of those that were not killed. Every boy wants to become a wringer—every boy, that is, except Palmer. But he can't let his hard-nosed, bully friends know that. Only his friend Dorothy knows his true feelings and she, like Penn Webb in *Crash,* is the butt of the gang's cruel jokes. The resolution of both books predictably honors what is good and kind but comes only as a result of some deep soul searching from both main characters.

To read more about this Conversation with Jerry and Eileen Spinelli, please visit Chapter 7 on our text's companion website at **www.prenhall.com/darigan**

Katherine Paterson is equally adept at capturing the dynamics of peer relationships. Her books pack a powerful punch, and the now-classic, Newbery-winning *Bridge to Terabithia* as well as her Newbery Honor book, *The Great Gilly Hopkins,* are must-read books for all children. In *Bridge to Terabithia,* we are introduced to 10-year-old best friends, Leslie and Jess. The two have created a make-believe kingdom in the wooded domain surrounding their homes where the two reign as queen and king. A simple swing on a rope over a dry creek bed allows them entrance. Nobody and nothing can touch them there. But tragedy strikes with the coming of a torrential spring rainstorm, and their world is shattered.

Gilly, the main character in Paterson's *The Great Gilly Hopkins,* is the perfect female counterpart to the rough-edged male antagonists found in Jerry Spinelli's books. Bouncing from foster home to foster home, young Gilly meets her match when she is introduced to Mame Trotter, "a huge hippopotamus of a woman." Under Trotter's roof, she attempts to push her way around through deception and manipulation. At each turn, however, she is met with understanding, love, and acceptance from both her foster mother and their blind African American neighbor, Mr. Randolph. This softens Gilly, helping her to become more accepting of others and tempers the dream she carries to be reunited with her birth mother.

Another book that we have found to be particularly effective as either a read aloud or a book read by a group of children in your classroom is Carol Fenner's *Randall's Wall.* Simply and in a straightforward manner, Fenner introduces us to the character Randall Lord, a destitute, ragamuffin, fifth-grade child shunned by all his classmates. The metaphorical wall he builds around himself protects him from the cruelty he experiences at the hands of his thoughtless peers. A quirky, independent girl in his class, Jean Worth Neary, "adopts" Randall, and with the help of Jean's family, begins to break down Randall's defenses and bring the family out of the depths of poverty.

In Jacqueline Woodson's *I Hadn't Meant to Tell You This,* we come to know Marie, a popular, well-to-do African American girl, and Lena, the poor white girl she is drawn to and subsequently befriends. When Marie learns that Lena is being sexually abused by her father, she is torn between informing the proper authorities and breaking the confidence she has promised to her friend. Lena's concern is that if this abuse were to come out publicly, she would be separated from her younger sister Dion, her only loving familial connection since her mother's death. Students will enjoy following the sisters in Woodson's sequel *Lena.*

Finally, Bruce Brooks's poignant novel *Vanishing* tells of Alice who, after her parents' divorce, gets bounced back and forth between her father and her mother. She falls ill and is hospitalized with a bad bout of bronchitis but, while there, decides to starve herself in an effort to keep from being returned to her mother and her cruel, insensitive stepfather. As her weight drops dangerously low and as she slips in and out of hallucinations, she is befriended by Rex, another patient in her ward who claims he is dying. Through this oftentimes humorous yet short-lived friendship, Alice understands how to take control of her life and, in the end, begins to make amends with her gruff stepfather.

Person Against Self

Inner struggles present themselves to us, and we are forced to deal with problems or issues that are often a result of something that is happening outside our own locus of control. In the end, we are the only ones who can arrive at a reasonable resolution. Issues like these range from the loss of a loved one, the pain of divorce, right vs. wrong, to simply standing up for the truth. These can often be the most intense conflicts we come to grips with because, in them, we are alone. At least, we often feel that way.

Books that deal with these inner conflicts, or what we refer to as "Person Against Self," first let children know that there have been others who have felt just as they do; just knowing that offers many some solace. Second, books further portray the fact that often there are people close to the main character, such as a sympathetic parent, neighbor, teacher, or school counselor, who can be used as a support during those trying times. In either case, the reader sees that all is not lost and that an adequate resolution to his or her own problems can result.

One major ingredient in this type of conflict is the "aloneness" the main character feels as he or she becomes wrapped up in the dilemma of the book. In Marion Dane Bauer's **On My Honor**, for example, young Joel feels totally isolated when his overcompetitive friend, Tony, accidentally drowns. The two, on a dare, swim out toward a sandbar in the treacherous Vermilion River in Illinois, but Joel is the only one who makes it safely. Feeling guilty over the incident, Joel hides Tony's bicycle and clothes, returns home, and attempts to cover up the tragic mishap by lying. He sequesters himself in his room but the latent "stink" of the river grows on him, as does his guilt. This novel faithfully re-creates the tremendous dissonance whirling around inside Joel, letting us, as readers, feel privy to his deepest fears and anxieties.

Ned Wallis feels much the same as Joel in Paula Fox's Newbery Honor book, **One-Eyed Cat.** After Ned receives an air rifle from his Uncle Hilary for his 11th birthday, Ned's father, the stolid Reverend James Wallis, forbids him to use it. Ned, however, disobeys his father and that night retrieves it from the attic. As he makes his way past the stable, he puts the rifle to his shoulder, aiming at nothing in particular, but sees "a dark shadow against the stones which the moon's light had turned the color of ashes." Before he can think, he fires. He has the uneasy feeling that someone has seen him, but he returns the rifle and is never punished for his disobedience. A few weeks later at the house of his neighbor, Mr. Scully, he comes across a one-eyed cat that seems to have "dried blood on his face." Tightly plotted and laced with rich language, this book offers a lesson about truth and honesty not to be forgotten.

Yet another book that accents the internal conflict of withholding the truth is Phyllis Reynolds Naylor's Newbery Medal winner, **Shiloh.** Eleven-year-old Marty Preston views his neighbor, Judd Travers, mistreating one of his dogs, a half-starved beagle. When the poor, ill-used foundling runs away and comes to Marty, the stage is set for some very difficult decisions to be made. Marty chooses to keep the dog and hide him in the woods near his home. He must then lie to his father in an effort to save the dog. Events unfold that make it necessary for him to confront both his lies and the mean neighbor, leading to a suspenseful climax of action. The sequels in the series will hold equal attraction for children and help sensitize them to the humane treatment of animals.

Authentic voice is the hallmark of Barbara Park's powerful novel **Mick Harte Was Here.** The opening section says it all . . .

> Just let me say right off the bat, it was a bike accident.
> It was about as "accidental" as you can get, too . . .
> I don't want to make you cry.
> I just want to tell you about Mick.
> But I thought you should know right up front that he's not here anymore.

From this startling introduction, we progressively learn more about the tomfoolery, as well as the fighting, the love, and the regret, that this brother and sister duo experience in a relationship cut short by Mick's unexpected death.

Darigan was reading **Mick Harte Was Here** to an undergraduate Language Arts class over the course of three class periods. They were studying "voice" in writing. That was the objective anyway. But for the most part, they all looked forward to the focus the book provided. They could escape the reality of their personal worlds for a moment and just sink into the story. The students naturally got comfortable as they settled in for the first 20 minutes of the class. Some students chose to stay in their desks, situated in a circle around the room, and others sat or lay back in the middle of the room, lounging on the carpeted floor in front of Darigan. As the book intensified, he noticed how these 20- and 30-year-old students, just like fifth graders, sidled closer and closer to him, as if drawn by the magnetic force of the written word. At the very climax of the book, when the main character, Phoebe, comes to grips with the loss of her brother, Darigan felt a

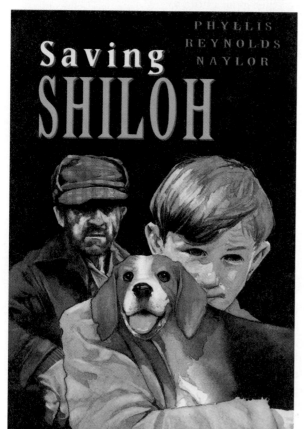

Cover from **Shiloh** by Phyllis Reynolds Naylor. Copyright © 1991 by Phyllis Reynolds Naylor. Jacket illustration copyright © 1991 by Lynne Dennis. Published by Atheneum Books for Young Readers. All rights reserved. Used by permission of Dilys Evans Fine Illustration.

Cover from **Shiloh Season** by Phyllis Reynolds Naylor. Copyright © 1996 by Phyllis Reynolds Naylor. Jacket illustration copyright © 1996 by Barry Moser. Published by Atheneum Books for Young Readers. All rights reserved. Reprinted by permission of Barry Moser.

Cover from **Saving Shiloh** by Phyllis Reynolds Naylor. Copyright © 1997 by Phyllis Reynolds Naylor. Jacket illustration copyright © 1997 by Barry Moser. Published by Atheneum Books for Young Readers. All rights reserved. Reprinted by permission of Barry Moser.

hand reaching out and lightly holding onto his ankle. Looking down, he saw one of the students laying at his feet, head resting on an outstretched arm with tears streaming down his face. It was hard to describe the impact this book had made on these young teachers-to-be.

Later that year, Darigan and a number of his students traveled to Nashville, Tennessee, and were fortunate to meet the author, Barbara Park, at the annual fall conference of the National Council of Teachers of English. They talked to her for quite a long time telling about how important *Mick Harte* was to them and how that shared experience meant so much to them. Books such as these are important catalysts in the formation of kind, sensitive citizens of all ages.

In a very unique book, author Jack Gantos presents a very real picture of the inner struggle inherent in being debilitated with Attention Deficit Hyperactive Disorder (ADHD). *Joey Pigza Swallowed the Key,* written in the first person, very convincingly allows us to see how the mood swings, self-doubt, and the constant physical reaction to "meds" work against this youngster. Joey can't quite seem to get a grip on what is appropriate behavior or how to accomplish it given his powerful inner urges. In class, one day, Joey makes up a game: He swallows his house key, attached to a string hanging around his neck, and pulls it back up, "like I was fishing for bottom feeders . . . Since I was doing it after lunch, I thought it was especially colorful because bits and pieces of food would stick to the key and around the string and I'd suck them off and reswallow them." When his teacher, appalled at this behavior, takes away the string and places the key in his T-shirt pocket, Joey unthinkingly repeats the act, but this time swallows the key only to realize he can't pull it back out. This incident, like many others throughout the book, allows us to see the severity of this child's disability and how he deals with it daily.

Person Against Nature

One of the most popular types of contemporary realistic fiction for both children and adults is the survival novel, or what we have categorized as conflict that accents "Person Against Nature." With this in mind, we broaden the category to comprise not only the rugged wilderness type of survival, but also various types of urban survival, and survival over physical illness.

Having written many wonderful books that cross a number of genres, Gary Paulsen seems to be the preeminent

Cover from *Mick Harte Was Here,* by Barbara Park. Copyright © 1995 by Barbara Park. Cover illustration © 1995 by John Nickle. Published by Alfred A. Knopf & Sons. All rights reserved. Reprinted by permission of the publisher.

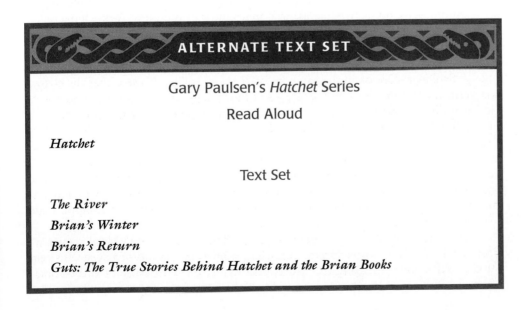

ALTERNATE TEXT SET

Gary Paulsen's *Hatchet* Series

Read Aloud

Hatchet

Text Set

The River

Brian's Winter

Brian's Return

Guts: The True Stories Behind Hatchet and the Brian Books

voice of the wilderness survival story. His series of books based on his Newbery Honor book, *Hatchet,* chronicles the adventures of 13-year-old Brian Robeson, who crash lands in the Canadian wilderness after the pilot of his Cessna 406 suffers a fatal heart attack. For the next 54 days, Brian is forced to survive with the use of only his wits and a small hatchet his mother has given him as a gift for the trip.

Forever changed, Brian is asked 2 years later to repeat his adventure in the sequel, *The River.* This time, government researchers want to learn what techniques Brian used to survive for so long with so little. He is accompanied by psychologist Derek Holtzer, who will collect data that will eventually inform both the space and military programs of the United States. Early in their trip, a freak summer storm blows in and when lightening strikes their shelter, it puts his new partner into a coma. It becomes evident to Brian that the only way to save Derek's life is to build a raft and float him down over 100 miles of river to the nearest trading post. This exciting sequel will be the natural next book for those who finish *Hatchet.*

Paulsen related to us not long ago that he had gotten an enormous amount of mail from children across the country asking the same question: "What if Brian *hadn't* been rescued after 54 days as happened in the first book, *Hatchet*?" Under normal circumstances, Paulsen stated, he wouldn't have given it much thought, but there was so much interest in the continued adventure of the 13-year-old Robeson that he wrote a companion sequel as if the boy was not rescued. In *Brian's Winter,* he takes on the most formidable force of nature—winter. In the conclusion of the series, Brian finds himself in high school, not fitting in and with a more isolated feeling among people than he had while alone in the woods. His return is recorded in the fourth and final book in the series, *Brian's Return.*

A relatively new voice in this genre comes from author Roland Smith. Known for many years now for his nonfiction picture books, Smith has branched out and addressed the intermediate novel audience with a number of fast-paced page-turners. *Thunder Cave, Jaguar,* and *The Last Lobo* all find young Jake Lanza, a hero with the same heart as Paulsen's Brian Robeson, surviving against great odds in books that additionally have a pro-environmental emphasis on saving endangered animals. *Sasquatch* tells of Dylan Hickock and his father's search for the Pacific Northwest rendering of Big Foot, known there as Sasquatch. All four novels are high-action and are great suggestions for the reluctant reader in need of an exciting adventure.

The flip side of the adventure story set in the wilderness is the survival novel set in the city. Paula Fox's *Monkey Island* and Felice Holman's *Slake's Limbo* both describe young boys who must make it on their own in the "wilds" of New York City. A more tempered variation on this theme is the ever popular classic *From the Mixed-up Files of Mrs. Basil E. Frankweiler,* by E. L. Konigsburg, in which a brother and sister team unravel a mystery while living clandestinely in the New York Metropolitan Museum of Art. Reaching out into the countryside is Cynthia Voigt's *Homecoming,* another modern classic that finds an entire family of children, who have also been abandoned by their mother, searching for a home and clues to their family identity.

A final type of book in the category of "Person Against Nature" has the characters in the novel again fighting "nature," but the kind of nature we refer to here is the kind that can be construed as a battle against a serious or fatal illness. For instance, in *Hang Tough, Paul Mather,* by Alfred Slote, we watch as Paul Mather, a gifted pitcher, attempts to play as much baseball as possible even though he has been diagnosed with leukemia and admonished by his parents and doctors to be very careful. Lois Lowry's first book, *A Summer to Die,* finds Meg terribly envious of her sister Molly's beauty and popularity. But when Molly, like Paul Mather, is also struck down with leukemia and eventually dies, Meg finds tremendous difficulty as she grieves and attempts to accept her sister's death.

Our final example of how nature takes its toll on humanity is in Margaret Mahy's Boston Globe/Horn Book Honor Book, *Memory.* This haunting tale begins with 19-year-old Jonny wandering the streets in an effort to make sense of and reconcile his sister's accidental death. On one of his nightly treks, he meets Sophie, an older

For further titles on the theme of "survival" with books by authors such as Jean Craighead George, Will Hobbs, John Marsden, and dozens of others, turn to the CD accompanying this text.

A CONVERSATION WITH. . .

Gary Paulsen

On Writing

I worked really hard to learn to write. I studied. I mean, I really studied hard. I read some books seven or eight times in a row, studying how the author did it. Like *A Movable Feast* by Hemingway; he writes in there about F. Scott Fitzgerald's talent being like the dust on a butterfly's wing. When the dust was gone, he kept beating his wings and couldn't understand why he couldn't fly. I thought, Jeez!, how could that man even think that? That is so eloquent and so beautiful and such an incredible way to look at something. And that's what I mean; I studied that—not just the words themselves, but how they were presented and how Hemingway wrote or how Dickens wrote or how some of Melville's stuff was like that or John Dos Passos in *The 42nd Parallel*.

On *Hatchet*

I flunked everything. Unfortunately, I skipped school and went to the woods. But the woods kept me sane, I think. Trapping and fishing and hunting when I was a young boy were the only things to me that had sanity to them. And I've been in two forced landings in bush plains. So a lot of that came into *Hatchet.*

And then, two things I specifically did for the book to make sure they worked. One is I started a fire with a hatchet and rock. It took me 4 hours. I just pounded this rock. I was sitting in the yard with all this tinder, I'd go out and get tinder like Brian did and I'd whack, whack, whack! Different rocks. And I finally got it to work. The other thing is I ate a raw turtle egg. I saw this snapper lay the eggs and I thought, well,

I've got this kid doing it, I'd better take a shot at it. I just cut the end off and I slurped it down. It got about halfway down my throat and it just hung there. I could not get it down. I always thought it's like if Vaseline could rot. Jeez, it was so foul!

On *The Island*

The Island is really about my son. He had these mental places he would go—islands. I would try to get him to change and come back to me, you know, to live like me. And finally I realized that he was right, and I went to his islands. He was 14 when I wrote the book and it was really about his life. He was a very sweet, shy, gentle kid, and he tried to help everybody. Tries to help everybody. He really wanted to have this place where he could be safe. An island he could go to. And I tried to keep him from going there. I thought it would be a wrong thing, but he's right. I went to his island and didn't make him come to mine; it was very great. It was very nice.

In fact, it was funny, the Charles Kuralt team came and did a show on me. Somebody in the production team had read *The Island,* and they had him up against the wall with the camera on him in the farm, and they asked him if he liked the book. At age 14 he was 6'2", so, I mean he's just this huge kid. And this producer said, "Didn't you know it was about you?" And there was this long stunned pause and he says, "No. I better read it. I might have to sue dad."

woman suffering from Alzheimer's disease, and befriends her. She lives alone with her cats in terrible squalor, and it is her lack of memories and his all-too-vivid memories that merge to find a resolution.

Person Against Society

Of the countless hurdles we face in our day-to-day lives, some of the larger issues boil down to a matter of "us against the world." There are many things that are simply out of our hands and are dictated by the whims of a frequently cruel society that operates beyond our immediate control. Racism, homelessness, poverty, families in distress, terrorism, and gang activity are all symptoms of an ailing society.

Of all the ills we face in society today, the misguided racism one group wages against another is the most insidious and counterproductive to humankind. Often, it takes only a bit of understanding or an opportunity to view, from the eyes of the "other," a new culture or a new perspective that leads to opening the door to acceptance. As we are reminded in the beginning quote to Sharon Creech's *Walk Two Moons,* "Don't judge a man until you've walked two moons in his moccasins." Trekking through the pages of a good book can certainly provide just that impetus to think in a different way about someone who is different.

To read more about this Conversation with Gary Paulsen, please visit Chapter 7 on our text's companion website at **www.prenhall.com/darigan**

Introducing:

A wonderful introduction to Maude Casey's book *Over the Water* with a similar theme is Allen Say's Caldecott Medal–winning *Grandfather's Journey.*

In Maude Casey's ***Over the Water,*** Mary, who is Irish but lives with her parents and siblings in London, can hardly tolerate her mother's simple family and their crude ways back home in Ireland. Yet in London, though the smartest in her class, Mary, herself, is perceived as being stupid by her British peers because she is Irish. During the summer of her 14th year, while making the annual visit across the Irish Sea in County Kilkinny, Mary works alongside her relatives and, listening to their stories, comes to understand her heritage and to accept who she is.

When characters like Mary look in on their own culture, critically analyzing and assessing it for its good and bad attributes, it adds authenticity and power to the story. This is the case with two other renegade characters, one from Peru and the other from Pakistan. In Joan Abelove's novel ***Go and Come Back,*** we meet Alicia, a young Peruvian girl who befriends a pair of anthropologists who have come to study her village and people. As she describes these strange New Yorkers, we see both our culture and hers in a new light. Describing the two scientists when they first arrive, she says, "They wore no beads, no nose rings, no lip plugs, no anklets. They didn't pierce their noses or their lower lips. They didn't bind their ankles or flatten their foreheads. They did nothing to make themselves beautiful." Alicia details the consistently "odd" behaviors of the two "old ladies," and whether the topic is marriage, stealing, life or death, the fresh first-person perspective jolts us into seeing ourselves as clearly as we see her culture.

Shabanu: Daughter of the Wind, by Suzanne Fisher Staples, offers yet another glimpse into a culture other than our own. Almost 12 years old, Shabanu, the daughter of a family of nomadic Pakistani camel herders, is promised, in an arranged marriage, to a middle-aged man who already has three wives. Rather than face such a fate, she makes up her mind, "I will not be beaten. I will not marry a man whose wives will make me their slave. I'll die first." Shabanu runs away, only to have her beloved camel break his leg in a foxhole and end her escape. When her father arrives, she has already accepted

---

ALTERNATE TEXT SET

Looking "In" on a Culture From the "Outside"

Read Aloud

Dangerous Skies, by Suzanne Fisher Staples

Text Set

Necessary Roughness, by Marie Lee

Burning Up, by Caroline B. Cooney

Waiting for the Rain, by Sheila Gordon

Star Fisher, by Laurence Yep

Child of the Owl, by Laurence Yep

Thief of Hearts, by Laurence Yep

her fate but promises herself she will not cry when he beats her for her disobedience. However, after he is done striking her, she relates, "I hear sobbing, as if from a great distance, and my knees crumple. Dadi catches me in his arms and buries his face against my bloody tunic. . . I realize it is Dadi sobbing, not me." Shabanu remains strong and learns much about the love of her father as well.

There are universal family problems, such as parents' separation and divorce, or dire economic circumstances that put families in acute distress. These, too, are poignantly addressed in books. For example, Anne Fine weaves an amazing set of tales in her book *Step by Wicked Step.* Five children, on a school field trip, are separated from their classmates and stuck for an entire night in an old castle. They come across an antique diary, which prompts them to tell about the profound effect divorce and remarriage have had on them all. The book does a wonderful job of sensitizing us to the issues related to family breakups, but further empowers children to start to "fix things." As Ralph, one of the children, states, "somebody has to make the effort."

Family problems such as homelessness and those in economic and emotional distress can be addressed with the novels in the next text set, many of which have been already discussed.

Finally, there are some extreme circumstances that many of us will hopefully never have to deal with in our lives, yet reading about these situations makes us more sensitive to troubles that exist outside our own realm of experience. Powerful books like *The Watcher,* by James Howe, allow us inside the head of Margaret, whose cerebral world hides the abuse her father lords over her. Martin Waddell's *The Kidnapping of Suzie Q* shows us the effects of a random abduction in a local supermarket. In Theresa Nelson's *Earthshine: A Novel,* sixth-grade Slim McGranahan leaves

Jacket design by Paul Lee from ***Dangerous Skies*** by Suzanne Fisher Staples. Jacket design © 1996 by Paul Lee. Copyright © 1996 by Suzanne Fisher Staples. Reprinted by permission of Farrar, Straus and Giroux, LLC.

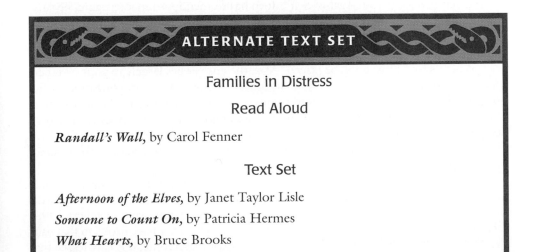

ALTERNATE TEXT SET

Families in Distress

Read Aloud

Randall's Wall, by Carol Fenner

Text Set

Afternoon of the Elves, by Janet Taylor Lisle

Someone to Count On, by Patricia Hermes

What Hearts, by Bruce Brooks

Monkey Island, by Paula Fox

The Great Gilly Hopkins, by Katherine Paterson

As a way of advertising the many titles in contemporary realistic fiction, you may want to dedicate a bulletin board to this genre. After covering the board with butcher paper, you can divide the space into the four previously mentioned categories: Person Against Self, Person Against Person, Person Against Nature, and Person Against Society. Then, as the children read books in a particular genre, they can record the titles and add their starred reviews (just like on Amazon.com) under the most appropriate category. This provides the other children in the classroom with the advertisement for other good books they can be on the lookout for.

her mother and most recent stepfather to live with her father and his "friend," Larry. But her dad is dying of AIDS. Gang life is poignantly and painfully depicted in Walter Dean Myers's **Scorpions** and the aforementioned ***The Outsiders,*** by S. E. Hinton.

A Word of Caution

It is important to remember, however, that these categories are neither as exclusive nor as rigid as some students (or teachers, for that matter) are led to believe. A single title may easily fall into several categories or may seem to defy definite assignment. Take, for example, Ben Mikaelsen's novel ***Rescue Josh McGuire.*** In this story set in the woods of Montana in early spring, young Josh notices a young black bear cub scurry into the forest after Josh's alcoholic father kills its mother out of season. Josh recovers the foundling and brings it back home, only to find that it will be confiscated by the state Fish and Game Department and eventually destroyed through scientific testing. He flees on a motorcycle to the safety of the mountains, taking both his dog and the cub. He is caught in an early freak snowstorm, has his dog attacked and hurt by a bear, and is injured, himself, in a motorcycle accident before he is found by police. On his return, his story is picked up by the media, and his cause to save his bear cub, highlighting the inhumane practices of animal testing, in general, is put to the test.

Is the conflict in this book best represented by "Person Against Person"? Certainly Josh's struggle with his father and the authorities would warrant such a suggestion. But what of "Person Against Society"? Clearly the notion of animal testing is accented and, though results from this practice are said to be for the betterment of society, do the results warrant destroying countless innocent animals? Or perhaps the conflict could be classified "Person Against Self": Josh has tremendous inner struggle, because each of his decisions seems to dig him deeper into trouble. However, the element of survival of Josh, his dog, and the bear in the great woods of the northwest would indicate that this book could fall under the category of "Person Against Nature."

Where should this book be placed? Alas, the answer lies largely in your own perspective. If you were a passionate animal rights advocate, your categorization of the book would be different than if you were married to or had a parent who was an abusive alcoholic like Josh's father. Remember that children come to us with their own perspectives, and choosing where a book should be placed is just as difficult for them as it is for us. In the end, the categorization is not nearly as important as the interaction the reader has with the book.

As a final teacher note, because we have chosen to organize contemporary realistic fiction around "conflict," the literature study dovetails nicely into the Writer's Workshop you probably have in place in your classroom. Considering what Fletcher (1993) refers to as "the classic story structure" where the main character has a problem that usually gets worse before it gets any better but is eventually overcome, it is easy to see that most of the personal narrative children do in their early stages is a natural spinoff of the "Person Against Person" type of conflict we describe. Therefore, noting it during literature study only reinforces the writing children do. In chapter 13, we will describe, in more detail, more reading and writing connections appropriate for your classroom.

A good way to assure that your students are reading widely across all genres is to duplicate a simple grid for each child. Along the left-hand column, leave plenty of space for the title of each book the child reads. Across the top, you can have each column represent the wide range of genres in children's literature, for example, contemporary realistic fiction, historical fiction, and poetry. By recording the students' progress, you can easily see if they are reading only a narrow band of books or across all genres—or somewhere in between.

Other Popular Types of Contemporary Realistic Fiction

Children do not come up to a librarian and ask, "Do you have another good book of contemporary realistic fiction? I'd particularly like something along the lines of 'Person Against Society.'" A child will, however, zero in on a particular type of book he or she has found within that genre, wanting another good title about animals or sports, a good humorous book, or a mystery. Stories in these areas have a proven appeal. Mysteries, for instance, have been at the top of children's preference lists since the 1920s, regardless of children's sex, ethnicity, or IQ (Haynes, 1988; Tomlinson & Tunnell, 1994). Teachers who prepare for the variety of students in an average classroom would do well to become familiar with some titles from each of these popular reading categories found within contemporary realistic fiction.

Animals

Many classic animal books are represented in contemporary realistic fiction. For instance, Sheila Burnford's *The Incredible Journey* chronicles the ordeal of two dogs and a cat as they travel 250 miles through the Canadian wilderness to reach their home. Other mainstays in animal stories include Allan Eckert's *Incident at Hawk's Hill*, Marguerite Henry's *Misty of Chincoteague*, Jim Kjelgaard's *Big Red*, and Sterling North's *Rascal*.

More contemporary animal novels include *Willa and Old Miss Annie* by Berlie Doherty, which finds young Willa, who has recently moved, convinced she will never find friends again, until she meets up with Miss Annie and her assemblage of animals. Betsy Duffey's *Throw-Away Pets* is a short beginning-reader novel that tells of two young girls, Evie and Megan, who find three abandoned pets and come up with resourceful ways to place then in suitable homes. In *Talking in Animal,* a multilayered novel about human and dog dilemmas by Terry Farish, we meet Siobhan, an 11-year-old who finds it difficult to accept the seriousness of her beloved dog's poor health. Also, she is finding it difficult to accept the imminent marriage of her activist friend who comes to the aid of hurt wild animals.

Homeless animals become the focus of two other animal books, one by Elizabeth Hall the other by Bill Wallace. Hall, in her *Child of the Wolves,* describes Granite, a husky pup, soon to be sold, running away into the Alaskan wilds but befriended by a wolf who has lost her own pups. Wallace's *Ferret in the Bedroom, Lizards in the Fridge* finds Liz, daughter of a zoologist, pleading to get rid of all the homeless critters her dad has accumulated, only to find that once they are gone, she misses them terribly.

Sports

Sport stories have been written about almost every imaginable event. Known for his large body of sport novels, Matt Christopher wrote about standard sports such as baseball, basketball, and football but also included hockey in his book *Face-Off* and motorcycle racing in *Dirt-Bike Racer.*

Other books that pack a punch are these three books by Chris Lynch: *Shadow Boxer, Iceman,* and *Slot Machine.* Bruce Brooks's Newbery Honor book, *The Moves Make the Man,* adds to the sports literature, as does Jerry Spinelli's *Crash,* all of which look more deeply than the average sports saga into characterization and the relationships these kids have with friends and family.

Bruce Brooks has also contributed nicely to the sports books category with his series about the Wolfbay Wings ice hockey team. Brooks uses sports as the launchpad for sophisticated plot and interpersonal relationships that make these deeper and more meaningful than the standard sports story. Featured are books about each of the major players of this rough and tumble team, including players such as ***Woodsie, Zip, Cody, Boot*** and ***Prince*** to name only a few.

Another string of books by Will Weaver finds young pitcher Billy Baggs involved in more than just baseball. Farming, friendships, and parent problems are all orbited around the sport of baseball to add depth that goes into extra innings in Weaver's trio, ***Striking Out, Farm Team,*** and ***Hard Ball: A Billy Baggs Novel.***

John Ritter has two baseball books that delve deeply into plot and characterization. In his ***Choosing Up Sides,*** set in the year 1921, we meet young Luke who has obvious signs of talent in baseball, his major downfall being that he is left-handed. His preacher father and the prevailing beliefs of the time consider left-handedness evil. In Ritter's ***Over the Wall,*** we find 13-year-old Tyler traveling from his troubled California home for the summer to stay with his aunt and uncle and to play baseball in Central Park. Getting his temper and emotions under control is more difficult than his attempts to connect with a fast curve ball and is the substance of this riveting story.

Finally, we note a perennial favorite of ours that, for decades, has engaged children: the previously mentioned ***Hang Tough, Paul Mather.*** This book remains fresh and timely despite its age. Slote's book takes a sensitive look at a young boy who comes up to bat against not only his opponents on the baseball diamond but also his own illness of leukemia.

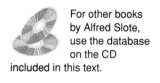
For other books by Alfred Slote, use the database on the CD included in this text.

Humorous Books

As we were going through the comments from our editor concerning the first draft of this book, we chuckled at a recurring question at the end of each and every section in this chapter on contemporary realistic fiction. "Any happy stories?" she kept asking. "Anything funny?" As we reviewed the books we had cited, we realized that all indeed *were* pretty laden with monumental personal issues and examined meaty social issues. As we mentioned earlier in our section on the importance of story, something has to happen for the reader to want to continue through a book, and it is conflict that drives the story. So, funny books? Sure! Here is an Alternate Text Set of books you may want to consider.

ALTERNATE TEXT SET

Tickling Your Funny Bone

Read Aloud

Heads or Tails, by Jack Gantos

Text Set

Bingo Brown, Gypsy Lover, by Betsy Byars

Bingo Brown and the Language of Love, by Betsy Byars

Anastasia Krupnik, by Lois Lowry

Harris and Me, by Gary Paulsen

The Agony of Alice, by Phyllis Reynolds Naylor

The Best Christmas Pageant Ever, by Barbara Robinson

Other books that are a nice blend of the humorous with some prevailing problems are Barbara Park's *The Kid in the Red Jacket,* Eve Bunting's *Nasty, Stinky Sneakers,* and Thomas Rockwell's *How to Eat Fried Worms.* Series books that will delight children are Robert Newton Peck's *Soup* books, Louis Sachar's "Wayside School" books, featuring the first *Sideways Stories from Wayside School,* and Barbara Park's many "Junie B. Jones" books, including *Junie B. Jones and the Stupid Smelly Bus.*

Mystery

Yet another popular type of contemporary realistic fiction is mystery. Murder and death are common subjects to be solved in novels for older children such as Avi's *Wolf Rider,* Mary Downing Hahn's *The Dead Man in Indian Creek,* and Ellen Raskin's *The Westing Game.* In the very beginning of *Wolf Rider,* 15-year-old Andy receives a phone call that is an unsolicited confession that the man at the other end of the line has just murdered his girlfriend. Interested in this, Andy investigates the mystery and makes some startling discoveries about who this man is, not to mention clarifying his own rocky relationship with his father.

In Mary Downing Hahn's mystery *Dead Man in Indian Creek,* Parker and his friend Matt discover a man in Indian Creek who has died of a drug overdose. Problems occur when Parker worries that his own mother may be involved. A mysterious death is also central to Ellen Raskin's *The Westing Game,* as young Turtle Wexler unscrambles key clues that reveal the real murderer of millionaire Sam Westing. Well-drawn characters and tight plotting make this book ever so much fun to read a second time to discover the details that were overlooked in the first reading.

Other mysteries of note are Lois Duncan's *I Know What You Did Last Summer* and Richard Peck's *Are You in the House Alone?* In both of these, young high school teens are tormented by mysterious characters. In Virginia Hamilton's *House of Dies Drear,* an African American professor and his family are tormented by the ghosts living in their rental house that was once a station on the Underground Railroad.

Not all of the titles listed under these headings are strictly contemporary realistic fiction. The majority of realistic fiction, either contemporary or historical, includes books that often cross genre lines. When a child likes mysteries, for example, it is important to find a good mystery. Whether the mystery has a fantasy component, such as the supernatural twist in Betty Ren Wright's *The Dollhouse Murders,* is of little consequence unless the child is searching specifically for a ghost story.

A small but important type of contemporary fiction does not fit the pattern where readers identify directly with the main character. For example, in Peggy Parish's *Amelia Bedelia* and the many stories that followed, there is little a youngster can identify with in this clueless maid other than the bonehead mistakes that she makes, reminding us of some silly things we have done. The humor of Amelia "icing the cake" by simply adding ice cubes and putting it in the freezer is enough to entertain and draw in readers.

Series Books

Let's face it: When we walk by and see you reading by the poolside or on the shore, you are not intent on finishing Dostoyevski's final novel. Undoubtedly you are reading another John Grisham or the latest Mary Higgins Clark. Books in series tend to be viewed unfavorably by literary critics but find continued popularity among readers (including adults). Series books tend to be formula fiction, written according to a recipe and suffering from predictable plots, relatively flat characters, and a writing style that tends toward the unimaginative. Strengths are that children may develop a familiarity with characters who appear in one book after another and also a comfortable

DID YOU KNOW?

Many years ago, when Avi and his wife had just moved into a new apartment in New Jersey, he really did receive such a phone call that was an admission of a supposed murder. At the time, Avi was a research librarian and his interest, like Andy's, was piqued. He attempted to unravel the mystery and actually contacted the presumed victim who, as it turned out, was a parole officer. In fact, there never was a murder, and a newspaper reporter friend convinced him to drop his search. But, Avi continued the investigation—this time it was internally and within the confines of his own fictional novel—which is probably far more interesting than the real incident . . . although we'll never know for sure.

DID YOU KNOW?

James Cross Giblin, Mary Downing Hahn's editor at Clarion Books, related this humorous story: A young boy who had read and loved *The Dead Man in Indian Creek* quipped that Mary should change her name to Mary "Drowning" Hahn.

To find out more about *Read 'em and Weep* and other library sources on the World Wide Web, visit Chapter 7 on the companion website at **www.prenhall.com/darigan**

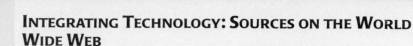

BOOKMARK

INTEGRATING TECHNOLOGY: SOURCES ON THE WORLD WIDE WEB

Numerous libraries have begun creating websites that encourage reading and provide resources for young readers. *Read 'em and Weep,* a section of Teen Territory at the Arlington, Virginia public library, is a good example of such a site, with summer reading contests, recommended books, and reviews written by teens. Picks by the teen advisory board and book reviews written by young adults make this site very student centered.

For further series books that children will want to investigate, look to the CD database accompanying this text. Here are some authors and characters you may want start with: Paula Danziger's books about Amber Brown, Hilary McKay's books about The Exiles, Jack Gantos's books about Jack, Cynthia Voigt's books about the Tillerman family, Lois Lowry's books about Anastasia Krupnik, Betsy Byars's three series about Herculeah Jones, Blossom Family, and Bingo Brown.

feeling from a plot and setting that vary little in each story. When reading from a series, young readers take fewer risks because the books are reasonably predictable. Therefore, series books often have a special appeal for the hesitant reader who is not totally secure with books and who fears striking out into the unknown.

Old series such as The Hardy Boys and Nancy Drew are still popular. Recent series that have captured thousands of devoted readers include The Baby-Sitters Club (Ann Martin), California Diaries (Ann Martin), Sweet Valley Twins (Francine Pascal), Goosebumps (R. L. Stine), Saddle Club (Bonnie Bryant), Pony Pals (Jean Bethancourt), Adventures of the Bailey School Kids (Debbie Dady and Marsha Thornton Jones), Danger.Com (Jordan Cray), and the Anamorphs (K. A. Applegate). Even the early grades have series, such as The Kids of Polk Street School (Patricia Reilly Giff) and The PeeWee Scouts (Judy Delton). With the possible exception of romance books, for which there seems to be an ever-insatiable appetite, readers tend to immerse themselves in a particular series until they reach a self-determined level of saturation or finish all the titles. As much as some teachers and librarians believe the weaker of the series books are somehow bad for a reader's literary health, no evidence exists to indicate that those who have indulged, even to extremes, tend to come to a bad end.

Romance Novels

The jury still seems to be out on romance books. Unlike other series, romance books appear under dozens of imprints and names, each with its own identifiable label that accurately signals the degree of sexual involvement in that series. Young readers of romance stories make the easy transition to romance books for adults that flood wire bookracks in endless waves. The number of romance titles and series continues to grow almost astronomically, with signs of continuing addiction detected in this series unlike any others. ***What You Don't Know (Sweet Valley Jr. High, No. 22),*** by Francine Pascal, was reviewed on Amazon.com by a 12-year-old who stated, "I love all of SVJH. And this book is no different." Our point exactly. These books *are* really not different. One is like the next.

Books like Lurlene McDaniel's duo ***Angel of Mercy*** and ***Angel of Hope*** are prototypic of these kinds of series with their overreliance on melodrama, generally flat characters, and fairly narrow views of issues. In the former title, McDaniel criticizes the Western missionaries for their superficial view on the native Ugandans but equally stereotypes the Africans, making this a shallow read. However, the love affair between Heather and Ian, as well as his death in an airplane crash, make this soap opera-ish book compelling as a quick read for teens. The latter title, not unlike any other book in any other series, furthers the plot in predictable ways, making for clichéd reading.

For a more insightful view of issues in Africa, for example, teens would be better to turn to Christina Kessler's ***No Condition is Permanent,*** which deals with female circumcision, or Nancy Farmer's Newbery Honor book, ***A Girl Named Disaster,*** where the main character, Nhamo, escapes an arranged marriage, and though she puts her life in grave danger, learns more about the luminous world of the African spirits.

▼▼▼▼▼▼▼

Categories of Contemporary Realistic Fiction

Depending on who cuts up the realistic fiction pie, the pieces might be as few as six general categories, as Tomlinson and Lynch-Brown (1996) note: families, peers, adolescent issues, survival and adventure, people with disabilities, and cultural diversity. Or the genre might be divided into as many as the following 24 more specific categories (Figure 7–1), as shown in Huck, Hepler, Hickman, and Kiefer (1997).

Why Create Categories?

Of the seemingly limitless ways you could choose to organize the titles in contemporary fiction, the value of creating and attending to certain categories is, first, to provide ourselves as teachers with a quick check to evaluate the breadth of our own personal reading. We all tend to read in narrow bands, either with a certain author in mind or within a single genre. For instance, we pick up everything we can find by an author such as Pat Conroy and devour it voraciously, and we can't wait until the newest Patricia Cornwell or Stephen King comes into print. When we see yet another book on

FIGURE 7–1 Web of contemporary realistic fiction.

If you *did* want to investigate "mysteries" using the CD that accompanies this text, you would simply search under the descriptor "mystery" and you would almost instantly come up with over 250 titles, both picture book and novel, from which to choose.

the United States Civil War, we can't rest until it finds a place on our shelf along with the rest in our collection. But, as we do for kids every day, *we* need to consciously nudge ourselves into new domains. Organizing and attending to our own reading in this genre assure that there will be no glaring gaps. So if, when reading, we see that we have read an abundance of survival stories yet very few mysteries, for example, we can ask our librarian or search the database included with this text for a few suggestions to beef up that particular subcategory.

Though it would appear to be a daunting task, we must be conversant with a variety of titles in *all* genres, including the categories of contemporary realism. As a consequence of this effort, we can make informed suggestions to our students to help satisfy their diverse reading interests. Further, we want to be sure that we don't allow our personal taste in reading to limit the breadth of titles we suggest to children. Time and again, teachers come to us saying that they never thought they would have liked fantasy or science fiction or survival stories. But now that they have sampled a few notable examples in that area, they have become "hooked." If we read only in a particular genre, such as historical fiction, or a narrow band of contemporary fiction, then we naturally recommend those books, short changing the other books and our students as well.

A second, and subsequent, value in categorizing books in this genre is that these classifications can be used as a tool for organizing, presenting, and discussing the myriad contemporary realistic fiction titles for children during their reading instruction. It helps children to see the overriding theme that binds the set of books you have chosen and offers a "common language" to use when talking about the books during literature circles. (For more information on reader's workshop and literature circles, see chapter 13.)

▼▼▼▼▼▼▼

Contemporary Realistic Fiction, Society, and the Age of Realism

Contemporary realism reflects society and the child's place in it. Contemporary novels written in the 1920s provided a snapshot of the American scene during that time, and novels written and set on the precipice of the new millennium do the same. The view of life in realistic stories from each decade is reflected in the mirror of societal mores and attitudes of that era. In books written around the time of World War I, for example, a pregnant woman would be identified as being "in a delicate condition," if she were identified at all. The word *pregnant* was rarely used in daily conversation and, consequently, rarely found in print. Life in the early 1900s definitely had pregnancies and other realities of human existence, including crime, great injustice, and pockets of ugliness, but these aspects of life were not a part of books written for children, because social attitudes dictated that they were unsuitable for children and therefore unavailable to young readers.

Until the mid-1960s, the world in children's books typically was presented without negative or earthy aspects. Geoffrey Trease (1983) lists some of the generally accepted restrictions that applied to the writing of children's books before 1960: no budding love affairs, no liquor, no supernatural phenomena, no undermining of authority, no parents with serious human weaknesses, no realistic working-class speech (including the mildest cursing).

But then the face of American society took on a new look because of upheavals such as the Civil Rights movement, Vietnam, and large cracks appearing in the traditional family structure. The effects were so widespread that children no longer could be kept in the dark (if they truly ever were). Evidence of the changes appeared on the front pages of newspapers, harsh realities were broadcast into the living rooms of the world on television newscasts, and no neighborhood was free from what S. E. Hinton (1967) referred to as "the social jungle."

INTEGRATING TECHNOLOGY: AUTHORS ON THE WORLD WIDE WEB

Kimberly Willis Holt, author of **My Louisiana Sky** (Boston Globe/Horn Book Award for fiction) and **Zachary Beaver Came to Town** (National Book Award for Young People's Literature), has created an aesthetically pleasing site that provides writing tips, biographical information, teacher's guides to her books, and information about the inspiration for each of her novels.

To find out more about Kimberly Willis Holt and other authors and illustrators on the World Wide Web, visit Chapter 7 on the companion website at **www.prenhall. com/darigan**

A new attitude accompanied the shift toward facing problems previously ignored: Children were viewed as citizens with rights beyond those granted by their parents. Some voices called for children to have full access to information, and young people achieved a new prominence in society. Following tradition, contemporary realistic fiction chronicled the current scene, and the child as consumer/citizen began to appear in books for young readers.

Contemporary realistic fiction is most often the genre in which the taboos of literature are tested. Changes in the content of children's literature typically appear first in this genre and then spread to others. Louise Fitzhugh's *Harriet the Spy* was a pivotal book when it appeared in 1964. It tells about a nontraditional girl who dressed in a sweatshirt, spied on neighbors, was neglected by her well-to-do parents, and underwent psychotherapy. All of these elements signaled a shift in the acceptable literary content of the day.

Controversy over the realities in these and other books spread widely. These changes, beginning in the 1960s and flourishing in the 70s, came to be called *new realism* (see chapter 2). The harsher parts of life simply had not been given center stage in books for young readers until then. When the taboos lifted, new books spewed forth problems and realities previously unseen in children's publishing. Topics such as death, divorce, drugs, abuse in all its forms, profanity, nontraditional lifestyles, and single-parent families not only were mentioned in the books but also became major themes.

Society continued to change. New problems arose, such as the plethora of recognized eating disorders such as bulimia and anorexia nervosa, inner-city survival, AIDS, teen suicide, gang life, random shootings, and white supremacy. Those new problems sprouted in contemporary books for children, and still newer problems continue to surface in both society and writing for young readers.

Because of the immediacy of the problems in realistic fiction, it traditionally has been the genre that attracts the most controversy. When a book deals with the issue of cocaine in a modern middle school, the emotional impact of the problem tends to be stronger than in a story treating the consequences of opium addiction in 18th-century China. Society was affected as drastically by drugs 200 years ago as today, but the middle school setting is closer to home both emotionally and physically. That closeness is celebrated as relevant and helpful by some people and abhorred as too stark and unnecessary by others, and thus the debate begins.

Didacticism

If the problem or a social issue in a book becomes more important than the story, the book suffers. This is true whenever the author uses the book as a means to drive home a point or present a moral, no matter how worthy the cause or noble the intent. As soon as the story ceases to be an experience, it becomes didactic—a lesson instead of a discovery. Didactic fiction in the past often was used to define proper behavior and belief, as we describe in chapter 2. Those earlier books lost their potential to become powerful reading experiences when they became vehicles for indoctrination. Yet in our enlightened modern times, current fiction can be equally as lopsided. Contemporary realistic fiction, which so often features modern problems, can be particularly prone to didacticism. When "problem novels" focus so narrowly on the problem—abuse, pregnancy, addiction—that they ignore the themes and issues raised by the situation, they generally offer a didactic quick-fix view of life.

Even when the social issue is largely agreed upon by readers as important, such as protecting the environment, the book becomes second-rate as soon as that issue overshadows the credibility of the characters and the believability of the plot. A book can be strengthened by its insights into contemporary issues and problems as long as those insights are secondary to the story. But using a book as a soapbox interferes with the impact of the reading experience, as in Chris Van Allsburg's *Just a Dream,* which is a thinly disguised lesson on ecology. Another example is Dr. Seuss's *Oh, the Places You'll Go!,* which sacrifices story to present in greeting-card style the message that one's potential is limitless.

Bibliotherapy

In its broadest definition, bibliotherapy is any kind of emotional healing that comes from reading books. Therapy from books falls into at least three categories: (1) the broad therapeutic feelings of recreation and gratification experienced by an individual reader, (2) the sense of connectedness felt by members of a group who read and share books, and (3) the particular information and insight books can provide in dealing with specific personal problems (Chatton, 1988).

The first two categories, recreation and connectedness, result naturally from reading. Those who have found compelling titles experience the first category as they discover the deep satisfaction, stimulation, and comfort that books can bring. The second category—connectedness—occurs when readers experience a book along with others, a new dimension to the group relationship. A teacher and classroom of children who read a book together are able to connect with one another in new ways when laughing, crying, or simply talking about their mutual experience.

It is in the third category—dealing with specific personal problems—where most difficulties arise. Because books can provide insight and comfort, adults sometimes are tempted to fix children's problems by insisting they read certain books to help them cope with those problems. If a boy is suffering because of his parents' divorce, for example, a well-meaning teacher might push him into a book about a child adjusting to life after a broken marriage. Because human beings are complex and unpredictable, the boy might not need or want to read about his own problem. He may be better served by a book that takes him far away from the painful reality at home. After all, "stories are not like mustard plasters to be applied for immediate relief where deepseated problems of behavior, attitudes and values exist" (Heaton & Lewis, 1955, p. 35). This sort of clinical bibliotherapy is, of course, best reserved for trained psychologists and psychotherapists, who can and do use books successfully in their practices. Other adults can serve children better simply by reading and recommending good books, and allowing personal insight, comfort, and the answering of troubling questions to come in their own natural and timely ways.

▼▼▼▼▼▼▼

The Place of Contemporary Realistic Fiction in the Classroom

As a note of caution, you must be ever mindful that though contemporary realistic fiction may be the single most popular genre in your classroom, you must temper that interest with the realities of your school and community. With the hard-hitting topics we have noted thus far and that only scratch the surface of this genre come tremendous potential for book challenges and censorship. One of our favorite books is ***Harris and Me,*** by Gary Paulsen. In this book chronicling the antics of the fun-loving, devil-may-care Harris who is constantly in trouble with his parents or, worse, his older sister Glennis, we are met with language that would not pass muster in most classrooms, fantastic frolics around the farm that go beyond anything you could imagine (though Gary assures us he and cousin did all this and more), all of which climax with Harris being duped into urinating on an electric fence to obtain a collection of what, in higher circles, might loosely be construed as "artistic anatomical studies." Though the book has not been censored or challenged, it has shocked many a teacher and would certainly need to be used with caution given the climate in your particular school setting. Only you, your librarian, and principal know what is "appropriate" to the culture of your school, but you must know that with this genre come risks you may need to prepare for.

The offerings of contemporary realistic fiction are as wide as life, helping to explain today's people, problems, and places. In this popular genre, young readers can find their own lives, recognize friends, and meet strangers who can show them different ways of living and thinking. Whether the appeal of a book lies in a skillful re-creation of current lifestyles or in a comfortable pattern found in a series, the best of contemporary realistic fiction always will examine human beings facing and overcoming the challenges of living today.

▼▼▼▼▼▼▼

Summary

In this chapter, we described the elements of contemporary realistic fiction, noting the importance of story and identification with the characters and settings as being key features that grab the student reader. We next looked at the types of conflict present in this genre, accenting Person Against Self, Person Against Person, Person Against Nature, and Person Against Society as major categories. Further, we noted other categories of interest to children with stories about animals, sports, good humorous books, and mysteries. We looked at the history of contemporary realistic fiction and noted how it has changed with the times. We also noted how didacticism, bibliotherapy, and controversial books affect your classrooms.

▼▼▼▼▼▼▼

Fifteen More of Our Favorites

Anderson, Laurie Halse. (1999). *Speak*. Farrar, Straus & Giroux. Speaking out at the "wrong" time by calling 911 from a teen drinking party makes Melinda a social outcast and has prompted her to rarely speak at all.

Avi. (1991). *Nothing but the truth*. Orchard. A ninth-grader's suspension for singing "The Star-Spangled Banner" during homeroom becomes a national news story.

Bunting, Eve. (1992). *Our sixth-grade sugar babies*. Lippincott. Vicki and her best friend fear that their sixth-grade project, carrying around 5-pound bags of sugar to learn about parental responsibility, will make them look ridiculous in the eyes of the seventh-grade boy they love.

Fenner, Carol. (1995). *Yolanda's genius*. McElderry. After moving from Chicago to Grand River, Michigan, fifth grader Yolanda, big and strong for her age, determines to prove that her younger brother is not a slow learner but a true musical genius.

Henkes, Kevin (1995). *Protecting Marie*. Greenwillow. Relates 12-year-old Fanny's love-hate relationship with her father, a temperamental artist, who has given Fanny a new dog.

Myers, Walter Dean. (1999). *Monster*. HarperCollins. While on trial as an accomplice to a murder, 16-year-old Steve Harmon records his experiences in prison and in the courtroom in the form of a film script as he tries to come to terms with the course his life has taken.

Nolan, Han. (1996). *Send me down a miracle*. Harcourt. A sleepy, God-fearing southern town erupts in chaos when a flamboyant artist from New York City returns to her birthplace for an artistic experiment.

Paulsen, Gary. (1988). *The island*. Orchard. Fifteen-year-old Wil discovers himself and the wonders of nature when he leaves home to live on an island in northern Wisconsin.

Pullman, Philip. (1988). *The ruby in the smoke*. Knopf. In 19th-century London, 16-year-old Sally, a recent orphan, becomes involved in a deadly search for a mysterious ruby.

Rawls, Wilson. (1961). *Where the red fern grows*. Doubleday. A young boy living in the Ozarks achieves his heart's desire when he becomes the owner of two redbone hounds and teaches them to be hunters.

Slepian, Jan. (1990). *Risk n' roses*. Philomel. In 1948, 11-year-old Skip moves to the Bronx and longs to shed her responsibility for her mentally handicapped older sister and concentrate on her new friendship with the bold and daring girl who seems to run the neighborhood.

Smith, Roland. (2001). *Zach's lie*. Hyperion. When Jack Osborne is befriended by his school's custodian and a Basque girl, he begins to adjust to his family's sudden move to Elko, Nevada, after entering the Witness Security Program.

Williams, Carol Lynch. (1997). *The true colors of Caitlynne Jackson*. Delacorte. Twelve-year-old Caity and her younger sister, Cara, must fend for themselves when their abusive mother storms out of the house with a suitcase and doesn't come back.

Wolff, Virginia Euwer. (1993). *Make lemonade*. Henry Holt. In order to earn money for college, 14-year-old LaVaughn babysits for a teenage mother.

Yolen, Jane, & Coville, Bruce. (1998) *Armageddon summer*. Harcourt Brace. Fourteen-year-old Marina and 16-year-old Jed accompany their parents' religious cult, the Believers, to await the end of the world atop a remote mountain, where they try to decide what they themselves believe.

▼▼▼▼▼▼▼▼

Others We Like

Animals

Cleary, Beverly (1991). *Strider* (Paul O. Zelinsky, Illus.). Morrow.

DiCamillo, Kate. (2000). *Because of Winn-Dixie*. Candlewick.

Haas, Jessie. (1996). *Be well, beware*. Greenwillow.

Henry, Marguerite. (1990). *King of the wind*. Macmillan. (Originally published by Rand 1947)

Keehn, Sally. (1999). *The first horse I see*. Philomel.

Mowat, Farley. (1962). *Owls in the family*. Little, Brown.

Paulsen, Gary. (1990). *Dogsong*. Bradbury.

Philbrick, W. Rodman. (1996). *The fire pony*. Scholastic.

Wallace, Bill. (1988). *Beauty*. Holiday House.

Humor

Blume, Judy. (1972). *Tales of a fourth grade nothing*. Dutton.

Cleary, Beverly. (1968). *Ramona the Pest*. Morrow.

Danziger, Paula. (1996). *Amber Brown wants extra credit*. Putnam. (See also the other Amber Brown books.)

Korman, Gordon. (1991). *I want to go home*. Scholastic.

Levy, Elizabeth. (1997). *My life as a fifth-grade comedian*. HarperCollins.

Lynch, Chris. (1997). *Ladies' choice*. HarperTrophy.

Manes, Stephen. (1982). *Be a perfect person in just three days!* Clarion.

McKay, Hillary. (1992). *The exiles*. Macmillan.

Naylor, Phyllis Reynolds. (1989). *Alice in rapture, sort of*. Atheneum.(See also the other Alice books.)

Mysteries

Bunting, Eve. (1992). *Coffin on a case*. HarperCollins.

Estes, Eleanor. (1951). *Ginger Pye*. Harcourt.

Kline, Suzy. (1995). *Orp and the FBI*. Putnam.

Nixon, Joan Lowry. (1986). *The other side of dark*. Delacorte.

Roberts, Willo Davis. (1975). *A view from the cherry tree*. Atheneum.

Stevenson, James. (1995). *The bones in the cliff*. Greenwillow.

Wallace, Bill. (1994). *Blackwater swamp*. Holiday House.

White, Ruth. (1995). *Belle Prater's boy*. Farrar, Straus & Giroux.

Yep, Laurence. (1998). *The case of the lion dance*. HarperCollins.

Problem Novels

Bauer, Marian Dane. (1986). *On my honor.* Houghton Mifflin.

Blume, Judy. (1970). *Are you there God? It's me, Margaret.* Bradbury.

Byars, Betsy. (1977). *The pinballs.* Harper & Row.

Cole, Brock. (1987). *The goats.* Farrar, Straus & Giroux.

Cooney, Caroline C. (1999). *Burning up.* Delacorte.

Griffin, Adele. (1997). *Split just right.* Hyperion.

Konigsburg, E. L. (1996). *The view from Saturday.* Atheneum.

Naidoo, Beverly. (1995) *No turning back.* HarperCollins.

Soto, Gary. (1995). *Boys at work* (Robert Casilla, Illus.). Delacorte.

Williams, Carol Lynch. (1993). *Kelly and me.* Delacorte.

Williams, Carol Lynch. (1998). *If I forget, you remember.* Delacorte.

Woodson, Jacqueline. (2000). *Miracle's boys.* Putnam.

Sports

Brooks, Bruce. (1984). *The moves make the man.* Harper & Row.

Brooks, Bruce. (2000). *Throwing smoke.* HarperCollins.

Christopher, Matt. (1988). *Tackle without a team.* Little, Brown.

Dygard, Thomas. (1993). *Game plan.* Morrow.

Slote, Alfred. (1990). *The trading game.* Lippincott.

Survival

Conly, Jane Leslie. (1998). *While no one was watching.* Henry Holt.

George, Jean Craighead. (1972). *Julie of the wolves.* Harper & Row.

Hill, Kirkpatrick. (1990). *Toughboy and Sister.* Macmillan.

Hobbs, Will. (1996). *Far North.* Morrow.

Marsden, John. (1995). *Tomorrow, when the war began.* Houghton Mifflin.

O'Dell, Scott. (1960). *Island of the blue dolphins.* Houghton Mifflin.

Sperry, Armstrong. (1940). *Call it courage.* Macmillan.

White, Robb. (1972). *Deathwatch.* Doubleday.

Easier to Read

Bulla, Clyde Robert. (1975). *Shoeshine girl.* Crowell. (Problem.)

Byars, Betsy. (1996). *Tornado.* HarperCollins. (Humor.)

Carrick, Carol. (1976). *The accident.* (Donald Carrick, Illus.). Seabury. (Problems.)

Cleary, Beverly. (1990). *Muggie Maggie.* Morrow. (Humor.)

Christopher, Matt. (1993). *The dog that stole home.* Little, Brown. (Sports.)

Clements, Andrew. (1996). *Frindle.* Simon & Schuster. (Humor.)

Conrad, Pam (1988). *Staying nine.* Harper & Row.

Conrad, Pam. (1998). *Don't go near that rabbit, Frank!* (Mark English, Illus.). HarperCollins. (Animal.)

Dahl, Roald. (1992). *The Vicar of Nibbleswicke.* Viking. (Humor.)

Giff, Patricia Reilly. (1996). *Good luck, Ronald Morgan.* Viking. (Humor.)

Hess, Karen. (1994). *Sable.* Henry Holt. (Animal.)

Keller, Holly. (1998). *Angela's top-secret computer club.* Greenwillow. (Mystery.)

Park, Barbara. (1982). *Skinnybones.* Knopf. (Humor.)

Peck, Robert Newton. (1974). *Soup.* Knopf. (Humor.)

Smith, Doris Buchanan. (1973). *A taste of blackberries.* Crowell. (Problem.)

Sobol, Donald. (1963). *Encyclopedia Brown, boy detective.* Nelson. (Mystery.)

Spinelli, Jerry. (1995). *Tooter Pepperday.* Random House. (Humor.)

Thomas, Jane Resh. (1981). *The comeback dog* (Troy Howell, Illus.). Houghton Mifflin. (Animal.)

Picture Books

Bunting, Eve. (1994a). *Smoky night* (David Diaz, Illus.). Harcourt Brace.

Bunting, Eve. (1994b). *Sunshine home* (Diane de Groat, Illus.). Clarion.

Bunting, Eve. (1996). *Going home* (David Diaz, Illus.). HarperCollins.

de Paola, Tomie. (1973). *Nana upstairs & Nana downstairs.* Viking.

Flournoy, Valerie. (1985). *The patchwork quilt* (Jerry Pinkney, Illus.). Dial.

Isadora, Rachel. (1991). *At the crossroads.* Greenwillow.

Polacco, Patricia. (1992). *Chicken Sunday.* Philomel.

Schertle, Alice. (1995). *Down the road* (E. B. Lewis, Illus.). Browndeer/Harcourt.

Shannon, David. (1995). *The amazing Christmas extravaganza.* BlueSky/Scholastic.

Sisulu, Elinor Batezat. (1996). *The day Gogo went to vote* (Sharon Wilson, Illus.). Little, Brown.

Viorst, Judith. (1995). *Alexander, who's not (do you hear me, I mean it!) going to move* (Robin Preiss Glasser, Illus.). Atheneum.

Yolen, Jane. (1992). *Letting Swift River go* (Barbara Cooney, Illus.). Little, Brown.

▼▼▼▼▼▼▼

Children's Literature References

Abelove, Joan. (1998). *Go and come back*. New York: Dorling-Kindersley.

Avi. (1986). *Wolf rider*. New York: Collier.

Avi. (1991) *Windcatcher*. New York: Bradbury Press.

Bauer, Marion Dane. (1986). *On my honor*. Boston: Houghton Mifflin.

Brooks, Bruce. (1984). *The moves make the man*. New York: HarperCollins.

Brooks, Bruce. (1992). *What hearts*. New York: HarperCollins.

Brooks, Bruce. (1997a). *Cody*. New York: Harper Trophy.

Brooks, Bruce. (1997b). *Woodsie*. New York: Harper Trophy.

Brooks, Bruce. (1997c). *Zip*. New York: Harper Trophy.

Brooks, Bruce. (1988a). *Boot*. New York: Harper Trophy.

Brooks, Bruce (1998b). *Prince*. New York: Harper Trophy.

Brooks, Bruce (1999). *Vanishing*. New York: HarperCollins.

Bunting, Eve. (1994). *Nasty, stinky sneakers*. New York: HarperCollins.

Burnford, Sheila. (1961). *The incredible journey*. Boston: Little, Brown.

Byars, Betsy. (1988). *The burning questions of Bingo Brown*. New York: Viking.

Byars, Betsy. (1989). *Bingo Brown and the language of love*. New York: Scholastic.

Byars, Betsy. (1990). *Bingo Brown, Gypsy lover*. New York: Viking.

Casey, Maude. (1994). *Over the water*. New York: Henry Holt.

Christopher, Matt. (1972). *Face-off*. Boston: Little, Brown.

Christopher, Matt. (1979). *Dirt-bike racer*. Boston: Little, Brown.

Cooney, Caroline B. (1999). *Burning up*. New York: Delacorte.

Corcoran, Barbara. (1974). *A dance to still music* (Charles Robinson, Illus.). New York: Atheneum.

Coy, John. (1996). *Night driving* (Peter McCarty, Illus.). New York: Henry Holt.

Creech, Sharon. (1994). *Walk two moons*. New York: HarperCollins.

Doherty, Berlie. (1994). *Willa and old Miss Annie*. Cambridge, MA: Candlewick.

Dowell, Frances O'Roark.(2000). *Dovey Coe*. New York: Atheneum.

Duffey, Betsy. (1993). *Throw-away pets*. New York: Viking.

Duncan, Lois. (1973). *I know what you did last summer*. Boston: Little, Brown.

Eckert, Allan. (1971). *Incident at Hawk's Hill*. Boston: Little, Brown.

Farish, Terry. (1996). *Talking in animal*. New York: Greenwillow.

Farmer, Nancy. (1996). *A girl named disaster*. New York: Orchard.

Fenner, Carol. (1991). *Randall's wall*. New York: McElderry.

Fine, Anne. (1996). *Step by wicked step*. Boston: Little, Brown.

Fitzhugh, Louise. (1964). *Harriet the spy*. New York: Harper & Row.

Fox, Paula. (1984). *One-eyed cat*. New York: Bradbury.

Fox, Paula. (1991). *Monkey Island*. New York: Orchard.

Gantos, Jack. (1994). *Heads or tails: Stories from the sixth grade*. New York: Farrar, Straus & Giroux.

Gantos, Jack. (1998). *Joey Pigza swallowed the key*. New York: Farrar, Straus & Giroux.

Gantos, Jack. (2000). *Joey Pigza loses control*. New York: Farrar, Straus & Giroux.

Gardiner, John Reynolds. (1980). *Stone fox*. New York: Scott, Foresman.

Gordon, Sheila. (1987). *Waiting for the rain*. New York: Orchard.

Hahn, Mary Downing. (1990). *The dead man in Indian Creek*. New York: Clarion.

Hall, Elizabeth. (1996). *Child of the wolves*. Boston: Houghton Mifflin.

Hamilton, Virginia. (1968). *The house of Dies Drear*. New York: Macmillan.

Hautzig, Esther. (1968). *The endless steppe*. New York: Crowell.

Henry, Marguerite. (1947). *Misty of Chincoteague*. New York: Rand.

Hermes, Patricia. (1993). *Someone to count on*. Boston: Little, Brown.

Hinton, S. E. (1967). *The outsiders*. New York: Viking.

Holman, Felice. (1974). *Slake's limbo*. New York: Scribner's.

Howe, James. (1997). *The watcher*. New York: Atheneum.

Jordan, Sherryl. (1999). *Raging quiet*. New York: Simon & Schuster.

Kerr, M. E. (1994). *Deliver us from Evie*. New York: HarperCollins.

Kessler, Christina. (2000). *No condition is permanent*. New York: Philomel.

Kjelgaard, Jim. (1945). *Big Red*. New York: Holiday House.

Konigsburg, E. L. (1967). *From the mixed-up files of Mrs. Basil E. Frankweiler*. New York: Atheneum.

Lee, Marie. (1996). *Necessary roughness*. New York: HarperCollins.

Lisle, Janet Taylor. (1989). *Afternoon of the elves*. Danbury, CT: Watts.

Lowry, Lois. (1977). *A summer to die* (Jenni Oliver, Illus.). Boston: Houghton Mifflin.

Lowry, Lois (1979). *Anastasia Krupnik*. Boston: Houghton Mifflin.

Lynch, Chris. (1993). *Shadow boxer*. New York: HarperCollins.

Lynch, Chris. (1994). *Iceman*. New York: HarperCollins.

Lynch, Chris. (1995). *Slot machine*. New York: HarperCollins.

Mahy, Margaret. (1987). *Memory*. New York: Dell.

Marsden, John. (1995). *Tomorrow, when the war began*. Boston: Houghton Mifflin.

McDaniel, Lurlene. (1999). *Angel of mercy*. New York: Bantam.

McDaniel, Lurlene. (2000). *Angel of Hope*. New York: Bantam.

McElfresh, Lynn. (1999). *Can you feel the thunder?* New York: Atheneum.

Mikaelsen, Ben. (1991). *Rescue Josh McGuire*. New York: Hyperion.

Miller, Frances A. (1980). *The truth trap*. New York: Dutton.

Myers, Walter Dean. (1988). *Scorpions*. New York: Harper & Row.

Naylor, Phyllis Reynolds. (1985). *The agony of Alice*. New York: Altheneum.

Naylor, Phyllis Reynolds. (1991). *Shiloh*. New York: Atheneum.

Naylor, Phyllis Reynolds. (1996). *Shiloh season*. New York: Atheneum.

Naylor, Phyllis Reynolds. (1997). *Saving Shiloh*. New York: Atheneum.

Nelson, Theresa. (1994). *Earthshine: A novel*. New York: Orchard.

North, Sterling. (1963). *Rascal*. New York: Dutton.

Park, Barbara. (1987). *The kid in the red jacket*. New York: Knopf.

Park, Barbara. (1992). *Junie B. Jones and the stupid smelly bus*. New York: Random House.

Park, Barbara. (1995). *Mick Harte was here*. New York: Knopf.

Parrish, Peggy. (1963). *Amelia Bedelia*. New York: HarperCollins.

Pascal, Francine. (2000). *What you don't know (Sweet Valley Jr. High, No. 22)*. New York: Scholastic.

Paterson, Katherine. (1977). *Bridge to Terabithia*. New York: Harper & Row.

Paterson, Katherine. (1978). *The great Gilly Hopkins*. New York: HarperCollins.

Paulsen, Gary. (1987). *Hatchet*. New York: Bradbury.

Paulsen, Gary. (1991). *The river*. New York: Delacorte.

Paulsen, Gary. (1993). *Harris and me*. San Diego: Harcourt Brace.

Paulsen, Gary. (1996). *Brian's winter*. New York: Delacorte.

Paulsen, Gary. (1999). *Brian's return*. New York: Delacorte.

Paulsen, Gary. (2001). *Guts: The true stories behind* Hatchet *and the Brian books*. New York: Delacorte.

Peck, Richard. (1978). *Are you in the house alone?* New York: Viking.

Peck, Robert Newton. (1974). *Soup*. New York: Knopf.

Raskin, Ellen. (1978). *The Westing game*. New York: Dutton.

Ritter, John. (1998). *Choosing up sides*. New York: Philomel.

Ritter, John. (2000). *Over the wall*. New York: Philomel.

Robinson, Barbara. (1972). *The best Christmas pageant ever* (Judith Gwyn Brown, Illus.). New York: HarperCollins.

Rockwell, Thomas. (1988). *How to eat fried worms*. New York: Dell.

Sachar, Louis. (1978). *Sideways stories from the Wayside School*. New York: Knopf.

Say, Allen. (1993). *Grandfather's journey*. Boston: Houghton Mifflin.

Seuss, Dr. (1990), *Oh, the places you'll go!* New York: Random House.

Shreve, Susan. (1991). *The gift of the girl who couldn't hear*. New York: Tambourine.

Slote, Alfred. (1973). *Hang tough, Paul Mather*. New York: Lippincott.

Smith, Roland. (1985). *Thunder Cave*. New York: Hyperion.

Smith, Roland. (1997). *Jaguar*. New York: Hyperion.

Smith, Roland. (1998). *Sasquatch*. New York: Hyperion.

Smith, Roland. (1999). *The last lobo*. New York: Hyperion.

Spinelli, Jerry. (1982). *Space station seventh grade*. Boston: Little, Brown.

Spinelli, Jerry. (1988). *Dump days*. Boston: Little, Brown.

Spinelli, Jerry. (1990). *Maniac Magee*. Boston: Little, Brown.

Spinelli, Jerry. (1996). *Crash*. New York: Knopf.

Spinelli, Jerry. (1997a). *The library card*. New York: Scholastic.

Spinelli, Jerry. (1997b). *Wringer*. New York: HarperCollins.

Staples, Suzanne Fisher. (1989). *Shabanu: Daughter of the wind*. New York: Knopf.

Staples, Suzanne Fisher. (1996). *Dangerous skies*. New York: Farrar, Straus & Giroux.

Van Allsburg, Chris. (1990). *Just a dream*. Boston: Houghton Mifflin.

Voigt, Cynthia. (1981). *Homecoming*. New York: Atheneum.

Waddell, Martin. (1994). *The kidnapping of Suzie Q*. Cambridge, MA: Candlewick.

Wallace, Bill. (1986). *Ferret in the bedroom, lizards in the fridge*. New York: Holiday House.

Weaver, Will. (1993). *Striking out*. New York: HarperCollins.

Weaver, Will. (1995). *Farm team*. New York: HarperCollins.

Weaver, Will. (1998). *Hard ball: A Billy Baggs novel*. New York: HarperCollins.

Williams-Garcia, Rita. (1995). *Like sisters on the homefront*. New York: Lodestar.

Woodson, Jacqueline. (1994). *I hadn't meant to tell you this*. New York: Delacorte.

Woodson, Jacqueline. (1999). *Lena*. New York: Delacorte.

Wright, Betty Ren. (1983). *The dollhouse murders*. New York: Holiday House.

Yep, Laurence. (1977). *Child of the owl*. New York: Harper & Row.

Yep, Laurence. (1991). *The star fisher*. New York: Morrow.

Yep, Laurence. (1995). *Thief of hearts*. New York: HarperCollins.

▼▼▼▼▼▼▼

Professional References

Chatton, B. (1988). Apply with caution: Bibliotherapy in the library. *Journal of Youth Services in Libraries, 1*(3), 334–338.

Darigan, D. (1999). Interviews with the 1999 CLA breakfast speakers: Jane Yolen, Kyoko Mori, Rita Williams-Garcia, and Joseph Bruchac. *Journal of Children's Literature, 25*(2), 80–89.

Dreyer, S. S. (1981–1995). *The bookfinder: A guide to children's literature about the needs and problems of youth aged 2–15.* 5 volumes. Circle Pines, MN: American Guidance Service.

Fletcher, R. (1993). *What a writer needs.* Portsmouth, NH: Heinemann.

Haynes, C. (1988). *The explanatory power of content for identifying children's literature preferences.* Unpublished doctoral dissertation, Northern Illinois University, DeKalb, IL.

Heaton, M. M., & Lewis, H. B. (1955). *Reading ladders for human relations* (Rev. ed.). Washington, DC: American Council on Education.

Hinton, S. E. (1967). Teen-agers are for real. *New York Times book review.* New York: New York Times.

Huck, C. S., Hepler, S., Hickman, J., & Kiefer, B. (1997). *Children's literature in the elementary school.* New York: Harcourt.

Monson, D., & Sebesta, S. L. (1991). Reading preferences. In J. Flood, J. Jensen, D. Lapp, & J. R. Squire (Eds.), *Handbook of research: Teaching the English language arts* (pp. 664–673). New York: Macmillan.

Norton, D. E. (1992). *The impact of literature-based reading.* New York: Macmillan.

Stephens, M. (1990). *A dictionary of literary quotations.* London: Routledge.

Tomlinson, C. M., & Lynch-Brown, C. (1996). *Essentials of children's literature.* Boston: Allyn & Bacon.

Tomlinson, C. M., & Tunnell, M. O. (1994). Children's supernatural stories: Popular but persecuted. In J. S. Simmons (Ed.), *Censorship: A threat to reading, learning, thinking* (pp. 107–114). Newark, DE: International Reading Association.

Trease, G. (1983). Fifty years on: A writer looks back. *Children's Literature in Education, 14*(3), 21–28.

HISTORICAL FICTION

8
CHAPTER
▼▼▼▼▼▼▼▼▼

If you want to cover
Prairie Life and Westward Expansion

Consider as a READ ALOUD

I Have Heard of a Land,
by Joyce Carol Thomas,
illustrated by Floyd Cooper

Black-Eyed Susan,
by Jennifer Armstrong,
illustrated by Emily Martindale

Consider as a TEXT SET

My Daniel,
by Pam Conrad

Prairie Songs,
by Pam Conrad

The Longest Ride,
by Denise Lewis Patrick

The Bone Wars,
by Katherine Lasky

Sarah, Plain and Tall,
by Patricia MacLachlan,
illustrated by Marcia Sewell

Mr. Tucket,
by Gary Paulsen

MR. TUCKET
by Gary Paulsen

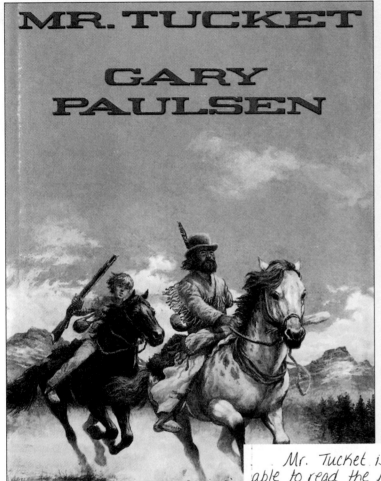

"I told him you were the toughest fighter in the Black Hills, that you were clever as the fox, that your heart was the heart of a mountain lion."

"You said all that about me?"

"Don't let it go to your head, Mr. Tucket. Indians don't take anybody's word on anything. Standing Bear says that he has a pretty tough boy in his village—"

"Oh, no . . ."

Excerpt from *Mr. Tucket* by Gary Paulsen

Student Response

Mr. Tucket is an engaging novel. I was able to read the book quickly because it was captivating and action packed. There, literally, was never a dull moment. For example, Mr. Tucket and Mr. Grimes are friends who travel together. Mr. Tucket trades with various Indian tribes in the area. Every time Mr. Grimes and Mr. Tucket venture to one of the indian camps Mr. Grimes boasts about Mr. Tucket's fighting ability. Therefore Mr. Tucket, who is fourteen years old, often finds himself rumbling with other fourteen year old boys.

Mr. Tucket is an extraordinary book. The way it is written makes you wish that it went on forever. Mr. Tucket is a distinguished book because of it's moral and the lesson that emerges.

Brandon, 10

To visit a classroom exploring the issues of Historical Fiction, please go to Chapter 8 of our companion website at **www.prenhall.com/darigan**

▼▼▼▼▼▼▼
Defining Historical Fiction

Historical fiction is a fitting companion to contemporary realistic fiction, which is why we consciously keep them together in this book. Both consider the lives of people in situations that *could* have happened but didn't. However, historical fiction relates those stories set in the near or distant past. Historical fiction bases its primary authenticity on historical fact and, when done well, offers the reader a glimpse of what the past was like without ever overwhelming him or her with ponderous research, figures, or statistics.

At the primary level, curricula have typically not included the formal study of history because concepts of time develop slowly in children. How can youngsters, who see next week as an eternity away or who ask if grandpa was around when the Pilgrims arrived, possibly gain an appreciation of their historical heritage? On the other hand, we have learned that teaching history through narrative, or story, *can* provide "a temporal scaffolding for historical understanding that is accessible even to quite young children" (Downey & Levstik, 1988, p. 338).

People tend to think in terms of narrative structures or story grammars, which basically involve characters formulating goals and then solving problems in order to achieve their goals. When historical settings are added to the mix, a natural segue to the past is opened.

▼▼▼▼▼▼▼
Elements of Historical Fiction

The Power of Story

Historical fiction can be a tremendously engaging reading experience for its own sake. The strong literary element in this genre captures readers and instantly transports them to the most unlikely places in *any* time. By simply opening the covers of a book, you could be a young girl sitting in a choir loft in 16th century Yorkshire, England, disguised as a boy and frantically wondering what you should do next. Beth Hilgartner's ***A Murder for Her Majesty*** is packed with intrigue as you begin to unravel the circumstances of your father's murder, which you have just witnessed, certain in the knowledge that the killers are agents of none other than Queen Elizabeth I herself. Or you could be pretending to be a boy in a similar situation but set in the American Civil War, as in Gloria Houston's exciting and romantic book, ***Mountain Valor.***

Because of this power in narrative, children and adults are more likely to process and remember historical information when it comes in the form of a good story (Armbruster & Anderson, 1984; Hidi, Baird, & Hildyard, 1982; McGowan & Guzzetti, 1991). For example, children can read "about" the loneliness and hardships associated with living on the prairie during the latter part of the 19th century, but they may not be able to identify with those abject conditions as presented in the social studies textbooks they read. In *America's Story,* the fifth-grade basal published by Harcourt Brace, the difficult circumstances of prairie life are characterized simply as living in dirty sod houses and having crops ruined by bad weather, fires, and insects. The abbreviated section covering this concept concludes with the bland statement, "Sometimes the hardships became so great that some people left their farms. But most stayed" (p. 485).

Breathing Life Into the Past

Good narrative allows students to vicariously "feel" what it would have been like as a child living through that period and viewing the adults' reactions to the times. In Eve Bunting's ***Dandelions,*** young Zoe comes face to face with the desperate isolation and loneliness her mother is beginning to feel as they arrive at their claim in the Nebraska

EVALUATING HISTORICAL FICTION

- Story: Is the story well developed and believable?
- Historical setting: Does the past come alive with details and historical events?
- People connection: Do characters come to life? Are they believable and well developed?
- Multiple perspectives: Are multiple historical perspectives presented, giving the reader a better sense of the times?
- Historical accuracy: Are the times portrayed accurately without undue sugar-coating and didacticism?
- Cultural authenticity: Are cultures accurately portrayed, showing the wide range of diversity present?

Territory. Rather than tell us about the state of women at that time, Bunting adeptly brings out that fact, as this short passage exemplifies. The family had gone to visit their nearest neighbors, and Zoe states:

> We started for the Swensons' the very next morning. It was hard to see their house; it was so much like the empty land around it. I think we would have missed it if Papa hadn't known exactly where he was going. I don't know how he did know, but Papa is smart.
>
> Mrs. Swenson came running toward us, and Papa stopped the wagon so Mama could get down. She and Mrs. Swenson met and hugged and cried.
>
> "Does Mama know her already?" I whispered to Papa.
>
> "No. But they are happy to see each other. It has been a long time since either of them has seen another woman." He sounded sad . . .

Maxim (1999) states that the use of books and story "make[s] the people, conditions, and events of the past seem well defined and real" (p. 472).

Teachers who share and encourage the reading of historical fiction in the form of picture books and novels are helping students learn historical facts but, more important, they are helping them see history as a vital and meaningful subject. Historical fiction can breathe life into what students may have considered irrelevant and dull. It allows them to see that their *present* is part of a *living past,* that people as real as themselves struggled with problems similar to their own, and that today's way of life is a result of what these people did to find solutions.

Where History Textbooks Fall Short

History textbooks, to their credit, present children with a sequential highlighting of history over time. From the pages of the textbook, we know what happened when and where. But they are *not* particularly effective in helping children make meaningful, personal connections with the past. In fact, studies report that students at all grade levels name social studies (history) as their most boring class and point to their textbooks as one of the major reasons (Fischer, 1997; Sewall, 1988). As far back as 1893, the National Education Association declared, "When the facts are chosen with as little discrimination as in many school [history] textbooks, when they are mere lists of lifeless dates, details of military movements . . . [t]hey are repellent" (Ravitch, 1985, p. 13).

The criticism from historians and educators today has not lessened (Loewen, 1995). "[History] textbooks have relied more and more on broken text and pictorial flash to hold student interest. Efforts to render textbooks 'readable'—at least by the standards of readability formulas—have contributed to their arid prose" (Sewall, 1988, p. 554).

To find out more about the America Memories Fellow Program and other historical fiction activities on the World Wide Web, visit Chapter 8 on the companion website at **www.prenhall.com/darigan**

BOOKMARK

INTEGRATING TECHNOLOGY: ACTIVITIES USING THE WORLD WIDE WEB

Jacob Have I Loved: America Memories Fellow Program is a project designed by Kathy Isaacs. Photographs from "America From the Great Depression to World War II," a section of American Memory, are used to provide visual images that can introduce and extend exploration of **Jacob Have I Loved,** by Katherine Paterson, a novel about jealousy set on an island in the Chesapeake Bay in the early 1940s.

One of history texts' biggest problems lies in the fact that they must cover so much material they cannot do justice to any event, person, or concept. For instance, Columbus is allowed only five paragraphs in Houghton Mifflin's fifth-grade history text (Bednarz et al., 1997), though the book also includes a brief excerpt from a historical novel about Columbus's first voyage. Harcourt Brace's textbook allows only 146 words to cover the Holocaust. Houghton Mifflin covers it in a single paragraph, and Macmillan/McGraw-Hill's book gives the subject five paragraphs and only 220 words (Banks et al., 1997). Couple these short offerings with "arid prose," and you have a formidable product that children look upon as "a kind of castor oil that one has to take—something that's good for you, maybe, but repulsive . . . rather than castor oil, history should be thought of as a tonic. It should wake us up, because it is the story of ourselves" (Freedman, 1993, p. 41).

Children's Literature Adds Breadth and Depth to Historical Study

Historical fiction, on the other hand, expands and brings to life the landmark as well as seemingly mundane events of the past, accenting the true "stories" in history.

While researching the novel that would one day become **Prairie Songs,** Pam Conrad came across Solomon Butcher's photographs in the Nebraska State Historical Society. She wrote, "The minute I saw all the pictures he had taken of Nebraska pioneers, I knew I wanted him to take a picture of the pioneer family in my book as well." With what little information she could gather, she proceeded to "make up" this man's character and "[he] came to life." This is how Conrad introduces him:

> Suddenly a wagon appeared, coming over the hill, a peculiar boxed type of thing, maybe like a gypsy wagon I had once seen, but it was smaller, and plain, and there was but one lonely man sitting in the seat . . .
>
> "Good afternoon, ladies." The man tipped his pale-gray hat to us. "And how are you this fine afternoon?" he asked, reining the horse to a halt. I began to think he might be a circus performer or a carnival act. He had smiling eyes and a block of a beard that covered the lower half of his face somewhat. He climbed down from his seat and extended his hand . . .
>
> "Pleased to meet you," he said, suddenly solemn and serious. "I truly am. Every time I ride along and come across a family at work or at play, I am deeply moved by the sight." He had placed his hat over his heart, and his eyebrows danced up and down with his words. "You are pioneers of Nebraska, pilgrims of the New World."

Butcher, whose vision was to record the oral and pictorial history of the people of Custer County in Nebraska during late 1800s, spent 7 years on the project and took more than 1500 photographs of pioneer life. He recorded family stories, anecdotes, and biographies. He photographed families sitting in front of their sod houses, tents,

Cover from *Prairie Songs* by Pam Conrad, illustrated by Darryl S. Zudeck. Published by Harper & Row, Publishers. Text copyright © 1985 by Pam Conrad. Jacket art © 1985 by Darryl S. Zudeck. Reprinted by permission of the publisher.

From *Prairie Visions: The Life and Times of Solomon Butcher.* Copyright © 1991 by Pam Conrad. Originally published by HarperCollins Children's Books, a division of HarperCollins Publishers. Photo reprinted by permission of the Nebraska State Historical Society.

and dugouts. He "preserved for all time, the faces and lives of the people of [the] county" (Conrad, 1985, p. 58), men, women, and children working the land, farmers fighting off locusts, and families living the prairie life. Conrad explains in her book *Prairie Visions: The Life and Times of Solomon Butcher,* "I loved Solomon Butcher, just as I loved Louisa and Lester and all the other characters that had come to me during the writing of *Prairie Songs.* Then one day, after my novel had been published, I was speaking (as a historical novelist) to a group of teachers in Grand Island, Nebraska. After the talk when I was signing books, a woman came over to me and asked me to sign two copies of *Prairie Songs,* one for herself and one for her neighbor—Solomon Butcher's daughter. A shiver ran through me. It was as though there had been a tug on my skirt and, turning around, I'd found Lester there." To Pam Conrad, this man, Solomon Butcher, had become real and because he had come to life for her, he comes to life for us on the written page.

Historical Fiction Makes the "People" Connection

If history is indeed the story of ourselves, then another limitation of history textbooks is that the people are missing! The best one-word definition of history is, in fact, "people." Without human beings, whose emotions and actions influence the times, there is no history. Ask anyone who has had a memorable history class to describe why it was good, and the reasons always include a focus on people, whether prominent or ordinary.

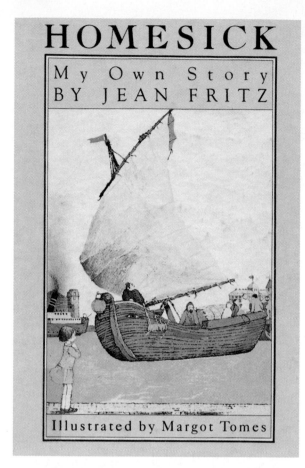

Illustrations by Margot Tomes, copyright © 1982 by Margot Tomes, illustrations, from **Homesick: My Own Story** by Jean Fritz. Used by permission of G. P. Putnam's Sons, a division of Penguin Putnam, Inc.

Jean Fritz, in her autobiographical novel, *Homesick,* recalls her first school experience with American history texts:

> Miss Crofts put a bunch of history books on the first desk of each row so they could be passed back, student to student. I was glad to see that we'd be studying the history of Pennsylvania. Since both my mother's and father's families had helped settle Washington County, I was interested to know how they and the other pioneers had fared. Opening the book to the first chapter, "From Forest to Farmland," I skimmed through the pages but I couldn't find any mention of people at all. There was talk about dates and square miles and cultivation and population growth and immigration and the Western movement, but it was as if the forest had lain down and given way to farmland without anyone being brave or scared or tired or sad, without babies being born, without people dying. Well, I thought, maybe that would come later.

But, it never did. Unfortunately, in many classrooms where the major resource for history is the textbook, the same is also true. The dreams, aspirations, and certainly the foibles of people constitute the "tonic" that makes history burst into life. If we want readers to come to that engaged stance we talk about in chapter 1, it is easy to see how good children's books can reach those ends.

Avi, in similar fashion to Pam Conrad's inclusion of the real Solomon Butcher, introduces the character of Edgar Allan Poe in his book *The Man Who Was Poe.* Most readers know Poe for his dark stories and poetry, which appear to be a direct result of the dark nature of his disturbed personality. Note how Avi introduces this man and allows us to make inferences into the true nature of his enigmatic character:

> A man, carpetbag in hand, made his way up College Hill, up from the sluggish river basin, battling the steep incline, the wind, and his own desire. He was not big, this man, but the old army coat he wore—black and misshapen, reaching below his knees—gave him an odd bulk. His face was pale, his mustache dark, his mouth set in a scowl of contempt. Beneath a broad forehead crowned by a shock of jet black hair, his eyes were deep, dark, and intense.
>
> Sometimes he walked quickly, sometimes slowly. More than once he looked back down the hill, trying to decide if he should return to the warm station and the train he had just left. There were moments he could think of nothing better. But he had traveled all day and was exhausted. What he wanted, what he needed, was a place where he could drink and sleep.
>
> And write. For the man was a writer very much in need of cash. A story would bring money. But of late he had been unable to write. Idea, theme, characters: he lacked them all.

We have a strong sense of who this man is and certainly of his dark nature.

Presenting History From Multiple Perspectives

Not only are people missing in history texts, but so, too, are varying historical perspectives. "To present history in simple, one sided—almost moralistic—terms, is to teach nothing worth learning and to falsify the past in a way that provides worse than no help in understanding the present or in meeting the future" (Collier, 1976, p. 138).

Indeed, history textbooks tend to approach topics from single perspectives; they have space to do little else (Foster, Morris, & Davis, 1996; Tunnell & Ammon, 1996). For instance, the American Revolution typically has been reported from the Whig perspective, which depicts "simple, freedom-loving farmers marching in a crusade to fulfill God's plan for a rationally ordered society based on the principles of liberty and equality" (Collier, 1976, p. 133). Certainly there were and are other points of view, however, and these are portrayed nicely in historical fiction. For example, the Loyalist perspective, which draws attention to the British position, can be seen in Scott O'Dell's *Sarah Bishop,* and the Progressive view, contrasted with the Whig standpoint, is seen in James Lincoln and Christopher Collier's *My Brother Sam Is Dead.*

By the same token, Columbus is presented in elementary-school textbooks only from a Eurocentric perspective. Of course, the Native Americans have a defensible point of view that deglorifies Columbus, but this perspective is covertly censored (Shannon, 1989) from textbook pages simply by not being mentioned. A welcome addition to this narrow view is Michael Dorris's *Morning Girl.* Dorris introduces the community of Taino people as they strive to coexist with the natural world on their Bahamian island. Sadly, the book ends with the arrival of Columbus and his ships. Morning Girl must stop herself from laughing at them because "the strangers had wrapped every part of their bodies with colorful leaves and cotton." However, she remembers, "One must always treat guests with respect . . . even when they are as brainless as gulls." The poignant epilogue to the book is the inclusion of a journal entry by Columbus himself describing these "simple" people who should make "good and diligent servants." Jane Yolen's *Encounter* furthers this perspective in picture book form describing the arrival of Columbus from the perspective a young Taino boy.

Unfortunately, "when a textbook is used as the only source of information, students tend to accept the author's statements without question" (Holmes & Ammon, 1985, p. 366). We know that history never has a single side to its story. Children's literature in the form of historical fiction and, as we see in chapter 10, historical nonfiction, is more likely to invite "the reader to enter into a historical discussion that involves making judgments about issues of morality. . . . What was it like to be a person here? What was the nature of good and evil in that time and place, and with whom shall my sympathies lie?" (Levstik, 1989, p. 137).

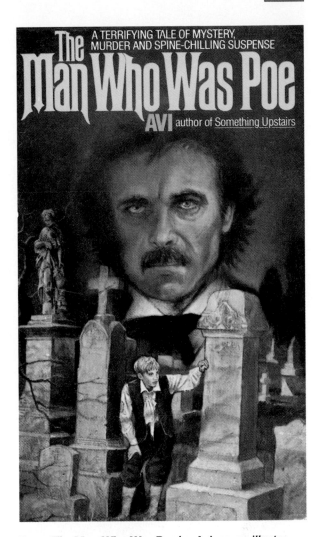

From *The Man Who Was Poe* by Avi, cover illustration by Ted Lewin. Published by Orchard books an imprint of Scholastic Inc. Text copyright © 1989 by Avi, illustration copyright © 1989 by Ted Lewin. Reprinted by permission.

To set the stage for this investigation of Columbus and his trip to the New World, you might want to contextualize the culture by reading a traditional folktale, such as Nina Jaffe's *The Golden Flower: A Taino Myth from Puerto Rico.*

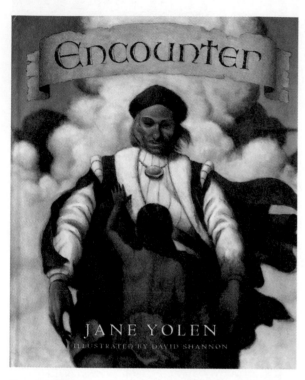

Cover from **Encounter** by Jane Yolen, illustrations
© 1992 by David Shannon. Reprinted by permission
of Harcourt.

From **Morning Girl** by Michael Dorris. Text Copyright
© 1992 by Michael Dorris. Reprinted by permission
of Hyperion Books For Children.

ALTERNATE TEXT SET

Historical Fiction by Mildred Taylor

Read Aloud

Mississippi Bridge

Text Set

Song of the Trees

Roll of Thunder, Hear My Cry

Let the Circle Be Unbroken

The Gold Cadillac

The Friendship

The Road to Memphis

The Well

Take, for example, Mildred Taylor's powerful novel *Mississippi Bridge*. Presenting a highly emotional picture of racism in the Deep South during the Great Depression era, Taylor engages the reader in the thought-provoking moral dilemmas of that time in the United States.

This sort of critical thinking about the story of ourselves involves the examination of conflicting viewpoints and making personal judgments. See our Alternate Text Set "Issues of Slavery and the American Civil War" for a number of pieces of historical fiction for young readers that approach slavery and the American Civil War from differing perspectives. Read as a class text set, these titles provide students with a concrete background that acts as the fodder for discussing, debating, and questioning the human motives behind the historical facts. All too often we ask children to converse about issues, such as slavery, when the only exposure they have had to the concept has been the sparse facts and examples provided in their social studies book. Adding good historical fiction to the curriculum gives them the context of the times, a feel for the "players" in the drama, and, therefore, a greater wherewithal to make educated arguments for their perspectives.

DID YOU KNOW?

During the United States Civil War, boys under the age of 16 who fought in this bloody battle were estimated to number from 250,000 to 420,000. How bloody was it? In the First Maine Heavy Artillery, 635 soldiers of their 900 were killed *in the first seven minutes* of battle, and a regiment from North Carolina had 714 of its 800 men killed at Gettysburg. Where did we get this information? From Jim Murphy's nonfiction offering, ***The Boy's War*** (p. 41). But to make these figures really spring to life, read Patricia Beatty's historical fiction book, ***Charley Skedaddle.***

ALTERNATE TEXT SET

Issues of Slavery and the American Civil War

Read Aloud

Shades of Gray, by Carolyn Reeder

Text Set

Turn Homeward, Hannalee, by Patricia Beatty

Charley Skedaddle, by Patricia Beatty

Jayhawker, by Patricia Beatty

Across Five Aprils, by Irene Hunt

Soldier's Heart, by Gary Paulsen

Lightning Time, by Douglas Rees

Running for Our Lives, by Glennette Tilley Turner and illustrated by Samuel Byrd

If you want to become acquainted with more titles about another Civil War topic, such as "The Underground Railroad," go to the children's literature database of this text.

What Makes Good Historical Fiction?

Historical fiction is identifiably different because, of course, it is set in the past. Generally, the main characters are fictional, but often they are based on real people and incidents that occurred in the past. Historical fiction is judged by the same criteria as any other piece of fiction. We discussed strength of character development and plot, writing style, definition of setting, and the handling of theme in detail in chapter 7, "Contemporary Realistic Fiction"; however, some considerations that are peculiar to this genre are worth noting.

To find out more about Small Planet Communications' Lesson Plan on The Civil War and other sources for historical fiction lesson plans on the World Wide Web, visit Chapter 8 on the companion website at **www.prenhall. com/darigan**

BOOKMARK

INTEGRATING TECHNOLOGY: SOURCES ON THE WORLD WIDE WEB

Lesson Plan on The Civil War is a well-developed unit plan on the Civil War created by Small Planet Communications. It includes genre study, a recommended booklist, links to primary documents, and a step-by-step template for students to create their own websites. Great resources are provided for integrating literature with archival information, music, writing, and history.

History Should Not Be Sugarcoated

When dealing with historical events, it is important to deal plainly with the truth. Several decades ago, some particularly unsettling truths were avoided or even revised in books written for children. The Age of New Realism in children's literature, which opened in the mid-1960s, began a trend that dictated more honesty in the writing of realistic and historical fiction. Topics that had often been avoided began to appear more frequently, such as the Japanese-American internment camps in the United States during World War II, as seen in Yoshiko Uchida's *Journey to Topaz,* and the frank treatment of the horrors of the slave trade in Paula Fox's *The Slave Dancer.*

Kathryn Lasky (1990) explains that an author of historical fiction has the responsibility to preserve what she calls "the fabric of time" by remaining faithful to the historical context in which a story is set. Lasky herself confronted the difficulty some readers have with that honesty after publication of her book *Beyond the Divide.* In her research, she learned that women in the Old West were constant targets of crime. They often were left alone and were vulnerable to rape and murder. And if they were raped, the women generally were ostracized, as happened with Serena Billings in *Beyond the Divide.* Lasky received a letter from an adult reader who was angry not so much because Serena was raped but because she was ostracized. The reader said, "[This] account did not set a good example for coping with the hurt and trauma that accompanies rape or for teaching young readers how they might cope with it" (Lasky, 1990, p. 164). Lasky responded by saying, "As a writer of historical fiction, I have an obligation to remain faithful, to remain accountable in my story telling, to the manners and mores and the practices of the period" (p. 165).

Indeed, much of the history of ourselves is unsavory. For example, the racism and bigotry toward African Americans, particularly prior to the Civil Rights movement in the 1960s, are a dark cloud in our nation's history. Yet much can be learned through books such as Evelyn Coleman's *Black Socks Only.* A young girl listens as her grandmother tells of her first solo trip to town whereupon she is attacked by a belligerent white man for drinking out of a water fountain that is posted "Whites Only." Though she removed her black patent leather shoes and stepped up with only her white socks on, she finds it hard to understand what she may have done that was wrong. In her defense, other Blacks step up and drink, calling the bluff of the bully and "from then on, nobody ever again saw the big white man who whipped us and the 'Whites Only' sign was gone from that water fountain forever."

The lessons history has to teach us will go unlearned if we forever soften or eliminate the message. Understanding and being sickened by Serena's treatment help us become more aware of righting the mistakes of the past. In the immortal words of George Santayana, "Those who cannot remember the past are condemned to repeat it."

Historical Accuracy Is Required

Because historical fiction is rooted in history, an infrastructure of accurate historical fact is necessary. When events are documented, they must not be altered. However, when fictionalizing history, authors may take some liberties. For example, they may create dialogue for famous individuals but should not put words into their mouths that don't match with their known attitudes and personalities. To serve the purpose of storytelling, for instance, in her book *Johnny Tremain,* Esther Forbes created conversations between Johnny Tremain and many of the well-known Sons of Liberty. What Paul Revere said to Johnny is certainly not factual, although it reflects what Forbes knew about Revere's attitudes and personal life. The fictional character of Johnny serves as a vehicle to unite in an efficient way the major people and the complex events of the Boston revolt, pulling fragmented occurrences together into a cohesive story. On the other hand, if Forbes had invented a surprise appearance of George Washington at the Boston Tea Party for dramatic effect, the reworking of the facts would have strained the story's historical credibility.

Not uncommonly, the main characters rub shoulders with real, historically prominent people, as we noted earlier in Avi's *The Man Who Was Poe* and Pam Conrad's *Prairie Songs.* Often, in the end material of a book, authors will place a note describing who was "real" and who was not, providing the reader with hints to the absolute authenticity of the overall piece.

Let's face it, though: Children seem to avoid "Author's Notes" as they were a double dose of castor oil. When they come to the end a book or story and see an "Afterword," it would seem the cover couldn't be slammed shut fast enough. Therefore, our job as teachers is to encourage the practice and directly model the benefit of reading such information. Take, for example, the read-aloud picture book we suggest at the beginning of this chapter. In *I Have Heard of a Land,* Joyce Carol Thomas articulates some very important insights about both the times and conditions African Americans faced during the westward expansion of the United States as well as rich details about her own family, who inspired this poetic text. When sharing this book with your class, be it university or elementary, a good idea would be to actually start at the *end* of the book by reading the first three paragraphs of the "Author's Note." This information sets the stage of the late 1800s, detailing why "many Blacks in the South were drawn to . . . land runs, in which they could stake a claim for free land." The teacher can then read the book aloud to the class, knowing they have a context for what they are about to see in Floyd Cooper's illustrations and hear in Thomas's text. After discussing comments and connections students make, the teacher can then go back to the end material and read the final four paragraphs, noting how this applied to the author's own family.

The Historical Period Must Come to Life

A historical period is brought to life when the author re-creates the physical environment, patterns of daily living, and spirit of the times. What was it like to live from day to day in Boston in 1775, or in London in 1215? What did a servant eat? What diseases were feared? Who went to school and who didn't? Mollie Hunter (1976), winner of Britain's Carnegie Award for her historical novel *The Stronghold,* feels that this sort of realism can best be communicated in writing when authors have come to know the place and time so well that they "could walk undetected in the past" (p. 43), waking in the morning to know the sort of bed they'd be sleeping in or reaching in their pockets to grasp familiar coins.

Creating this atmosphere in a novel also depends on avoiding modern terms. Joan Blos (1985), author of the Newbery Award–winning *A Gathering of Days,* points out that authors of historical novels struggle with the compromises that must be made in maintaining strict historical validity and says that sometimes the rules require bending to make a story readable. For example, an overabundance of archaic speech in a story of the Middle Ages may derail a young reader. However, she says, "historical material and thought lack validity if expressed in modern phrases, idioms,

To find out more about Patricia Reilly Giff and other authors of historical fiction on the World Wide Web, visit Chapter 8 on the companion website at **www.prenhall. com/darigan**

BOOKMARK

INTEGRATING TECHNOLOGY: AUTHORS ON THE WORLD WIDE WEB

Some publishers create wonderful websites that can supplement and extend the reading of children's books. Random House has an in-depth web page for *Patricia Reilly Giff,* which includes an excellent teacher's guide for *Lily's Crossing,* a real-audio message from the author, a prereading activity, thematic and interdisciplinary connections, and related books.

or linguistic rhythms," as in this example relating to the American Revolution: "Peering out of her bedroom window, Deeny saw bunches of Hessians heading for the green" (1985, p. 39). "Bunches" to describe groups of people is an informal, modern use of the word that is out of place in a colonial American setting.

Re-creating the spirit of the times may be the most important and most difficult challenge an author faces. To understand the motivating factors that led individuals or groups of people to make decisions that altered the patterns of life or the course of political history is not a simple affair. What stirred the winds of change or suppressed them? The spirit of the times fueled the rebellion against the Crown or encouraged the acceptance of slavery, but as is true in today's world, not everyone was moved by the spirit in the same way. Tories resisted the American Revolution, and young men and boys enlisted in the American Civil War for a variety of reasons other than the standard historical textbook stance—to abolish slavery. Take, for example, a short scene in Harold Keith's Civil War novel, **Rifles for Watie.** Young 16-year-old Jeff Bussey has finally joined ranks with the Union Army, and the new volunteers are waiting in line for the quartermaster to issue uniforms and supplies. They strike up a conversation about why they joined.

> "My family's Union. Mammy didn't want me to go to no war. But we knowed the bushwhackers was hid out in the brush, stealin' money and hosses and chokin' boys my age when they found 'em. I didn't wanta git choked. I runned away. I wanted to run away sooner."
>
> "I jined fer a frolic," laughed a tall fellow from Republic County with warts on his face. He turned to his messmate, a blond boy from Fort Scott. "Why did you come in?"
>
> "Wal, by Jack, because they told me the rebels was cuttin' out Union folks' tongues and killin' their babies. After I got here I found out all it was over was wantin' to free the niggers," complained another, disgustedly.
>
> "I decided I'd jest as well be in the army as out in the bresh. Now I'm about to decide I'd druther be in the bresh," snorted another.

These varying perspectives are what led to the conflicts that initiated change and are the very sort of spirit that should permeate good historical stories.

History Revealed Through the Eyes of a Young Protagonist

Although young main characters seem a requirement for most children's fiction, historical novels have an especially pressing need for them. Young readers are accosted with a study of history that generally ignores people their age—people like themselves—and in almost every case, no children are ever mentioned. Therefore, the gap between themselves and the dusty past widens. A young protagonist who is inserted into the tumultuous times of the Boston revolt or the difficult period of the Great Depression allows

ALTERNATE TEXT SET

Living in Medieval Times

Read Aloud

Lost Magic, by Amoss Berthe

Text Set

Fire, Bed and Bone, by Henrietta Branford

A Door in the Wall, by Marguerite DeAngeli

Robin's Country, by Monica Furlong

Black Horses for the King, by Anne McCaffrey

Mary, Bloody Mary, by Carolyn Meyer

The Ramsay Scallop, by Francis Temple

The Queen's Own Fool, by Jane Yolen

young readers to experience history through the senses of someone who views life the way they do—as a child.

Jane Yolen (1989) tells of being invited to talk to a group of eighth graders about the Holocaust. Horrified, the students asked her if she made "all that stuff up." The realities of Europe in the 1930s and 40s were so far outside their realm of experience that they thought this story of such massive human suffering was a fabrication; people couldn't do such things to one another. Yolen's answer to this problem is found in her writing.

Her novel *The Devil's Arithmetic* uses the fantasy technique of time travel to transport a 14-year-old American Jewish girl of the 1980s back to World War II Poland. As a youngster disconnected with her own past, Hannah is allowed to experience personally the spirit of the times and ask questions such as "How could you be so dumb as to believe those Nazis when they say you are only being resettled?" Says Yolen, "Children are mired in the present. . . . [So, by] taking a child out of that *to-day* in a novel, [with] a child protagonist that the reader identifies fully with, and throwing the child backwards or forwards in time, the reader too is thrown into the slipstream of yesterday or tomorrow. The reader becomes part of that 'living and continuous process,' forced to acknowledge that we *are* our past just as we *are* our future" (1989, p. 248). Truly seeing history through the eyes of someone their own age, Yolen states, "is a straight road into memory, an experiential act for an understanding of the past. It is once-upon-a-very-real-time, making history immediate and accessible for the young reader, letting them see backwards through a clear lens" (1989, p. 247).

From *The Devil's Arithmetic* by Jane Yolen, cover illustration by Viqui Maggio, copyright © 1988 by Viqui Maggio, cover illustration. Used by permission of Viking Kestrel, a division of Penguin Putnam, Inc.

Whether bringing a modern child back in time or creating a young protagonist who is born to that time, authors of historical fiction are able to give their young audience a sense of connecting with the past.

Giving Appropriate Attention to Historical Detail

Telling a good story is still the essence of historical fiction. Authors may be tempted to cram in as many details from their historical research as possible, which can make the writing laborious and destroy the sense of story. Joan Blos (1985) notes two ways that an author may give in to this temptation. First, she refers to "the overstuffed sentence" (or paragraph or chapter). This is characterized by the sentence that is loaded with far too many intrusive clauses of historical explanation:

> Zeke was eager to get to the corner. He wanted to be certain that when the procession came by he could see President Abraham Lincoln who, with his running mate, Senator Hannibal Hamlin of Maine . . . (1985, p. 38)

Second, an author may launch into inappropriate, overblown descriptions. Blos explains that a good litmus test for this would be to ask whether a contemporary character would "carry on" about a similar detail and gives this example:

> Sam's mother adjusted one of the four round dials that adorned the front of the white enamelled stove, turning it from High to Simmer, and waiting a minute to be sure that the heat had been reduced. (1985, pp. 38–39)

Cultural Authenticity Is a Must

We are so fortunate to have such diversity in the body of children's literature. However, we must be ever wary of cultural authenticity and work diligently to provide the best and most accurate literature for our children. In recent years, the scrutiny that has been weighed upon publishers has significantly improved the authenticity of books available for children of all ages. As we mention in chapter 7, on contemporary realistic fiction, great effort has been placed on getting books right. Certainly authors like Mildred Taylor, who writes of her own family's experience in the South during the Great Depression in books such as ***Roll of Thunder, Hear My Cry, Mississippi Bridge,*** and ***The Well,*** has a special connection to both the issues and the people. Taylor is writing as an insider—an African American writing about the African American experience. Laurence Yep does likewise from his own Chinese American perspective in ***Child of the Owl,*** its sequel, ***Thief of Hearts,*** and ***The Star Fisher.***

However, to play devil's advocate and for the sake of academic argument, consider that the main characters in all three of Yep's wonderful books are female. Can he adequately write from the voice of a girl but not be female? As we stated before, it is the great writer who can transcend culture, gender, and, in the case of historical fiction, time. In these particular cases, we think Yep does so admirably well. Again, we caution that we as teachers and librarians always be on guard for books that are inaccurate or stereotypic.

To read more of the Conversation with Karen Cushman, please visit Chapter 8 on our text's companion website at **www.prenhall.com/darigan**

▼▼▼▼▼▼▼▼

Types of Historical Fiction

A Story That Occurs Before the Life of the Author

Most historical stories are of the type that are set completely in the past, in a period the author has not personally experienced. This means that the author relies completely on historical research rather than personal experience in creating the story. Examples of this variety of historical novel are four of Karen Cushman's novels: ***Catherine, Called Birdy, The Midwife's Apprentice, The Ballad of Lucy Whipple,*** and ***Matilda Bone.***

A CONVERSATION WITH . . .

Karen Cushman

Over the years I thought a lot about writing and I always had a lot of ideas. I'd have ideas for non-fiction, sometimes fiction and I'd say to my husband, Phil, "I've got this great idea for a book." I would tell him everything but that would be the end of it; the pressure would be off. One time on vacation I woke up and I said, "I have this great idea for a book." Phil said, "You've been saying this for 25 years now and I've never seen a word on paper. I refuse to listen but I'll read it if you'll write it down." He gave me his stenographer's pad and a pen and I wrote seven pages, which was the full summary of *Catherine, Called Birdy.* The whole thing was there, including the title. Once it was written down I felt some kind of commitment to it. I wanted to see what happened to this girl. I wanted to see it turned into a whole story. To this day I take those seven pages with me when I talk to school children and show them that it's not enough just to have an idea, even if it's a good idea. You have to take a stand; have a commitment, write it down, and put it into action.

From there, *Catherine* took on a life of her own. I couldn't ask anybody what happened to her because I was the one who had to make it all up. Over the next three and half years I did research and writing.

I started out researching in academic libraries like UC Berkeley. I thought that this was the place I needed to go. But the background information there only told me about battles and treaties, the church, economics, and the men in power at the time. I found that my training in museum studies helped me glean the information I wanted; to look at objects and ideas and find out what they had to say about the everyday life of ordinary people. I wanted to know what the women were doing. How they baked bread without a bread machine, where they went to the bathroom, and what they did for fun. Luckily I found that a lot of that information in bookstores.

It seems that recently there has been a growing interest in history and that a lot of the primary sources from that time have been reprinted. I was able to find a whole host of tidbits: about keeping house in the 14th century or how one would travel during those times. A number of older libraries around Berkeley and Oakland had a lot of books dated from the 1920s and 1930s that dealt with everyday life in the 13th century. Sometimes these sources didn't have answers but they would pose further questions.

I was determined not to make Catherine a 20th century young person in the 13th century. I wanted her to be a bit of an aberration, not exactly fit in, but still to really see things mostly through the lens of the 13th century. She had to realize that she didn't have an alternative to this planned marriage; that she actually couldn't go off on the road by herself or go on crusade. I also wanted the other characters to be real.

I researched the clothing, foods, and festivals of the times. I looked at expectations, beliefs, and values because they were so different from our times. For example, people weren't monsters because they went to public executions. Then it was an accepted form of entertainment. Further, in *The Midwife's Apprentice* there was no expectation that there should be a place to care for this homeless child, Alyce. She didn't have that expectation, nor did society.

In the case of my main character in *The Ballad of Lucy Whipple* I couldn't find a whole lot of material on women and girls during the Gold Rush. I found that especially interesting in this area of California where I live because this is where the Gold Rush actually happened. So we drove out to Gold Rush country and looked through the archives. There was a lot of information about miners, the letters they wrote and on the process of mining but there wasn't much about women and children. So I went to the material culture; right to the objects. I looked at real tents and saw first-hand what size they were so I could imagine being in it in the rain and freezing cold with people living inside. I walked through those dusty streets on an August day and looked out at the mountains. By looking at the objects that were left from the Gold Rush we were able to learn a lot about living conditions, which I think is important for learning or teaching anything.

I tell kids that when I went to England I was in a castle that had a dungeon and they let us handle some of the "implements of destruction." I lifted, or tried to lift, this sword that was like 75 lbs. It was black and you could see the hammer marks left in the blade that was not especially sharp. It presented a very different image of Robin Hood lithely leaping up and down the stairs sword in hand. With these things sword fights were more likely hacking contests where the last person who could lift the weapon probably was the winner. They had to have taken a long time and must have been quite brutal. I learned that from this object. That all came from my museum background not only looking at the everyday life but at the objects of everyday life.

Reprinted in part with permission from a previously printed article: Darigan, D. (1998). A breakfast with the author: Karen Cushman. *Journal of Children's Literature, 23* (2), 108–113.

A CONVERSATION WITH. . .

Cynthia DeFelice

My books often start when I read or find out about something that is unbelievable, fascinating, weird, or really exciting; something that happened in the past that I wasn't aware of. Before I wrote **Weasel,** for example, I learned of the "Removal Act," passed by Congress in 1830 during the Westward Expansion, which "removed" Native Americans to the Indian Territories. If they didn't go peacefully, they were often killed. That was the little seed that started that book.

In **Nowhere to Call Home,** I read a statistic that blew my mind: During the Depression, there were an estimated 250,000 kids riding the rails as hobos. A quarter of a million teenagers! I began my research thinking this could be a fascinating story to tell. And you know, as with anything, the more I found out about it, the more interesting it became. I feel that if I can go back to a place and time in the past and get excited about it, then I have hope I will be able to get my young readers excited about it, too.

My husband, kids, and I do a lot of nature trips, backpacking, hiking, and bird watching. We had been to the Everglades a couple of times and learned that back in the 1900s, the very birds we were looking at were nearly wiped out by what were called "plume hunters." At the time, it was the fashion for ladies to wear hats that were decorated with bird feathers, or even that had the whole dead bird plopped right on top of the hat! It seemed so bizarre, and this practice led many species right to the brink of extinction. Thus came the idea came for **Lostman's River.**

The inspiration for **The Apprenticeship of Lucas Whitaker** came one Sunday when my husband handed me a page out of the *New York Times* and said, "This is right up your alley." The article had to do with the discovery of a strange folk medical practice from the mid-1800s. It was discovered when, in 1990, the Connecticut state archeologist unraveled a story behind a series of graves whose occupants had been unearthed as a cure for consumption, or what we now refer to as tuberculosis, and then later "laid to rest."

I am often asked about some of the grisly details I portray in my books. I explain to children that if I wrote in the book, "Well, there was this guy named Weasel. He was really mean and evil and did bad things," I'd get the big yawn.

When writing, however, you are trying to show and not tell. So when you read that Ezra, one of the protagonists, has no tongue, and you become aware that Weasel has cut it out with a knife, then I don't have to *tell* you Weasel is evil. You *feel* it in your heart, in your mind, and in your gut.

I think it is most important for readers to create their own images. For example, I particularly love the hardcover jacket of **Weasel** because in it we don't see Weasel's face at all. Dennis Nolan did a wonderful jacket showing Weasel's back as he is standing over Nathan, with his patch of white hair blowing in the wind. It is obvious something bad is happening. Nathan's face is fabulous. You can see he is angry and frightened, while trying, at the same time, to be brave and determined. But you don't see Weasel's face, so every child reading the book gets to take that image as far as he or she can stand or is comfortable with. It has been interesting to me to hear kids' reactions to the paperback jacket. They say, "Is that supposed to be Weasel? That guy doesn't look scary enough." And I love that because in their imaginations he is more frightening than any picture can make him.

In a movie, someone else's images are thrust on you, and you have no choice about what to see. In a book, you can make the images your own.

To read more of this Conversation with Cynthia DeFelice, please visit Chapter 8 on our text's companion website at **www.prenhall. com/darigan**

Great care must then be taken by the author to research both the people and the times to present an accurate portrayal. Author Patricia Beatty was particularly attentive to this in her research. As noted in her books ***Turn Homeward, Hannalee, Be Ever Hopeful, Hannalee,*** and ***Jayhawker,*** she offers readers copious notes describing her research, definitions of terms, and clear indications about what was real and what was fiction.

Contemporary Novels Become Historical Fiction With the Passage of Time

When Marie McSwigan wrote ***Snow Treasure*** during World War II, it was a contemporary novel based on the heroic true story of Norwegian children who smuggled gold bullion on their sleds past Nazi guards in broad daylight. They hid the gold in a snow cave, from which it was later secreted away by the British. Every one of today's schoolchildren and most of their teachers were not yet born when this event occurred. *Snow Treasure* is now most firmly in the realm of historical fiction.

Sometimes it is difficult to decide whether certain books are contemporary or historical, and often the determining factor can be found in the age of the reader. Eve Bunting's powerful picture book *The Wall* tells of a father and son going to the Vietnam War Memorial in Washington, D.C. to find the name of the boy's *grandfather*. For those of us who lived through those traumatic and turbulent times, there is a bit of astonishment involved in the knowledge that, indeed, many contemporary grandfathers *did* fight and die in that ill-fated conflict. The Vietnam War may be contemporary for adult readers but ancient history to a fourth- or fifth-grader.

DID YOU KNOW?

With regard to her book **The Apprenticeship of Lucas Whitaker,** DeFelice told us a couple of sixth-grade boys were very surprised one day because as they were scooting down a gravel embankment of a construction site, they noticed two human skulls rolling right along with them. It turns out that the digging had unearthed some of those old graves and when the state archeologist examined the remains, they confirmed this bizarre folk practice.

An Author's Life Chronicled in a Fictional Format

Another variety of historical fiction is unusual because the author recounts episodes from his or her own life. The story is a fictionalized account of the time period and the events experienced by the author but written years later. The Little House books (*The Little House in the Big Woods, Little House on the Prairie,* etc.) by Laura Ingalls Wilder are books of this type.

Cover from **When I Was Your Age: Original Stories About Growing Up.** Cover © 1996 Candlewick Press, Inc. Reproduced by permission of the publisher Candlewick Press, Inc., Cambridge, MA.

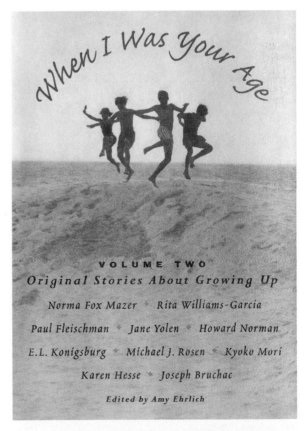

Cover from **When I Was Your Age, Volume Two.** Cover © 1999 Candlewick Press, Inc. Reproduced by permission of the publisher Candlewick Press, Inc., Cambridge, MA.

Another example of this variety of historical fiction is a pair of very creative books edited by Amy Ehrlich. ***When I Was Your Age: Original Stories About Growing Up*** and ***When I Was Your Age: Volume Two*** present short stories by 20 noted children's authors based on stories from their own lives. Ehrlich charged the writers to construct a story that "doesn't have to be literally true in every detail but should be located in time and space in your own childhood" (Ehrlich, 1996, p. 6). The result of this project is a stunning variety of tales by James Howe, Katherine Paterson, Avi, Laurence Yep, Jane Yolen, E. L. Konigsburg, Joseph Bruchac, and Paul Fleischman, to name only a few.

The Protagonist Travels Back Into History

Time travel, a feature of fantasy rather than realism, has been used as a mechanism to transport contemporary characters into the past and then later return them to their own time. Everything else in this type of historical novel conforms to the realistic nature of the genre. As mentioned earlier, Jane Yolen's ***The Devil's Arithmetic*** is an example of this type, as are Elvira Woodruff's ***The Orphan of Ellis Island,*** Jeanette Ingold's ***The Window,*** and Caroline B. Cooney's trilogy, ***Both Sides of Time, Out of Time,*** and ***Prisoner of Time.***

A Story Based on Accurate Historical Accounts

Sometimes the story's focus is not on events in history but rather on a wholly imaginary plot that is accurately set in a particular period and place from the past. Examples are Karen Cushman's engaging ***The Ballad of Lucy Whipple,*** set during the California Gold Rush days of the 1840s; Wilson Rawls's immortal dog story, ***Where the Red Fern Grows,*** set in the Ozarks of Oklahoma in the 1920s; Maude Casey's heartbreaking ***Over the Water,*** set in the Irish countryside during the 1940s; and Avi's stunning duet ***Beyond the Western Sea: The Escape from Home*** and ***Lord Kirkle's Money.***

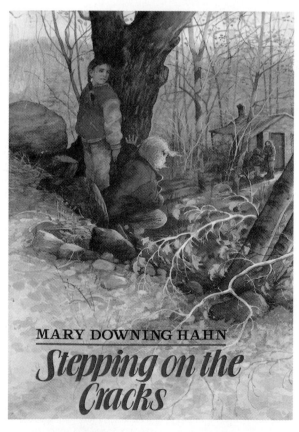

Cover from ***Stepping on the Cracks,*** by Mary Downing Hahn. Jacket illustration © 1991 by Diane de Groat. Reprinted by permission of Houghton Mifflin Company. All rights reserved.

Protagonists Experiencing Real Historical Events

Other times, the story's plot can involve the protagonist in significant historical events. In Esther Forbes's ***Johnny Tremain,*** for instance, the fictional main character becomes involved in the Boston Tea Party and the Battles of Lexington and Concord. Sook Nyul Choi's ***The Year of Impossible Goodbyes*** describes the recruitment of young Korean girls by the military who were extricated from their homes during the Japanese occupation of that country during World War II and sold into prostitution in Seoul. A final example lies in Theodore Taylor's ***The Bomb,*** which deals with the aftermath and subsequent effect on the local populace of the U.S. government's testing of atomic bombs on the Bikini Atoll in the western Pacific Ocean.

A Balance Between Fiction and Reality

Most often, however, a balance is reached with a combination of historical settings, fictional, yet realistic personages of the times, and a compelling story line. Mary Downing Hahn's ***Stepping on the Cracks*** offers such a blend. Eleven-year-old Margaret deals with some very important moral dilemmas when she finds that the neighborhood bully whom she fears yet totally despises is hiding his brother, a World War II deserter, in a hideout in the woods. Her own brother, Jimmy, is risking his life overseas fighting Hitler, and though Margaret should shun such a turncoat, she feels a great desire to help protect and nurse the ailing brother back to health. In the process, she learns much about war, and herself, and becomes more sympathetic as a result of her kindness and caring.

▼▼▼▼▼▼▼

Summary

In this chapter, we first noted that the power of story must engage the reader and then breathe life into the past. We discussed how, unlike textbooks, historical fiction can add depth and breadth to any period, making it spring alive for the reader. Historical fiction makes solid people connections and offers multiple historical perspectives. We discussed that historical and cultural accuracy are necessary and that books in the genre should not present a sugar-coated version of the period. However, we noted that teachers should help children avoid books that have too much historical detail that may tend to bog them down. Finally, we discussed the variety of types of historical fiction, naming books that occurred before the authors' life, books written as contemporary fiction that have become historical with the passage of time, an author setting his or her life in a fictional format, characters traveling back in time, a fictional story based on historical accounts, and protagonists facing real historical events.

▼▼▼▼▼▼▼

Fifteen More of Our Favorites

Alexander, Lloyd. (2001). *The Gawgon and the boy.* Dutton. Readers are introduced to a wild and eccentric cast of young David's family members, including his old Aunt Annie, the eponymous Gawgon, and mixes fantasy, raucous humor, and splendid shenanigans in this book about real "schooling."

Anderson, Laurie Halse. (2000). *Fever 1793.* Simon & Schuster. In 1793 Philadelphia, sixteen-year-old Matilda Cook, separated from her sick mother, learns about perseverance and self-reliance when she is forced to cope with the horrors of a yellow fever epidemic.

Bunting, Eve. (1996). *S.O.S. Titanic.* Harcourt. Fifteen-year-old Barry O'Neill, traveling from Ireland to America on the maiden voyage of the Titanic, finds his life endangered when the ship hits an iceberg and begins to sink.

Bunting, Eve. (1995). *Spying on Miss Müller.* Clarion. At Alveara boarding school in Belfast at the start of World War II, thirteen-year-old Jessie must deal with her suspicions about a teacher whose father was German and with her worries about her own father's drinking problem.

Cormier, Robert. (1998). *Heroes.* Delacorte. After joining the army at fifteen and having his face blown away by a grenade in a battle in France, Francis returns home to Frenchtown hoping to find—and kill—the former childhood hero he feels betrayed him.

Fleischman, Paul. (1993). *Bull Run.* Harper. Northerners, Southerners, generals, couriers, dreaming boys, and worried sisters describe the glory, the horror, the thrill, and the disillusionment of the first land battle of the Civil War.

Fleischman, Paul. (1991). *The borning room.* HarperCollins. Lying at the end of her life in the room where she was born in 1851, Georgina remembers what it was like to grow up on the Ohio frontier.

Giff, Patricia Reilly. (2000). *Nory Ryan's song.* When a terrible blight attacks Ireland's potato crop in 1845, twelve-year-old Nory Ryan's courage and ingenuity help her family and neighbors survive.

Holm, Jennifer. (1999). *Our only May Amelia.* As the only girl in a Finnish American family of seven brothers, May Amelia Jackson resents being expected to act like a lady while growing up in Washington state in 1899.

Meyer, Carolyn. (1996). *Gideon's people.* Harcourt. Torn between youthful rebellion and their traditional heritages, two boys from very different cultures—one Amish, one Orthodox Jew—discover just how similar they really are.

Paulsen, Gary. (1993). *Nightjohn*. Delacorte. A 12-year-old slave girl receives brutal treatment when she is taught to read.

Peck, Richard. (1998). *A long way from Chicago*. Dial. A boy recounts his summer trips to rural Illinois during the Great Depression to visit their larger-than-life grandmother.

Speare, Elizabeth George. (1958). *The witch of Blackbird Pond*. Houghton Mifflin. In 1687 in Connecticut, Kit Tyler—who feels out of place in the Puritan household of her aunt and befriends

an old woman the community thinks is a witch—suddenly finds herself standing trial for witchcraft. Winner of the Newbery Medal.

Watkins, Yoko Kawashima. (1986). *So far from the bamboo grove*. Lothrop. A young Japanese girl, her older sister, and her mother struggle to escape the dangers of an angry Korea as World War II ends.

White, Ruth. (1996). *Belle Prater's boy*. Farrar, Straus & Giroux. With the support of her resourceful cousin, Woodrow, 12-year-old Gypsy tries to solve a tragic family mystery.

▼▼▼▼▼▼▼▼

Others We Like

Anderson, Rachel. (1995). *Black water*. Henry Holt.

Armstrong, William H. (1969). *Sounder*. HarperCollins.

Armstrong, William H. (1971). *Sour land*. HarperCollins.

Berry, James. (1991). *Ajeemah and his son*. HarperCollins.

Brink, Carol Ryrie. (1935). *Caddie Woodlawn*. Macmillan.

Bunting, Eve. (1996). *S.O.S. Titanic*. Harcourt.

Curtis, Christopher Paul. (1995). *The Watsons go to Birmingham—1963*. Delacorte.

Curtis, Christopher Paul. (1999). *Bud, not Buddy*. Delacorte.

Farmer, Nancy. (1996). *A girl named Disaster*. Orchard.

Fleischman, Paul. (1991). *The Borning Room*. HarperCollins.

Forbes, Esther. (1943). *Johnny Tremain*. Houghton Mifflin.

Gauch, Patricia Lee. (1975). *Thunder at Gettysburg*. Putnam.

Greene, Bette. (1973). *The summer of my German soldier*. Dial.

Lasky, Kathryn. (1994). *Beyond the burning time*. Scholastic (Blue Sky).

Lowry, Lois. (1989). *Number the stars*. Houghton Mifflin.

McGraw, Eloise. (1961). *The golden goblet*. Coward.

O'Dell, Scott. (1986). *Streams to the river, river to the sea: a novel of Sacagawea*. Houghton Mifflin.

Orlev, Uri. (1984). *The island on Bird Street*. Houghton Mifflin.

Peck, Richard. (2000). *A year down yonder*. Dial.

Siegal. Aranka. (1981). *Upon the head of the goat: A childhood in Hungary, 1939–1944*. Farrar, Straus & Giroux.

Taylor, Theodore. (1969). *The cay*. Doubleday.

Yep, Laurence. (1977). *Dragonwings*. Harper & Row.

Easier to Read

Avi. (1997). *Finding Providence: The story of Roger Williams*. HarperCollins.

Bishop, Claire Huchet. (1980). *Ten and twenty*. Penguin Puffin. (Original work published 1952)

Bulla, Clyde Robert. (1956). *The sword in the tree*. Crowell.

Coerr, Eleanor. (1977). *Sadako and the thousand paper cranes*. Putnam.

Fleischman, Sid. (1986). *The whipping boy*. Morrow.

Gardiner, John. (1980). *Stone fox*. Crowell.

Herman, Charlotte. (1990). *The house on Walenska Street*. Dutton.

Picture Books

Gauch, Patricia Lee. (1974). *This time, Tempe Wick?* (Margot Tomes, Illus.). Coward.

Goble, Paul. (1987). *Death of the iron horse*. Bradbury.

McCully, Emily Arnold. (1996). *The bobbin girl*. Dial.

Polacco, Patricia. (1994). *Pink and Say*. Philomel.

Sewall, Marcia. (1986). *The Pilgrims of Plimoth*. Atheneum.

Tsuchiya, Yukio. (1988). *Faithful elephants: A true story of animals, people and war*. (Ted Lewin, Illus.). Houghton Mifflin.

Turner, Ann. (1985). *Dakota dugout*. (Ronald Himler, Illus.). Macmillan.

Uchida, Yoshiko. (1993). *The bracelet*. (Joanna Yardley, Illus.). Philomel.

Winter, Jeanette. (1988). *Follow the drinking gourd*. Knopf.

For a more comprehensive list of historical fiction titles, consult the CD-ROM that accompanies this text.

▼▼▼▼▼▼▼▼

Children's Literature References

Amoss, Berthe.(1993). *Lost magic*. New York: Hyperion.

Armstrong, Jennifer. (1995). *Black-eyed Susan*. New York: Crown.

Avi. (1984). *The fighting ground*. Philadelphia: Lippincott.

Avi. (1989). *The man who was Poe*. New York: Orchard.

Avi. (1996a). *Beyond the western sea: Lord Kirkle's money*. New York: Orchard.

Avi. (1996b). *Beyond the western sea: The escape from home*. New York: Orchard.

Beatty, Patricia. (1984). *Turn homeward, Hannalee*. New York: Morrow.

Beatty, Patricia. (1987). *Charley skedaddle*. New York: Morrow.

Beatty, Patricia. (1988). *Be ever hopeful, Hannalee*. New York: Morrow.

Beatty, Patricia. (1991). *Jayhawker*. New York: Morrow.

Blos, Joan. (1979). *A gathering of days*. New York: Scribner's.

Branford, Henrietta. (1998). *Fire, bed and bone*. Cambridge, MA: Candlewick.

Bunting, Eve. (1990). *The wall* (Ronald Himler, Illus.). New York: Clarion.

Bunting, Eve. (1995). *Dandelions* (Greg Shed, Illus.). San Diego: Harcourt Brace.

Casey, Maude. (1994). *Over the water*. New York: Henry Holt.

Choi, Sook Nyul. (1991). *The year of impossible goodbyes*. Boston: Houghton Mifflin.

Coleman, Evelyn. (1996). *Black socks only*. Morton Grove, IL: Albert Whitman.

Collier, James Lincoln, & Collier, Christopher. (1974). *My brother Sam is dead*. New York: Four Winds.

Collier, James Lincoln, & Collier, Christopher. (1981). *Jump ship to freedom*. New York: Delacorte.

Conrad, Pam. (1985). *Prairie songs*. New York: Harper & Row.

Conrad, Pam. (1989). *My Daniel*. New York: Harper & Row.

Conrad, Pam. (1991). *Prairie visions: The life and times of Solomon Butcher*. New York: Harper & Row.

Cooney, Caroline B. (1995). *Both sides of time*. New York: Random House.

Cooney, Caroline B. (1996). *Out of time*. New York: Random House.

Cooney, Caroline B. (1998). *Prisoner of time*. New York: Random House.

Cushman, Karen. (1994). *Catherine, called Birdy*. New York: Clarion.

Cushman, Karen. (1995). *The midwife's apprentice*. New York: Clarion.

Cushman, Karen. (1996). *The ballad of Lucy Whipple*. New York: Clarion.

Cushman, Karen. (2000). *Matilda Bone*. New York: Clarion.

DeAngeli, Marguerite. (1949). *A door in the wall*. New York: Doubleday.

DeFelice, Cynthia. (1990). *Weasel*. New York: Atheneum.

DeFelice, Cynthia. (1994). *Lostman's river*. New York: Macmillan.

DeFelice, Cynthia. (1996). *The apprenticeship of Lucas Whitaker*. New York: Atheneum.

DeFelice, Cynthia. (1999). *Nowhere to call home*. New York: Farrar, Straus & Giroux.

Dorris, Michael. (1992). *Morning girl*. New York: Hyperion.

Ehrlich, Amy. (1996). *When I was your age: Original stories about growing up*. Cambridge, MA: Candlewick.

Ehrlich, Amy. (1999). *When I was your age: Volume two*. Cambridge, MA: Candlewick.

Forbes, Esther. (1943). *Johnny Tremain*. New York: Houghton Mifflin.

Fox, Paula. (1973). *The slave dancer*. New York: Bradbury.

Fritz, Jean. (1982). *Homesick: My own story*. New York: Putnam.

Furlong, Monica. (1995). *Robin's country*. New York: Knopf.

Hahn, Mary Downing. (1991). *Stepping on the cracks*. New York: Clarion.

Hilgartner, Beth. (1986). *A murder for Her Majesty*. Boston: Houghton Mifflin.

Houston, Gloria. (1994). *Mountain Valor*. New York: Philomel.

Hunt, Irene. (1964). *Across five Aprils*. New York: Follett.

Hunter, Mollie. (1974). *The stronghold*. New York: Harper & Row.

Ingold, Jeanette. (1996). *The window*. San Diego: Harcourt Brace.

Jaffe, Nina. (1996). *The golden flower: A Taino myth from Puerto Rico* (Enrique O. Sanchez, Illus.). New York: Simon & Schuster.

Keith, Harold. (1957). *Rifles for Watie*. New York: Crowell.

Lasky, Kathryn. (1983). *Beyond the divide*. New York: Macmillan.

Lasky, Kathryn. (1988). *The bone wars*. New York: Morrow.

Lasky, Kathryn. (1996). *True north: A novel of the Underground Railroad*. New York: Scholastic.

MacLachlan, Patricia. (1985). *Sarah, plain and tall*. New York: Harper & Row.

McCaffrey, Anne. (1996). *Black horses for the king*. San Diego: Harcourt Brace.

McSwigan, Marie. (1942). *Snow treasure*. New York: Dutton.

Meyer, Carolyn. (1999). *Mary, bloody mary*. San Diego: Harcourt Brace.

Murphy, Jim. (1990). *The boy's war*. New York: Clarion.

O'Dell, Scott. (1980). *Sarah Bishop*. New York: Houghton Mifflin.

Patrick, Denise Lewis. (1999). *The longest ride*. New York: Henry Holt.

Paulsen, Gary. (1995). *Mr. Tucket*. New York: Delacorte.

Paulsen, Gary. (1998). *Soldier's heart*. New York: Random House.

Rawls, Wilson. (1961). *Where the red fern grows*. Garden City, NY: Doubleday.

Reeder, Carolyn. (1989). *Shades of gray.* New York: Macmillan.

Rees, Douglas. (1997). *Lightning time.* New York: DK Ink.

Rinaldi, Ann. (1997). *An acquaintance with darkness.* San Diego: Harcourt Brace.

Taylor, Mildred. (1975). *Song of the trees.* New York: Dial.

Taylor, Mildred. (1976). *Roll of thunder, hear my cry* (Jerry Pinkney, Illus.). New York: Dial.

Taylor, Mildred. (1981). *Let the circle be unbroken.* New York: Dial.

Taylor, Mildred. (1987a). *The friendship.* New York: Dial.

Taylor, Mildred. (1987b). *The gold Cadillac* (Michael Hays, Illus.). New York: Dial.

Taylor, Mildred. (1990a). *Mississippi bridge.* New York: Dial.

Taylor, Mildred. (1990b). *The road to Memphis.* New York: Dial.

Taylor, Mildred. (1995). *The well.* New York: Dial.

Taylor, Theodore. (1995). *The bomb.* San Diego: Harcourt.

Temple, Francis. (1994). *The Ramsay scallop.* New York: Orchard.

Thomas, Joyce Carol. (1998). *I have heard of a land* (Floyd Cooper, Illus.). New York: HarperCollins.

Turner, Glennett Tilley. (1994). *Running for our lives.* New York: Holiday House.

Uchida, Yoshiko. (1971). *Journey to Topaz.* New York: Scribner's.

Yep, Laurence. (1977). *Child of the owl.* New York: Harper & Row.

Yep, Laurence. (1991). *The star fisher.* New York: Morrow.

Yep, Laurence. (1995). *Thief of hearts.* New York: HarperCollins.

Yolen, Jane. (1988). *The devil's arithmetic.* New York: Viking Penguin.

Yolen, Jane. (1992). *Encounter* (David Shannon, Illus.). San Diego: Harcourt Brace.

Yolen, Jane. (2000). *The queen's own fool.* New York: Philomel.

Wilder, Laura Ingalls. (1932). *Little house in the big woods.* New York: Harper.

Wilder, Laura Ingalls. (1935). *Little house on the prairie.* New York: Harper.

Wisler, G. Clifton. (1995). *Mr. Lincoln's drummer.* New York: Dutton.

Woodruff, Elvira. (1997). *The orphan of Ellis Island.* New York: Scholastic.

▼▼▼▼▼▼▼

Professional References

Armbruster, B. B., & Anderson, T. H. (1984). Structures for explanation in history textbooks, or what if Governor Stanford missed the spike and hit the rail? In R. C. Anderson, J. Osborn, & R. J. Tierney (Eds.), *Learning to read in American schools* (pp. 181–194). Hillsdale, NJ: Erlbaum.

Banks, J. A., Beyer, B. K., Contreras, G., Craven, J., Ladson-Billings, G., McFarland, M. A., & Parker, W. C. (1997). *United States: Adventures in time and place.* New York: Macmillan/McGraw-Hill.

Bednarz, S., Clinton, C., Hartoonian, M., Hernandez, A., Marshall, P. L., & Nickell, M. P. (1997). *Build our nation.* Atlanta: Houghton Mifflin.

Blos, J. (1985, November). The overstuffed sentence and other means for assessing historical fiction for children. *School Library Journal,* 38–39.

Boehm, R. G., McGowan, T., McKinney-Browning, M. C., & Meramontes, O. B. (1997). *America's story.* Vol. 2. Orlando, FL: Harcourt Brace.

Collier, C. (1976). Johnny and Sam: Old and new approaches to the American Revolution. *The Horn Book, 52,* 132–138.

Darigan, D. (1998). A breakfast with the author: Karen Cushman. *Journal of Children's Literature, 23*(2), 108–113.

Downey, M. T., & Levstik, L. S. (1988, September). Teaching and learning history: The research base. *Social Education,* 336–342.

Fischer, B. (Ed.). (1997). The bottom line. *NEA Today, 16*(4), 9.

Foster, S., Morris, J. W., & Davis, O. L. (1996). Prospects for teaching historical analysis and interpretation: National curriculum standards for history meet current history textbooks. *Journal of Curriculum and Supervision, 11*(4), 367–385.

Freedman, R. (1993). Bring 'em back alive. In M. O. Tunnell & R. Ammon (Eds.), *The story of ourselves: Teaching history through children's literature* (pp. 41–47). Portsmouth, NH: Heinemann.

Hidi, S., Baird, W., & Hildyard, A. (1982). That's important but is it interesting? Two factors in text processing. In A. Flammer & W. Kintsch (Eds.), *Discourse processing* (pp. 63–75). Amsterdam: Elsevier-North Holland.

Holmes, B., & Ammon, R. (1985). Teaching content with trade books: A strategy. *Childhood Education, 61*(5), 366–370.

Hunter, M. (1976). *Talent is not enough.* New York: Harper & Row.

Lasky, K. (1990). The fiction of history: Or, what did Miss Kitty really do? *The New Advocate, 3*(3), 157–166.

Levstik, L. (1989). A gift of time: Children's historical fiction. In J. Hickman & B. Cullinan (Eds.), *Children's literature in the classroom: Weaving Charlotte's web* (pp. 135–145). Needham Heights, MA: Christopher-Gordon.

Loewen, J. (1995). By the book. *The American School Board Journal, 182*(1), 24–27.

Maxim, G. (1999). *Social studies and the elementary school child.* Upper Saddle River, NJ: Merrill/ Prentice Hall.

McGowan, T., & Guzzetti, B. (1991). Promoting social studies understanding through literature-based instruction. *The Social Studies, 82*(1), 16–21.

Ravitch, D. (1985). The precarious state of history. *American Educator, 9*(4), 11–17.

Sewall, G. T. (1988, April). American history textbooks: Where do we go from here? *Phi Delta Kappan,* 553–558.

Shannon, P. (1989). Overt and covert censorship of children's books. *The New Advocate, 2*(2), 97–104.

Tunnell, M. O., & Ammon, R. (1996). The story of ourselves: Fostering new perspectives. *Social Education, 60*(4), 212–215.

Yolen, J. (1989). An experiential act. *Language Arts, 66*(3), 246–251.

MULTICULTURAL AND INTERNATIONAL CHILDREN'S BOOKS

by Deborah Thompson

College of New Jersey

9

CHAPTER

▼▼▼▼▼▼

If you want to cover
Grandmothers: Wit, Wisdom and Love

Consider as a READ ALOUD

Halmoni's Day,
by Edna Coe Bercaw,
illustrated by Robert Hunt
(Asian American—Korean)

Consider as a TEXT SET

Abuela, by Arthur Dorros,
illustrated by Elisa Kleven (Latino)

Luka's Quilt, by Georgia Guback
(Native Hawaiian)

Faraway Home, by Jane Kurtz,
illustrated by E. B. Lewis
(African American—Ethiopian)

Chinatown, by William Low
(Asian American—Chinese)

Sitti's Secrets, by Naomi Shihab Nye,
illustrated by Nancy Carpenter
(Arab American—Palestinian)

Rainy's Powwow, by Linda Theresa Raczek,
illustrated by Gary Bennett (Native American)

We Had a Picnic This Sunday Past,
by Jacqueline Woodson,
illustrated by Diane Greenseid

WE HAD A PICNIC THIS SUNDAY PAST
by Jacqueline Woodson

Got up at four this morning to make this chicken. Best batch I ever fried. These biscuits just as tasty. Can't chew for swallowing, can hardly swallow 'cause you'll be too busy reaching for more.

Excerpt from *We Had a Picnic This Sunday Past* by Jacqueline Woodson

Student Response

Julia   age 7

I liked the part, when Gandma
Me, and Paulette said Hmph

My favorite cariter was Gandma
becaus she lived to brag.

To visit a classroom exploring the issues of Multicultural and International Literature, please go to Chapter 9 of our companion website at **www.prenhall.com/darigan**

> If the United States is a "melting pot," it could be getting harder to stir. Racial and ethnic minorities now account for one-fourth of the U.S. population. By 2015,[1] projections indicate that minorities will make up one-third of all Americans—a phenomenon already seen among children and youth. (Pollard, 1999)

The quote above comes from the 1999 United States Population Data Sheet. Pollard notes something that we in public education have known for quite some time: The winds of change and diversity are blowing, rapidly changing the look and lay of the American landscape. The browning of America will continue to increase, especially Latinos and Asians (Population Reference Bureau, 2001), until people of color who call the United States home constitute the majority—a collective majority, but a majority nonetheless. Is there any better argument for the continued growth and use of multicultural children's literature?

Multicultural and international books offer many positive experiences to readers of all hues in at least three ways. Books about specific cultures and nations can

- foster an awareness, understanding, and appreciation of people who seem at first glance different from the reader;
- present positive and reassuring representations of a reader's own cultural group;
- introduce readers to the literary traditions of different world cultures or cultural groups in America.

The values that are derived from reading literature in general hold true for reading multicultural literature. Bishop (1987) lists three understandings about a multicultural society that are realized through the use of literature in general, and multicultural literature specifically:

1. Readers can connect to others' experiences common to all our emotions, needs, and desires.
2. Readers can understand and learn to appreciate and celebrate the *differences* among us.
3. Readers can develop an understanding of the effect of social issues and forces on the lives of ordinary individuals. (pp. 60–61)

Furthermore, research shows that the use of multicultural literature enhances the reading comprehension and problem-solving skills of all children (Foster, 1987). Multicultural literature can empower young readers. Being exposed to divergent thought and language patterns, value systems, and ways of living can sharpen sensitivities to the differences and similarities of us all (Matsuyama & Jensen, 1990). Well-written books that express multicultural themes or that are international in their origins can have a profound effect on readers, prompting a global outlook as well as an understanding that even though members of the human family have more similarities than differences, those differences are invitations for discovery and appreciation.

▼▼▼▼▼▼▼▼

What's in a Term? Of Parallel Cultures and Multiethnic Literature

Multicultural books typically focus on the lives and customs of people from parallel cultures. The growing use of the term "parallel cultures" suggests a sea change in the way we think about the cultures from which multicultural literature evolves. Cai and

---

[1]The minority population of Canada is on a similar trajectory. It is estimated that by 2016, 20% of Canada's population and 25% of its youth population will be minority (Esses & Gardner, cited in Bainbridge, Pantaleo, & Ellis, 1999).

Sims Bishop (1994) borrowed the term from Virginia Hamilton who used it in her 1986 Boston Horn Book Award acceptance speech for *Anthony Burns: The Defeat and Triumph of a Fugitive Slave*. Cai and Sims Bishop note: "Although the term may not be perfectly suited as a substitute for the uncomfortable term *minority,* it has the advantage of according equal status to the cultures designated as parallel" (p. 70). The authors also note that the relevant definition of *parallel* is not a derivative of the geometric denotation, meaning lines (or cultures) that never touch (or interact). Nor does the term evolve from Havel's definition meaning cultures that cannot or may not reach out to the public through the nonprint media (Vladislav, 1987). Here *parallel* denotes equality, not in the Orwellian sense, but as in all cultures are equal, with no one culture dominating or subordinating the others.

Although individuals use the terms *multiethnic* and *multicultural* interchangeably, they are not synonymous. We can think of *multiethnic literature* as a focused term that refers to the literature of people of color who reside in North America—mainly the United States. On the other hand, *multicultural literature* is a global term that comprises not only literature about people of color within the United States and Canada—African Americans, Native Americans, Asian Americans, and Latinos—but also literature from and about other cultural groups both within and beyond the United States and Canada, such as women; religious groups (e.g., Jews, Catholics, Moslems, Mormons, and the Amish); people with disabilities; the elderly; gays, lesbians, and transgendered individuals; the homeless; and people from regional cultures, such as Cajuns and Appalachians. However, as we expand our reading and book lists, it is important to remember that *culture* and *race* are not synonymous terms; for example, there is no such thing as *the* African American culture or *the* Native American culture. Neither culture nor race is monolithic. There are many different subcultures subsumed under a particular culture. Members of a particular racial group can belong to many different cultural groups. Quality multicultural children's literature can help us all think more broadly about all races and cultures, provided these books portray their subjects honestly.

▼▼▼▼▼▼▼

The Need for Multicultural Books

Xenophobia, the mistrust or fear or, worse, ignorance of people who are strangers or foreigners, is at the root of our worldwide inability to live together in peace. Parents and society may purposely or inadvertently program children to mistrust, fear, or even hate certain groups of people who are unlike them. Teaching children at an early age "about the [positive] differences and similarities between [*sic*] people will not singularly ensure a more gentle and tolerant society; but might act as a prerequisite to one" (Sobol 1990, p. 30). Candy Dawson Boyd (1990) makes it clear that we cannot begin too early to give our children a multicultural perspective:

> We know that there's a substantial body of research on the development of racial consciousness begun in 1929, and what does it tell us? It tells us that children develop negative attitudes towards other people as they take on the culture of their parents. It tells us that by age three, racial awareness is evident. *Three.* [Emphasis added] And that by age ten, racial attitudes have been crystallized.

Furthermore, Aboud (cited in Bainbridge, Pantaleo, & Ellis, 1999) suggests that children's attitudes toward diversity tend to stay constant unless altered by life-changing events. Yet, children in early adolescence "are not too old for significant attitudinal changes. Counteraction is therefore possible" (Sonnenschein, 1988, p. 265).

Literature can be one of the most powerful tools for combating the ignorance that breeds xenophobic behavior. "For decades experienced educators have reported success stories about using children's literature to broaden attitudes toward people from a variety of cultures" (Hansen-Krening, 1992, p. 126). Rudine Sims Bishop

(1992), who has long been a champion of the well-written multicultural book, believes that "literature is one of the most powerful components of a multicultural education curriculum, the underlying purpose of which is to help make the society a more equitable one" (p. 40). In support of this view, she quotes James Baldwin: "Literature is indispensable to the world. . . . The world changes according to the way people see it, and if you alter, even by a millimeter, the way a person looks at reality, then you can change it" (Sims, 1982, p. 1). Indeed studies have indicated that students' prejudices have been reduced because of their involvement with good multicultural books (Darigan, 1991; Pate, 1988).

Certainly, children of parallel cultural groups need books that bolster self-esteem and pride in their heritage. And children of all groups, especially from those of privilege, need books that sensitize them to and educate them about people from cultural and racial groups different from their own.

▼▼▼▼▼▼▼

Judging Multicultural Literature

As with all books, multicultural books must measure up to the criteria used to judge literature in general (see chapter 2). Racial and cultural stereotyping must be avoided. Stereotypes are alienating because they perpetuate a simplified, biased, and often negative view of groups of people—all African Americans are poor, all Latinos are lazy, all Native Americans live in the past, all women work as secretaries or in the home, all Asians are secretive and sly, all Jews are entrepreneurs. Though common elements often link the lives and the daily practices of members of cultural groups, it is important to communicate that every group is made up of individuals who have their own set of personal values, attitudes, and beliefs. In books written for children, characters who are from cultural minorities need to be represented as real individuals. This necessarily means that authors must create minority and majority group characters who are multidimensional and who fall along the spectrum of human behavior from good to evil.

Cultural details need to be represented accurately in literature. These may include the use of dialects[2] or idioms, descriptions of ethnic foods, customs, and clothing, and religious beliefs and practices. Of course, sensitivity to subcultures within a group is also important. For example, customs vary among the different factions of Judaism—Hasidic Jews are strictly orthodox as evidenced by dress codes and other identifiable practices, but Reform Jews are much less bound by religious law. In the same way, customs and lifestyles vary greatly among the many Native American tribes. Spanish-speaking groups are not alike, even in the Spanish they speak: Cubans are not like Mexicans, who are not like Puerto Ricans, who are not like Panamanians, etc.

However, additional criteria focusing on the multicultural themes and content area are also necessary to consider. The Council on Interracial Books for Children (1981) created guidelines that are frequently cited.

1. *Check* the illustrations. Look for stereotypes, tokenism and the roles of minority characters. One of our favorite picture books, Mary Hoffman's *Amazing Grace,* has come under fire for the picture of Grace dressed as Hiawatha. She is in a full-feathered headdress, sitting ramrod straight, legs crossed (as many elementary teachers are wont to say—Indian style) and arms across her chest. Reese (1997) is correct that we shouldn't celebrate one culture at the expense of another, but it is wrong to censor the book; we can use the picture as a launching point for discussion of how Native Americans are portrayed in books, television, and movies. Students deconstruct illustrator Caroline Binch's notion of how Native Americans look in modern times based not only on her illustration of Hiawatha, but also by her own admission to loving cowboys and

To learn more about the controversy over *Amazing Grace,* visit Chapter 9 on the companion website at **www.prenhall.com/darigan**

---

[2]In examining selected books with African American characters who use "Ebonics," we have found that few authors, no matter what their race, have a full command of this complex, rule-governed dialect.

Indians when she was young. Students can also consider how the British Binch may have acquired her stereotypical views of Native Americans—television (BBC or American import), reading materials, movies. We can then examine other books she illustrated, for example, **Billy the Kid, Hue Boy** or **Boundless Grace,** to check to see if there she has illustrated other stereotypical images.

2. *Check* the story line. What are the standards for success? How are problems solved? Who solves the problem? What are the roles of women?

3. *Look* at the lifestyles. Where do the minority characters live? Are cultural customs, clothing, mores, etc. accurate? In which century is the story placed, for example, are all Native American stories set in the past? Do all African Americans live in public housing? Are all Latinos migrant workers? In the introduction to the paperback edition of his book *Our Kind of People: Inside America's Black Upper Class,* Lawrence Graham notes that he received lots of negative feedback from both whites and African Americans. He states: "The stereotype of the working class black or the impoverished black is one that whites, as well as blacks, have come to embrace and accept as an accurate and complete account of the black American experience" (Graham, 2000, p. ix). As revealed in the book, there have been African American millionaires since the late 1800s, thus there should be books that have African Americans who are rich, not because they have played basketball or sing rap songs, but because their forebears earned their fortunes through genius and fortitude.

She was Hiawatha, sitting by the shining Big-Sea-Water. . .

From **Amazing Grace** by Mary Hoffman, illustrated by Caroline Binch, copyright © 1991 by Mary Hoffman, text. Copyright © 1991 by Caroline Binch, illustrations. Used by permission of Dial Books for Young Readers, a division of Penguin Putnam, Inc.

A more egregious stereotyping of lifestyles involves Native Americans. First, they barely exist as characters in contemporary fiction. If they do live in modern America, their families are often nonexistent or dysfunctional. They may live with foster families because of the dysfunctional immediate family, or there may be one lone Native American student being forced to shoulder the burdens of an entire student body of racist Anglo students. When they do appear in books, the settings of the books are often in the past. Reese (1996) cites an occasion that when introduced to a Native American visitor to her classroom, a four-year-old stated: "Indians aren't people. They are all dead." The late Michael Dorris (1993) noted that as a child, he refused to read books about Native Americans or with Native American characters because he found the characters to be too typecast. In these books: "Indian kids were too busy making clay pots or being fascinated by myths of the origins of the universe to be much fun" (p. 219). His friends did not think or act like any of the Indians in those books, so he shunned those books completely.

4. *Weigh* the relationships among the characters. Who possesses the power, takes leadership roles, or makes important decisions?

5. *Note* the heroes. Ask, "Whose interest is a particular hero really serving?"

6. *Consider* the effect on a child's self-image, for example, is white associated with things good, black with things evil?

7. *Consider* the author's or illustrator's background. What qualifies the author or illustrator to deal with the subject? Innumerable times we have reviewed books with multicultural characters or themes and have found them lacking a certain ring of authenticity. When checking credentials, we find it amazing that the author or illustrator knew a person like the book's character and decided to write a book about him or her. A child's cursory observations of a trusted family helper do not provide the adult with all the necessary information needed to write about anyone, especially in a book for children.

8. *Check* out the author's perspective.

9. *Watch* for loaded words related to race, religion, and gender.

10. *Look* at the copyright date.

To generate a list of titles about one ethic group, consult the accompanying CD-ROM.

For more information on Jump at the Sun publishers, go to Chapter 9 on the companion website at **www.prenhall. com/darigan**

To learn more about Lee and Low publishers, visit Chapter 9 on our companion website at **www.prenhall.com/darigan**

Consult the accompanying CD-ROM to compile a text set of Cinderella variants from around the world.

▼▼▼▼▼▼▼

Issues in Multicultural Literature

Even as we embark upon a new century and a new millennium, multicultural literature still elicits negative or uninformed responses from teachers, administrators, and the general public. Some of the outcry comes from those comfortable with privilege, and all that having privilege entails, who think recognizing and teaching about other cultures is a zero sum game, that is, if we recognize and teach about other cultures, then our culture will lose out. Others, ignoring how borders have been reduced and barriers have fallen because of technology, still fall back on the very weak argument of not having "those types of children in my class" as a reason for not using multicultural literature. These arguments are hollow, and they should be tossed in the trash bin of outmoded ideas and beliefs.

A real issue in multicultural children's literature is availability of titles. Experts note that books about or by African Americans make up about 2–3% of the American juvenile titles produced each year; the title production for Asian Americans, Latinos and Native Americans is even less. That means that in 1998, of the approximately 3086 American juvenile book titles published (Bogart, 1999), only about 100 titles were about or by African Americans. There were even fewer numbers of titles written by and about other ethnic groups.

Steps have been taken to improve upon the dismal numbers listed here. Several imprints are now devoted exclusively to publishing multicultural titles. For example, in 1998, Jump at the Sun, launched by Andrea Davis Pinkney, became the first African American children's imprint at a major publisher (Hyperion). Even in its infancy, the imprint has been very successful, with Brian Pinkney's receiving the 2000 Coretta Scott King Illustrator's Award for *In the Time of the Drums,* by Kim L. Siegelson. Other engaging Jump at the Sun titles are the lively and affirming collaboration from bell hooks and Chris Raschka, *Happy to be Nappy,* Sharon Flakes's stunning first novel, *The Skin I'm In,* Peter Mandel's rollicking *Say Hey! A Song of Willie Mays,* Andrea Davis Pinkney's absorbing *Silent Thunder,* and Doreen Rappaport's *Freedom River,* provocatively illustrated by Bryan Collier.

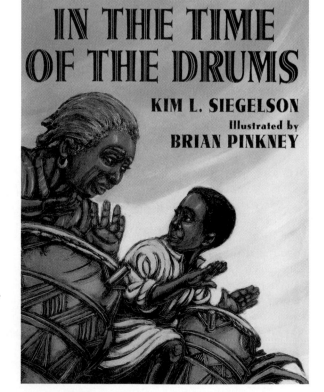

Cover art from ***In the Time of the Drums,*** by Kim L. Siegelson. Illustrated by Brian Pinkney. Text copyright © 1999 by Kim L. Siegelson. Illustrations copyright © 1999 by Brian Pinkney. Reprinted by permission of Hyperion Books for Children.

Happy with hair all short and strong.

Happy with locks that twist and curl.

From ***Happy to be Nappy*** by bell hooks. Text copyright © 1999 by bell hooks. Illustrations copyright © 1999 by Chris Raschka. Reprinted by permission of Hyperion Books for Children.

Lee and Low, established in 1991, is an independent children's book publisher specializing in multicultural titles. This imprint, too, has been rewarded for producing a myriad of laudable multicultural titles, including ***Night Golf***, by William Miller, ***In Daddy's Arms I Am Strong*** (an award-winning book of poetry illustrated by Javaka Steptoe, son of the late John Steptoe, award-winning children's book illustrator), and Ken Mochizuki's ***Passage to Freedom: The Sugihara Story***. As with Jump at the Sun, Lee and Low fills a niche in the market heretofore poorly served by the larger publishing houses—publishing quality stories for and about children of color. They also make a special effort to work with illustrators of color.

Other small imprints are also bringing new voices and illustrators to the world of children's literature. Rising Moon (Northland) specializes in books that feature Native Americans, mainly of the West and Southwest. Shen's Books specializes in multicultural Cinderellas, including ***Jouanah: A Hmong Cinderella*** and ***Angkat: The Cambodian Cinderella***, both retold by Jewell Reinhart Coburn. Children's Book Press in San Francisco publishes titles that celebrate stories that evolve from the diverse cultures that make up this country.

However, the large publishing houses are not ceding the market to these specialized imprints. They, too, are making efforts to bring works from new authors and illustrators of color to the public's reading habits. Still, there is much room for growth in this area of publishing. More authors and illustrators of color are needed, particularly Native Americans and Latinos, as well as books representing the mentally and physically challenged cultures.

Cover art from ***Jouanah: A Hmong Cinderella*** adapted by Jewell Reinhart Coburn with Tzexa Cherta Lee. Illustration copyright © 1996 by Anne Sibley O'Brien. Published by Shen's Books. Reprinted by permission of Shen's Books.

To find out more about "Gathering a Life Story" and other activities on the World Wide Web, visit Chapter 9 on the companion website at **www.prenhall.com/darigan**

INTEGRATING TECHNOLOGY: ACTIVITIES USING THE WORLD WIDE WEB

Writer, teacher, and storyteller *Sheldon Oberman* provides some very useful resources on his personal website. There are play versions of several of his writings, including **The Always Prayer Shawl.** He provides numerous guides, activities, and lessons. One of the most interesting sections involves the process of "Gathering a Life Story." Oberman provides a detailed procedure for collecting and writing a life story. Adapted to fit the grade level and the context, this site can be an incredible bridge between literature, writing, and community.

Who Can Write My Story? Insiders and Outsiders and Writing With a "Double Voice"

Cover are from **Sounder,** by William H. Armstrong. Illustrations copyright © 1969 by James Barkley. Used by permission of HarperCollins Publishers.

Few issues in multicultural children's literature resonate with so many people as does the issue of cultural authenticity. This issue, above all others in multicultural literature, touches raw nerves, engenders point/counterpoint articles in scholarly journals, and elicits pronouncements from scholars on both sides of the issue and exclusionary edits from major book-related organizations. At issue is who can write for whom or, as Jacqueline Woodson (1998) asks: "Who can tell my story?" (p. 34). If one follows the cardinal rule—write about what you know—then the answer to Woodson's question would be: only those who have lived the experiences to be portrayed—an insider. Insider status, then, would be the prerequisite for all writing, especially for and about a particular cultural or racial or religious group.

There are many experts who feel that books portraying a specific culture can be written only by members of that culture; outsiders need not make the attempt. For instance, William Armstrong's Newbery-winning novel, *Sounder,* portrays the lives of a poor family of African American sharecroppers. Armstrong is not an African American, and critics charge that there is no way he could understand the nuances of living the lives of African American sharecroppers. "Someone who does not share the specific culture remains an outsider, no matter how astute or well-meaning their intentions" (Wilson, 1990, p. A25).

At the same time, others believe that if outsiders make concentrated efforts not only to understand but also to inhabit a different cultural world, then they may indeed be able to write with cultural authenticity (Gates, cited in Bishop, 1992). Of course, some rare authors seem to have a particular gift for "imagining other's lives" (Horn, 1993, p. 78). Horn makes her case by highlighting the immense talents of Eudora Welty, who could write in the voice of a myriad of characters and lend authenticity to each. But for every Welty or Baldwin, there are authors whose clumsy attempts at writing as insiders fall flat, thus highlighting the dangers of writing outside one's sphere of understanding.

Henry Louis Gates (1988) does not subscribe to the insider/outsider dichotomy, but he does argue that African American authors (and, by extension, other authors of color) write with what he terms a "double voice." This double voice arises from African American authors having been steeped in both the Western literary tradition—the Western canon—and the oral tradition of black vernacular. By virtue of having to succeed in both their home cultures and the majority culture, African American writers and, indeed, other authors of color create two-toned or two-voiced texts (Gates, 1988). The notion of double voice can also be extended to those authors of color who grew up in the bilingual world of San Francisco's Chinatown or the barrios in Los Angeles. It is the double voice that allows a Taylor, a Hamilton, a Yep, a Bruchac, or a Soto to write with such power. It is the double voice that gives the rhythm and depth to Giovanni's, Wong's, or Greenfield's poetry.

For example, Mildred Taylor's award-winning books about the Logan family exude the rich double voice that Gates describes. Her writing is clearly literary, but it is permeated with the power of words, phrases, and characters' thoughts and actions that can arise only from her other voice. One can hear the voice of Taylor the writer and the voice of Taylor who was steeped in the stories of her father. In *Roll of Thunder, Hear My Cry,* we can feel the emotion radiating from the page as we discover along with Little Man that on his first day of school he does not get a new book, but instead an old, worn out, discarded book that was considered in poor condition when it was last assigned to a white student. His first day of school excitement is cruelly dashed. Not only does he not receive a new book, when he rejects the offending book, his teacher tells him he is not showing his appreciation to the [good] white folks for providing his class with books. To make matters worse, the book had the word "nigra" (a corrupted pronunciation of "Negro" used by whites to show their contempt for blacks) stamped on the ragged inside cover:

> As he stared at the book's inside cover, his face clouded, changing from sulky acceptance to puzzlement. His brows furrowed. Then his eyes grew wide, and suddenly he sucked in his breath and sprang from his chair like a wounded animal, flinging the book across the floor and stomping madly on it.

There are "outsiders" who do very credible jobs of writing in the voice of another. Two that come to mind are Beverley Naidoo and Mary E. Lyons. Naidoo's *Journey to Jo'burg* and *Chain of Fire* capture the passion and the humiliation of South Africa's apartheid system. A refugee from the system herself, Naidoo infused in her lead character, Nalidi, the anger and the incredulity of being separated from her mother or being forced to leave her home. Naidoo writes with power about this very strange society, where the majority was forced by the minority to live in squalid conditions. They could not vote or share in the riches of the land on which they once lived freely. Gates (cited in Bishop, 1992) would say that Naidoo has made an effort "to understand, to learn, to inhabit" a 12-year-old native South African's world.

 To create a text set of Mildred Taylor books, consult the accompanying CD-ROM.

Cover from *Journey to Jo'burg* by Beverly Naidoo. Illustrations copyright © 1986 by Eric Velasquez. Published by HarperTrophy. Reprinted by permission of HarperCollins Publishers.

Lyons specializes in biographies of African American artists and authors. Her writing is so fluid, and she does such a seamless job in writing about Zora Neale Hurston, Harriet Jacobs, and Mary Evans, that she is often mistakenly listed as an African American author on different websites.

▼▼▼▼▼▼▼

Culturally Neutral, Culturally Generic, and Culturally Specific Books

Awareness about the types of multicultural books that exist may be helpful in judging and selecting books for libraries and classrooms. Certainly they include folktales, biographies, historical novels, informational books, fantasy, picture books, and contemporary realistic fiction. However, Rudine Sims Bishop (1992) suggests that there are three general categories of books relating to or involving people of color: neutral, generic, and specific. Each type of book has its place in all children's reading experiences.

Culturally Neutral Books

Culturally neutral children's books include characters from cultural minorities but are essentially about other topics—jobs, events, the alphabet, early concepts, or vocations. Sims notes that into this category fall mostly picture books. Practically any picture book about "things" can be considered culturally neutral. These books can be found in most genres. For example, Margaret Miller's ***Can You Guess?*** is a concept book; Neil Johnson's photographic essay ***All in a Day's Work: Twelve Americans Talk About Their Jobs*** is an information book. Miller's book asks a series of questions with various hues of children serving as models for the possible answers. Johnson's book focuses on 12 types of jobs, and he interviews and photographs people filling these jobs. Among those found in the book are people of color.

The I Want to Be Series, authored by Stephanie Maze and Catherine Grace O'Neill (***I Want to Be . . . a Fashion Designer, I Want to Be . . . an Engineer, I Want to be . . . a Firefighter,*** etc.), is an intermediate/middle level series of information books that examines the various types of careers young people can pursue. By depicting workers from diverse ethnic groups in these careers, the authors show that any and all careers are open to everyone, people of color and women included. Each book also includes a multicultural array of famous individuals who have become successful chefs, dancers, or fashion designers.

ALTERNATE TEXT SET

Culturally Neutral Books

Read Aloud

Underground Train, by Mary Quattlebaum

Text Set

C is for City, by Nikki Grimes

Next Stop Grand Central, by Maira Kalman

A Summery Saturday, by Margaret Mahy

Shelley Rotner's ***Action Alphabet*** shows children of various hues, shapes, and sizes participating in all types of physical activities. Byron Barton's ***Machines at Work*** and Vicki Cobb's ***Skyscraper Going Up!*** feature work crews that include both people of color and women.

Neutral books randomly place multicultural faces among the pages in order to make a statement about the value of cultural diversity. Sometimes, the diversity is required because of the book's setting; for example, Quattlebaum's ***Underground Train*** is set in Washington, D.C. Similarly, in ***C Is for City***, there is intent to place diversity front and center, not only because of the subject matter—New York City—but also because both author and illustrator are African Americans. Although culturally neutral books are ostensibly about places, things or events, Bishop (1992) notes that these books can be "evaluated on the basis of their accuracy, visual and literary artistry, and possible omissions" (p. 46).

Culturally Generic Books

Generic books focus on characters representing a cultural group, but few specific details are included that aid in developing a cultural persona. Instead, these characters are represented as functioning in members of a large common culture, such as the mythical American "melting pot." These books carry universal themes where our similarities are more in focus than our differences. Examples of these books include Dolores Johnson's ***What Kind of Babysitter Is This?*** and ***The Best Bug to Be***, Phyllis Rose Eisenberg's ***You're My Nikki***, Anne Matthews Martin's ***Rachel Parker, Kindergarten Show-off***, ***Subway Sparrow***, by Leyla Torres, ***Where Does the Trail Lead?***, by Albert Burton, and ***Sand Castle***, by Brenda Shannon Yee. The main characters in most of these books are children of color, but the books contain no culturally specific materials. In these books, children are interacting with other children, their parents, or routines in which all children engage on a daily basis.

Ann Morris has created a culturally generic series (the All Around the World series) of picture books that feature things common to people the world over. Houses, bread, hats, weddings, and tools are among the topics she covers. Morris's books show young readers the commonalities that connect all cultures.

Pat Cummings illustrates and sometimes writes books that show life in middle-class African American families. Among the titles she has illustrated or written are ***Just Us Women***, by Jeannette Caines, ***Storm in the Night***, by Mary Stolz, ***Jimmie Lee Did It!***, and ***Willie's Not the Hugging Kind***, by Joyce Durham Barrett.

 To create an Ann Morris text set, consult the CD-ROM that accompanies this text.

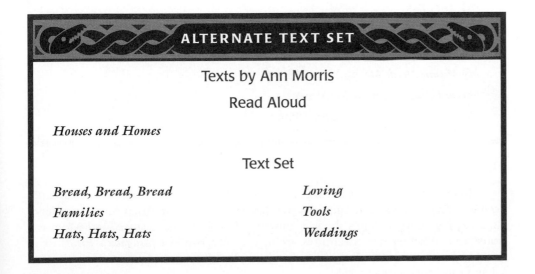

ALTERNATE TEXT SET

Texts by Ann Morris

Read Aloud

Houses and Homes

Text Set

Bread, Bread, Bread	*Loving*
Families	*Tools*
Hats, Hats, Hats	*Weddings*

Above the train, above my head, a green light turns to red.

Pat Cummings Picture Books

Read Aloud

My Aunt Came Back

Text Set

Angel Baby

Clean Your Room, Harvey Moon!

C.L.O.U.D.S.

I Need a Lunchbox, by Jeannette Caines

Just Us Women, by Jeannette Caines

My Mama Needs Me, by Mildred Pitts

Storm in the Night, by Mary Stolz

Two and Too Much, by Mildred Pitts

Juanita Havill and illustrator Anne Sibley O'Brien have created a series about a young middle-class African American girl, Jamaica, who has an Asian American friend, Brianna. Big brother thinks she is a nuisance. Dad is a businessman, and Mom is a housewife. Whether her adventures are at the playground (*Jamaica's Find*) or in school (*Jamaica and the Substitute Teacher*), all of Jamaica's experiences are universal and can happen to any child.

The traffic halts; the people cross.

From ***Underground Train*** by Mary Quattlebaum. Illustrations copyright © 1997 by Cat Bowman Smith. Published by Yearling Books. Reprinted by permission of Bantam Doubleday Bell.

The multitalented Angela Johnson has written a series of picture books that features African American children participating in a variety of family events. Each book is universal in its theme—leaving friends and loved ones in the old city neighborhood to move to a new suburban neighborhood (*The Leaving Morning*), the delight of the youngest of three siblings (*One of Three*), enjoying quality time with Grandpa (*When I Am Old With You*) or Mama (*Tell Me a Story, Mama*), or the pleasure in imitating big sister (*Do Like Kyla*). Although these books represent universal themes, there is a rhythm and a beat to Johnson's writing and her illustrators (usually David Soman) that let the reader know these are unmistakably African American children at work and play.

Johnson's novels for older readers, such as *Toning the Sweep* and *Heaven*—for which she has won the Coretta Scott King Award—focus on a variety of themes, some of which are rooted in the African American experience. Others, such as *Humming Whispers,* examine the world of mental illness, in particular, schizophrenia.

Some books become culturally generic through an editor's decision. For example, Australian Mem Fox's *Sophie* is a story with universal appeal—the bonds of love between a child and her grandfather. The illustrator selected for this story was African American Aminah Brenda Lynn Robinson. The editor could have easily selected an Asian American or Latino or Native American or European American illustrator. Each book would have had the overall universal appeal, but with the "cultural" nuances that the illustrator would have woven into the pictures. Similarly, Zolotow's *Do You Know What I'll Do?* has been revised and newly illustrated. The person selected for this newly illustrated version is African American illustrator Javaka Steptoe, whose bold ethnic illustrations leap from each page.

Culturally generic books show the universality of experiences among peoples. They show us how small the planet really is and how common tasks, events and foods, etc., connect across boundaries of language, culture, race, and religion. This does not mean that because these books possess universal themes that they should not be held

DID YOU KNOW?

When illustrator James Ransome, who illustrated Angela Johnson's ***Do Like Kyla,*** visited a local independent bookstore in West Chester, Pennsylvania, where Darigan lives, he and his mother went to hear Ransome speak and get their books autographed. As Darigan's mother, a former third-grade teacher, was leafing through a copy of Ransome's ***Sweet Clara and the Freedom Quilt,*** she kept coming back to the full title page showing a country scene. She noted aloud that it reminded her of the cotton fields that stretched out in all directions from her grandma's farmhouse when she was a third grader back in North Carolina. Ransome, who was in earshot, looked up and wondered, "Where in North Carolina?" She responded, "Near Rich Square." Ransome's face lit up and he said, "That's where I grew up, too." It turns out that not only did they grow up in the same town, they both went to school in Rich Square—except that Ransome went in an integrated situation, and the elder Darigan went during times of racial segregation.

ALTERNATE TEXT SET

The Jamaica Series

Read Aloud

Jamaica and Brianna

Text Set

Jamaica and the Blue Marker
Jamaica's Find
Jamaica and the Substitute Teacher
Jamaica Tag-Along

ALTERNATE TEXT SET

Angela Johnson Picture Books

Read Aloud

Do Like Kyla

Text Set

Down the Winding Road   *Tell Me a Story, Mama*
The Leaving Morning   *The Wedding*
One of Three   *When I Am Old With You*
Shoes Like Miss Alice's

to the same standards as other books. Just as with cultur-ally neutral books, it is important that readers still scruti-nize these titles and others like them for evidence of char-acters with realistic, nonstereotypical qualities.

Culturally Specific Books

Culturally specific children's books incorporate cultural details that help define characters. Cultural themes are evident, if not prevailing, in fictional plots or nonfiction content. Of course, the artwork in picture books will ex-press many of these cultural details. It is in this category of multicultural literature that cultural authenticity is par-ticularly important.

More so than in any other category of multicultural book, topics in culturally specific books must be accurate and portrayed with sensitivity and understanding. Whether fiction or nonfiction, these books must be true to their subjects. The Holocaust, the Civil Rights move-ment, the enslavement of African peoples, the disenfran-chisement of Native American peoples, or the internment of Japanese Americans during World War II are among the topics that must be carefully researched and presented so as not to add to existing misconceptions or create new ones. The publishers of Just Us Books (1995) note that a good multicultural book should be so designed to "open the reader's mind and guide him or her on a journey to-wards knowledge and awareness of self and others."

Spotlight on Selected Authors and Illustrators of Culturally Specific Books

The novels and retold folktales of Joseph Bruchac give readers an authentic look at certain Native American cul-tures. Bruchac's *Eagle Song* is a quick but solid reading about a modern Native American boy—Iroquois—who lives in Brooklyn. His mother is a social worker and his

When *Do You Know What I'll Do?* was revised in 2000, these Garth Williams illustrations were re-placed by art from Javaka Steptoe that highlights the culturally generic, universal appeal of the text. Illustration from *Do You Know What I'll Do?* by Charlotte Zolotow. Illustrations copyright © 1958 by Garth Williams. Used by permission of HarperCollins Publishers.

ALTERNATE TEXT SET

Children of the Holocaust

Read Aloud

Let the Celebrations BEGIN!, by Margaret Wild

Text Set

Hilde and Eli: Children of the Holocaust, by David A. Adler

Star of Fear, Star of Hope, by Jo Hoestlandt

Rose Blanche, by Christophe Gallaz and Roberto Innocenti

Flowers on the Wall, by Miriam Nerlove

The Lily Cupboard, by Shulamith L. Oppenheim

To look more closely at this discussion about cultural authenticity, visit Chapter 9 of our companion website at **www.prenhall.com/darigan**

A CONVERSATION WITH. . .

Joseph Bruchac

When my wife and I went to Africa, we found ourselves in the middle of an African culture where we were not treated differently because of the color of our skin. And I think for the first time in my life, outside of America I began to look at African faces and not see them first as African but see the common humanity there. In Ghana, people would describe each other by the color of their skin, but not pejoratively. Someone might say, "My friend so-and-so has very dark skin." But it wasn't a prejudiced description. It was simply a description of the way a human being looked. I began to see beyond that racial mask that clouds people's eyes. So I think that was a wonderful experience for me.

Then the second aspect of this is that I saw a tribal culture, a culture that was based on community, and family, and extended family, which is like the old tribal cultures that Native American people come from that still exists to a greater or lesser degree in Native communities. And there was a familiarity to it that really touched me.

I have been taught by numerous people to see things as a circle. And in that circle the small child is at the start, and as you go around the circle you come to the adolescent and the adult and then the elder. The elder is close to the small child in that circle. Can you picture that? Those are the things that we don't respect in our culture. We are putting our elders away. We are ignoring our elders, we are separating them from our families and we are putting our children away from us. And we are doing so now in ways we never used to do before. The number of children who are on Ritalin they do not really need—they are just children. If they are fidgeting, so what? Kids fidget. If they have limited attention spans, guess what? So did Albert Einstein. I think it is a very dangerous cultural matrix where you have the separation of elders from families and the drugging of children to get what you regard as good behavior. I know Ritalin is important for some kids. But to me, it is a symptom of something that is deeply, deeply wrong. And we need to restore what is truly the value of family, which is respect for all aspects of that circle—especially the elder and the child. And another thing, too: People are scared of adolescents. People will cross the street to avoid walking near a group of teenagers. We've heard of the self-fulfilling prophecy. If kids are told they are dangerous, they begin to think they are dangerous. It is a strange time that we are in now.

And I truly believe that one of the ways we can see that balance again is by listening to story. By telling our stories, by sharing our stories, by hearing the old stories and the new ones. That is why a book like **When I Was Your Age** is so important to me—because it shares those stories and connects together those generations in a very special way. I have worked with some of the supposedly worst people in our culture. For 8 years, I ran a college program inside a maximum-security prison, and I have worked in youth detention centers. I have done storytelling workshops in these places and I have seen people transform. Maybe not permanently, maybe forever—I don't know—but transformed through the hearing and the telling of a story. It touches the heart and it changes the way we relate to the world when we understand our lives as story.

To read more of this Conversation with Joseph Bruchac, please visit Chapter 9 on our text's companion website at **www.prenhall.com/darigan**

father is a construction worker. This book is useful because there are so few that portray modern Native Americans who live and work in cities just as people from other cultural groups do. The prolific Bruchac has written nonfiction, novels, and picture books, including *Sacajawea, Lasting Echoes: An Oral History of Native American People, A Boy Called Slow, Children of the Longhouse,* and *Crazy Horse's Vision.*

Picture books depicting modern Native American boys and girls and their families are sorely needed. The majority of picture books with Native American themes are folktales. Virginia Driving Hawk Sneve has written a commendable series (The First Americans published by Holiday House) that presents thumbnail sketches of selected Native American groups. Each book begins with a myth or legend related to the group highlighted, and ends with members of the featured group today—as modern Americans in dress, occupation, recreational pursuits, etc.

Other Native American authors and illustrators of note include author/illustrator Shonto Begay (*Navajo: Visions and Voices Across the Mesa*), author Michael Dor-

---

ALTERNATE TEXT SET

The First Americans Series

Read Aloud

The Iroquois: A First Americans Book

Text Set

The Apaches: A First Americans Book

The Cherokees: A First Americans Book

The Cheyennes: A First Americans Book

The Hopis: A First Americans Book

The Navajos: A First Americans Book

The Nez Perce: A First Americans Book

The Seminoles: A First Americans Book

For the complete list of Reese's recommended books about Native Americans, please visit Chapter 9 of our companion website at **www.prenhall.com/darigan**

ris (*Guests, Morning Girl, Sees Behind Trees, The Window*), author Louise Erdrich (*The Birchbark House*), illustrator S. D. Nelson (*Crazy Horse's Vision, The Gift Horse: A Lakota Story*), and illustrator Redwing T. Nez (*Forbidden Talent*).

Native American scholar Debbie Reese, a member of the Nambe Pueblo, has compiled a list of recommended books about (some by) Native Americans. She includes among these titles *Pueblo Storyteller* and *Potlatch,* by Diane Hoyt-Goldsmith, *Pueblo Boy,* by Marcia Keegan, *Earth Daughter,* by George Ancona, and *A Boy Becomes a Man at Wounded Knee,* by Ted Wood.

Laurence Yep is the award-winning author of *Dragonwings* and *Dragon's Gate.* He also writes from his own experiences growing up in San Francisco's Chinatown. His *Later, Gator* is a funny exposé of life as a big brother to a "perfect" younger brother. There are loads of laughs and love on every page. Yep continues the family fun and brotherly love in *Cockroach Cooties.*

Janet Wong is a Chinese-Korean American. Her poetry is edgy and honest, born of the complexities of both her heritage and growing up in a racist society. Particularly revealing are her collections of poems where she displays all sides of her heritage—Chinese, Korean, and American—*Good Luck Gold* and *A Suitcase of Seaweed; and Other Poems.*

Korean illustrator Chris K. Soentpiet is building a very impressive portfolio. His stunning illustrations have graced such books as Marie Bradby's *More Than Anything*

From *Crazy Horse's Vision,* by Joseph Bruchac, illustrations by S. D. Nelson. Text copyright © 2000 by Joseph Bruchac, illustrations copyright © 2000 by S. D. Nelson. Published by Lee & Low Books Inc. Reprinted by permission of Lee & Low Books Inc.

To find out more about Virginia Hamilton and other authors and illustrators on the World Wide Web, visit Chapter 9 on the companion website at **www.prenhall.com/darigan**

B O O K M A R K

INTEGRATING TECHNOLOGY: AUTHORS ON THE WORLD WIDE WEB

Virginia Hamilton, author of over 30 books for children, including **M.C. Higgins, the Great** and **Zeely,** has a website full of information about her life and her books. The Virginia Hamilton Conference, which explores children's literature in light of cultural awareness, cultural pride, and the issues surrounding the concept of culture, is also highlighted on this website. There are also plenty of surprises, including numerous frog jokes, and a wonderful presentation of Hamilton's recent visit to South Africa.

Else, Haemi Balgassi's *Peacebound Trains, Molly Bannaky*, by Alice McGill, and *Something Beautiful,* by Sharon Dennis Wyeth. He has won the IRA Award twice: for *More Than Anything Else* and *Molly Bannaky.* He won the 1996 Society of Illustrators Gold Medal for *Peacebound Trains.*

Latinos (Hispanics) hail from many parts of the globe, with each group having its own customs, beliefs, attitudes, and dialect of Spanish. Just as with other ethnic groups, one book will not fit all. Writers Gary Soto and Rudolfo Anaya and photoessayist George Ancona are Mexican Americans, and their works reflect this heritage—Soto's *Neighborhood Odes,* and Anaya's *Farolitos for Abuela* and *Maya's Children: The Story of La Llorona* are but a few of the titles readers will find enjoyable. Cuban-born Alma Flor Ada was awarded the Pura Belpré Award for *Under the Royal Palms: A Childhood in Cuba.* Her alphabet book *Gathering the Sun* is a lively and colorful text written in both Spanish and English. George Ancona's photo essays focus on many cultures. Some of his most recent works highlight the lives of Spanish-speaking children who live in various regions of the world—America's big cities (*Barrio: José's Neighborhood*) and our southern neighbor (*Mayeros: A Yucatec Maya Family* and *Charro: The Mexican Cowboy*). Latino illustrator Raul Colón has illustrated books across cultures, including Pat Mora's *Tomás and the Library Lady,* Jane Resch Thomas's *Celebration!,* a story about an African American

ALTERNATE TEXT SET

Virginia Hamilton

Read Aloud

The People Could Fly

Text Set

The Bells of Christmas

Drylongso

In the Beginning

Her Stories

Many Thousand Gone

A Ring of Tricksters

When Birds Could Talk & Bats Could Sing

family; Naomi Shihab Nye's *Habibi,* the story of a young Palestinian girl's life after her family moves from the United States to her father's native land; and Deborah Hopkinson's *A Band of Angels,* a fictionalized account of the Fisk Jubilee Singers.

Finally, we turn to one of the most honored children's authors in the world: Virginia Hamilton. Hamilton's books sing with the vitality of all the cultures, literary and oral, in which she is rooted. She has a way with words that is stunning—few books are as finely written as one of her earliest award-winning books, *The Planet of Junior Brown,* or her *The Magical Adventures of Pretty Pearl,* which is an intricate weaving of historical fiction and fantasy that elicits vivid images in the reader's mind. Hamilton is well known for her novels, but she also writes shorter works and anthologies.

▼▼▼▼▼▼▼

The Growth of Multicultural Literature

Metaphorically, America has proudly referred to herself as a "melting pot." This quaint Eurocentric term has been traced to a playwright who viewed America as "God's crucible . . . for all races of Europe" (Tiedt & Tiedt, 1990, p. 7). For years, children's literature perpetuated the portrait of America as a melting pot for Europeans without being challenged. Those rare books that did have minority characters generally portrayed them badly or ignored them completely. Minority characters appeared in illustrations but were not part of the central story; they served as obvious "window dressing." However, when African American author Arna Bontemps won a Newbery Honor in 1949 for *Story of the Negro* and became the first African American to appear on the Newbery list, he ushered in the real beginning of change for all cultural groups. Though few other minority authors or illustrators appeared on award lists during the next two decades, more of their work was being produced. Also, books by majority culture authors that presented less stereotyped images of minority cultures appeared and received awards. *Song of the Swallows* by Leo Politi won the Caldecott Award in 1950 and was the first Caldecott winner with a Hispanic American protagonist. *Amos Fortune, Free Man,* by Elizabeth Yates, *Secret of the Andes,* by Ann Nolan Clark, and *. . . And Now, Miguel,* by Joseph Krumgold, won the Newbery in 1951, 1953, and 1954 respectively; and *The Snowy Day,* by Ezra Jack Keats, won the Caldecott in 1963. Although these books may fail to pass muster in terms of cultural sensitivity and authenticity now, when they were written, they represented bold steps toward presenting minority protagonists positively.

As the Civil Rights movement gained momentum in the 1960s, awareness of and sensitivity to minorities increased. Nancy Larrick called attention to the lack of minority characters in children's books in her landmark article in the September 11, 1965 issue of *Saturday Review.* In that article, "The All-White World of Children's Books," Larrick noted that publishers of children's literature had participated in a cultural lobotomy on the country, and in conjunction with children's authors, had excluded blacks from visibility in history and literature in order to make them appear as rootless people. The publishing and library worlds increased their efforts to include more African Americans in children's books. Accordingly, publishers flooded the market with books purporting to reflect the black experience. Books about other invisible protagonists—women, Asians, Hispanics, Native Americans, the physically or mentally challenged—also were being included. However, quantity did not necessarily mean quality.

In 1966, the Council on Interracial Books for Children (CIBC) was founded. Its publications pointed to racial stereotypes that were still prevalent among this new crop of multicultural books. Its efforts with publishers helped to promote and get into print the works of authors and illustrators of color, especially African Americans. In fact, for a number of years, the CIBC sponsored an annual contest for unpublished writers and illustrators of color and saw to it that the winners' works were published.

ALTERNATE TEXT SET

Children Around the World

Read Aloud

Children Just Like Me, by Susan Elizabeth Copsley, Barnabas Kindersly, Anabel Kindersley, Harry Belafonte

Text Set

Kanu of Kathmandu: A Journey of Nepal, by Barbara A. Margolies

Rehema's Journey: A Visit in Tanzania, by Barbara A. Margolies

Children of Belize, by Frank Staub

The Children of the Tlingit, by Frank Staub

How My Family Lives in America, by Susan Kuklin

The authors and illustrators who were given their start by the CIBC are some of the best known today in the world of multicultural children's literature: African Americans Mildred Taylor and Walter Dean Myers, Native American author Virginia Driving Hawk Sneve, and Asian American writers Ai-Ling Louie and Minfong Ho. In 1969, the Coretta Scott King Award was established to recognize the distinguished works of African American authors and illustrators. In 1996, the Pura Belpré Award was established. This biennial award honors Latino writers and illustrators whose work best portrays, affirms, and celebrates the Latino cultural experience in a work of literature for youth.

Authors and illustrators of color have begun to be recognized by many of the awards committees. In 1975, Virginia Hamilton won the Newbery Award for ***M. C. Higgins, the Great,*** the first African American to be so honored. In 1977, Mildred D. Taylor won the Newbery for ***Roll of Thunder, Hear My Cry.*** In 2000, Christopher Paul Curtis scored

---

Jerry Pinkney—***Mirandy and Brother Wind, John Henry, Talking Eggs, The Ugly Duckling***

Brian Pinkney—***Faithful Friend, Duke Ellington***

Carole Byard—***Working Cotton***

John Steptoe—***Mufaro's Beautiful Daughters, The Legend of Jumping Mouse***

Christopher Myers—***Harlem***

Faith Ringgold—***Tar Beach***

Ed Young—***The Emperor and the Kite, Seven Blind Mice***

Allen Say—***The Boy of the Three-Year Nap***

Donald Crews—***Freight Train, Truck***

Tom Feelings—***Moja Means One, Jambo Means Hello***

Taro Yashima—***Crow Boy***

FIGURE 9–1   Caldecott Honor award winners.

There is a growing body of award-winning illustrators of color. They have won Caldecotts, Coretta Scott King Illustrator Awards, and other illustrator awards of note as testaments to their achievements. Some, such as Jerry Pinkney, David Diaz, Donald Crews, Ed Young, and Allen Say, are well established and internationally known. Below are 15 additional noteworthy illustrators of color. Some are well known, and others are beginning to build impressive portfolios of illustrated books.

Brian Pinkney

Faith Ringgold

Javaka Steptoe

Jan Spivey Gilchrist

Jean and Mou-sien Tseng

Carole Byard

Francisco X. Mora

Chris K. Soentpiet

E. B. Lewis

Floyd Cooper

James Ransome

Sheila Hamanaka

S. D. Nelson

Synthia St. James

Christopher Myers

FIGURE 9–2 A baker's dozen plus two: Notable illustrators of color.

a double win with the Newbery Medal and the Coretta Scott King Award, both for ***Bud, Not Buddy.*** Curtis became the first author to win both of the top writing awards in the same year, and he became the first African American male to win the Newbery. Leo Dillon is the only African American illustrator to win the Caldecott Award. He and his wife, Diane, won for Verna Aardema's ***Why Mosquitoes Buzz in People's Ears*** in 1976 and repeated the next year with ***Ashanti to Zulu: African Traditions,*** by Margaret Musgrove. Asian American illustrators Ed Young and Allen Say have both won the Caldecott Award; Young won for ***Lon Po Po*** and Say for ***Grandfather's Journey.*** Latino artist/illustrator David Diaz won the Caldecott for ***Smoky Night,*** by Eve Bunting. Numerous authors and illustrators of color have won the Caldecott and Newbery Honor awards (see Figures 9–1 and 9–2).

Since the 1960s, more authors from minority cultural and racial groups have been writing for children and appear consistently on best books lists and awards lists. Still, there is much room for growth in this area of publishing. Several publishing houses and imprints are producing high-quality multicultural literature for children.

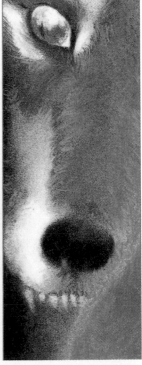

From ***Lon Po Po*** by Ed Young, copyright © 1989 by Ed Young. Used by permission of Philomel Books, a division of Penguin Putnam, Inc.

DID YOU KNOW?

There is a wonderful reference you may want to investigate when choosing International Literature for children: In his *Children's Books from Other Countries,* our friend and colleague Carl Tomlinson, has compiled a grouping of 724 titles representing 29 countries. Further, he shows how to share these wonderful international books with children in curricular units, in read alouds, and in thematic units that connect books from the U.S. with those from abroad.

▼▼▼▼▼▼▼

International Books, or the Widening World[3]

Just as multicultural books dealing with American society assist in creating a bridge of understanding, international books can help children gain an appreciation and understanding of our global society. The history and culture of other countries as well as their literary traditions are illuminated through books that have their origins outside the United States.

English Language Titles

The most common international books are English language titles written and published in another English-speaking country, such as England, Canada, Australia, and New Zealand. Because these books need no translation, they can be acquired and marketed readily in the United States.

Long before J. K. Rowling and Harry Potter became worldwide phenomena, savvy young readers were devouring C. S. Lewis's **Chronicles of Narnia,** Brian Jacques's Redwall series, Philip Pullman's mysteries and fantasies, Rosemary Sutcliffe's historical fiction, and Susan Cooper's award-winning fantasies.

Australian Mem Fox is one of the best-known English language authors. Her books are staples in classrooms across the United States. **Possum Magic** and **Koala Lou** introduce readers of all ages to the land down under. **Wilfred Gordon McDonald Partridge** is a gentle story of a young boy who helps an Alzheimer's patient recall her years past. Breathes there a more ferocious (or tender-hearted) pirate than Boris (**Tough Boris**) or a more observant and fearless hen than Hattie (**Hattie and the Fox**)?

Although revised for an American readership, Hoffman's **Amazing Grace** and **Boundless Grace**[4] originated as British picture books. Few first novels score like Michelle Magorian's **Good Night, Mr. Tom,** the story of a young London World War II evacuee who learns about love and friendship in the household of a country curmudgeon. Also set during World War II in Britain is Robert Westall's **Blitzcat.** Cat lovers everywhere will enjoy this engaging story of a cat that goes out in search of her "human" who has left to fight for King and Country. During her journey, she interacts with other humans and greatly influences their lives.

Jamaican-born James Berry writes across the genres. He has enchanted us with his poetry (**When I Dance**), haunted us with images of the West Indian slave trade and its consequences (**Ajeemah and His Son**), and entertained us with short stories and folktales from his native Jamaica (**A Thief in the Village**).

Translated Titles

Although translated books are less plentiful in this country, this area of publishing is growing. These foreign language books have been written and printed in other countries. American publishing companies then acquire the rights to publish them, and they are translated into English. A limited number of foreign language children's books from other countries are released in the United States in translated form.

One consideration when judging translated books is the quality of the translation. Though the flavor of the country needs to be retained, the English text must be fluent and readable, yet not too "Americanized." Often a few foreign words and phrases may be left in to provide readers a feel for the culture and the language, but too many can be troublesome for children.

One standout translated title that has found a favorable audience in the United States is Christina Bjork's **Linnea in Monet's Garden.** It is a delightful story of a

---

[3]We like Hazel Rochman's term (1993) that describes the expanding boundaries of our cultures, experiences, and reading habits.
[4]The British title is **Grace and Family.** Although the setting in both **Amazing Grace** and **Grace and Family** is clearly in the United Kingdom, in **Boundless Grace,** Grace and her family live in New York.

ALTERNATE TEXT SET

Books by James Berry

Read Aloud

A Thief in the Village and Other Stories from Jamaica

Text Set

Anancy Spiderman
Everywhere Faces Everywhere
Isn't My Name Magical? Brother and Sister Poems
When I Dance
The Future Telling Lady
First Palm Trees
Ajeemah and His Son

ALTERNATE TEXT SET

Australian Books

Read Aloud

Possum Magic, by Mem Fox

Text Set

The Bamboo Flute, by Gary Disher
Big Rain Coming, by Katrina Germain
The Burnt Stick, by Anthony Hill
Dreamtime: Aboriginal Stories, by Oodgeroo
My Place, by Nadia Wheatley
Where the Forest Meets the Sea, by Jean Baker

young girl whose love of art, particularly Monet, is enhanced after viewing his paintings in Paris and then visiting his gardens in Giverny. ***Rose Blanche,*** by Gallaz and Innocenti, and ***Hiroshima No Pika,*** by Toshi Maruki, are Batchelder Award winners that have given American readers a realistic look at how World War II harmed the lives of innocents both in Europe and Japan. Other recommended titles include the 1995 Batchelder Award winning book, ***The Boys from St. Petri,*** by Bjarne Reuter, an action-filled novel about the Nazi resistance movement in Denmark. Uri Orlev's award winning novel, ***Island on Bird Street,*** centers on the hardships of hiding from the Nazis in a Warsaw ghetto. Ruud van der Rol and Rian Verhoeven's ***Anne Frank Beyond the Diary: A Photographic Remembrance*** gives readers new insight into this famous Holocaust victim's brief life.

To find out more about the IBBY and other sources on the World Wide Web, visit Chapter 9 on the companion website at **www.prenhall. com/darigan**

BOOKMARK

INTEGRATING TECHNOLOGY: SOURCES ON THE WORLD WIDE WEB

The International Board on Books for Young People (*IBBY*) is "a non-profit organization which represents an international network of people from all over the world who are committed to bringing books and children together." The website provides extensive information about the organization and its activities, which includes the Documentation Centre of Books for Disabled Young People, International Children's Book Day, the Hans Christian Andersen Awards, and the journal *Bookbird*. The IBBY site is extended and supported by the websites of the national affiliates, including the *USBBY*. Thirteen national affiliates from Austria to Venezuela have websites, and for those interested in international children's books, these sites are invaluable.

Promoting International Children's Books

There is an ever increasing exchange of children's books among countries, but most of the international books published in the United States come from Europe. Each year since 1966, publishers from around the world have attended an international book fair in Bologna, Italy, where they share their books and work out agreements for publishing them in other countries. An important book fair that highlights authors of color is the Zimbabwe International Book Fair. It is the largest book fair in sub-Saharan Africa. Although a major focus of this fair is reading materials for adults, there is a small cadre of publishers who also feature children's titles.

Since World War II, a number of organizations, publications, and awards have been established to promote the idea of an international world of children's books. In 1949, the International Youth Library was founded in Munich, Germany; it has become a world center for the study of children's literature. In 1953, the International Board on Books for Young People (IBBY) was established, and soon after, in 1956, the organization created the first international children's book award.

The Hans Christian Andersen Medal is awarded biennially to an author whose lifetime contribution to the world of children's literature is considered outstanding. In 1966, a separate award for illustration was added to the Hans Christian Andersen Medal, and IBBY also began publishing *Bookbird,* a journal linking those interests in international children's books. In 1968 in the United States, the American Library Association established the Mildred Batchelder Award (see Figure 9–3). This award is given to the American publisher of the most noteworthy translated children's book of the year.

The Apprentice (Spain—1994)

Secret Letters from 0 to 10 (France—1999 Honor)

Sister Shako and Kolo the Goat: Memories of My Childhood in Turkey (Turkey—1995 Honor)

The Baboon King (Holland—2000)

The Lady with the Hat (Israel—1996)

The Friends (Japan—1997)

Vendela in Venice (Sweden—2000 Honor)

FIGURE 9–3   Some recent Batchelder Award winners.

▼▼▼▼▼▼▼

Summary

With the increased emphasis on well-written multicultural and international children's books, teachers and parents have another means by which they can help children avoid the pitfalls of ignorance that breed intolerance, hatred, and conflict. Through sharing these books with their children, parents too can become better informed about cultures and countries about which they know little. With technology shrinking our international borders, we cannot afford to allow either ignorance or xenophobia to stifle our growth at the start of the 21st century.

▼▼▼▼▼▼▼

Fifteen More of Our Favorites

Novels

Choi, Sook Nyul. (1991). *The year of impossible goodbyes*. Houghton Mifflin. A young Korean girl survives the oppression of the Japanese and Russian occupations of North Korea of the 1940s, to later escape to freedom in South Korea.

Mori, Kyoko. (1993). *Shizuko's daughter*. Henry Holt. After her mother's suicide when she is 12, Yuki spends years living with her distant father and his resentful new wife, cut off from her mother's family, and relying on her own inner strength to cope with the tragedy.

Myers, Walter Dean. (1999). *Monster*. HarperCollins. While on trial as an accomplice to a murder, 16-year-old Steve Harmon records his experiences in prison and in the courtroom in the form of a film script as he tries to come to terms with the course his life has taken. (Winner of the first Michael Printz Award for Young Adult readers.)

Soto, Gary. (1998). *Petty crimes*. Harcourt Brace. A collection of short stories about Mexican American youth growing up in California's Central Valley.

Taylor, Mildred. (1990). *Mississippi bridge*. New York: Dial. During a heavy rainstorm in rural 1930s Mississippi, a 10-year-old white boy sees a bus driver order all the black passengers from the bus to make room for the late-arriving white passengers.

Yep, Laurence. (1977). *Child of the owl*. HarperCollins. A twelve-year-old girl who knows little about her Chinese heritage is sent to live with her grandmother in San Francisco's Chinatown.

Yep, Laurence. (1991). *The star fisher*. Morrow. A Chinese-American family finds it hard to adjust when they move from Ohio to West Virginia in the 1920s.

Picture Books

Ancona, George. (1993). *Powwow*. Harcourt Brace. A photo essay on the pan-Indian celebration called a powwow, this particular one being held on the Crow Reservation in Montana.

Bruchac, Joseph. (2000). *Squanto's journey: The story of the first Thanksgiving* (Greg Shed, Illus.). Harcourt Brace. Squanto recounts how in 1614 he was captured by the British, sold into slavery in Spain, and ultimately returned to the New World to become a guide and friend for the colonists.

Cooper, Floyd. (1996). *Mandela: From the life of a South African statesman*. Philomel. From his boyhood days in the South African countryside, to his time as leader of the African National Congress, to his 27 years in prison, Mandela firmly resisted injustices wherever he saw them.

Hamilton, Virginia. (2000). *The girl who spun gold*. Scholastic. A West Indian variant of the traditional story of "Rumpelstiltskin." Simple colloquial language combined with stunningly detailed illustrations, bordered in gold, makes this book a welcome addition to the folktale genre.

Hopkinson, Deborah. (1993). *Sweet Clara and the freedom quilt* (James Ransome, Illus.). Knopf. A young slave stitches a quilt with a map pattern that guides her to freedom in the North.

Lee, Jeanne M. (1991). *Silent lotus*. Farrar, Straus & Giroux. Although she cannot speak or hear, Lotus trains as a Khmer court dancer and becomes eloquent in dancing out the legend of the gods.

Polacco, Patricia. (1994). *Pink and Say*. Philomel. Say Curtis describes his meeting with Pinkus Aylee, a black soldier, during the Civil War, and their capture by Southern troops.

Soto, Gary. (1995). *Chato's kitchen* (Susan Guevara, Illus.). Putnam. To get the "ratoncitos," little mice, who have moved into the barrio to come to his house, Chato the cat prepares all kinds of food: fajitas, frijoles, salsa, enchiladas, and more.

▼▼▼▼▼▼▼

Others We Like

African and African American

Novels

Bryan, Ashley. (1998). *Ashley Bryan's African tales, uh-huh*. Atheneum.

Draper, Sharon M. (1997). *Forged by fire*. Atheneum.

Fenner, Carol. (1995). *Yolanda's genius*. McElderry.

Forrester, Sandra. (1995). *Sound the jubilee*. Lodestar.

Hamilton, Virginia. (1995). *Her stories: African American folktales, fairy tales and true tales* (Leo Dillon & Diane Dillon, Illus.). Scholastic.

Hamilton, Virginia. (1999). *Bluish*. Scholastic.

Hanson, Joyce. (1989). *The gift-giver*. Clarion.

Hanson, Joyce. (1994). *The captive*. Scholastic.

Haskins, James. (1995). *Black Eagles: African Americans in aviation*. Scholastic.

Johnson, Angela. (1998). *Gone from home*. DK Ink.

Lester, Julius. (1995). *Othello: A novel*. Scholastic.

Mead, Alice. (1998). *Junebug and the reverend*. Farrar, Straus & Giroux.

Myers, Walter Dean. (1988). *Scorpions*. HarperCollins.

Myers, Walter Dean. (1992). *Somewhere in the darkness*. Scholastic.

Naidoo, Beverley. (1995). *No turning back*. HarperCollins.

Tillage, Leon Walter. (1997). *Leon's story*. Farrar, Straus & Giroux.

Woodson, Jacqueline. (1995). *From the notebooks of Melanin Sun*. Scholastic.

Picture Books

Aardema, Verna. (1996). *The lonely lioness and the ostrich chicks* (Yumi Heo, Illus.). Knopf.

Aardema, Verna. (1999). *Koi and the kola nuts* (Joe Cepeda, Illus.). Atheneum.

Battle-Lavert, Gwendolyn. (1995). *Off to school* (Gershom Griffith, Illus.). Holiday House.

Coleman, Evelyn. (1996). *White socks only* (Tyrone Geter, Illus.). Albert Whitman.

Cooper, Floyd. (1994). *Coming home: From the life of Langston Hughes*. Philomel.

Echewa, T. Obinkaram. (1999). *The magic tree: A folktale from Nigeria*. Morrow.

Flournoy, Valerie. (1985). *The patchwork quilt* (Jerry Pinkney, Illus.). Dial.

Grimes, Nikki. (2000). *Is it far to Zanzibar?* (Betsy Lewin, Illus.). Lothrop.

Isadora, Rachel. (1991). *At the crossroads*. Greenwillow.

Johnston, Tony. (1996). *The wagon* (James E. Ransome, Illus.). Tambourine.

May, Kathy L. (2000). *Molasses man* (Felicia Marshall, Illus.). Holiday House.

McGill, Alice. (1999). *Molly Bannaky* (Chris K. Soentpiet, Illus.). Houghton Mifflin.

McKissack, Patricia C. (1989). *Nettie Jo's friends* (Scott Cook, Illus.). Knopf.

McKissack, Patricia C. (1997). *Ma Dear's apron* (Floyd Cooper, Illus.). Atheneum.

Mitchell, Margaree King. (1993). *Uncle Jed's barbershop* (James Ransome, Illus.). Simon & Schuster.

Myers, Christopher. (1999). *Black cat*. Scholastic.

Pinkney, Andrea Davis. (1994). *Dear Benjamin Banneker* (Brian Pinkney, Illus.). Harcourt Brace.

Wright, Courtni C. (1994). *Jumping the broom*. Holiday House.

Asian and Asian American

Novel

Haugaard, Erik Christian. (1991). *The boy and the samurai*. Houghton Mifflin.

Ho, Minfong. (1991). *The clay marble*. Farrar, Straus & Giroux.

Hoobler, Dorothy, & Hoobler, Thomas. (1999). *The ghost in the Tokaido Inn*. Philomel.

Kim, Helen. (1996). *The long season of rain*. Henry Holt.

Lord, Bette Bao. (1984). *In the year of the boar and Jackie Robinson*. Harper & Row.

Salisbury, Graham. (1994). *Under the blood-red sun*. Delacorte.

Uchida, Yoshiko. (1981). *A jar of dreams*. McElderry.

Yep, Laurence. (1977). *Child of the owl*. Harper & Row.

Yumoto, Kazumi. (1999). *The spring tone*. Farrar, Straus & Giroux.

Picture Books

Armstrong, Jennifer. (1993). *Cin Yu Min and the ginger cat* (Mary Grandpré, Illus.). Crown.

Choi, Sook Nyul. (1997). *Yummi and Halmoni's trip* (Karen Dugan, Illus.). Houghton Mifflin.

Climo, Shirley. (1993). *Korean Cinderella* (Ruth Heller, Illus.). New York: HarperCollins.

Heo, Yumi. (1996). *The green frogs*. Houghton Mifflin.

Mochizuki, Ken. (1993). *Baseball saved us* (Dom Lee, Illus.). Lee and Low.

Mochizuki, Ken. (1995). *Heroes* (Dom Lee, Illus.). Lee and Low.

Uchida, Yoshiko. (1993). *The bracelet* (Joanna Yardley, Illus.). Philomel.

Yep, Laurence. (1997). *The dragon prince: A Chinese beauty and the beast tale* (Kam Mak, Illus.). HarperCollins.

Young, Ed. (1995). *Night visitors*. Philomel.

Hispanic American (Latino)

Novels

Carlson, Lori M. (1994). *An island like you: Stories of the barrio*. Orchard.

Martinez, Floyd. (1997). *Spirits of the high mesa*. Arte Público Press.

Mikaelsen, Ben. (1993). *Sparrow hawk red*. Hyperion.

Paulsen, Gary. (1987). *The crossing*. Orchard.

Ryan, Pam Munoz. (2000). *Esperanza rising*. Scholastic.

Soto, Gary. (1990). *Baseball in April*. Harcourt Brace.

Soto, Gary. (1997). *Snapshots from the wedding*. New York: Putnam.

Picture Books

Ancona, George. (1993). *Pablo remembers: The fiesta of the Day of the Dead*. Lothrop.

Dorros, Arthur. (1991). *Abuela* (Elisa Kleven, Illus.). Dutton.

Horenstein, Henry. (1997). *Baseball in the barrios*. Harcourt Brace.

Lomas Garza, Carmen. (1996). *In my family/en mi familia*. Children's Book Press.

Mora, Pat. (1992). *A birthday basket for Tia* (Cecily Lang, Illus.). Macmillan.

Soto, Gary. (1993). *Too many tamales* (Ed Martinez, Illus.). Putnam.

Soto, Gary. (2000). *Chato and the party animals* (Susan Guevara, Illus.). Putnam.

Turner, Robyn Montana. (1993). *Frida Kahlo: Portraits of women artists for children*. Little, Brown.

Native American

Bruchac, Joseph. (1992). *Thirteen moons on turtle's back: A Native American year of moons* (Thomas Locker, Illus.). Philomel.

Bruchac, Joseph. (1994). *A boy called Slow* (Rocco Baviera, Illus.). Philomel.

Bruchac, Joseph. (1996). *Legends of Native American sacred places*. Dial.

Casler, Leigh. (1994). *The boy who dreamed of an acorn* (Shonto Begay, Illus.). Philomel.

Cohen, Caron Lee. (1988). *The mud pony* (Shonto Begay, Illus.). Scholastic.

dePaola, Tomie. (1983). *The legend of the Bluebonnet: A tale of Texas*. Putnam.

dePaola, Tomie. (1988). *The legend of the Indian paintbrush*. Putnam.

Ekoomiak, Normee. (1988). *Arctic memories*. Henry Holt.

Freedman, Russell. (1992). *Indian winter* (Karl Bodmer, Illus.). Holiday House.

Goble, Paul. (1994). *Iktomi and the buzzard*. Orchard.

Goble, Paul. (1999). *Paul Goble gallery: Three Native American stories*. Simon & Schuster.

Left Hand Bull, Jacqueline. (1999). *Lakota hoop dancer* (Suzanne Haldane, Photog.). Dutton.

Lunge-Larsen, Lise, & Preus, Margi. (1999). *The legend of the lady slipper* (Andrea Arroyo, Illus.). Houghton Mifflin.

Sneve, Virginia Driving Hawk (Ed.). (1989). *Dancing teepees: Poems of American Indian youth* (Stephen Gammell, Illus.). Holiday House.

Stevens, Janet. (1993). *Coyote steals the blanket: A Ute tale*. Holiday House.

Religious Cultures

Ammon, Richard. (1996). *An Amish Christmas* (Pamela Patrick, Illus.). Atheneum. (Christian—Amish)

Ammon, Richard. (1998). *An Amish wedding*. (Pamela Patrick, Illus.). Atheneum. (Christian—Amish)

Barrie, Barbara. (1990). *Lone star*. Delacorte. (Jewish)

Cormier, Robert. (1990). *Other bells for us to ring*. Delacorte. (Christian—Catholic)

Demi. (1996). *Buddha*. Henry Holt. (Buddhist)

Demi. (1997). *Buddha stories*. Henry Holt. (Buddhist)

Demi. (1998). *The Dalai Lama*. Henry Holt. (Tibet)

Fisher, Leonard Everett. (1995). *Moses*. Holiday House. (Christian)

Gerstein, Mordicai. (1999). *Noah and the great flood*. Simon & Schuster. (Christian)

Highwater, Jamake. (1994). *Rama: A legend*. Henry Holt. (Hindu)

Kimmel, Eric A. (2000). *The jar of fools: Eight Hanukkah stories from Chelm* (Mordicai Gerstein, Illus.). Holiday House. (Jewish)

Oberman, Sheldon. (1994). *The always prayer shawl* (Ted Lewin, Illus.). Boyds Mills. (Jewish)

Osborne, Mary Pope. (1996). *One world, many religions: The ways we worship*. Knopf.

Rylant, Cynthia. (1986). *A fine white dust*. Bradbury. (Christian—Protestant)

Wisniewski, David. (1996). *Golem*. Clarion. (Jewish—Winner of Caldecott Medal)

Yolen, Jane, & Coville, Bruce. (1998). *Armageddon summer*. Harcourt Brace. (Religious cult experience)

Various Other World Cultures

Eboch, Chris. (1999). *The well of sacrifice*. Clarion. (Mayan)

Farmer, Nancy. (1996). *A girl named Disaster*. Orchard. (African)

Giff, Patricia Reilly. (2000). *Nory Ryan's song*. Delacorte. (Irish)

Heide, Florence Parry, & Gilliland, Judith Heide. (1990). *The day of Ahmed's secret*. Lothrop. (Egyptian)

Staples, Suzanne Fisher. (1989). *Shabanu: Daughter of the wind*. Knopf. (Pakistani)

Staples, Suzanne Fisher. (1993). *Haveli*. Knopf. (Pakistani)

Wisniewski, David. (1992). *Sundiata: Lion King of Mali*. Clarion. (Mali)

International Books Reading List

English Language Books

Aiken, Joan. (1995). *Cold Shoulder Road*. Delacorte. (UK.)

Fine, Anne. (1996). *Step by wicked step*. Little, Brown. (UK.)

Fox, Mem. (1983). *Possum magic* (Julie Vivas, Illus.). Harcourt Brace. (Australia.)

Harrison, Ted. (1993). *O Canada*. Ticknor. (Canada.)

Mahy, Margaret. (1995). *The other side of silence*. Viking. (New Zealand.)

Park, Ruth. (1980). *Playing beatie bow*. Macmillan. (Australia.)

Sutcliff, Rosemary. (1990). *The shining company*. Farrar, Straus & Giroux. (UK.)

Westall, Robert. (1991). *The kingdom by the sea*. Farrar, Straus & Giroux. (UK.)

Translated Books

Lindgren, Astrid. (1983). *Ronia, the robber's daughter*. Viking. (Sweden.)

Orlev, Uri. (1991). *The man from the other side*. Houghton Mifflin. (Israel.)

Richter, Hans Peter. (1972). *I was there*. Henry Holt. (Germany.)

Zei, Aldi. (1979). *The sound of dragon's feet*. Dutton. (Greece.)

Because women and people with disabilities historically have had minority status, we have included some recent titles dealing with the rights and accomplishments of both groups.

Women

Colman, Penny. (1995). *Rosie the riveter: Women working on the home front in World War II*. Crown.

Cushman, Karen. (1994). *Catherine, called Birdy*. Clarion.

Dash, Joan. (1996). *We shall not be moved: The women's factory strike of 1909*. Scholastic.

Fradin, Dennis Brindell, & Fradin, Judith Bloom. (2000). *Ida B. Wells: Mother of the civil rights movement*. Clarion.

Fritz, Jean. (1995). *You want women to vote, Lizzie Stanton?* Putnam.

Hansen, Joyce. (1998). *Women of hope: African Americans who made a difference*. Scholastic.

Keenan, Sheila. (1996). *Scholastic encyclopedia of women in the United States*. Scholastic.

Lauber, Patricia. (1988). *Lost star: The story of Amelia Earhart*. Scholastic.

Macy, Sue. (1996). *Winning ways: A photohistory of American women in sports*. Henry Holt.

Macy, Sue. (Ed.). (2001). *Girls got game*. Henry Holt.

McDonough, Yona Zeldis. (2000). *Sisters in strength: American women who made a difference* (Malcah Zeldis, Illus.). Henry Holt.

Meltzer, Milton M. (1998). *Ten queens: Portraits of women of power* (Bethanne Andersen, Illus.). Dutton.

Oneal, Zibby. (1990). *A long way to go* (Michael Dooling, Illus.). Viking.

Pinkney, Andrea Davis. (2000). *Let it shine: Stories of black women freedom fighters* (Stephen Alcorn, Illus.). Harcourt Brace.

Rappaport, Doreen, & Callan, Lyndall. (2000). *Dirt on their skirts: The story of the young women who won the world championship* (E. B. Lewis, Illus.). Dial.

Thimmesh, Catherine. (2000). *Girls think of everything: Stories of ingenious inventions by women* (Melissa Sweet, Illus.). Houghton Mifflin.

People With Disabilities

Bloor, Edward. (1997). *Tangerine*. Harcourt Brace. (Blindness)

Girnis, Meg. (2000). *ABC for you and me* (Shirley Leamon Green, Photog.). Albert Whitman. (Down's Syndrome)

Maguire, Gregory. (1994). *Missing sisters*. McElderry. (Physical disabilities)

McKenzie, Ellen Kindt. (1990). *Stargone John* (William Low, Illus.). Henry Holt. (Emotional disabilities)

McMahon, Patricia. (2000). *Dancing wheels* (John Godt, Photog.). Houghton Mifflin. (Physical disabilities)

Millman, Isaac. (2000). *Moses goes to school*. Farrar, Straus & Giroux. (Deafness)

Morpugo, Michael. (1996). *The ghost of Grania O'Malley*. Viking. (Cerebral palsy)

Shreve, Susan Richards. (1991). *The gift of the girl who couldn't hear*. Tambourine. (Deafness)

St. George, Judith. (1992). *Dear Dr. Bell . . . your friend, Helen Keller*. Putnam. (Deafness and blindness)

For a more comprehensive list of multicultural titles, consult the CD-ROM that accompanies this text.

▼▼▼▼▼▼▼

Children's Literature References

Aardema, Verna. (Reteller). (1975). *Why mosquitoes buzz in people's ears* (Leo Dillon & Diane Dillon, Illus.). New York: Dial.

Ada, Alma Flor. (1997). *Gathering the sun* (Simon Silva, Illus.). New York: Lothrop.

Ada, Alma Flor. (1999). *Under the royal palms: A childhood in Cuba*. New York: Atheneum.

Adler, David A. (1994). *Hilde and Eli: Children of the Holocaust* (Karen Ritz, Illus.). New York: Holiday House.

Albert, Burton. (1991). *Where does the trail lead?* (Brian Pinkney, Illus.). New York: Simon & Schuster.

Ananya, Rudolfo. (1997). *Maya's children: The story of La Llorona* (Maria Baca, Illus.). New York: Hyperion.

Ananya, Rudolfo. (1998). *Farolitos for Abuela* (Edward Gonzales, Illus.). New York: Hyperion.

Ancona, George. (1995). *Earth daughter: Alicia of Acoma Pueblo*. New York: Simon & Schuster.

Ancona, George. (1997). *Mayeros: A Yucatec Maya family*. New York: Lothrop.

Ancona, George. (1998). *Barrio: José's neighborhood*. San Diego: Harcourt Brace.

Ancona, George. (1999). *Charro: The Mexican cowboy*. San Diego: Harcourt Brace.

Andersen, Hans Christian. (1999). *The ugly ducking* (Jerry Pinkney, Reteller & Illus.). New York: Morrow.

Armstrong, William F. (1969). *Sounder* (James Barkley, Illus.). New York: HarperCollins.

Baker, Jean. (1987). *Where the forest meets the sea*. London: Walker.

Balgassi, Haemi. (1996). *Peacebound trains* (Chris K. Soentpiet, Illus.). New York: Clarion.

Barrett, Joyce Durham. (1989). *Willie's not the hugging kind* (Pat Cummings, Illus.). New York: HarperCollins.

Barton, Byron. (1987). *Machines at work*. New York: Crowell.

Begay, Shonto. (1995). *Navajo: Visions and voices across the mesa*. New York: Scholastic.

Bercaw, Edna Coe. (2000). *Halmoni's day* (Robert Hunt, Illus.). New York: Dial.

Berry, James. (1986). *A thief in the village and other stories from Jamaica*. New York: Viking.

Berry, James. (1988). *Anancy spiderman*. New York: Henry Holt.

Berry, James. (1991a). *Ajeemah and his son*. New York: HarperCollins.

Berry, James. (1991b). *When I dance* (Karen Barbour, Illus.). San Diego: Harcourt Brace.

Berry, James. (1993). *The future-telling lady and other stories*. New York: HarperCollins.

Berry, James. (1994). *Celebration song: A poem* (Louise Brierly, Illus.). New York: Simon & Schuster.

Berry, James. (1996). *Everywhere faces everywhere* (Reynolds Ruffin, Illus.). New York: Simon & Schuster.

Berry, James. (1999a). *First palm trees: An Anancy story* (Greg Couch, Illus.). New York: Simon & Schuster.

Berry, James. (1999b). *Isn't my name magical? Brother and sister poems* (Shelly Hehenberger, Illus.). New York: Simon & Schuster.

Björk, Christina. (1985). *Linnea in Monet's garden* (Lena Anderson, Illus.; Joan Sandin, Trans.). Stockholm: R&S Books.

Björk, Christina. (1999). *Vendela in Venice* (Inga-Karin Eriksson, Illus.; Patricia Crampton, Trans.). Stockholm: R&S Books.

Bontemps, Arna. (1948). *Story of the Negro*. New York: Viking.

Bradby, Marie. (1995). *More than anything else* (Chris K. Soentpiet, Illus.). New York: Orchard.

Bruchac, Joseph. (1994). *A boy called Slow* (Rocco Baviera, Illus.). New York: Philomel.

Bruchac, Joseph. (1996). *Children of the longhouse*. New York: Dial.

Bruchac, Joseph. (1997a). *Eagle song* (Dan Andreasen, Illus.). New York: Dial.

Bruchac, Joseph. (1997b). *Lasting echoes: An oral history of Native American people*. San Diego: Silver Whistle/Harcourt.

Bruchac, Joseph. (1999). The snapping turtle. In Amy Ehrlich (Ed.), *When I was your age* (pp. 162–183). Cambridge, MA: Candlewick.

Bruchac, Joseph. (2000a). *Crazy Horse's vision* (S. D. Nelson, Illus.). New York: Lee & Low.

Bruchac, Joseph. (2000b). *Sacajawea*. San Diego: Harcourt Brace.

Bunting, Eve. (1994). *Smoky night* (David Diaz, Illus.). San Diego: Harcourt Brace.

Caines, Jeannette. (1988). *I need a lunchbox* (Pat Cummings, Illus.). New York: Harper & Row.

Caines, Jeannette. (1982). *Just us women* (Pat Cummings, Illus.). New York: HarperCollins.

Choi, Sook Nyul. (1993). *Halmoni and the picnic* (Karen M. Dugan, Illus.). Boston: Houghton Mifflin.

Clark, Ann Nolan. (1952). *Secret of the Andes* (Jean Charlot, Illus.). New York: Viking.

Cobb, Vicki. (1987). *Skyscraper going up!* New York: Crowell.

Coburn, Jewell Reinhart (Reteller). (1998). *Angkat: The Cambodian Cinderella* (Eddie Flotte, Illus.). Auburn, CA: Shen's Books.

Coburn, Jewell Reinhart, with Tzexa Cherta Lee. (1996). *Jouanah: A Hmong Cinderella* (Anne Sibley O'Brien, Illus.). Auburn, CA: Shen's Books.

Crews, Donald. (1978). *Freight train.* New York: Greenwillow.

Crews, Donald. (1980). *Truck.* New York: Greenwillow.

Cummings, Pat. (1985). *Jimmie Lee did it!* New York: Lothrop.

Cummings, Pat. (1986). *C.L.O.U.D.S.* New York: Lothrop.

Cummings, Pat. (1991). *Clean your room, Harvey Moon!* New York: Bradbury.

Cummings, Pat. (1998). *My aunt came back.* New York: HarperCollins.

Cummings, Pat. (2000). *Angel baby.* New York: HarperCollins.

Curtis, Christopher Paul. (1995). *The Watsons go to Birmingham—1963.* New York: Delacorte.

Curtis, Christopher Paul. (1999). *Bud, not Buddy.* New York: Delacorte.

Dalokay, Vedat. (1994). *Sister Shako and Kolo the goat: Memories of my childhood in Turkey* (Güner Ener, Trans.). New York: Lothrop.

Disher, Gary. (1993). *The bamboo flute.* New York: Ticknor & Fields.

Dorris, Michael. (1992). *Morning girl.* New York: Hyperion.

Dorris, Michael. (1994). *Guests.* New York: Hyperion.

Dorris, Michael. (1996). *Sees Behind Trees.* New York: Hyperion.

Dorris, Michael. (1997). *The window.* New York: Hyperion.

Dorros, Arthur. (1991). *Abuela* (Elisa Kleven, Illus.). New York: Dutton.

Eisenberg, Phyllis Rose. (1992). *You're my Nikki* (Jill Kastner, Illus.). New York: Dial.

Erdrich, Louise. (1999). *The birchbark house.* New York: Hyperion.

Feelings, Muriel. (1971). *Moja means one: Swahili counting book* (Tom Feelings, Illus.). New York: Dial.

Feelings, Muriel. (1974). *Jambo means hello: Swahili alphabet book* (Tom Feelings, Illus.). New York: Dial.

Flake, Sharon G. (1998). *The skin I'm in.* New York: Jump at the Sun/Hyperion.

Fox, Mem. (1983). *Possum magic* (Julie Vivas, Illus.). San Diego: Harcourt Brace.

Fox, Mem. (1985). *Wilfred Gordon McDonald Partridge* (Julie Vivas, Illus.). Brooklyn, NY: Kane/Miller.

Fox, Mem. (1987). *Hattie and the fox* (Patricia Mullins, Illus.). New York: Simon & Schuster.

Fox, Mem. (1989). *Koala Lou* (Pamela Lofts, Illus.). San Diego: Harcourt Brace.

Fox, Mem. (1994a). *Sophie* (Aminah Brenda Lynn Robinson, Illus.). San Diego: Harcourt Brace.

Fox, Mem. (1994b). *Tough Boris* (Kathryn Brown, Illus.). San Diego: Harcourt Brace.

Fox, Mem. (1996). *Wombat divine* (Kerry Argent, Illus.). San Diego: Harcourt Brace.

Gallaz, Christophe, & Innocenti, Roberto. (1985). *Rose Blanche* (Roberto Innocenti, Illus.; Martha Conventry & Richard Craglia, Trans.). Mankato, MN: Creative Education.

Germain, Katrina. (2000). *Big rain coming* (Bronwyn Bancroft, Illus.). New York: Clarion.

Greenfield, Eloise. (1988). *Nathaniel talking* (Jan Spivey Gilchrist, Illus.). New York: Black Butterfly Books.

Greenfield, Eloise. (1991). *Night on Neighborhood Street* (Jan Spivey Gilchrist, Illus.). New York: Dial.

Grimes, Nikki. (1995). *C is for city* (Pat Cummings, Illus.). New York: Lothrop.

Guback, Georgia. (1994). *Luka's quilt.* New York: HarperCollins.

Guy, Rosa. (1991). *Billy, the great* (Caroline Binch, Illus.). New York: Delacorte.

Hamilton, Virginia. (1971). *The planet of Junior Brown.* New York: Macmillan.

Hamilton, Virginia. (1974). *M. C. Higgins, the great.* New York: Macmillan.

Hamilton, Virginia. (1983). *The magical adventures of Pretty Pearl.* New York: Harper & Row.

Hamilton, Virginia. (1985). *The people could fly: American black folktales* (Leo Dillon & Diane Dillon, Illus.). New York: Knopf.

Hamilton, Virginia. (1988). *In the beginning: Creation stories from around the world* (Barry Moser, Illus.). San Diego: Harcourt Brace.

Hamilton, Virginia. (1989). *The Bells of Christmas* (Lambert Davis, Illus.). San Diego: Harcourt Brace.

Hamilton, Virginia. (1992). *Drylongso* (Jerry Pinkney, Illus.). San Diego: Harcourt Brace.

Hamilton, Virginia. (1993). *Many thousand gone: African Americans from slavery to freedom* (Leo Dillon & Diane Dillon, Illus.). New York: Knopf.

Hamilton, Virginia. (1995). *Her stories: African American folktales, fairy tales, and true tales* (Leo Dillon & Diane Dillon, Illus.). New York: Scholastic.

Hamilton, Virginia. (1996). *When birds could talk & bats could sing: The adventures of Bruh Sparrow, Sis Wren & their friends* (Barry Moser, Illus.). New York: Scholastic.

Hamilton, Virginia. (1997). *A ring of tricksters: Animal tales from America, the West Indies and Africa* (Barry Moser, Illus.). New York: Scholastic.

Havill, Juanita. (1987). *Jamaica's find* (Anne Sibley O'Brien, Illus.). Boston: Houghton Mifflin.

Havill, Juanita. (1989). *Jamaica tag-along* (Anne Sibley O'Brien, Illus.). Boston: Houghton Mifflin.

Havill, Juanita. (1993). *Jamaica and Brianna* (Anne Sibley O'Brien, Illus.). Boston: Houghton Mifflin.

Havill, Juanita. (1995). *Jamaica and the blue marker* (Anne Sibley O'Brien, Illus.). Boston: Houghton Mifflin.

Havill, Juanita. (1999). *Jamaica and the substitute teacher* (Anne Sibley O'Brien, Illus.). Boston: Houghton Mifflin.

Hill, Anthony. (1995). *The burnt stick* (Mark Sofilas, Illus.). Boston: Houghton Mifflin.

Hoestlandt, Jo. (1995). *Star of fear, star of hope* (Johanna Kang, Illus.). New York: Walker.

Hoffman, Mary. (1991). *Amazing Grace* (Caroline Binch, Illus.). New York: Dial.

Hoffman, Mary. (1995). *Boundless Grace* (Caroline Binch, Illus.). New York: Dial.

hooks, bell. (1999). *Happy to be nappy* (Chris Raschka, Illus.). New York: Jump at the Sun/Hyperion.

Hopkinson, Deborah. (1999). *A band of angels: A story inspired by the Jubilee Singers* (Raul Colón, Illus.). New York: Atheneum.

Hoyt-Goldsmith, Diane. (1991). *Pueblo storyteller* (Lawrence Migdale, Photog.). New York: Holiday House.

Hoyt-Goldsmith, Diane. (1997). *Potlatch: A Tsimshian celebration* (Lawrence Migdale, Photog.). New York: Holiday House.

Johnson, Angela. (1989a). *Tell me a story, Mama* (David Soman, Illus.). New York: Orchard.

Johnson, Angela. (1989b). *When I am old with you* (David Soman, Illus.). New York: Orchard.

Johnson, Angela. (1990). *Do like Kyla* (James Ransome, Illus.). New York: Orchard.

Johnson, Angela. (1991). *One of three* (David Soman, Illus.). New York: Orchard.

Johnson, Angela. (1992). *The leaving morning* (David Soman, Illus.). New York: Orchard.

Johnson, Angela. (1993). *Toning the sweep.* New York: Orchard.

Johnson, Angela. (1995a). *Humming whispers.* New York: Orchard.

Johnson, Angela. (1995b). *Shoes like Miss Alice's* (Ken Page, Illus.). New York: Orchard.

Johnson, Angela. (1998). *Heaven.* New York: Simon & Schuster.

Johnson, Angela. (1999). *The wedding* (David Soman, Illus.) New York: Orchard.

Johnson, Angela. (2000). *Down the winding road* (Shane W. Evans, Illus.). New York: DK Ink.

Johnson, Dolores. (1991). *What kind of babysitter is this?* New York: Macmillan.

Johnson, Dolores. (1992). *The best bug to be.* New York: Macmillan.

Johnson, Neil. (1989). *All in a day's work: Twelve Americans talk about their jobs.* Boston: Little, Brown.

Kalman, Maira. (1999). *Next stop Grand Central.* New York: Putnam.

Keats, Ezra Jack. (1962). *The snowy day.* New York: Viking.

Keegan, Marcia. (1991). *Pueblo Boy: Growing up in two worlds.* New York: Dutton.

Kindersley, Barnabas, & Kindersley, Anabel. (1995). *Children just like me: A unique celebration of children around the world.* Foreword by Harry Belafonte. London: Dorling Kindersley.

Krumgold, Joseph. (1953). *. . . And now Miguel* (Jean Charlot, Illus.). New York: Crowell.

Kuklin, Susan. (1992). *How my family lives in America.* New York: Bradbury Press.

Lester, Julius. (Reteller). (1994). *John Henry* (Jerry Pinkney, Illus.). New York: Dial.

Llorente, Pilar Molina. (1993). *The apprentice* (Johanna H. Prins & Johanna W. Prins, Trans.). New York: Farrar, Straus & Giroux.

Low, William. (1997). *Chinatown.* New York: Henry Holt.

Magorian, Michelle. (1981). *Good night, Mr. Tom.* New York: Harper & Row.

Mahy, Margaret. (1998). *A summery Saturday morning* (Selina Young, Illus.). New York: Penguin Putnam.

Mandel, Peter. (2000). *Say hey! A song of Willie Mays* (Don Tate, Illus.). New York: Jump at the Sun/Hyperion.

Martin, Ann Matthews. (1992). *Rachel Parker, kindergarten show-off* (Nancy Poydar, Illus.). New York: Holiday House.

Maruki, Toshi. (1980). *Hiroshima No Pika* (Kurita-Bando Literary Agency, Trans.). New York: Lothrop.

Maze, Stephanie, & O'Neill, Catherine Grace. (1997a). *I want to be . . . an astronaut.* San Diego: Harcourt Brace.

Maze, Stephanie, & O'Neill, Catherine Grace. (1997b). *I want to be . . . a dancer.* San Diego: Harcourt Brace.

Maze, Stephanie, & O'Neill, Catherine Grace. (1997c). *I want to be . . . an engineer.* San Diego: Harcourt Brace.

Maze, Stephanie, & O'Neill, Catherine Grace. (1999a). *I want to be . . . a chef.* San Diego: Harcourt Brace.

Maze, Stephanie, & O'Neill, Catherine Grace. (1999b). *I want to be . . . a firefighter.* San Diego: Harcourt Brace.

Maze, Stephanie, & O'Neill, Catherine Grace. (2000). *I want to be a . . . fashion designer.* San Diego: Harcourt Brace.

McGill, Alice. (1999). *Molly Bannaky* (Chris K. Soentpiet, Illus.). Boston: Houghton Mifflin.

McKissack, Patricia C. (1988). *Mirandy and Brother Wind* (Jerry Pinkney, Illus.). New York: Knopf.

Miller, Margaret. (1993). *Can you guess?* New York: Greenwillow.

Miller, William. (1999). *Night golf* (Cedric Lucas, Illus.). New York: Lee & Low.

Mitchell, Rita Phillips. (1993). *Hue boy* (Caroline Binch, Illus.). New York: Dial.

Mochizuki, Ken. (1997). *Passage to freedom: The Sugihara story* (Dom Lee, Illus.). New York: Lee & Low.

Mora, Pat. (1997). *Tomás and the library lady* (Raul Colón, Illus.). New York: Knopf.

Morgenstern, Susie Hoch. (1998). *Secret letters from 0 to 10* (Gill Rosner, Trans.). New York: Viking.

Morris, Ann. (1989a). *Bread, bread, bread* (Ken Heyman, Photog.). New York: Lothrop

Morris, Ann. (1989b). *Hats, hats, hats* (Ken Heyman, Photog.). New York: Lothrop.

Morris, Ann. (1990). *Loving* (Ken Heyman, Photog.). New York: Lothrop.

Morris, Ann. (1992a). *Houses and homes* (Ken Heyman, Photog.). New York: Lothrop.

Morris, Ann. (1992b). *Tools* (Ken Heyman, Photog.). New York: Lothrop.

Morris, Ann. (1995). *Weddings.* New York: Lothrop.

Morris, Ann. (2000). *Families.* New York: HarperCollins.

Musgrove, Margaret. (1976). *Ashanti to Zulu: African traditions* (Leo Dillon & Diane Dillon, Illus.). New York: Dial.

Myers, Walter Dean. (1997). *Harlem* (Christopher Myers, Illus.). New York: Scholastic.

Naidoo, Beverley. (1986). *Journey to Jo'burg: A South African story* (Eric Valasquez, Illus.). New York: Lippincott.

Naidoo, Beverley. (1989). *Chain of fire* (Eric Valasquez, Illus.). New York: Lippincott.

Nelson, S. D. (1999). *The gift horse: A Lakota story.* New York: Abrams.

Nerlove, Miriam. (1996). *Flowers on the wall*. New York: McElderry.

Nye, Naomi Shihab. (1994). *Sitti's secrets* (Nancy Carpenter, Illus.). New York: Four Winds.

Nye, Naomi Shihab. (1997). *Habibi* (Raul Colón, Illus.). New York: Simon & Schuster.

Oodgeroo. (1993). *Dreamtime: Aboriginal stories* (Bronwyn Bancroft, Illus.). New York: Lothrop.

Oppenheim, Shulamith L. (1992). *The lily cupboard* (Ronald Himler, Illus.). New York: HarperCollins.

Orlev, Uri. (1984). *Island on Bird Street* (Hillel Halkin, Trans.). Boston: Houghton Mifflin.

Orlev, Uri. (1995). *The lady with the hat* (Hillel Halkin, Trans.). Boston: Houghton Mifflin.

Pinkney, Andrea Davis. (1997). *Duke Ellington: The Piano Prince and his orchestra* (Brian Pinkney, Illus.). New York: Hyperion.

Pinkney, Andrea Davis. (1999). *Silent thunder: A Civil War story*. New York: Jump at the Sun/Hyperion.

Politi, Leo. (1949). *Song of the swallows*. New York: Scribner's.

Quattlebaum, Mary. (1997). *Underground train* (Cat Bowman Smith, Illus.). New York: Doubleday.

Quintana, Anton. (1999). *The baboon king* (John Nieuwenhuizen, Trans.). New York: Walker.

Raczek, Linda Theresa. (1999). *Rainy's powwow* (Gary Bennett, Illus.). Flagstaff, AZ: Rising Moon.

Rappaport, Doreen. (2000). *Freedom river* (Bryan Collier, Illus.). New York: Jump at the Sun/Hyperion.

Reuter, Bjarne. (1994). *The boys from St. Petri* (Anthea Bell, Trans.). New York: Dutton.

Ringgold, Faith. (1991). *Tar beach*. New York: Crown.

Rotner, Shelley. (1996). *Action alphabet*. New York: Atheneum.

Rosa-Casanova, Sylvia. (1997). *Mama Provi and the pot of rice* (Robert Roth, Illus.). New York: Atheneum.

Say, Allen. (1993). *Grandfather's journey*. Boston: Houghton Mifflin.

San Souci, Robert D. (Reteller). (1989). *The talking eggs* (Jerry Pinkney, Illus.). New York: Dial.

San Souci, Robert D. (Reteller). (1995). *The faithful friend* (Brian Pinkney, Illus.). New York: Simon & Schuster.

Siegelson, Kim L. (1999). *In the time of the drums* (Brian Pinkney, Illus.). New York: Jump at the Sun.

Sneve, Virginia Driving Hawk. (1993a). *The Navajos: A first Americans book* (Ronald Himler, Illus.). New York: Holiday House.

Sneve, Virginia Driving Hawk. (1993b). *The Sioux: A first Americans book* (Ronald Himler, Illus.). New York: Holiday House.

Sneve, Virginia Driving Hawk. (1994a). *The Nez Perce: A first Americans book* (Ronald Himler, Illus.). New York: Holiday House.

Sneve, Virginia Driving Hawk. (1994b). *The Seminoles: A first Americans book* (Ronald Himler, Illus.). New York: Holiday House.

Sneve, Virginia Driving Hawk. (1995a). *The Hopis: A first Americans book* (Ronald Himler, Illus.). New York: Holiday House.

Sneve, Virginia Driving Hawk. (1995b). *The Iroquois: A first Americans book* (Ronald Himler, Illus.). New York: Holiday House.

Sneve, Virginia Driving Hawk. (1996a). *The Cherokees: A first Americans book* (Ronald Himler, Illus.). New York: Holiday House.

Sneve, Virginia Driving Hawk. (1996b). *The Cheyennes: A first Americans book* (Ronald Himler, Illus.). New York: Holiday House.

Sneve, Virginia Driving Hawk. (1997). *The Apaches: A first Americans book* (Ronald Himler, Illus.). New York: Holiday House.

Snyder, Dianne. (1988). *The boy of the three-year nap* (Allen Say, Illus.). Boston: Houghton Mifflin.

Soto, Gary. (1992). *Neighborhood odes* (David Diaz, Illus.). San Diego: Harcourt Brace.

Steptoe, Javaka (Compiler). (1997). *In Daddy's arms I am tall: African Americans celebrating fathers*. New York: Lee & Low.

Steptoe, John. (Reteller). (1984). *The story of Jumping Mouse*. New York: Lothrop.

Steptoe, John. (Adapter). (1987). *Mufaro's beautiful daughters*. New York: Lothrop.

Stolz, Mary. (1988). *Storm in the night* (Pat Cummings, Illus.). New York: HarperCollins.

Taylor, Mildred D. (1976). *Roll of thunder, hear my cry*. New York: Dial.

Thomas, Jane Resh. (1997). *Celebration!* (Raul Colón, Illus.). New York: Hyperion.

Torres, Leyla. (1993). *Subway sparrow*. New York: Farrar, Straus & Giroux.

van der Rol, Ruud, & Verhoeven, Rian. (1993). *Anne Frank beyond the diary: A photographic remembrance* (Tony Langham & Plym Peters, Trans.). New York: Viking.

Walter, Mildred Pitts. (1983). *My mama needs me* (Pat Cummings, Illus.). New York: Lothrop.

Walter, Mildred Pitts. (1990). *Two and too much* (Pat Cummings, Illus.). New York: Bradbury.

Watts, Jeri Hanel. (1997). *Keepers* (Felicia Marshall, Illus.). New York: Lee & Low.

Westall, Robert. (1989). *Blitzcat*. New York: Scholastic.

Wheatley, Nadia. (1992). *My place* (Donna Rawlins, Illus.). Brooklyn, NY: Kane/Miller.

Wild, Margaret. (1991). *Let the celebrations BEGIN!* (Julie Vivas, Illus.). New York: Orchard.

Wilder, Kathryn, (Reteller). (1995). *Forbidden talent* (Redwing T. Nez, Illus.). Flagstaff, AZ: Northland.

Williams, Sherley Anne. (1992). *Working cotton* (Carole Byard, Illus.). San Diego: Harcourt Brace.

Wong, Janet S. (1994). *Good luck gold and other poems*. New York: McElderry.

Wong, Janet S. (1996). *A suitcase full of seaweed; and other poems*. New York: McElderry.

Wood, Ted, with Wanbli Numpa Afraid of Hawk. (1991). *A boy becomes a man at Wounded Knee*. New York: Walker.

Woodson, Jacqueline. (1997). *We had a picnic this Sunday past* (Diane Greenseid, Illus.). New York: Hyperion.

Wyeth, Sharon Dennis. (1998). *Something beautiful* (Chris K. Soentpiet, Illus.). New York: Doubleday.

Yashima, Taro. (1955). *Crow boy*. New York: Viking.

Yates, Elizabeth. (1950). *Amos Fortune, free man* (Nora Unwin, Illus.). New York: Aladdin.

Yee, Brenda Shannon. (1999). *Sand castle* (Thea Kliros, Illus.). New York: Greenwillow.

Yep, Laurence. (1975). *Dragonwings.* New York: Harper & Row.

Yep, Laurence. (1993). *Dragon's Gate.* New York: HarperCollins.

Yep, Laurence. (1995). *Later, gator.* New York: Hyperion.

Yep, Laurence. (2000). *Cockroach cooties.* New York: Hyperion.

Yolen, Jane. (1967). *The emperor and the kite* (Ed Young, Illus.). Cleveland, OH: World Publishing.

Young, Ed. (1989). *Lon Po Po: A Red-Riding Hood story from China.* New York: Philomel.

Young, Ed. (1992). *Seven blind mice.* New York: Philomel.

Yumoto, Kazuki. (1996). *The friends* (Cathy Hirano, Trans.). New York: Farrar, Straus & Giroux.

Zolotow, Charlotte. (2000). *Do you know what I'll do?* (Rev. ed.). (Javaka Steptoe, Illus.). New York: HarperCollins.

▼▼▼▼▼▼▼

Professional References

Bainbridge, J. M., Pantaleo S., & Ellis, M. (1999). Multicultural picture books: Perspectives from Canada. *The Social Studies, 90,* 183–188.

Bishop, R. S. (1987). Extending multicultural understanding through children's books. In B. E. Cullinan (Ed.), *Children's literature in the reading program* (pp. 60–67). Newark, DE: International Reading Association.

Bishop, R. S. (1992). Multicultural literature for children: Making informed choices. In V. J. Harris (Ed.), *Teaching multicultural literature in grades K–8* (pp. 37–53). Norwood, MA: Christopher-Gordon.

Bogart, D. (Ed.). (1999). *The Bowker annual: Library and trade almanac* (44th ed.). New Providence, NJ: R. R. Bowker.

Boyd, C. D. (1990, June). Presentation given at the American Booksellers Association and Trade Exhibit. Las Vegas, NV. (cassette recording).

Cai, M., & Bishop, R. S. (1994). Multicultural literature for children: Towards a clarification of the concept. In A. H. Dyson & C. Genishi (Eds.), *The need for story: Cultural diversity in classroom and community* (pp. 57–71). Urbana, IL: National Council of Teachers of English.

Council on Interracial Books for Children. (1981). 10 quick ways to analyze children's books for racism and sexism. On-line at http://www.birchlane.davis.ca.us/library/10quick.htm

Darigan, D. (1991). *The effects of teaching reading aloud on elementary children's attitudes toward African Americans,* unpublished dissertation, University of Oregon, Eugene, Oregon.

Dorris, M. (1993). The way we weren't. In H. Rochman (Ed.), *Against borders: Promoting books for a multicultural world* (pp. 219–220). Chicago, IL: ALA Books/Booklist Publications.

Foster, F. S. (1987, April). *Ethnic children's literature in the schools.* Paper presented at the First Annual Conference of the Society for the Study of the Multi-ethnic Literature of the United States. Irvine, CA. (ERIC Document Reproduction No ED 291 842)

Gates, H. L., Jr. (1988). *The signifying monkey: A theory of African American literary criticism.* New York: Oxford University Press.

Graham, L. O. (2000). *Our kind of people: Inside America's black upper class.* New York: Harper Perennial.

Hansen-Krening, N. (1992). Authors of color: A multicultural perspective. *Journal of Reading, 36,* 124–129.

Horn, M. (1993, February 15). Imaging other's lives. *U.S. News & World Report, 114,* 78–81.

Just Us Books. (1995). What is an authentic multicultural book? On-line at http://:www.mpec.org/WhatIs.html

Larrick, N. (1965, September 11). The all-white world of children's books. *Saturday Review, 48,* 63–65, 84–85.

Matsuyama, U., & Jensen, K. (1990). Asian and Asian American literature for adolescents. *Journal of Reading, 33*(4), 317–320.

Pate, G. S. (1988). Research on reducing prejudice. *Social Education 52*(4), 287–291.

Pollard, K. (1999). U.S. diversity in more than black and white. *1999 United States data sheet.* On-line at http://www.prb.org/pubs/usds99.htm

Population Reference Bureau. (2001). America's diversity and growth: Signposts for the 21st century. On-line at http://www.prb.org/pubs/population_bulletin/bu55-2/55_2_Racial_Ethnic_Diversity.html

Reese, D. (1996). Teaching young children about Native Americans. *ERIC Digest.* http://ericeece.org/pubs/digests/1996/rees96.html

Reese, D. (1997). Native Americans in children's literature. In V. J. Harris (Ed.), *Using multiethnic literature in the K–8 classroom* (pp. 155–192). Norwood, MA: Christopher Gordon.

Rochman, H. (1993). *Against borders: Promoting books for a multicultural world.* Chicago: ALA Books/Booklist Publications.

Sims, R. (1982). *Shadow and substance: Afro-American experience in contemporary children's fiction.* Urbana, IL: NCTE.

Sobol, T. (1990). Understanding diversity. *Educational Leadership, 48*(2), 27–30.

Sonnenschein, F. M. (1988). Countering prejudiced beliefs and behaviors: The role of the social studies professional. *Social Education, 52*(4), 264–266.

Tiedt, P. L., & Tiedt, I. M. (1990). *Multicultural teaching: A handbook of activities, information, and resources.* Boston: Allyn & Bacon.

Vladislav, J. (Ed.). (1987). *Vaclav Havel, or living in truth: Twenty-two essays published on the occasion of the awarding of the Erasmus Prize to Vaclav Havel.* London: Faber & Faber.

Wilson, A. (1990, September 26). I want a black director. *The New York Times,* p. A 25.

Woodson, J. (1998). Who can tell my story? *The Horn Book, 74*(1), 34–38.

INFORMATIONAL BOOKS

10
C H A P T E R
▼▼▼▼▼▼▼

If you want to cover
Let's Fly

Consider as a READ ALOUD

Bald Eagle, by Gordon Morrison

Consider as a TEXT SET

A Nest Full of Eggs,
by Priscilla Belz Jenkins,
illustrated by Lizzy Rockwell

Falcons Nest on Skyscrapers,
by Priscilla Belz Jenkins,
illustrated by Megan Lloyd

From Caterpillar to Butterfly,
by Deborah Heiligman,
illustrated by Bari Weissman

How Do Birds Find Their Way?,
by Roma Gans, illustrated by Paul Mirocha

Zipping, Zapping, Zooming Bats,
by Ann Earle, illustrated by Henry Cole

ZIPPING, ZAPPING, ZOOMING BATS
by Ann Earle, illustrated by Henry Cole

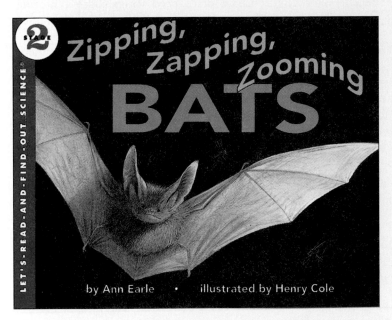

Many bats hunt insects. They eat lots of insects. Each night a bat chomps half its own weight in bugs. If you weigh 60 pounds, that's like eating 125 peanut-butter-and-jelly sandwiches every day.

Don't be scared if a bat flies past your head. It won't get into your hair. It's probably catching a juicy mosquito.

Excerpt from *Zipping, Zapping, Zooming Bats* by Ann Earle, Illustrated by Henry Cole

"I drew a picture of a bat that's looking at pretty butterflies. Some bats might eat butterflies, but this bat I drew won't. He just likes to admire the colors on their wings. My bat likes to eat beetles, mosquitoes, and grasshoppers. He is smiling because he is a friendly bat and he won't hurt you. I learned that bats have special ways of hearing. And they can change the shape of their wings, and zig zag fast to catch lots of bugs to eat. Now I know that bats are very gentle and I won't be scared if a bat flies past me. Grown-ups shouldn't be scared either. I think it would be fun to have a bat for a pet, but my mommy won't let me get one. She won't let me have Pokemon stuff either." [Taylor's drawing says "People should like bats"]

Student Response

TAYLOR

PEEPL SHUD LIC BATS

As never before, informational books provide sources for accurate and practical home and classroom instruction. Evidence that these books are finding their place in the world of children's literature includes the establishment of the Orbis Pictus Award in 1989, the prize given each year by the National Council of Teachers of English for the outstanding nonfiction book. The Orbis Pictus Award is an indication of what teachers and children have discovered about today's informational books: They not only teach us about the world but also make pleasurable reading.

But it hasn't always been that way. For 20 years, we have asked college students majoring in elementary education for their immediate personal reaction to the term *informational books.* Only a few students in 2 decades have identified informational books as either desirable or interesting. Most have responded negatively. Author Margery Facklam says many adults share this view. "Nonfiction is utilitarian—like underwear and hot water heaters—the kinds of things you *have* to buy when you'd really like caviar and cruisers. Libraries have to buy nonfiction so kids can write reports" (Facklam, 1990, p. 27). What are informational books, and what is it about them that lacked in appeal for these thousands of college students preparing to teach children and for many librarians?

To visit a classroom exploring Informational Books, please go to Chapter 10 at **www.prenhall.com/darigan**

▼▼▼▼▼▼▼

Informational Books—Fact and Fiction

Informational books are catalogued as nonfiction and, at their best, present children with current and accurate knowledge about some part of the universe—past or present. Take, for example, the text set of "Let's Fly" books that open this chapter. In Gordon Morrison's ***Bald Eagle,*** we are presented with beautiful, full-color illustrations that complement a highly readable text concerning development of two newborn eagles from fledgling to adulthood. Detailed pen-and-ink drawings and marginal notes add extra information and make this book suitable for readers of all ages. The other paperback books listed in this set focus on other flying animals such as bats and butterflies, and look at bird habitat and migration patterns. The information in these as well as in all other nonfiction is verifiable where authors cite sources from the library, letters or journals, or firsthand, observable fact. Expository writing—the form of language that explains and conveys information—is used for creating nonfiction.

As already discussed in chapter 7, fiction represents the other side of the literary coin and so, tells a story. Its purpose is not to present information but to engage readers in the lives of characters who are facing a dilemma. Fiction may be a total invention springing completely from the writer's imagination, but it may also contain accurate information from the world. Even if fiction does contain verifiable fact, that information is always secondary to the story. Narrative writing, then—the form of language used to tell a story—is used for fiction.

Nonfiction books for children are divided into two main categories, biography (see chapter 11) and informational books. The Dewey Decimal System, still used in most children's libraries, organizes all knowledge into 10 major categories, each labeled with a number from 000 to 900. Fiction is in the 800s; the rest of the numbers designate nonfiction. The content of this genre is endless: everything about history, animals, space, technology, geography, music, sports, religion, jokes, folktales, geology, cooking, and so on until all topics and subjects known to humankind are listed.

So, the question becomes, "If the contents of this genre include everything in this interesting and vibrant cosmos, why don't college students flock to informational books?" We think that at least three factors may help explain their largely negative responses.

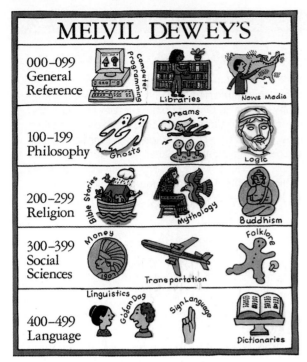

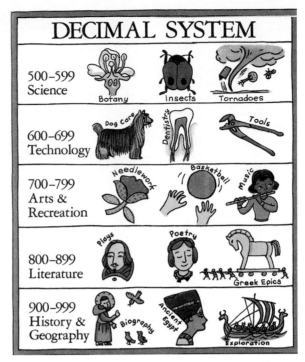

Illustrations from ***Books and Libraries,*** by Jack Knowlton. Illustrations copyright © 1991 by Harriet Barton. Used by permission of HarperCollins Publishers.

Informational Books Are Traditionally Not Used for Pleasure Reading

When a baby is born, parents who have learned that books can stimulate the intellect of their child and provide bonding experiences begin reading almost immediately to the newborn. Because of the high cost of picture books, they learn early to use the local library, where appropriate titles have been collected on shelves labeled something like "First Books," "Beginning Books," or "Easy Reading."

What is the subject matter of the hundreds of books they read to their newborn for pleasure? Almost without exception, they come from fiction. All those desirable skills, attitudes, and memories that come from early reading are typically associated with fiction. The fact is, reading nonfiction aloud for pleasure generally doesn't happen . . . but it should. According to Beverly Kobrin (1988), "By their nature, [children] are information sponges. They want to know about the real world" (p. 12).

Now, you probably already think you know where we're going with this. But, no, we're not going to ask you to throw the proverbial baby out with the bath water . . . or the fiction by reading nonfiction exclusively. In fact, we strongly suggest you continue reading lots of fiction to your children, but you might want to start interjecting a bit of nonfiction from time to time into your child's early reading diet. Later in this chapter, we provide you with the titles and tools to begin that process of adding informational books to your daily reading regimen.

A Reputation for Being Boring

A lingering impression that informational books are crammed with facts, have a few stiff, black-and-white drawings or photographs, and look more like old textbooks than anything else is pervasive (Kobrin, 1988). We readily admit that a good number of informational books published years ago did have less appeal. When we were teaching

To find out more about science trade books for children and other sources for informational books on the World Wide Web, visit Chapter 10 on the companion website at **www.prenhall.com/darigan**

BOOKMARK

INTEGRATING TECHNOLOGY: SOURCES ON THE WORLD WIDE WEB

As part of Project Primary, a collaborative project designed to help integrate student-centered science activities at the primary level in Ohio schools, Dr. Amy McClure created a section of the site that shows how to use informational books with children when exploring science. The section of the website on *science trade books for children* includes Criteria for Selecting and Evaluating Nonfiction Literature, Reading Aloud Nonfiction, Readers Theatre with K–2 Students, Mini-Lessons for Helping Children Learn from Nonfiction Texts, Semantic Mapping, Group Summarizing, and a wonderful listing of Exemplary Science Books for Grades K–3.

elementary school and asked our students to do country reports, for example, our young charges seemed to be forever returning from the school library with pathetic looks on their faces. In their hands were books that looked as if they had predated the American Civil War. No matter that the population of their country had doubled since the book was written or that its name had changed since the book's creation. Admittedly, there are some pretty pathetic books still sitting on library and classroom bookshelves.

But even from "way back then," notable exceptions delighted and rewarded readers. For example, *The I Hate Mathematics! Book,* by Marilyn Burns, from the Brown Paper School series published by Little, Brown, immediately captures a reader's attention. It feeds the reader's initial interest with a lively writing style, fascinating math games and puzzles, and unexpected connections between the young reader's world and math principles.

The good news is that a major transformation has occurred during the past 20 years: Attractive and appealing informational books are no longer the exception. In fact, no other genre in children's literature has made such dramatic advances in gaining readers' attention as has informational books. Note titles such as the *Scholastic Kid's Almanac for the 21st Century,* Eileen Christelow's *What Do Authors Do?,* and Barnabas and Anabel Kindersley's *Children Just Like Me.* These bright, colorful books beg children to sample their contents and supply readers with information not available in any textbook.

When a reader already has an interest in a topic, virtually any book with new information will be appealing to them. If second-grade Halley, for example, loves tree frogs, she will embrace almost any book she can find about these darling amphibians. But Kendra, one of her classmates, has always had a particular aversion to "those slimy little creatures." A book like Joy Cowley's *Red-Eyed Tree Frog* might just be the effective informational book to create an interest and help her overcome her dis-

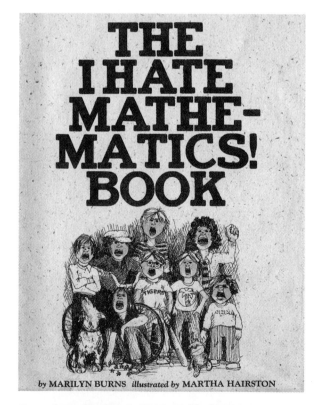

Cover from *The I Hate Mathematics! Book,* by Marilyn Burns, illustrated by Martha Hairston. Copyright © 1975 by the Yolla Bolly Press. Published and reprinted by Little, Brown & Company.

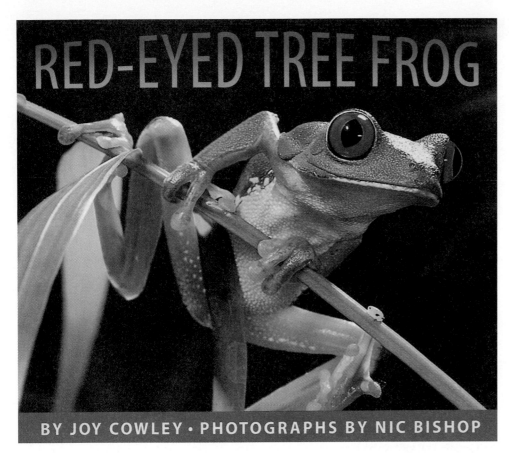

taste for the little critters. So, the purpose of these books is not merely to present data but also to stir a reader's interest in a subject.

As with *The I Hate Mathematics! Book,* what makes a book appealing to the average reader generally is not the topic but how it is handled. In the right hands, any topic is potentially exciting. Take mushrooms, for example. We suppose most kids would rather "leave" them, but in Katya Arnold and Sam Swope's *Katya's Book of Mushrooms,* vibrant watercolor illustrations bordered in Arnold's characteristic woodblock style provide children with the necessary nudge to investigate these interesting fungi. Varieties of mushrooms that the two authors mention range from ones we may be a bit familiar with such as chanterelles, puffballs, and truffles to the more exotic varieties such as stinkhorns, hawk wings, and boletes. Readers may not become mushroom eaters from reading this book, but they could very well become mushroom hunters as a result of reading this fine informational text.

Now, if a not-so-hot topic can be made interesting within the pages of a good book, the converse is also true: In the wrong hands, any topic can become deadly dull. On this point, fiction and nonfiction have much in common. Skilled writers, regardless of the genre, create interest by the smooth and artistic ways they shape their books.

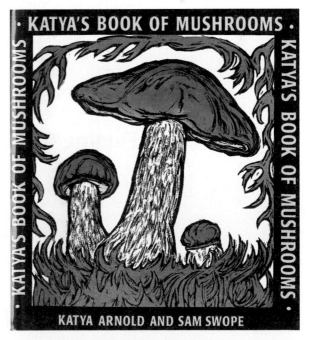

- Topic: Is the topic timely, interesting, unusual, or unique?
- Format and design: Is the book attractively designed, and does it engage our interest?
- Details: Are there compelling details that pique our interest?
- Subject choice: Does the subject for the book provide an unusual viewpoint or make fascinating comparisons?
- Precision: Is the book accurate, authentic in its perspective, and a reliable resource?

Informational Books? *Why Bother?*

One of our colleagues was startled to learn that we didn't all have the Internet at home. "How will your kids do their homework?" she worried. "How can they do their reports if you don't have access to the World Wide Web?"

"Jeez, maybe they could use *books?*" was our counter.

Surprised, she stared off into space and responded, "I never would have thought of that."

Over and over again, we have found that in the time it took for our own children to log on, find an appropriate search engine, list the request for information and start to narrow their topic, we had already located and pulled numerous books from our own shelves perfect for the task at hand. (And this was *before* we had developed the database that accompanies this text.) As a courtesy to our children's infatuation with New-Age technology, we would allow them another half hour or so of jumping around on the Net to let them find and print some information. In the end, what we had neatly stacked on a chair in the corner of the office . . . something known as books, became the major resources for their reports.

Certainly there is a lot available with respect to electronic media. Some of it is perfectly good, but we have found that much of what is out there is not particularly kid-friendly. Information is presented without much support of illustrations, figures, or maps. Suffice it to say that the going trend in the minds of our youth (and that's all the way through college-age students) is that it is easier and far more convenient to gather information and materials electronically, forsaking books altogether.

▼▼▼▼▼▼▼▼

Finding Good Informational Books

As we mentioned earlier, both the writer of fiction and the writer of nonfiction must shape their books to engage and sustain children's interest. But beyond that, they must approach their task from different viewpoints. Fiction writers create their own interesting worlds, whereas nonfiction authors report on the real one in interesting ways. Says Margery Facklam (1990):

> With fiction, you start with the embryo and build a person's life. You begin with, "What if?" and create a whole world. You work from the inside out. With nonfiction, you start with a complete life—or an invention, or an historical event, or an animal—and take it apart layer by layer to find out what made it happen, or what makes it work. You work from the outside in, like peeling away the layers of an onion. (p. 28)

The writer of compelling nonfiction does not simply collect and display facts but weaves information and details into a vision that reveals the subject in a way readers will find irresistible. Take Jim Murphy's wonderful book ***Across America on an Em-***

igrant Train, which chronicles the life of the young Robert Louis Stevenson, the author who would eventually write classics such as *Treasure Island, A Child's Garden of Verses,* and *The Strange Case of Dr. Jekyll and Mr. Hyde.* Stevenson sets off from his homeland in Scotland having to travel across the United States to California. He had been informed that the woman whom he loved was suffering from what was thought to be a fatal "brain fever." The book chronicles his trip in great detail and you would think, "This is going to be really dry." But Murphy maintains a conversational, narrative tone and intersperses facts about Stevenson and his life with diary entries, historical tidbits, and information of the day. This reads like a novel yet is pure nonfiction at its best.

▼▼▼▼▼▼▼

What Makes Good Nonfiction Informational Books?

How do adults recognize nonfiction books that will spark curiosity in elementary students? After a lot of years of experience working with children and countless hours reading nonfiction, we figure we can tell the potential of an informational book by picking it up and thumbing through it for no more than 3 minutes. But the "time on task" isn't the key here; you can do this, too. If, after that short amount of time, you are not "caught up" with the text or the format, or if you just can't say, "There is something about this book I like . . ." then chances are this will probably not grab younger readers either. In fact, we think the "catching" comes during the first minute and is generally for one of the following five reasons: (1) attractive format and design, (2) compelling details, (3) fascinating comparisons, (4) unusual subjects or viewpoints, and (5) personalized content.

Attractive Format and Design

Conventional wisdom cautions us against making a hasty decision about books. Remember the old maxim: "Don't judge a book by its cover." Yet, children will pass over books that appear boring or unrewarding in a split second. Beverly Kobrin's motto is, "Say NO to ugly books" (Kobrin, 1988, p. 59). An informational book may, indeed, have solid and thoughtful content, but if it does not look interesting, it seldom gets the chance to work on a child unless someone else points out the strengths. Two elements that give a book that chance are color and design.

Color

A common appeal of attractive books today comes from the extensive use of colored artwork and photographs. Recent technological developments in the printing process have resulted in color being less expensive than in the past and the result is a wealth of stunning illustrations and photographs that enrich nonfiction books as we have never seen before. Take, for example, Lynn Curlee's *Rushmore,* which describes in word and picture the carving of George Washington, Thomas Jefferson, Theodore Roosevelt, and Abraham Lincoln into the side of Mount Rushmore over the period of time from 1925 through 1941. Curlee's bright, crisp acrylic paintings bring to life the historic construction of one of the world's most magnificent stone carvings.

Design

In years past, nonfiction books looked more like textbooks than they do today. Books for older children were built of substantial chapters with information that seemed to drone on. Thinner informational picture books were brief and predictable. Although the content in earlier informational books was largely accurate and dependable, it did little to awaken interest or stir the reader's imagination.

Cover from ***Rushmore,***
by Lynn Curlee. Copyright
© 1999 by Lynn Curlee.
Jacket illustration © 1999
by Lynn Curlee. Reprinted
by permission of Scholas-
tic Inc.

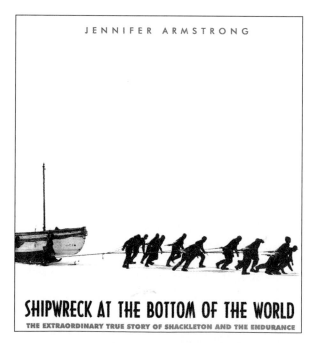

Cover from ***Shipwreck at the Bottom of the World,*** by
Jennifer M. Armstrong. Copyright © 1998 by Jennifer M. Armstrong. Jacket photograph courtesy of
The Scott Polar Research Institute. Used by permission of Crown Children's Books, a division of Random House. All rights reserved.

Currently, informational books for children are designed especially to catch the eye. Careful attention is
given to making both the cover and the contents visually
appealing. Jennifer Armstrong's book, ***Shipwreck at the
Bottom of the World: The Extraordinary True Story of
Shackleton and the Endurance,*** describing the brave
1914 expedition to Antarctica, is a perfect example. Note
the almost totally white cover. It immediately grabs our
attention, and the sepia-toned photograph, spanning the
bottom third of the cover and showing the crew struggling to drag a heavy lifeboat across the ice, leads our eye
to the title. In fact, the photo was flip-flopped from the
original that showed the men straining from the right to
the left. This directional change was wise because it very
naturally invites us to open the cover and begin to read.

Other eye-catching covers that will make books
jump off the shelves are Penny Colman's ***Corpses,
Coffins, and Crypts: A History of Burial, Mummy Mysteries: Tales from North America,*** by Brenda Z. Guiberson, and David Getz's ***Frozen Man*** and ***Frozen Girl.***

The increased use of illustrations and photographs
inside the book has further resulted in many new titles
appearing in picture book format. Large, slender volumes skillfully mix text and illustration to make the content appealing across the grades. For younger children,
Bruce McMillan's crisp photographic essays present

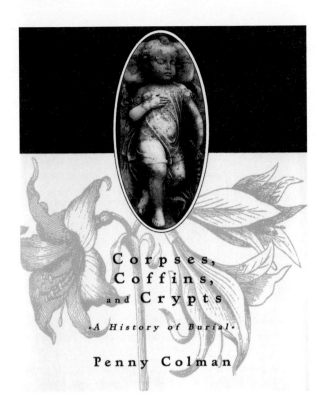

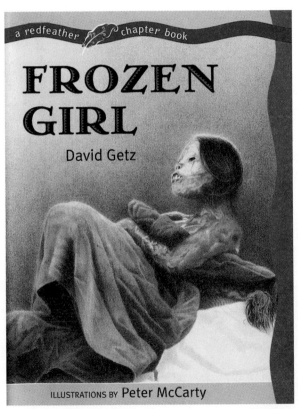

Cover from ***Corpses, Coffins, and Crypts: A History of Burial,*** by Penny Colman. Text copyright © 1997 by Penny Colman. Cover photograph © 1997 by Penny Colman. Published by Henry Holt and Company, Inc. Reprinted by permission of the publisher. All rights reserved.

Cover from ***Mummy Mysteries: Tales from North America,*** by Brenda Z. Guiberson. Copyright © 1998 by Brenda Z. Guiberson. Jacket photo copyright © 1998 by Brenda Z. Guiberson. Published by Henry Holt and Company, Inc. Reprinted by permission of the publisher. All rights reserved.

Cover are by Peter McCarty from ***Frozen Girl*** written by David Getz. illustrations copyright © 1998 by Peter McCarty. Reprinted by permission of Henry Holt and Company, LLC.

preschool and primary children with beautiful examples of engaging informational books such as his *Night of the Puffins, Puffins Climb, Penguins Rhyme,* and *Jelly Beans for Sale.*

No longer the exclusive property of the very young, many contemporary picture books are geared for the upper elementary child, and even beyond, by presenting more sophisticated views of the subject matter and dealing with it in depth. Consider, for instance, the recent books taking an interest in the Mexican fiesta *El Día de Los Muertos,* or the Day of the Dead. This three-day celebration, held yearly at the end of October and the beginning of November, remembers and honors those who have died but who return to Earth each year to share in a feast with the living. The three books by authors George Ancona, (*Pablo Remembers: The Fiesta of the Day of the Dead*), Kathryn Lasky, (*Days of the Dead*), and Diane Hoyt-Goldsmith (*Day of the Dead: A Mexican-American Celebration*) all use crisp, bright photography to illustrate their spin on this celebration. Tony Johnston, on the other hand, relies on the paintings of Jeanette Winter with equal effectiveness in her *Day of the Dead.*

One successful approach to informational books was developed in the late 1970s when Usborne Books in England targeted older readers as an appropriate audience for picture books. In Usborne picture books, content is divided into distinct topics, each with its own focus or viewpoint treated fully on one double-page spread. *The Usborne Young Cartoonist,* for instance, presents information to the young artist about drawing cartoons and caricatures. One double-page spread shows the reader first how to draw faces, detailing happy faces, sad and angry faces, as well as many other expressions. In the next spread, the reader is shown how to draw figures from different sides and viewpoints. Turn the page, and you are shown how to draw those same figures in motion.

Every double-page spread can be read independently. The text is nonsequential and appears in a bite-size cluster near each illustration rather than in full paragraphs in columns. This format invites browsing and satisfies the reader, who can begin anywhere on the page and read as little or as much as desired—finishing only one sentence, skipping randomly throughout, or consuming the entire book.

Other publishers have adopted and fine-tuned this concept. Dorling Kindersley, another British publisher (known as DK Publishing in the United States), kept the

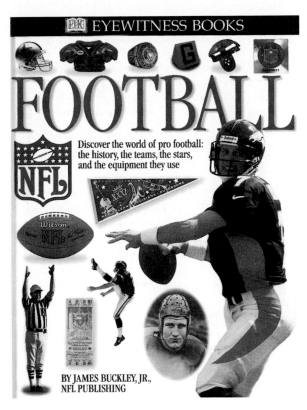

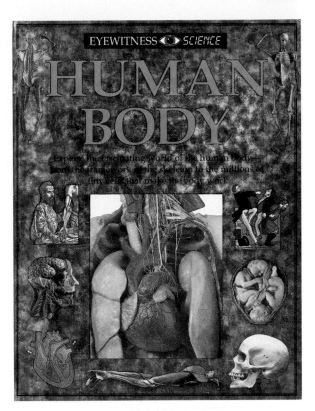

idea of the double-page spread but uses photographs almost exclusively, varying the layout, and adding more white space. The photographs of each item, trimmed at the borders like paper-doll cutouts or shot in front of a white screen, are displayed on a pure white background that highlights them dramatically. In addition, Dorling Kindersley included not only individual titles but also a number of distinct series: general information, art, science, and nature for younger readers.

With the right format and layout, books written even for the very young can capture the attention of young and old alike. *Color Zoo* is a concept book of shapes aimed at preschoolers—one shape die-cut from the center of each heavy page. By overlaying three shapes at a time, Lois Ehlert creates the face of an animal, which changes to a different animal as each page is lifted. Keeping the same set of eyes, the lion (turn the page) becomes a mouse, which (turn the page) becomes a fox. The young reader practices not only identifying the shapes but also seeing how different animal faces contain those shapes.

Compelling Details

Information becomes interesting when details are included. Details in nonfiction make the difference between showing and telling, just as they do in fiction, but in nonfiction that difference becomes the key to whether the reader will become interested in a new subject or totally ignore it. Without sufficient details, it is difficult for the reader to become involved in a subject and experience a kinship with it. Details come in a variety of types, including quotations, anecdotes, and little-known facts.

Quotations. ***The Boys' War,*** by Jim Murphy, focuses on the Civil War from the viewpoint of boys who were 16 years old or younger. It was estimated that between 250,000 and 420,000 boys served in that conflict. Imagining the glory of battle, young soldiers instead found fear and disillusionment that resulted in their loss of innocence, as is illustrated in a letter written by Private Henry Graves:

> I saw a body of a man killed the previous day this morning and a horrible sight it was. Such sights do not effect [*sic*] me as they once did. I can not describe the change nor do I know when it took effect, yet I know that there is a change for I look on the carcass of a man with pretty much the same feeling as I would do were it a horse or dog.

The words of the young soldier put a face on the weariness and desensitization described in a general way by the author.

Some informational books have little or no author narrative, using only quoted material. Over the years, noted author Milton Meltzer has provided intermediate readers with poignant and pithy oral histories that bring an era or issue to life using the voices of real people. In his *The American Revolutionaries: A History in Their Own Words, 1750–1800* and *Voices from the Civil War,* Meltzer adds only a brief paragraph or two to set the stage for a particular topic, then he presents excerpts from diaries, speeches, newspaper articles, memoirs, and letters to breathe life into and add depth to these major events in American history.

Other notable examples of this personalized view of historical events come from the brief, concise picture book *I Was Dreaming to Come to America: Memories from the Ellis Island Oral History Project.* A variety of men and women comment on their immigration to the United States that is complemented with dramatic, hand-painted collage illustrations by the selector, Veronica Lawlor. Here is a quote from Helen Cohen, a Polish immigrant who arrived in the United States in 1920 at the age of 20:

> I said I wish one day I'll be in America. I was dream to come to America . . . And I was dreaming, and my dream came true. When I came here, I was in a different world. It was so peaceful. It was quiet. You were not afraid to go out in the middle of the night . . . I'm free. I'm just like a bird. You can fly and land on any tree and you're free.

Yet another powerful oral history creates the same effect with Barry Denenberg's *Voices from Vietnam.* The stories of so many involved in this protracted conflict, ranging from political and military leaders to soldiers to the Vietnamese citizenry, are starkly told and detail how the war weighed on their lives for so many years.

Anecdotes. The power of anecdotes lies in the description of a person who has firsthand experience. Anecdotes can come from surprising sources. During the 1800s in the American South, slaves purposely were kept illiterate and consequently did not keep many written records. Despite that law, some did learn to read and write, as did many blacks who were free. In Milton Meltzer's *The Black Americans: A History in Their Own Words,* we read the words of Solomon Northrup, a free black who was kidnapped in New York and taken to New Orleans, where he was sold on the auction block. Other blacks were auctioned the same day, including a woman named Eliza who had two children. One, her son, was purchased separately.

> She kept on begging and beseeching them, most piteously, not to separate the three. Over and over again she told them how she loved her boy. A great many times she repeated her former promises—how very faithful and obedient she would be; how hard she would labor day and night, to the last moment of her life; if he would only buy them all together. But it was of no avail; the man could not afford it. The bargain was agreed upon, and Randall must go alone. Then Eliza ran to him; embraced him passionately; kissed him again and again; told him to remember her—all the while her tears falling in the boy's face like rain. . . .
>
> The planter from Baton Rouge, with his new purchase, was ready to depart.

DID YOU KNOW?

The Laura Ingalls Wilder Award is given by the American Library Association every 3 years to an author or illustrator whose body of work is deemed to have made a substantial and lasting contribution to literature for children. Milton Meltzer, whom we have just cited here, is the most recent recipient for the over 100 books he has authored during his career. For more information on this prestigious award, consult Appendix B or visit their website at www.ala.org

"Don't cry, mama. I will be a good boy. Don't cry," said Randall, looking back, as they passed out the door.

What has become of the lad, God knows. It was a mournful scene indeed. I would have cried myself if I had dared.

The human drama in this heartbreaking scene, which must have been repeated thousands of times, has greater impact because it is recounted by one who was there.

Little-known facts. Little-known facts hold elements of both mystery and discovery. There seems to be a "wow" factor associated with this sort of trivia. Rowland Morgan's book *In the Next Three Seconds . . .* offers a multitude of "wows." Did you know that in the next 3 *seconds,* 95 trees will be cut down—to make the liners for disposable diapers? Or did you know that in the same time period, Americans will throw away 3,000 aluminum beverage cans? No? Well, you might be surprised to find out that in the next 3 *minutes,* the people on the planet Earth will take enough aspirin to fill six railroad cars. In the next 3 *hours,* Americans will throw away 99 miles of plastic pens and a stack of 350,000 horizontally laid cigarette lighters, which is as high as Oregon's Mount Hood. Lengthening the time a bit more, we find that in the next 3 *days,* Britons will flush away enough toilet paper to stretch to the moon . . . and back. Do you have any idea what might happen in the next 3 weeks, 3 years, 3 decades, or 3 centuries? This fascinating and often disquieting treatise on consumption, world wildlife, health, population, and general Earthly conditions will produce many "wows."

Little-known facts also help breathe life into a certain historical period, a time of discovery, or an explanation of some phenomenon. They create interest in topics the reader often has not considered worth pursuing. For example, *Stephen Biesty's Cross-Sections: Man of War,* by Richard Platt, explores the little-known facts of life aboard a British warship during the Napoleonic era, when sailing ships ruled the world's oceans. Men on these vessels were at sea for long periods. With no refrigeration, the kinds of food were limited—salt pork, dried peas, salt beef, oatmeal, beer in sealed barrels, and hard, moldy cheese. Fresh bread was out of the question, but each ship had a store of unleavened bread called hardtack, which was something like very thick crackers. Unfortunately, weevils and black-headed maggots liked hardtack, too. Sailors inadvertently chewed them up in their bites of hardtack. The sailors found "black-headed maggots were fat and cold, but not bitter . . . like weevils." Weevils were impossible to dislodge, but the cook knew how to get rid of the black-headed maggots: He placed a raw fish on a plate on top of the hardtack. When it was completely covered with maggots, he threw the fish into the sea, replacing it as necessary until no more maggots appeared. The hardtack then was easier to eat.

The human face of the Holocaust is starkly presented in *Tell Them We Remember: The Story of the Holocaust,* by Susan D. Bachrach, and *Kinderlager: An Oral History of Young Holocaust Survivors,* by Milton J. Nieuwsma. Bachrach presents a broad view of the large-scale slaughter of the millions of people murdered by the Germans—more than 1 million of whom were children and teenagers. Bachrach adds captioned photographs of some of those who went through this horror and relates their firsthand stories. For example, Sándor Braun tells of the time when "a camp guard, promising extra food, entered his barracks holding a violin, and asked if anyone could play. Sándor and two others volunteered. The first two prisoners did not please the guard, and they were both killed before Sándor's eyes. Sándor, however, played the 'Blue Danube' waltz, and received an extra ration of food for his performance."

In Nieuwsma's book, we are provided with the individual voices of those who survived the Nazi death camps in the special section of Auschwitz known as the *Kinderlager.* Three powerful oral histories describe the events leading up to the mass deaths that transpired in that horrendous place. For instance, young Frieda Tenenbaum tells of her close encounter with death one day in October of 1944. The infamous Dr. Josef Mengele had separated the prisoners and they were waiting for hours, naked, at the doors of the *Badeanstalt* (bathhouse).

From ***In The Next Three Seconds*** ... by Rowland Morgan, illustrated by Rod and Kira Josey, copyright © 1997 by Rowland Morgan, text; illustrations copyright © 1997 by Rod and Kira Josey. Used by permission of Lodestar Books, an affiliate of Dutton Children's Books, a division of Penguin Putnam, Inc.

Finally the guard told us to get dressed. I found my shoes and gray flannel dress and put them on. Mama took my hand again, and I followed her up the stairs.

Nobody told us why we didn't go through the iron door. We just lay in our bunk and waited for the next day to come.

Years later I learned what saved us. On October 7, 1944, the *Sonderkommando,* a prisoner detail charged with cremating the corpses after gassing, blew up the ovens in Crematorium IV. Several prisoners, including a woman named Roza Robota, had smuggled dynamite in for that purpose. They were condemned to death by hanging. Before the trapdoor opened, Roza shouted in Hebrew, *"Hazak v'ematz!"* (Be strong, have courage!).

Little-known facts create interest in familiar topics as well as in new ones. In ***Zipping, Zapping, Zooming Bats,*** by Ann Earle, for example, we learn that in Bracken Cave, located in Texas, there are 20 million Mexican free-tailed bats in residence. That fact, in and of itself, is pretty amazing but even more interesting is that every night, these bats consume 250 tons of insects. Further, Earle states that the average bat eats

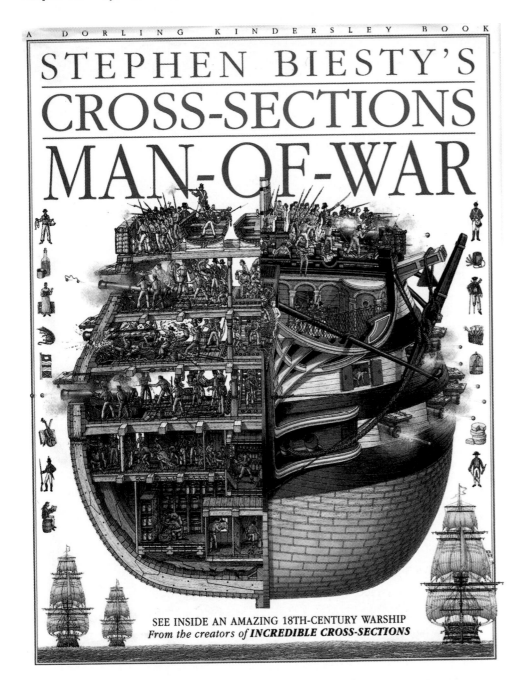

Cover from ***Cross-Sections Man-of-War*** by Stephen Biesty. Copyright © 1993 by Dorling Kindersley Limited, London. Published by permission of Dorling Kindersley.

half its weight in bugs every night. She compares that to a child who weighs 60 pounds—that's like eating 125 peanut butter and jelly sandwiches every day.

Little-known facts have such an attraction that some books are devoted exclusively to them. ***The Do-It-Yourself Genius Kit,*** by Gyles Brandreth, is a slip-cased set of four very small paperback books, each listing an assortment of odd bits of information, such as the only place in the world where one can see the sun rise over the Pacific Ocean and set in the Atlantic. Any ideas?

Although the facts in these trivia books often appear in random order, a regular sprinkling of such information spices up the classroom by giving students things to think about. Further, it acts as a stimulus to send them to additional sources to verify ideas they find incorrect. So here is a quiz: Who is basketball's top scorer? Many kids would bet on Michael Jordan or Magic Johnson. Referring to ***Scholastic Kid's Almanac for the 21st Century,*** we find that, in fact, Michael Jordan's paltry 26,710 career points is fifth behind the likes of . . . well, who would *you* guess? Who are the top scorers?

ALTERNATE TEXT SET

Always to Remember—The Holocaust

Read Aloud

The Children We Remember, by Chana Byers Abells

Text Set

Kinderlager: An Oral History of Young Holocaust Survivors, by Milton J. Nieuwsma

Tell Them We Remember: The Story of the Holocaust, by Susan D. Bachrach

Anne Frank: Beyond the Diary, by Ruud van der Rol & Rian Verhoeven

Smoke and Ashes: The Story of the Holocaust, by Barbara Rogasky

Never to Forget: The Jews of the Holocaust, by Milton Meltzer

We Remember the Holocaust, by David Adler

Okay, we'll spill the answer to you, but only for the purpose of making a point. Elvin Hayes and Moses Malone inched Jordan out with 27,313 and 27,409 points respectively. The second highest scorer was Wilt Chamberlain, with 31,419 points, and the highest scorer of all time was the great Kareem Abdul-Jabbar, with a whopping 38,387 points. Today's elementary child was born well after Wilt the Stilt retired in 1973 and even after Kareem's career was over in 1989. For that reason alone, they may not know much about these great players of the past—but, guess what? Information about both is *also* housed in these wonderful nonfiction books. Just a small question like this and the subsequent search for the answers reminds us just how broad and interesting this world is.

Fascinating Comparisons

Okay class, take out a piece of paper. It is time for another quiz.

> Question #1: If you were to count from 1 to 1 million, how long do you think it would take you? How long would it take you to count from 1 to 1 billion? How about to 1 trillion?
>
> Question #2: If you put a million goldfish in a bowl, how big would the bowl have to be? How big a bowl would you need to hold a billion? How about a trillion?
>
> Question #3: If you had $100 in pennies and you had to stack them up, how tall would that stack be?

You may want to search the CD-ROM that accompanies the text for books by Aliki, Jim Arnosky, Marilyn Burns, Gail Gibbons, or Seymour Simon.

Ready to learn the answers? They are easily found in David Schwartz's trio of books, *How Much is a Million?*, *If You Made a Million,* and *On Beyond a Million.* (We have also placed them at the end of the chapter on p. 366 just in case you don't want to get out of bed and head to the library.) Schwartz uses fascinating comparisons to bring these huge numbers into perspective.

Schwartz has used the idea of comparisons as the entire focus in his book *If You Hopped Like a Frog.* Here he takes many common animals and then compares their capabilities and capacities to those of us humans. For instance, if *you* could hop like a frog, you would be able to "jump from home plate to first base in one mighty leap." "If you swallowed like a snake . . . you could gulp a hot dog thicker than a telephone pole." "If you scurried like a spider . . . you could charge down an entire football field

in just two seconds." A concise afterword provides the more sophisticated reader with additional information about Schwartz's claims.

Human beings are not always able to assimilate abstract concepts or those that are particularly complex. Topics and issues such as kindness, the plight of endangered species, divorce, war, digestion (or indigestion for us oldsters), and enormous numbers become more understandable when comparisons bring the fuzzy areas into sharp focus. Working in much the same manner as metaphor or simile, fascinating comparisons create instant and powerful images. Surely, you will see the hinged jaw of a snake in an entirely different way after reading the amazing comparison Schwartz has conjured up.

Seymour Simon, a former science teacher who has written over 100 informational books for young readers, frequently uses comparisons to clarify his content. Let's face it, light-years and the gargantuan numbers used in astronomy are often hard to get a handle on, but Simon's use of comparison helps make these figures far more understandable. In **Saturn,** he mentions that the ringed planet is much larger than Earth. How much larger? "If Saturn were hollow, about 750 planet Earths could fit inside." In **Destination: Jupiter,** a more recent book in this series and written 13 years later, he wisely continues with a parallel comparison. As we know, Jupiter is the largest of the planets in our solar system. He states, "If Jupiter were hollow, more than thirteen hundred planet Earths could fit inside."

Yet another helpful comparison comes in his book **The Universe.** How do we fit within the planetary scheme of things? Simon asks us to think of our "complete" address showing where we live—within the universe. It might look like this:

Your name
Street, city or town, zip code, country
Planet Earth
Solar System
Milky Way Galaxy
The Universe

This provides the young reader (in fact, all of us) with a sequential listing of our ever expanding place in the cosmos. Simon completes this thought by mentioning, "There's no zip code for the universe, of course, but if there was one, it might be ∞—the symbol for infinity."

Fascinating comparisons can also be found in the illustrations as well as the text. Note Linda Vieira's book **The Ever-Living Tree: The Life and Times of a Coast Redwood,** illustrated by Christopher Canyon, as a notable example. Vieira provides information about the growth of this giant, long-lived tree and at the same time inserts historical events that occurred along its 2,500-year life span. This clever blend of science with history offers the reader a fresh perspective that provides an incredible context for understanding the growth of these ancient behemoths. For example, even the endpapers present a pictorial bar graph comparing age and size as this giant tree grows from a 30-foot seedling to a towering 300-foot giant. As we begin reading the body of text, Vieira notes the friendly conditions present on the North American continent for the redwood's growth. To provide a historical context, Vieira discusses Alexander the Great who, also at the time the redwood was a seedling, was perfecting the use of the catapult for battle. Illustrator Canyon very cleverly shows Alexander, a line of elephants he used as beasts of burden, and his troops marching across the bottom of the page.

Some of the other landmark events during this tree's life come at a mere 539 years old when The Great Wall in China was being built, and later at the mature age of 2,000, Christopher Columbus was traveling across the Atlantic in search of a trade route to China. This play between the growth of the tree and the historical happenings around the world as it matures puts the development of this ancient treasure into perfect perspective.

The digestive process is made clearer in the classic ***Blood and Guts*** by Linda Allison's use of a simile. She notes that after food leaves the stomach as "a mashed-up, milky liquid," it travels on into the small intestine,

> . . . a long, curly tube with a shaggy lining. It is equipped with its own set of digestive juices for final food breakdown. The walls of this tube hug and push the food along in an action called peristalsis (perry STAL sis).
>
> Peristalsis puts the squeeze on food muscles in the intestinal wall. They contract and relax, forcing the food around and through. It's the same way you might squeeze a tube of toothpaste.

The wonder of food moving through intestines becomes clearer by comparing the process to moving toothpaste in a tube.

Unusual Subjects or Viewpoints

Some subjects are so unusual that they offer appeal simply by being presented. Often the title of the book treating an unusual subject or viewpoint is enough to entice readers to pick it up.

> ***Toilets, Toasters & Telephones: The How and Why of Everyday Objects,*** by Susan Goldman Rubin
>
> ***Gold: The True Story of Why People Search for It, Mine It, Trade It, Steal It, Mint It, Hoard It, Shape It, Wear It, Fight and Kill for It,*** by Milton Meltzer
>
> ***Animals Eat the Weirdest Things,*** by Diane Swanson
>
> ***Now You See It, Now You Don't: The Amazing World of Optical Illusions,*** by Seymour Simon

Books on unusual subjects generally appeal to a wide range of readers. Michelle Byam's ***Arms and Armor*** is an Eyewitness picture book study of selected weapons and protection against weapons humans have developed since earliest times. The photographs and text are simple enough to appeal to the middle grades and complete enough to satisfy adults.

Stone axes are no surprise, nor are the variety of swords and knives used throughout history. But Byam presents some unusual inventions we have used, and continue to use, to hurt each other. For example, the African throwing knife from Zaire is an odd arrangement of sharp edges and five irregularly placed points with one handle. "When thrown, the knife turns around its center of gravity so that it will inflict a wound on an opponent whatever its point of impact." Another unusual weapon is the Apache pistol used around 1900 in Paris. It has a six-shot cylinder but no barrel, so it was accurate

Introducing:

TEACHING IDEAS

Children in your class may want to investigate some natural oddity and write their own informational book about it. For example, they may read a fact like this one from Seymour Simon's ***Gorillas:*** "Chest beating is a way a gorilla shows his strength while avoiding an actual attack." This may prompt a research project for a child to see what other animals bluff like the gorilla or what animals use bombastic tactics to scare away their adversaries.

A CONVERSATION WITH. . .

David M. Schwartz

I was outside, looking up on a clear night at a sky full of stars, and having a flashback to my childhood when I used to find the stars so awesome. That was back in the days when "awesome" actually meant something—filled with awe or capable of filling someone with awe—whereas now it means anything better than pretty good. I found the stars to be awesome because I'd contemplate the distances to them, you know. How even the closest star to our solar system had to be measured in light-years. While light traveled 186,000 miles per second, in 1 second light could travel the distance that was more than seven times around the earth. One second—and the closest star was 4.2 light-years from us! The thought that stars were so far and that they were so big!

All that stuff came back to me on that night. I thought about how kids don't really fill themselves with awe. One of my favorite activities as a child was to find out information that would boggle my brain and then just think about it and let it sink in and just revel in that feeling of amazement. I didn't know too many kids who did that and I thought, well, maybe I can write a book that kind of brings some of those feelings back to kids. So that was **How Much is a Million?**

I could tell you a little story about the origin of most of my books. Here's one: **If You Hopped Like A Frog** came out of my childhood in a certain way. When I was a kid, people would say if you could be any animal, what animal would you like to be? I usually would say, "I'd like to be a frog," partly for the shock value, but partly also because I truly was fascinated by the hopping ability of frogs. I would ride my bike as a child of maybe 10 or so, ride my bike to this pond not too far from my house and sit on the shore

and watch the frogs jump. I would be amazed at how they could hop so far, compared to their own size. At one point I figured it out proportionately that a frog was hopping 20 times its own length. And then I imagined applying that to my own body proportions. I figured that a 4-foot-6 child could hop, if he hopped like a frog, 90 feet— which is the distance from home plate to first base. So, I thought "wouldn't that be great?" On the baseball field I could use a little extra hop.

When I was at a school, I showed a picture of a frog hopping to the group of teachers, and I worked out the math. I told them how you simply look at this frog and say it hops 5 feet—end of story. Or, you could say it's 3 inches long and it hops 5 feet, so how many of its own lengths is it hopping? Then you could do the math—and it's hopping 20 times its own length. Then I pondered, "what if you could hop like a frog? What if you could hop 20 times your own length?" One of them came up to me afterwards and said, "You know I love that example of the frog; you should do a book like that."

Now, normally people come up to me tell me they have a great idea for a book I ought to write and I usually listen politely and say, "That is a great idea! But, you know, you ought to write that book." But this time, after listening to the idea, instead I said, "Okay, thank you. I think I will." And I did. The dedication in the book is "To all the creative math-loving teachers who give me inspiration and especially to Kim Shepherd of Dallas, who gave me this idea."

---

only at point-blank range. Instead of a barrel, it sports a folding dagger ideal for stabbing, and the pistol grip is a set of brass knuckles—three weapons in one.

The unusual topics described in these new informational titles are just as engaging to adults as they are to children. In fact, you wonder if many of the topics were chosen as the result of an adult's interest and subsequent investigation—then later made accessible to children. At first glance, a book like George Ancona's *Cutters, Carvers, & the Cathedral* or Charlotte Foltz Jones's *Yukon Gold: The Story of the Klondike Gold Rush* would appear to be more of an adult topic of interest. However, the simplicity with which the subjects are handled and the engaging nature of the books easily draw children in.

Another adult author successful with children is David Feldman, who asks questions and finds answers about why the world is as it is. His series of 11 books (for example, *How Do Astronauts Scratch an Itch?*) explores what he calls "imponderables,"

To read more of this Conversation with David M. Schwartz, please visit Chapter 10 on our text's companion website at **www.prenhall.com/darigan**

ALTERNATE TEXT SET

Books by David Feldman

Read Aloud

How Do Astronauts Scratch an Itch?

Text Set

Do Penguins Have Knees? An Imponderables Book

How Does Aspirin Find a Headache? An Imponderables Book

What Are Hyenas Laughing At, Anyway? An Imponderables Book

Why Do Clocks Run Clockwise? An Imponderables Book

Why Do Dogs Have Wet Noses? An Imponderables Book

and during the exploring, teaches children as a by-product how to observe, question, and discover. For example:

> Why do some ice cubes come out cloudy and others come out clear?
> Why don't birds tip over when they sleep on a telephone wire?
> How does the Campbell Soup Company determine which letters to put in their alphabet soup? Is there an equal number of each letter? Or are the letters randomly inserted in the can?
> Why don't crickets get chapped legs from rubbing their legs together? If crickets' legs are naturally lubricated, how do they make that sound?
> What flavor is bubble gum supposed to be? Why is bubble gum usually pink?
> Why do we have to close our eyes when we sneeze?

Personalized Content

A good informational book is not just a bucket of facts but a personal tour of a subject. The format and design, the details, the comparisons, and even the topics reflect the individuality of the author and illustrator. What we have not mentioned is that authors of good informational books teach the same way good classroom teachers teach: They examine a subject, think about things, make discoveries, and then share a personal view about what they have learned. Skilled authors of informational books personalize content using the techniques already described, but they also may provide readers with a new, personal perspective on old subjects and may take readers along on an eyewitness journey.

New Perspective

When subjects have been around a while, particularly as a part of the curriculum, they sometimes take on a familiarity that produces yawns. Quality informational books prove those prejudices groundless, reminding us it is not the subject that is dull but the presentation. For instance, the eight parts of speech are still taught in most classrooms, although learning about them generally does not rivet students to their seats. Ruth Heller has created a number of picture books to present the parts of speech, using polished meter and stunning illustrations to introduce them in a fresh way. The following text comes from the first 10 pages of ***A Cache of Jewels and Other Collective Nouns.***

A word that means a collection of things,
like a
CACHE
of jewels
for the crowns of kings . . .
or a BATCH of bread all warm and brown,
is always called a COLLECTIVE NOUN.
a SCHOOL of fish
a GAM of whales
a FLEET of ships
with
purple sails . . .

From **A Cache of Jewels and Other Collective Nouns** by Ruth Heller, copyright © 1987 by Ruth Heller. Used by permission of Grosset & Dunlap, a division of Penguin Putnam, Inc.

You may want to refer to chapter 4, "Poetry," or the CD-ROM that accompanies this text for a complete listing of Ms. Heller's books in this series.

In **Bridges Are to Cross,** by Philemon Sturges, we learn that the reason for bridges goes well beyond the simple notion that they are used to "get to the other side." In this beautiful book of paper-cut illustrations by Giles Laroche, we learn not only about the different varieties of bridges whose construction was driven by function but also of bridges from around the world that were castles, forts, aqueducts, and canals, to name only a few. Bright double-page spreads contain boxed information in simplified form noting the bridge, its location, and when it was built. Below this is a more detailed paragraph offering further insights about the structure. Describing the Brooklyn Bridge constructed in 1883, Sturges states, "This bridge soars across the across the East River on woven webs of wire." Specific information includes, "Since the East River is not surrounded by cliffs, stone towers were built to hold the twisted steel wire cables. Here it is shown as it would have looked in the 1880s, when its towers were among the tallest structures in the city."

The human body is the same today as it has been for thousands of years, but Jonathan Miller's views in **The Human Body** show its characteristics in a new light. As we open the pop-up book, the front of a skull snaps into shape about 5 inches off the page, the left half showing bone and the right half a variety of muscles. Anatomically accurate but looking slightly macabre, the jaw moves up and down when the cover is wiggled, and readers can peer down from the open top of the skull to locate the brain. Using pull tabs, slides, and folds, additional pages show how sounds vibrate the bones in the ear, demonstrate how fibers slide over one another when muscles flex, and allow readers to lift all torso muscles to reveal the stomach and ribs, raise the ribs to expose the lungs, and fold back the lungs to show the heart.

First-Person Accounts

Another form of personalized content is the first-person account. Reminiscent of the old Jacques Cousteau undersea programs on Public Television, the author actually experiences something and then writes about it. Often written in the first person, the resulting book has the feel of a personal tour: "As we near the sunken ship, we swim past a school of friendly groupers . . . " These narratives are not a recounting of information but an experience where reader and author seem to discover together. For instance, we watch Bianca Lavies as she tries to improve the soil in her home garden by making a compost pile. But what is garbage to Bianca Lavies becomes a banquet for a host of organisms from microscopic bacteria to earthworms and snails, an army of new guests she photographs and describes in **Compost Critters.** The human element and progressive changes she witnesses in her compost pile personalize the way nature creates rich soil.

The same power of personal story is in **Buried in Ice: The Mystery of a Lost Arctic Expedition,** by Owen Beattie and John Geiger. The authors take the reader on their journey to discover what happened to two ships chasing after the Northwest Passage in 1845. From a frozen and perfectly preserved crewman buried on an island in the

Canadian Arctic, the authors determined the fate of the ships and their crews. The reader is present as the mystery slowly unravels, and the authors discover that the crew may have perished from lead poisoning due to a newly developed canning process for preserving rations in the mid-1800s.

In *The Search for the Right Whale,* Scott Kraus and Ken Mallory document in text and photographs the work of a team of scientists from the New England Aquarium in Boston to determine migration patterns of a small species of whales called right whales. Using a ship and helicopter, they followed a pod of whales they could identify by their individual markings caused by whale lice. The marine biologists successfully determined when and where the whales traveled, and the reader is present for all the discoveries.

Finally, Wilborn Hampton reports in his *Kennedy Assassinated! The World Mourns* the story he followed as a cub reporter with the United Press International in Dallas, Texas during the aftermath of the assassination of U.S. President John F. Kennedy. This unique story provides an inside view of what went on during those calamitous days following one of the most momentous events in recent history.

▼▼▼▼▼▼▼

Considerations for Choosing Quality Informational Books

The basis of all informational books is accuracy. The books exist to introduce the reader to the world or to present something particular about it, so the content must be factual and dependable. But in the past, authors and editors seemed not to be as concerned about absolute accuracy as they are today—factual liberties in informational books for children were winked at. In the name of the readers' immaturity or the need to capture interest, elements were allowed in nonfiction that technically were not accurate. Most compromises involved making animals and objects more human-like. Wild animals in a life-cycle book might have been given names, for instance, making them seem more like pets than denizens of their own world. Or motives were attributed to animals that made them seem human (anthropomorphism): "The deer *wondered* when the snow would melt so he could find grass to eat."

Caution Against Anthropomorphism

Today's nonfiction books for young readers are less likely to take liberties with the facts. Yet, because of their creativity, artistry, and the author's need to find an appealing angle to pique children's interest, some books may seem to slip into the domain of anthropomorphism, where the author gives human characteristics to animals or inanimate objects. Often these books are not even intended to be nonfiction, though outwardly they give every appearance of being so. Because they speak with such authority and are chock full of facts, they can be misplaced in this category. Take Pam Conrad's book, *Call Me Ahnighito,* which describes the discovery, excavation, and subsequent move of a great meteorite from Greenland, where it landed, to a museum in New York City. Conrad describes the point when the huge stone had been wrenched from the ground, after which it declares, "What joy I felt, free at last!" Further it (the meteorite) states, "I hoped these new people would take me with them . . . but . . . they abandoned me." Well, as much as we enjoyed this story, as accurate as the details are, and as much as we love this gifted and talented author, this book—if used as an informational reference—inches right to the edge of being misleading.

In *Baby Lemur,* by Susan Hellard, we are presented with what appears, at first glance, to be a nonfiction book. But a number of "tip-offs" almost immediately make us think otherwise. First, we find that the baby lemur has a name—Liam. Second, there is dialogue between mother and child. Eventually, we learn that the mother thinks it is

To find out more about Fred Bortz and other authors and illustrators on the World Wide Web, visit Chapter 10 on the companion website at **www.prenhall.com/darigan**

BOOKMARK

INTEGRATING TECHNOLOGY: AUTHORS ON THE WORLD WIDE WEB

Fred Bortz, author of **To The Young Scientist: Reflections on Doing and Living Science** and other award-winning science tradebooks, has created an extensive and informative website, *Dr. Fred's Place,* related to his own and other authors' books on science and technology. This well-designed site includes a science project discussion board, a section entitled "Ask Dr. Fred," information about his books, and recommendations of other science-related tradebooks. The website is part of the Cherry Valley Books, so the books mentioned can be ordered directly from the site.

time for him to do things for (him)self and when the other little lemurs want Liam to play games such as "Pull the Tail" and "Hunt the Berry," he hangs back, clinging to his mother's side. In the end, of course, he makes the leap into becoming more grown-up and independent while knowing all the time that his mother will always be there for him. This charming little book uses lemurs as the vehicle to personify growing up and for the preschool reader but, like Conrad's text just mentioned, it should not be mistaken for an informational text.

Check for Accuracy

Readers can often recognize the accuracy of an informational book by looking at the author's notes and introductions, references, acknowledgments, the author's credentials, and the basic book format. Scrutinizing these features can provide the reader with an insight into how much (or little) the author did his or her homework.

ALTERNATE TEXT SET

Books by James Cross Giblin

Read Aloud

The Century That Was: Reflections on the Last One Hundred Years

Text Set

The Mystery of the Mammoth Bones: And How It was Solved

Be Seated: A Book About Chairs

From Hand to Mouth: Or, How We Invented Knives, Forks, Spoons and Chopsticks & The Table Manners to Go With Them

The Riddle of the Rosetta Stone

The Truth About Unicorns

When Plague Strikes: The Black Death, Smallpox, AIDS

A CONVERSATION WITH . . .

James Cross Giblin

For the past year, I've been working on an autobiography for Adolf Hitler for ages 10 and up that will be the same length as my Charles Lindbergh biography. It has been a very demanding project. Exciting because it takes me back to my own boyhood. I was 8 when we got into World War II and 12 when it ended, and so I remember vividly hearing my parents talking about Stalingrad and I remember how shocked and upset I was by the first photos in *Life* magazine of the concentration camps when they were liberated in the spring of 1945. Those photos were really horrible for an impressionable 11-year-old. I remember asking my mother, "Are these people?" I couldn't believe the piles of corpses I saw in the photos of Auschwitz.

The best ideas for a writer come from some deep source within that you want to explore for your own sake, first of all, and then for your readers. For me, all my books have been searches for discovery. I didn't know anything about the history of the Black Death 'til I wrote **When Plague Strikes.** So, I'm kind of a self-taught historian. I figure I'm a good person to write about complex subjects or complex people for the young people my books are aimed at because in a way, I'm discovering the subject and then trying to bring it to life for them. So a writer of nonfiction for children has to be a translator in a way, a translator of difficult material. Research is like an iceberg: Only a little bit of it shows on the surface. But as I have also said before, I think you can feel its presence even if it doesn't go on and on for pages. It lends authority to the material.

You almost have to be an actor when you are writing nonfiction for kids. When I was a kid, I did quite a bit of acting and I know when I was working on Lindbergh, I kept trying to think, "Well, if I were in a play acting the part of Charles Lindbergh, what would be the core? What would be the thing that I would fix on to try to build the character around?" And I decided that throughout his life it was his stubbornness. He was a very stubborn man. When he decided to do something, whether it was to fly to Paris or to speak out for that controversial isolationist policy at the beginning of World War II, he was stubborn to the point where he wouldn't listen to anybody else. And sometimes that had a very positive result and sometimes it didn't.

The author of nonfiction must translate the material for young readers and then, just as important, it must excite them. I don't think it should just sit there on the page being quietly informative. It doesn't stick with a reader.

Once I've made the overall plan for my book, I bury myself in books. I wish you could see my office. I try to buy the books myself rather than photocopy them at the library. I like to be free to mark in the margins and thoroughly deface some books when I'm working on something. Most of my books are histories. I don't do a lot of interviewing. If I were writing about space exploration I'd want to interview the people involved.

There is one last thing that I feel brings nonfiction to life, and that is the specific details and the telling anecdotes that relate to the topic. For example, Hitler's last public appearance was to pin a medal on a 14-year-old boy who had thrown a grenade at a Russian tank. The boy had been brought down into the bunker and this was the last, what we would now call a photo op, for Hitler. He pinned the medal on the boy and an attaché said the boy was so excited to meet Hitler but he was also so exhausted that as soon as the medal was pinned on him he fell over in a corridor of the bunker sound asleep and they had to carry him out. I love that story and will include it in the book. I found that to be so indicative of the state of not only Hitler but Germany at the time, and that is the kind of thing I am always looking for—I think all good writers do.

To read more of this Conversation with James Cross Giblin, please visit Chapter 10 on our text's companion website at **www.prenhall.com/darigan**

As we mention in chapter 7, "Historical Fiction," however, children tend to avoid author notes like the plague. The fact of the matter is that a quick glance often provides the student with the context of the particular topic and an idea of the degree of the research and sources that the author culled in developing the book. For example, in her book *Growing Up in Coal Country,* Susan Campbell Bartoletti notes that she was prompted to discover more about the stories of the coal mining Pennsylvanians when she heard her husband's grandparents discussing it at the dinner table.

Massimino's and Pearl's stories fascinated me, and I wanted to hear more. I took a tape recorder and sought out stories from other relatives. I placed notices in newspapers and church bulletins and found other people who invited me into their living rooms and told me their stories.

> I read old mining inspection records, newspapers, magazines, and books. In museum archives, I searched through boxes of interview transcripts and listened to recorded interviews. I studied old photographs.

Bartoletti's introduction tells us that she sought out both personal stories and documented information, but further it gives us an overall sense that her subject was well researched and that we can trust her data.

An author's listing of references can be very helpful in determining whether or not the book has been well researched. For instance, Milton Meltzer is meticulous in his investigation and lists references in all of his books. In his book *Weapons & Warfare: From the Stone Age to the Space Age,* he notes almost two dozen books in his bibliography; students can use this inventory to do further research or, at the least, rest assured that the author did his work.

Author acknowledgments often lead the reader to understand where the research was done, further adding to the authenticity of the work. We like to think that it is not really as important to look at *who* the author is thanking—we wonder who all of these people are, anyway—as it is to know *where* those people thanked come from. For example, in Charlotte Foltz Jones's book *Yukon Gold: The Story of the Klondike Gold Rush,* which we mentioned earlier, a glance at the acknowledgments shows that she was helped by people in the libraries of Alaska, Denver, Vancouver, and the University of Washington. Further, the acknowledgments include the Western History Department, the Museum of History and Industry, the National Park Service, and the Washington State Historical Society. With input from these "gold rush" centers, one can infer that careful research was carried out.

Currency of the Information

Children may be confused by references to the dinosaur called the *Brontosaurus* or by an unusually low number of rings attributed to Saturn. For the times in which certain nonfiction texts were written, it is quite likely the information they present was, indeed, considered accurate. But research and scientific study march on, and books do become dated with time. Does that mean we should throw them away? We always find it hard to toss away books. Better to use them as a springboard for comparison and further research.

Author's Credentials

Regarding the author's credentials, we would immediately want you to wonder, "Who is this person, anyway?" What makes him or her "the" person to write a book such as this—at least, "a" person to write it? And can his or her work be trusted? Answers to these questions may first come from the author biography on the dust jacket of the book. What makes Sandra Markle, for instance, an expert when it comes to writing a nonfiction book about the swift-swimming, slithery reptile in her book *Outside and Inside Alligators*? Glancing at the back flap tells us that she has authored more than four dozen nonfiction books. *So far, so good.* She is a former elementary science teacher. *Now we're talking; a teacher!* Further, she has been a consultant on science specials at CNN and has published classroom materials for the Children's Television Workshop. Finally, she has directed the development of an interactive science curriculum that is available on Internet. *Okay, we say, she has a pretty good science track record.* Any more questions? Well, we might wonder where she received her academic training. How far did she get? Is she one of *those* Ph.D. types? All in all, we should feel pretty comfortable about her work given these credentials.

Resources Within the Book

Another way to tell how much an author puts into a book is to note the book's basic format. For example, does the book contain a table of contents, an index, a glossary, or additional appendixes? Now, we caution you that not having one or all of these doesn't make a book bad from the start; there are, of course, many variables involved in a book's organization. But if we want our young readers to have the freedom to peruse the book for facts that are interesting to them or for a report they are doing, an index would be very helpful. If there are words that are likely to be new to the student because of the content or that are in some way difficult to pronounce, a glossary comes in very handy. These features all make up a sound piece of nonfiction.

In the end, the truth is that the average reader—even an adult reader—doesn't know for certain that all the information in any particular children's informational book is correct. And taking time to check the accuracy with other sources is laborious. We are, after all, reading the book to learn this information. If you are concerned about a book's accuracy, we would encourage you to cross-reference your sources to gain a consistent picture of the topic you are investigating.

So the bottom line for us is that in today's world of publishing, knowing how careful authors, illustrators, and editors are when publishing a book, we feel pretty comfortable that everybody has done their appropriate homework to make a book that is accurate and error free. Certainly, there are instances where mistakes slip through or inaccuracies get printed, but given a wary eye, we maintain the position to take the word of the author until other evidence shows us we should not.

▼▼▼▼▼▼▼

Types of Informational Books

The bulk of children's informational books produced today focuses on a single subject in a straightforward manner. Table 10-1 lists a few examples.

 Using the database accompanying this text, you may want to choose a topic of interest to you and trim the list to meet your own classroom needs.

The depth of detail varies according to the format; certainly a picture book covers less ground than a text that is formatted as chapter book. The target audience also influences how specifically a subject is covered. When discussing penguins, for example, you would want to use a simple book like Bruce McMillan's **Puffins Climb, Penguins Rhyme** for toddlers, but for older children, you would want to provide them with the details in Gail Gibbons's **Penguins!** or Dorothy Hinshaw Patent's **Looking at Penguins.**

Although all types of informational books tend to keep focused and stick to one subject, similar approaches, presentation, or treatments occur frequently enough that categories begin to emerge. The following categories of informational books can appear in either picture book or chapter book format: activity books (craft, how-to, experiment), concept books, journals and interviews, photo essays, pop-ups, reference books, series, social histories, and survey books.

Topic	Title and copyright	Author
animal noses	**Bizarre & Beautiful Noses**	The Santa Fe Writer's Group
plagues	**When Plague Strikes: The Black Death, Smallpox, AIDS**	James Cross Giblin
prehistoric cave paintings	**Painters of the Caves**	Patricia Lauber
tracking whale migrations	**The Search for the Right Whale**	Scott Kraus and Ken Mallory
superstitions	**Cross Your Fingers, Spit in Your Hat**	Alvin Schwartz

TABLE 10–1   Single-subject informational books.

Activity Books

Activity books invite the reader to engage in a specific activity beyond the reading. Classic types of activity books include science experiments, how-to and craft books, cookbooks, and art activity books. Take, for example, Barbara Valenta's ***Pop-O-Mania: How to Create Your Own Pop-Ups,*** which is a pop-up book that describes how to make pop-up books . . . and more. Readers learn how to use slides, flaps, spirals, and spinners to create books, holiday cards, and invitations. ***Make Believe: A Book of Costume and Fantasy*** comes with a plastic box of costume jewelry and invites readers to become their own heroes, sports stars, ballerinas, monsters, and meanies easily and inexpensively. Gwen Diehn's ***Making Books That Fly, Fold, Wrap, Hide, Pop Up, Twist, and Turn: Books for Kids to Make*** provides the history of various kinds of books plus instructions for making them: a magic carpet book from the Far East, which unfolds one piece at a time until the whole is exposed; a travel journal with a secret middle page for private messages; and a traveling museum book with places to collect bits of information found in field study. Today's offerings in activity books seem practically unlimited.

Concept Books

The first type of informational book a child sees is usually a concept book. The concept book is a simplified picture book that presents basic knowledge about one topic in a way both understandable and interesting for the small child learning basic information about the world. Concept books often invite the young reader to engage in some activity to reinforce the idea being presented, such as picking out which object is small and which is large in Margaret Miller's ***Big and Little.*** Identifying the circles and squares from familiar surroundings occurs in Tana Hoban's ***So Many Circles, So Many Squares,*** and noticing three-dimensional shapes is highlighted in her ***Cubes, Cones, Cylinders, & Spheres.***

N. N. Charles has collaborated with Caldecott illustrators Leo and Diane Dillon in yet another concept book, titled ***What Am I? Looking Through Shapes at Apples and Grapes.*** In this book, the young reader is prompted to look through die-cut shapes and choose a fruit based on an engaging couplet. For example, in the first double-page spread, the child looks through a square on the right side behind which is a deep red. The text reads, "I'm red, I'm round, I fall to the ground. What am I?" Turning the page, we see the answer, the apple in question, and a tree loaded with apples.

Getting a bit more sophisticated, the young reader can enjoy ***The Busy Building Book,*** by Sue Tarsky and illustrated by Alex Ayliffe. Showing in a simplistic way how a new office building is constructed, this book very cleverly provides a number of levels at which the reader or listener can participate depending on his or her own sophistication. Initially, we are met with bright endpapers showing construction vehicles that are labeled by name and part. Each spread depicts part of the process of building one of these giant buildings; the text is split between large bold print, which gives the gist of the page, and a smaller font that explains this step in building in more detail. For example, for the younger child, you could simply read the bold caption, "Excavate!", discuss all the different machines shown, and move on to the next spread. For the older, more sophisticated reader, the description of how workers dig the foundation is explained, so the reader has the opportunity to learn some of the specifics of the process.

A final grouping of concept books by Ann Morris must be included. Using crisp photographs, simple concepts such as ***Work, Play,*** and ***Shoes Shoes Shoes*** are beautifully illustrated and explained. Further, Morris shows us how men, women, and children work, for example, around the world. As a final feature, the last spread of these books contains a simple index of each photograph, telling where it was taken and a more detailed explanation of its content. Finally, the last page shows a world map indicating where all these pictures were taken. These books are the perfect first informational books.

Cover from ***Work,*** by Ann Morris. Jacket Photograph © 1998 by John Eastcott/Yva Momatiuk. Text copyright © 1998 by Ann Morris. Published by Lothrop, Lee & Shepard Books. Reprinted by permission of the publisher. All rights reserved.

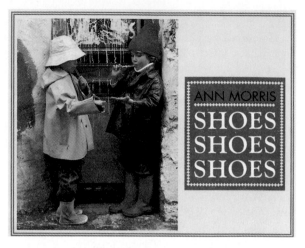

Cover from ***Shoes Shoes Shoes,*** by Ann Morris. Text copyright © 1995 by Ann Morris. Front jacket photograph © 1995 V. Winckler/Rapho photographique. Published by Lothrop, Lee & Shepard Books. Reprinted by permission of the publisher. All rights reserved.

Cover from ***Play,*** by Ann Morris, copyright © 1998 by Ann Morris. Used by permission of HarperCollins Publishers.

Journals and Interviews

Journals and interviews are the two most common kinds of books based on primary sources. *I, Columbus: My Journal 1492–3,* by Peter Roop and Connie Roop, offers edited but accurate selections from the log of Columbus's first voyage. Milton Meltzer uses journals from more than one person to paint a specialized picture of an era or event. ***Voices from the Civil War*** is a mosaic created from the journals of those who participated in or were affected by America's bloodiest conflict. Interviews, like journals, offer information directly to the reader with only a minimum of author manipulation.

ALTERNATE TEXT SET

More Voices From the American Civil War

Read Aloud

North Star to Freedom: The Story of the Underground Railroad, by Gena K. Gorrell

Text Set

Now Is Your Time! The African-American Struggle for Freedom, by Walter Dean Myers

A Separate Battle: Women and the Civil War, by Ina Chang

Civil War: A Library of Congress Book, by Martin W. Sandler

For Home and Country: A Civil War Scrapbook, by Norman Bolotin and Angela Herb

Till Victory is Won: Black Soldiers in the Civil War, by Zak Mettger

Civil War! America Becomes One Nation, by James I. Robertson, Jr.

Photo Essays

Photo essays employ . . . well, photographs. Seems like a no-brainer, doesn't it? But the key to the success of a book in this category is the artist's ability to capture the emotion of the moment and to verify the information the text is intended to describe. Photographs accompany the text on almost every page in a photo essay, as in Dorothy Hinshaw Patent's *Fire: Friend or Foe.* Here Patent discusses how forest fires affect both human and wild life. With the aid of William Munoz's crisp, clear photographs, the book points out the positive and negative effects fire has on our planet and offers clear descriptions of the breadth and magnitude of one of nature's most powerful forces. The photographs in Kathryn Lasky's *Shadows in the Dawn: The Lemurs of Madagascar* perform a similar function in extending the information in the text by showing how lemurs move, relate to one another in their society, and respond to the death of an infant lemur. Walter Dean Myers uses period photographs, many from his own vast collection, to illustrate the life of African Americans in his *One More River to Cross.* Spare text tells the story of the heartache, joy, and pain of being black in America, but it is the photographic display that captures and rivets the point home.

Two books that complement the Alternate Text Set on the Civil War just listed are two books by Raymond Bial. In his *The Underground Railroad* and *The Strength of These Arms: Life in the Slave Quarters,* Bial provides crisp, colorful photographs of historical sites, interspersing them with period photographs, line drawings, and maps that paint an accurate portrait of the life, conditions, and times of slaves during the 19th century.

Considering text that is more simplified, there is Ken Robbins's *Autumn Leaves,* which describes for the younger reader what fall is all about: why leaves change color and what many of the common trees in America look like as autumn overtakes them. Close-up photographs of 13 leaf types are juxtaposed with a larger picture of the entire tree to accent the beauty of one of the most breathtaking times of the year. William Jaspersohn presents a very thorough overview of one of the greatest institutions in the world: the public library. In his book, *My Hometown Library,* he uses photographs and words to explain the history of libraries, how they work, and many of the features they offer readers of all ages.

Cover by Jennie Maizels, from ***The Amazing Pop-Up Grammar Book*** by Jennie Maizels, and Kate Perry, copyright © 1996 by Jennie Maizels, illustrations and lettering. Text © 1996 by Kate Perry. Paper engineering copyright © 1996 by Damian Johnston. Used by permission of Dutton Children's Books, a division of Penguin Putnam, Inc.

The Art of Science: A Pop-Up Adventure in Art. Text © 1999 by Martin Jenkins; Concept and paper engineering © 1999 by Jay Young. Reproduced by permission of the publisher Candlewick Press Inc., Cambridge, MA, on behalf of Walker Books Ltd., London.

Pop-Up and Three-Dimensional Books

Once pop-up books were largely for entertainment, but today a number of excellent informational books appear in pop-up format. Ron van der Meer's series of seven pop-up titles, including ***The Architecture Pack*** and ***Music Pack,*** present overviews of a variety of subjects ranging from art and music to architecture and math. Jay Young's ***The Art of Science: A Pop-Up Adventure in Art*** very cleverly addresses how science has informed art. Each double-page spread pops up to provide the reader with hands-on activities that show how the melding of these two disciplines has produced some of the great innovations in visual art. Included are pop-ups of a stereoscope and a camera obscura. Batteries are not included, so you will need a 9-volt cell to experiment with the last spread, which describes how "interactive artists" work and offers the child an opportunity to create his or her own art using wire.

Jennie Maizels and Kate Petty have addressed an unexpected topic with this format in ***The Amazing Pop-Up Grammar Book.*** Flaps, pull-tabs, and pop-up landscapes address parts of speech and punctuation with a whole new flair. As a final note, Robert Sabuda has done it again. This time, the master of three-dimensions has easily bested his lovely ***ABC Disney*** with ***The Wonderful Wizard of Oz: A Commemorative Pop-Up.*** A pop-up tornado, a replica of the Emerald City itself (supplied with green glasses with which to view it), and even the hot air balloon that whisks

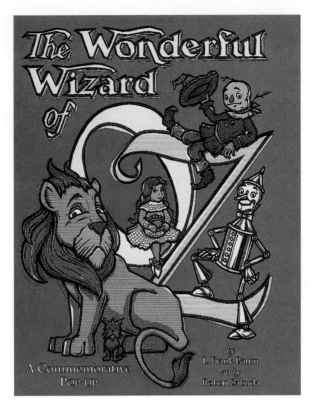

Reprinted with the permission of Little Simon, an imprint of Simon & Schuster Children's Publishing Division from *The Wonderful Wizard of Oz: A Commemorative Pop-Up* by L. Frank Baum, art by Robert Sabuda. Copyright © 2000 Robert Sabuda.

Dorothy back to Kansas are only three examples of engineered wonders Sabuda has created. This book, which includes small, multiple-page, inset texts that pop up as well, will cause you to gasp with every turn of the page, so stunning are they and a fitting contribution to the 100-year anniversary of this classic book.

Taking the pop-up book one step further, DK Publishing has introduced the Eyewitness 3-D books. Using the same basic concept as the stereopticon, readers use a mirrored divider (provided with each book) that splits a double image on each page and produces a remarkable three-dimensional likeness of a variety of geological forms in *3-D Rocks and Minerals* and various anatomical features in their *3-D Human Body*. Scholastic has also moved into the 3-D world with their series of Discovery Box books. In their *Pyramids,* they include a 32-page booklet as well as all the pieces to build Khufu's Great Pyramid at Giza (in miniature, of course), showing the burial chamber and secret passageways.

Reference Books

Although some children may spend time browsing in reference books or occasionally reading them from beginning to end, young readers generally go to reference books for isolated bits of specific knowledge. For example, if a child needed to know more about what it was like to live during World War II, he or she might search through the 14 pages of information included in *The United States in the 20th Century* by David Rubel. The book, which chronicles major eras during the past 100 years, contains double-page spreads that are neatly organized into four major categories: "Politics," "Life in the [specific time period, such as World War II]," "Arts and Entertainment," and "Science and Technology." Also featured is a spotlight on a famous person, an event, or a trend of special importance during that time period. This comprehensive reference source provides interesting and informative thumbnail sketches of the 20th century in a readable format. Also from Scholastic is the *Encyclopedia of the United States at War.* This book focuses on major conflicts the United States faced throughout its relatively short history. The text, chock-full of historical tidbits, also includes insert information about specific characters from history as well as featured items of human interest and

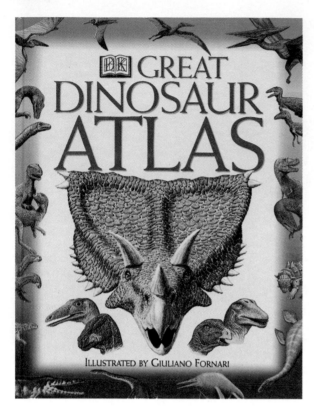

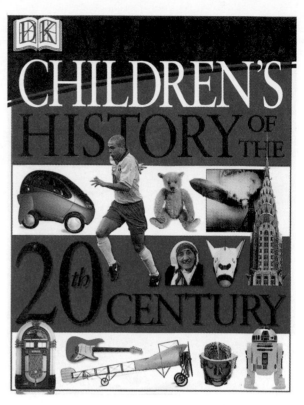

Cover from **The Great Dinosaur Atlas,** written by William Lindsay, illustrated by Giuliano Fornari. Copyright © 2000 by Dorling Kindersley Limited. Published by DK Publishing, Inc. Reprinted by permission of the publisher. All rights reserved.

Cover from **Millennium: Children's History of the 20th Century,** written by Simon Adams, Robin Cross, Ann Kramer, Haydn Middleton, Sally Tagholm. Copyright © 2000 by Dorling Kindersley Limited, London. Published by DK Publishing, Inc. Reprinted by permission of the publisher. All rights reserved.

techniques of war. A final example of a book that belongs in every fifth-grade classroom is Lila Perl's *It Happened in America: True Stories from the Fifty States.* State reports always seem to work their way into the curriculum at this level, and the use of this book will bring them to life when children include many of the interesting facts noted about each of the states in the union. For example, did you know that Pennsylvania is the Home of the Prairie Schooner or that in the early 1800s, Frederic Tudor, the Ice King, shipped 180 tons of ice to India, which he harvested from local Massachusetts lakes? Incidental facts such as these makes each state's profile even more rich and enjoyable.

The current trend to make reference books attractive and readable adds a new dimension: reference books as recreational reading. The Eyewitness series, published by DK Publishing and Knopf and often labeled as identification books, is an example of the new generation of colorful, engaging reference tools. Children will want to look at William Lindsay's *DK Great Dinosaur Atlas* as well as titles such as *Eyewitness Spy, Eyewitness Mummy,* and *Eyewitness Horse,* to name only a few in the list.

Series

School libraries traditionally have informational books in series, partly because subject areas studied in school provide ready-made topics. For example, elementary schools frequently have a series of books about the United States, one title per state, which students use most often for doing reports. Although the information in these traditional series is generally acceptable, their appeal can be low depending on the age of the set.

Fortunately, today's informational series books have been conceived and executed by those who go beyond simply listing information to seeing inside it. Their views are accurate and up-to-date, and the books convey excitement about the topics. For example,

BOOKMARK

INTEGRATING TECHNOLOGY: ACTIVITIES USING THE WORLD WIDE WEB

Scholastic's **The Magic School Bus** was recently awarded the National Conservation Achievement Award for Education presented by the National Wildlife Federation (NWF) for its "outstanding efforts to educate children about science and the environment, and to build a foundation for the conservationists of tomorrow." Information about the science-related series by Joanna Cole and Bruce Degen is provided. On the website, there is also a kid's art gallery and an activities lab related to the Magic School Bus books (as well as the TV show, videos, and CD-ROMs). Some of the sections are quite constructivist and student centered, such as the Storytelling activity.

To find out more about The Magic School Bus and other activities on the World Wide Web, visit Chapter 10 on the companion website at **www.prenhall.com/darigan**

the enormously popular *Magic School Bus* series is composed of 10 titles, plus 6 more based on separate episodes from the animated TV series. In these, Ms. Frizzle takes her class on field trips in a special bus that can change size and function as it travels through various parts of the universe, the human digestive system, the earth's crust, a hurricane, the solar system, and the generators and electric wires that bring power to their town.

Another very interesting series from Scholastic books comes in their "Scholastic Question and Answer Series" (see Alternate Text Set below). Many things we all wonder about are answered in these intriguing volumes. For example, some common and some not-so-common questions about the human body, weather, insects, and the stars and the planets are addressed.

On the math front, there is yet another very popular series written by Stuart J. Murphy, known as MathStart. In these books, the author has built a story around a particular math concept that engages the reader in a way a simple math text cannot.

For other titles in the *Magic School Bus* series, you can access the database that accompanies this textbook.

ALTERNATE TEXT SET

Scholastic Question and Answer Books by Melvin and Gilda Berger

Read Aloud

Do All Spiders Spin Webs?

Text Set

Do Stars Have Points?

Why Don't Haircuts Hurt?

Can It Rain Cats and Dogs?

How Do Flies Walk Upside Down?

Do Whales Have Belly Buttons?

Why Do Volcanoes Blow Their Tops?

Do Tarantulas Have Teeth?

Do Tornadoes Really Twist?

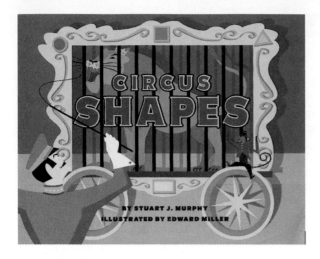

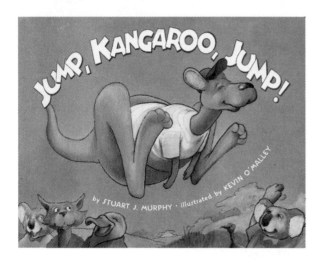

Cover from **Circus Shapes** by Stuart J. Murphy, illustrated by Edward Miller. Jacket art © 1998 by Edward Miller III. Text copyright © 1998 by Stuart J. Murphy. Published by HarperCollins Children's Books. Reprinted by permission of the publisher. All rights reserved.

Cover from **Every Buddy Counts** by Stuart J. Murphy, illustrated by Fiona Dunbar. Text copyright © 1997 by Stuart J. Murphy. Illustrations copyright © 1997 by Fiona Dunbar. Cover art © 1997 by Fiona Dunbar. Published by HarperCollins Children's Books. Reprinted by permission of the publisher. All rights reserved.

Cover from **Jump, Kangaroo, Jump!** by Stuart J. Murphy, illustrated by Kevin O'Malley. Text copyright © 1999 by Stuart J. Murphy. Jacket art © 1999 by Kevin O'Malley. Published by HarperCollins Children's Books. Reprinted by permission of the publisher. All rights reserved.

For a complete listing of all the MathStart, books go to Chapter 10 on the companion website at **www.prenhall. com/darigan**

For a more complete listing of books by author/illustrator Gail Gibbons, you can visit the database that accompanies this book.

In these leveled books, a wide variety of illustrators present information addressing myriad math concepts. For the preschool level, Murphy covers recognizing shapes in his *Circus Shapes,* illustrated by Edward Miller, and counting in *Every Buddy Counts,* illustrated by Fiona Dunbar. At the upper level, he addresses fractions with *Jump, Kangaroo, Jump!,* illustrated by Kevin O'Malley, estimating in *Betcha!,* illustrated by S. D. Schindler, and algorithms in *Too Many Kangaroo Things to Do!,* also illustrated by Kevin O'Malley, which discusses multiplying.

Construed more loosely, we have book series that are more author specific. For example, Gail Gibbons's work over the years has been an extraordinary contribution to nonfiction. Though her books don't come in specific, linear series such as the example we noted of one book for every state in the union, she does tend to have books that fit together in nice categories. Her books on animals, such as *Gulls, Gulls, Gulls, The Honey Makers,* and *Soaring with the Wind: The Bald Eagle,* are musts for any classroom library. Her books on space, such as *Stargazers, The Planets,* and *The Moon Book,* present a very consumable view of the stars and solar system for the young reader.

Social Histories

A look at an event, era, or prevailing attitude in the past is sometimes called social history. In *The Boys' War,* which we described earlier, Jim Murphy shows the Civil War from the point of view of participants under the age of 16. *Children of the Dust Bowl:*

The True Story of the School at Weedpatch Camp, by Jerry Stanley, documents the plight of migrant workers who came to California during the Depression. In Stanley's *I Am An American,* he looks at the Japanese internment in the United States during World War II, and his *Hurry Freedom* focuses on African Americans during the California Gold Rush of 1849. *Give Me Liberty!,* by Russell Freedman, outlines the events and political ramifications that led up to the framing of the Declaration of Independence. *Immigrant Kids,* also by Freedman, shows what life was like for those children who left their homes to find new lives in America.

Social histories can be narrative accounts or a collection of documentary accounts. Whatever the format, the goal is best expressed by Milton Meltzer: "To meld eyewitness accounts with my narrative to create a dramatic history that will illuminate fundamental issues and bring to life the people who shape them" (1993, p. 27).

Survey Books

Survey books present an overview of a broad subject. Even when in picture book format, they are often thicker than most other informational children's books because they cover so much material. Although reminiscent of an encyclopedia, survey books are usually far more captivating. For example, Martin W. Sandler's series of books, *Cowboys, Pioneers,* and *Inventors,* all Library of Congress Books, presents each subject using period photographs, paintings, and insert quotations as well as lively text that explains each topic fully. Dorothy Hinshaw Patent and William Munoz team up once again to offer a very important overview of our global environment in their book *Biodiversity.* Covering the miracle of our diverse planet, how humans affect it, and how we can preserve it, this volume presents the subject in an unsettling yet beautiful way and begs readers to take action to save our planet.

▼▼▼▼▼▼▼

Summary

In this chapter, we began by looking at a number of issues and stereotypes surrounding informational books, such that they have been perceived as boring, not traditionally for pleasure reading, and not a good alternative to all the information that can be accessed on the Internet. We looked at what makes for a good informational book, including attractive format and design, compelling details, fascinating comparisons, unusual subject or viewpoints, and personalized content. We noted that when we consider quality informational books, accuracy, authenticity, and reliability should be taken into account. We looked last at the different types of informational books available today, which include activity books, concept books, journals and interviews, photo essays, pop-up books, reference books, series, social histories, and survey books.

▼▼▼▼▼▼▼

Fifteen More of Our Favorites

Bartoletti, Susan Campbell. (1999). *Kids on strike!* Houghton Mifflin. Describes the conditions and treatment that drove working children to strike, from the mill workers' strike in 1834 and the coal strikes at the turn of the century to the children who marched with Mother Jones in 1903.

Bowen, Gary. (1994). *Stranded at Plimoth Plantation 1626.* HarperCollins. The fictional account of the daily activities of 13-year-old Christopher, whose ship crashes on Plimoth Plantation and who must wait until further passage to Jamestown becomes available.

Carrick, Carol. (1993). *Whaling days* (David Frampton, Illus.). Clarion. Surveys the whaling industry, ranging from hunting in colonial America to modern whaling regulations and conservation efforts.

Hansen, Joyce, & McGowan, Gary. (1998). *Breaking ground breaking silence: The story of New*

York's African burial ground. Henry Holt. Describes the discovery and study of the African burial site found in Manhattan in 1991, during excavation for a new building, and what it reveals about the lives of black people in Colonial times.

Isaacson, Philip M. (1993). *A short walk around the pyramids & through the world of art.* Knopf. Introduces tangible and abstract components of art and the many forms art can take, including sculpture, pottery, painting, photographs, and even furniture and cities.

Irvine, Joan. (1992). *How to make super pop-ups.* Beech Tree. Step-by-step instructions with clear diagrams for making a variety of pop-ups, including giant designs for stage sets.

Kenna, Kathleen. (1995). *A people apart.* Houghton. A heartfelt, understanding profile of a rarely photographed people, the Old Order Mennonites, who live a life in which time has seemed to have stood still.

McKissack, Patricia C., & McKissack, Fredrick L. (1999). *Black hands, white sails: The story of African-American whalers.* Scholastic. A history of African-American whalers between 1730 and 1880, describing their contribution to the whaling industry and their role in the abolition movement.

Maestro, Betsy. (1999). *The story of clocks and calendars: Marking a millennium.* Lothrop.

Discusses the story of time-keeping: how, over thousands of years, calendars and clocks came to be.

Schwartz, David. (1995). *Yanomami: People of the Amazon.* (Victor Englebert, Photog.). Lothrop. Stunning photoessay gives readers a glimpse of the lives of the vanishing people known as the Yanomami located where Brazil meets Venezuela, deep in the Amazon rain forest.

Simon, Seymour. (1997). *Strange mysteries.* Morrow. Describes nine strange phenomena and possible explanations for them, including the day it rained frogs, an atomic explosion that occurred 40 years before the atom bomb, and an eerie crystal skull. (Orginal work published 1980)

Smith, Roland, & Schmidt, Michael J. (1998). *In the forest with the elephants.* Harcourt. Describes how elephants are trained to help in the timber camps of Myanmar, formerly known as Burma, and their important contribution to the selective and sustainable harvesting of teak there.

St. George, Judith. (1999). *In the line of fire: Presidents' lives at stake.* Holiday House. Historical account that focuses on the four slain United States presidents, giving ample coverage to their assassinations, assailants, and their successors in office.

▼▼▼▼▼▼▼

Others We Like

Adams, Simon. (2000). *World War II.* (Andy Crawford, Photog.). Dorling Kindersley.

Arnosky, Jim. 1988 (1977). *I was born in a tree and raised by the bees.* Bradbury.

Ashanbranner, Brent. (1996). *A strange and distant shore: Indians of the Great Plains in exile.* Cobblehill/Dutton.

Bachrach, Susan D. (2000). *The Nazi Olympics.* Little, Brown.

Blumberg, Rhoda. (1985). *Commodore Perry in the land of the Shogun.* Lothrop.

Boyne, Walter. (1988). *The Smithsonian book of flight for young people.* Atheneum.

Brust, Beth Wagner. (1994). *The amazing paper cuttings of Hans Christian Andersen.* Ticknor & Fields.

Calabro, Marian. (1999). *The perilous journey of the Donner party.* Clarion.

Cohn, Amy L. (Compiler). (1993). *From sea to shining sea: a treasury of american folklore and folk songs.* (Illustrated by eleven Caldecott Medal and four Caldecott Honor Book artists.) Scholastic.

Cone, Molly. (1992). *Come back, Salmon* (Sidnee Wheelwright, Photog.). Sierra Club.

Fleischman, Paul. (1996). *Dateline: Troy.* (Gwen Frankfeldt & Glen Morrow, Illus.). Candlewick.

Fradin, Dennis Brindell. (1999). *Is there life on Mars?* McElderry.

Frances, Neil. (1988). *Super flyers.* Addison-Wesley.

Garelick, Mae. (1995). *What makes a bird a bird?* Mondo.

Herb, Angela M. (1996). *Beyond the Mississippi: Early westward expansion of the United States.* New York: Lodestar.

Irvine, Joan. (1992). *How to make super pop-ups.* Beech Tree.

Isaacson, Philip M. (1988). *Round buildings, square buildings, and buildings that wiggle like a fish.* Knopf.

Jones, Charlotte Foltz. (1996). *Accidents may happen: Fifty inventions discovered by mistake.* Delacorte.

Jones, Frances. (1992). *Nature's deadly creatures.* Dial.

Kaner, Etta. (1989). *Balloon science.* Addison-Wesley.

Kaniut, Larry. (1983). *Alaska bear tales.* Alaska Northwest Books.

Klutz Press Editors. (1992). *Kids/shenanigans: Great things to do that Mom and Dad will just barely approve of.* Klutz Press.

Krementz, Jill. (1981). *How it feels when a parent dies.* Knopf.

Krementz, Jill. (1984). *How it feels when parents divorce.* Knopf.

Lanier, Shannon, & Feldman, Jane. (2000). *Jefferson's children: The story of one American family.* Random House.

Lasky, Kathryn. (1998). *Shadows in the dawn: The lemurs of Madagascar.* (Christopher Knight, Photog.). Harcourt.

Lauber, Patricia. (1986). *Volcano: The eruption and healing of Mount St. Helens.* Bradbury.

Lauber, Patricia. (1989). *The news about dinosaurs.* Bradbury.

Levine, Ellen. (2000). *Darkness over Denmark: The Danish resistance and the rescue of the Jews.* Holiday House.

Macaulay, David. (1993). *Ship.* Houghton Mifflin.

Macaulay, David. (2000). *Building big.* Houghton Mifflin.

Macdonald, Fiona. (1998). *A child's eye view of history.* Simon & Schuster.

Maestro, Betsy. (2000). *Struggle for a continent: The French and Indian Wars, 1689–1763.* HarperCollins.

Mallory, Kenneth. (1998). *A home by the sea: Protecting coastal wildlife.* Harcourt.

McKissack, Patricia, McKissack, Fredrick L. (1994). *Christmas in the big house, Christmas in the quarters.* (John Thompson, Illus.). Scholastic.

Patterson, Francine. (1985). *Koko's kitten.* Scholastic.

Pringle, Laurence. (2001). *A dragon in the sky: The story of a green darner dragonfly.* (Bob Marshall, Illus.). Orchard.

Roehrig, Catharine. (1990). *Fun with hieroglyphics.* Viking.

Rosenthal, Paul. (1992). *Where on Earth: A geografunny guide to the globe.* Knopf.

Rubel, David. (2001). *Encyclopedia of the presidents and their times.* Scholastic.

Ruth, Maria Mudd. (1998). *Firefighting: Behind the scenes.* (Scott Sroka, Photog.). Houghton.

Simon, Seymour. (1979). *Pets in a jar.* Puffin.

Storring, Rod. (1998). *A doctor's life: A visual history of doctors and nurses through the ages.* Dutton.

Swanson, Diane. (1994). *Safari beneath the sea: The wonder world of the north Pacific coast.* (Royal British Columbia Museum, Photog.). Sierra Club.

Tunnell, Michael O., Chilcoat, George W. (1996). *The children of Topaz: The story of a Japanese American internment camp based on a classroom Diary.* Holiday House.

Walker, Barbara M. (1979). *The little house cookbook: Frontier foods from Laura Ingalls Wilder's classic stories.* (Garth Williams, Illus.). Harper.

Warren, Andrea. (1996). *Orphan train rider: One boy's true story.* Houghton.

Zotti, Ed. (1993). *Know it all! The fun stuff you never learned in school.* Ballantine.

Easier to Read

Bare, Colleen Stanley. (1989). *Never kiss an alligator.* Dutton.

Fritz, Jean. (1987). *Shh! we're writing the constitution.* (Tomie dePaola, Illus.). Putnam.

Getz, David. (1994). *Frozen man.* (Peter McCarty, Illus.). Holt.

Grover, Wayne. (1993). *Dolphin adventure.* Greenwillow.

Martin, James. (1993). *Tentacles.* Crown.

Peters, David. (1986). *Giants of land, sea & air: Past & present.* Knopf.

Simon, Seymour. (1979). *Animal fact/animal fable.* (Diane de Groat, Illus.). Crown.

Snedden, Robert. (1996). *Yuck!: A big book of little horrors—micromarvels in, on, and around you!* Simon & Schuster.

Sobol, Donald J., & Sobol, Rose. (1991). *Encyclopedia Brown's book of strange but true crimes* (John Zielinski, Illus.). Scholastic.

Picture Books

Aliki. (1979). *Mummies made in Egypt.* Harper.

Appelbaum, Diana. (1993). *Giants in the land* (Michael McCurdy, Illus.). Houghton Mifflin.

Berger, Melvin, & Berger, Gilda. (2001a). *Can you hear a shout in space?: Questions and answers about space exploration* (Vincent Di Fate, Illus.). Scholastic.

Berger, Melvin & Berger, Gilda. (2001). *What makes an ocean wave?: Questions and answers about oceans and ocean life* (John Rice, Illus.). Scholastic.

Burleigh, Robert. (1991). *Flight: The journey of Charles Lindbergh.* (Mike Wimmer, Illus.). Philomel.

Chorlton, Windsor. (2001). *Wooly mammoth: Life, death, and rediscovery.* Scholastic.

Curlee, Lynn. (1998). *Into the ice: The story of Arctic exploration.* Houghton Mifflin.

Fisher, Leonard Everett. (1999). *Gods and goddesses of the ancient Maya.* Holiday House.

Gibbons, Gail. (1999). *Bats.* Holiday House.

Gibbons, Gail. (2000). *Apples.* Holiday House.

Heller, Ruth. (1995). *Behind the mask: A book about prepositions.* Grosset & Dunlap.

Hirst, Robin, Hirst, Sally. (1990). *My place in space.* (Roland Harvey with Joe Levine, Illus.). Orchard.

Lasky, Kathryn. (2001). *Interrupted journey: Saving endangered sea turtles* (Christopher G. Knight, Photog.). Candlewick.

Lewin, Ted & Lewin, Betsy. (2000). *Elephant quest.* HarperCollins.

Macaulay, David. (1975). *Pyramid.* Houghton Mifflin.

Parsons, Alexandra. (1990). *Amazing mammals.* Dorling Kindersley.

Singer, Marilyn. (2000). *On the same day in March: A tour of the world's weather.* (Frané Lessac, Illus.). HarperCollins.

Spier, Peter. (1980). *People.* Doubleday.

▼▼▼▼▼▼▼

Publishers of Informational Books

Three publishers of nonfiction books for young readers merit special notice. Each produces such interesting books and so many titles that consulting their catalogs is perhaps the easiest way to find books appropriate for individual libraries and classrooms.

Usborne Books pioneered the now-popular format of presenting one aspect of a subject on a double-page spread, complete with many illustrations and snippets of text. Turn the page, and find another focus. Usborne now has over 100 nonfiction series for children of different ages and interests. Catalog: EDC Publishing, P.O. Box 470663, Tulsa, OK 74147-0663. Phone: (800) 475-4522.

DK Publishing, Inc. (formerly Dorling Kindersley), has more than 20 informational series for young readers plus a wealth of single titles as well as some fiction. DK is noted for fine photography, appealing layout, and information that is intriguing as well as accurate. Catalog: DK Publishing, Inc., 95 Madison Avenue, New York, NY 10016. Phone: (212) 213-4800 ext. 291.

Eyewitness Books and Eyewitness Junior Books are series from DK Publishing but more than 100 titles of these series were published only by Knopf/Random House and not listed or sold by DK (the contract was made before DK had a U.S. office). Catalog: Random House Publishing, 400 Hahn Road, Westminster, MD 21157. Phone: (800) 733-3000.

Klutz Press specializes in the zany, clever, and innovative—in both format and subject. Many of the 71 books published for children come with some sort of manipulative, like the hair bows, ribbons, and clips that accompany *Hair: A Book of Braiding and Styles* (Johnson, 1995) and the eight bricks of different-colored clay that are a part of *The Incredible Clay Book: How to Make and Bake Zillions of Permanent Clay Creations* (Sherri Haab and Laura Torres, 1994). Catalog: Klutz Press, 455 Portage Avenue, Palo Alto, CA 94306. FAX: (650) 857-9110. Phone: (650) 857-0888.

Informational Series

For each series of informational books mentioned next, two sample titles are included. The number in parentheses indicates how many titles were in that series as of summer 1998. That number naturally will change with time but provides a general idea of the series size.

Brown Paper School Books (19 titles). Hands-on activities and compelling views of both traditional and nontraditional subjects.
Booth, Jerry. (1988). *The big beast book.* Little, Brown.
Burns, Marilyn. (1976). *The book of think (or how to solve a problem twice your size).* Little, Brown.

Extremely Weird (16 titles) and *Bizarre & Beautiful* (5 titles). Illustrated with lavish photographs, each title in these two similar series presents unusual animals or strange physical characteristics of animals.
Lovett, Sarah. (1993). *Extremely weird snakes.* John Muir.
Santa Fe Writers Group. (1993). *Bizarre & beautiful noses.* John Muir.

Imponderables (11 titles). Explanations of events, traditions, and happenings in everyday life. Written for adults; devoured by children.
Feldman, David. (1996). *How do astronauts scratch an itch?* Harper.
Feldman, David. (1993). *How does aspirin find a headache?* Harper.

Inside Story (15 titles). Detailed cutaway views of the building and function of historical structures and other engineering marvels.
MacDonald, Fiona. (1996). *The Roman colosseum.* Peter Bedrick.

Steedman, Scott. (1993). *A frontier fort on the Oregon Trail.* Peter Bedrick.

Let's Read-and-Find-Out Science (77 titles—24 Stage 1 [preschool and kindergarten]; 53 Stage 2 [grades 1–3]). Science concepts for preschool through third grade.
Esbensen, Barbara Juster. (1993). *Sponges are skeletons.* (Holly Keller, Illus.). Harper. (Stage 2.)
Otto, Carolyn. (1996). *What color is camouflage?* (Megan Lloyd, Illus.). Harper. (Stage 1.)

A Library of Congress Book
Sandler, Martin W. (1994a). *Cowboys.* HarperCollins.
Sandler, Martin W. (1994b). *Pioneers.* HarperCollins.
Sandler, Martin W. (1995a). *Immigrants.* HarperCollins.
Sandler, Martin W. (1995b). *Presidents.* HarperCollins.
Sandler, Martin W. (1996a). *Inventors.* HarperCollins.
Sandler, Martin W. (1996b). *Civil War.* HarperCollins.

Ann Morris Books (10 titles)
Morris, Ann. (1995). *Shoes shoes shoes.* Lothrop.
Morris, Ann. (1998a). *Play.* Lothrop.
Morris, Ann. (1998b). *Work.* Lothrop.
Time Quest Books (8 titles). In-depth looks at disasters and historical mysteries.
Reeves, Nicholas. (1992). *Into the mummy's tomb: The real-life discovery of Tutankhamen's treasures.* Scholastic.
Tanaka, Shelley. (1996). *On board the Titanic: What it was like when the great liner sank.* Scholastic.

What Makes a . . . a . . .? (10 titles). Each title focuses on the style, subject matter, and contribution of one famous artist.
Mühlberger, Richard. (1993). *What makes a Monet a Monet?* Viking.
Mühlberger, Richard. (1994). *What makes a Picasso a Picasso?* Viking.

Children's Literature References

Abells, Chana Byers. (1986). *The children we remember.* New York: Greenwillow.
Adler, David A. (1989). *We remember the Holocaust.* New York: Henry Holt.
Allison, Linda. (1976). *Blood and guts.* Boston: Little, Brown.
Ancona, George. (1995). *Cutters, carvers & the cathedral.* New York: Lothrop.
Armstrong, Jennifer. (1998). *Shipwreck at the bottom of the world: The extraordinary true story of the Shackleton and the Endurance.* New York: Crown.
Arnold, Katya, & Swope, Sam. (1997). *Katya's book of mushrooms* (Katya Arnold, Illus.). New York: Holt.
Bachrach, Susan D. (1994). *Tell them we remember: The story of the Holocaust.* Boston: Little, Brown.
Bartoletti, Susan Campbell. (1996). *Growing up in coal country.* Boston: Houghton.
Baum, Frank L. (2000). *The wonderful wizard of Oz: A commemorative pop-up* (Robert Sabuda, Illus.). New York: Little Simon.
Beattie, Owen, & Geiger, John. (1992). *Buried in ice: The mystery of a lost Arctic expedition.* New York: Scholastic.
Berger, Melvin, & Berger, Gilda. (1998a). *Do stars have points?* (Vincent Di Fate, Illus.). New York: Scholastic.
Berger, Melvin, & Berger, Gilda. (1998b). *Why don't haircuts hurt?: Questions and answers about the human body* (Karen Barnes, Illus.). New York: Scholastic.
Berger, Melvin, & Berger, Gilda. (1999a). *Can it rain cats and dogs?: Questions and answers about weather* (Robert Sullivan, Illus.). New York: Scholastic.
Berger, Melvin, & Berger, Gilda. (1999b). *Do tarantulas have teeth?: Questions and answers about poisonous creatures* (Jim Effler, Illus.). New York: Scholastic.
Berger, Melvin, & Berger, Gilda. (1999c). *Do whales have belly buttons?: Questions and answers about whales and dolphins* (Higgins Bond, Illus.). New York: Scholastic.
Berger, Melvin, & Berger, Gilda. (1999d). *How do flies walk upside down?: Questions and answers about insects* (Jim Effler, Illus.). New York: Scholastic.
Berger, Melvin, & Berger, Gilda. (1999e). *Why do volcanoes blow their tops?: Questions and answers about volcanoes and earthquakes* (Higgins Bond, Illus.). New York: Scholastic.
Berger, Melvin, & Berger, Gilda. (2000a). *Do all spiders spin webs?: Questions and answers about spiders* (Roberto Osti, Illus.). New York: Scholastic.
Berger, Melvin, & Berger, Gilda. (2000b). *Do tornadoes really twist?: Questions and answers about tornadoes and hurricanes* (Higgins Bond, Illus.). New York: Scholastic.
Bial, Raymond. (1995). *The underground railroad.* Boston: Houghton Mifflin.
Bial, Raymond. (1997). *The strength of these arms: Life in the slave quarters.* Boston: Houghton Mifflin.
Blackbirch Graphics. (1999). *Scholastic kid's almanac for the 21st century.* New York: Scholastic.

Bolotin, Norman, & Herb, Angela. (1995). *For home and country: A Civil War scrapbook.* New York: Lodestar.

Brandreth, Gyles. (1989). *The do-it-yourself genius kit.* New York: Penguin.

Burns, Marilyn. (1975). *The I hate mathematics! book.* Boston: Little, Brown.

Byam, Michelle. (1988). *Arms and armor.* New York: Knopf.

Chang, Ina. (1991). *A separate battle: Women and the Civil War.* New York: Lodestar.

Charles, N. N. (1994). *What am I? Looking through shapes at apples and grapes* (Leo Dillon & Diane Dillon, Illus.). New York: Scholastic.

Christelow, Eileen. (1995). *What do authors do?* New York: Clarion.

Colman, Penny. (1997). *Corpses, coffins, and crypts: A history of burial.* New York: Holt.

Conrad, Pam. (1995). *Call me Ahnighito* (Richard Egielski, Illus.). New York: HarperCollins.

Cowley, Joy. (1999). *Red-eyed tree frog* (Nic Bishop, Illus.). New York: Scholastic.

Curlee, Lynn. (1999). *Rushmore.* New York: Scholastic.

Denenberg, Barry. (1995). *Voices from Vietnam.* New York: Scholastic.

Diehn, Gwen. (1998). *Making books that fly, fold, wrap, hide, pop up, twist, and turn: Books for kids to make.* Ashville, NC: Lark Books.

Earle, Ann. (1995). *Zipping, zapping, zooming bats* (Henry Cole, Illus.). New York: HarperCollins.

Editions Gallimard Jeunesse. (1999). *Pyramids.* New York: Scholastic.

Ehlert, Lois. (1989). *Color zoo.* New York: Lippincott.

English, June A., & Jones, Thomas D. (1998). *Scholastic encyclopedia of the United States at war.* New York: Scholastic.

Feldman, David. (1987). *Why do clocks run clockwise? An imponderables book.* New York: Harper & Row.

Feldman, David. (1992a). *Do penguins have knees? An imponderables book.* New York: HarperCollins.

Feldman, David. (1992b). *Why do dogs have wet noses? An imponderables book.* New York: HarperCollins.

Feldman, David. (1993). *How does aspirin find a headache? An imponderables book.* New York: HarperCollins.

Feldman, David. (1995). *What are hyenas laughing at, anyway? An imponderables book.* New York: Putnam.

Feldman, David. (1996). *How do astronauts scratch an itch?* New York: Putnam.

Freedman, Russell. (1980a). *Give me liberty! The story of the Declaration of Independence.* New York: Holiday House.

Freedman, Russell. (1980b). *Immigrant kids.* New York: Dutton.

Getz, David. (1994). *Frozen man* (Peter McCarty, Illus.). New York: Holt.

Getz, David. (1998). *Frozen girl* (Peter McCarty, Illus.). New York: Holt.

Gibbons, Gail. (1992). *Stargazers.* New York: Holiday.

Gibbons, Gail. (1993). *The planets.* New York: Holiday.

Gibbons, Gail. (1997a). *Gulls, gulls, gulls.* New York: Holiday.

Gibbons, Gail. (1997b). *The honey makers.* New York: Morrow.

Gibbons, Gail. (1997c). *The moon book.* New York: Holiday.

Gibbons, Gail. (1997d). *Soaring with the wind: The bald eagle.* New York: Morrow.

Gibbons, Gail. (1998). *Penguins!* New York: Holiday House.

Giblin, James Cross. (1987). *From hand to mouth: Or, how we invented knives, forks, spoons and chopsticks & the table manners to go with them.* New York: Crowell.

Giblin, James Cross. (1990). *The riddle of the Rosetta Stone.* New York: Crowell.

Giblin, James Cross. (1991). *The truth about unicorns.* New York: HarperCollins.

Giblin, James Cross. (1993). *Be seated: A book about chairs.* New York: HarperCollins.

Giblin, James Cross. (1995). *When plague strikes: The black death, smallpox, AIDS.* New York: HarperCollins.

Giblin, James Cross. (1999). *The mystery of the mammoth bones: And how it was solved.* New York: HarperCollins.

Giblin, James Cross. (2000). *The century that was: Reflections on the last one hundred years.* New York: HarperCollins.

Gorrell, Gena K. (1996). *North star to freedom: The story of the underground railroad.* New York: Delacorte.

Guiberson, Brenda Z. (1998). *Mummy mysteries: Tales from North America.* New York: Holt.

Hampton, Wilborn. (1997). *Kennedy assassinated! The world mourns.* Cambridge: Candlewick.

Heiligman, Deborah. (1996). *From caterpillar to butterfly* (Bari Weissman, Illus.). New York: HarperCollins.

Hellard, Susan. (1999). *Baby lemur.* New York: Holt.

Heller, Ruth. (1987). *A cache of jewels and other collective nouns.* New York: Grosset & Dunlap.

Hoban, Tana. (1998). *So many circles, so many squares.* New York: Greenwillow.

Hoban, Tana. (2000). *Cubes, cones, cylinders, & spheres.* New York: Greenwillow.

Jackson, Donna M. (1996). *The bone detectives: How forensic anthropologists solve crimes and uncover mysteries of the dead* (Charlie Fellenbaum, Photog.). Little, Brown.

Jaspersohn, William. (1994). *My hometown library.* Boston: Houghton Mifflin.

Jenkins, Pricilla Belz. (1995). *A nest full of eggs* (Lizzy Rockwell, Illus.). New York: HarperCollins.

Jenkins, Pricilla Belz. (1996). *Falcons nest on skyscrapers* (Megan Lloyd, Illus.). New York: HarperCollins.

Jones, Charlotte Foltz. (1999). *Yukon gold: The story of the Klondike gold rush.* New York: Holiday.

Kindersley, Barnabas, & Kindersley, Anabel. (1995). *Children just like me.* New York: DK.

Klutz Press Editors. (1993). *Make believe: A book of costume and fantasy.* Palo Alto, CA: Klutz Press.

Kraus, Scott, & Mallory, Ken. (1993). *The search for the right whale.* New York: Crown.

Lasky, Kathryn. (1998). *Shadows in the dawn: The lemurs of Madagascar* (Christopher G. Knight, Photog.). San Diego, CA: Harcourt Brace.

Lauber, Patricia. (1998). *Painters of the caves.* Washington, DC: National Geographic Society.

Lavies, Bianca. (1993). *Compost critters.* New York: Dutton.

Lawlor, Veronica. (1995). *I was dreaming to come to America: Memories from the Ellis Island oral history project.* New York: Viking.

Maizels, Jennie, & Petty, Kate. (1996). *The amazing pop-up grammar book.* New York: Dutton.

Markle, Sandra. (1998). *Outside and inside alligators.* New York: Simon & Schuster.

McMillan, Bruce. (1995a). *Night of the puffins.* San Diego: Harcourt Brace.

McMillan, Bruce. (1995b). *Puffins climb, penguins rhyme.* San Diego: Harcourt Brace.

McMillan, Bruce. (1996). *Jelly beans for sale.* New York: Scholastic.

Meltzer, Milton. (1976). *Never to forget: The Jews of the Holocaust.* New York: Harper Trophy.

Meltzer, Milton. (1984). *The black Americans: A history in their own words.* New York: Crowell.

Meltzer, Milton. (1987). *The American revolutionaries: A history in their own words, 1750–1800.* New York: Crowell.

Meltzer, Milton. (1989). *Voices from the Civil War.* New York: Crowell.

Meltzer, Milton. (1993). *Gold: The true story of why people search for it, mine it, trade it, steal it, mint it, hoard it, shape it, wear it, fight and kill for it.* New York: HarperCollins.

Meltzer, Milton. (1996). *Weapons & warfare: From the stone age to the space age.* New York: HarperCollins.

Mettger, Zak. (1994). *Till victory is won: Black soldiers in the Civil War.* New York: Lodestar.

Miller, Jonathan. (1993). *The human body.* New York: Viking.

Miller, Margaret. (1998). *Big and little.* New York: Greenwillow.

Morgan, Rowland. (1997). *In the next three seconds . . .* (Ron Josey & Kira Josey, Illus.). New York: Lodestar.

Morris, Ann. (1995). *Shoes shoes shoes.* New York: Lothrop.

Morris, Ann. (1998a). *Play.* New York: Lothrop.

Morris, Ann. (1998b). *Work.* New York: Lothrop.

Morrison, Gordon. (1998). *Bald eagle.* Boston: Houghton Mifflin.

Murphy, Jim. (1990). *The boys' war: Confederate and Union soldiers talk about the Civil War.* New York: Clarion.

Murphy, Jim. (1992). *The long road to Gettysburg.* New York: Clarion.

Murphy, Jim. (1993). *Across America on an emigrant train.* New York: Clarion.

Murphy, Jim. (1995). *The great fire.* New York: Scholastic.

Murphy, Jim. (1998). *Gone-a-whaling: The lure of the sea and the hunt for the great whale.* New York: Clarion.

Murphy, Stuart J. (1996). *Too many kangaroo things to do!* (Kevin O'Malley, Illus.). New York: HarperCollins.

Murphy, Stuart J. (1997a). *Betcha!* (S. D. Schindler, Illus.). New York: HarperCollins.

Murphy, Stuart J. (1997b). *Every buddy counts* (Fiona Dunbar, Illus.). New York: HarperCollins.

Murphy, Stuart J. (1998). *Circus shapes* (Edward Miller, Illus.). New York: HarperCollins.

Murphy, Stuart J. (1999). *Jump, kangaroo, jump!* (Kevin O'Malley, Illus.). New York: HarperCollins.

Myers, Walter Dean. (1991). *Now is your time! The African-American struggle for freedom.* New York: HarperTrophy.

Myers, Walter Dean. (1995). *One more river to cross: An African American photograph album.* San Diego: Harcourt.

Nieuwsma, Milton J. (1998). *Kinderlager: An oral history of young Holocaust survivors.* New York: Holiday House.

Oldershaw, Cally. (1999). *3D rocks and minerals.* New York: DK.

Parsons, Alexandra. (1990). *Amazing mammals.* New York: Dorling Kindersley.

Patent, Dorothy Hinshaw. (1993). *Looking at penguins* (Graham Robertson, Photog.). New York: Holiday House.

Patent, Dorothy Hinshaw. (1996). *Biodiversity* (William Munoz, Photog.). New York: Clarion.

Patent, Dorothy Hinshaw. (1998). *Fire: Friend or foe* (William Munoz, Photog.). New York: Clarion.

Perl, Lila. (1992). *It happened in America: True stories from the fifty states* (Ib Ohlsson, Illus.). New York: Holt.

Platt, Richard. (1993). *Stephen Biesty's cross-sections: Man of war.* New York: Dorling Kindersley.

Robbins, Ken. (1998). *Autumn leaves.* New York: Scholastic.

Robertson, James I., Jr. (1992). *Civil War! America becomes one nation.* New York: Knopf.

Rogasky, Barbara. (1988). *Smoke and ashes: The story of the Holocaust.* New York: Holiday House.

Roop, Peter, & Roop, Connie. (1990). *I, Columbus: My journal, 1492–3.* New York: Walker.

Rubel, David. (1995). *The United States in the 20th century.* New York: Scholastic.

Rubin, Susan Goldman. (1998). *Toilets, toasters & telephones: The how and why of everyday objects* (Elsa Warnick, Illus.). San Diego: Harcourt.

Sabuda, Robert. (1998). *ABC Disney: An alphabet pop-up.* New York: Disney Press.

Sandler, Martin W. (1994a). *Cowboys.* New York: HarperCollins.

Sandler, Martin W. (1994b). *Pioneers.* New York: HarperCollins.

Sandler, Martin W. (1996a). *Civil War: A Library of Congress book.* New York: HarperCollins.

Sandler, Martin W. (1996b) *Inventors.* New York: HarperCollins.

Santa Fe Writer's Group. (1993). *Bizarre & beautiful noses.* Santa Fe, NM: John Muir.

Schwartz, Alvin. (1974). *Cross your fingers, spit in your hat: Superstitions and other beliefs.* Philadelphia: Lippincott.

Schwartz, David. (1985). *How much is a million?* (Steven Kellogg, Illus.). New York: Lothrop.

Schwartz, David. (1989). *If you made a million* (Steven Kellogg, Illus.). New York: Lothrop.

Schwartz, David. (1999a). *If you hopped like a frog* (James Warhola, Illus.). New York: Scholastic.

Schwartz, David. (1999b). *On beyond a million: An amazing math journey* (Paul Meisel, Illus.). New York: Doubleday.

Simon, Seymour. (1985). *Saturn.* New York: Morrow.

Simon, Seymour. (1998a). *Destination: Jupiter.* New York: Morrow.

Simon, Seymour. (1998b). *The universe.* New York: Morrow.

Simon, Seymour. (1998c). *Now you see it, now you don't: The amazing world of optical illusions.* New York: Morrow.

Simon, Seymour. (2000). *Gorillas.* New York: HarperCollins.

Stanley, Jerry. (1992). *Children of the dust bowl: The true story of the school at Weedpatch Camp.* New York: Crown.

Stanley, Jerry. (1994). *I am an American.* New York: Crown.

Stanley, Jerry. (2000). *Hurry freedom: African Americans in gold rush California.* New York: Crown.

Sturges, Philemon. (1998). *Bridges are to cross* (Giles Laroche, Illus.). New York: Putnam.

Swanson, Diane. (1998). *Animals eat the weirdest things.* New York: Holt.

Tarsky, Sue. (1997). *The busy building book* (Alex Ayliffe, Illus.). New York: Putnam.

Valenta, Barbara. (1997). *Pop-o-mania: How to create your own pop-ups.* New York: Dial.

van der Meer, Ron. (1994). *Music pack.* New York: Knopf.

van der Meer, Ron, & Sudjic, Deyan. (1997). *The architecture pack.* New York: Knopf.

van der Rol, & Verhoeven, Rian. (1993). *Anne Frank: Beyond the diary.* New York: Viking.

Vieira, Linda. (1994). *The ever-living tree: The life and times of a coastal redwood* (Christopher Canyon, Illus.). New York: Walker.

Walker, Richard. (1999). *3D human body.* New York: DK.

Young, Jay. (1999). *The art of science: A pop-up adventure in art.* Cambridge, MA: Candlewick.

▼▼▼▼▼▼▼▼

Professional References

Facklam, M. (1990). *Writing nonfiction.* Speech given at the Highlights Writer's Conference, Chautauqua, NY, 12 July.

Kobrin, B. (1988). *Eyeopeners! How to choose and use children's books about real people, places, and things.* New York: Viking.

Meltzer, M. (1993). Voices from the past. In M. O. Tunnell & R. Ammon (Eds.), *The story of ourselves: Teaching history through children's literature* (pp. 27–30). Portsmouth, NH: Heinemann.

Answers to David Schwartz's math quiz (see p. 340):
To count to a million, saying each number completely and going nonstop, would take 23 days. To reach a billion would consume 95 years, and counting to a trillion, over 200,000 years. A stack of $100 in pennies would be 50 feet tall and, of course, you would have 10,000 of them. Finally, a 1 with 100 zeros after it is called a "googol."

BIOGRAPHY

11

CHAPTER

If you want to cover
People Who Made a Difference

Consider as a READ ALOUD

America's Champion Swimmer:
Gertrude Ederle,
by David A. Adler,
illustrated by Terry Widener

Consider as a TEXT SET

Bard of Avon,
by Diane Stanley and Peter Vennema,
illustrated by Diane Stanley

Cleopatra,
by Diane Stanley and Peter Vennema

Mandela,
by Floyd Cooper

Mary McLeod Bethune,
by Eloise Greenfield,
illustrated by Jerry Pinkney

A Picture Book of Sojourner Truth,
by David Adler,
illustrated by Gershom Griffith

A Weed is a Flower: The Life
of George Washington Carver,
by Aliki

SOJOURNER TRUTH
by David A. Adler, illustrated by Gershom Griffith

A Picture Book of
Sojourner Truth

David A. Adler

illustrated by Gershom Griffith

Sojourner Truth called slave owners sinners who soon would be punished by God. She laughed at the idea that women were weaker than men. "Look at me," she said. "I have plowed and planted . . . and ain't I a woman?" She even pulled up her sleeve and showed the audience her muscular arm. "Sisters," she said, "if women want any rights, more than they got, why don't they just take them, and not be talking about it?"

Excerpt from *A Picture Book of Sojourner Truth* by David A. Adler, illustrated by Gershom Griffith

Student Response

Riley 7

I mowed and planted and ain't I a women?

To visit a classroom exploring the issues of Biography, please go to Chapter 11 of our companion website at **www.prenhall.com/darigan**

To one degree or another, we all seem to have a taste for learning more about great or important people; who they are and what makes them tick. This predisposition translates into the natural interest children show when they pick up biographies and autobiographies about contemporary heroes or historical figures they may be studying in school. The titles that we use to open this chapter provide you with a good example of the latter. These books represent the stories of the extraordinary things real people from the past have accomplished. These people, in most cases, were ordinary folks who went on to write, lead their fellow citizens, invent, or carry out great physical feats. Because of that, they are remembered in biography. After all, the word "biography" comes from the Greek *bio-,* meaning life, and *-graphy,* which means to write—writing somebody's life.

▼▼▼▼▼▼▼

What Is Biography?

There are many permutations within this category of "writing somebody's life," or the genre of biography. But among all the variations, these books provide readers with essential facts, anecdotes, and stories about a particular person's life. If well written, these books set the person firmly in the place and times in which he or she grew up. Take, for example, Cheryl Harness's *Mark Twain and the Queens of the Mississippi.* This lively picture book biography provides readers with as much information about Twain (the

ISLAND No.10 was a rebel stronghold until April 7, 1862. Now the U.S. forces controlled the river south to MEMPHIS which fell to U.S. gunboats. June 6, 1862

U.S. General Ulysses S. Grant

The Civil War ended Sam's pilot days in the spring of 1861. Battles and blockades ended regular shipping on the Mississippi River. Sam was ordered to pilot "ironclad" gunboats for the Union but he did not want to fight against his home state of Missouri, whose governor sided with the South. He drilled for a while with a band of pro-South volunteers, but unhappy, out-of-a-job Sam didn't really want to fight the Union soldiers of the U. S. Government either, so when his big brother, Orion, asked him to go west with him, Sam left the river and the war behind. "I retired to private life, to give the Union cause a chance," said Sam wryly.

Reprinted with the permission of Simon & Schuster books for Young Readers, an imprint of Simon & Schuster Children's Publishing Division from *Mark Twain and the Queens of the Mississippi* by Cheryl Harness. Copyright © 1998 Cheryl Harness.

pseudonym he used for his real name, Samuel Clemens) as it does about the times. For example, when Harness discusses how young Sam Clemens's riverboat days ended as a consequence of the battles and blockades of the Civil War, she also includes a map and handwritten annotations that provide historical highlights of the effect the war had on the river. This contextualizing of the times allows young readers to more ably understand a period well beyond their own life experiences.

As we mentioned in chapter 2, the Age of New Realism began to change the face of children's books beginning somewhere in the 1960s. Until then, juvenile biographies generally were fictionalized, sometimes at the expense of honesty and accuracy. Publishers, librarians, and educators felt that children would not read a biography unless it looked and read like a novel. These *fictionalized biographies* are less common today and, instead, fictional accounts of a person's life are often written and classified as historical fiction. Examples include **Upon the Head of the Goat,** Aranka Siegal's powerful autobiographical story of her family's Holocaust ordeal. Sook Nyul Choi presents a harsh indictment of the Japanese military as she describes their occupation of Korea during World War II in her novel **Year of Impossible Goodbyes.** Kyoko Mori fictionalizes her own mother's suicide and the resulting sadness and shame she felt growing up in Japan in her book **Shizuko's Daughter.**

The *authentic biography,* written as true nonfiction, is today's trend in biographies for young readers. Although crafted in expository form rather than in narrative form (as with novels), authentic biographies can be as vigorous and entertaining as good fiction. Milton Meltzer, known for his biographies and informational books about history and

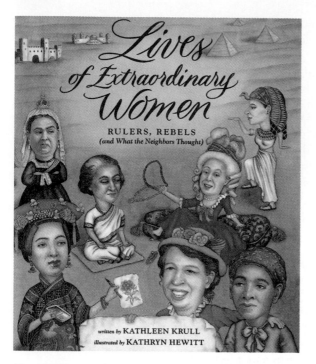

Lives of Extraordinary Women: Rulers, Rebels (and What the Neighbors Thought) by Kathleen Krull, Illustrations © 2000 by Kathryn Hewitt. Reprinted by permission of Harcourt.

social change, says, "I think I've used almost every technique fiction writers call on (except to invent the facts) in order to draw readers in, deepen their feeling for people whose lives may be remote from their own, and enrich their understanding of forces that shape the outcome of all our lives" (quoted in Donelson & Nilsen, 1989, p. 259).

Note the stylistic flair Russell Freedman gives to these paragraphs in his *Lincoln: A Photobiography*:

Today it's hard to imagine Lincoln as he really was. And he never cared to reveal much about himself. In company he was witty and talkative, but he rarely betrayed his inner feelings. According to William Herndon, his law partner, he was "the most secretive—reticent—shut-mouthed man that ever lived."

In his own time, Lincoln was never fully understood even by his closest friends. Since then, he had become as much a legend as a flesh-and-blood human being. While the legend is based on truth, it is only partly true. And it hides the man behind it like a disguise.

The vast majority of biographies for children are written as *individual biographies,* which deal with the life of a single subject. Most of what we describe in this chapter centers on the individual biography. Another brand of biography is the *collective biography,* which contains a number of short biographical pieces about subjects who have a common trait. For example, Russell Freedman's *Indian Chiefs* looks at the lives of six prominent Native American leaders, including Sitting Bull and Chief Joseph. Bo Zaunders introduces eight adventurers in his *Crocodiles, Camels, & Dugout Canoes.* Included are sketches of people such as the author Richard Burton, Ernest Shackleton, and Antoine de Saint-Exupéry (author of *The Little Prince*).

In another selection, biographical poetry features 14 young women "who made a difference" such as Amelia Earhart, Rachel Carson, and Mary Jane McLeod, in *All*

ALTERNATE TEXT SET

Biographical Sketches by Kathleen Krull

Read Aloud

Lives of Extraordinary Women: Rulers, Rebels (and What the Neighbors Thought)

Text Set

Lives of the Musicians: Good Times, Bad Times (and What the Neighbors Thought)

Lives of the Writers: Comedies, Tragedies (and What the Neighbors Thought)

Lives of the Artists: Masterpieces, Messes (and What the Neighbors Thought)

Lives of the Athletes: Thrills, Spills (and What the Neighbors Thought)

EVALUATING BIOGRAPHY

- ▌ Authenticity: Is the biography accurate? Does the biographer acknowledge his or her sources, and does he or she include direct quotes?
- ▌ Objectivity: Is the biographer objective about his or her subject? Does he or she paint a complete picture of the subject, listing both good and bad traits?
- ▌ Writing style: Is the biography readable and not just a listing of facts?
- ▌ Subjects: Is the person about whom the biography is written worthy of this profile?
- ▌ Book design and layout: Is the book attractively constructed and engaging to the reader?
- ▌ Type of biography: Does the biography fall clearly into a discernible category, such as autobiography, picture book biography, and simplified biography?

by Herself, by Ann Whitford Paul. A very interesting grouping of collective biographies appears in Katherine Leiner's *First Children: Growing Up in the White House.* Included are the humorous, as well as the serious, anecdotes about the 17 families who lived in the Executive Mansion.

Often collective biographies hit the mass-market bookshelves and feature popular, current personalities, such as sports heroes, actors, and rock stars. Although this sort of collective biography may not be well written because of the hurried nature of getting it to press before these folks fall out of the public eye, the interest level for many young readers is high.

▼▼▼▼▼▼▼▼

Considerations for Selecting Biographies for Young Readers

Authenticity

Because biography is a special brand of nonfiction, good biographies must exhibit certain characteristics that vary from those in fiction. Naturally, the need for authenticity cannot be ignored. Authenticity involves several factors. First, and most basic, is that the information in a biography must be accurate. Often biographers will acknowledge their sources of information as a way of letting their readers know that plenty of research went into their writing. John B. Severance, for example, lists detailed acknowledgments, indexes, and bibliographies in his insightful portraits of great leaders, such as *Thomas Jefferson: Architect of Democracy* and *Gandhi: Great Soul.*

BOOKMARK

INTEGRATING TECHNOLOGY: SOURCES ON THE WORLD WIDE WEB

An annual annotated book list created by the National Council for the Social Studies (NCSS) in cooperation with the Children's Book Council (CBC) is available on the website *Notable Children's Trade Books in the Field of Social Studies.* Bibliographies for K–8 books published in 1997, 1998, and 1999 are available. The books are divided into subcategories such as "Global Connections" and "Time, Continuity, and Change." The listings are quite extensive.

To find out more about Notable Children's Trade Books and other sources on the World Wide Web, visit Chapter 11 on the companion website at **www.prenhall. com/darigan**

Also, authors of authentic biographies must take care with the use of direct quotes. Jean Fritz (1988) makes it clear that she does "not use quotation marks unless I have a source" (p. 759). For instance, in **Can't You Make Them Behave, King George?,** George's mother is quoted as saying, "Stand up straight, George. Kings don't slouch." Although these words may sound fabricated, Fritz found them in **King George III** by John Brooke. Of course, fictionalized biographies take greater liberties with the words spoken by the characters, which is why they often are classified as historical fiction today.

Objectivity

However, it must be noted that authenticity has its less exacting side. It is impossible for biographers to be totally objective; their personal perspectives will always color the ways in which they present their subjects. Interpretation of events must be based soundly in fact, but once again, there is always more than one side to a story. Subjectivity can't be avoided totally because authors are only human. For example, if an author were a Holocaust survivor, writing an objective biography of Adolf Hitler would be difficult. A civil rights activist might have trouble writing an honest biography about Martin Luther King, Jr., a biography that would show King's weak points as well as his strong ones. As Newbery-winning author James Daugherty (1972) has said, "when you're writing biography you're also writing autobiography." In other words, how biographers feel about their subjects affects, at least subtly, the portrayal.

As you might guess, when people write about their own lives, the problem with objectivity is even more acute. However, *autobiography* provides the unique viewpoint of self-revelation. What writing about oneself loses in objectivity it gains in wholeness. No one has as complete a view of a life as the one who has lived it. Biographers who write of others' lives can never get inside their subjects' heads and hearts, although this distance may allow for a more balanced and objective view.

On the other hand, a biographer ought to avoid making blatant personal judgments and should allow the actions and words of the subject to speak for themselves. For instance, Jean Fritz presents Christopher Columbus as an arrogant, egotistical individual in her brief biography **Where Do You Think You're Going, Christopher Columbus?** Note, however, that she never states, "Christopher Columbus was a self-absorbed egomaniac." Instead, she allows the reader to come to that conclusion through reading Columbus's words and deeds. The perfect example of this is when he robbed Rodrigo, one of his sailors, of the promised prize for spotting land first. "Columbus said no, he had, himself, sighted land when he'd seen a light at ten o'clock. How could it be otherwise? Surely God, who had gone to so much trouble to bring him here, meant him to have the honor."

One of the shortcomings in some juvenile biographies is that the authors may glorify the subjects, to turn them into idols or make them larger than life. This is a form of stereotyping that can actually alienate readers from the subject of a biography instead of helping them know the subject as a real person. To present a balanced view means looking at the blemishes as well as the strong points. Instead of conveying the message, for instance, that Abraham Lincoln was born virtually perfect, a more positive and effective message for young readers is that Lincoln had many of the same human weaknesses as the rest of us, but he was able to rise above them to do great things.

Russell Freedman's Newbery-winning *Lincoln: A Photobiography* provides a nice blend of the man's imperfections as well as his strong points. We see a Lincoln who was self-effacing, who stood bravely to sign the Emancipation Proclamation (though it was popular with nearly no other politicians), and who wrote the Gettysburg Address. But we also see the Lincoln whose law office was a colossal mess. "He was moody, lapsing into long brooding silences" and suffered from severe depression much of his life. And he argued with his wife. "When Mary lost her temper, the neighbors would hear her furious explosions of anger." We like this Lincoln better than the one on a pedestal because we recognize him as more like one of us. Note how human and vulnerable Lincoln appears when forced to end his courtship of Mary Todd:

> Early in 1841, Lincoln broke off the engagement. He had known bouts of depression before, but now he plunged into the worst emotional crisis of his life. For a week, he refused to leave his room. People around town said that he had thrown "two cat fits and a duck fit." He had gone "crazy for a week or two." To his law partner Stuart, who was serving a term in Congress, Lincoln wrote: "I am the most miserable man living. If what I feel were equally distributed to the whole human family, there would not be one cheerful face on earth."

Writing Style

Biographies should, of course, conform to the other standards of good writing. Just presenting facts is not enough. Heavens, if we wanted just the facts we would go to an encyclopedia, a biographical dictionary, or the Internet. But just as we have talked about the importance of *voice* in the writing of narrative, we find that the author's voice in nonfiction must be just as strong—maybe even stronger. That voice is present in nonfiction may be the most important factor about whether a child reads on or not (Meltzer, 1993, p. 29).

But what is voice? Ralph Fletcher likens it to the "*intimacy* between writer and subject"; it's the author "pulling in close, cozying up to the subject" (p. 72). On the other hand, Patricia Lee Gauch (personal communication, 2000) counters that voice, in the end, is "letting go." So which is it, you ask, pulling in close or letting go?

In our minds, it is both. First, the author must get close to the subject. That happens during the research phase of the book. Immersing oneself in every aspect of the character, then, engenders that intimacy. Knowing what the person wore, where he or she lived, what he or she liked and disliked all allow the author to "cozy up" to the subject. Once the author has sufficiently steeped him- or herself in that character, like a hot tea pot sitting atop the stove on a cold winter morning, then and only then can he or she "let go" and write about that person with passion. It is the blended soul of the subject and the author that must spring forth on the page, come alive, and engage the reader. If that doesn't happen, the reader will close the book and both the author and the subject will remain forgotten.

Take, for example, Patricia McMahon's profile, *One Belfast Boy.* Notice how her prose jumps from the page, giving us a flavor of both boy and setting in just her introductory paragraph:

> Liam Leathem walks through the winter light of his neighborhood, Turf Lodge, in the city of Belfast, Northern Ireland. He pulls on his blue stocking cap, the one he always wears, cold or no. Up ahead he spots a group of kids younger than his eleven years. The gang is throwing rocks at a wall, a wall covered with words. The graffiti

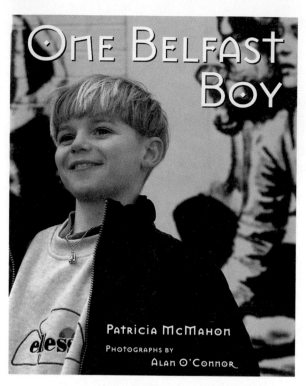

Cover from *One Belfast Boy,* by Patricia McMahon, photographs by Alan O'Connor. Jacket photograph copyright © 1999 by Alan O'Connor. Reprinted by permission of Houghton Mifflin Company. All rights reserved.

proclaims WE SHALL NEVER BE DEFEATED. Other slogans read IRA and TIOC-FAIDH ÁR LA. All the rock throwers, whether they speak Airish or not, know that these last words proclaim OUR DAY WILL COME.

Another important consideration in writing style is the perspective that the author chooses to tell his or her story. Biography is most often written in the third person omniscient. This means someone else, a distant third party, is telling the story, which allows the teller to remain a bit detached yet knowledgeable. Again, the voice of the teller is of utmost importance. Consider Diane Stanley's description of Joan's home as she was growing up, in *Joan of Arc.*

Jacques d'Arc, Joan's father, was something of a leader in the village, and the family lived in a stone house next door to the church. But do not imagine anything grand. It had a dirt floor, and the rooms were musty and damp. There were no bathrooms, and no one in the village was likely to be very clean.

Stanley delivers her first sentence, which is a mere description of Joan's father's position in the community and where they lived. Then she very deftly, but simply, pulls us in by telling us, "But do not imagine anything grand." It is just as if she were telling this story to a group of people, but then she turns her head right toward us and almost parenthetically states, "But do not imagine anything grand."

Another stylistic choice authors adopt is to tell their stories from the point of view of a child or minor character who can then discuss the biographical subject from an "I was there so I can tell you" perspective. Judith Byron Schachner employs this technique in her book *Mr. Emerson's Cook.* Describing the great Ralph Waldo Emerson is Annie Burns, a domestic newly arrived from Ireland who cooked and cleaned for the great philosopher and poet. Annie Burns, who was actually Schachner's great grandmother, tells about her struggles in getting Emerson to eat because of "an overactive imagination and a meddlesome Mother Nature."

Subject Matter

This may sound rather simplistic, but *who* the biography is about is a very important factor as well. No matter what genre we are reading, we want to give our children the best literature that is available. Specific to our subject at hand, this means providing kids with well-written biographies about subjects who truly warrant being written about.

In the middle of the last century, biographies were basically dominated by a handful of characters in American and world history who were as predictable as changing of the seasons. A plethora of books that discussed the great presidents, scientists, and a handful of athletes were about the extent of the material available. Today, we are seeing biographies that cut a wide swath, allowing our students to sample an extremely diverse population.

If you look back at this chapter's opening text set, notice that four of the six paperback selections are about people of African descent. This kind of choice encourages children to read widely about a variety of people (both female and male) and many diverse cultures. In keeping with this philosophy, you will notice that throughout this chapter we refer to a very wide range of personalities as an example of this.

This diversity turns out to be a distinct advantage to *all* children in *all* cultures. For example, it is important for a white sixth-grade child to read about figures such as Mexican muralist Diego Rivera, in Anne E. Neimark's *Diego Rivera: Artist of the*

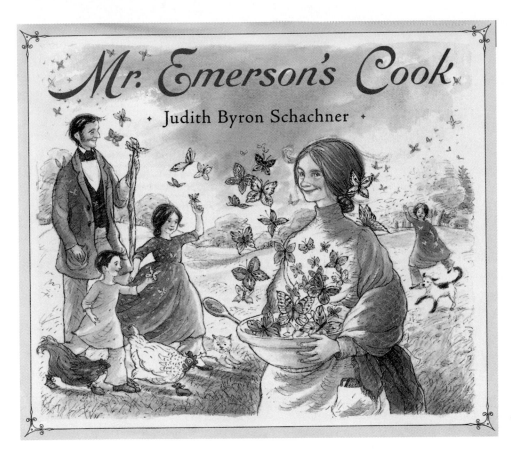

Cover from *Mr. Emerson's Cook* by Judith Byron Schachner, copyright © 1998 by Judith Byron Schachner. Used by permission of Dutton Children's Books, a division of Penguin Putnam, Inc.

People. Clearly that same child would also benefit tremendously from reading about African American poet Langston Hughes, in Audrey Osofsky's *Free to Dream: The Making of a Poet.* Also, reading about pianist Clara Schumann, in Susanna Reich's *Clara Schumann: Piano Virtuoso,* gives all children, no matter what race they may be, a sense of a great woman who was able to manage a very successful musical career as well as raise eight children in a time in history that was not nearly so supportive of females working outside the home as it is now. Providing these richly written biographies to children opens up a world and culture they quite possibly never realized existed.

On the other hand, a Mexican American child reading about Diego Rivera or an African American child reading about Langston Hughes gets the opportunity to see his or her own culture represented in a book. Further, it models notable examples to which they can also aspire.

Finally, the advantage we share in this golden age of children's literature, with so many books at our fingertips, is that many biographies have been written about less well-known figures who have nonetheless contributed significantly to humankind. Take, for instance, Pam Conrad's book *Prairie Visions: The Life and Times of Solomon Butcher.* Conrad chronicles the life of this entrepreneur, so taken by the tenacity of the sod farmers of Nebraska that he single-handedly photographed the citizens of Custer County, wrote up their homespun tales, and produced them as a book serving as a lasting memorial to these hardworking pioneers.

A name that doesn't command nearly the notoriety of a Picasso or Winslow Homer is that of the colonial painter and scientist Charles Wilson Peale. Janet Wilson's detailed biography, *The Ingenious Mr. Peale,* demonstrates the greatness of this self-taught portrait painter and natural historian who captured almost every great leader in the American Revolution in oil on canvas. This book (along with a fictional biography by Michael O. Tunnell that focuses on a small episode in Peale's life, called *The Joke's On George,* illustrated by Kathy Osborn) deepens the knowledge children have of this man who contributed so much to the American colonies of the time.

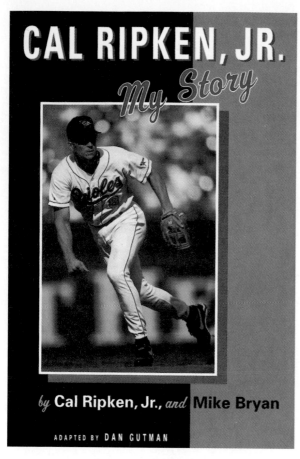

Cover from **Cal Ripken, Jr.: My Story** by Cal Ripken, Jr., and Mike Bryan. Adapted by Dan Gutman. Copyright © 1999. Reprinted by permission of Dial Books for Young Readers.

Mary E. Lyons has chosen yet another American painter, Clementine Hunter, and produced a dramatic re-creation of her life and work taken from Hunter's own words written in newspaper and magazine articles. In her **Talking With Tebé: Clementine Hunter, Memory Artist,** we are introduced to this self-taught folk artist who captured the backbreaking work of the Louisiana plantation in her simple, bright paintings.

Finally, Jerry Stanley introduces us to a character who gets only passing references in the social studies texts (if any at all), Annie Clemenc, in his **Big Annie of Calumet: A True Story of the Industrial Revolution.** Describing the determination and heroism of this powerful woman, Stanley tells Annie's story against the backdrop of the 1913 Michigan miners' labor strike waged at the powerful Calumet and Hecla Mining Company.

Book Design and Layout

To some children, informational books, biography in particular, tend to have a less compelling story line, therefore the design of the book is of utmost importance. We reiterate Beverly Kobrin's admonishing in the last chapter when she says, "Say no to ugly books!" Kids *do* judge books by their covers; let's face it.

Cover

Let's start with the cover. Just as we mentioned with informational books in the last chapter, the cover must immediately engage readers. It must pique their interest so

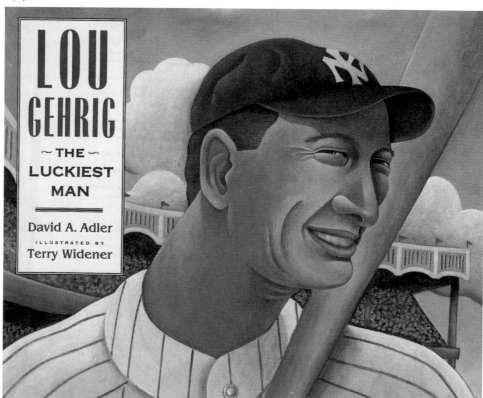

Cover from **Lou Gehrig: The Luckiest Man,** by David A. Adler, illustrations copyright © 1997 by Terry Widener. Reprinted by permission of Harcourt.

they will naturally delve inside for all the goodies the book holds. Photographs of people doing what they were noted for is the first, best way to reach that end. Whether it is Cal Ripkin, Jr. digging to his right to snag a hot ground ball, as shown in **Cal Ripkin, Jr.: Play Ball!,** by Ripkin himself and Mike Bryan, or a photo of Tomie de-Paola welcoming us in his front door in Barbara Elleman's **Tomie dePaola: His Art and His Stories,** these crisp, colorful portraits beg us to enter.

In many other successful biographies, close-up paintings seem to be the attention grabber that makes us want to open the cover and read. Look at Terry Widener's extra-large cover illustration in **Lou Gehrig: The Luckiest Man,** by David Adler. It accents the larger-than-life persona of the Iron Horse of professional baseball who set a world record with his 2,130 consecutive games.

On a more aesthetic level, we see how Peter Sís encourages us to enter the world of Galileo in his Caldecott Honor book, **Starry Messenger.** Notice how this cover is perfectly symmetrical from top to bottom with the title and author's name, as well as side to side with the enlarged castle blocks interrupted only by the window opening in dark blue. The figure of Galileo is offset to the left, BUT notice he has his telescope pointed to the right and is focused on turning the cover to open the book. Inside, a quick glance at the dark endpapers bordered with symbols of this scientist's turbulent life has only one bright spot—Galileo, once again looking to the right, the way we turn the page and read.

Internal Design

Once readers are inside, it is essential that the layout does not look like sterile, bland social studies books of the past. Boring line drawings and poorly reproduced photographs have given way to bright illustrations, less text, and a real attention to design. Notice how a wonderfully designed book makes us want to turn to the next page. For instance, in Mary Azarian's Caldecott-winning *Snowflake Bentley,* the biography of photographer Wilson Bentley written by Jacqueline Briggs Martin, we see young Willie reveling in a Vermont snowstorm. You can see in the illustrations how Azarian has started the road behind Bentley and see the way it slopes down from behind the barn, widens, and runs off the right-hand side of the page. We are amply invited to turn the page, just as we would continue down the road. Attention to subtle details such as these makes a ho-hum read into a humdinger.

▼▼▼▼▼▼▼

Types of Biography

Worthwhile biographies, then, must first engage young readers with eye-catching cover and design, and keep their interest with fresh prose and a riveting perspective that brings the subjects to life. In addition, the subject

Jacket design from **Starry Messenger,** text and illustrations by Peter Sís, copyright © 1996. Reprinted by permission of Farrar, Straus and Giroux, LLC.

From **Snowflake Bentley** by Jacqueline Briggs Martin, illustrated by Mary Azarian. Text copyright © 1998 by Jacqueline Briggs Martin. Illustrations copyright © 1998 by Mary Azarian. Reprinted by permission of Houghton Mifflin Company. All rights reserved.

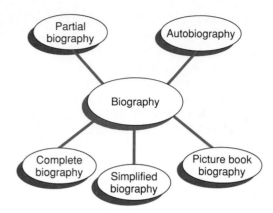

FIGURE 11–1
Web of biography.

must be worthy of being presented in a biography and the story must be told in an authentic, accurate, and objective way.

Russell Freedman, whose book ***Lincoln: A Photobiography*** won the Newbery Medal, explains that this fan letter expresses the highest praise a biographer can receive and the heights each biographer strives for. "Dear Mr. Freedman," a young boy wrote in a letter, "I read your biography of Abraham Lincoln and liked it very much. Did you take the photographs yourself?" (Freedman, 1993a, p. 41).

> Did you take the pictures yourself? he asks. That youngster came away from my book with the feeling that Abraham Lincoln was a real person who must have lived the day before yesterday. That's exactly the response I'm aiming for. After all, the goal of any biographer, any historian, is to make the past seem real, to breathe life and meaning into people and events that are dead and gone. (1993a, p. 41)

Of course, not all biographies are historical. Contemporary individuals also are the topics of biographies, and certainly autobiographies. Yet, the goal of the biographer ought to be the same—"to breathe life and meaning into people and events" (Freedman, 1993a, p. 41).

In order for us to narrow the field into subcategories, you may want to think of biography at the center of a web that would look like the graphic organizer we have placed in Figure 11–1. The scope of a biography is often dictated by format, the age of the intended readers, and the purpose of the biography itself. The specific subsets we describe here are autobiography, picture book biography, simplified biography, complete biography, and partial biography.

Autobiography

First, in *autobiography,* a living person, usually somebody well known or famous, writes about his or her own life. Beverly Cleary, author of ***Ramona*** and the many other Ramona books, ***Dear Mr. Henshaw,*** and ***The Mouse and the Motorcycle,*** has written an enormously successful autobiography in her ***A Girl From Yamhill: A Memoir.*** This book chronicles her early years growing up in Oregon as well as her high school and young adult years.

Lois Lowry's more recent autobiography, ***Looking Back: A Book of Memories,*** provides photographs and short snippets about the life of this Newbery-winning author who brought us ***Number the Stars*** and ***The Giver,*** as well as ***Anastasia Krupnik*** and the many subsequent Anastasia books. Lowry has very neatly set off her memoirs with quotes from her books that show how her life directly connected to her works. When she talks, for example, about living at her grandfather's house when she was 6 years old and her father had gone away during World War II, she ties that memory directly to the setting from her first novel, ***Autumn Street.*** In this extremely engaging

Cover from *A Girl from Yamhill: A Memoir,* by Beverly Cleary. Used by permission of Random House Children's Books, a division of Random House, Inc.

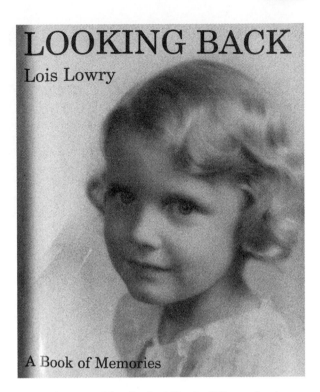

Cover from *Looking Back: A Book of Memories,* by Lois Lowry. Copyright © 1998 by Lois Lowry. Reprinted by permission of Houghton Mifflin Company. All rights reserved.

book, she shares many of the secrets of her life such as her divorce, her beautiful yet underappreciated "Kate or Allie dress," even the recent tragic death of her grown son. Family photographs set off virtually every double-page spread and add to the charm of this life story.

Betsy Byars has presented the memoirs of her life and her own spin on writing in her book *The Moon and I.* In it, she relates many humorous anecdotes about her life, such as the time she noticed a big blacksnake in the rafters of her front porch. The big fella had been watching over her for an hour while she sat, rocking, and editing a manuscript—later he would be named "Moon." Like Lois Lowry, Byars has inserted quite a number of family photos, which, in this case, are included in a center section and not interspersed throughout the text.

Further, Byars discusses her writing—where it comes from and what her process is. After discussing the important elements of story, such as writing plot, characters, and setting, she notes that a good book must have some "good scraps." She says, "Plenty of good scraps are as important in making a book as in making a quilt. I often think of my books as scrapbooks of my life, because I put in them all the neat things that I see and read and hear."

When discussing her book *Night Swimmers,* she talks about how her characters were just not coming alive. In fact, she states, "They just floated around the swimming pool, getting waterlogged." It was not until one of those little scraps entered her consciousness that she realized *who* these people were and that once she named them properly, they naturally came to life. In the book, she had named the children's father Shorty Anderson, a man who runs an all-night garage. The names

To find out more about Biography Writing with Pat and Fred McKissack and other activities on the World Wide Web, visit Chapter 11 on the companion website at **www.prenhall.com/darigan**

BOOKMARK

INTEGRATING TECHNOLOGY: ACTIVITIES USING THE WORLD WIDE WEB

From the "writing with writers" homepage at Scholastic, which is truly one of the more cutting-edge ideas included on a publishing house website, students can actually learn about the writing process from authors they have read and enjoyed. In *Biography Writing with Pat and Fred McKissack,* the student learns now to research and write a biographical sketch. Children can complete the workshop on their own but a teacher's guide is also provided, which does a great job of relating the workshop to standards, and providing detailed ideas on how to integrate the workshop into the classroom. The site even explains how to vary the plan depending on whether you have one computer for the entire classroom, several computers, a lab, or no computers at all. Either way, a certificate signed by the McKissacks can be downloaded and presented to students when they finish the workshop.

she had given these sodden kid characters were George, Barbara, and Henry. However, it all came together one night while she was watching the Grand Ole Opry. She realized that this dad was really the embodiment of the country singer Little Jimmy Dickens. And if that were the case, then he would have naturally named his children after country stars. So the kids' names were changed to Retta for Loretta Lynn, Johnny for Johnny Cash, and Roy for the legendary Roy Acuff. Only then did the characters jump off the page.

Finally, author Alma Flor Ada offers readers an overview of her youth in her book ***Under the Royal Palms: A Childhood in Cuba.*** Chronicling her early years, she includes joyful memories such as the friendship she had with her beloved dance teacher that sustained her during a horrible school year. She also describes sad remembrances, such as that of the untimely death of her uncle Medardo who loved to fly but crashes right in front of her and her family. Interlaced throughout the text is cultural and historical information about Cuba, a country few know much about.

We often see autobiographies that appear to be penned by a famous person; however, in many of these cases, there is also listed (in a little finer print) a coauthor or a "written with" author. Let's be honest: Greats like Cal Ripkin, Jr. show off their stuff on the playing field, not in front of a computer. So the help of writers Mike Bryan and Dan Gutman makes his intermediate-level biography, ***Cal Ripken, Jr.: My Story,*** as enjoyable as seeing Ripken on third base on a hot and sunny afternoon in Camden Yards. Such is also the case with Olympic gold medalist and professional figure skater Brian Boitano. In ***Boitano's Edge: Inside the Real World of Figure Skating,*** he describes his life and the grueling realities of skating. The book, written *with* (but penned mostly by) Suzanne Harper, includes rich details about skating, the life of professional touring, the moves, and the competitive rules of the sport.

Picture Book Biographies

Picture book biographies, usually intended for the young and early intermediate readers, are brief and often carry more illustration than text. Generally set in 32 pages, the standard length for picture books, such biographies provide an overview, focusing on the highlights of the subject's life. A picture book biography series by David Adler is an example of the authentic, illustrated biographies in this category.

Picture book biographies written for a more sophisticated reader logically include more text and deal with the characters and events in that subject's life in more depth. Take the books created by Diane Stanley and Peter Vennema as a prime example. This couple's titles (they are married), such as ***The Bard of Avon: The Story of William Shakespeare, Charles Dickens: The Man Who Had Great Expectations,*** and ***Cleopatra,*** contain details not possible to cover in a simplified picture book biography. For instance, when Vennema describes Dickens's famous *Pickwick Papers,* a serial that launched him into literary fame, he is able to actually note where the idea came from. He discusses how tragedy turned into great fortune, and quite possibly where, many years later, Walt Disney got all his entrepreneurial ideas for marketing a good book. All we can say is step aside, *Lion King*—let the Pickwickians show you how marketing should be done! If you really want to know the details to these statements, you'll just have to get to your library and read ***Charles Dickens*** by Vennema and Stanley. Other books by Diane Stanley alone are her ***Leonardo da Vinci*** and the previously mentioned, superb ***Joan of Arc.*** These texts are enjoyed by children in the middle and upper grades and aren't so long that they become daunting to the reader.

To find almost two dozen biographies written by author David Adler, refer to the database that accompanies this text.

Simplified Biography

Simplified biographies are aimed at the newly independent, intermediate readers and appear as picture books or as short chapter books. Typically, these books include frequent illustrations, and though their content is not as inclusive as the complete biography, they certainly go into much more detail than what we find in the garden variety picture book. A wonderful example of this type of book, centering on the Revolutionary War era, is a series authored by Jean Fritz and illustrated by a wide variety of famous children's illustrators. Fritz has brought to life many of the central figures in this battle between America and England with her engaging style and her adherence to interesting details. She discusses, for instance, the exorbitant lifestyle of John Hancock, with his garish clothing and his home decorated with comforts beyond imagination, in ***Will You Sign Here, John Hancock?*** She describes the reaction in Boston when England repealed the Stamp Act:

> Such news called for a celebration, and who was the Number One Celebrator?
>
> John Hancock, of course. He festooned his house with flags, piled his tables high with food, lighted up windows (all 54 of them), and when the townspeople gathered on the Common, John Hancock threw open his doors for one of the grandest parties Boston had ever had. For those who couldn't fit in the doors, he rolled out a 126-gallon cask of Madeira wine. Then he set off fireworks—huzza! huzza!

Other series of simplified biographies include the Dell Yearling Biographies in paperback and written by a variety of authors. David Adler also writes a series called A First Biography, which includes many of the same subjects as his picture book biography series but for a slightly older audience. Viking's Women of Our Time series, written by a variety of well-known authors, focuses on influential women such as Sandra Day O'Connor, Margaret Mead, Laura Ingalls Wilder, and Mother Teresa.

DID YOU KNOW?

In the 1970s, illustrator Trina Schart Hyman had done one of Jean Fritz's short American history novels and was working on a second, ***Will You Sign Here, John Hancock?*** when she became only too aware that reviewer Virginia Kirkus was not only panning her books, but "viciously stomping on them. It appeared that she was out to get me," Hyman told us. So in the graveyard illustration on page 43, she played a literary joke. On the tombstones she printed real names and epitaphs. But on one, very close to the front, she wrote, "Here lies Virginia Kirkus. A nasty soul is its own reward." If you can find a first edition of this book, you will see it—every subsequent edition had the epitaph deleted.

Complete Biographies

Although complete biographies may be in simplified, picture book, or lengthy chapter book format, their purpose is to span the *complete* life of a subject. Russell Freedman's work is a notable example. His complete biographies include three that appear on the Newbery list: ***Lincoln: A Photobiography, The Wright Brothers: How They Invented the Airplane,*** and ***Eleanor Roosevelt: A Life of Discovery.*** Jean Fritz has written a number of complete biographies that are also noteworthy. Titles

ALTERNATE TEXT SET

Books by Jean Fritz

Read Aloud

Will You Sign Here, John Hancock? illustrated by Trina Schart Hyman

Text Set

And Then What Happened, Paul Revere? illustrated by Margot Tomes

Why Don't You Get a Horse, Sam Adams? illustrated by Trina Schart Hyman

Where Was Patrick Henry on the 29th of May? illustrated by Margot Tomes

What's the Big Idea, Ben Franklin? illustrated by Margot Tomes

Can't You Make Them Behave, King George? illustrated by Tomie de Paola

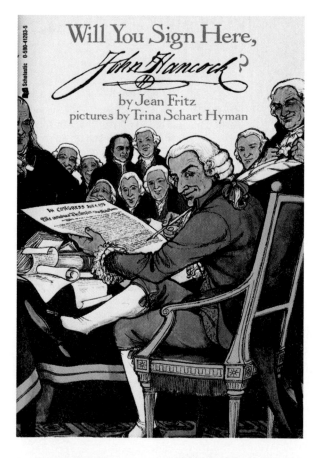

From *Will You Sign Here, John Hancock?* by Jean Fritz, pictures by Trina Schart Hyman, copyright © 1976 by Trina Schart Hyman, illustrations. Used by permission of Coward-McCann, a division of Penguin Putnam, Inc.

include *The Great Little Madison, Make Way for Sam Houston, Harriet Beecher Stowe and the Beecher Preachers,* and *Bully for You, Teddy Roosevelt!* Catherine Reef also has a nice pair of biographies in her *Walt Whitman* and *John Steinbeck.*

Another example of the complete biography comes in Jane Resh Thomas's treatment of Queen Elizabeth in her *Behind the Mask: The Life of Queen Elizabeth I.* Specific details of the times and the intrigue that surrounded the 16th-century English court make this book jump alive. As Thomas states, "Medical knowledge was sketchy and treatment primitive in Tudor England. Physicians 'bled' people for all sorts of maladies, using leeches or slitting veins and collecting the blood in basins. One 'cure' was to swallow a live spider in molasses. As treatment for another condition, a pullet, a live young chicken, was tied to the patient's body until the bird died." Information like this spices up the reading and contextualizes the times for those young readers with little background knowledge.

Mary E. Lyons has prepared a stunning biography of one of the major figures in the Harlem Renaissance in her *Sorrow's Kitchen: The Life and Folklore of Zora Neale Hurston.* Describing Hurston's life growing up at the turn of the century in a small town in Florida, moving on to her migration north with hundreds of thousands of other African Americans during the triumphant and turbulent times of the Harlem Renaissance, Lyons brings to life one of America's great novelists and folklorists.

B O O K M A R K

INTEGRATING TECHNOLOGY: AUTHORS ON THE WORLD WIDE WEB

Mary Lyons is a well-known author of both fiction and nonfiction, and many of her books are biographical, focusing on figures such as Zora Neale Hurston and Harriet Jacobs. On her well-designed website, *The Lyon's Den: Books for Young Readers by Mary Lyons,* in addition to information about the books, there are reviews and activities. There is biographical information as well as a section on how Lyons became a writer. She also encourages e-mail.

To find out more about Mary Lyons and other authors and illustrators on the World Wide Web, visit Chapter 11 on the companion website at **www.prenhall.com/darigan**

Partial Biographies

Partial biographies have a more focused purpose than complete biographies: They cover only a segment of the subject's life, as in Alan Schroeder's *Satchmo's Blues,* illustrated by Floyd Cooper. This biography focuses on the young Louis Armstrong and his attempts to get his very first trumpet from a local New Orleans pawn shop for the price of $5.00. Another book by Schroeder, this one illustrated by Caldecott Honor artist Jerry Pinkney, is *Minty: A Story of Young Harriet Tubman.* This book describes Harriet, or Minty as she was called as a youngster, and all the heartache and disappointment she suffered as a house slave and later in the field. This fictionalized biography sets the stage for Tubman to eventually run away only to return to the South again and again, helping hundreds of slaves escape to the North.

Barbara Cooney's lovely picture book, *Eleanor,* describes the formative years of probably the most famous of all First Ladies of the United States, Eleanor Roosevelt. Young Eleanor grew up a lonely and shy child. She was motherless at age 8 and grew up in her grandmother's home until she was shipped off to boarding school outside London, England. There, she was befriended by the headmistress, Mlle. Souvestre, who opened up an entire new world to the young Totty, as she was called then. Eleanor returned "poised, and confident, brave, loyal, and true." Cooney's portrayal very adequately describes, as Schroeder's books did, the experiences that led these great personages to be who they eventually became.

Finally, a bittersweet biography comes from the tragically premature sickness and death of tennis great Arthur Ashe. In *Daddy and Me: A Photo Story of Arthur Ashe and His Daughter, Camera,* we see how, despite Ashe's declining health as a victim of the AIDS virus, he was still able to spend quality time with his beloved daughter. Lovely black-and-white photographs taken by his wife, Jeanne Moutoussamy-Ashe, add to the poignancy of this sad story.

Having students write a biography is a wonderful way for them to become more knowledgeable about a famous contemporary or historical character. It helps to cement their knowledge about that person and, at the same time, provides them with the opportunity for an authentic writing activity. Because the partial biography is more akin to the length of paper that they will be writing, and because it focuses on only a short span of a person's life, it makes the perfect model for intermediate readers to use when preparing their own biographies. After they have read a complete biography, they can do further research in the library and on the Internet, then as a response they can write their own partial biographies. Like the examples we have given here, the genre is open to some fictionalization, so they could use all the information at their disposal to create a very engaging snippet of a person's life.

▼▼▼▼▼▼▼

Typical Personalities in Biographies

Because famous personalities are usually the focus of adult and juvenile biographies, it is easy to organize biographies by either the careers of the individuals or some other factor responsible for their fame. We have assembled all of our biographies, sorted them in various ways, and arrived at the following categories. As you begin to read more and more books in this genre, you, too, will start to come up with ways to sort these wonderful books.

Scientists and Inventors

Thomas Alva Edison is perhaps the most popular inventor in juvenile biographies. Over the years, other scientists and inventors featured in juvenile biographies have included Albert Einstein, George Washington Carver, the Wright Brothers, and Madame Curie.

 If you want to obtain titles about these famous historical figures, you can refer to the database that accompanies this text.

Two marvelous additions to biography for children come from Leonard Everett Fisher. In both ***Alexander Graham Bell*** and ***Gutenberg,*** Fisher has chosen to use dark, heavily shadowed illustrations, rendered in gradations of black and white, offering an old-world flavor to these significant historical figures. Illustrator Kevin Hawkes does the opposite in Kathryn Lasky's ***The Librarian Who Measured the Earth,*** with his brightly colored paintings, also in acrylics. His illustrations take us back 2,000 years to a time when the Greek Eratosthenes was young; even as a baby, he was inquisitive. He wanted more than anything else to discover the answers to his many questions, and eventually he accurately measured the circumference of the earth.

Wendy Towle offers a great addition to biography with her book ***The Real Mc-Coy: The Life of an African-American Inventor,*** which chronicles the life of the little-known Elijah McCoy. In the late 1860s, while working as an oilman for the Michigan Central Railroad, he saw a need for an automatic oil cup that would drip oil when it was needed. He invented and patented one that was so successful that train engineers wanted only the one Elijah had designed—the "real McCoy," which is where that phrase was coined. McCoy went on to invent the portable ironing board, a lawn sprinkler, and an improved rubber heel for shoes, to name just a few inventions.

Yet another inventor is remembered in Laurie Carlson's ***Boss of the Plains.*** John Batterson Stetson moved west during the Colorado Gold Rush and found that the scorching sun blistered his face for want of a hat with more protection than his derby had provided. He set out to design a hat that was "big and picturesque." When a horseman galloped into town and saw the strange-looking lid atop John's head, he reached into his pocket and offered him five dollars for it on the spot. Stetson decided to move back east to Philadelphia, where he produced the most popular hat west of the Mississippi River.

Finally, Ralph C. Staiger introduces intermediate readers to Renaissance scientist ***Thomas Harriot: Science Pioneer*** in his comprehensive complete biography. At a time when scientific thought was met with great skepticism, Harriot's theories prompted new ways of thinking in mathematics and astronomy. A man who isn't as well known as William Shakespeare or Sir Walter Raleigh, he nevertheless deserves to be remembered for his innovative accomplishments.

Political Leaders

The category of political leaders includes United States presidents and congress members as well as kings, queens, and other monarchs. The publishing of this type of biography can be influenced by current elections, coups, or other swings in power. On the eve of a presidential election, especially when no incumbent is running, some publishers will have biographies of both candidates ready for printing. When the results are announced, the winner's biography goes into immediate production and the loser's . . . well, you get the idea.

There is fierce competition in the arena of current juvenile biographies, but subjects such as George Washington and Abraham Lincoln are standard and lasting fare. We have already mentioned Russell Freedman's *Lincoln: A Photobiography* for the older reader. Two further examples for the younger reader are Edith Kunhardt's *Honest Abe,* with the bright folk art illustrations by Malcah Zeldis, and Myra Cohn Livingston's poetic version, *Abraham Lincoln: A Man for the People.*

Other American leaders are remembered in Dennis Fradin's *Samuel Adams: The Father of American Independence* and Russell Freedman's *Franklin Delano Roosevelt,* both wonderful examples of the complete biography. For general information about those who have served in the Oval Office, you may want to refer to Martin W. Sandler's *Presidents,* which provides a comprehensive view of the presidency, the men who served, and what they did outside their job . . . well, not everything. For a really refreshing picture of the one of the most powerful political positions in the world, you will need to read Judith St. George's *So You Want to Be President?* Tickle-your-funny-bone illustrations by David Small add to the uproariously funny facts you'll learn in this book. "Do you have pets? All kinds of pets lived in the White House . . . Theodore Roosevelt's children didn't just have pets, they ran a zoo. They had dogs, cats, guinea pigs, snakes, mice, rats, badgers, raccoons, parrots, and a Shetland pony called Algonquin. To cheer up his sick brother, young Quentin once took Algonquin upstairs in the White House elevator!"

Cover copyright © 2000 by David Small, illustrations, from *So You Want to be President?* by Judith St. George, illustrated by David Small. Used by permission of Philomel Books, a division of Penguin Putnam, Inc.

Other royal figures are remembered in biographies. Diane Stanley and Peter Vennema's stunning *Cleopatra* provides a beautifully illustrated and detailed portrait of the young Queen of Egypt, her ambitions, and her tragic end. Robert Sabuda brings us yet another Egyptian monarch with *Tutankhamen's Gift,* which offers young readers the backdrop of the young pharaoh's short life. Continuing through the death of his father, the cruel reign of his older brother Amenhotep IV, and his eventual rise to the throne, Sabuda shows how this young king was able to rebuild the temples and the people's faith.

People in the Arts: Artists, Musicians, and Dancers

The category of people in the arts has, over time, experienced a swing to the trendy side. For example, many musicians and actors popular with young people do not really measure up over time and are quickly forgotten. *Like, who was the rock group The Strawberry Alarm Clock anyway, man?* Yet, there is a market for the quickly done, reasonably brief biographies of figures in our popular culture, heavily illustrated with photographs.

On the other hand, the likes of Beethoven, Norman Rockwell, and Isadora Duncan seem to warrant and get serious attention by biographers. For example, Barbara Nichol's *Beethoven Lives Upstairs* presents a dialogue (in the form of letters) between nephew Christoph and his uncle about one of the greatest composers of all times, Ludwig Von Beethoven—who lives upstairs. Artist Norman Rockwell is remembered in Beverly Gherman's *Norman Rockwell: Storyteller with a Brush* with a clear view of the man and loads of color and black-and-white examples of his artwork. Famed and highly spirited dancer Isadora Duncan is portrayed well in *Isadora Dances.* The unconventional ideas of this innovative dancer receive their just rewards in this simple, but beautiful, book by Rachel Isadora. Though artists and authors are subjects that are less trendy for children, they portray the lasting goodness in the arts that carry on after the teen heartthrobs have long been forgotten.

Artists are an equally popular subject in juvenile biography. Carolyn Croll beautifully renders a glimpse of the delicate watercolor art of Pierre-Joseph Redouté in *Redouté: The Man Who Painted Flowers.* From the series "Portraits of Women Artists for Children" is Robyn Montana Turner's *Mary Cassatt.* Photography is also admired in yet another book in that same series and by the same author in *Dorothea Lange.* Here we see some of the most dramatic documentary photographs ever of migrant farm workers taken during the Great Depression. A more comprehensive companion to this is Elizabeth Partridge's *Restless Spirit: The Life and Works of Dorothea Lange.* Finally, African Americans are the focus of George Sullivan's *Black Artists in Photography, 1840–1940.* Herein we meet six photographers who changed the face of the medium over a hundred-year period. A last note on artists that will engage all children, both old and young, is this "autobiography," *Walt Disney's Mickey Mouse: My Life in Pictures,* by Russell Schroeder, that offers a retrospective from the 1920s to the present of probably the best-known cartoon character of all time.

In music, two legends are remembered with Roxanne Orgill's *If I Only Had a Horn: Young Louis Armstrong* and Andrea Davis Pinkney's Caldecott Honor book, *Duke Ellington,* illustrated by her husband, Brian Pinkney. In writing, two other men are remembered in Kathryn Lasky's *A Brilliant Streak: The Making of Mark Twain* and Jim Murphy's *Into the Deep Forest with Henry David Thoreau.*

DID YOU KNOW?

Basho was a famous Japanese poet known for his charmingly simple haiku. In the book *Grass Sandals,* by Dawnine Spivak and illustrated by Demi, we are given a biographical sketch of this man concerning a particular incident in his life. Restless, he decided to take a journey, and on foot traversed the entire country. He recorded his observations in poem form, and Spivak has added one to each double-page spread to accent her narrative. This is the perfect book to lead children back to Chapter 4, "Poetry."

Sports Personalities

A few sports figures, such as Babe Ruth, Jim Thorpe, Jackie Robinson, and Babe Didrickson Zaharias, withstand the test of time and appear in serious biographies for young readers. Others may be well remembered in years to come, and still others are forgotten except by the baseball, football, or basketball aficionado. Again, a trendy element exists in sports biography, almost to the point of dominating the subject. Watch for the slick, photograph-laden biographies that immediately appear after each Olympics, such as those about the reigning women's gymnast.

Bill Littlefield's *Champions: Stories of Ten Remarkable Athletes* offers profiles of 10 greats in sports such as baseball, soccer, boxing, and tennis. Another collective biography is Jonah Winter's *Fair Ball!: 14 Great Stars from Baseball's Negro Leagues,* which features players that most children won't remember but should know for their lasting contribution to the sport. Probably the greatest success story of all times in baseball, or any other sport for that matter, is that of Jackie Robinson. Beginning in the Negro Leagues, as well, Robinson broke through the color barrier as the first African American to play in the major leagues. Derek T. Dingle ably introduces readers to this icon in sports history with his *First in the Field: Baseball Hero Jackie Robinson.*

Explorers and Frontiersmen

As expected, a rash of Columbus biographies appeared during the quincentennial commemoration of his monumental voyage. They have provided broad coverage and varied perspectives on the motives for and impact of Columbus's mission. For example, Milton Meltzer's *Columbus and the World Around Him* is a frank, perhaps even critical, exposé of Columbus's shortcomings, and Kathy Pelta's *Discovering Christopher Columbus: How History Is Invented,* though more complimentary, examines how historian biases and the infusion of myth into history have slanted Columbus's story.

For a view of the exploration and the taming of the wild, wild West, we first find Steven Kroll's biography *Lewis and Clark: Explorers of the American West,* which details the 2½-year expedition beginning on May 14, 1804 and that eventually arrives at the Pacific Ocean in May 1805. Andrew Glass brings us yet another profile of a great man from the West in his *A Right Fine Life: Kit Carson on the Santa Fe Trail.* For a multicultural perspective, we see by the previously mentioned team of Andrea and Brian Pinkney *Bill Pickett: Rodeo-Ridin' Cowboy.*

ALTERNATE TEXT SET

Let's Fly

Read Aloud

Flight, by Robert Burleigh, illustrated by Mike Wimmer

Text Set

Good-bye, Charles Lindbergh, by Louise Borden, illustrated by Thomas B. Allen

Grandpa Is a Flyer, by Sanna Anderson Baker, illustrated by Bill Farnsworth

The First Air Voyage in the United States: The Story of Jean-Pierre Blanchard, by Alexandra Wallner

Lindbergh, by Chris L. Demarest

Fly, Bessie, Fly, by Lynn Joseph, illustrated by Yvonne Buchanan

The beginnings of a thematic unit: As you begin to read widely, you start to see books fall into certain categories. It might be books about survival, both in the woods and in the city. Or you may see books that are centered on dragons or secrets—that is the beginning of a thematic unit of study. One theme would be books based on famous people who have flown, which are listed in the preceding Alternate Text Set. You can begin with this listing, use the database that accompanies the book, and discuss your ideas with your colleagues to tap their expertise as well. You are on your way to a thematic unit. See chapter 15 for more information.

Often we think of explorers as being from the past. However, our modern astronauts and oceanographers are no less intrepid in pushing back our remaining frontiers and are worthy subjects of current biographies, such as is found in Don Brown's *One Giant Leap: The Story of Neil Armstrong.*

Humanitarians

Jane Addams, Albert Schweitzer, Florence Nightingale, and Mother Teresa are interesting subjects for young readers because of their daring and selfless deeds. The heroic qualities of humanitarians add special appeal to their stories. A few Americans who have changed our social consciousness are remembered in biography and are well worth mentioning. Jean Fritz's *You Want Women to Vote, Lizzie Stanton?* presents the great women's suffragist and champion for equality among men and women as well as for blacks and whites in a much more detailed fashion than do her earlier biographies of the Revolutionary War era figures, such as *What's the Big Idea, Ben Franklin?*

Cover from *Lindbergh,* by Chris L. Demarest. Copyright © 1993 by Chris L. Demarest. Used by permission of Crown Children's Books, a division of Random House, Inc.

A CONVERSATION WITH . . .

Russell Freedman

When I choose a topic for a book, I have to have an authentic personal interest in it, I have to believe that the subject has some redeeming value, and that I am going to be able to say something that is worth saying and worth all the work. As well, I have to believe that there is an audience for it, so it can't just be something that I am interested in.

I think that every time you write a biography or about a historical event, you are rewriting history. There are as many versions of what happened as there are people writing about it and no one accurate version, no one clearly accurate view of reality. There are as many realities as there are people observing it. Not only are you using fictional techniques in an authentic way, you are using quotations from diaries and journals and everything in order to substitute for dialogue. You are using dramatized scenes that the reader can visualize even though nothing is fictionalized. Through your selection of the material, you are, in a manner of speaking, distorting reality; you can't write about it otherwise.

For example, when I was working on the Eleanor Roosevelt book, I was fascinated. I don't know how many biographies I read of Eleanor Roosevelt, but each one was about a different person. That is especially true about Lincoln. You can pick any decade and read a Lincoln biography, from the 30s, from the 20s, from the 60s, and it is about a different person because each generation brings a different set of values and a different agenda to the subject. I never think that when I am writing a biography that that is the one and only version of that person's life. It is the way that I understand the subject, and it is what I want to say about that person. What is the simile about the fisherman with the net? You are trawling and when you pull in the net you get a lot of good stuff. But most of what is down there in the water is left behind. Then you sift through the net and pick out what you want and throw everything else overboard. You wind up with 1% of the potential catch. And is that the truth about that person's life? Or is it what you came up with through your process of selectivity? It isn't true of only biographies, but of any kind historical writing. That makes it quite fascinating, knowing that. I think that you are always rewriting history: My books are history according to Russell Freedman.

Right now, I am doing a book now on Confucius that was suggested to me by Arthur Levine, editor of the Harry Potter books. I jumped at the chance because I really felt I needed a fresh subject. It is terrific and I love it; tremendous fun. It's factual because he was a real person, but there is so much mythology about him and so little hard knowledge that really you can do anything. That has given me a lot of creative leeway. Confucius was a remarkable person.

There is a definite group of children who are history buffs out there. I think they are a minority, but when I think back to my own elementary school days, I don't think most kids were readers; but those of us who were readers were avid readers and within that group we, too, had a group of nonfiction readers. Is it genetic predisposition to nonfiction; who knows? There are kids who read history, and I do believe they are going to be the ones who are going to be important. You know what Confucius said? He said, "Isn't it a joy to make practical use of something you have learned?" And that is what reading is all about.

To read more of this Conversation with Russell Freedman, please visit Chapter 11 on our text's companion website at **www.prenhall.com/darigan**

Judith Bentley offers yet another view of equal rights across cultures with her *"Dear Friend": Thomas Garrett & William Still, Collaborators on the Underground Railroad.* In this book, we see the partnership between Garrett, a white man living in the slave state of Delaware, and Still, a free black man living in Philadelphia, and their efforts they called "friends of humanity" in aiding slaves north to resettle in Canada.

Another social reformer is found in Russell Freedman's **Kids at Work: Lewis Hine and the Crusade Against Child Labor.** Hine, a teacher and photographer, exposed the unfair treatment of children during the Industrial Age in America with his in-depth investigation and his camera. Classic photographs of children in mills and mines belong to this true modern crusader.

People Who Overcome Tremendous Odds

Biographies of people who overcome tremendous odds focus on a different sort of heroism. Many biographies have been published about Helen Keller (including her autobiography), and her story of struggling to overcome nearly insurmountable physical difficulties continues to be popular reading for children and young adults.

Other compelling stories along this line include Russell Freedman's ***Out of Darkness: The Story of Louis Braille.*** This concise overview of Braille's life presents young readers with the man who brought reading and writing to the blind. Breaking through the color barrier during the 1960s was little Ruby Bridges, who recalls her involvement to integrate her school in New Orleans in ***Through My Eyes.*** This powerful autobiography will bring the troubles of those turbulent times to children of the present in this picture book retrospective. Bridges serves as a beacon of hope for civil rights here and around the world. Another not-so-famous person who was captive to a vicious and violent overseer is found in ***The True Adventure of Daniel Hall,*** by Diane Stanley. Daniel Hall, who went to sea at the age of 14, never suspected all the troubles and trials he would encounter in the next years. Setting sail on a whaling ship out of New Bedford, Massachusetts, he came to realize his captain was a cruel and moody man. Deserting ship, he came on land in Siberia where survival became his only concern as he battled hunger, wild animals, and the constant cold.

From ***The True Adventure of Daniel Hall*** by Diane Stanley, copyright © 1995 by Diane Stanley. Used by permission of Dial Books for Young Readers, a division of Penguin Putnam, Inc.

Ordinary People

A more recent trend in juvenile biography is the book that focuses on someone who is not particularly famous or globally known such as a government leader, a famous athlete, or the latest teen heartthrob. Now that is not to say that the people about whom these books are written don't do something pretty special in the end; quite the contrary. In fact, if that were the case, we would all have biographies written about us and our mundane lives. The point here is that the characters examined in this category of book are basically ordinary folks who, for some reason, do or create something quite noteworthy. Take, for example, Philip Simmons, a blacksmith from Charleston, South Carolina. Blacksmithing is an old and reputable trade—but in Mary E. Lyons's ***Catching the Fire: Philip Simmons, Blacksmith,*** we see the ordinary turned into true craftsmanship. Simmons has created some absolutely stunning works of art with just his anvil, his hammer, a hunk of iron, and an abundance of skill and talent. Notice the beautiful gate in the photograph on p. 392 that is functional yet a work of art all at the same time.

In Robert D. San Souci's ***Kate Shelley: Bound for Legend,*** we are introduced to a young girl—totally ordinary in every way, described as good-natured and sturdy, hardworking and an inveterate reader. In fact, she had to take over the family chores and responsibility with her father being dead and her mother in very poor health. However, during a torrential rainstorm, one of the engines used to push trains up the steep incline at the Honey Creek Bridge, near Kate's house, slipped off, taking the bridge with it. Knowing a train wreck of tremendous proportions would occur when the midnight train came through, Kate realized that if she didn't somehow warn the people, an even more terrible disaster would occur. With lantern in hand, she forged ahead, crossing the nearly 700 feet of bridge spanning the Des Moines River on her hands and knees. Single-handedly, she averted what would have been a devastating train wreck and became a local hero for her courageous actions.

Quinceañera: Celebrating Fifteen, by Elizabeth King, introduces readers to the most popular Mexican and Aztec custom for girls coming of age and, in particular, to the biggest party of Cindy Chávez's life. Using just one girl as an example, the detailed

Front and back cover from ***Catching The Fire: Philip Simmons, Blacksmith*** by Mary E. Lyons. Front jacket photo © 1997 by John Michael Vlach. Back jacket photo © 1997 by Mannie Garcia. Reprinted by permission.

text and color photographs of this stunning book describe this celebration that has roots back to pre-Columbian Central America.

Sara Hoagland Hunter relates the heroic story of the more than 800 Navajo men who served in World War II using their native language as a code to fool Japanese forces in her book, ***The Unbreakable Code***. In this fictional biography, a grandfather describes the activities of the "unbreakable code" system that allowed the American forces to take Iwo Jima and eventually win the war.

Jerry Stanley's ***Children of the Dust Bowl: The True Story of the School at Weedpatch Camp*** describes the efforts of Leo Hart, superintendent of the Weedpatch Camp, a sensitive and perceptive advocate of the "Okies" during the Dust Bowl. This is a 1940s version of the Jaime Escalante "Stand and Deliver" story, but with larger numbers and probably lower odds for success. Despite that, as the Weedpatch "community" built a sophisticated and functioning school for these Oklahoma expatriates. The reader sees the great influence Hart had on the success this school enjoyed. Books like these give children the sense that everyone, not just the big names from history, has a story and can make a contribution.

Children's Authors and Illustrators

One growing category in children's biography is, rightly, the profile on the very people who write and illustrate the books we read. These very talented people are already important to us as educators, but to make them into full-fledged stars to avid young readers is our goal. Wouldn't it be nice to have a child aspire to be as kind as someone like Bill Martin, Jr. or Steven Kellogg, as funny as David Wisniewski, or as creative and talented as Jan Brett? (Rather *that* than imitating some of the highly deviant and disrespectful behaviors we see in the news from numerous athletic stars and musicians in the mainstream!)

Three major stars in children's literature are featured in books that are great for kids, yet can be just as elegant

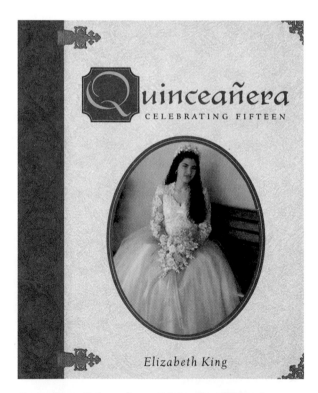

Cover from ***Quinceañera: Celebrating Fifteen*** by Elizabeth King, copyright © 1998 by Elizabeth King. Used by permission of Dutton Children's Books, a division of Penguin Putnam, Inc.

Tea time? Teachers in the Kennett Square Consolidated School District in Pennsylvania have a wonderful idea when it comes to biography. As the children read throughout their elementary years, and particularly during sixth grade, they focus on one author. After digesting as many books by that person as they can, they do an in-depth study of that author, learning all they can about his or her life. In the spring, they have their annual "Tea," where each child dresses up as the author and takes on the persona of that person. As they "mill" and "chat," guests are encouraged to ask any of the many "authors" anything and the children answer as if they really were those people. This is something all the children in the district look to as a major culminating experience in their elementary careers.

on your own coffee table. The first is *The Art of Eric Carle,* which provides a comprehensive autobiography of the illustrator of books such as *The Very Hungry Caterpillar* and *Brown Bear, Brown Bear, What Do You See?* Next is *Bill Peet: An Autobiography,* winner of the Caldecott Honor and a very readable profile on the man who started at Walt Disney Studios and made movies such as *101 Dalmations* and *Cinderella,* then later published nearly 40 books for children—all of which are still in print. Finally, Barbara Elleman has provided us with yet another comprehensive view of an author/illustrator in her *Tomie dePaola: His Art & His Stories.* This book takes us into the home and studio of the creator of *Strega Nona* and over 200 other books for children and is a handsome addition to any teacher's collection.

Intermediate readers will enjoy the biographies of two other important figures in children's literature, with *E. B. White: The Elements of a Writer,* by Janice Tingum, and Caldecott Honor artist Ted Lewin's autobiographical sketch in *Touch and Go: Travels of a Children's book Illustrator.* A growing series that provides ample information on some of the great authors of our time for children is produced by The Learning Works. Featured are the authors in the Alternate Text Set below.

Another series of books features illustrators designed with a very interesting format. Over the years, Pat Cummings has compiled the answers to questions we all would ask one of these illustrators if only given the chance. For example, wouldn't you love to ask Chris Van Allsburg, the man who did *The Polar Express* and *Jumanji,* "Where do you get your ideas?" "Who influenced you?" and "What do you do all day?" In her books, *Talking With Artists, Talking With Artists: Volume Two,* and *Talking With Artists: Volume Three,* answers to those questions and more from many of your very favorite children's book illustrators are presented. Six more artists are featured in Leonard Marcus's *A Caldecott Celebration: Six Artists and Their Paths to the Caldecott Medal,* featuring Robert McCloskey, Maurice Sendak, and William Steig, to name only a few.

ALTERNATE TEXT SET

Learning Works Biographies of Children's Authors

Avi, by Lois Markham

Jean Craighead George, by Alice Cary

Lois Lowry, by Lois Markham

Katherine Paterson, by Alice Cary

Gary Paulsen, by Stephanie True Peters

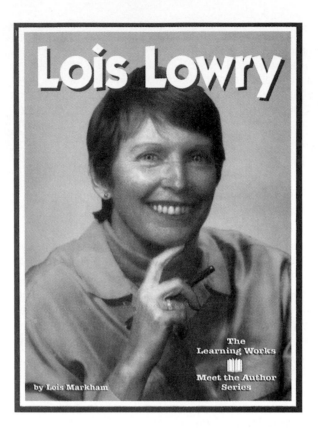

Cover of **Lois Lowr**y by Lois Markham, copyright © 1995 The Learning Works, Huntington Beach, CA 92649.

Thus far, we have discussed only contemporary authors and illustrators, but Alexandra Wallner has done two profiles on past authors in her *Laura Ingalls Wilder,* which features the woman who wrote all the *Little House on the Prairie* books, and the creator of Peter Rabbit, *Beatrix Potter.* Further, Joan W. Blos has adapted an autobiographical note by Margaret Wise Brown, author of the well-loved *Goodnight Moon,* in *The Days Before Now.*

Finally, brief and very interesting autobiographical sketches appear about a host of authors and illustrators in Lee Bennett Hopkins's *Pauses: Autobiographical Reflections of 101 Creators of Children's Books.* You can learn wonderful anecdotes, such as how Robert McCloskey plied his ducks with red wine to make them stay still so he could draw them for his Caldecott Honor book, *Make Way For Ducklings.* Finally Paula W. Graham has compiled dozens of interviews with notable authors such as Bruce Coville, Jacqueline Woodson, and Naomi Shihab Nye in her *Speaking of Journals.* In this volume, the authors discuss their journals, diaries, and sketchbooks.

▼▼▼▼▼▼▼

Summary

In this chapter, we first described and defined biography. We then noted that most of biography written today is known as authentic biography, featuring individual profiles or collective pieces about particular subjects who have common traits. We noted that when considering biographies for your young readers, you need to pay close attention to authenticity, objectivity, writing style, subject matter, and book design and layout. We noted the various categories of biography—autobiography, picture book biographies, simplified biography, complete biography, and partial biography. Finally, we described the typical personalities biographers tend to describe in today's books for children, which include scientists and inventors, political leaders, people in the arts such as artists, musicians, and dancers, sports personalities, explorers and frontiersmen, humanitarians, people who overcome tremendous odds, ordinary people, and children's authors and illustrators.

▼▼▼▼▼▼▼

Fifteen More of Our Favorites

Aronson, Marc. (2000). *Sir Walter Ralegh and the quest for El Dorado.* Clarion. Recounts the adventurous life of the English explorer and courtier who spelled his name "Ralegh" and who led many expeditions to the New World. (Winner of the first Robert F. Sibert Award for most distinguished informational book).

Corey, Shana. (2000). *You forgot your skirt, Amelia Bloomer!* (Chesley McLaren, Illus.). Scholastic. Women's rights activist Amelia Bloomer reconsiders the restrictive clothes considered proper in 19th-century America with a new design of her own.

Demi. (1996). *Buddha.* Henry Holt. Recounts the life of Siddhartha, born into luxury but taking on a remarkable spiritual journey ending later in his life under a bodhi tree where he became an "Enlightened One," or Buddha.

Freedman, Russell. (1996). *The life and death of Crazy Horse.* Holiday House. A biography of the Oglala leader who relentlessly resisted the white man's attempt to take over Indian lands.

Freedman, Russell. (1999). *Babe Didrikson Zaharias: The making of a champion.* Clarion. A biography of Babe Didrikson, 1911–1956, who broke records in golf, track and field, and other sports, at a time when there were few opportunities for female athletes.

Giblin, James Cross. (2000). *The amazing life of Benjamin Franklin* (Michael Dooling, Illus.). Scholastic. A handsome picture book biography noting the accomplishments as well as difficulties of this great American.

Krull, Kathleen. (1996). *Wilma unlimited: How Wilma Rudolph became the world's fastest woman* (David Diaz, Illus.). Harcourt. A biography of the African American woman who overcame crippling polio as a child to become the first woman to win three gold medals in track in a single Olympics.

Lasky, Kathryn. (2000). *Vision of beauty: The story of Sarah Breedlove Walker* (Nneka Bennett, Illus.). Candlewick. A biography of Sarah Breedlove Walker who, though born in poverty, pioneered hair and beauty care products for black women, and became a great financial success.

Meltzer, Milton. (1990). *Columbus and the world around him.* Watts. Covers the voyages of Columbus, the terrible impact of the Spaniards on the Indians, and the ultimate cultural influence of the Native Americans on their white conquerors.

Myers, Walter Dean. (1999). *At Her Majesty's request: An African princess in Victorian England.* Scholastic. Biography of the African princess saved from execution and taken to England, where Queen Victoria oversaw her upbringing and where she lived for a time before marrying an African missionary.

Paulsen, Gary. (1990). *Woodsong.* Bradbury. (Autobiography.) For a rugged outdoor man and his family, life in northern Minnesota is a wild experience involving wolves, deer, and sled dogs. Includes an account of the author's first Iditarod, a dogsled race across Alaska.

Spinelli, Jerry. (1998). *Knots in my yo-yo string: The autobiography of a kid.* Knopf. This Italian-American Newbery medalist presents a humorous account of his childhood and youth in Norristown, Pennsylvania.

Stanley, Diane. (2000). *Michelangelo.* HarperCollins. A biography of the Renaissance sculptor, painter, architect, and poet, well known for his work on the Sistine Chapel and St. Peter's Cathedral in Rome.

Stanley, Fay. (2001). *The last princess: The story of Princess Ka'iulani of Hawai'i* (Diane Stanley, Illus.). HarperCollins. Recounts the story of Hawaii's last heir to the throne, who was denied her right to rule when the monarchy was abolished.

Stevenson, James. (1992). *Don't you know there's a war on?* Greenwillow. (Autobiography, picture book.) The author recalls his childhood efforts to win the Second World War, including planting a victory garden, collecting tin foil, and looking for spies.

▼▼▼▼▼▼▼

Others We Like

Brown, Don. (1993). *Ruth Law thrills a nation.* Houghton Mifflin.

Cox, Clinton. (1997). *Fiery vision: The life and death of John Brown.* Scholastic.

Demi. (1998). *The Dalai Lama.* Henry Holt. (Picture book biography).

Fleischman, Sid. (1996). *The abracadabra kid.* Greenwillow. (Autobiography.)

Freedman, Russell. (1998). *Martha Graham: A dancer's life.* Clarion.

Gerrard, Roy. (1988). *Sir Frances Drake: His daring deeds.* Farrar, Straus & Giroux. (Picture book biography.)

Gold, Alison Leslie. (2000). *A special fate: Chiune Sugihara, hero of the Holocaust.* Scholastic.

Golenbock, Peter. (1990). *Teammates* (Paul Bacon, Illus.). Harcourt. (Picture book biography.)

Govenar, Alan. (2000). *Osceola: Memories of a sharecropper's daughter.* Hyperion.

Hyman, Trina Schart. (1981). *Self-portrait: Trina Schart Hyman.* Addison-Wesley. (Autobiography, picture book.)

Marrin, Albert. (2000). *Sitting Bull and his world.* Dutton.

Meltzer, Milton. (1993). *Lincoln: In his own words* (Stephen Alcorn, Illus.). Harcourt.

Morpurgo, Michael. (1999). *Joan of Arc* (Michael Foreman, Illus.). Harcourt.

Myers, Walter Dean. (1993). *Malcolm X: By any means necessary.* Scholastic.

Parks, Rosa (with Jim Haskins). (1992). *Rosa Parks: Mother to a movement.* Dial. (Autobiography.)

Pelta, Kathy. (1991). *Discovering Christopher Columbus: How history is invented.* Lerner.

Severance, John. (1996). *Winston Churchill: Soldier, statesman, artist.* Clarion.

Szabo, Corinne. (1997). *Sky pioneer: A photobiography of Amelia Earhart.* National Geographic.

Uchida, Yoshiko. (1991). *The invisible thread.* Messner. (Autobiography.)

Van Meter, Vicki, with Dan Gutman. (1995). *Taking flight: My story by Vicki Van Meter.* Viking.

Collective Biographies

Jacobs, William J. (1996). *Great lives: World religions.* Atheneum. (See other titles in the Great Lives series.)

Krull, Kathleen. (1999). *They saw the future: Oracles, psychics, scientists, great thinkers, and pretty good guessers.* Atheneum.

Meltzer, Milton. (1998). *Ten queens: Portraits of women of power.* Dutton.

Monceaux, Morgan, & Katcher, Ruth. (1999). *My heroes, my people: African Americans and Native Americans in the west.* Farrar, Straus & Giroux.

Provensen, Alice. (1995). *My fellow Americans: A family album.* Browndeer/Harcourt. (Picture book biography.)

Rylant, Cynthia. (1996). *Margaret, Frank, and Andy: Three writers' stories.* Harcourt.

Turner, Glennette Tilley. (1989). *Take a walk in their shoes.* Dutton.

Easier to Read

Coerr, Eleanor. (1977). *Sadako and the thousand paper cranes.* Putnam.

dePaola, Tomie. (1999). *26 Fairmount Avenue.* Putnam. (Winner of Newbery Honor and part of the Fairmount Avenue book series).

Kramer, S. A. (1995). *Ty Cobb: Bad boy of baseball.* Random House.

Kraske, Robert. (1989). *Harry Houdini: Master of magic.* Scholastic.

Mayo, Margaret. (2000). *Brother sun, sister moon: The life and stories of St. Francis.* Little, Brown.

Meaderis, Angela Shelf. (1994). *Little Louis and the jazz band.* Lodestar/Dutton.

Osborne, Mary Pope. (1987). *The story of Christopher Columbus, admiral of the ocean sea.* Dell. (See other books in the Dell Yearling Biography series.)

Picture Books

Blos, Joan. (1991). *The heroine of the Titanic: A tale both true and otherwise of the life of Molly Brown* (Tennessee Dixon, Illus.). Morrow.

Blos, Joan W. (1996). *Nellie Bly's monkey* (Catherine Stock, Illus.). Morrow. (Fictional biography told from the perspective of Bly's monkey.)

Coerr, Eleanor. (1993). *Sadako* (Ed Young, Illus.). Putnam.

Cooney, Barbara. (1996). *Eleanor.* Viking.

Crews, Donald. (1991). *Bigmama's.* Greenwillow. (Autobiography.)

Demi. (1991). *Chingis Khan.* New York: Holt.

dePaola, Tomie. (1994). *Christopher: The holy giant.* Holiday House.

dePaola, Tomie. (1995). *Mary: The mother of Jesus.* Holiday House.

Fisher, Leonard Everett. (1995). *Moses.* Holiday House.

Gerstein, Mordicai. (1999). *Noah and the great flood.* Simon & Schuster.

Gilliland, Judith Heide. (2000). *Steamboat!: The story of Captain Blanche Leathers.* DK Ink.

Johnson, D. B. (2000). *Henry hikes to Fitchburg.* Houghton Mifflin.

Kellogg, Steven. (1988). *Johnny Appleseed.* Morrow.

Mandel, Peter. (2000). *Say hey!: A song of Willie Mays* (Don Tate, Illus.). Hyperion.

Myers, Walter Dean. (2000). *Malcolm X: A fire burning brightly* (Leonard Jenkins, Illus.). HarperCollins.

Winter, Jeanette. (1999). *Sebastian: A book about Bach.* Browndeer/Harcourt.

▼▼▼▼▼▼▼

Children's Literature References

Ada, Alma Flor. (1998). *Under the royal palms: A childhood in Cuba.* New York: Atheneum.

Adler, David A. (1989). *A picture book of Martin Luther King, Jr.* New York: Holiday House.

Adler, David A. (1990). *A picture book of Thomas Jefferson.* New York: Holiday House.

Adler, David A. (1991a). *A picture book of Christopher Columbus.* New York: Holiday House.

Adler, David A. (1991b). *A picture book of Eleanor Roosevelt.* New York: Holiday House.

Adler, David A. (1993). *A picture book of Anne Frank.* New York: Holiday House.

Adler, David A. (1994). *A picture book of Sojourner Truth* (Gershom Griffith, Illus.). New York: Holiday House.

Adler, David A. (1996). *A picture book of Thomas Edison.* New York: Holiday House.

Adler, David A. (1997). *Lou Gehrig: The luckiest man* (Terry Widener, Illus.). San Diego: Gulliver.

Adler, David A. (2000). *America's champion swimmer: Gertrude Ederle* (Terry Widener, Illus.). San Diego: Harcourt Brace.

Aliki. (1988). *A weed is a flower: The life of George Washington Carver.* New York: Simon & Schuster.

Ancona, George. (1990). *Riverkeeper.* New York: Macmillan.

Baker, Sanna Anderson. (1995). *Grandpa is a flyer* (Bill Farnsworth, Illus.). Morton Grove, IL: Albert Whitman.

Bentley, Judith. (1997). *"Dear Friend": Thomas Garrett & William Still, collaborators on the Underground Railroad.* New York: Dutton.

Blos, Joan W. (1994). *The days before now: An autobiographical note by Margaret Wise Brown* (Thomas B. Allen, Illus.). New York: Simon & Schuster.

Boitano, Brian, & Harper, Suzanne. (1997). *Boitano's edge: Inside the real world of figure skating.* New York: Simon & Schuster.

Borden, Louise. (1998). *Good-bye, Charles Lindbergh* (Thomas B. Allen, Illus.). New York: McElderry.

Bridges, Ruby. (1999). *Through my eyes.* New York: Scholastic.

Brooke, John. (1972). *King George III.* New York: McGraw-Hill.

Brown, Don. (1998). *One giant leap: The story of Neil Armstrong.* Boston: Houghton Mifflin.

Brown, Margaret Wise. (1947). *Goodnight moon* (Clement Hurd, Illus.). New York: Harper.

Burchard, Peter. (1995). *Charlotte Forten: A black teacher in the Civil War.* New York: Crown.

Burleigh, Robert. (1991). *Flight* (Mike Wimmer, Illus.). New York: Philomel.

Byars, Betsy. (1980). *The night swimmers* (Troy Howell, Illus.). New York: Delacorte.

Byars, Betsy. (1991). *The Moon and I.* New York: Simon & Schuster.

Carle, Eric. (1971). *The very hungry caterpillar.* New York: Crowell.

Carle, Eric. (1996). *The art of Eric Carle.* New York: Philomel.

Carlson, Laurie. (1998). *Boss of the plains: The hat that won the West* (Holly Meade, Illus.). New York: DK.

Cary, Alice. (1996). *Jean Craighead George.* Santa Barbara, CA: The Learning Works.

Cary, Alice. (1997). *Katherine Paterson.* Santa Barbara, CA: The Learning Works.

Choi, Sook Nyul. (1991). *Year of impossible goodbyes.* Boston: Houghton Mifflin.

Cleary, Beverly. (1965). *The mouse and the motorcycle* (Louis Darling, Illus.). New York: Morrow.

Cleary, Beverly. (1983). *Dear Mr. Henshaw* (Paul O. Zelinsky, Illus.). New York: Morrow.

Cleary, Beverly. (1984). *Ramona* (Alan Tiergreen, Illus.). New York: Morrow.

Cleary, Beverly. (1988). *A girl from Yamhill: A memoir.* New York: Morrow.

Conrad, Pam. (1991). *Prairie visions: The life and times of Solomon Butcher.* New York: HarperCollins.

Cooney, Barbara. (1996). *Eleanor.* New York: Viking.

Cooper, Floyd. (1996). *Mandela.* New York: Philomel.

Croll, Carolyn. (1996). *Redouté: The man who painted flowers.* New York: Putnam.

Cummings, Pat. (1992). *Talking with artists.* New York: Bradbury Press.

Cummings, Pat. (1995). *Talking with artists: Volume two.* New York: Simon & Schuster.

Cummings, Pat. (1999). *Talking with artists: Volume three.* New York: Clarion.

Demarest, Chris L. (1993). *Lindbergh.* New York: Crown.

dePaola, Tomie. (1975). *Strega Nona: An old tale.* New York: Prentice Hall.

Dingle, Derek T. (1998). *First in the field: Baseball hero Jackie Robinson.* New York: Hyperion.

Elleman, Barbara. (1999). *Tomie dePaola: His art & his stories.* New York: Putnam.

Fisher, Leonard Everett. (1993). *Gutenberg.* New York: Macmillan.

Fisher, Leonard Everett. (1999). *Alexander Graham Bell.* New York: Atheneum.

Fradin, Dennis. (1998). *Samuel Adams: The father of American independence.* New York: Clarion.

Freedman, Russell. (1987a). *Indian chiefs.* New York: Holiday House.

Freedman, Russell. (1987b). *Lincoln: A photobiography.* New York: Clarion.

Freedman, Russell. (1990). *Franklin Delano Roosevelt.* New York: Clarion.

Freedman, Russell. (1991). *The Wright brothers: How they invented the airplane.* New York: Holiday House.

Freedman, Russell. (1993). *Eleanor Roosevelt: A life of discovery.* New York: Clarion.

Freedman, Russell. (1994). *Kids at work: Lewis Hine and the crusade against child labor.* New York: Clarion.

Freedman, Russell. (1997). *Out of darkness: The story of Louis Braille.* New York: Clarion.

Fritz, Jean. (1973). *And then what happened, Paul Revere?* (Margot Tomes, Illus.). New York: Coward.

Fritz, Jean. (1974). *Why don't you get a horse, Sam Adams?* (Trina Schart Hyman, Illus.). New York: Scholastic.

Fritz, Jean. (1975). *Where was Patrick Henry on the 29th of May?* (Margot Tomes, Illus.). New York: Scholastic.

Fritz, Jean. (1976a). *What's the big idea, Ben Franklin?* (Margot Tomes, Illus.). New York: Putnam.

Fritz, Jean. (1976b). *Will you sign here, John Hancock?* (Trina Schart Hyman, Illus.). New York: Scholastic.

Fritz, Jean. (1977). *Can't you make them behave, King George?* (Tomie de Paola, Illus.). New York: Scholastic.

Fritz, Jean. (1980). *Where do you think you're going, Christopher Columbus?* New York: Putnam.

Fritz, Jean. (1982). *Homesick: My own story.* New York: Putnam.

Fritz, Jean. (1986). *Make way for Sam Houston.* New York: Putnam.

Fritz, Jean. (1988). *And then what happened, Paul Revere?* (Margot Tomes, Illus.). New York: Scholastic.

Fritz, Jean. (1989). *The great little Madison.* New York: Putnam.

Fritz, Jean. (1991). *Bully for you, Teddy Roosevelt!* New York: Putnam.

Fritz, Jean. (1994). *Harriet Beecher Stowe and the Beecher preachers.* New York: Putnam.

Fritz, Jean. (1995). *You want women to vote, Lizzie Stanton?* (DyAnne DiSalvo-Ryan, Illus.). New York: Putnam.

Gherman, Beverly. (2000). *Norman Rockwell: Storyteller with a brush.* New York: Atheneum.

Giblin, James Cross. (1997). *Charles A. Lindbergh: A human hero.* New York: Clarion.

Glass, Andrew. (1997). *A right fine life: Kit Carson on the Santa Fe trail.* New York: Holiday House.

Graham, Paula W. (1999). *Speaking of journals: Children's book writers talk about their diaries, notebooks, and sketchbooks.* Honesdale, PA: Boyds Mills Press.

Greenfield, Eloise. (1977). *Mary McLeod Bethune* (Jerry Pinkney, Illus.). New York: HarperCollins.

Harness, Cheryl. (1998). *Mark Twain and the queens of the Mississippi.* New York: Holiday.

Hopkins, Lee Bennett. (1995). *Pauses: Autobiographical reflections of 101 creators of children's books.* New York: HarperCollins.

Hunter, Sara Hoagland. (1996). *The unbreakable code* (Julia Miner, Illus.). Flagstaff, AZ: Northland.

Isadora, Rachel. (1998). *Isadora dances.* New York: Viking.

Joseph, Lynn. (1998). *Fly, Bessie, fly* (Yvonne Buchanan, Illus.). New York: Simon & Schuster.

King, Elizabeth. (1998). *Quinceañera: Celebrating fifteen.* New York: Dutton.

Kroll, Steven. (1994). *Lewis and Clark: Explorers of the American West* (Richard Williams, Illus.). New York: Holiday House.

Krull, Kathleen. (1993). *Lives of the musicians: Good times, bad times (and what the neighbors thought)* (Kathryn Hewitt, Illus.). San Diego: Harcourt Brace.

Krull, Kathleen. (1994). *Lives of the writers: Comedies, tragedies (and what the neighbors thought)* (Kathryn Hewitt, Illus.). San Diego: Harcourt Brace.

Krull, Kathleen. (1995). *Lives of the artists: Masterpieces, messes (and what the neighbors thought)* (Kathryn Hewitt, Illus.). San Diego: Harcourt Brace.

Krull, Kathleen. (1997). *Lives of the athletes: Thrills, spills (and what the neighbors thought)* (Kathryn Hewitt, Illus.). San Diego: Harcourt Brace.

Krull, Kathleen. (1998). *Lives of the presidents: Fame, shame (and what the neighbors thought)* (Kathryn Hewitt, Illus.). San Diego: Harcourt Brace.

Kunhardt, Edith. (1993). *Honest Abe* (Malcah Zeldis, Illus.). New York: Greenwillow.

Lasky, Kathryn. (1994). *The librarian who measured the Earth* (Kevin Hawkes, Illus.). Boston: Little, Brown.

Lasky, Kathryn. (1998). *A brilliant streak: The making of Mark Twain* (Barry Moser, Illus.). San Diego: Harcourt Brace.

Leiner, Katherine. (1996). *First children: Growing up in the White House* (Portraits by Katie Keller). New York: Tambourine.

Lewin, Ted. (1999). *Touch and go: Travels of a children's book illustrator.* New York: Lothrop.

Littlefield, Bill. (1993). *Champions: Stories of ten remarkable athletes* (Bernie Fuchs, Illus.). Boston: Little, Brown.

Livingston, Myra Cohn. (1993). *Abraham Lincoln: A man for all the people* (Samuel Byrd, Illus.). New York: Holiday House.

Lowry, Lois. (1979). *Anastasia Krupnik.* Boston: Houghton Mifflin.

Lowry, Lois. (1980). *Autumn Street.* Boston: Houghton Mifflin.

Lowry, Lois, (1989). *Number the stars.* Boston: Houghton Mifflin.

Lowry, Lois. (1993). *The giver.* Boston: Houghton Mifflin.

Lowry, Lois. (1998). *Looking back: A book of memories.* Boston: Houghton Mifflin.

Lyons, Mary E. (1990). *Sorrow's kitchen: The life and folklore of Zora Neale Hurston.* New York: Scribner's.

Lyons, Mary E. (1997). *Catching the fire: Philip Simmons, blacksmith.* Boston: Houghton Mifflin.

Lyons, Mary E. (1998). *Talking with Tebé: Clementine Hunter, memory artist.* Boston: Houghton Mifflin.

Marcus, Leonard. (1998). *A Caldecott celebration: Six artists and their paths to the Caldecott medal.* New York: Walker.

Markham, Lois. (1995). *Lois Lowry.* Santa Barbara, CA: The Learning Works.

Markham, Lois. (1996). *Avi.* Santa Barbara, CA: The Learning Works.

Marrin, Albert. (1987). *Hitler.* New York: Viking Kestrel.

Martin, Bill, Jr. (1970). *Brown bear, brown bear, what do you see?* (Eric Carle, Illus.). New York: Henry Holt.

Martin, Jacqueline Briggs. (1998). *Snowflake Bentley* (Mary Azarian, Illus.). Boston: Houghton Mifflin.

McCloskey, Robert. (1941). *Make way for ducklings.* New York: Viking.

McMahon, Patricia. (1999). *One Belfast boy* (Alan O'Connor, Photog.). Boston: Houghton Mifflin.

Meltzer, Milton. (1990). *Columbus and the world around him.* New York: Watts.

Mori, Kyoko. (1993). *Shizuko's daughter.* New York: Henry Holt.

Moutoussamy-Ashe, Jeanne. (1993). *Daddy and me: A photo story of Arthur Ashe and his daughter, Camera.* New York: Knopf.

Murphy, Jim. (1995). *Into the deep forest with Henry David Thoreau* (Kate Kiesler, Illus.). New York: Clarion.

Neimark, Anne E. (1992). *Diego Rivera: Artist of the people*. New York: HarperCollins.

Nichol, Barbara. (1993). *Beethoven lives upstairs* (Scott Cameron, Illus.). New York: Orchard.

Nye, Naomi Shihab. (1999). *Speaking of journals*. New York: Simon & Schuster.

Orgill, Roxane. (1997). *If I only had a horn: Young Louis Armstrong* (Leonard Jenkins, Illus.). Boston: Houghton Mifflin.

Osofsky, Audrey. (1996). *Free to dream: The making of a poet*. New York: Lothrop.

Partridge, Elizabeth. (1998). *Restless spirit: The life and work of Dorothea Lange*. New York: Viking.

Paul, Ann Whitford. (1999). *All by herself* (Michael Steirnagle, Illus.). San Diego: Harcourt Brace.

Peet, Bill. (1989). *Bill Peet: An autobiography*. New York: Houghton Mifflin.

Pelta, Kathy. (1991). *Discovering Christopher Columbus: How history is invented*. Minneapolis: Lerner.

Peters, Stephanie True. (1999). *Gary Paulsen*. Santa Barbara, CA: The Learning Works.

Pinkney, Andrea D. (1996). *Bill Pickett: Rodeo-ridin' cowboy* (Brian Pinkney, Illus.). San Diego: Harcourt Brace.

Pinkney, Andrea D. (1998). *Duke Ellington* (Brian Pinkney, Illus.). New York: Hyperion.

Reef, Catherine. (1995). *Walt Whitman*. New York: Clarion.

Reef, Catherine. (1996). *John Steinbeck*. New York: Clarion.

Reich, Susanna. (1999). *Clara Schumann: Piano virtuoso*. New York: Clarion.

Ripken, Cal, Jr., & Bryan, Mike (1995). *Cal Ripken, Jr.: Play ball!* New York: Dial.

Ripken, Cal. Jr., & Bryan, Mike. (1999). *Cal Ripken, Jr.: My story*. New York: Dial.

Sabuda, Robert. (1994). *Tutankhamen's gift*. New York: Aladdin.

Sandburg, Carl. (1928). *Abe Lincoln grows up*. New York: Harcourt Brace.

Sandler, Martin W. (1995). *Presidents: A Library of Congress book*. New York: HarperCollins.

San Souci, Robert D. (1995). *Kate Shelley: Bound for legend* (Max Ginsburg, Illus.). New York: Dial.

Schachner, Judith Byron. (1998). *Mr. Emerson's cook*. New York: Dutton.

Schroeder, Alan. (1996a). *Minty: A story of young Harriet Tubman* (Jerry Pinkney, Illus.). New York: Dial.

Schroeder, Alan. (1996b). *Satchmo's blues* (Floyd Cooper, Illus.). New York: Doubleday.

Schroeder, Russell. (1997). *Mickey Mouse: My life in pictures*. New York: Disney Press.

Schwartz, Harriet Berg. (1996). *When Artie was little* (Thomas B. Allen, Illus.). New York: Knopf.

Severance, John B. (1997). *Gandhi: Great soul*. New York: Clarion.

Severance, John B. (1998). *Thomas Jefferson: Architect of democracy*. New York: Clarion.

Siegal, Aranka. (1981). *Upon the head of the goat*. New York: Farrar, Straus & Giroux.

Sís, Peter. (1996). *Starry messenger*. New York: Farrar, Straus & Giroux.

Staiger, Ralph C. (1998). *Thomas Harriot: Science pioneer*. New York: Clarion.

Stanley, Diane. (1995). *The true adventures of Daniel Hall*. New York: Dial.

Stanley, Diane. (1996). *Leonardo da Vinci*. New York: Morrow.

Stanley, Diane. (1998). *Joan of Arc*. New York: Morrow.

Stanley, Diane, & Vennema, Peter. (1993a). *The bard of Avon: The story of William Shakespeare* (Diane Stanley, Illus.). New York: William Morrow.

Stanley, Diane, & Vennema, Peter. (1993b). *Charles Dickens: The man who had great expectations* (Diane Stanley, Illus.). New York: William Morrow.

Stanley, Diane, & Vennema, Peter. (1994). *Cleopatra* (Diane Stanley, Illus.). New York: William Morrow.

Stanley, Jerry. (1992). *Children of the dust bowl: The true story of the school at Weedpatch Camp*. New York: Crown.

Stanley, Jerry. (1996). *Big Annie of Calumet: A true story of the Industrial Revolution*. New York: Crown.

St. George, Judith. (2000). *So you want to be president?* (David Small, Illus.). New York: Philomel.

Sullivan, George. (1996). *Black artists in photography, 1840–1940*. New York: Dutton.

Thomas, Jane Resh. (1998). *Behind the mask: The life of Queen Elizabeth I*. New York: Clarion.

Tingum, Janice. (1995). *E. B. White: The elements of a writer*. Minneapolis, MN: Lerner.

Towle, Wendy. (1993). *The real McCoy: The life of an African-American inventor* (Wil Clay, Illus.). New York: Scholastic.

Tunnell, Michael O. (2001). *The joke's on George* (Kathy Osborn, Illus.). Honesdale, PA: Boyds Mill.

Turner, Robyn Montana. (1992). *Mary Cassatt: Portraits of women artists for children*. Boston: Little, Brown.

Turner, Robyn Montana. (1994). *Dorothea Lange: Portraits of women artists for children*. Boston: Little, Brown.

Van Allsburg, Chris. (1981). *Jumanji*. Boston: Houghton Mifflin.

Van Allsburg, Chris. (1985). *The polar express*. Boston: Houghton Mifflin.

Wallner, Alexandra. (1995). *Beatrix Potter*. New York: Holiday House.

Wallner, Alexandra. (1996). *The first air voyage in the United States: The story of Jean-Pierre Blanchard*. New York: Holiday House.

Wallner, Alexandra. (1997). *Laura Ingalls Wilder*. New York: Holiday House.

White, Ryan. (1991). *Ryan White: My own story*. New York: Dial.

Wilder, Laura Ingalls. (1935). *Little house on the prairie* (Garth Williams, Illus.). New York: Harper.

Wilson, Janet. (1996). *The ingenious Mr. Peale*. New York: Atheneum.

Winter, Jonah. (1999). *Fair ball! 14 great stars from baseball's Negro leagues*. New York: Scholastic.

Wolf, Bernard. (1978). *In this proud land: The story of a Mexican American family*. Philadelphia: Lippincott.

Zaunders, Bo. (1965). *Crocodiles, camels, & dugout canoes* (Roxie Munro, Illus.). New York: Dutton.

▼▼▼▼▼▼▼
Professional References

Daugherty, J. (1972). *James Daugherty.* Videocassette. Weston, CT: Weston Woods.

Donelson, K. L., & Nilsen, A. P. (1989). *Literature for today's young adults.* Glenview, IL: Scott, Foresman.

Fletcher, R. (1993). *What a writer needs.* Portsmouth, NH: Heinemann.

Freedman, R. (1993). Bring 'em back alive. In M. O. Tunnell & R. Ammon (Eds.), *The story of ourselves:*

Teaching history through children's literature (pp. 41–48). Portsmouth, NH: Heinemann.

Fritz, J. (1988). Biography: Readability plus responsibility. *The Horn Book, 64* (6), 759–760.

Meltzer, M. (1993). Voices from the past. In M. O. Tunnell & R. Ammon (Eds.), *The story of ourselves: Teaching history through children's literature* (pp. 27–32). Portsmouth, NH: Heinemann.

UNIT 3

Using Good Books in the Classroom

MOTIVATING CHILDREN TO READ

12

CHAPTER

▼▼▼▼▼▼▼

If you want to cover
Kids Just About Like Me

Consider as a READ ALOUD

The Graduation of Jake Moon,
by Barbara Park

Consider as a TEXT SET

Wringer,
by Jerry Spinelli

Seedfolks,
by Paul Fleischman

Children Just Like Me,
by Barnabas and Anabel Kindersley

Absolutely Normal Chaos,
by Sharon Creech

Frindle,
by Andrew Clements

One-Eyed Cat,
by Paula Fox

THE GRADUATION OF JAKE MOON
by Barbara Park

Student Response

Eating dinner with James had become one of the most dreaded parts of my week. James may be older than me, but he has no scruples. Not even one. Which is not to say that I'm overflowing with scruples, myself. But no matter how low I go, James goes even lower.

Excerpt from *The Graduation of Jake Moon* by Barbara Park

I have really enjoyed this book. <u>The Graduation of Jake Moon</u> by Barbara Park is a great book. Why? Because it is a book about a 12-year-old boy named Jake Moon. His grandfather, Sherman Kelly Moon, (or Skelly for short) has Alzheimer's disease. This book, about a very serious topic, has been made funny because of Jake's attitude towards it. Barbara Park combines humor into it and here are some of my favorite parts: Jake does not get along well with his 13-year-old cousin, James. James is <u>VERY</u> rich & he lives with his mother. Sunday night is "Family Dinner Night" at Jake's house. Mrs. Park describes the very <u>not</u> close relationship between Jake and James, which is hysterical. Skelly has a couple of embarrassing moments throughout the 12 chapters. I recommend this book!

Grace
Age 12

To visit a classroom exploring the issues of Motivating Children to Read, please go to Chapter 12 of our companion website at **www.prenhall.com/darigan**

Back when T. H. Bell served as Secretary of the United States Department of Education, he traveled around the country observing schools to find ways to make them better. His experiences led him to identify three areas for improvement that are as timely today as they were then. Change must necessarily take place, and Bell (1982) stated that "the first [area] is in student motivation." He explained that *nothing* of any consequence is learned without the consent and involvement of the learner. Students have to *want* to know something in order to acquire it genuinely. Sure, they may read assigned material or learn specific facts, storing the data temporarily to, say, pass a test. But for the long term, students must see how the books they have read and the information they have learned connect with their own needs and interests. If teachers are to make a difference in current educational practice, they must pay more attention to students' attitudes.

Bell went on to identify the second area in need of improvement, which was student motivation. And the third area in need of scrutiny? You got it: student motivation. In short, he said there is *nothing* so important in improving schools as motivating our students.

Unfortunately, in practice, motivation in educational circles often means carefully planning an activity so the students *appear* to choose it when actually the whole thing was the teacher's idea. We think that this definition borders more closely on manipulation. Genuine motivation is a personal decision that comes from the heart.

Alas, there is never a guarantee that a teacher's most genuine efforts will motivate anyone. The best we can do, however, is offer sincerely and continually, and hope that students will resonate to what they see and hear. No one can predictably orchestrate real motivation in another human being, but speaking with honesty, passion, and genuine enthusiasm increases the odds that change will take place.

We hope that after reading through unit 2 in this book and after the corequisite wide reading you have done in trade books, you, yourself, have been bitten by the reading bug and have an increased desire to actively read on your own. Perhaps you have begun to talk to your colleagues across the hall and at other grade levels about specific titles you've enjoyed. Hopefully, you are also discussing with your colleagues how, in general, using real books in your room is something you are working toward and want to continue to refine. But finally, and most important, we hope you are sharing the concomitant enthusiasm you have gained for reading with your children in your class every day.

It is not uncommon in schools where a literature base is the standard for us to hear teachers chatting about the latest title they've read as their classes come shuffling in after recess. For example, you'll hear teachers say, "You know, Blanche, I just finished Lois Lowry's newest book over the weekend, *Gathering Blue*—I think I like it better than *The Giver*—and *you* know how much I loved that book!" The teacher then turns to her class and enthusiastically reminds, "Okay kids, now that you are all back from recess get to your seats quickly so we can see what happens next in our read aloud, *Crash*" (by Jerry Spinelli). And in the very same breath, she turns back to her colleague, "And you know, Blanche, I'm trying to figure out how to work this into my modern fantasy unit for next spring . . . what do you think?" This is the kind of discussion that emerges all up and down the halls when literature is valued and supported.

DID YOU KNOW?

Lois Lowry's enormously successful book **The Giver** was certainly the center of great controversy. Readers, both children and adults, disputed whether the protagonist, Jonas, dies at the end of the book as he sleds down the hill into "Elsewhere." The answer? Lowry herself discussed this at a speech we attended; her book **Gathering Blue** is a companion to **The Giver** and hints at Jonas's existence at its end. Lowry says there is a planned third book that links the characters in both books. So, Jonas does indeed live.

Now it may be that you're one of those who still hasn't been bitten by that reading bug—which is entirely possible. So many of our students, both at the undergraduate and graduate levels, come up to us and pour out their hearts concerning the dread, distaste, and dislike they have always had for reading, particularly as a child; naturally, it transfers to them as adults. Many confess that they haven't read a book in years . . . or, sad to say, ever! So if you are in that category, don't you dare beat yourself up about it. We would encourage you, however, just like that ill-tempered third grader sitting in the back corner of the room, to go back to the shelves, find a book that is concerned with a topic that is interesting to you, and give reading another chance. We do know that in the end, if reading real books for real purposes is to be the accepted norm in your classroom, then *you* have to be the Number 1 advo-cate for literacy—*you* have to be passionate about books if you expect your children to be turned on to them as well.

So what we investigate in this chapter on motivating children to read is three-fold. We first take a close look at how the motivation to read can be encouraged in your classroom. Second, we discuss how your role as teacher is critical to that motiva-tion, and, finally, provide you with specific classroom organizational techniques and considerations that can make reading the accepted, standard activity of choice.

▼▼▼▼▼▼▼
Motivation Is the Key to Engaged Reading

As we said earlier, it is a very difficult task to motivate anybody to do anything. Think of the lengths you go to in just getting your sixth-grade child to wash the dishes or, worse yet, how about trying to get your "significant other" to take out the trash? So we admit that what we are attempting to do here is daunting. Knowing that fact, our goal here is simple: We want to *increase* the odds that children will become engaged readers. The questions we must ask ourselves, then, are these: "What can we do to mo-tivate children to read? How can we encourage them to become lifelong lovers of lit-erature?"

Typically, we meet a lot of teachers, especially in the early levels of our literacy and children's literature courses, who believe that the motivational process is handled best by finding a "cute" idea in a book of black-line masters that can be found at a lo-cal teacher's supply store. "It's all there," they tell us, "you don't even have to buy a picture book or novel for *this* wonderful activity."

Well, we've looked at dozens of such books and at hundreds of activities, and quite frankly, we're unimpressed. Here is an example of one of these packaged lesson plans that targets John Chapman, probably better known to you as Johnny Appleseed. Included in this "dynamic" two-page packet (which you are free to duplicate for school use) is:

- a "story"
- a game
- a cooking recipe
- a sequencing work sheet

The "story" contains a mere three short paragraphs barely explaining anything concerning who this famous American folk hero was, what he did, or what prompted him to do it. Following the "story," the teacher is given the opportunity to play a silly relay game with his or her class, which can then be followed by the making of "apple pancakes (recipe included)." Assuming they need something to busy themselves while the apple pancakes are being cooked, there is included (for no extra charge) a work sheet containing six pictured frames that need to be numbered, colored, cut out, and then pasted back together in sequential order.

Herein lies the idea many teachers unfortunately believe to be representative of literature-based instruction. But here is the main point—the entire lesson includes NO reading by children. What little reading the teacher does is represented by only 116 words. Hmm. Is there something wrong with this picture?

Now, granted, the children will sit and listen to the "story." The fact is, it will be over before they even have had a chance to get antsy. The game, touted for its "large motor skills," has nothing to do with reading. The cooking . . . well, with as many food metaphors as we have used in this book, we are hardly ones to complain . . . however, the cooking still has nothing to do with reading—there isn't even a ready-to-duplicate recipe for the kids to follow along with. As far as the work sheet is concerned, there, again, is no reading required. And sad to say, kids are so enculturated by the "cut and paste" syndrome, these days, that they hardly think twice about doing it. For them, it

To find out more about student-created author projects, visit Chapter 12 on the companion website at **www.prenhall.com/darigan**

BOOKMARK

INTEGRATING TECHNOLOGY: AUTHORS ON THE WORLD WIDE WEB

There is certainly enough interesting information available on many authors that students can create their own biographical projects. In fact, this sort of project can help students think about both the literature they read and the people who write it in new and exciting ways. On the *Author, Author* website, students at Nichols Middle School in Evanston, IL explore literature and compare their favorite authors. Students are asked to locate information about one of their favorite authors, including at least 10 interesting facts, a quote, an excerpt, and appropriate graphics. The students do a great job compiling, creating, and documenting their projects.

is a simple school kind of activity. Now, we ask you this: Do ANY of these materials really motivate children to read?

We think there are a lot of options (thoughout this unit) to this sort of senseless busy work. But one alternative stands out among the many others as being superior in motivating children to pick up a book and read. This one alternative we're talking about is easy, it's cheap, and it has been proven to work.

But before we tell you what it is, let's first take a look at the report issued by the Commission on Reading back in 1985 (Anderson, Hiebert, Scott, & Wilkinson, 1985) for help. Some of the biggest names in reading got together; they studied and synthesized all the research pertaining to reading and issued a comprehensive report on the results. They looked at how reading emerges, how it is nurtured, and what we as teachers and parents can do to promote it. This commission was funded by the U.S. Department of Education and organized by The National Academy of Education, The National Institute of Education, and The Center for the Study of Reading. What were their findings? It's simple; they state: "The single most important activity for building the knowledge required for eventual success in reading is *reading aloud* to children" (p. 23—our emphasis). They go on to say, "There is *no substitute for a teacher who reads children good stories.* It whets the appetite of children for reading. . . . It is a practice that should continue throughout the grades" (p. 51).

How can something so simple be of such great value, you ask? Fortunately for us all, the research is quite clear on this point. For young children, reading aloud aids in linguistic development, increases their knowledge of vocabulary, and affects their active use of language. For school-age children, Chomsky (1972) found that reading aloud produced higher linguistic competence, and Feitelson, Kita, and Goldstein (1986) found that it significantly increased phoneme development. For African American children, Cullinan, Jagger, and Strickland (1974) found that reading aloud substantially increased usage of standard English structures without reducing the level of proficiency in native Black English. Numerous studies showed that reading aloud produces significant gains in children's reading comprehension while it further increases children's knowledge of story structure, increases attention span, and broadens their horizons. Yet despite a plethora of research to support the use of reading aloud in classrooms, research indicates that this strategy is not widely prevalent in our schools (Darigan, 1991).

Reading aloud to children every single day, many times a day, WORKS! As an instructional technique, it is beyond compare. In chapter 14, we outline exactly how you can fit reading aloud effectively into your reading instruction. But first, let's analyze why reading aloud is the ultimate motivational tool. Our pal Jim Trelease (1995) has made the perfect connection on the matter and says it far more succinctly than we.

Want motivation? Think of one of the most successful businesses in modern times—McDonald's. "This fast food chain has been in business for more than 30 years, and never once has it cut its advertising budget. Every year, McDonald's spends more money on advertising than it did the previous year, which comes to more than $1 million *per day* just for advertising"(p. 45).

If McDonald's is at the top of the heap, then why do they continue to advertise? Look at their bottom line for the answer. "Every time we read aloud to a child or class, we're giving a commercial for the pleasures of reading" (Trelease, 1995, p. 45). If the corporate honchos living under the Golden Arches refuse to rest on their laurels and cut programming, neither should we. We need to advertise reading daily in our classrooms and homes by reading aloud.

You may recall the old adage, "You can take a horse to water but you can't make him drink." Well, those "cute" apple-of-our-eye lesson plans won't motivate children to drink from the pool of literature that awaits them. Reading aloud is central to engaging children in the joys and rewards of reading. This has been a key activity for all three of us in our own elementary teaching careers. Most recently, in Darigan's fifth-grade classroom out in Oregon, he read aloud—in one single year, mind you—23 novels, and they quit counting picture books at 150. This, by the way, was in a class where his initial literacy survey showed that EVERY single student "disliked" reading. In answer to "Who reads aloud to you?" they singularly answered, "My teacher." When asked if they liked it, they unanimously responded, "No!" By the end of the year, the answers had shifted in exactly the opposite direction. All 24 favored reading and "loved" to have him read to them.

Let's return to Johnny Appleseed and those absurd black-line masters. You might, instead, consider reading aloud one or all of the following titles in your classroom. They will provide the fodder for subsequent discussions, comparisons, and critical literary analysis. And if you want to make applesauce, apple pancakes, apple fritters—all the better! (In fact, we'd love it if you'd send the recipes to us c/o Merrill/Prentice Hall.) But for our teaching success, it is essential that literature lead the way, only later to be followed by activities and extensions.

Beyond reading aloud, there are numerous other considerations to be taken into account in motivating children to read. The bulk of the rest of the chapter identifies those ideas, activities, and techniques. In the next section, we look at what we, as teachers and parents, can do to help students find the books they like and that are appropriate for them. Next, we see what can be learned from readers who are motivated already.

ALTERNATE TEXT SET

Johnny Appleseed

Read Aloud

The True Tale of Johnny Appleseed, by Margaret Hodges, illustrated by Kimberly Bulcken Root

Text Set

Johnny Appleseed, by Reeve Lindbergh, illustrated by Kathy Jakobsen

Johnny Appleseed, by Steven Kellogg

The Real Johnny Appleseed, by Laurie Lawlor, illustrated by Mary Thompson

Then we show you how to get students quickly into books, and finally take a critical look at reading incentive programs as a means of motivating children to read.

Helping Students Find Books They Like

Perhaps one of the most common ways to get children motivated and on the road to reading is to identify their interests and then locate books on those subjects. We have found that an initial "interest inventory" given at the beginning of the school year helps you to learn more about each child as a reader and what his or her specific interests are. We have included one such instrument in Figure 12-1, which is an adaptation of the one we found way back in graduate school, so we're not certain who developed it.

Use the database that accompanies this text as your first resource for books to use in your classroom. For example, when we entered the descriptor "humor" and searched for all the titles in our database, we almost instantaneously came up with over 300 picture books and novels in that category. Looking for a book? Do yourself a favor and crank up the CD-ROM!

Another thing we encourage you to do is to have regular one-on-one conferences during your Reader's Workshop time with each of your children just to get to know them better. For example, we kept a large, three-ring binder with a separate section for each student. Whenever we learned something new or potentially important about that child, we jotted it on a self-sticking note and stashed it in the file. As the year progressed, we began to see some striking patterns. So when we did the one-on-one conferences, we would just pull out the interest inventory and add the extra information right on that document. Then, whenever necessary and at a quick glance at the file, we could refresh our memories on what the children were specifically interested in.

When you learn, for example, that a child enjoys a good joke, you could steer him or her to Katy Hall's ***Really, Really, Really Bad Jokes*** and Rick Walton's ***Really, Really Bad Summer Jokes.*** Then, to raise the level of humor a few notches, you could recommend hilarious picture books like David Wisniewski's ***The Secret Knowledge of Grown-ups*** and ***Tough Cookie.*** As far as novels are concerned, you could then lead them to books in the text set we recommend in chapter 7, "Tickling Your Funny Bone."

This method of matching books to children's interests works well, by and large, but we admit it has a few drawbacks. In a regular library, all the books on any particular topic soon get exhausted. You know how children seem to have their interests clump together—it sort of becomes a reading feeding frenzy? For instance, many second graders are tremendously interested in dinosaurs, and every fifth grader, these days, can't seem to wait to get their hands on the newest Harry Potter. In either circumstance, *good luck* trying to find either of these groupings on the library shelves—those are the books that are always checked out! This, then, puts the onus on the teacher to redirect the child to another area of interest.

As if that weren't problem enough, we have found, probably more important, a certain "other" sector of children who just simply *do not know* what they are interested in. Compounding the problem is that these kids generally have little background in choosing books and so they tend to fall between the cracks and end up with no good choices. Unfortunately, these children are usually the ones who need books the most. Here, again, what is a teacher to do?

Finding out what each of your children is interested in AND helping them choose an appropriate book are a tall order. Here is an anecdote that may help to assuage some

We found "Let's Do Lunch" to be a particularly effective way to get to know the kids in our classroom. Once or twice a week, and with individuals or in small groups, we invited the students in our class "in" for lunch. They either pulled their brown bags out of their backpacks or carried their trays back to the classroom. All we had to do was sit back, and listen, and if need be, we asked only a few pertinent questions about their families, their interests, what they did in their spare time, and what their dreams and aspirations were. This made them feel so special, and it afforded us the opportunity to see our students in a totally different light. Try it, and you will find that you discover so much about them as learners and particularly as human beings.

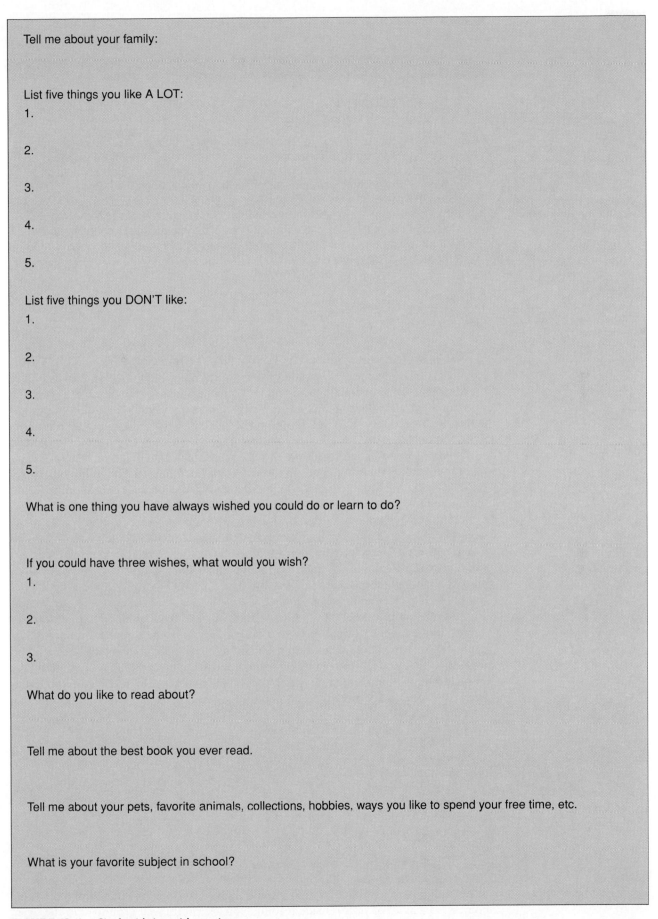

Tell me about your family:

List five things you like A LOT:
1.

2.

3.

4.

5.

List five things you DON'T like:
1.

2.

3.

4.

5.

What is one thing you have always wished you could do or learn to do?

If you could have three wishes, what would you wish?
1.

2.

3.

What do you like to read about?

Tell me about the best book you ever read.

Tell me about your pets, favorite animals, collections, hobbies, ways you like to spend your free time, etc.

What is your favorite subject in school?

FIGURE 12-1 Student interest inventory.

To find out more about Aaron Shepard's Reader's Theater Page and other lesson plans on the World Wide Web, visit Chapter 12 on the companion website at **www.prenhall. com/darigan**

BOOKMARK

INTEGRATING TECHNOLOGY: ACTIVITIES USING THE WORLD WIDE WEB

One way to motivate children to read is to work with various ways of approaching the written word. Stressing the interactive, oral, and dramatic qualities of literature can often motivate students who are not normally active readers, and it can provide a different way of approaching literature for those who are already avid readers. *Aaron Shepard's Reader's Theater Page* is a website that explains Reader's Theater, gives tips on how to carry it out, and, most important, provides numerous scripts (both original adaptations of folktales and Reader's Theater scripts adapted from other books). Shepard, who is also an author of picture books, provides scripts and downloadable color posters for many of his books.

of your fears. Quite a number of years ago—in fact, *many* years ago—in Darigan's sixth-grade class in Los Angeles, his students spent a full hour every Thursday afternoon in the library, both for instruction and for checking out books for the next week. Darlene, a young Mexican American girl, always quickly chose the thickest of novels and would be first in line to go back to the classroom. Later, during Silent Sustained Reading, she would sit bolt upright, her eyes glued to the page, but it didn't take long for Darigan to detect that poor Darlene could barely read a single word on the page, let alone maintain the thread of the story. The next week, when he attempted to aid her in a better book selection, he found that his own limited knowledge of books at that time (as we said, it was a long, long time ago) restricted his ability to help her.

Ah, but in stepped the hero of the day: the school librarian. She knew exactly what was in her collection, and with Darigan's knowledge of Darlene's interests as well as a good idea of her approximate reading level, the two were able to provide the girl with a number of titles from which she could choose. Everyone was a winner, but most pleased was Darlene because she was proudly able to read and enjoy a book, her book—perhaps for the first time in her life.

Returning to our steadfast belief in the power of reading aloud, we want to reiterate how this practice can motivate both of the aforementioned groups of students—those who would benefit from expanding their areas of interest and those who seemingly have none. When a teacher reads aloud and presents that "commercial" for story and books and reading, it opens worlds students never believed existed. Here is what poet David McCord has to say about it:

> Books fall open,
> you fall in,
> delighted where
> you've never been;
> hear voices not once
> heard before,
> reach world on world
> through door on door. . .

The question, now, is where do you start? If you are anything like we were at your stage of the game, you feel like the old saying, "Goodness, I know only enough to be dangerous." Well, cut yourself some slack! After reading this book up to this point as well as all of your outside reading, you are pretty well grounded in the overall scope of children's literature. But now you might find yourself saying, "Geez, I just finished Sharon Creech's **Walk Two Moons** and loved it. Now, I see that including her

We've found that the way to cover a lot of ground, especially during the school year, as far as the number of books you can read is concerned, is to have two or three titles going at the same time. We know this sounds crazy and you say you can't do it, but hear us out. You should personally be reading a book every day during Silent Sustained Reading; why not pick a children's book? For teaching purposes in either Reader's or Writer's Workshop, you should also have an ongoing novel you are reading aloud to the class. There is book number two. At home, you should either be reading aloud to your own kids (no matter how old they are) or your roommate or significant other while *he or she* does the dishes (sort of a New-Age Tom Sawyer trick). And, of course, you should have a book on the bedstand. Gosh, that is four books, and they *all* could be children's. We found that when we were teaching elementary school, we were reading somewhere in the neighborhood of 100 novels a year. So see, you can catch up pretty quickly.

newest book *The Wanderer,* I still have five more books on her list to read. Then there is Lois Lowry and James Howe and Lloyd Alexander and Avi and . . . . Yikes, I'll never catch up!"

You see, the more you *know,* the more you realize you *don't* know—our parents probably told us that but we were too "smart" to listen. Anyway, before you have a heart attack, let's put this into perspective. We have *all* been at the beginning stages. And if you'd only applaud all the accomplishments you made thus far and build on that solid base, you'd feel a lot better about yourself and treat yourself with a lot more respect. Consider that thus far this term, you have done quite a lot of reading.

So (and this is the long way of getting around to this) the first step in choosing books for the children in your classroom is to recommend your personal favorites. When teachers introduce as well as read from books they genuinely like, students are more likely to be motivated for two reasons. First, those books are generally better books than kids would choose in the sense that they usually are more solidly crafted and contain more levels where children can make connections. Second, when teachers recommend books that are personally meaningful, a genuine and irresistible enthusiasm accompanies their words. When you talk about books you like, your sincerity and conviction often influence those who listen.

But don't be fooled; no source or method is foolproof. Even picking books exclusively from lists of award winners such as the Caldecott and Newbery carries no guarantee children will respond positively to them. Again, you ought to strongly consider using the database included with this text as a matter of course when choosing books. Because you can search by topic, author, illustrator, and theme, to mention only a few descriptors, you can begin with a fairly large number of selections on any one subject and then limit it from there. We have recently combed the over 14,000 titles and added award designations. Of course, the biggies like the Newbery and Caldecott are included, but for the specific use of you and the children in your classes, we have added almost two dozen other awards and we have listed state award winners, which are truly the voice of children and their preferences.

Nothing we offer children is more important than an adult who reads. As mentioned in Chapter 1, children end up doing what we do, not what we say, and all the admonitions about the importance of reading in their lives fall on deaf ears if they view us as people who do not take our own advice. When we speak from our own experience, however, our words are more honest and persuasive. Why do you think we include so many stories from when we were classroom teachers? We can't convince children of the beauty of mathematics unless that vision comes from our own hearts and minds. We can't paint a believable picture of how appealing life is in the desert unless we have lived there and loved it. And we largely waste our time singing the virtues of reading when the last book we read was 5 years ago . . . or more.

In summary, teachers have a choice in motivating children to become lifelong readers. They can either preach on the joys of reading, or they can model for the youngsters what a reader who enjoys reading does. By regularly reading aloud to children each day, by modeling that you read during Silent Sustained Reading time, and by making reading a priority in your school day, you make a difference. In the end, what teachers do ultimately will depend on how much they truly believe in the importance of reading (Perez, 1986, p. 11).

Learning From Motivated Readers

A group of college-age Americans was living in Germany, trying to learn German but making slow progress. An old hand offered a piece of advice that made an enormous difference: "If you want to speak like the Germans, listen to the way Germans speak." Embarrassingly simple and obvious, it changed the course of their learning, which until then had been too formal and academic.

We adapt that advice for this chapter: "If we want students to be motivated readers, let's look at how motivated readers read." Teachers sometimes believe that students need careful preparation to read a book or that they have to be bribed or prodded into reading. Yet some children jump right into books, reading without the benefit of preparatory steps or the intervention of either a carrot or a whip. Two principles underlie the motivation of these eager readers: First, reading is personal, and second, reading is a natural process. The following common characteristics of motivated readers reflect these two principles.

1. Motivated readers read not for others but for their own purposes. They read what is important to them and know real reading is not to answer someone else's questions or fill out a work sheet.
2. Motivated readers have personal and identifiable likes and dislikes in books: subject matter, authors, illustrators, formats, styles, and so on.
3. Motivated readers feel rewarded during the reading process. They find immediate pleasure in the book and don't read because they will need it next year.
4. Motivated readers do not feel trapped by a book. They can put it down without guilt when it no longer meets their needs.
5. Motivated readers feel free to talk about what they read from their own point of view. They are not hesitant about passing judgment on a book.
6. Motivated readers read at their own rate. They skip, scan, linger, and reread as is necessary or desirable.
7. Motivated readers don't feel obligated to remember everything they read. They find reading worthwhile even if they can't recall every concept or idea, and they allow themselves to skip over words they don't know as long as they understand the idea or story.
8. Motivated readers read broadly, narrowly, or in between, depending on how they feel.
9. Motivated readers develop a personal attachment to books they like.
10. Motivated readers find time—better yet, they *make* time—to read regularly.

Motivated readers don't look over their shoulders as they read. They are in charge. We adults shouldn't get excited when they put down books without finishing them. We shouldn't make ourselves crazy when they devour what we think are worthless books or when their taste does not reflect our own or when they read very narrowly.

Yet teachers with the best of intentions can interfere with motivated readers. Often the most difficult hurdle is simply getting out of their way. Whatever an adult does that keeps the child from becoming involved with the book is something to be avoided. It is easy to spot mind-numbing exercises that treat the book as merely a repository of facts to be mined, and those practices should be avoided. But even the right principles can be followed with too much fervor, as is evident in the following two examples:

Rose Napoli is an experienced, dedicated teacher who became enthusiastic during a summer institute about trade books and their use in the classroom. She returned to her teaching inflamed with ideas about allowing students to choose their own books, providing time for them to read, and initiating discussions based on their personal responses. The trouble was that her enthusiasm was so strong she simply overpowered the children. She jumped immediately into questions about their involvement with the stories and so peppered them with requests for their feelings that even those children who initially responded began to keep quiet. Only when she began to let students talk from their own perspectives, and sincerely listened to them, did the children start to respond honestly. In time, the simplistic but honest comments became more complex and perceptive, and Rose eventually found the kind of student involvement she earlier had tried to force (Calkins, 1986, pp. 243–249).

Gordon Whiting (personal communication, 1991), a professor at Brigham Young University, prided himself on allowing his 9-year-old daughter adequate rein in selecting the books she would read. He was pleased to see her choose The Little House series and was not bothered when she finished them all and began immediately to reread the seven titles in the slipcase. She read them a third time, then a fourth. When she began a fifth reading, he wondered if she wouldn't be served better by reading something else but said nothing. As she started the sixth time, he had to hold his tongue. When she picked up the first book to begin a seventh reading, he could keep his peace no longer. He did not forbid her to read them again but insisted she read one different book before returning to the series. Result? She quit reading. Chances are good that she would have moved to other titles in her own time, but clearly she was getting something from the series that caused her to read the books again and again. We simply don't know what goes on in the heads of children when they are immersed in a book. If they are to become motivated readers, we must allow them to be in charge.

Get Students Quickly Into Books

We can learn a useful lesson about reading, oddly enough, from TV. Why do people watch it so much? Because it is so good? Hardly; we watch it because it is so easy. It is generally located in a central place in the home; it is highly visible, and simple to use. Figure it this way: If the TV were stored in a basement closet and we had to haul it upstairs every time we wanted to see a program, we might decide to bring it out only on weekends. But then again, we more likely would find something better to do instead.

How does this TV tidbit transfer to motivating kids to read? When we make reading easier, we find more children reading. We need to make books as easy and accessible as TV tends to be in our homes. We need to read aloud daily, many times a day. Books need to be handy. We must hold them up, read passages, and help get students to see all the goodies contained inside. So teachers reading aloud to their classes, thereby displaying the joys and benefits as well as modeling effective and efficient reading behaviors, is a first step.

Next, in an effort to make reading easier, we need to take yet another hint from the Report on the Commission on Reading (Anderson et al., 1985). Besides setting up a literate classroom environment, allowing an adequate amount of time to read and write, we need to "maintain a brisk pace and *keep rates of success high* [emphasis added]" (p. 118). Let's try this example on for size: We've been told that the average adult should be able to bench-press his or her own weight—whether that's true or not, for

To find out more about the Internet Public Library and other sources on the World Wide Web, visit Chapter 12 on the companion website at **www.prenhall.com/darigan**

BOOKMARK

INTEGRATING TECHNOLOGY: SOURCES ON THE WORLD WIDE WEB

The Youth division of the *Internet Public Library* contains book reviews by kids, story hours, on-line stories, an "Ask the Author" section in which children can submit questions to celebrated authors such as Lois Lowry and Katherine Paterson, and biographies of authors and illustrators. The site is interactive and student centered and can further motivate readers to explore literature in interesting ways. "Weblink," an Internet newsletter for kids, is also located at this site.

the sake of argument, let's say bench-pressing your weight is a reasonable standard. Therefore, if you are a pixie-sized 100-pounder, you should be able to press 100 pounds. For those of us who are more than double that weight we, too, should be able to press . . . well, let's not go there! But that's our point exactly! Nobody would expect any of the three of us to bench-press our weight the first time. The reasonable course would be to set up a training routine and to work up slowly in both repetition and weight. Why, then, do we expect children to metaphorically "read" their own weight— all the time, every time? *Oh, since Johnny is in fifth grade he MUST be reading fifth-grade materials.*

From this point, many teachers go on to say that not only do we need to have kids reading at grade level, we need to push them, stretch them, lest they get lazy. Well, if we go back to the weight-lifting example, we say to these same teachers, "Okay, you are a seemingly fit 30-year-old woman weighing 145 pounds. But you need to push yourself tonight. Get on the bench! We'll bump the bar up to 175. It will be good for you!" Now it is true that we may, indeed, pump a bit more iron on a day when we've had an extra half a bowl of Wheaties, but we generally don't push ourselves either on the bench or in the reading we do. The lesson here is to engage children at *their* fluency level—maybe a bit more, but certainly not at their frustration level.

Finally, we need to handle children and books the way we would handle children and basketball. How do kids learn the game? We provide them with a hoop and a ball and let them play. There's no need to first recite the history of the game, learn about the manufacturing of basketballs, or study the specifications of different backboards or breakaway rims. Give them the ball, and let them "just do it." (Now, that is not to say that discussion during reading isn't necessary to give the kids added depth of experience, the same way a wise coach can improve play on the court. We talk more about that in chapter 14.) An interesting book does not need elaborate introductions or preparations any more than an appealing movie needs a narrator to set the stage for the viewer. We open the cover and read.

Reading Incentive Programs

To focus on individual reading in the classroom and inspire students to spend time with books, teachers sometimes provide an incentive by using a chart or other visual record of each child's reading. Often thematic, the chart may be called "Shoot for the Moon," with a rocket ship for each child lined up at the bottom and a moon at the top. For every book read, the rocket ship advances an inch. Or paper ice cream cones may line the back wall; every time a child reads a book, the title is written on a paper ice cream scoop and placed on the cone. When every cone has 10 scoops, the class has an ice cream party.

Incentive programs often revolve around prizes as well as charts. Some are generated by teachers, like the ice cream party, and others come from businesses, such as coupons good for pizza. Alfie Kohn (1992) states that although it may be conceived and carried out with the very best of intentions, an outside or extrinsic motivator simply cannot take the place of an activity we find rewarding in itself (p. 59). Further, and specific to reading, some research shows that extrinsic rewards actually can hinder the development of intrinsic motivation to read (Lepper, Greene, & Nisbett, 1973). Yet other conflicting research reports that extrinsic rewards do not necessarily have a negative impact on intrinsic motivation to read, at least in the areas of attitude, time on task, and performance (Cameron & Pierce, 1994).

Teachers need to be aware, however, that when they offer a prize as a reward for reading, they must to be able to determine when the prize overshadows the book. Teachers should ask, "How can I know if the student is reading for the prize or for the love of the book?" If they are not sure of the answer, then teachers should examine the situation more closely to know if the reward is getting in the way. As soon as the prize becomes more important than the reading, the incentive program is no longer a friend but has become the enemy. If teachers are sure students are motivated primarily by the books, then nothing is wrong with cashing in on the free pizzas. But one reward, and one reward only, keeps people reading over time: the reading itself. Over the long haul, people turn to books because the books are enjoyable and worthwhile.

An example of an incentive program going astray was clear when a male student came up after class to tell about the contest sponsored by his school when he was in the third grade. Whoever read the most books over three months would win a bicycle. This student burned with the idea of owning the bike and read during every free moment at school and home. He read more than every one of the other fourth, fifth, and sixth graders and he won the bicycle. During the schoolwide assembly when the principal presented him the prize, his fine example was held up to the rest of the students as stellar and enviable. Finishing the story, he said, "Since winning the bike, I have not read one book except those required by my classes." The reading champion of the school ended up being a nonreader. To win a bicycle, he simply engaged in a competitive activity involving books.

One problem with the moon shot and the ice cream cones is that these programs do not help those who need it most. We never have seen a reading chart without finding a few race cars still at the starting line or bookworms waiting for additional body segments; these belong to the children in every class who need books the most. They do not read easily, are not doing well in school, and receive little or no encouragement at home. And because they are not doing well at school, the chart meant to inspire instead condemns, revealing at a glance the names of those children who are failures and who, yet again, have blown it. They *know* they'll never win, so there isn't much point to trying.

At the other end of the spectrum are the handful of achievers whose rockets take off in a blinding blast. They shoot to the moon, continue beyond the mark to the top of the wall, and then make a turn at the ceiling toward the opposite wall. These competitive types can't stand to lose. Like the boy who won the bike, their compulsion to win often overshadows the pleasures of reading, and they tend to zoom through book after book at home with thoughts like "I'll get that Ruthie! I'll bet I'm reading more pages tonight than she is." As if possessed, these readers exhibit the same drive whether the contest is skipping rope or gathering leaves. Born to win, they sail through stacks of books with little benefit.

The majority of the children, the regular kids, go along with a reading incentive plan for a while. Then they are inclined to drift away from the chart, particularly after an initial goal is met or teacher support wanes. Except in rare cases, these three groups—the nonreaders, the cutthroat competitors, and the regular kids—tend to be badly served by a system that places the game before the book.

Group motivation and record keeping are another matter. The teacher who requires students to keep records of their personal reading can tally each week's reading and then display the increasing total, for example, in a thermometer where the temperature rises with continued reading or simply in a growing line that snakes around the top of the walls. These visual summaries provide bragging rights to *everyone* in the class, as opposed to the individual successes offered by the race car or ice cream chart. When a goal is reached, *everyone* participates in the victory, even those kids who have read few or no books. No one except the teacher need know or even be aware of the amount each child reads. No additional stigma is placed on those who are not performing. The teacher now has the opportunity to work individually with those students who need extra time and attention.

The Teacher as the Predominant Example of Literacy

In motivating children to read, the most important element in the equation is a teacher who reads. The power of a teacher's example, as described in chapter 1 as well as earlier in this chapter, appears here as a reminder. "The key to developing a personal love of books is a teacher who communicates enthusiasm and an appreciation of literature through his attitudes and examples" (Wilson & Hall, 1972, p. 341). How does the teacher best demonstrate this? By reading, of course. From everyday sessions of reading aloud and silent sustained reading to making a wide variety of books readily available to the class, the teacher is key to the entire process. Four useful ways for the teacher to structure time for that essential interaction with books are (1) reading aloud, (2) silent reading, (3) bringing books to kids, and (4) going to the library. We discuss these next.

Reading Aloud

There are few absolutes in education, more particularly in children's literature. Whether we like and appreciate the illustrations in a particular book or the story line an author writes in a novel is certainly a fairly subjective matter. As we note in many of the genre chapters, determining if a book falls into one specific category as opposed to another is also up for debate. But one of the constants we are absolutely certain of is that of the importance of the teacher reading aloud to his or her class. We are dead certain on this point. In fact, we open every one of our college classes with a read aloud book, and whether you are teaching at the university level all the way down to the primary grades and preschool, we would hope that you do, too.

But good experiences reading aloud don't just happen. They occur when certain principles are followed.

1. You should honestly like the books you read aloud. The difference in reading a book aloud only because it is handy and reading a book aloud because it is loved is enormous.

2. Don't read aloud unfamiliar books unless you are willing to accept the consequences. The temptation is great to "learn the book" as you share it with the class, but too many drawbacks can occur. First, you may soon realize that you do not like the book. This one you can get out of gracefully because you can demonstrate the importance of having courage to model putting the book away for a later date or forever. Second, you may have unpleasant surprises in store—words you are not comfortable saying aloud and didn't know were coming up in the next sentence, a character with negative traits who shares a name with a child in your class, or something in the plot you wish you had known about earlier. Third, you have a much more difficult time dramatizing the book or emphasizing highlights because you don't know them until you are right on top of them; then it is too late. Finally, and most important, your enthusiasm for the story probably will be weak because you are learning at the same time as the children.

3. Teachers should do the oral reading aloud themselves. Even if a child is skilled enough to read the book out loud, the teacher's participation carries an important message to the class; that is, "Our teacher *wants* to be a part of this activity, so it *must* be important." In addition, students get to see a teacher's personal involvement in books that, through time, generally will include both laughter and tears. Children learn much more than the story when an adult reads aloud.

4. Don't expect all students to like every book. Tell your class, "We will read many books in here this year. No one will like them all. I expect that everyone will find some they do like." In Darigan's Oregon fifth-grade class, he started Barbara Brooks Wallace's **Peppermints in the Parlor** sometime in early October to coincide with the school's Halloween celebration. After a full week of reading and being well into the fourth chapter, the kids were clearly not engaged in the book. As a group, they decided that maybe they would be better off halting then and there and going on to Roald Dahl's **Matilda.**

Interestingly enough, somewhere in mid-spring, the class had just finished an ongoing novel and as the group was pondering what book should come next, one child asked, "What ever happened to that **Peppermints in the Parlor** book you started, Dr. D?" "Yeah," another chimed in, "We really liked that!" Darigan pulled it off the shelf and within three weeks had not only reread to where they had stopped but finished the entire book to boot. The kids were thrilled—but then they were finally ready.

5. Establish your own rules for read-aloud time. Some teachers allow students to draw; others don't. Some are not concerned when children fall asleep; others are. Still others allow students to go the water fountain or bathroom, whereas others don't. If anything bothers a teacher, it must be fixed, or the distraction will weaken the reading experience.

Silent Reading

Students need a portion of their daily schedule to be reserved for reading books that are personal and self-selected. Silent Reading is a practice commonly seen in classrooms across the country. At Hillcrest Elementary School in Elgin, Illinois, the school halted its regular daily operation for silent reading. The *whole* school! In fact, each of the school's staff—the lunchroom and playground supervisors, custodians, the nurse, the principal, and secretaries—would go into the classrooms to demonstrate their reading as well. At 12:30, everything halted while 20 minutes was dedicated to the enjoyment of reading. And what a message that sent each and every student. One day, they would have Mr. Fonte, the head custodian, sitting in a corner reading and the next Dr. Johnson, the principal, might drop in for a read. Whether it be just in your classroom or schoolwide, Silent Sustained Reading is a must.

Silent reading is often referred to by one of the following acronyms: SSR (*S*ustained *S*ilent *R*eading), DEAR (*D*rop *E*verything *A*nd *R*ead), and SQUIRT (*S*uper *Q*uiet *U*n*I*nterrupted *R*eading *T*ime). One summer, though, a fellow teacher and graduate student told us about OTTER (*O*ur *T*urn *T*o *E*njoy *R*eading), which is more to our liking. Whatever you call it, the rules are easy: For the allotted time, everyone reads—*including* the teacher. But be forewarned, SSR is not an automatic and immediate success. To make it work, have a bit of patience. We list some of the essentials:

1. The teacher *must* read. When a number of SSR programs were evaluated, findings indicated the program failed when the teacher did not participate (McCracken & McCracken, 1978, pp. 406–408). If the teacher does not read, the message to the students is perfectly clear: "This is only a school assignment, important for you but not for me." Beyond modeling a love of reading, one of the distinct advantages of SSR is that it provides the teacher time to catch up on new children's books. Don't get us wrong: Your reading should be self-selected as well, and does not have to be limited only to titles appropriate for children. Anything personally interesting to you is fair

game—well, almost anything. However, when a student recommends a favorite book and the teacher actually reads it, the positive results are overwhelming.

Don't fall into the habit of using SSR time to talk to your neighbor, take attendance, correct papers, or complete any other such clerical tasks. When Darigan (1991) was conducting the research for his dissertation, he observed classrooms in a variety of settings: suburban, rural, and inner city. In the latter, he watched a third-grade teacher wander around the classroom during SSR with a huge roll of orange carnival tickets. When she "caught" a child reading, she (rather loudly) slapped a ticket on his or her desk—to be redeemed at a later date for candy or school supplies. All she had to do was sit down and read and she would have had far better results.

2. Use an old egg timer to keep track of the clock. More times than we would like to remember as classroom teachers, we had been so engrossed in a book that we became oblivious to the clock and ended up missing a special or were, yet again, late for lunch. Set the timer for the allotted amount of time; when it "dings," remember to give the kids another minute or two to find a good place to stop.

And keep this in mind: Just because you are teaching sixth graders, it doesn't necessarily mean they can begin the year reading for 20 to 25 minutes. Like training for a running event, you need to build up to race pace slowly. What if we were to ask you to go out and run a 6-minute mile—right now, today. Gasp! More logically, we would ask you to walk the track for 10 minutes. You would perhaps do that for a week, then the next week alternate two walking laps with half a running lap. Over time, and at your pace, you would be running the entire time. This is true with SSR, as well. Start with as little as 6 to 8 minutes (even with the older kids) and build their reading endurance from there.

3. If a child starts a book (as we mentioned with the earlier example of ***Peppermints in the Parlor***) and after a reasonable time remains uninterested in it, make sure he or she knows that finishing is not required.

4. The teacher makes no assignments for the books read during SSR. Students may choose to use a book they read during SSR for an assigned activity, but they are not required to report on SSR books. To monitor the books and number of pages our students read, we provided them with weekly bookmarks so at the end of SSR they could record what and how much they read each day. Again, no grade was given for this; it was just useful information to be included in their portfolios.

DID YOU KNOW?

This simple yet powerful tool for literacy still isn't being widely used. Trelease (1995) states, "I personally surveyed 300 teachers in four states: Does their school have a time set aside for SSR? Only 28 of the 300 teachers said yes. This is supported by the 1992 NAEP report showing that more than half of all students have no SSR. It also helps explain why test scores have stagnated for twenty years and why we have so few lifetime readers" (p. 194).

5. Anticipate possible distractions or interruptions, and let students know what you will do about them. Fine-tuning SSR is extremely important to its success. Because you can't anticipate every possible difficulty, being clear on as many sticking points as possible makes for a smoother reading time. For example, we always had SSR right after lunch recess. But BEFORE the kids left for lunch in the cafeteria, however, we made sure they had ample reading materials *on their desks* before they lined up. When they returned, they got a quick drink, went to the bathroom, and then everybody could read uninterruptedly.

You need to decide if the children have to stay in their seats during the entire reading time. Some teachers have no problem with students' moving about; others do not allow them to wander about for any reason. We always let one table, one row, or a predetermined fifth of the roster sit wherever they wanted during SSR. With big pillows, carpet squares, and lots of "under the table" places, the once-a-week treat was always something the kids looked forward to.

6. If students have taken their books home the night before and forgotten to bring them back, you must be prepared for how to handle that. You might have a box or plastic carton of picture books, short stories and novels, or magazines available so appealing reading material is not difficult to locate.

7. If a student has a pressing question during SSR, it is best left until the period is over. As we have said already, this time is also for the teacher who does not want to be interrupted.

8. ALWAYS end the SSR session with a brief and informal discussion of what has been read that day—sort of a "book review" or the "top pick of the day." Sample the class for volunteers or randomly ask specific students what they enjoyed reading. These reviews work much like the McDonald's commercials we noted earlier. Once, in his fifth-grade class, when Darigan was reading a library edition of David Wiseman's *Jeremy Visick* and when SSR came to an end, he was just bursting to tell the class what a wonderful book he was reading and what he liked about it. Later, just before school was letting out, young Joe came up and asked if he could borrow the book when Darigan was done. "Of course," he said. "It isn't due back for another week and a half." Well, after Joe read it, he lent it to Austin, who was followed by Adam. The book came back 4 weeks and three readers later. Darigan gladly paid the minimal library fine, knowing the book had been well appreciated.

Bringing Books to Kids

As we said before, the love of reading cannot be generally taught; it relies on children's direct contact with specific titles, certain subjects, and particular authors. Again, this exposure is largely dependent on the modeling done by the knowledgeable teacher and/or parent. To grab and keep students' attention, an enormously wide variety of books of different formats and levels of difficulty need to be available in the elementary classroom. All the grades need fiction, nonfiction, and poetry. Every lower grade needs some chapter books. Every upper grade needs some picture books. The most sincere and devoted intentions to help children become readers turn to dust if books are not handy for teachers to read aloud, to introduce to the class, and generally for students to pick over for silent reading time. Later in the chapter in the section "Building a Classroom Library," we suggest specific ways to acquire books and build your own collection.

The bottom line here is for you, as teacher, to put books at the top of your agenda. If reading, and by this we mean reading for its own sake, does not appear on the daily schedule, the message to students is clear: "We do not value personal reading in this classroom."

Daily Book Introductions

Simply releasing children into a world filled with books does not make them readers. Like sixth-grade Darlene, whom we mentioned earlier in this chapter, those students who have no interest in books, no reading habit, and no idea about what they are looking for tend to easily gloss over and ignore the wealth of superb titles at their disposal. It is, therefore, up to the teacher to bridge the gap between book and child, and one successful way is for the teacher to introduce new titles to the students.

There are many ways to introduce books, but simply holding up the book so students can see what it looks like and telling them something about the book are really all that is necessary. Predictably, teachers are most successful when introducing books they have read and liked, but it is possible to introduce books the teacher does not yet know. By reading the blurb on the back of paperbacks or on the inside flap of hardbacks, enough information is available to present the book to the class. In addition, you may want to turn on the PBS book-introduction programs *Reading Rainbow* and *Cover to Cover.*

You should make a book introduction time a regular, daily part of your schedule. Be aware that the number of books presented to the students on any one day can vary. For example, during the first week or two of the school year, you may want to introduce five or more books per day to ensure that enough books are known to get the students started. After that, a book or two every day works fine. The point is to provide students with some titles they can look forward to trying out.

Going to the Library

If your elementary school has a library, you should plan to get your children there regularly. Because of the innovation of flexible scheduling, some teachers elect not to sign their entire class up for the weekly library period. After a few introductory visits, students cycle into the library singly or in pairs, before and after school, at lunch, or during the school day as the need arises.

If you do visit the library as a class, it is best that you stay there for the entire period and circulate among your students, helping them find good books. Yes, we are aware that it is your planning period. But the more titles your children are exposed to, the more excitement is generated for books, and further, the more successful the library visit will be.

But even with your presence in the library, be prepared to have students wander aimlessly and make small disturbances. Giving them specific directions before entering can help eliminate trouble and streamline the process. These three directions from a teacher to the students work as well as any:

1. *Try 'em on.* Your job is to find books that fit you. One way to pick a good chapter book, for example, is to turn somewhere near the middle and start reading. If you read three or four pages and find the story interesting, this could be a good choice. Also, give your book the five finger test: As you read one page, put up a finger for every word you don't know. If, at the end of the page, you have all five fingers up, it might be that this book is too difficult for you.
2. *Check 'em out.* Check out the books that appeal to you.
3. *Read 'em.* Sit down and read your books until we all are ready to go back to class.

Creating a Reading Atmosphere

A classroom where reading is valued will have an atmosphere that gives evidence that books are important. That message may be delivered in a number of ways:

1. Make the emotional climate in your room safe but exciting. Students need to know that their reactions to books will be accepted and not belittled. Teachers hope students will reflect their involvement with print but will not expect them to mirror their taste. And the emphasis will be on making personal connections and new discoveries.
2. Promote the idea that you want your classroom to become a community of readers. Your focus should be on developing the group's attitude that reading is a pleasurable way of making discoveries about the world in fiction as well as nonfiction. Everyone in the classroom community will have the chance to select reading materials that reflect personal choices and interests.
3. Liven up that room. Ask for old displays (dumps, they're called in the business) or posters from bookstores. Tack up children's drawings inspired by books. Display books and book jackets. The more "face out" books you display, the more books you'll "sell." Guaranteed! Write publishers for their free, attractive materials—posters, postcards, bookmarks—to decorate the walls. Check publisher offerings in the *CBC Features* brochure from the Children's Book Council, mentioned in Appendix A.
4. Keep the classroom library visible, not tucked in a corner or behind locked cabinet doors. Have books become a part of the classroom's interior decorating scheme.
5. As your personality and classroom space permit, allow students to do their free reading in places other than at their desks. You may want a reading center—a place designated for pleasure reading that has pillows, a comfortable chair or couch, or other homey furnishings. But as we mention in the section on Silent Reading, make sure everyone gets to use the reading center equally. If it becomes the domain of those who finish their work first, those who need it most never get the chance to use it.

▼▼▼▼▼▼▼

Organizing Your Class for the Optimal Acceptance of Reading

Teachers whose desire it is to make reading a natural part of the educational landscape will want to plan their classrooms so books fit smoothly and easily into the school day and their children's lives at home. Two areas to consider when organizing the ideal reading classroom are making and nurturing that all-important parent-teacher connection, and building a classroom library.

Nurture the Parent-Teacher Connection

Except for the often painfully polite back-to-school evenings, parents and teachers usually have contact only when there is trouble. As a result, teachers and parents have a natural hesitancy to communicate (much to the delight of many children who would prefer keeping their two worlds separate). The teacher who decides to bridge this traditional gap between school and home can do so with relative ease and much positive effect on children and their reading.

Teachers need to initiate the contact, either through a letter or a meeting with each child's parents. To gain support for your approach to reading, that contact should deal with two points: communicating with parents and informing them of your program, and requesting their support.

Communicate with Parents

You should communicate to the parents the benefits of regular, daily reading all year long (both in school *and* at home). Include your own views on the advantages of reading aloud and daily silent reading, and the benefits of having an abundance of reading materials on hand. Make available information about the local public library and their services and encourage parents to take advantage of this free community resource.

Next, you need to explain how reading instruction will proceed in your classroom and how that may be different from what parents have seen in previous grades. Teaching reading using children's literature can, at the outset, appear to be random and haphazard. You need to assure parents that what you are doing is based on sound theory and pedagogy and that not only will their children learn to read more efficiently, but they will enjoy it as well. In the next chapter, we detail how the Reader's Workshop should proceed, and if you are not already infusing these techniques into your classroom, you may want to begin trying a literature-based unit to see how exciting this kind of teaching can be.

Request Parental Support

You should request parental support for each child's personal reading at home. Parents can help their child in the following ways:

- Encourage their child to read regularly at home. And by that we don't mean sitting at the kitchen table with the child reading aloud, being absolutely certain to recite every word perfectly. We are talking about silent reading—but at home. Setting aside a certain time for the entire family is helpful. If one of the requirements of the children in your class is to read daily outside of school, be certain to mention that and ask for parental support.

- Talk with their child about the books being read both at school and at home.

- Read *to* the child every day. If the parents are having trouble in choosing books that are appropriate, have them contact the school or public librarian or send them your extra copy of Jim Trelease's *The Read-Aloud Handbook* (1995), which you have reserved for just this purpose.

- Buy books for their child's birthdays and for special holidays, along with the games and toys. Further, you can encourage parents to support their child in buying from school-sponsored book fairs and the monthly classroom book clubs when possible.
- Help the child create a place in the bedroom to keep personal books.
- Read regularly where their child can see them with a book. Periodically make it a point to tell the child about what they are reading.
- Volunteer to come to the classroom and assist children in their reading.

Building a Classroom Library

Every classroom needs its own library. Even if the school has a fine offering of books in an attractive central library or media center, each classroom should have a collection of conspicuously displayed titles. Two main reasons underscore the need for classroom libraries, one practical and one philosophical. The *practical* reason is that if books are present and prominent, they can be found easily and used for sustained silent reading, for browsing, or for answering personal questions as well as those arising from classroom discussions. The *philosophical* reason is that the presence of trade books in a classroom speaks volumes about their central place in the learning process. Simply by being there, shelves of real books—not textbooks—in a classroom give evidence of the teacher's commitment to immediate and lifelong learning. If a teacher talks about the importance of reading but only a few books are visible, the message rings hollow to young ears.

A love of reading can't be taught in the abstract any more than a love of good food can be taught through the lecture method. Until we hold the books in our own hands, or slide the steaming forkful of chicken Kiev between our own open lips, we can't truly know the reward of either print or entrée. Hence, we need the books close at hand—right there in the classroom—to sample and respond to.

The obvious truth is that we don't love the *act* of reading. If we did, any page filled with words would thrill us. We would be equally delighted by random IRS directives, last year's text on quantum mechanics, a current issue of *Guns & Ammo,* and directions for Danish cross-stitching. What we do love is a particular book. Perhaps the writings of a particular author. Maybe a particular subject. Because a book holds no attraction simply because it is filled with words, we need enough titles within arm's length to appeal to a wide audience.

How many books do we need so children in our classrooms can feast on the titles, authors, or subjects they love? One third-grade teacher reported he had 25 books or so—"More than I could use." Then he began using trade books in his reading program and boosted the classroom library to over 400—"Not nearly enough," he said.

How many are enough? The multimillionaire John D. Rockefeller reportedly was asked how much money was enough. His reply: "Just a little bit more." Teachers who seek to expand their classroom libraries tend to respond similarly. After you get started, it seems impossible to drive past a bookstore without "just a quick look at what's new." Our significant others groan (but smile inwardly) at yet another book purchase. "How could you need more books?" they ask. "Just a little bit more," we smile.

The greatest obstacle to building a classroom library is impatience. Once convinced of the value in having books close at hand, most teachers want their collections to mushroom *right now*. The enthusiasm and desire are understandable but sometimes harmful. It simply takes time—usually years—to get the kinds and numbers of books a teacher wants. The point is to begin building the collection and learn to resist the natural feelings of discouragement because it doesn't grow faster.

Imagine you recently signed your first teaching contract and just arrived at your new school. After meeting the principal, you find your classroom, which is stark and empty, and then look for the library. The school does not have one. You are fresh out of college and own 15 trade books. What next?

The greatest strength of good teachers is a willingness to persevere no matter the odds. Good teachers make do. If services or materials are lacking, they use what is available and make it work. If no money is in the supply budget, they still find some way to give students what they need. Good teachers enter the profession because they want to make a difference and will not be stopped because conditions are sometimes below par. This make-do attitude is a blessing to the profession and the lives of children.

When confronted with a shortage of trade books, however, you must go against the tradition of good teachers who accept substandard situations and do their best. If a lack of trade books in the classroom is viewed without alarm—"I guess I'll have to get along without books"—the make-do attitude is a curse instead of a blessing. Finding books is *imperative*. A teacher who accepts empty bookshelves as a given, making no attempt to fill them, deprives children of the most powerful classroom tool for convincing them of the value of reading. To become readers, children must have constant access to books. And teachers must find ways to provide those titles.

Having decided to fill the shelves, a teacher needs to concentrate on two areas: finding free books and finding money to buy books. Even in tight economic times, both are possible.

Acquiring Free Books

With ingenuity and grit, a teacher can bring books into the classroom from a variety of sources, such as the following. Note the pluses (+) and minuses (−) of each.

Borrow from the school library. The fastest and easiest way to get books on classroom shelves is to borrow them from the school library or media center. Regulations vary, but teachers generally can check out large numbers of books for classroom use. Some teachers do not allow these library books to go home, whereas others develop a checkout system.

> + Effortless way to get many books into the classroom. Good selection of titles.
> − Books need to be returned to the library. Teacher is responsible for lost books.

Borrow from the public library. Another quick way to get books on the shelf is to visit the public library and borrow as many titles as allowed. Many libraries have special arrangements for classroom teachers, which often include a longer checkout time and an easier checkout system. If your town has no local library, you generally are served by some other library—in a neighboring town, a county system, a bookmobile, or the state library.

Often you'll be pleasantly surprised at the huge selection your library has to offer and, of course, these books aren't brand new. Like the Velveteen Rabbit, they have been loved to tatters—but that is good sign. Those cherished books are the most precious. Ann Jonas, author and illustrator of **Round Trip,** once told us that she really enjoyed autographing new books—"After all, it means I've sold a book." she said. "But what I really love is when a kid brings in one of my books that is worn and the cover is hanging by a thread. Then I know the book has been well-loved."

> + Wide selection of materials. Immediate availability.
> − Transporting books back and forth. Teacher is responsible for lost books. Usually a 6-week maximum checkout time.

Ask students to bring books from home. Many children in the classroom have books at home that are appropriate for classroom reading. Often, they are willing to share these books with others for the year. Before they bring their personal books, ask students to write their names in each book in at least two places. Tell them to leave treasured books at home because they can be damaged or lost even when students take pains to treat them carefully. During the final week of the school year, these books are to be returned to their owners.

+ Less work for the teacher than any other method. Students feel ownership in their library and like to recommend their personal titles to others.
− Inevitably, some books will be damaged or will disappear.

Acquire bonus titles from book clubs. When students order from a book club (Trumpet, Scholastic, Troll, Weekly Reader), the teacher receives points that can be used to order free books. Regularly using a book club helps students not only by focusing on book reading and ownership but also by adding substantially to the classroom library with the bonus books. Some clubs even have extra teacher catalogs offering big books, classroom sets, recommended packages of preselected books, or individual titles for good reading.

Also, you can return the favor for children ordering through the book clubs by using some of those bonus points to obtain a book that can be given to them as gifts, say at winter break, birthdays (or half-birthdays), or at the end of the year.

+ Bonus books are often attractive and always new.
− Somewhat limited selection.

Request birthday books. If it is a classroom custom for parents to provide a treat on their child's birthday, the teacher can request that a book be donated to the classroom library instead. Inscribing the child's name and birth date inside the front cover helps personalize the gift and make it more noteworthy. Be sure parents do not think they need to spend a great deal; paperbacks are perfectly acceptable as birthday books. These birthday books might be placed on a special shelf.

+ Encourages parents to participate in building the library. Children leave a legacy for others.
− Can introduce a small degree of competitiveness.

Acquire library discards. All libraries undergo a periodic weeding process. Books that are deleted from the collection for the most part are simply not being circulated and though they may be out of print, that doesn't mean they are "bad" books. In fact, we often find rare treasures among these discards. The titles taken from the shelves are usually sold for a dollar or less. It is possible that a library will donate these discards to a school. Ask the library director.

+ Little or no cost. Immediate delivery.
− Many titles are discarded for a good reason; be selective in your choices.

Hold a book drive. A book drive is an organized request for people to donate their unwanted books to your classroom or school. Book drives normally yield hundreds of books appropriate for the classroom, and also raise money for the purchase of new books. Although they take some planning and also demand energy for sorting and disposing of books, the rewards of a book drive make the time and effort worthwhile.

Plan the book drive for a Saturday morning from 9:00 to noon. About 6 weeks before, talk to the class about the need for books and the idea of having people donate their unwanted titles. Secure or draw a large map of the area around your school or the areas your students will canvass. Organize the students into pairs, and assign each pair to cover a certain part of the neighborhood. Write a flyer explaining the book drive, and have each pair deliver it about 3 weeks before the drive. Have them deliver a reminder flyer on the Thursday or Friday immediately before the book drive.

Sign up a parent volunteer to oversee each pair of students during the flyer deliveries and during the book drive itself so students can take the books to a car. Begin no earlier than 9:00 A.M.; we understand that somewhere, somebody actually sleeps that late . . .

When all the books are in your classroom, your task is to divide them into two piles: keep and not keep. The books you don't wish to keep may be turned into capital for buying more titles.

Trade the unwanted books at a used bookstore for titles you would like. Or speak to the manager of a thrift store about a 2-for-1 deal: If you have 600 books, offer to donate them for 300 of your choosing. Everyone is a winner! If the store doesn't have 300 you want, take a credit for the remainder, which you will pick up over time.

Books also can be sold many ways, but the object is to get rid of the books as quickly and as easily as possible. Resist tedious and cumbersome methods such as yard sales, flea markets, back-to-school-night sales, and classified ads. One of the most efficient ways is to sell them to a used bookstore. The drawback is that you will not get top dollar.

Another efficient way yields more money. After getting permission, sell them outside a mall or large grocery store on a Saturday morning, charging one price for paperbacks and one for hardcover books. When business slows down, sell by the pound or line them as you would on a shelf and sell by the inch. Naturally, students handle all the transactions, having practiced selling (and weighing and measuring, when necessary) and making change. If the students are too young, simply have people pick the books they like and pay the students what they think is appropriate for a cause as worthy as the education of the town's children.

+ Provides boxes of free books and money for purchasing additional titles. Students practice skills in map reading, talking to adults, selling, measuring, weighing, and making change.
− A good deal of planning and labor is involved.

Raising Money for Books

All requests for raising money need to be cleared with the principal. Sometimes you may be unaware of conditions or rules that affect your plans. To ensure maximum success, the principal must support your efforts for soliciting funds.

Ask the principal. Resist the urge to think this is a totally senseless act, even though the principal just asked the faculty to cut back on copier paper because money is tight this year. Schools are budgeted organizations and have to keep some money in reserve for unforeseen problems. Usually some funds will remain near the end of the fiscal year. Because budgeted monies are spent instead of returned, a worthy project has a high chance of getting funded at that time.

To increase the chance for support from the principal, acknowledge that money is short, look at the expenditures made for your classroom, and identify purchases you can do without. If you are allotted $600 for basal materials, for example, you may not need to spend the whole amount because you plan on using trade books to teach some of your reading program. Perhaps you can get by without a basal workbook. That amounts to a savings of $240 that could be used to buy children's books (30 students times $8 per book). Or commit to using 10 fewer reams of copier paper (and stick to that).

Principals often are edgy about requests for money because so many teachers simply ask. When your idea is stated clearly in writing *and* accompanied by your willingness to cut present expenses, your chances of getting the money are greatly improved.

Solicit donations from local businesses. Businesses generally are supportive of community needs, particularly when they receive publicity for their support. Plan with the children how to provide publicity for businesses, such as the following ideas:

▪ Insert a bookplate naming the contributing business inside the front cover of each book.
▪ Submit before-and-after articles to the local newspaper, mentioning the names of all that contributed.

- Identify the businesses in a detailed article to appear in the school newsletter, which goes to each home and encourages parents to patronize those that have donated to the program.
- Make printed thank-you cards that can be posted on the wall of the business.
- Create a classy certificate to present to each donor. Put the certificate in a frame, suitable for immediate hanging.
- List all contributors on a permanent plaque to hang in your school.

Then create several donating options that the children can present to businesses when they visit. Adapt your options to fit local conditions. For donations up to $25, for example, a business will be mentioned in a newspaper article, in the school newsletter, and will receive a thank-you card. A donation up to $50 adds a bookplate for each title bought with that money and a place on the permanent plaque. Up to $75 includes the certificate, and up to $100, a framed certificate with an official seal identifying maximum contribution.

Identify the businesses most likely to contribute. Have children practice their sales approach long and well with the samples of bookplates and certificates before meeting with the owners. Children should call to ask for an appointment. Have the children make the sales pitch in pairs or threes. Keep in mind that it is *much* harder to turn down 9-year-old brown eyes than to say no to an adult teacher.

Ask the PTA/PTSA/PTO. The Parent/Teacher Association is committed to improving the school and generally hosts some kind of fund-raiser as a part of its duties. Write a plan that shows how you will strengthen teaching and learning by using more trade books in the curriculum. You are likely to merit closer consideration if you propose the idea along with other teachers, showing how all of you can share or rotate the books to get maximum use from them.

Host a book fair. Bringing tables full of new books to the school for student browsing and buying is called a book fair. Usually book fairs run a number of days, with each class visiting the buying area twice—once to look around and another time to buy the books. The plus of a book fair is that a percentage of the total sales goes to the school, generally from 20 to 40%, depending on the volume. Books are available from local bookstores (it's always nice to have a local bookstore support the project and bring a salesperson), local news distributors (check the Yellow Pages under "Magazines—Distributors"), and national companies. Three of the large national book fair companies are Scholastic Book Fairs (phone: 800-325-6149 for the number of the your local representative), Troll Book Fairs (phone: 800-446-3194), and Trumpet Book Fairs (phone: 800-347-3080).

Ask local service clubs. Service organizations such as Rotary, Kiwanis, Sertoma, Lions, Eagles, and B.P.O.E. are interested in being a part of and improving the community. Requesting $200 to $300 for a particular improvement in a school is reasonable. Follow the group's specific procedures. If you are invited to a meeting, prepare the children so they make the bulk of the presentation.

Request grants. Ask about district and state programs for improving instruction. Develop an approach that genuinely fits your personality and curriculum goals. For instance, if you are particularly fond of social studies or feel a need to strengthen your social studies instruction, propose a plan that relies more heavily on trade books to involve students and improve their social studies learning.

Hold fund-raisers. Avoid commercial programs that prey on schools. Most people feel held hostage by children who ask them to buy overpriced jewelry or very small bars of expensive chocolate—and quite frankly, the market is swamped by such programs these days. A good fund-raiser should enable the children to learn something. For example, one principal taught photography and darkroom procedures to sixth-grade students. Those children then organized a portrait program for families, set up appointments, shot the pictures, developed, printed, and sold them. Another teacher taught students how to make salt-and-pepper centerpieces for picnic tables, which they then constructed and sold.

Have children earn money for books. Instead of asking children to bring money for books, contact parents and ask for support in having their child work at home doing extra chores for a standard price. Parents could pay, perhaps a dollar an hour, for good, honest labor.

Staff a student store. During lunch, your class could sell school supplies and treats to the student body, keeping profits for books. Students help plan and conduct the daily business. Sometimes this gets approval more easily when it is for a specified period of time, say, one day a week for an entire month.

Appeal to local contributors. Ordinarily, when you request money to buy trade books for your classroom, you will have to write some kind of rationale or proposal. Ask about and follow the procedure of each particular benefactor. If a benefactor has none, present a clear, attractive, professional-looking, but brief (one page is fine) request at the time you ask for funds. Include a specific dollar amount you seek, what kinds of books and how many you will buy, and the benefit those books will bring to your students and teaching. Frankly, if you can't make it clear how these books will benefit your students, you don't deserve the money.

Where to Buy Books

Books are available from a variety of places. Following are some recommended sources, including the pluses (+) and minuses (−) of each.

Book clubs. Two of the best are The Trumpet Club, P.O. Box 604, Holmes, PA 19043. Phone: (800) 826-0110; and Scholastic Book Club, 730 Broadway, New York, NY 10003. Phone: (800) 724-2424. Each has separate clubs according to grade levels.

+ Inexpensive. Relatively quick turnaround time—no more than 2 weeks, if you call in the order.
− Limited titles, like any book club. Some books are a slightly smaller size than regular bookstore editions.

Bookstores. Ask about educational discounts (if you can't get at least 20%, look elsewhere). Inquire about minimum orders (some stores give no discounts on small purchases). Take the school's tax-exempt number to avoid paying sales tax.

+ Immediate availability.
− Discount is small. Availability limited to stock on hand.

Local paperback wholesalers. Cities with populations over 100,000 are likely to have a paperback distributor. Look in the Yellow Pages under "Magazines—Distributors." Those listed generally carry a line of paperbacks, including children's books, and sell at a substantial discount to teachers who pay with a school check or purchase order. Call first for details.

+ Books available today. Can do your own book club or book fair.
− Paperback wholesalers are found only in larger metropolitan areas.

Mail-order discounted new paperbacks. For any order totaling a minimum of either 25 books or $100, a 30% discount is available through The Booksource, 1230 Macklind Avenue, St. Louis, MO 63110. Phone: (800) 444-0435. FAX: (800) 647-1923. A new catalog is available every August and lists 7,500 titles; 20,000 more are in stock at their warehouse. (Send them a list, and they will type it up and return it at no charge with current prices for your final selections.) Shipping charges are between 5 and 8%. You can buy most titles prebound (made into hardcover) for about twice the cost of the regular paperback.

+ No one offers a better discount on single titles. Titles are organized in the catalog by subject and also alphabetically by author and title. Library processing is available. Books for all ages are available.
− No advantage for small orders under 25 titles or $100 (for those, use a local bookstore and get a 20% discount).

Paperback publishers. Many paperback publishers sell books to teachers for a greatly reduced price but ship only to schools—no private addresses. Often the procedures for requesting copies are announced in publishers' catalogs. If not, ask each for its specific guidelines. Two examples follow:

Bantam Doubleday Dell

Bantam Doubleday Dell offers a special price of $3 per paperback (hardcovers are half price) with its examination copy offer. This is available to teaching professionals to help in evaluating Bantam Doubleday Dell books for classroom adoption.

Only one copy per title per teacher is permitted. For catalogs, which contain titles and specific ordering information, send a self-addressed label (typed or printed clearly) with your request (specify grades K–3, 4–5, or 6–8) to Bantam Doubleday Dell, 2451 Wolf Road, Des Plaines, IL 60018-2676.

Send your request (including your name, address, and each book's title and ISBN number on school letterhead) and a check made payable to Bantam Doubleday Dell Examination Copy Department at the preceding BDD address.

Avon Books

Avon Books has slightly different procedures: Teachers still send requests on school letterhead and prepay with each order, but they are limited to six titles at a time. Paperbacks up to $4.99 are $1.50; those $5.00 and over are half price. Include a $2 shipping and handling fee with each order. To receive a catalog, call (800) 223-0690. Send requests for books to Avon Books, Customer Service Department, Box 767, Dresden, TN 38225.

> \+ Inexpensive.
> − Limited to titles of each particular publisher.

Sources of remaindered books. When books go out of print, publishers frequently sell the remaining copies in bulk to a remainder house; these books are referred to in the business as "remainders." These books are then available at tremendous savings, often discounted 80% from the original price. One of the easiest sources to use is University Book Service. Different catalogs list books for elementary, junior high, high school, and general audiences. Specify which catalog or catalogs you want. Catalogs quote reviews and offer detailed information about each book. University Book Service, P. O. Box 728, Dublin, OH 43017. Telephone number: (800) 634-4272.

> \+ Enormous savings on new books. Helpful evaluations. Not limited to
>   institutional sales; individuals can buy for private use.
> − Limited selection.

Sources of used books. Some bookstores specialize in used books and have decent ones for greatly reduced prices. Thrift stores have better prices, but the pickings tend to be slimmer. Garage sales? Spotty.

> \+ Very inexpensive.
> − Very limited selection.

Reading Is Fundamental. Reading Is Fundamental (RIF) will not help build a classroom library, but it does provide books to give to students. RIF is a federally funded, nonprofit organization with the goal of increasing book ownership among students, particularly those with special needs (defined as meeting 1 criterion from a list of 10, including below-average reading skills, eligibility for free or reduced-price lunch, emotionally disturbed, without access to a library, and having disabilities). When 60% of the children in a school or special school program qualify, RIF will give 75% of necessary funds to buy paperback books for all students in the qualifying group (25% of the money must be provided locally). RIF provides 100% of the necessary funds for children of migrant or seasonal farm workers. Deadlines for submitting applications are January 14 and October 1. Contact: Reading Is Fundamental (RIF), 600 Maryland Avenue, Suite 600, Washington, DC 20024. Phone: (202) 287-3220.

Finally—You Have Your Classroom Library

Once a classroom has a library, the teacher has to make some decisions about its use. Should those books be limited to reading in the classroom, or can students take them home? Are they on their honor to return the books, or should there be some kind of checkout system? How many is each child allowed to check out? How long may children keep the books? Does every book need a card pocket? Does the teacher serve as class librarian, or can children handle the job?

No universal answers exist for these questions. Each teacher has to devise a system that is personally comfortable. One fact every teacher can count on: If children borrow books from a classroom library, some titles will be lost. Period. The only way not to lose books is to keep students from touching them. For peace of mind, accepting this inevitability is essential. Yet few titles are lost to calculated theft. Most missing books are due to students' misplacing them or simply forgetting to return them. So some kind of system is recommended to help students remember they have a book from the classroom library. The easiest system is to have the students themselves write their names, dates, and book titles on a form attached to a clipboard or filed in a folder. As students return books, they draw a line through their names and the other information. Appointing one or more students as librarians also works well.

Protecting and Preserving Paperbacks

Many teachers do nothing to prolong the life of paperbacks, believing the books will wear out anyway. Some simple procedures can keep books looking better for a longer time, however. Asking parent volunteers to cover the books with clear contact paper yields good results. Even easier is to use the taping machine many libraries have to repair the spines of hardbacks. Paperbacks wear most quickly along the edges. A paperback can be reinforced by running a strip of four-inch clear tape along the center of the spine, folding it over onto the front and back covers. Trim tape flush with the top and bottom of the book. Do the same to the front edges of both covers, folding the tape half to the inside and half to the outside. Now the spine and front edges of the covers are protected, prolonging significantly the looks and increasing substantially the life of the book.

When pages fall out of paperbacks, the best method for restoring them is to buy a tube of clear silicon bathtub caulk (shaped like a toothpaste tube, not one of the large cylindrical variety used in caulking guns unless you are repairing hundreds of books). By barely cutting the tip, you can run a very small bead of caulk along the back of a page if it has fallen completely out or along the spine if the back is broken. Reattach the siliconed pages, apply pressure with a rubber band or the weight of other books, and leave for a day. Those pages never will come loose again. Other glues tend to crack, but the silicon caulk, with both strength and a little flexibility, will do its job beyond your retirement.

No matter how bad the economic times, it is possible for a teacher to find free books and money for books. With perseverance and patience, any teacher can build an enviable library that will help turn kids into readers. And with little effort and expense, the books can be reinforced and repaired to offer dozens and dozens of readings.

The ideas in this chapter come from years of classroom experience, both ours and others. Unfortunately, following them to the letter will not guarantee that every child will become a reader. No reading approach, person, or program has a 100% conversion rate with children. Simply expect that some tough nuts to crack will not fall in love with books, no matter what you do. Implementing these ideas, however, will increase the odds that children will read more and read better.

Summary

In this chapter, we have discussed the major motivating factors in getting children to read. In the end, the key to success lies largely with you, as their teacher. We looked at ways motivated readers behave and applied that knowledge to helping those less inclined to become engaged in reading and discussed ways to get kids quickly into books. We talked about the limitations of reading incentive programs. We then noted concrete ways the teacher can get children into books, such as reading aloud to them, offering them regular, daily silent reading time, bringing good books *to* the children, and regularly visiting the library. We talked about a number of ways to organize your classroom for the children's optimal acceptance of reading, such as keeping parent/teacher lines of communication open and building a solid, comprehensive classroom library. Finally, we gave you some hints on how to protect and manage your classroom library.

▼▼▼▼▼▼▼▼

Children's Literature References

Clements, Andrew. (1996). *Frindle*. New York: Simon & Schuster.

Creech, Sharon. (1990). *Absolutely normal chaos*. New York: HarperCollins.

Creech, Sharon. (1994). *Walk two moons*. New York: HarperCollins.

Creech, Sharon. (2000). *The wanderer*. New York: HarperCollins.

Dahl, Roald. (1988). *Matilda*. New York: Viking.

Fleischman, Paul. (1977). *Seedfolks*. New York: HarperCollins.

Fox, Paula. (1984). *One-eyed cat*. New York: Bradbury.

Hall, Katy. (1999). *Really, really, really bad jokes* (M. Lester, Illus.). Cambridge, MA: Candlewick.

Hodges, Margaret. (1997). *The true tale of Johnny Appleseed* (Kimberly Bulcken Root, Illus.). New York: Holiday House.

Jonas, Ann. (1983). *Round trip*. New York: Greenwillow.

Kellogg, Steven. (1988). *Johnny Appleseed* (Kathy Jakobsen, Illus.). Boston: Little, Brown.

Kindersley, Barnabas, & Kindersley, Anabel. (1995). *Children just like me*. New York: DK.

Lawlor, Laurie. (1995). *The real Johnny Appleseed* (Mary Thompson, Illus.). Morton Grove, IL: Albert Whitman.

Lindbergh, Reeve. (1990). *Johnny Appleseed*. (Kathy Jakobsen, Illus.) Boston: Little, Brown.

Lowry, Lois. (1993). *The giver*. Boston: Houghton.

Lowry, Lois. (2000). *Gathering blue*. Boston: Houghton.

McCord, David. (1966). *All day long: Fifty rhymes of the never was and always is* (Henry B. Kane, Illus.). Boston: Little, Brown.

Park, Barbara. (2000). *The graduation of Jake Moon*. New York: Atheneum.

Spinelli, Jerry. (1996). *Crash*. New York: Knopf.

Spinelli, Jerry. (1997). *Wringer*. New York: HarperCollins.

Wallace, Barbara Brooks. (1980). *Peppermints in the parlor*. New York: Atheneum.

Walton, Rick. (1999). *Really, really bad summer jokes* (Jack Desrocher, Illus.). Cambridge, MA: Candlewick.

Wiseman, David. (1981). *Jeremy Visick*. Boston: Houghton.

Wisniewski, David. (1998). *The secret knowledge of grown-ups*. New York: Lothrop.

Wisniewski, David. (1999). *Tough cookie*. New York: Lothrop.

▼▼▼▼▼▼▼▼

Professional References

Anderson, R. C., Hiebert, E. H., Scott, J., & Wilkinson, I. A. G. (1985). *Becoming a nation of readers*. Champaign-Urbana, IL: Center for the Study of Reading.

Bell, T. H. (1982). Speech to faculty of College of Education at Brigham Young University, Provo, Utah, 21 October.

Calkins, L. M. (1986). *The art of teaching writing*. Portsmouth, NH: Heinemann.

Cameron, J., & Pierce, W. D. (1994). Reinforcement, reward, and intrinsic motivation: A meta-analysis. *Review of Educational Research, 64,* 363–423.

Chomsky, C. (1972). Stages in language development and reading exposure. *Harvard Educational Review, 42,* 196–217.

Cullinan, B. E., Jagger, A. M., & Strickland, D. (1974). Language expansion for black children in the primary grades: A research project. *Young Children,* 98–111.

Darigan, D. L. (1991). *The effects of teachers reading aloud on elementary children's attitudes toward black Americans*. Unpublished doctoral dissertation.

Feitelson, D., Kita, B., & Goldstein, Z. (1986). Effects of listening to series stories on first graders' comprehension and use of language. *Research in the Teaching of English, 20*(4), 339–356.

Kohn, A. (1992). *No contest: The case against competition*. Boston: Houghton.

Lepper, M. R., Greene, D., & Nisbett, R. E. (1973). Undermining children's intrinsic interest with extrinsic rewards: A test of the "overjustification" hypothesis. *Journal of Personality and Social Psychology, 28,* 129–137.

McCracken, R. A., & McCracken, M. J. (1978). Modeling is the key to sustained silent reading. *The Reading Teacher, 31,* 406–407.

Perez, S. A. (1986). Children see, children do: Teachers as reading models. *The Reading Teacher, 40,* 8–11.

Trelease, J. (1995). *The read-aloud handbook.* New York: Penguin.

Wilson, R. & Hall, M. A. (1972). *Reading and the elementary school child.* New York: Van Nostrand Reinhold.

TEACHING READING USING CHILDREN'S LITERATURE

13
CHAPTER

▼▼▼▼▼▼▼

If you want to cover

*Books Written
by Betsy Byars*

Consider as a READ ALOUD

The Midnight Fox

Consider as a TEXT SET

*The Burning Questions of Bingo
Brown*

The Computer Nut

The Not-Just-Anybody Family

The Pinballs

Tornado

The 18th Emergency

TORNADO
by Betsy Byars, illustrated by Doron Ben-Ami

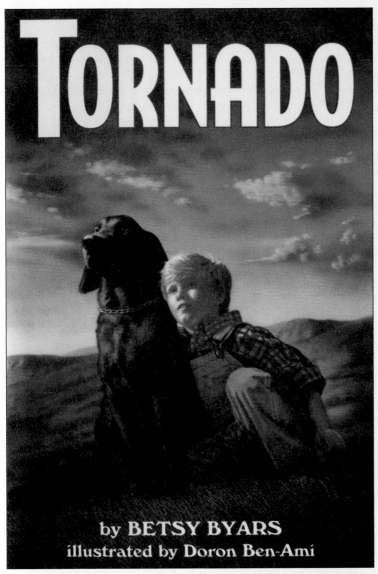

TORNADO

by BETSY BYARS
illustrated by Doron Ben-Ami

Tornado took one step forward. He stretched out his neck. He took the card. He took the card! *I remember it to this day. It was the three of hearts. The dog was standing there with the three of hearts in his mouth!*

Excerpt from *Tornado* by Betsy Byars, illustrated by Doron Ben-Ami

Student Response

Jonathan   age 9

I liked Tornado because of all the good stories about the boy and his dog Tornado. I especially liked how Tornado can do a good card trick.

To visit a classroom exploring the issues of Teaching Reading Using Children's Literature, please go to Chapter 13 of our companion website at **www.prenhall.com/darigan**

Dan Darigan, then a fifth-grade teacher in Springfield, Oregon, is leading his class through a text set of five books all written by Newbery author Betsy Byars. As he finishes the fifth chapter in *The Midnight Fox,* he closes the book, and putting it in his lap begins the discussion with, "What do you think so far?" In fact, he does this with every book he reads aloud, whether it is a picture book or an ongoing novel like this one. The invitation prompts a lively discussion about how self-centered the main character is.

After a number of children respond, Darigan gets to what he has planned as the actual "objective" of the lesson, which is a closer look at *characterization*. He focuses the class with, "What more do we know about Tom after our reading today? Think about what new information we have learned concerned with his emotional state of mind, his family, what he looks like, and how he has changed." But before the children have a chance to begin talking, he continues: "Turn to the person sitting next to you and tell them what you think." As the children chatter away about what they deem to be the changes in Tom, the main character, Darigan leans over to listen to the pair closest to him. This is a wonderful way to break their silence. After all, they have been sitting and listening for almost 15 minutes, as well as another few minutes in discussing their general reactions, which is a lot of time to expect them to remain silent and focused. This "pair work" allows every student a voice and blows a bit of steam off so they can sit and talk just a bit longer.

Next he gets the group back together with, "Let's go back to our web and see what we can add. Who'll get us started? Karen . . . ?" (See Figure 13-1.)

As children verbalize additional information, Darigan records their responses on the graphic organizer the class has been building on a large sheet of butcher paper. Karen notes, "I think that Tom is beginning to like living on the farm because he's interested in the black fox he has seen."

"Why do you say that?" asks Darigan.

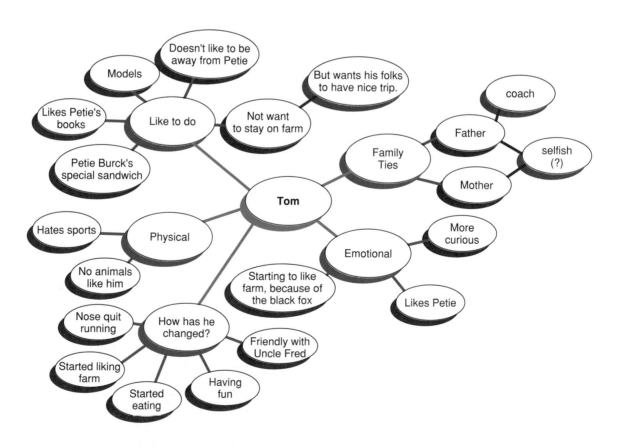

FIGURE 13-1   Class web for *The Midnight Fox.*

"Well, even though he didn't write about it as a P.S. in his letter to his friend Petie back home, I really think he thought it was important. Like the way 'War' was a huge headline in his dad's newspaper—he thought 'Fox' should be a big headline."

"Right on!" Darigan jots in green marker a brief paraphrase of what she said *starting to like the farm because of the fox.* Darigan chooses a different color marker each day to show the progression of accomplishment. He rereads it (for the auditory learners) and tracks it word for word (for the visual learners—even though they are in fifth grade) and then goes on to the next student.

When the class has exhausted all the major points, he tells them, "Now today, when you read in your own book by Betsy Byars, I want you to continue focusing on how *your* main character has changed. Then the first thing you'll do after reading today is to record that information in your notebooks."

The workshop continues with students *and* teacher spending 15 minutes reading their Betsy Byars books at their seats. Because it is near the beginning of the school year, Darigan knows they can't sustain a much longer time and, in fact have built up from 8 minutes per session when they began back in September.

After the silent, independent reading time is over, Darigan has them spend a few minutes with their learning logs (spiral notebooks he purchased on special at a local drug store for 29 cents apiece), jotting additions they have noticed in their reading that day. In Figure 13-2, you'll notice Doug's web—invented spelling and all. He is reading Byars's book *The Computer Nut* and has dutifully followed the example modeled during the minilesson.

Finally, the students get together in their book groups, organized by title, and informally discuss what they liked, what questions they have about what they have read, and what they think might happen next.

DID YOU KNOW?

In our classes, we often add anecdotes about what this author said or that illustrator did. Students are forever wondering how we know so many. The fact is, authors and illustrators for children are very accessible. How? Professional conferences! For example, while crossing the street in Orlando, Florida during the International Reading Association's Annual Convention a few years back, we spied Betsy Byars stuck on the boulevard waiting to cross. We said hello, told her how much we loved her work, and our conversation ended up lasting 15 minutes. We learned so much about her and her work. You, too, can meet authors and illustrators by attending these wonderful conferences, both local and national. (See Appendix A for organizations such as IRA, ALA, and NCTE that hold regular conferences concerning children's literature.)

▼▼▼▼▼▼▼▼

How Should Reading Be Taught?

How should reading be taught, and with what sorts of materials? Phonics or sight words or context clues? Basals or trade books? Do "real" books come later, after a child has mastered decoding skills? Or might the child start with real books from the library or book club and learn skills as needed in a so-called natural context? What are the best ways of leading a child to literacy?

The traditional method of teaching reading in America's classrooms has been to use the reading textbook, the basal reader. Shirley Koeller (1981, p. 553) reveals that 95 to 99% of teachers relied on the basal to teach reading in 1958. Although the percentage is not quite as high today, basal readers still are used in more than 90% of schools (Reutzel & Cooter, 1996, p. 339).

Those who use literature-based reading instruction instead of basal programs boast stunning levels of success with all types of students and particularly with disabled and uninterested readers. We have used the expression *real books* more than once, a term that now seems to be generally accepted in the literature about reading instruction. So-called artificial materials—such as workbooks, skill cards, textbooks, and basal readers—are the sort that children can get only through teachers. Children would seldom read a textbook by choice, much less a workbook or skill card, and neither would an adult. Real reading materials, on the other hand, are the sorts of things people read because they want to. Comic books, *Sports Illustrated for Kids,* and a McDonald's sign all count as real reading materials, although children's trade books such as *Charlotte's Web,* by E. B. White, and *Where the Wild Things Are,* by Maurice Sendak, are most commonly identified for use in literature-based or individualized reading instruction.

FIGURE 13-2
Doug's web for ***The Computer Nut***.

The Studies

A number of controlled studies have compared literature-based reading with basal and mastery-learning reading instruction, and others have simply looked at growth within classrooms that use literature-based reading programs. A landmark study by Cohen (1968), for example, used a control group of 130 second-grade students who were taught using traditional basal reader instruction and compared those students with 155 children in an experimental group using a literature component along with regular instruction. The schools in New York City were selected because of academic retardation likely due to the students' low socioeconomic backgrounds. The experimental treatment consisted mainly of reading aloud to children from 50 carefully selected children's trade picture books—books without the controlled vocabulary or fixed sentence length that existed in abundance in the 1960s but are rarely published today—and then following up with meaning-related activities. The children were encouraged to read the books anytime. Metropolitan Achievement Tests and Free Association Vocabulary

BOOKMARK

INTEGRATING TECHNOLOGY: SOURCES ON THE WORLD WIDE WEB

The *International Reading Association* website includes vast amounts of information about literacy, reading, and children's literature. IRA journals, including *Reading Research Quarterly,* the *Journal of Adolescent & Adult Literacy,* and *The Reading Teacher,* now have an on-line component; *Reading Online* is a wonderful journal that appears solely on the Internet.

To find out more about the International Reading Association and other reading organizations on-line, visit Chapter 13 on the companion website at **www.prenhall. com/darigan**

Tests were administered in October and June, and the experimental group showed significant increases over the control group in word knowledge ($P<.005$), reading comprehension ($P<.01$), vocabulary ($P<.05$), and quality of vocabulary ($P<.05$). When the six lowest classes were compared, the experimental group showed an even more significant increase over the control group. Cohen's study was replicated a few years later by Cullinan, Jaggar, and Strickland (1974), yielding basically the same results.

Another controlled study that warrants a closer look was conducted by Eldredge and Butterfield (1986), whose initial study involved 1,149 second-grade children in 50 Utah classrooms. They compared a traditional basal approach to five other experimental methods, including two that used variations of a literature-based program. Using a variety of techniques that included an instrument for evaluating phonics skills developed and validated by Eldredge, the Gates-MacGinitie Reading Test, and A Pictorial Self-Concept Scale, the researchers discovered that 14 of 20 significant differences among the different instructional methods favored the literature approach teamed with a series of special decoding lessons also developed by Eldredge—lessons taking no more than 15 minutes daily. The other literature-based group also placed highly. Eldredge and Butterfield (1986) concluded that "the use of children's literature to teach children to read had a positive effect upon students' achievement and attitudes toward reading— much greater than the traditional methods used" (p. 35; also see Bader, Veatch, & Eldredge, 1987, p. 65).

▼▼▼▼▼▼▼▼

Reader's Workshop: At First Glance

One of the major advantages of Reader's Workshop is that as a consequence of its very structure, readers naturally become efficient, effective, and independent. Reader's Workshop gives you ample opportunity for instruction, time for children to practice reading, and plenty of opportunities for reflection, by both you and the students, concerning what they have learned and accomplished. The way we look at it, the successful workshop facilitates children in becoming truly engaged readers. We know we've reached our goal when we get students who, like those in the cartoon shown here, have the wherewithal to know when instant replays are necessary and will take as many as need be—for the sheer pleasure of it—just like they would take a second helping of strawberries and chocolate sauce.

FAMILY CIRCUS

10-27

"Know what I like about books? You can have as many instant replays as you want."

In this chapter, we explain what we have found to be theoretically practical. So often from our vantage, we see two distinct perspectives. On one hand, there is the scholar who knows what the theory and research state regarding effective and efficient reading instruction. On the other hand, we have the teacher who doesn't want to be bothered. "Just show me what will work. Show me what I can do tomorrow." Because the three of us think we have a hand in both worlds, perhaps we can help mediate this duality.

Essential Elements of Reader's Workshop

What we have just seen in this brief classroom vignette of Reader's Workshop is how this model of teaching allows and supports what we consider four aspects essential to sound reading instruction:

1. It provides time for the teacher to teach new concepts and reinforce those already introduced.
2. It gives students time to practice the specific skill or strategy taught that day while further allowing them to learn globally within the context of a real reading event.
3. It provides the students time for reflection both in what they have read and their process in going about it.
4. It provides the students with a nonjudgmental forum of peers with which to interact about their individual responses to the book.

All teachers who are anywhere on the continuum, ranging from a highly skills-based, traditional perspective to a full-blown literature-based approach, could say, "Sure, we do all that. We teach and reinforce new concepts, give kids time to practice those concepts, and then give them feedback on how they did. We do that every day." And strictly speaking, they are right.

Here Is the Difference

Let's say that instead of reading, you were going to teach a child how to play baseball. How would you go about it? Common sense indicates that you start by teaching the basics. So you would probably want to start by teaching the rules of baseball. They'd need to know, for instance, general rules such as three strikes and you're out, four balls and you draw a walk. Further, they would need to know more specific rules: If a ball is hit on the ground down the foul line and tails off into foul territory after it passes first base, the ball is still fair. Then there are rules that lie in between general and specific. How about the infield fly rule?

After they had mastered all the rules of the game, you should probably show them how to swing the bat. Then you'd need to teach them how to throw the ball. At these early stages, it is very important that they do it perfectly, so you will want to spend an abundant amount of time on getting their swing and throw just right. Finally, they need to know how to slide into a base.

Now that all the basics have been covered, you certainly would want to try to pull some strings to get the children on an all-star team. After all, they know the rules, all of the basic elements of the game. But don't settle for just an instructional league team; you want them to play up with the older kids and only the best. You know that if you push them, push them hard early on. That will get them to improve much faster. Who knows, they may make it to the majors someday!

Now, if you were to really teach children baseball in such a ludicrous manner, how do you suppose they would perform? The answer is obvious: It would be disastrous. What is missing here?

You've got it! The kids have yet to play the game. And we all know that they need hours and hours and hours of just playing the game. And as they play, they learn the game and all its nuances.

So, why don't more of us teach reading this way? Some seem to think that if we teach them all the rules, then have them practice all the skills *in isolation,* they are going to be able to put it all together and not only be able to read, but also *want* to read and be good at it.

It may seem we have strayed a long way from reading instruction, but our point is this: We need to engage children in real reading. Just as in baseball, where we would encourage them to simply play the game, in reading, we need encourage them and provide them the time to read. In baseball, we would want to give them a few hints along the way, such as how to make their batting stance better; likewise, we would want to offer kids tips on how to be more efficient and strategic in their reading. Further, we allow their peers open interaction so that they can naturally teach each other the nuances of the game. So, too, with reading.

Traditional Classrooms

For the sake of argument, let's look at how reading instruction might play out in a very traditional classroom because we've already seen a more holistic, literature-based classroom in the opening vignette. The traditional teacher might teach a lesson that comes from one of the required district textbooks. For example, he or she might need to cover characterization, the same skill we noted in the opening vignette. Typically, the teacher would relate to the children the major points to focus on when thinking about character. Perhaps the teacher would connect it to the most recent story they had read from the basal reader. Next the teacher hands out a work sheet to reinforce the concept of characterization that contains a number of paragraphs all focusing on a variety of traits related to characterization, with multiple-choice questions designed to test whether each trait was mastered by the student. The lesson on "characterization" would thus have been taught, the concept practiced, students given the opportunity to demonstrate whether they have gotten it or not.

Comparing Approaches

If we compare this traditional approach with the literature-based lesson we described earlier, we can see some notable differences. First of all, in the literature-based vignette, the read aloud that opened the lesson was highly motivating and interesting to the students. They were engaged in the story specifically and in reading in general. Darigan then capitalized on that by having the children discuss what *they* liked about the story. Remember? He asked, "What do you think so far?" It was the initial, personal response he was after. Beyond being engaging and interesting, the read aloud and the subsequent discussion about characterization provided the students with a model they could relate to when doing their own assignment (Barrentine, 1996). The literature-based lesson then provided the children with a block of uninterrupted time to "practice" reading—with the specific focus on characterization. This "gentle touch" kind of teaching floats an idea just under the surface, allowing the reader to grab hold of it when it bobs by.

Further, and you may have already noticed this, the lesson validated a far wider variety of viewpoints than could be assessed in a multiple-choice format. The children were allowed to talk about their opinions, and because Darigan chose to have them talk in pairs first, *every* child got his or her chance.

The literature-based lesson provides a broader context on which to base skills and strategies; in this example, the concept of characterization. The difference in what a novel can say and articulate as opposed to a single paragraph on a work sheet is enormous. This longer, more detailed form allows readers to more fully investigate particular elements, skills, and strategies in their reading and then cements them solidly as foundation to their reading knowledge.

Because there was time allotted for open-ended, peer-led conversation about the books, the topics the children discussed in the literature-based example were specific to each novel in the set and were dynamic and thought provoking. Discussions were motivating and produced their own energy. For instance, a child would state that what he or she considered to be fact could be countered by another who said something to the contrary. Both would then need to delve back into their books to find proof of their positions. Aha! That is called "rereading for a purpose," yet another objective covered but not planned!

▼▼▼▼▼▼▼

Reader's Workshop: The Model

Granted, few of us are at either of the extreme ends of the spectrum we have just described, being purely traditional or purely literature-based; most of us are in the middle somewhere. But hopefully, you are moving in the direction of literature-based instruction. The following is a discussion about how to put this into place in your classroom.

In Reader's Workshop, we allow for an easy give-and-take between playing the game and learning the skills of the game. From our baseball example, we can see how this means that we adapt the reading materials and instruction for each individual child, let him or her read independently, and then allow opportunities for response.

Adapting Instruction

At baseball practice, the coach works with the players to help them hone their skills. For example, if being able to catch grounders is a problem, they will spend time practicing it again and again. But the wise coach will keep in mind two things. First of all, he or she will vary hitting to each of the players. For example, a brand new 10-year-old player will get a slow, bounding grounder that will be hit close enough to him to field with reasonable ease. The veteran 12-year-old, on the other hand, will get a much harder hit ball, close to the ground and more difficult for her to handle. With either kid, the ball will be hit within reach. The coach adapts to the individual capabilities of each player. Second, the coach attempts to make this practice duplicate game conditions as much as possible. When the coach hits a grounder to second base, he or she expects the fielder to scoop it up and throw it to first base for the force out, just like in a game.

So applying this analogy to our reading instruction, we learn that we must keep reading materials within easy reach of the child and that no matter what, we do our best to simulate real reading conditions. This means selecting books for children whose text they can negotiate with ease. The natural consequence of this is that it replicates real reading events and that children will be reading and responding for real and authentic purposes.

At this point, we have explained the whole and now want to look at the component parts of Reader's Workshop, show how they fit together, and prompt you to think about how you might make it work in your own classroom situation. Thus far in this section, we have practiced what we preach: We began by describing the big picture, the whole story detailing the classroom portrait of Darigan's Reader's Workshop. That description was, in a sense, our read aloud—it was the "story" you would read to your kids that serves as the overall backdrop for your lesson. We need to provide learners with the whole picture first to give them a context for their learning. But, as Weaver (1994) states, we need to begin whole-to-part and then modulate back and forth part-to-whole, which is where we are right now. We describe the parts, only to go back to applying them to the whole once again.

For Reader's Workshop to be successful, the structure must be predictably evident for your students. By that we mean the classroom routine must be consistent from day to day. What we have found most effective, and Atwell (1987, 1998) agrees, is to divide your workshop into three distinct components: the minilesson, independent reading, and response.

Minilesson	Independent Reading	Response
5–15 minutes	15–30 minutes	10–15 minutes

Next, we describe each component in detail. Note, too, that we have listed a span of time for each. Bear in mind that these times are variable and dependent on the grade level you are working with and, of course, how long you have been doing the workshop with your kids. As you might expect, the younger children would need shorter times, whereas the older kids could sustain their attention spans for a longer period of time. But, as we noted with Sustained Silent Reading in chapter 12, just because you are working with sixth graders, don't kid yourself into thinking that they can stay on task for 30 minutes for independent reading on the first day—just because they are older. As with anything that taxes the mind or body, we must work slowly toward a total fitness level.

Minilesson

The minilesson is the time set aside each day at the beginning of your Reader's Workshop for the teacher to explicitly teach. As you will see, it ensures you a "teachable moment" every day, allowing you the opportunity to introduce and demonstrate to children strategies and skills that efficient, effective readers go through in the act of reading. Further, it primes the pump of their reading consciousness to later use those concepts when they read independently.

Importance of the Read Aloud

We believe that every minilesson should be introduced with a read aloud. What better way to discuss a literary point than to use literature as an example? The read aloud itself can be done from a picture book, or it can be an ongoing novel that accompanies your text set that follows the theme or in some way relates to what you are studying.

Throughout this book, we have prefaced each of our text sets with one or more read aloud books for that very reason. If you want to explore the theme of homelessness and families in distress, it makes total sense that the class can share in the theme through read alouds like Eve Bunting's picture book *Fly Away Home* followed by the reading of Cynthia Voigt's novel *Homecoming.*

The minilesson allows you to:

1. address the obvious and immediate needs of the students in your class;
2. address the major skills and strategies articulated in virtually every state curriculum and reading program in the market;
3. predispose your students to what you are going to teach them.

Minilesson Example

Here is how we think your minilesson should proceed. First, you settle in with the kids and read aloud the book you selected. When you come to a good stopping point with your ongoing novel or to the end of your picture book, open the door for a short discussion concerning the reactions your kids are having. This conversation should flow naturally. Try not to get in the middle of it too soon; allow the children to lead the way. All you need do is keep the conversation going with good questioning and rephrasing of what has been said, always attempting to help them make connections.

Too often we see our college students and even their cooperating teachers jump headfirst into their lesson without allowing adequate time to debrief the story. Heavy duty books such as Katherine Paterson's ***Bridge to Teribithia***, ***Monster***, by Walter Dean Myers, and ***Shiloh***, by Phyllis Reynolds Naylor, beg to be talked about and processed. Please make it a point to spend time every day discussing the affective part of the story before you move on to your lesson.

For example, if you were reading Wilson Rawls's classic, ***Where the Red Fern Grows***, and you've finished the very saddest part of the book, you wouldn't gloss over the tragedy and begin your lesson on "similes and metaphors"! Get to the heart and emotion first. Let us tell you, it is really a good thing to show your own emotions when reading these kinds of books. That is one of the wonderful things books can offer us: the opportunity to identify with powerful emotions.

Begin Addressing Your Lesson Objectives

Once you have accomplished this all-important debriefing, a relief for both you and the class, you can then move on to your objective for that lesson.

Spend *only minutes* discussing the skill or strategy you want to accent. You can use what you just read to show them direct analogies and examples relating specifically to the skill you are teaching. Then you can send them on their way to read and figure out how it applies to their own book.

Minilessons Should Be Based on the Immediate Needs of the Students

When Darigan was working on a text set of novels in his fifth-grade class focusing on the United States Civil War, he noticed that, based on their learning log responses, many of the students in his class were having trouble summarizing completely. Further, many were hard-pressed to state their opinions about what they had read, and found it difficult as well to make connections from what they had read to their own lives or to other similar books they had read on the subject.

Miles had written the response shown in Figure 13-3 in his learning log based on his first day's reading of Carolyn Reeder's powerful Civil War novel, ***Shades of Gray***. As a background to his response, you need to know that in the story the main character, young Will, has suffered the loss of his parents and family through war, disease, and grief. Having to move in with his aunt and uncle was quite a change for him because, unlike his own family, Uncle Jed and his wife were not supportive of the Confederate cause; in fact, Uncle Jed refused even to fight for the South.

As you can see, Miles read a total of 20 pages and barely wrote as many words in his response. Had Miles's log been among only a few in the class that brief, Darigan would have placed a note in the margin commenting on how he wanted the quality of the response to improve. Something positive, yet firm and directive such as, "I loved how you picked up on that part of the story, but since it has been so long since I read

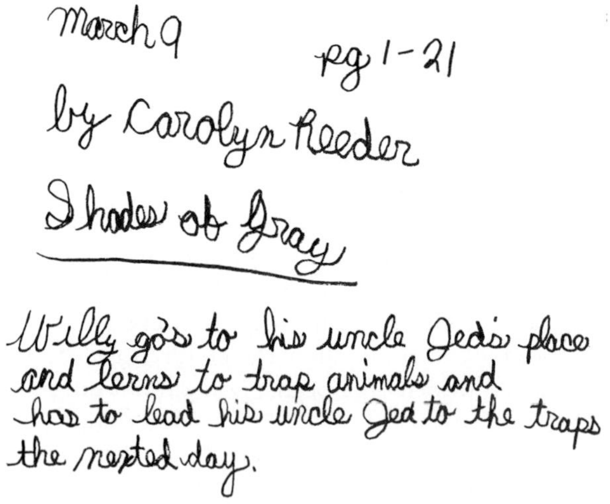

FIGURE 13-3
Miles's first response to
Shades of Gray.

> March 9   pg 1-21
>
> by Carolyn Reeder
>
> Shades of Gray
> _____
>
> Willy goes to his uncle Jed's place and lerns to trap animals and has to lead his uncle Jed to the traps the nexted day.

this book, I'd like to know more than just about Will's trip to the 'trap lines.' Please give me more details. What else happened?" Then he would have insisted that Miles write/rewrite the entry before he returned to reading his book "the nexted day."

However, all the responses he read appeared weak. To make matters worse, his own professional reading at the time included the book edited by Kathy Gnagey Short and Kathryn Mitchell Pierce, *Talking About Books: Creating Literate Communities* (1990). In it, Carol Gilles reports on the seventh-grade learning-disabled students she observed for 6 months and what the quality of their discussions were. She was able to detect clear patterns in their responses that included the following four categories: kids talked about the book, talked about the reading process, talked about making connections between the book and themselves, and talked about the group's process or routine (p. 56). The kids in Darigan's class hadn't even written a passable summary, and here were learning-disabled students only 2 years older analyzing their process and making significant connections!

Darigan was really frustrated by this, but rather than abandon his beliefs, he decided to go back to what he knew about teaching and learning—this is where knowing theory and the research to back it up comes in very handy. Based on the students' need, his minilesson the next day dealt with the quality of the responses the kids were writing. After his read aloud from Belinda Hurmence's *A Girl Called Boy,* he met the issue head-on and spent a few minutes discussing the weak responses he had seen from many of them the night before. Then he said, "Here is an example of what I want you to do." He placed on the overhead *his* written response from the day before when he, too, was reading. Uncovering ONLY the "Summary" section, he read the response aloud to them (Figure 13-4). He told the kids he wanted a *far* more detailed summary from them—much like what he had showed them.

He continued, "I also want to know what you think about this book. Let me give you another example," he said. Then he uncovered and read the opinion he had written (again, see Figure 13-4). When he finished reading his response, he looked out on that group who sat there dumbstruck. They couldn't believe they would have to write *that* much. "That is the kind of response I want to see after you read today."

March 10

p. 95–103

Summary:

During this reading time, Lije met with Mrs. Gaines and took off for Missouri to start his spying career. After they crossed the river, they came to a small tavern and inquired about how to find the bushwhackers or the group of men fighting to keep slavery alive. Mrs. Gaines said that her grandson (really Lije) was no good for learning and was more suited for raiding the homes of the Jayhawkers or the men who steal slaves out of freedom.

Opinion:

This book is really wonderful. There is a lot of action and it tells the story of a boy about the age of our class. I can really "feel" the hardships of the Tulley family. After the death of Lije's father, the burning of their house by Bushwhackers and the splitting up of their family, it seems the tragedy must end sometime soon.

I think it may be a good possibility for a read aloud after **A Girl Called Boy.**

FIGURE 13-4 Darigan's log entry.

March 9   pg 1-21

by Carolyn Reeder

<u>Shades of Gray</u>

Will go's to his uncle Jed's place and lerns to trap animals and hos to lead his uncle Jed to the traps the nexed day. March 10   pg. 20-44
Summary.
Will's cousin Meg took Will fishing and Will met some boys at the pond and Will caught a bass at the pond.
Will's Uncle Jed asked Will if he was ready to lead him to the traps today and Will said he wasn't reddy yeat.
I like this book alot. I like the way the disciles Will and Uncle Jed and everybody else in the book.

FIGURE 13-5   Miles's next learning log response.

How did the kids respond? There was improvement shown from *every* child in the class that very first day. Here is Miles's next learning log response (Figure 13-5)—it is far from what Darigan would have found exemplary, but clearly progress had been made from one day to the next. Notice that Miles almost tripled the number of words he wrote. He penned a beefier summary than the previous day, and noted the beginnings of an opinion focusing on his feelings about the book as well as the author's ability to describe characters thoroughly. What a difference one single minilesson can make!

Responding to the needs of the students is the first and best way to determine what you should teach in a minilesson. You may have had only a limited experience working with children in a classroom setting, perhaps less teaching reading. Every day can be a mad guessing game as to what you should address in every subject area—not just reading.

Use the Scope and Sequence

You may want to look either in the front or in the back of the teacher's edition to your adopted basal program for what is referred to as the "Scope and Sequence." This grid can be about four or five pages in length, and it outlines all of the major reading skills and strategies addressed in the entire series, grades kindergarten through 8. It further informs you at what grades those same skills are to be introduced, reinforced, and finally tested and mastered.

We are not advocating that you use this program devotedly, but its Scope and Sequence can be of great help to you. It can be used to inform you of which skills and strategies you need to address in your minilessons and how well you can expect your students to learn them.

First, make certain that your minilesson grows out of the needs of the students (either apparent needs or skills and strategies found in the Scope and Sequence). Continue using the literature you have chosen for your unit. Use the read aloud as the exemplar for your lesson's objective, then have the children "practice" that skill or strategy while they read.

We recommend that you make a nice, clean photocopy of the Scope and Sequence and then staple it inside your weekly lesson plan book. As you teach a skill or strategy, note the date in the first box after its listing. We present a "mock-up" of what we are talking about in Figure 13-6. As the year progresses and as you hop around in the Scope and Sequence, you will be able to see clearly where you are going a little

Skill or Strategy	K	1	2	3	4	5	6	7	8
Sequencing	1/7	•	•	•	•	•	•	•	•
Cause and Effect	1/11	1/12	•	•	•	•	•	•	•
Paraphrasing	1/15	1/16	•	•	•	•	•	•	•
Making Predictions	1/8	1/9	•	•	•	•	•	•	•
Summarizing	1/13			•	•	•	•	•	•
• indicates that this is a grade where the skill or strategy is tested									

FIGURE 13-6   Scope and sequence.

heavy and what areas you have hardly touched upon. Either way, it will make you aware that you need to address those skills within the context of real reading events.

Based on the needs of the students, you model, through your read aloud, an important skill or strategy that will make them better readers. This is the "prompt" for them to investigate and "practice" that skill while they are reading in their own books. You've had your say; now it is time for the children to take over.

Independent Reading

Independent reading, the second component of Reader's Workshop, is the time when students read silently and alone from their books for a sustained period of time.

The Minilesson Influences Reading

Recall that the minilesson is presented to lay the foundations of their thinking about the given objective of that day's lesson—in the case of our opening classroom vignette, the focus was *characterization*. Were Darigan not to have directed the class toward that one element, it is likely that many would have simply become wrapped up in the story they were reading and pay no heed to this element—and that is not an altogether bad thing, mind you. However, our duty as teachers is to broaden and deepen our students' reading abilities. We want our students to think more deeply about what they have read, to reread portions of text, if necessary, to clarify their thought processes and predictions, and to improve their overall comprehension and recall of details (Robb, 2000, p. 155).

In short, independent reading is the minilesson put into action. So when we look back at the lesson Darigan taught at the beginning of this chapter, where *characterization* was the main objective addressed, students were expected to read their books keeping characterization particularly in mind, then take that concept and apply it to their book. Doug's web (Figure 13-2) is an example of how he interacted with the text over a period of a few days.

Time to Develop Proficiency

Just as they do in baseball, kids need to be allowed a lot of time to approximate "mastery," fluency, and proficiency in their reading. Playing the game or reading the book holds so many rewards. Every day in school should provide many opportunities for children to read for pleasure and enjoyment as well as to answer their own inquiries.

Replicate Real Reading

Finally, the practice involved in the reading event should, as closely as possible, replicate real reading. Work sheets with fill-in-the-blank answers don't hold a candle to reading real stories. So, like the coach who works on ground balls within the context of a double play, the reading teacher prompts the reader within the context of a good story.

We know this may all sound a bit too simplistic to really work, but remember, independent reading is reading with the major objective that the students focus on or attend to what you have just taught in your minilesson. Now granted, the students are still reading to "find out what happens next" but they are *also* reading for a specific purpose; your minilesson objective. They will be looking, for instance, at how the character is changing within the story, how the author has used simile or metaphor to deepen understanding, or how the foreshadowing in one chapter plays itself out 50 pages later.

Teacher Modeling

When we talk about independent reading time with teachers, they take a sigh of relief and tell us, "Good, I could sure use that extra time when

DID YOU KNOW?

Before going any further, we want to make certain you understand that independent reading is NOT to be confused with Sustained Silent Reading. They are two different animals. *Both* should occur in your classrooms *every single day,* but the latter is self-selected reading for pleasure. Independent reading, within the context we describe in Reader's Workshop, is the specific time set aside *every* day for nothing other than the reading of books for instructional purposes. If we return to our baseball metaphor, Sustained Silent Reading is the pickup, sandlot variety of baseball, and independent reading is the organized Little League version, which includes both practice and games.

Independent reading can provide children with:

1. time to develop their own literacy proficiency;
2. an opportunity to replicate a real reading event;
3. the model of their own teacher reading; and
4. a nonthreatening forum to build their reading stamina.

they are reading to do my individual testing, conferencing, and meetings with those kids who need the help the most. I might even be able to grade a paper or two." We certainly know what you mean, and we commiserate with you. There never seem to be enough hours or minutes in the day. But we would defer to the research, particularly that of Shirley Brice Heath in her book *Ways With Words* (1983).

Your modeling the pleasures and stimulation of reading by the simple virtue of the fact that *you are reading yourself* will, in the long run, do more to make those children readers than all the diagnostic instruments and activities you can muster (Tunnell & Jacobs, 1989). *You* need to read along with them and then join in their conversations (McCracken & McCracken, 1978). Let them know how your book is affecting *you*. If you like it (or hate it—or somewhere in between), they need to know that and they need to know why. Share with them how your book is like (or unlike) the ones they are reading as well as the ongoing read aloud. Holdaway (1982) notes that teachers presenting new material (books) with wholehearted enjoyment is an essential element for the success of shared reading. The power of this modeling is essential to sparking their interest and maintaining it throughout the year—and eventually their lifetimes—making them lifelong readers.

So, don't fall victim to using independent reading time as your catch-up—either with your work or your neighbor across the hall. Read *along* with the kids and get involved. You may find out that your example will prompt them to have even stronger opinions than you do about books and reading.

Build Up to a Comfortable Time Limit

Remember that as with Sustained Silent Reading, you need to build your class up slowly as far as the time they spend reading is concerned. You want to have them read only for a time limit that is comfortable. You can gauge that by just observing them. They will start to show signs of reading fatigue—chairs and desks start to squeak around on the floor, feet shuffle, they stare over the top of their books instead of in it, and they whisper behind the perceived protection of their books. That's when you quietly inform them they have only "one minute to find a comfortable place to stop." As we noted in chapter 12, use a kitchen timer and, as their endurance gets greater so, too, will their time on task. You will find they "build up strength" quickly.

Response to Reading

Response is the child's reflection and explanation of what he or she has gotten as a result of reading the text. This information can be used to carry on a dialogue with the student about the content, and it can be used to direct and inform our next instructional move.

As noted before and is demonstrated in Figure 13-4, Darigan made it a point always to have his kids record specific information for each entry in their learning log.

They always needed to write the date, the pages they had read that day, and a short but concise summary of what they had read. This information, followed by the general reactions they noted, gave him a good idea of how they were progressing through their books and what they were getting out of them.

As a quick review, in Reader's Workshop, we provide children with a minilesson that will help guide their reading, focusing on a particular skill or strategy. Next we give them time during independent reading to work with that skill or strategy. Finally, we allow time for response, which helps them process what they have read and demonstrate their learning.

We are aiming to initiate in children real and authentic responses to the content of what they have read.

Coloring, cut-and-paste activities and work sheets that ask simple recall questions do not bring about real and authentic responses. We know that many teachers rely on these kinds of responses; some quite heavily. We think there is an alternative.

Authentic Responses

Let us give you a nonbook example of what we mean here. Think about the last movie you saw. When the credits began to roll (or the commercials started to play if you were at home), did you turn to your friend, roommate, or significant other and ask, "Who were the main characters?" "What happened first?" "What happened second?" "How do you think Jack felt when his dog died?"

Of course, you didn't! You would have started right off on the important things that tugged at your heart, convinced or didn't convince you, angered you, made you think, or confused you. Sequencing the order of events, for example, would come *only* if you were unsure of how the plot of the mystery unfolded. Main characters' names would come up only if you happened to forget one's influence on the overall plot. So, too, we would want children to respond to the books and stories they read.

Two Kinds of Responses

How do we get kids to talk thoughtfully and intelligently? We see these responses coming in two venues. One is written responses—often recorded in journals or learning logs, and the other is oral responses—usually referred to as "literature circles" or "book groups." In either case, you need to copiously model during selected minilessons how you want the children to respond, what the overall workshop guidelines are, what responses are appropriate and which ones are not, and what kind of behavior is and isn't acceptable during literature circles in particular.

Written Responses to Literature: Learning Logs

We have found that having the children produce written responses to their reading is an effective strategy in their learning. The mere process of having to put their thoughts down on paper forces them to think at a much higher level and makes them articulate their positions as well as defend them with concrete examples from what they have read.

As we noted earlier in the chapter with the vignette on the Civil War book **Shades of Gray,** the written responses Darigan received significantly informed his teaching. Literally in black and white, you see where you need to concentrate your efforts based on the responses you get.

So let's look at some of the basics of response. After independent reading is over, you want the children to move naturally into the response section of the lesson and tell you what they have learned. You want them to reflect on what they read, preferably with regard to the minilesson you opened the workshop with. Responses can be recorded in spiral notebooks, composition books, or any other similar booklet. Darigan simply used five or six sheets of duplicating paper folded in half, covered with a sheet of colored construction paper, and stapled two or three times on the spine. This produced a little booklet that was small and handy for the children to use, and it also allowed him to have a different color for each text set they read throughout the year. For example, "A 'Little' Fantasy," which we note later in the chapter, was covered in purple, and the historical fiction books on the U.S. Civil War were covered in yellow.

Dialogue journals. Nancie Atwell discussed this response mode in great detail in her *In the Middle: Writing, Reading, and Learning with Adolescents* (1987) and it is where many of our ideas come from. She noted that touching base with each reader in any classroom situation was difficult at best and extremely problematic in the middle school situation. A teacher at that level might see over 75 students in a day. She came up with what she referred to as the "dialogue journal" (1987, p. 165) as a means of response allowing a literary conversation to take place between the teacher and each student. In the dialogue journal, the student writes his or her reactions to what was read and the teacher later responds just as if he or she were sitting at a dining room table and in the middle of a heated discussion. This written "dialogue" is reasonably easy, doesn't take all that much time to do, and gives the teacher a good sense of what is going on in the child's reading.

We know that the use of children's written responses to their reading is not as authentic as what we do in real life. But we want to open up a forum for kids to respond openly to what they have read. In a class of 25 to 30 kids, that is difficult; in five to six middle school sections, it is downright impossible. There isn't enough time in the day or hands in the classroom to manage such an undertaking. So we take Atwell's lead and attempt to create an environment for children's literature responses that resembles the way adults might respond if they were sitting together debriefing a movie or play they'd just seen: The free-flowing discussion would hinge on reactions, concerns, and questions that were brought to mind by the film or performance. No guided questions or prompts are necessary.

So, this is how the process plays out in your classroom: You complete independent reading by telling the children they have 2 minutes left to read and need to find a place to logically halt for the day. Then have them get out their learning logs and write. As we noted earlier, Darigan had his students write the page numbers they had read that day, a short, succinct summary of the story, followed by a response to the minilesson that would indicate to what extent they got the objective of the lesson.

Managing the children's responses. After the writing and if you have time, you may want to hold short literature discussions (which we describe in the next section), or you can simply collect the logs and move on to your next subject area. You are probably wondering how you can manage all those responses—especially if you are teaching in a team situation where you are solely responsible for all the reading or in a middle school situation with a large number of sections. A good point. We suggest that you make life easy and collect only about one-third of your logs to respond to every night. If you find a child who is struggling or is not writing up to expectations, you can read it again the next night and until you have that child back on track and up to speed. The second night, you will pull another one-third of the class and respond to them. Obviously, on the third night you will have read and responded to the entire class, and the cycle starts anew with that first third.

Keep in mind that you don't need to write as much back to the child as he or she writes to you. All you want to do is get a flavor of what they are getting from their reading, which will inform your instruction. Then you want to respond in such a way that the student feels he or she is being "heard." We find brief comments in the margins and a summary sentence or two at the end of their comments to have a powerful effect on the quality of the student's response and will serve as the communication link that keeps the dialogue going.

Oral Responses to Reading: Literature Circles

If the only response children made to their reading were in the form of writing, the process would get laborious quite quickly and they would soon lose interest. They also need the opportunity to discuss what they have read, to question, and to pull apart the text within group conversations. The opportunity should also be provided for them to share what they have learned with others who are reading different books. This format has been referred to as Grand Conversations (Peterson & Eeds, 1994) by some, book groups by others, and what we, along with Gunning (2000), Hill, Johnson, and Schlick Noe (1995), and Daniels (1994), call Literature Circles.

We have found that these circles sustain and enhance your reading program and add a spark of love for reading (Klein, 1995). But, as with anything good, these discussions do not come easily or naturally to children in the beginning. In an open exchange with little support or direction, the topic soon falls by the wayside and dissolves into chitchat. We offer here some suggestions on the "how to," which will help you get started in Literature Circles.

To find out more about Literature Circles/Club de Lecture and other sites with teaching ideas, visit Chapter 13 on the companion website at **www.prenhall.com/darigan**

BOOKMARK

INTEGRATING TECHNOLOGY: ACTIVITIES USING THE WORLD WIDE WEB

Literature Circles/Club de Lecture is a wonderful project from Montreal in which both second-grade English speakers and second-grade French immersion classes use the Literature Circle process to create a website filled with book reviews and art work. An article by Maureen Baron published in *Reading Online* describes the project and its outcomes, providing an opportunity to analyze and perhaps replicate parts of the project.

A Literature Circle Minilesson

As we said, these groups can fall apart quickly if the children don't have the where-withal to sustain them. The perfect venue for teaching successful Literature Circles is the minilesson. During this time, you are "teaching" children how to respond thoughtfully, honestly, and to each other in a supportive nature. You are helping them develop a sense of what is important in literature so they can notice it in their own reading. Further, you are showing them how to communicate that knowledge to their peers (Daniels, 1994; Hill, Johnson, & Schlick Noe, 1995).

This is how your minilesson might look: You continue to read aloud from your ongoing novel as an introduction to your lesson. Your objective that day might center on connections the children have made to their own lives and to other books they have read. We suggest that you select five or six children and move them into a small circle, along with yourself, in the middle of the room and have the other children sit around you in a fishbowl setting.

The ground rules are these:

1. Those who are sitting in the inner circle are the only ones who can talk; the outside circle is made up of observers only. Let them know that they will get their chance for input later.
2. Further, the inner circle should be reminded to avoid, at all costs, "putting down" any other child in the group.
3. Finally, students should do their best to stay on the topic at hand and to have substantiation for the points that they make.

Inner circle conversation. By having the children in the inner circle talk, you can model what and how they are to do this when set loose on their own. You control the conversation while at the same time allowing for a free flow of ideas. In regard to the topic we suggested, connections they have made from the read aloud to their own lives and to their books, you can open the exchange with their general impressions of the book thus far. The moment a child makes one of those connections, you jump right on it, saying, "You're right, Josh! *The Midnight Fox* is like *The Pinballs* because the main characters feel alone and not cared for. What made you say that?" After Josh articulates his stance, you want to applaud his opinion and his ability to back it up. Make a big deal about it. The feeling will sink in to the entire class how important it is to state a point of view and be able to back it up.

You will undoubtedly encounter a child who makes a statement that is inaccurate or whose response doesn't make total sense. This is a crucial point in the miniles-son, because the way you deal with it here, in this controlled forum, will set the tone for other such responses in Literature Circles for the rest of the year. As delicately and gently as possible, probe what the child meant and see how he or she made the connection. Again, applaud the child's efforts. Most often there is some logical connection the student made, and that is what you want to applaud. If students misread part of the text, assure them you've done the same many times before.

Group debriefing. After inner-circle book discussion has reached its end, you will want to debrief with the entire class and talk about both content discussed and the process. At this point, the folks in the outside circle have the opportunity to add their input. You may begin, "Did any of you in the outside circle have a point of view that was not voiced in our small group?" Surely hands will shoot up. "What did you want to say?" Give a few children the opportunity to state their views. At this point, you can assure them that their opinions will be heard and that this can be done more ably in many smaller groups instead of one big group. But, assure them that if they are going to do this, a few very important things must be regarded.

Discuss that they must stay on topic and allow everybody an opportunity to talk. You will further want to remind them that these discussions are to be conducted in a safe atmosphere and that everybody's opinion counts. Put-downs will not be tolerated. After the children have learned the procedures, they can move on to specific discussion skills that will enhance their group exchange and will help deepen their subsequent reading.

Adding depth to the conversation. Often children haven't had the opportunity to express many opinions, so they don't know how to respond naturally and authentically. Enter another minilesson! Harvey Daniels has done much to articulate and hone these discussions based on his work in *Literature Circles* (1994). In this book, he describes how teachers can lead children to deeper and more meaningful discussions. He notes different roles students can play in both fiction and nonfiction discussions. Daniels has found that if these roles are taught and reinforced, they become part of the fiber of the child's response system.

Thus, after being taught the role of "connector," for example, students will very naturally start to make those all-important connections to their lives and to other books and events, to other books the same author has written, to name just a few. Then, he suggests, the teacher moves on to other roles with which to become familiar.

Touch base. You may want to keep a few other considerations in mind while holding Literature Circles. This, again, is not time for you to tutor kids with special needs, grade papers, or talk to your neighbor across the hall. You need to circulate among the groups, adding commentary when necessary, asking probing questions where pertinent, but most often you need to touch base with each group and simply get out of the way and allow the discussions to flow. Your presence will help kids stay on task and keep discussions going when a lull has come over the group.

We offer this as a final note of advice that might come in handy: Darigan always felt as though he didn't have enough time with the book groups in his fifth-grade classroom, and keeping his class of "more than difficult charges" on task was often a challenge. He fell into a strategy that helped manage his Literature Circles; though he doesn't remember where he picked it up, he found it worked wonders in keeping the children on the topic. First, he went to the school librarian and borrowed six small tape recorders. Then he handed one to each group just before they met in their circles. He told them to speak clearly and not to interrupt each other because he wouldn't be able to hear all that went on in the group if they did. The introduction of tape recorders added a whole new dynamic to the discussions. He found that the children were far more attentive and on task than they would have otherwise been—knowing that they were being recorded. The fact of the matter is that there weren't enough hours in the day to listen to all that tape, but the kids managed themselves better from then on. When Darigan was able to "listen in," he learned quite a bit about the group dynamics, what content was covered, and how kids were responding to the books they read.

▼▼▼▼▼▼▼

Book Selection—Revisited

At this point, you are probably wondering how you can organize, assemble, and accumulate all the books necessary to get Reader's Workshop successfully off the ground. And you are correct in assuming that this is a major concern. A very large part of the

High Student Choice	Equal Choice	High Teacher Choice
Individual Copies	**Text Sets**	**Core Books**

FIGURE 13-7 Book selection and choice.

success of your workshop has to do with book selection. We now look at a variety of constructs to reach that end. Of all the possibilities that are out there for the literature-based teacher, there are three basic variations in overall book selection:

1. *Core books*. This organizational permutation provides for *whole-class instruction* in which every child in your class is reading the same book and is often referred to as a core book (Cooper, 2000).
2. *Individual copies*. When every child in your class is reading from a different book, individual copies are in place (Atwell, 1987). This construct provides for individual instruction and allows the teacher to accommodate every child with reading material that is at his or her fluency level.
3. *Text sets*. Using multiple copies of a variety of titles that are centered on a particular theme or genre is the hallmark of text sets (Harste, Short, & Burke, 1988). This is a nice compromise between core books and individual copies and capitalizes on the strengths of both.

Each category certainly has strengths and a few drawbacks. By looking at book selection from all three angles, you can decide the best course for your class and your particular situation.

Ownership Is the First Issue

It's wise to look at these categories in book selection from the perspective of who is doing the choosing. If you look at Figure 13-7, you will see that on the right side of the continuum, which includes core books, teachers have the majority of choice when it comes to what will be read. All students read the same book at the same time and it is the teacher, in essence, who does the choosing. At the other end of the continuum, the students have the greatest choice when reading in individual copies.

One thing we know about reading is that choice and ownership are important elements for ultimate success in reading. So, why not let kids read only what they want? Well, the fact of the matter is that we as teachers do know significantly more than our charges—though they would like to think otherwise—so our input is necessary. Shouldn't we use what we know to encourage what is best for them? Let's look closely at each category so you can see the high points as well as the shortcomings of each. Then you can make a decision about what is best for your classroom situation.

Core Books

We start with core books only because we see this most often in the schools we visit around the country. We define core books as a single title that is to be read by everyone in the entire class. For example, all students in the fifth grade may read **Sign of the Beaver,** by Elizabeth George Speare, and all students in second grade may read **My Father's Dragon,** by Ruth Stiles Gannett. In many ways, this is the easiest way to teach. Simply put, the teacher selects a title and everyone reads it. You have one book, one lesson plan, and you don't have to juggle groups, worrying about giving attention to one and busy work to the rest of the class. Everyone in class is virtually on the same page, and everybody can join in on the discussion. The result is that it levels the reading playing field (Cooper, 2000).

Sounds pretty good, doesn't it? But keep in mind that we aren't on a Ford assembly line, stamping out parts and putting together a station wagon or coupe. In your class, you have a variety of makes, models, and years. So adapting to those differences is essential, and core books lock you into a specific book at a definite reading level.

Often we see school districts demanding core books in their overall curriculum. These range from three to four titles that every child will read at every grade level throughout the district to lists that have grown to include so many titles that there is little room for anything else.

The good news in this is that often the *district* will purchase the books instead of that cost coming out of your own pocket. The bad news is that you may be "stuck" with a book you don't care for or that the kids can't read. In one district, a teacher was in love with E. B. White's ***The Trumpet of the Swan***. His charisma and dogged support for the book led to its being added to the fourth-grade curriculum district wide. Now, if you have read this book, you know that it is a tough one for fourth graders. Certainly the love and energy this teacher had for it led the class successfully through the book, whereas other teachers down the hall grimaced and dragged their classes along chapter by chapter, grumbling all the way.

Drawbacks to Core Books

The downside to core books is that you are inevitably going to have children in your class who can't read the book because it is just too difficult for them. This variable, of course, depends on the group you have each year. One year, you may be very successful using a book like Avi's ***The Barn*** with your fourth graders only to find that the following year, it is just too difficult or the topic too sophisticated for them to grab hold of.

Readability. You must consider readability seriously. Some classes are more readily able to negotiate text than others are—or you may find that within a particular class, you have five or six who cannot read the book you put in front of them.

Buddy reading. So the question becomes, "What do you do to accommodate those children having difficulties?" Buddy reading, paired reading (Topping, 1989), or, more properly, *neurological impress* is a strategy where a less able reader is paired with one who is more able and allowed to simultaneously see and hear print. Together they read the text and when the tutee comes to a word he or she doesn't know, the tutor reads it and then the tutee must repeat it. Topping found this to be of significance for all readers. In Chomsky's (1978) study, children "read" in the trade book while following along with the recorded version on audiocassette. Eldredge and Butterfield (1986) used reading dyads (pairs) or triads (groups of three), teaming poor readers with average readers. The readers sat together and read aloud from the same book; the faster reader touched words as they were read and the slower reader repeated them. Groups changed every few days, and as proficiency was gained, the slower reader began to read silently, using the better reader as a word resource.

Even the use of Big Books, as suggested by Holdaway (1982) and White, Joseph, and Rorie (1986), allows for a form of neurological impress. Big Books usually are trade picture books that have been reproduced in a format large enough to be seen from 20 feet away. With Big Books, teachers can have their students follow their fluent reading.

But if you do too much of that, parents may start complaining; wondering who is being paid to teach, you or their kid. They have a valid point, we think.

Books on tape. Another strategy for those children who are really struggling with the text is to use an audiotape of the book so the child can "read along" with the text in a listening center or at home. Again, not a bad idea—but then it is incumbent on you to purchase the tape or to record the entire novel or book aloud—and where do you find time and money for that? Also, keep in mind that it is a good thing if they are listening to the book, but they are not really reading, are they?

Sophistication of Subject

Beyond the difficulty of negotiating the text, you may find classes who can easily read the text you put in front of them but are not yet ready for the content of the book. Again, with ***The Barn,*** teachers have told us that even though the children in their classes can read the words, they are often thrown into fits of uncomfortable laughter when, for instance, young Ben must "clean" his father, who is in a coma. "For there I was, nine years of age, having to undress my father and clean his privates both back and front. What shame I felt that *he* should be like a baby to *me*, who was his youngest son!" The maturity level of your class can often dictate what books are appropriate each year.

Adapting Instruction

The obvious retooling to the core book approach is to choose a book that is low enough for everyone—or almost everyone in your class—and that contains a more bland content so that reading by the masses is possible. But by introducing a book like this, do we potentially sacrifice the readers who are more sophisticated? Clearly, there are some problems with "dumbing down" the book selection.

In the long run, we think you ought to defer to text sets and individual copies (which we explain next) over core books. There are simply too many problems with trying to make one book "fit" an entire class to justify their regular use. But, keep in mind that we aren't opposed to a judicious use of a core book—especially at the beginning of the year.

You may want to open the school year with a core book so that you can model many of the strategies and ensuing extension activities children will be responsible for. For example, after reading a few chapters together in a core book, you could introduce how to make a diorama. A few chapters later, you could show them how to create a book poster advertising the book, adding a comprehensive "review." This supports their learning and adequately prepares them for these sorts of activities when they are working more independently in text sets and individual copies throughout the rest of the year.

Individual Copies

Look at the other end of the continuum: individual copies. This is a collection of books, again centering on a theme or genre, where single titles, usually gathered from the classroom, school, and public libraries, make up the bulk of the selections. This category allows the children by far the most choice. With individual copies, children can select from dozens upon dozens of books. In Darigan's fifth-grade class, for instance, when the kids were studying the United States Civil War, the classroom was flooded with a huge number of books. He personally owns somewhere around 60 individual novel-length books, both fiction and nonfiction, that deal with that conflict alone. Added to that, he borrowed from both the school and local public libraries, collecting well over 100 books for the kids to choose from and enjoy.

Advantages of Individual Copies

Individual copies have some very distinct advantages. For instance, kids have greater choice both in content and in fit for readability. With the wider selection available to them, students can choose a book more to their liking. For example, the girls in Darigan's class tended to choose books where a girl was the main protagonist, and the boys likewise aligned themselves with books where boys were the main protagonists.

Self-selection

Children's attitudes toward reading seem to be affected positively by allowing them to select their own reading materials. Every study examined included a time when students at every age level were encouraged to find and read books of their own choosing. Though sometimes books were read together (as with Big Books), each classroom had a large library from which children could select their own books. Sustained Silent Reading is unsuccessful unless children are allowed to read books of their own choosing.

Self-selection of reading materials allows students to choose books that match their interests, and interest is not a factor to be ignored in education. Several studies undertaken by one group of researchers pinpointed what helps children recall information from their reading. Two of the factors were readability—making the language

simple and easy to understand—and reader interest. The experiments concluded that "interest accounted for an average of thirty times as much variance in sentence recall as readability" (Anderson, Shirley, Wilson, & Fielding, 1987, p. 289). In other words, what the researchers called the "interestingness" of text is 30 times more powerful than the readability of text when it comes to comprehending and remembering information from print. Because children have different interests, teachers may miss the advantages of a powerful instructional tool if they ignore "interestingness" by not allowing ample opportunity for children to learn from self-selected books. Also, one of the continuing problems of basal readers, when used as the major resource for reading instruction, is that opportunities for self-selection are limited.

Further, when children choose their books with individual copies, they have a wider range of readability levels. Within his collection, Darigan had books that ranged as low as third grade and as high as eighth grade. With the careful guidance of the teacher, children can select books that will be of interest and that they will be able to negotiate easily.

Another advantage of individual copies is that the price is always better because you can almost always depend on your librarian to help you collect the supply of books—in part or whole. And because you need only one of each title, it is right up the library's alley.

Drawbacks to Individual Copies

There is also a downside to individual copies. We can hear your concerns already:

▌ How will I be able to read all of those books before I hand them out to the kids?

▌ How will I be able to monitor and manage 27 kids reading 27 different books?

▌ Won't I be putting myself in jeopardy if I give a kid a book I, personally, haven't read?

Again, all of these are good questions.

Reading every book. As for reading all the books your students are reading, let's face it, we all have lives. Don't we? You will not, nor could you possibly, read all the individual copies your students are reading. So first of all, you need to get comfortable with that notion.

Monitoring and managing. Our sense is that first of all, you *will* be able to manage these books and the children's responses with relative ease. Look at the section later in this chapter covering "Response," which will give you some concrete hints on ways to manage and monitor these books.

If you are worried that students will try to pull the wool over your eyes by writing fictitious responses, you can rest assured that their attempts will be as obvious as a sore thumb.

On the other hand, we have found that the distance you have from the book can work to your advantage. Because you do not know specific details about the book, children will need to explain what they have read (both orally and in writing) in a more coherent fashion because you won't be filling in the gaps with your own prior knowledge of the story.

Jeopardy of book challenges. If your librarian (who will undoubtedly have collected many, if not all, of the books in your set of individual copies) has recommended a book, you can rest assured that it will be supported and shouldn't be open to challenge. Even if it does come up for a challenge, you have the full support of the American Library Association and the International Reading Association in such matters. Because most librarians purchase books for their collection based on reviews and because those reviews tend to flag titles with potential difficulties, you are generally safe by using books they have selected. In communities where book challenges have become commonplace, if a book might appear to be offensive, your librarian will probably not purchase it.

Text Sets

The middle road in book selection comes in the form of text sets. Because we have opened each chapter with a text set, you can probably guess where our hearts lie. After first describing text sets and giving you some further examples of the possibilities, we'll plunge into their potential advantages and limitations.

Text sets, originally described by Harste, Short, and Burke (1988), are defined as a grouping of books where you have multiple copies of a number of different titles. In other practical terms, depending on the size of your class, you would make available for your students five or six copies of five or six different books that are bound together by some unifying element.

You may ask, "What might that element be?" We see three overarching categories that can be addressed in your classroom. Actually, during the course of the chapters thus far, we have included all three. Any guesses as to what they are? Take a minute and look back over the text sets from the very beginning of the book and see if you can discern what these groupings might be. Look for commonalities. What seems to take shape?

The answer? We see text sets delineated by three considerations:

1. books created by a specific author or illustrator
2. books that are related by genre
3. books that are grouped by theme

You may have implicitly picked up some or all of those categories.

ALTERNATE TEXT SET

Centered on a Specific Author or Illustrator

Books by Eric Carle

Read Aloud

The Grouchy Ladybug
Do You Want To Be My Friend?
Papa, Please Get the Moon for Me

Text Set

The Very Hungry Caterpillar	*The Very Lonely Firefly*
The Very Quiet Cricket	*The Very Clumsy Click Beetle*
The Very Busy Spider	

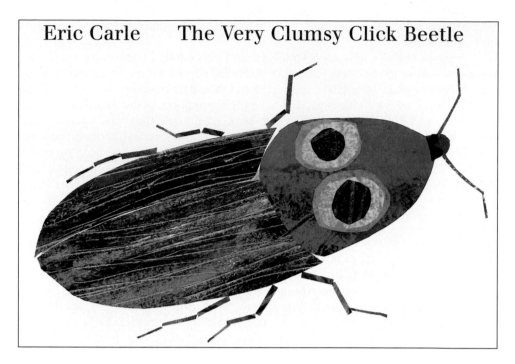

Eric Carle   The Very Clumsy Click Beetle

From ***The Very Clumsy Click Beetle*** by Eric Carle, copyright © 1999 by Eric Carle. Used by permission of Philomel Books, a division of Penguin Putnam, Inc.

DID YOU KNOW?

Eric Carle's distinctive style of art is a collage technique he developed using hand-painted tissue paper and cutting out individual shapes and gluing them onto another piece of paper. His process is captured on video in ***Eric Carle: Picture Writer.*** Visit your local library or bookstore for a copy. You will find many others featuring your favorite authors and illustrators such as Bill Martin, Jr., Gerald McDermott, Gary Paulsen, and Betsy Byars.

We opened this chapter with an example of a text set *by author*, including some of the books written by Newbery Medal–winning author Betsy Byars. At the primary level, you may want to concentrate on a specific *illustrator* such as Tomie dePaola, Jan Brett, and Eric Carle. For example, with the choice of author and illustrator Eric Carle, you could use the three books we list as read alouds. As we mentioned earlier in the discussion on minilessons, the read aloud books set the stage for the children's independent reading and prepare them for the lesson you are going to teach. The books we have chosen make a nice comparison to the text set, which Carle himself considers his "very" books (Carle, 1993). These books, then, would make up bulk of your text set.

ALTERNATE TEXT SET

Centered on a Specific Genre

A "Little" Fantasy

Read Aloud

The Indian in the Cupboard, by Lynne Reid Banks

Text Set

Redwall, by Brian Jacques

The Cricket in Times Square, by George Seldon

The Castle in the Attic, by Elizabeth Winthrop

The Fairy Rebel, by Lynne Reid Banks

The Littles, by John Peterson

Examples of text sets that are related *by genre* have essentially opened every chapter in part 2 of this book. Yet another one that Darigan used with his fifth graders illustrates the flexibility text sets offer you as a teacher in regard to meeting the readability needs of your class. For example, he chose books in this text set that came from the genre of modern fantasy and further dealt with characters that were tiny people or animals. Therefore he titled the set "A 'Little' Fantasy."

Note how each of the books in this grouping is at a distinctly different reading level. Mind you, we don't put a whole lot of stock in readability formulas, but they can be of use in generally predicting a book's difficulty and helping you level books for your class. We have listed the titles for "A 'Little' Fantasy" here in descending order, from a quite sophisticated level for fifth grade to a book that is often seen at second grade.

Brian Jacques's *Redwall* would have to be placed at a high sixth-grade level based on its readability, not to mention its prodigious length at 349 pages—a meaty selection for the average fifth grader, indeed. George Seldon's *The Cricket in Times Square* is listed at a sixth-grade level, and *The Castle in the Attic,* by Elizabeth Winthrop, is right about at a fifth-grade level. *The Fairy Rebel,* by Lynne Reid Banks, comes in at about fourth grade, and John Peterson's *The Littles* is somewhere around a high second-grade readability. Keep in mind how convenient this is for the children in your class. We know that the children in your room aren't all reading "on level"; that is why core books are so problematic. With a range such as the one we have listed here, we can meet the readability needs of every child in the class. A bit later in this chapter, we tell you how to match children with books; suffice it to say here that we are creating flexible grouping possibilities based on reading levels.

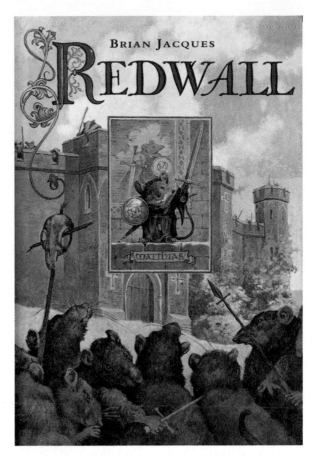

Illustrations by Gary Chalk, copyright © 1986 by Gary Chalk, from **Redwall** by Brian Jacques. Used by permission of Philomel Books, a division of Penguin Putnam, Inc.

ALTERNATE TEXT SET

Cenetered on a Particular Theme

The Journey to Self-Discovery

Read Aloud

Walk Two Moons, by Sharon Creech

Text Set

Nowhere to Call Home, by Cynthia DeFelice

Joey Pigza Swallowed the Key, by Jack Gantos

Split Just Right, by Adele Griffin

The Watcher, by James Howe

Wringer, by Jerry Spinelli

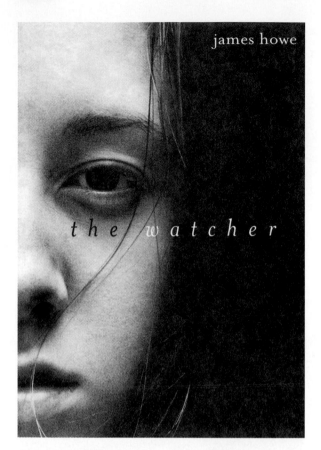

james howe

t h e   w a t c h e r

Cover from ***The Watcher*** by James Howe. Jacket photograph © 1997 by Betsy Imershein. Reprinted by permission of Atheneum books for Young Readers, an imprint of Simon & Schuster Children's Publishing Division.

Books can also be selected *by theme.* As you and your students read each day, the connections you collectively make are remarkable, and the vision of a potential set of books that could turn into a text set often unfolds on its own. Jacobs and Darigan did just such a brainstorming session and arrived at a theme-related text set that turned into a symposium they presented at the International Reading Association's annual convention in Indianapolis, Indiana. Titling the set "The Journey to Self-Discovery," they included the books listed on the preceding page that could be used at the upper elementary level and certainly at the middle school level. It merely grew out of a discussion they had recently about books they loved reading that went above and beyond the average problem novel.

This grouping of books details the difficulties of growing up. Crossing the lines of time and culture and personal circumstance, these books are all hard-hitting commentaries on the problems children face as they grow up. Again, there is a range of sophistication in both readability and content that would make book selection more appropriate for all the children in your class.

So, text sets have a tremendous amount of flexibility as far as meeting the readability needs of your students is concerned, they are fairly easy to identify, and they allow your students some choice while you have a major amount of input as well. All in all, they are a great way to organize literature study in your classroom (Gunning, 2000). We think, over the long haul, they are the best way to proceed and would hope that most of your units are designed with this structure in mind.

The Disadvantage to Text Sets

There is a downside to using text sets, however. To identify the books in your set is one thing; obtaining them is completely another. In chapter 12, we discussed loads of creative ways to get books. Obtaining multiple copies of multiple titles can be an expensive proposition. Take the average price of a paperback and multiply it by 30 and you have quite a chunk of change. One further way beyond the suggestions in the last chapter we found to be helpful is to combine your own resources with that of your local library systems, both school and public. For Darigan's "A 'Little' Fantasy" unit, for example, he purchased about half the books out of his own pocket after he had obtained the other half of the copies from his own school library and the two local public libraries in his area. This saves you, or whatever funding source you have tapped, a lot of money and, in the end, models yet another good use of the library.

Developing Your Own Text Sets

By now, you have been able to sample a number of the text sets we have put forth in the book. But your next questions probably resemble these:

- How do I do this on my own?
- How can I design these text sets to reflect the interests of my children and me and meet the needs of my curriculum?

Teacher as Reader . . . Again

We assure you, we are getting closer to the answer to these questions. But the basis of the solution to both answers resides almost wholly in you. First and foremost, it is incumbent on you to be an overt and joyful reader. As we noted in chapter 1, the benefits of your own wide reading will be returned to you and your students in further knowledge and an authentic excitement for the act. The more *you* read and the more connections *you* make, the deeper the connections will be with the kids.

You need to read widely, both at home and at school, so you can start choosing books not only that you like, but also that you think your children will like. You've already begun that journey by simply reading this far in our textbook. Hopefully, you have sampled books here and there as you coursed through the genre chapters. Now, *you* need to read for a real purpose, the selection of books for successful class text sets. And don't misunderstand; this doesn't mean you have to read a zillion books. The journey begins with a first step: reading one book you really like. Here is a scenario of how you might go through the process.

Let's say for the sake of argument that you are a fifth-grade teacher. During Sustained Silent Reading, you have just finished Mary Downing Hahn's book ***Time for Andrew: A Ghost Story.*** "Aha!" you say to yourself, "this is something I would love to share with my students. And I *do* like the idea of text sets. I want to use this for the read aloud—but where do I go for the other five or six books?"

Back to the Database

Enter, stage left, accompanied by a fanfare of music, are Darigan, Jacobs, and Tunnell singing together: The database that accompanies this book! Remember? Of course you do; we have been singing this refrain for hundreds of pages. Now, you are using it for a real purpose, not just a class assignment.

So you have defined a category that is directly related to an area of your interest and one that you are certain your children will like. Later, we address themes related to your curriculum. Here, though, we are focusing on a text set with the most powerful energy force in the classroom in the driver's seat—you. It is your energy and your passion for the set that will carry the unit to uncommon heights.

Reviewing the three categories of text sets—by author, by genre, and by theme—let's start by creating a potential text set based on Mary Downing Hahn as an author. Searching her name in the database, you will come up with a minimum of 12 titles. That certainly is enough for a set. We suggest that you print out the entire list of annotations, spread them out on a table, and look at the whole group. A closer inspection might lead you to think that given her body of work, at least as represented here, the topics are too varied in both genre and subject matter, not to mention that she has written a few books that are way above your grade level. So it's back to the drawing board.

But remember, it was ***Time for Andrew: A Ghost Story*** that you liked. So, looking back at your list, you notice she has written a number of ghost stories, at least five of them. But, again, on closer inspection, you notice that her book ***Look for Me By Moonlight*** has a 16-year-old protagonist AND deals with vampires AND is for grades seven and up. Not a good choice for your class. That leaves you with four books, which is really too few for the average classroom; having groups of no more than five children is really the best (Gambrell & Almasi, 1996).

Not to be daunted, you go back to the drawing board once again. Perhaps you could drop the idea of "featuring" Mary Downing Hahn in an author study, still use the books you like of hers, and then search by the theme of "ghosts." That will render other suggestions by other authors—over 200 titles, in fact. *Now* you may have a text set in the making. By limiting that list of "ghost" stories, you can put together a powerful text set.

Go down the hall and show the list to your colleagues. Better yet, head into the library and ask your librarian what he or she thinks. By honing this list to five or six titles, you will have one bang-up grouping of books that your kids will really enjoy.

Looking back at your process, by virtue of your reading just one book, you have taken a book you love, tapped the database as well as other "experts" like yourself who provided you input on further books, and you are now on your way to a great text set. Before it is all said and done, you'll undoubtedly read more books within this theme.

To find out more about Judy Blume and other authors and illustrators on the World Wide Web, visit Chapter 13 on the companion website at **www.prenhall.com/darigan**

BOOKMARK

INTEGRATING TECHNOLOGY: AUTHORS ON THE WORLD WIDE WEB

Judy Blume has a wonderful site with loads of information on Judy, her books, and the writing process. A reader's guide and an on-line discussion board for **Summer Sisters** are included. Blume provides answers to frequently asked questions, and she also encourages e-mail and snail mail, some of which is posted on her website. She also includes the thought-provoking introduction to her edited volume *Places I Never Meant To Be: Original Stories By Censored Writers.* Sooner or later, every teacher will have to address the concerns of parents who seek to remove certain books from their child's classroom, and this essay will help prepare them for conversations with parents.

Your children will benefit from this wide reading. See how easy it was? It started with your simply reading one book you loved.

Beyond the Database

We have a couple of other suggestions that might prove helpful. *Book Links: Connecting Books, Libraries, and Classrooms* is a publication of the American Library Association that comes out six times a year and is a rich resource for literature study. In their "Classroom Connection" section, *Book Links* offers at least a half dozen themed units for both primary and intermediate classrooms. The authors of these already-researched areas have chosen a theme, read every book related to that theme, and then trimmed the list down to the very best titles; usually no more than 30 to 40 books. These themes are generally global enough to fit into your curriculum.

Of course, the downside in using *Book Links* is that it limits you to the topics the journal itself has identified in each of its issues. The upside is that each theme has been extremely well researched in culling the best books for children. If you want to get a listing of all the topics they have published, you can hit the next resource, the Internet. By accessing ALA through the Internet, you can get a printout of every article they have published since the very beginning of *Book Links* back in 1989.

A Final Review of Book Selection Options

Looking back on all the ground we've covered concerning book selection, allow us a final word on the three categories we have identified, their advantages, and their disadvantages. Clearly, core books allow for easier selection (with only one title you have to choose) and they give the teacher most of the choice. Cox and Zarillo (1993) are strong advocates of individual titles. On the other hand, though they require more in-depth research for titles, they give children much more choice, which is a strong motivating factor (Atwell, 1998). Text sets, as we have shown, offer an in-between alternative, with the best of both teacher and student needs answered.

▼▼▼▼▼▼▼▼

Getting Text Sets Started in Your Classroom

Now, the following questions may have popped into your mind:

▪ Now that I've made the leap to accept text sets into my classroom routine, how am I supposed to manage them?
▪ How do children select their books? Etc.

These are all very important considerations, and ones that will either make or break your Reader's Workshop using text sets.

Follow the Reader's Workshop Format

Even on the very first day of Reader's Workshop when using text sets, you are going to continue to use the predictable format we described earlier in the chapter that uses these three elements: minilesson, independent reading, and response. We first take a look at how to proceed on your first day with a new text set when students select their books, and then we move to the day-to-day administration of the workshop.

The First Day

We like to address the book selection using the very same format as with any lesson in Reader's Workshop: We present a minilesson, allow for independent reading, and finally ask students to respond. It follows the routine you have already set in place and is consistent with every other reading lesson you have presented.

Ownership Is Essential

But let's first get back to that ownership issue we mentioned earlier and how it plays out in the use of text sets. We said that text sets have a unique position on that continuum of ownership (see Figure 13-7 on page 451) because they offer the teacher choice while at the same time allowing children a variety of alternatives.

You, as the teacher, have chosen an overarching topic of organization centered on a particular author or illustrator, a genre, or a theme. You have further selected a read aloud book to introduce each lesson and a number of titles that you will feature to the students, much like the ice cream list at the local sweet shop. The children are told about all the available flavors and afforded a little sample of each, after which they make their choice. When this process is completed, we hope they will respond as if they just received a delightful double-dip of ice cream. In this group, they are in an informal setting to read, to discuss just exactly what it was they liked or didn't like about their book.

The Minilesson: Introducing the Text Set

We use the minilesson to introduce the topic and the new titles in the text set to the children. The procedure is quite simple: As with any good minilesson, you begin by introducing the author, genre, or theme with your read aloud book. Let's use the text set we opened this chapter with as an example.

Introduce the Read Aloud

When the kids are settled and ready, you begin, "Today, we are going to start reading a grouping of books by the author Betsy Byars. For the read aloud, I have selected her wonderful book *The Midnight Fox*. Hmm, given just this title, what do you think this book is going to be about? Talk to the person sitting next to you and tell them what you think." After a brief moment allowing both people in the pair to share, you go on.

Examine the Book Cover

"Now, let's look at the cover of the book." Slowly scan the book's cover across the class so the children can see it. "How does this new information add to your predictions? Once again, talk to the person sitting next to you and tell them what you think." After each child shares, make sure to ask them why they think the way they do. "What is it that makes you think that way?" This forces them to think more critically, using references in the text as well as connections they have made to other books that are similar and to events in their own lives.

After this discussion has exhausted itself, you will want to add, "The caption on the cover says, 'Can Tom save the beautiful fox from his uncle's shotgun?' This certainly adds fuel to the fire. Now what do you think?"

Begin Reading Aloud

After taking responses from a few, you can begin reading. "The first chapter," you say, "is titled 'Bad News.' "

> Sometimes at night when the rain is beating against the windows of my room, I think about that summer on the farm. It has been five years, but when I close my eyes I am once again by the creek watching the black fox come leaping over the green, green grass. She is as light and as free as the wind, exactly as she was the first time I saw her.

"What do you think? How are your predictions based only on the cover illustration altered by this first paragraph?" The kids will certainly pick up on the freedom the fox seemingly has and be satisfied that though the fox is going to be in trouble, in the end it will survive and be free. Undoubtedly, though, a few of the children will recall the chapter's title, "Bad News," and wonder if that is an introduction to the problem or portent of what is to happen.

"Let's read on," you say.

> Or sometimes it is that last terrible night, and I am standing beneath the oak tree with the rain beating against me . . .

"Now, what do you think?" you query. Survey the kids' reactions, which will surely point toward some sort of disaster. You continue, "Let's read on . . . "

> The lightning flashes, the world is turned white for a moment, and I see everything as it was—the broken lock, the empty cage, the small tracks disappearing into the rain. Then it seems to me that I can hear, as plainly as I heard it that August night, above the rain, beyond the years, the high, clear bark of the midnight fox.

"Wow," you say. "*Now* what do you think?"

Breaking Up the Reading

Your classroom text set is off to a great beginning. The children's interest has been piqued and they are ready to hear the rest of the first chapter and move right into the text set. What you have done in this little vignette is to provide the impetus to move forward on a study of literature in a very natural way. Again, the read aloud is key to that motivation.

But notice how the introductory reading was broken up into consumable parts to allow the children to process their own understanding of the book. By prompting them to think about what they expect will happen in the book, you are building some very important connections for their independent reading. Goodman, Goodman, and Bridges-Bird (1990) tell us that reading is nothing more than "tentative information processing" and that as we read along in a text, we predict, both in words and in content, what is going to come next. When they come to something that doesn't make sense, fluent readers backtrack to find out where they went wrong. Teaching children to predict, based on what they know already about the text or the situation, helps support that tentative information processing and improves their ability to negotiate text and their reading comprehension.

Book Talks

Next come the book talks. We have always opened these exciting days at the beginning of a new literature study by having the books all laying out for the kids to see. Then, one by one, we tell them a bit about each. All you simply have to do is hold the book

In the case of Betsy Byars or any number of big-name authors, you may want to work in video footage showing this author at work and talking about his or her process. You can check the companion website that accompanies this book to see what resources we have included. Beyond that, you can access professional video productions offering portraits of children's literary luminaries through Trumpet or Scholastic Book clubs. See chapter 12 for specific addresses.

up so they can see the cover and tell them what the book is about. As we said about book talks in chapter 12, your knowledge of the book can be no more than what you have read on the back cover. This gives the children a point of comparison and aids them in making some educated decisions.

Be careful that you don't "oversell" one title at the expense of another. It may be that you have read already read Betsy Byars's *The Pinballs* in its entirety and loved it. If you make the mistake of talking too much about that book, telling them specifics about the characters and highlighting memorable scenes, the entire class will follow your lead and want to select that book. The problem is that your text sets have only six copies of a particular title, and you'll have some pretty disappointed kids if half the class lists it as their number one choice. A word to the wise, then, would be to give each book the same amount of "advertisement" and let the kids choose from there.

Introducing the Text Set: Independent Reading

Children Sample

After the book talks are completed, it is time for the kids to go to work and begin their own selection process. You simply let the kids loose with the books you have selected for them to choose from. Their task is to peruse each book (like they would taste a little spoonful of each ice cream) to see which ones are most appealing and, just as important, which ones they can read independently. During this time, you can circulate throughout the classroom, informally chatting with the students and offering a bit of advice.

Adapt to Reading Abilities

Use this time to make suggestions for those students who will need a bit more guidance. For instance, there is inevitably a child in the room who is a weak reader but who will choose the most difficult book to try and save face or to be included in the "in group." Suggest a title that would be within his or her range and yet still appealing. By the same token, you will find a whole host of strong students who are first in line to choose the easiest book on the list.

It may be wise for the children to do a "five finger test" on each book. Ask them to randomly read a page, any page, and when they come up against a word they don't know, they simply raise a finger on their hand. If, before they have reached the end of the page, they have all five digits up, then the book may just be too difficult for them and they should select one more at their level.

Also remind them that they should be choosing books based on their *own* interest, *not* the interests of their group of friends. So often each clique will get together and decide they will all read one title or another. Unfortunately, even within that small group, there is going to be a natural spread of reading levels, and some children will find their book way too difficult or too easy. Then the dynamic benefits of the text set are lost to peer pressure.

After the children have completed their examination of the books within the text set, they move out of independent reading to their own selection, which comes loosely under the category of response.

Introducing the Text Set: Response

During the independent reading time, while the students are poring over the books and as you circulate around the classroom, hand out a small slip of paper to each child. They need not be any larger than one-fourth of the standard 8 1/2 X 11 inch sheet—in fact, we used to cut up unused duplicated copies from the recycling bin into fourths for just this purpose.

Ask the children to place their name at the top of the slip of paper and then list their first, second, and third choices for books. That's it. They have responded and you can go on about the day. Reader's Workshop is completed for the first day.

Now, at a later time, your job is to match titles with kids. In this sense, you still have the final say on who receives what book. So the kids who want to clump together can be broken up; those who choose a book that is too hard or too easy can be gently placed into one more at their level.

Teacher Makes the Final Choices

In the comfort of your own home, or wherever you choose to do this, lay out all the slips of paper and group them according to first choices. You'll see that they are pretty evenly distributed (unless you sold one book too strongly or gave another only a mediocre review). No matter what, there will always be some shifting that will need to occur. For example, you may have eight children interested in Betsy Byars's book *The 18th Emergency* and only six copies available. You probably don't want any more than six in a group anyway, so two of those children will need to receive their second choice.

Beyond trimming the groups for suitable size, you will also find that children who don't get along particularly well may end up in the same group as well. Rather than destroy the literature study with acerbic remarks and in-fighting, you can easily switch one of the students to his or her second choice. Daniels (1994) refers to this as "massaging" the groups for both suitable size and the potential each group has for its productivity.

You will further find children, as we mentioned before, reading at a very basic level who choose a book that is far too difficult for them. Again, you can move them to their second or third choice so they are allowed a text that is more readable for them. Daniels (1994) goes on to say that students' receiving their third choice is a far better motivator than no choice.

The same holds true for those more fluent readers or those gifted students we mentioned earlier who quite often choose the easiest text in the list. They, too, can have their first choice swapped for one that is more suited to their reading level.

On the second day of the text set unit, you can proceed with your minilesson followed by independent reading, where you hand out all the books to the students.

▼▼▼▼▼▼▼▼

A View of Reader's Workshop at the Primary Grades

Clearly the face of reading instruction must change when working with the beginning readers in the primary grades. We like to think that instruction at this level is setting the stage for later independent reading. But, according to Tunnell and Jacobs (1989), the reading of "real" texts in a holistic, literature-based curriculum offers significantly better results than falling back to basal programs. We steadfastly adhere to the use of "real" books in lieu of these programs with only a small diversion into prepackaged programs that merely give children a quick jump-start on reading.

How do we set the stage? Don Holdaway spelled out the beginnings in his book *The Foundations of Literacy* (1979). There he introduced what is known as the

"Shared Book Experience," which, in essence, replicated the lap reading many parents do with their children every day. With a child on his or her lap, the parent reads enthusiastically, pointing out various concepts about print and story illustration, and demonstrates how reading "works." Parents naturally track the words as they read across the page, and the child begins to understand the concept of directionality, or the notion that words in the English language go from left to right, top to bottom, and front to back. Using enlarged texts, teachers can do the very same thing. We refer to them as Big Books now, but the procedure is the same. Using a pointer, the teacher tracks the words across the page and makes explicit how print works.

Just as parents naturally encourage their child to join in on the fun of reading the text, the teacher, too, beckons the class to participate. The class may be reading Janet and Allan Ahlberg's book *Each Peach Pear Plum*. The teacher will track with the pointer the first and second lines,

> Each peach, pear, plum,
> I spy Tom Thumb.

At this point, the teacher will want to ask, "Where do we go next? Who can tell me?"

When it is clear that it is the next page, the teacher will then ask, "Now that we are on a new page, where do we start? Which way do we go? When we get to the end of the first line, where do we go?" All of these questions and their responses explicitly teach the basic concepts about print and how it works. The teacher continues to read:

> Tom Thumb in the cupboard,
> I spy Mother Hubbard . . .

Here, the teacher will want to stop before turning the page to see if the children can predict what the next words will be. What he or she is attempting to make explicit to the class is the pattern the text is taking. Bill Martin (1972) refers to this as "interlocking text." Because of the repetition, the last words in one line become the first words in the next. They lock together, and knowing that aids the reader to predict with great accuracy how the next line will start.

> Mother Hubbard in the cellar,
> I spy _____.

"What do you think she spies?" The class will chime in together, "Cinderella!"

Lessons such as these are the framework of reading and engage children joyfully in the pleasures and benefits.

Success of literature-based programs is well documented. Disabled readers are brought into the world of literacy (and not just decoding) using real books. When children learn that reading and books are worthwhile, they will spend more self-initiated time in books, as Fielding, Wilson, and Anderson (1984) point out. Children who participate in this self-initiated practice (some children read from 10 to 20 times more than others) make more progress because frequent personal reading improves the automaticity of basic reading skills. Unfortunately, in a study of after-school activities of fifth-grade children, Fielding and her colleagues (1984) discovered that only 2% of free

Simona Lynch

When my first graders come in at the beginning of the year, they are at varied reading levels. Last year, I had kids that didn't know their alphabet letters, let alone sounds, and I also had kids who were reading on actually a fourth- or fifth-grade level. Of course their comprehension wasn't at all sophisticated, but they could pick up a book and read print from a fifth-grade book.

I started with basic sight words that came from a variety of sources and that I knew would be appropriate for the beginning of first grade: the Dolch word list, our basal reader, and words I know are going to be important to them. Color words are a big deal, for example. But since most of them couldn't read yet, we did a lot of predictable poetry. They read the poem over and over; memorizing the poem, really. And by doing this they began to learn concepts about print such as tracking, directionality, and the notion of "wordness."

We did a variety of poems where colors are prominent words. Whenever a color word came up, we matched the word with the color. For example, if we read the word "blue" we printed the word in blue, and so forth. Next we made strip books from the poems.

Strip books are little books made out of little strips of paper, and the kids make their own book. It is a repetitive book set up in a pattern. I modeled an example on the overhead that went like this: Let's just say we were doing the color yellow; I would have a yellow cover and would call it "My Yellow Strip Book." Inside, the first page would say, "I see a yellow _____." They all had picture dictionaries and they looked through them to find a picture of, say, a pencil. They would draw a picture of a pencil in their book and write the word "pencil" in the blank. Because the words I also wanted them to learn were "the" and "a," I would use the sentences, "I can see *the* _____" or "I can see *a* _____," where every page alternated but their picture changed. If the kids were real fluent writers and readers, they had up to 15 pages, but my beginning ones would pump out only one or two pages.

Jeremy, one of my lowest kids, actually had no confidence in reading and this was the activity that made him feel he could do it. At the beginning of the year, he came to me and the first thing he said was, "I can't do anything." I knew right away that I had to change that. So using the strip books he memorized the text, having the picture there to help him, and he thought he was reading. The other teachers who came in would say, "Oh Jeremy, I heard you were reading, let me hear your book." After four or five teachers did this, he just knew he could read. I mean, he wasn't reading in its purest sense yet, but just getting over that hurdle gave him great confidence.

Next, we went into nursery rhymes and came to the book **Each Peach Pear Plum.** We read the book and did a number of activities with it. Each child had blank "I Spy" books. I put all 20 of their names in a bag,

and my own. They came up and picked someone's name, and I started it off with "Each Peach, Pear, Plum I spy . . . Michelle on the playground playing on a toy with _____." They had to rhyme with "toy." So Michelle would write, "Each Peach, Pear, Plum I spy Suzy out on the playground playing on a toy with the 'boys.'" It is something simple and basic, but it got them looking at words and thinking how to find a word that rhymes.

Next we did a word of the day. If the word was, for example, "cat," I might say, "What does a cat do?" "What does a cat look like?" "Where does a cat live?" "What does a cat eat?" After brainstorming a lot of ideas, we would pick one sentence together from this discussion and I would write it on the overhead. They then recorded that sentence in their book, and would read it to me or an aid, tracking it all the way. They drew a picture to match their sentence.

By the second or third month, I was able to do cloze sentences with them. I started out where the word of the day might be "school." I might say, "In school, we learned how to _____." They would have to finish it. We kept the same the same brainstorming procedure and I would ask, "What are some things we do in school?" "What kind of things do we find in school?" By December, they were able to write their own sentences.

From there we did "Word Pockets." It was just a piece of construction paper that I folded over, leaving a little tab, and I laminated it so it had a little pocket. They had an envelope with letters and these could be held in their word pockets. We worked on word families, and individually or in pairs, this reinforced their idea of rhyming words.

We also had reading groups; I found that managing time in these was one of the hardest things to do. This past year, I was lucky because I had two aids, and a practicum student, which made my job a lot easier. We chose books cited in *Guided Reading,* by Fountas and Pinnell. With the use of running records and word inventories, we got baseline data on the kids and quickly got them into leveled materials that were appropriate for them. We worked on sequencing and comprehension. We then had literature circles, which was challenging to these kids. The groups varied, and I tried to meet with them at least two to three times a week. Those who were not readers I met with every day.

We planned around these books, and did a lot of thematic planning, branching out to find other books that matched the theme. Over time, they started reading. On Dr. Seuss day, they were reading. Jeremy read the first chapter in his pre-primer. David, another one of my slower students, picked up a book and simply started reading. I knew he could do it but I cried; I simply bawled. He was so worried to see me that way and asked what he had done wrong. I told him, "David, you did everything right." It was the best feeling, and it is why I love teaching first grade.

time is spent reading (a daily average of 9.2 minutes). Fifty percent of the children read only 4 minutes or less each day, and 30% read 2 minutes or less (10% did not read at all). It is no surprise that television watching consumed most of their after-school time (an average of 136.4 minutes daily). Yet, these researchers concluded that

> among all the ways children can spend their leisure time, average minutes per day reading books was the best and most consistent predictor of standardized comprehension test performance, size of vocabulary, and gains in reading achievement between second and fifth grade. (Fielding, Wilson, & Anderson, 1984, p. 151)

Greaney (1980) reviewed studies concerning leisure reading and discovered that "a number of studies have reported significant relationships between amount of leisure reading and level of pupil attainment" (p. 339). One of the studies Greaney points to was conducted decades ago by LaBrant (1936). His longitudinal study reported that students who completed a 6-year free reading program were, 24 years later, reading significantly more than most other groups to which they had been compared.

Fielding, Wilson, and Anderson (1984) note that reading trade books deepens knowledge of the forms of written language. Early experiences with the richness and variety found in children's books seem to give children reason to read, teaching them, as Trelease (1985) explains, not only "how to read, but to want to read" (p. 6).

For these reasons, it is easy to see that literature-based programs give purpose and pleasure to the process of learning to read, making skills instruction more meaningful, and in the end turning out lifelong readers.

▼▼▼▼▼▼▼▼

Summary

In this chapter, we gave an overall picture of how to teach reading in the classroom using children's literature. We accented Reader's Workshop as the model we regard most highly for engaging children in authentic reading events. We first discussed the overall structure of the workshop, including minilessons, independent reading time, and opportunities for response. We then looked at book selection from the vantage point of organizing your classroom with the greatest efficiency, noting the advantages and disadvantages to core books, individual copies, and text sets. We discussed how to get the workshop started in the first week of school and provided an outline of strategies for the teacher who is just beginning to test the waters in this process. Finally, we discussed how to get the workshop started in the primary classroom where independent reading and writing are still not realized but manageable.

▼▼▼▼▼▼▼▼

Children's Literature References

Ahlberg, Janet, & Ahlberg, Allan. (1978). *Each peach pear plum: An I-spy story.* New York: Viking.

Avi. (1994). *The barn.* New York: Orchard.

Banks, Lynne Reid. (1981). *The Indian in the cupboard.* New York: Doubleday.

Banks, Lynne Reid. (1989). *The fairy rebel.* New York: Camelot.

Bunting, Eve. (1991). *Fly away home* (Ronald Himler, Illus.). New York: Clarion.

Byars, Betsy. (1968). *The midnight fox.* New York: Viking.

Byars, Betsy. (1973). *The 18th emergency.* New York: Viking.

Byars, Betsy. (1977). *The pinballs.* New York: Harper & Row.

Byars, Betsy. (1984). *The computer nut.* New York: Viking.

Byars, Betsy. (1986). *The not-just-anybody family.* New York: Delacorte.

Byars, Betsy. (1988). *The burning questions of Bingo Brown.* New York: Viking.

Byars, Betsy. (1996). *Tornado.* New York: HarperCollins

Carle, Eric. (1971a). *Do you want to be my friend?* New York: Crowell.

Carle, Eric. (1971b). *The grouchy ladybug.* New York: Crowell.

Carle, Eric. (1971c). *The very hungry caterpillar.* New York: Crowell.

Carle, Eric. (1985). *The very busy spider.* New York: Putnam.

Carle, Eric. (1986). *Papa, please get the moon for me.* Saxonville, MA: Picture Book Studio.

Carle, Eric. (1990). *The very quiet cricket.* New York: Philomel.

Carle, Eric. (1993). *Eric Carle: Picture writer.* New York: Philomel.

Carle, Eric. (1995). *The very lonely firefly.* New York: Philomel.

Carle, Eric. (1999). *The very clumsy click beetle.* New York: Philomel.

Creech, Sharon. (1994). *Walk two moons.* New York: HarperCollins.

DeFelice, Cynthia. (1999). *Nowhere to call home.* New York: Farrar, Straus & Giroux.

Gannett, Ruth Stiles. (1948). *My father's dragon.* New York: Knopf.

Gantos, Jack. (1998). *Joey Pigza swallowed the key.* New York: Farrar, Straus & Giroux.

Griffin, Adele. (1997). *Split just right.* New York: Hyperion.

Hahn, Mary Downing. (1994). *Time for Andrew: A ghost story.* New York: Clarion.

Hahn, Mary Downing. (1995). *Look for me by moonlight.* New York: Clarion.

Howe, James. (1997). *The watcher.* New York: Atheneum.

Hurmence, Belinda. (1982). *A girl called Boy.* Boston: Houghton Mifflin.

Jacques, Brian. (1986). *Redwall.* New York: Philomel.

Myers, Walter Dean. (1999). *Monster.* New York: HarperCollins.

Naylor, Phyllis Reynolds. (1991). *Shiloh.* New York: Atheneum.

Paterson, Katherine. (1977). *Bridge to Terabithia.* New York: Crowell.

Peterson, John. (1970). *The Littles.* New York: Scholastic.

Rawls, Wilson. (1961). *Where the red fern grows.* New York: Doubleday.

Reeder, Carolyn. (1989). *Shades of gray.* New York: Macmillan.

Seldon, George. (1960). *The cricket in Times Square* (Garth Williams, Illus.). New York: Farrar, Straus & Giroux.

Sendak, Marice. (1963). *Where the wild things are.* New York: Harper & Row.

Speare, Elizabeth George. (1983). *The sign of the beaver.* Boston: Houghton Mifflin.

Spinelli, Jerry. (1997). *Wringer.* New York: HarperCollins.

Voigt, Cynthia. (1981). *Homecoming.* New York: Atheneum.

White, E. B. (1952). *Charlotte's web.* New York: Harper & Row.

White, E. B. (1970). *The trumpet of the swan.* New York: Harper & Row.

Winthrop, Elizabeth. (1985). *The castle in the attic.* New York: Holiday House.

▼▼▼▼▼▼▼▼

Professional References

Anderson, R. C., Hiebert, E. H., Scott, J. A., & Wilkinson, I. A. G. (1985). *Becoming a nation of readers: The report of the commission on reading.* Washington, DC: National Institute of Education.

Atwell, N. (1998). *In the middle: New understandings about writing, reading, and learning.* Portsmouth, NH: Heinemann. (Original work published 1987)

Bader, L. A., Veatch, J., & Eldredge, J. L. (1987). Trade books or basal readers? *Reading Improvement, 24,* 62–67.

Barrentine, S. J. (1996). Engaging with reading through interactive read-alouds. *The Reading Teacher, 50,* 36–43.

Chomsky, C. (1978). When you still can't read in third grade: After decoding, what? In J. Samuels (Ed.), *What research has to say about reading instruction* (pp. 13–30). Newark, DE: International Reading Association.

Cohen, D. (1968). The effect of literature on vocabulary and reading achievement. *Elementary English, 45,* 209–213, 217.

Cooper, J. D. (2000). *Literacy: Helping children construct meaning.* Boston: Houghton Mifflin.

Cox, C., & Zarillo, J. (1993). *Teaching reading with children's literature.* Upper Saddle River, NJ: Merrill/Prentice Hall.

Cullinan, B., Jaggar, A., & Strickland, D. (1974). Language expansion for black children in the primary grades: A research report. *Young Children, 29,* 98–112.

Daniels, H. (1994). *Literature circles: Voice and choice in the student-centered classroom.* York, ME: Stenhouse.

Eldredge, J. L., & Butterfield, D. (1986). Alternatives to traditional reading instruction. *The Reading Teacher, 40,* 32–37.

Fielding, L. G., Wilson, P. T., & Anderson, R. (1984). A new focus on free reading: The role of trade books in reading instruction. In T. E. Raphael (Ed.), *The contexts of school based literacy* (pp. 149–160). New York: Random House.

Gambrell, L. B., & Almasi, J. F. (1966). *Lively discussions! Fostering engaged reading.* Newark, DE: International Reading Association.

Goodman, Y., Goodman, K., & Bridges-Bird, L. (1990). *The whole language catalog.* Glencoe, IL: McGraw-Hill.

Greaney, Vincent. (1980). Factors related to amount and type of leisure reading. *Reading Research Quarterly, 15*(3), 337–357.

Gunning, T. G. (2000). *Creating literacy instruction for all children.* Boston: Allyn & Bacon.

Harste, J. C., Woodward, V. A., & Burke, C. L. (1988). *Creating classrooms for authors: The reading-writing connection.* Portsmouth, NH: Heinemann.

Heath, S. B. (1983). *Ways with words: Language, life, and work in communities and classrooms.* New York: Cambridge University Press.

Hill, B. C., Johnson, N. J., & Noe, K. L. S. (1995). *Literature circles and response.* Norwood, MA: Christopher-Gordon.

Holdaway, D. (1979). *The foundations of literacy.* Sydney, Australia: Ashton Scholastic.

Holdaway, D. (1982). Shared book experience: Teaching reading using favorite books. *Theory Into Practice, 21,* 293–300.

Klein, A. (1995). Sparking a love for reading: Literature circles with intermediate students. In B. C. Hill, N. J. Johnson, & K. L. S. Noe (Eds.), *Literature circles and response* (pp. 71–84). Norwood, MA: Christopher-Gordon.

LaBrant, L. L. (1936). *An evaluation of free reading in grades ten, eleven and twelve.* Columbus, OH: Ohio State University Press.

Martin, B., Jr., & Brogan, P. (1972). *Sounds of a young hunter.* Teachers Edition. New York: Holt, Rinehart and Winston.

McCracken, R., & McCracken, M. (1978). Modeling is the key to sustained silent reading. *The Reading Teacher, 31,* 406–408.

Peterson, R., & Eeds, M. (1994). *Grand conversations: Literature groups in action.* Ontario: Scholastic.

Reutzel, D. R., & Cooter, R. B., Jr. (1996). *Teaching children to read: From basals to books.* Upper Saddle River, NJ: Merrill/Prentice Hall.

Robb, L. (2000). *Teaching reading in middle school: A strategic approach to teaching reading that improves comprehension and thinking.* New York: Scholastic Professional Books.

Short, K. G., & Pierce, K. M. (1990). *Talking about books: Creating literate communities.* Portsmouth, NH: Heinemann.

Topping, K. (1989). Peer tutoring and paired reading: Combining two powerful techniques. *The Reading Teacher, 42,* 488–494.

Trelease, J. (1985). *The read aloud handbook.* New York: Viking/Penguin.

Tunnell, M. O. & Jacobs, J. S. (1989). Using "real" books: Research findings on literature-based reading instruction. *The Reading Teacher, 42,* 470–477.

Weaver, C. (1994). *Reading process and practice: From socio-psycholinguistics to whole language* (2nd ed.). Portsmouth, NH: Heinemann.

White, J. H., Vaughan, J. L., & Rorie, I. L. (1986). Picture of a classroom where reading is for real. *The Reading Teacher, 40,* 84–86.

Evaluation and Assessment

14
CHAPTER

If you want to cover

The Ups and Downs of School

Consider as a READ ALOUD

Thank You, Mr. Falker,
by Patricia Polacco

Consider as a TEXT SET

Joey Pigza Swallowed the Key,
by Jack Gantos

Anastasia Krupnik,
by Lois Lowry

There's a Boy in the Girl's Bathroom,
by Louis Sachar

Nothing But the Truth,
by Avi

Stargone John,
by Ellen Kindt McKenzie

THANK YOU, MR. FALKER
by Patricia Polacco

Student Response

PATRICIA POLACCO

Thank you, Mr. Falker

To visit a classroom exploring the issues of Evaluation and Assessment, please go to Chapter 14 of our companion website at **www.prenhall. com/darigan**

Jennifer ushered her parents into the classroom and, as rehearsed, helped them to their seats. She was dressed in a two-piece outfit with a skirt and top whose collar and cuffs were delicately graced with blue flowers. It was the first time she had worn anything other than hand-me-down jeans and threadbare T-shirts all year. Her mother also wore a dress, her stepfather a shirt and tie. From the way he tugged at his collar it appeared he, too, was not used to such finery.

However, this was a special day. After all, this was the day of Jennifer's first *real* parent conference. The day she and her fifth-grade teacher, Dr. Darigan, and her parents met to see all that she had done since the beginning of school. She had been preparing for this all year but these last 2 weeks had been the hardest—and the most fun. Her portfolio, an accumulation of work samples, test scores, photographs, painted a picture of her as a learner.

Darigan had his students keep all their work in a partitioned accordion folder by subject, making sure they dated and added anecdotal notes detailing what each of the assignments were. When conference time came around, they sorted through all of the papers and, as Jennifer recognized, were able to see their improvement in reading, writing, and other subjects.

"Look at how short and simple my sentences were at the beginning of the year," she remarked. "I really got better. We read lots of picture books, and I figured out how stories worked. It's like you could see that there was always a problem for someone to solve and then they solved it.

"Dr. D made us write our own books for Mrs. Ahle's first graders down the hall. We made sure we added a problem and then had to figure out how to fix it. Now, I see problems everywhere. I can see them in every chapter of the novels I'm reading. Like in the one I'm reading right now [*Turn Homeward, Hannalee,* by Patricia Beatty], Hannalee and her mother are all scared because the Yankee soldiers are marching south and the Confederate soldiers are burning the bridge outside of town to keep them away. They are trying to figure out what to do next—but her mom is real scared! They gotta figure out what to do."

With determined pride and confidence, Jennifer explains, during their 20-minute conference, what she sees as her strong points, what she could improve on, and where she has grown. Darigan adds comments along the way to support her statements, including standardized test scores from last year, and unit and chapter tests taken this year. But the test scores, though good enough, pale in comparison to the authentic and realistic growth that is demonstrated in this portfolio conference.

After teachers have embraced the concept of literature study and its significant value in bringing children to literacy, these questions inevitably come up:

1. How am I going to evaluate my students? How do I know they've gotten it?
2. How can I use my assessments to generate positive student attitudes to reading?
3. How do I form a complete profile on each of my students?

Reader's Workshop is not a program that lends itself particularly well to multiple-choice, true-false, or fill-in-the-blank tests that can be easily scored. In this chapter, we attempt to answer these questions, as well as provide you with some specific advice for meaningful assessment and evaluation. What we hope will occur is that the teacher and child will have a much better understanding of the child's individual progress, and that he or she will find a mentor in the teacher, as did many of the children in the chapter's text set, "The Ups and Downs of School."

▼▼▼▼▼▼▼

Evaluating Children's Reading

Reading gets more attention than any other part of the curriculum in the elementary school. And for good reason: Reading is the basic skill needed for survival and continued learning in a literate society. As such, the evaluation of a child's reading has always been an important part of the public school. Parents and educators alike are concerned with how well our children are doing in this consequential area.

Although a host of definitions identify what reading is, the explanation in *Becoming a Nation of Readers* (Anderson, Hiebert, Scott, & Wilkinson, 1985) is as clear and comprehensive as any.

■ Skilled reading is constructive. Becoming a skilled reader requires learning to reason about written material using knowledge from everyday life and from disciplined fields of study.

■ Skilled reading is fluent. Becoming a skilled reader depends on mastering basic processes to the point where they are automatic, so that attention is freed for the analysis of meaning.

■ Skilled reading is strategic. Becoming a skilled reader requires learning to control one's reading in relation to one's purpose, the nature of the material, and whether one is comprehending.

■ Skilled reading is motivated. Becoming a skilled reader requires learning to sustain attention and learning that written material can be interesting and informative.

■ Skilled reading is a lifelong pursuit. Becoming a skilled reader is a matter of continuous practice, development, and refinement. (pp. 17–18)

Traditional Methods

To determine how well a child is reading, an accurate evaluation should at least touch on each point in this list. Until recent years, however, the standard procedure for evaluating reading was limited to administering a national test. These tests report a child's reading level in specific and tidy numbers. If a boy is reading at 4.2, for instance, that translates into his reading at the same mean level as the average American child in fourth grade, second month of instruction. Such a score would please the parents and teacher of a boy in second grade but not be such good news for the parents and teacher of a child just finishing sixth.

Although standardized tests still are used widely, we now know that reading is not so easily evaluated. Standardized reading tests measure only a narrow spectrum of total reading (Gillet & Temple, 2000; Johnston, 1984). They are restricted to easily measurable elements of the reading process, particularly recall of information, some literal thinking, and some vocabulary matching. Because standardized tests reflect only this limited view, they are no longer trusted as the definitive measure of a child's current reading abilities (Cambourne & Turbill, 1990). National tests (1) are inconsistent with our knowledge of reading processes; (2) don't capture the complexities of reading acquisition and learning; (3) require students to engage in decontextualized tasks with ecologically invalid materials; and (4) offer teachers little help in guiding and directing students' reading instructional programs in classrooms (Baumann & Murray, 1994).

Work sheets also carry a caution: Although widely used, they do not help students learn to read or help them read better. Their use is not related to year-to-year gains in reading proficiency (Leinhardt, Sigmond, & Cooley, 1981; Raphael & McMahon, 1994; Rosenshine & Stevens, 1984). Too often, they are used to keep students quiet and busy, are poorly designed, and demand only the most perfunctory level of attention from students (Anderson et al.,

1985, p. 76). Workbook and skill-sheet use should be cut back to the minimum (Reutzel & Cooter, 2000).

Observing and Record Keeping Are Key

How, then, can a teacher know how well a child is reading? The five points we mentioned from *Becoming a Nation of Readers* can be checked by:

- listening to the child read aloud;
- talking with the child about the content; and
- observing the child reading.

Observations in each area should be included in an anecdotal reading record for each child. This personalized record keeps track of and compares the child's progress from one grading period to the next. Anecdotal records are idiosyncratic for each child, identifying precisely the strengths and weaknesses of each child's reading abilities. They also contain teacher observations about the child's broader orientation to reading, including difficulty or ease in finding interesting titles, attention span, involvement in books, and any other telling observations. As such, anecdotal reading records tell much more about the particular child's reading abilities and growth or regression than statistically normed tests (Wood & Algozzine, 1994, chapter 7).

Listen to the Child Read Aloud

The quickest way to evaluate reading skills is to listen to the child read aloud a passage of text for the first time. Most of the individual skills of reading are evident in this oral reading, and a teacher can identify areas of strength and weakness by observing how the child decodes and the child's fluency, which includes rate, expression, and smoothness. How well the child can decode is evident in which words cause him or her difficulty and how the child unlocks the pronunciation. The rate should approximate normal speech. Expression, which should be as varied as the content demands, reveals how well the child understands and interacts with the text. And smoothness shows the child's confidence and competence in reading for meaning.

If you follow along on a separate copy of the text as the student reads, you can mark the child's specific errors, or, as Goodman (1990) refers to them, miscues—deviations from the expected responses to the print. Further, you can jot down other observations about the child's behavior, and this all becomes part of the student's anecdotal reading record. We have found Rhodes and Shanklin's Classroom Reading Miscue Assessment (1993), also referred to as CRMA, of particular help for the general population of your classroom, along with a modified version of Goodman's Miscue Analysis (1985) for specific cases of children who are struggling.

Before beginning either the CRMA or the Modified Miscue Analysis, make certain the child is comfortable and in a place that will have little to no distractions. You need to inform the child that you are going to listen to him or her read. Say that you

will be taking a few notes as he or she reads. You need to further explain that if the child comes to a word or phrase that he or she cannot unlock, you will not be able to help. He or she will just need to skip over the problem area and go on. Lastly, the child needs to know that after reading the selection, he or she is going to retell you everything he or she remembers about the text. Because the stage is set with all the expectations, the child will not be surprised at any of the procedures.

Classroom Reading Miscue Assessment

Simply stated, Rhodes and Shanklin (1993) suggest that when using the CRMA, the teacher just listens to the child read and records whether he or she is maintaining semantic meaning for each sentence. Using a T-Chart (see Figure 14–1), the teacher places one hash mark per sentence in either the "yes" column or the "no" column, indicating whether or not the child read the sentence and was able to keep the essential meaning intact. They caution that the sentence need not be read perfectly. After the child has finished each entire sentence, you determine whether the essential semantic meaning was maintained. This inventory helps you to discover what strategies the child is using and gives you a beginning picture of the meaning he or she is making of the text.

For example, the child may see the sentence, "When the girl got to her *house* after baseball practice it was bustling with activity." But she may read, "When the girl got to her *home* after baseball practice it was bustling with activity." Substituting *home* for *house* is semantically acceptable and, therefore, the teacher would place a hash mark under the "yes" column of the T-Chart. However, if the child were to read, "When the girl got to her *horse* after baseball practice it was bustling with activity" and further made no attempt to self-correct this miscue, the teacher would assume that semantic meaning was not made and thus mark the response under the "no" column.

CRMA retelling. After the child has completed the selection, you would then ask him or her to do a retelling of the story to determine what meaning was made. You would expect that the child could tell you about the characters and their development, the plot and sequence of events, and some general connections made to his or her life and to other similar books. Some probing may be necessary, but the teacher should be wary not to place words in the student's mouth. Your intent is to get the child to recall and articulate everything he or she can remember about what was just read.

In these one-on-one settings, you can use the CRMA to listen to each child in your class read. During this time, you can assess his or her general reading abilities. If you do two or three assessments every day, you can cover the entire class in a matter of two to three weeks. It is suggested that these be done at the beginning of the year, repeated mid-year, and done again at the end of the year to show growth and development over time. As you can see, this instrument gives you a good picture of how the child is handling the text with a minimum of effort.

Modified Miscue Analysis

When parents wonder how their child is doing, the most helpful response a teacher can give is to ask them to listen to the child read aloud. Even the untrained adult can get a fairly accurate impression of the child's skill in recognizing familiar words, figuring out new words, and interacting with the text when hearing the child read. What we introduce here is a more sophisticated system to analyze these deviations from the expected response to the text.

For those students who are having a particularly difficult time, you can do a more in-depth analysis using our version of a modified miscue analysis. Rest assured that there will almost always be a small handful of such children in each class every year you teach, and this instrument helps you to see what strategies the child is using as well as what the child further needs to do to become an efficient, fluent reader. What we have done is glean the best from the Miscue Analysis (Goodman, 1967; Rhodes & Shanklin, 1993), the Informal Reading Inventory (Burns, 1998), and the Running Record (Clay, 1985).

Scoring codes you need to use. Again, you are going to have a child read aloud for you. The material used can be from a trade book, a story from a basal reader, or more simply, a selection from a published IRI form. Your intent is to have the child read the material and make a minimum of 25 miscues. This time, it is of great importance that you audiotape-record the child's reading so you can return to it to document the exact responses the child has made. On a separate sheet, you take the script of what the child

Yes	No
///	//

FIGURE 14–1 T-Chart.

Note: For a little practice in doing a CRMA, you can access the Companion Website that accompanies this text and listen to Kendra read text from *The Adventures of King Midas,* by Lynne Reid Banks. Voice, text, and T-Chart are included.

DID YOU KNOW?

Lynne Reid Banks has written a number of other books you may know. We have cited her throughout this book, but her series beginning with *The Indian in the Cupboard* has been most popular. You may want to read them all. The final book, *The Mystery of the Cupboard,* provides both a good story and the historical roots of the magic medicine cabinet that gives life to small plastic toys.

has read and record any deviations that child has made from the text. Using the following codes, you can highlight:

1. *omissions* by circling the omitted word(s)
2. *insertions* by using a ^ and writing the word above
3. *substitutions* by crossing out the substituted word and writing what was substituted above

These three deviations constitute the bulk of the miscues we suggest you score. Beyond these, you may want to mark other notable reading behaviors; though they are not scored as miscues, it is a good idea to record them for your own information. You may begin to see a pattern. For example, you may see that many words are being sounded out or that the child retreats, continuously repeating text in an effort to unlock its meaning. Mark such behaviors in the following ways:

Words *sounded out* with (SO)
Words *repeated* with ® _____
Words *self-corrected* with (SC)

With this analysis, you are attempting to discern what the child is doing with the text he or she is given. What strategies is the child using? What does he or she find difficult? When you establish what the child knows and what the child is struggling with, you can more ably consider the next steps in your instruction.

Recording data. After the child has read the selection, you will need to fill out the form shown in Figure 14–2 to analyze better the miscues the child has made.

In the first column (Text), you need to write what the text actually says, and in the second column (Reader), you record what the reader reads. For example, the sentence reads, " 'I been a slave all my life, Tommy' said Jeff sitting up in the hay." The child, however, may read, " 'I been a slave all my life, Tommy' said Jeff *still* up in the hay." You would place "sitting" in the first column and "still" in the second.

After you have entered all your data, you will want to analyze each miscue for its quality. In column A, you want to decide if the miscue was ESL- or dialect-related. In other words, did the child's language strengths affect the way the text was read? In column B, you want to look at the entire sentence in which the miscue occurs and determine if, given what the child read, the sentence's meaning was left intact. (This should look familiar—it is essentially what you recorded in your CRMA.) In column C, you mark whether the miscue was corrected. This is important because it sheds light on how closely the child is attending to both the actual text and the meaning. Finally, in column D, you mark whether the miscue was *either* meaning-preserving (column B) or whether it was self-corrected (column C).

Now, it may seem that column D is redundant; just a repetition of columns B and C. And in a way, it is. Column D merely acts as a summary of columns B and C, providing the teacher with information about the ability of this child in his or her attempt to make meaning. A "yes" in Column D would indicate that the child has *either* substituted a meaningful word *or* self-corrected the miscue that he or she made. The more checks in the "yes" column, the more meaning the child is making. However, you may come across a child with a large amount of miscues on the "no" side of the ledger. This would indicate that either meaning is not being made or the child is only attempting to "sound out" words, forsaking meaning altogether. Your goal, as teacher, is to help the child read strategically so that you see more and more of those "yes" checks in column D.

These data will allow you to begin to see patterns in the child's reading, where his or her strengths lie as well as where he or she needs to be supported. A tally of each column and a calculation of the percentages for each will give you a basis for your instruction and can be used to compare to subsequent Modified Miscue Analyses that you perform during the rest of the school year.

Talk with the Child About the Content—Retelling

The child's understanding of content is often evident during discussions in small groups or even with the entire class. By directing questions to a specific student, the

Reader's Name _____ Date _____ Reading Selection _____ _____		A. Was the miscue dialect-related or ESL-related? (Used only if applicable)		B. Was the essential meaning of the *sentence* left intact?		C. Was the miscue corrected?		D. Was the miscue *either* meaning-preserving OR corrected?	
Text	**Reader**	**Yes**	**No**	**Yes**	**No**	**Yes**	**No**	**Yes**	**No**
1.									
2.									
3.									
4.									
5.									
6.									
7.									
8.									
9.									
10.									
11.									
12.									
13.									
14.									
15.									
16.									
17.									
18.									
19.									
20.									
21.									
22.									
23.									
24.									
25.									
Totals									
Percents									

Adapted from "Miscue Analysis Form" (Constance Weaver, *Reading Process and Practice: From Socio-Psycholinguistics to Whole Language.* 2nd edition. Portsmouth, NH: Heinemann. 1994).

FIGURE 14–2 Miscue analysis form.

teacher can infer how well that student understood the story or information from the reading. It is impossible to keep records for all children in all discussions, but when something noteworthy occurs, it is wise to record it in the child's anecdotal record.

Asking the child to tell you about the passage or story just read can check comprehension. The teacher should be looking for evidence of understanding of the text in literal elements (detail, sequence, vocabulary) and nonliteral elements (main idea, cause and effect, and inference). If the child hesitates, the teacher then can ask leading questions that deal with the content or element in question. The forms in Figure 14–3 will aid you in recording the child's retelling for both narrative and expository texts.

Whether in one-on-one interviews or in discussions, anecdotal records of comprehension should be kept periodically for each child. Note the ease (or hesitation) of response, the degree of completeness, the literal and nonliteral elements that the student voluntarily included in a response as well as responses indicating a lack of understanding.

Observe the Child Reading

Watching the child read provides information about skills as well as motivation. Children whose lips move or whose fingers follow each line of print are not reading as fluently as they will be with more practice and confidence. Teachers can assess student motivation by observing how focused children are when they search the classroom library for a book, how quickly they get ready to read when it is time for Sustained Silent Reading (SSR), how well they stay on task, how long they stay on task, and how often and how eagerly they discuss what they read with their teacher or peers.

Measuring the Amount of Reading

If teachers want to evaluate students' growth in overall reading abilities, they will want to measure the time their students spend reading in books of their own choosing. Of all outside school activities, the best predictor of reading growth in children between the second and fifth grades is the average number of minutes per day they spend reading books (Anderson et al., 1985, p. 77). Stephen Krashen (1991) confirmed that students who spend time reading strengthen their reading skills considerably. He examined a number of studies that compared growth in reading as a result of direct reading instruction with progress made when students simply read books.

In face-to-face comparisons, reading is consistently shown to be more efficient than direct instruction. Other studies confirm that direct instruction has little or no effect. The only conclusions we can draw from these findings can be stated easily: Reading is a powerful means of developing literacy, of developing reading comprehension ability, writing style, vocabulary, grammar, and spelling. Direct instruction is not (Krashen, 1991, p. 22).

While reading meaningful text, children practice all the subskills of the reading act. Naturally, the more children read, the better readers they become. Bernice Cullinan (1981) illustrates this principle with the following model: Reading skills improve with practice, as does the ability to perform any task we repeat over and over. The more we read, the better we get at reading. The better we get at reading, the more pleasure we find in it. And the more pleasure it gives us, the more we practice—with the result that we get better. (See Figure 14–4.)

Although some see a conflict between emphasizing skills instruction and focusing on engaged personal reading, there really is no conflict between the two. The aim of both approaches is to have students become more proficient, skilled, experienced readers.

Note: For a little practice in doing a Modified Miscue Analysis, you can access the Companion Website that accompanies this text and listen to Kendra read text from **The Drinking Gourd** by F. N. Monjo. Voice, text, and form are all included.

Narrative Text Note: Indicate any probing with a "P"	All	Some	None
Character recall			
Character development			
Setting			
Relationship of events			
Plot			
Theme			

Overall retelling			

Reader's retelling transcription:

Retelling summary: ☐ many details, logical order ☐ some details, some order ☐ few details, disorder

Expository Text Note: Indicate any probing with a "P"	All	Some	None
Major concepts			
Generalizations			
Specific information			
Logical structuring			
Overall retelling			

Reader's thumbnail transcription:

Retelling summary: ☐ many details, logical order ☐ some details, some order ☐ few details, disorder

FIGURE 14–3 Retelling scoring sheets.

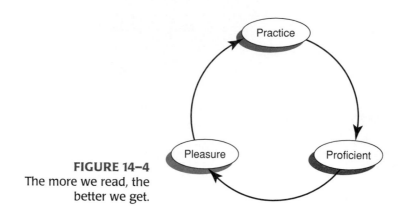

FIGURE 14–4
The more we read, the better we get.

Record Keeping

If reading more helps children read better, one way to evaluate progress is to keep track of how much each child reads. This information then makes it evident that the reader is practicing measurable reading skills as well as interacting with print. The three measurable parts of the individual reading activity are books, pages, and time. When children know that their reading is being recorded (and often teachers suggest a minimum or guideline), then keeping track only of the number of books presents a problem because books vary so much in length. In an effort to make things fairer, some teachers count total pages. Yet pages are hardly uniform. Because of their size and number of words, a page in one children's novel may have 60 words, whereas a page in another may have 450. The most democratic method of offering a goal and keeping a record is to look at the time spent reading. If a slow reader and a fast reader spend the same 20 minutes reading, the fast reader naturally will cover more ground, but they put forth equal effort.

In an effort to get students reading on their own, two teachers, unknown to each other and half a nation apart, created similar reading programs. Kemie Nix of Atlanta, Georgia, and Katie Blake of Provo, Utah, both knew that students who read successfully only at school run the risk of losing the reading habit once June rolls around. Each reasoned that teaching children to find reading time in their own world, unaffected by the schedules and bells of the classroom, would increase their chances of becoming self-motivated readers. Samples of the record-keeping forms are reproduced here. (See Figure 14–5.) By having the children pay attention to what they read, how much they read, and how much time they spent every day, students, for the first time, were aware of their own reading habits, and both teachers found that they adjusted accordingly. For example, when the children missed a day or two, both teachers noted that they naturally picked up the slack and read as part of their daily routine.

The similarities of the plans are remarkable. Both focus on students' finding their own meaning in books outside of class and provide a nudge in that direction by reminding them to read regularly. Both give readers complete control over their reading materials. Perfection is reading 5 days per week. Students do not have to report on the books they read. They read for short periods of time, and the results of their reading are reported only to the teacher, not displayed on a wall for all to see.

Each plan differs slightly from the other. Blake assigned a specific number of minutes by grade level; Nix left the required time spent reading to each teacher's discretion. For Blake, daily reading time could be either a child's private reading, or a parent's reading to the child, or the child's reading to the parent. Blake's record-keeping system is visible in the home (she recommends putting the form on the refrigerator) and can be used easily by all students, including those in kindergarten through second grade; Nix's reading record stays in the school and is more difficult for younger children (K–2) to handle. Once individual teachers understand the principles in these two plans, they can use them to structure a program of their own.

I read: _____   Extra time: _____   Monday,
I did not read: _____
Author: _____   Title: _____

I read: _____   Extra time: _____   Tuesday,
I did not read: _____
Author: _____   Title: _____

I read: _____   Extra time: _____   Wednesday,
I did not read: _____
Author: _____   Title: _____

I read: _____   Extra time: _____   Thursday,
I did not read: _____
Author: _____   Title: _____

I read: _____   Extra time: _____   Weekend,
I did not read: _____
Author: _____   Title: _____

I read: _____   Extra time: _____   Monday,
I did not read: _____
Author: _____   Title: _____

I read: _____   Extra time: _____   Tuesday,
I did not read: _____
Author: _____   Title: _____

I read: _____   Extra time: _____   Wednesday,
I did not read: _____
Author: _____   Title: _____

I read: _____   Extra time: _____   Thursday,
I did not read: _____
Author: _____   Title: _____

I read: _____   Extra time: _____   Weekend,
I did not read: _____
Author: _____   Title: _____

FIGURE 14–5   Kemie Nix's out-of-school reading program.

In addition to the daily reading record, each child should maintain a list of titles and authors read that year. These data, along with a compilation of how many minutes the children have read in SSR and how many titles the teacher has read aloud, are formidable. In a world that sometimes seems driven by scientific research and statistical data, the number of books read, the number of pages, and amount of time spent reading can sometimes be overlooked. Yet these numbers are hard data that show genuine growth.

Kemie Nix's Out-of-School Reading Program
Atlanta, Georgia

1. Students read books of their own choosing, but daily reading at home is a part of classroom requirements.

2. Teacher makes booklet of forms for entire period of record keeping. For a school year, do the following:
   a. Make one form without dates.
   b. Duplicate number needed for one complete booklet. Because one form records 2 weeks of reading, 18 are needed for a 36-week year.
   c. Type in dates for entire year. One copy is now finished.
   d. Now duplicate—one for each student.
   e. Put in inexpensive folder secured by brads.

3. Booklets are kept in one spot in classroom and filled out daily by each student.

4. Student checks "I read" if required time was spent reading the previous day.

5. If student misses a day, the reason for not reading is to be written in the space for that day.

6. Reading does not have to be made up. Goal is to make reading delightful and easy, and no one performs without missing occasionally.

7. Grading is according to teacher prerogative. Nix uses "Excellent" for not missing, "Very Good" for missing one day, and "Good" for missing two days. Missing three or more days simply cancels the week—counts neither for nor against student.

8. Progress is checked each week by teacher, preferably with student in a one-minute visit. Whole class can open booklets on desks with teacher circulating.

9. Students write title and name of author each day, even if book takes a number of days to finish. No ditto marks. Writing the titles and authors results in students developing more confidence and competence in knowing and talking about books.

10. Include a lined page at the front of the booklet to record each title and author as books are finished. Teachers can assess progress at a glance, and students often are surprised to see how many books they have read.

FIGURE 14–5   *continued*

Children With Reading Problems

Increasing the amount of reading will not automatically increase the reading abilities of all children, though Krashen and McQuillan note "there is strong evidence that free voluntary reading is effective in developing literacy" (1998, p. 410). About 85% of the children in a given classroom will improve their reading skills markedly just from spending additional time with good books. The remaining 15% will need more specific help (McCormick, 1987, p. 12). Those 15% have problems in at least one of three areas: context clues, sight reading, and phonics. Roughly two thirds of that 15% have difficulty with context clues and sight reading and can be helped by more contact with

meaningful language, partly solved by increased involvement with trade books. The remaining third of that 15%
need additional phonics help. When encouraged and allowed to spend more time with books of their own choosing, 85% of all students will respond favorably and grow in
their reading abilities. The teacher then has more time to
focus on those three to five children—the remaining
15%—who need special attention.

The Ohio Reading Recovery program, reported by
Boehnlein (1987) to be an American version of New
Zealand's Reading Recovery program, is specifically targeted at beginning readers who have a profile that will
make failure likely. Results of a controlled study match
those of the New Zealand findings, which are best en-
capsulated in this remarkable statement:

> After an average of 15 to 20 weeks, or 30 to 40 hours of instruction, 90% of the
> children whose pretest scores were in the lowest 20 percent of their class catch up
> to the average of their class or above and *never need remediation again.* (Boehn-
> lein, 1987, p. 33)

The Ohio Reading Recovery program confirmed that gains are maintained, and
when compared to control groups, the Reading Recovery children "not only made
greater gains than the other high risk children who received no help, but they also made
greater gains than the children who needed no help" (Boehnlein, 1987, p. 33). Continued success has placed this program at the forefront in the field when it comes to helping readers who are experiencing great difficulties (Deford, Lyons, & Pinnell, 1991).

Another experiment dealing with literature-based reading and children at high
risk of failure, the Open Sesame program, was conducted at P.S. 192 on New York
City's west side (Larrick, 1987). Ninety-two percent of the children in P.S. 192 came
from non-English-speaking homes, 96% were below the poverty level, and 80% spoke
no English when entering school. The Open Sesame program began with 225 kindergarten students and gave them an opportunity to read in an unpressured, pleasurable
way—no basals, no workbooks. Immersion in children's literature and language experience approaches to reading and writing were the major instructional thrusts, and
skills were taught primarily in meaningful context as children asked for help in writing. As the year concluded, all 225 students could read their dictated stories and many
of the picture books shown in class. Some were even reading on a second-grade level.
School officials were so impressed that they made a written commitment to extend the
program gradually through sixth grade. The following year, all 350 first graders were
happily reading English—60% on or above grade level. In fact, only 3 of the 350 failed
to pass district comprehension tests, and those 3 had been in the United States less
than 6 months.

McIntyre and Freppon (1994) found in a 2-year study that children learned alphabetic concepts and basic skills necessary for reading and writing in both a skills-
based classroom and a whole language classroom. The difference was that in the latter setting, children were able to learn through reading and writing of actual texts and
not through synthetic, isolated events.

▼▼▼▼▼▼▼

Ways to Generate Positive Reader Response

Although increased skills come as a by-product of increased reading, many teachers
are interested in what can be done to involve the hearts and minds of children in the
books that they read.

▪ How can we help them become more interested in their reading?

▪ What can we do to get them to respond favorably to books?

Before we get to the specific approaches and activities, it is important to understand the principles that lead to successful involvement with books. Madeleine L'Engle (1980) outlined perhaps the main characteristic we teachers want to capitalize upon.

> Readers usually underestimate their own importance. If a reader cannot create a book along with the writer, the book will never come to life. Creative involvement: That's the difference between reading a book and watching TV.
>
> In watching TV, we are passive—sponges; we do nothing. In reading we must become creators, imagining the setting of the story, seeing the facial expressions, hearing the inflection of the voices. The author and reader "know" each other; they meet on the bridge of words. (pp. 37–38)

We want readers to "create a book along with the writer." We want them to live in the book and to be active in their experience and response.

Reading Aloud as a Model of "Living in the Book"

We have said this throughout this book, but it bears repeating: The teacher who joyfully and passionately reads aloud to his or her class daily plants those seeds of love for reading that will bear abundant fruits as the readers mature. When students can see the benefits and feel the pull of story every day, they are far more likely to become interested in reading (May, 1998).

Favorable Response

To keep them from being sponges, we must provide them the assignments and activities that allow the kind of reading to take place where reader and author "meet on the bridge of words."

If an activity allows and encourages readers to respond in a way that L'Engle calls "creative involvement," the assignment is generally a plus. When used with self-selected books, such an activity is helpful when it adheres to three principles: (1) students choose the books they wish to respond to, (2) students choose the activities, and (3) students read most books without any obligation to respond.

Even when students are enthusiastic about a certain way of responding to books, teachers need to remember that variety is the key to keeping them involved. No response or activity designed to involve readers with their books works for long. Students may love recording their personal thoughts in a reading journal, but if it is required for every book, the idea wears thin. As one teacher said, "What I want when they finish reading ***Tuck Everlasting*** is a gleam in their eyes." If assigned responses—like the traditional book report—dim that gleam, they need to be rethought.

The traditional book report (focusing on elements of fiction, including plot, characters, setting, style, and theme) has done more to kill the love of reading in Americans ages 9 to 18 than any other idea to come from the schools (Root, 1975). Cunningham and Allington (1999) state that when adults were asked to respond to their own elementary school experiences, book reports were the "most commonly mentioned 'turn-off' " (p. 44). Traditional book reports are almost universally detested. Ask any American group how many had to write traditional book reports in school (many hands go up), and then ask how many remember the task with fondness (hardly a hand rises). They continue to be used because some teachers demand tangible evidence that the child has read the book. Of course, it is possible for students to write reports on books they have not read. Any sixth grader can offer a variety of ways: Rent the movie. Read the front flap. Talk to someone about the book. Use someone else's old book report. Read about the book in *Junior Plots*. Or, for the daring, invent the book—title, author, plot, characters—the entire thing. The only defense for traditional book reports is that they foster imagination by teaching kids to cheat creatively.

The following response options offer alternatives to the traditional book report.

Group Responses

Grand Conversations

For those books or poems everyone has read or has had read to them, discussions can provide the opportunities for meaningful responses. Peterson and Eeds (1994) call this approach "grand conversations," which are characterized by teachers participating fully in the discussion where they model and share their thought processes and personal interpretations about the story. The teacher is not the central focus, however, and needs to be careful that adult comments do not become pronouncements. The spotlight is on the book and the readers' responses. The teacher simply participates by being a voice with the students (Eeds & Peterson, 1997; Wells, 1995). Teachers allow and encourage students to share their personal responses, providing open-ended prompts when necessary for group discussion: "What did you notice in the story?" "What do you remember from the story?" "Does anything in the story remind you of your own life?" "Did you find anything in the story that was funny?"

Grand conversations can also include the discussion of literary merit and technique. As long as the questions do not have one right answer, so that the talk is truly a discussion, children can become involved. "What hints did the author drop to prepare us for the ending?" "Are there any facts or details in the book that let us know Josh was not to be trusted?" "Can you find an image—a picture in your mind—put there by the author that helps you to see the castle clearly?"

Teachers must be prepared for discussion that goes beyond their own preparation and understanding. In grand conversations, even a 6-year-old can notice something an experienced teacher has missed.

When discussing William Steig's *Sylvester and the Magic Pebble*, 6-year-old Tracy responded to an illustration showing Sylvester using the magic pebble to abruptly stop a rainstorm as ducks in the background peer skyward in confusion. Tracy shared with her teacher examples of things she thought were funny:

DID YOU KNOW?

Despite the tremendous success of *Sylvester and the Magic Pebble,* the book has had its detractors. Over the years, a number of our students have told us that they have heard of groups who wanted to ban the book for its illustrations. At first, we were dumbfounded. What could be so horrible about this lovely little modern fantasy? Was it that Sylvester Duncan and his parents were donkeys, and readers were thinking only of the three-letter equivalent? No, it was simply that the police who came to help find Sylvester when he was missing were drawn as pigs. Perhaps the movement toward Political Correctness started longer ago than we thought.

Tracy:	When Sylvester finds the red pebble—and the ducks are cute. . . .
Teacher:	The what?
Tracy:	The ducks are cute. . . .
Teacher:	The ducks are cute. They've got their bills up in the air like they're just enjoying the sunshine, having a grand time, uh-huh. . . .
Tracy:	Or else they're thinking, "How'd that happen?"
Teacher:	How'd what happen?
Tracy:	The rain started, then stopped.
Teacher:	Yes! Of course they're thinking that!
Tracy:	They go—"It started a little while ago—what happened?"

The teacher was looking at the picture but had not noticed the ducks. She was dumbfounded that a 6-year-old had picked up on a subtle point of interpretation that an adult had overlooked (Peterson & Eeds, 1994, pp. 17–18).

Literature Circles

After observing a number of small groups of elementary school children discussing books, Harvey Daniels (1994) identified specific kinds of responses that kept reappearing. He then named these responses, for example: Discussion Director—assumed the role of keeping things moving along; Connector—centered on connections to parts of the child's life or other books beyond the one being discussed; Vocabulary Enricher—noticed the author's specific word choices. Using a small group of students, Daniels explained the clearly defined roles, allowed the children to practice them, and then assigned each member of the group to play a particular role in a discussion. They changed roles over a 2-week period, allowing them both to participate and to observe as each child centered on just one aspect of a discussion. The idea of a literature circle is to make students aware of the kinds of responses that are possible, give them practice with each, and move as quickly as possible to the desired end: All participants play all the roles in genuine discussions of books.

Reading Groups

The teacher forms small groups of readers by having multiple copies of a number of books and then telling the entire class about five or six of the titles. Each student is then allowed to choose one that sounds interesting. Those reading the same book naturally belong to one group.

Because children read at different rates and with different intensities, one problem in choreographing small-group responses is having everyone read the same book without making it seem like work. One member of a group may finish the book overnight, whereas another might take a couple of weeks to get to the last page. One way to allow for this natural difference is to plan for small-group responses to take about 3 weeks. Let students read at their natural rates, and those who finish first can move on to other titles during SSR or at home, wherever the reading is being done. Those who are moving more slowly have 2 weeks to complete the book, and then the group responds sometime during the third week.

To provide necessary variety, the teacher can offer the groups four or five response options for the first 3-week period. Then the next time, each group may be allowed to choose from one section of the possibilities listed in Figure 14–6. The time after that, the students might come up with their own plan. The idea is that the responses are always honest and varied. And for that reason, small reading groups should not be in constant session but should have liberal vacations between the 3-week periods.

Individual Reader Responses

No matter how interesting and varied reader responses might be, readers do not want to make even an informal response to every book they read. If you finish a particularly gripping novel out on the beach one hot and sunny summer day, you don't automatically jump up and head for a closet in search of a shoe box to construct a diorama as a response to the book. Most likely you turn to your friend or significant other and tell him or her a bit about what you've just read, highlighting the details and your favorite parts. If you had to do a project for every book you read, you'd soon lose your desire to read. Think about how this applies to the primary student who reads a book a day: Insisting that students do something with every title is sure to backfire. In fact, most of the books a person reads should be left alone—the reading is sufficient.

But every so often, perhaps a few times every grading period, teachers can ask students to respond to a book they have read by completing an activity. Allowing the students to select the title and to have some choice in the method of response are both essential if the response is to have any real meaning to the reader. Again, the list in Figure 14–6 provides some alternatives, but students may come up with their own ways to respond to the books they read.

Can We Undo Failure?

What about children who have already failed? Chomsky (1978), in a research report aptly titled "When You Still Can't Read in Third Grade: After Decoding, What?" addressed the plight of the young "stalled" reader who, for better than 1 year, had made absolutely no progress in reading. In a middle-class suburban community near Boston, she worked with five third-grade children who had average IQs and no apparent language or speech problems but who always had been remedial reading students, had hated reading, and had made no progress in reading since first grade. Abandoning the intensive decoding program, the researcher instead asked the children to listen to tape-recorded stories from real books, and return often to each title until the story was memorized. The neurological impress method (child simultaneously sees and hears print)

Writing Activities

1. Rewrite part of the story, telling it from the viewpoint of a different character.
2. Write an advertisement for the book. Identify where the advertisement will be displayed.
3. Write a poem based on the book.
4. Make up riddles about the book or any parts of it.
5. Write a rebus of the book's title, a short summary, or a certain scene in the book.
6. Develop a word game based upon the book (word scramble, crossword puzzle, acrostic).
7. Write a letter to the author, particularly if you enjoyed the book or have a question. (Send the letter to the publisher of the book and it will be forwarded.)
8. Write an imaginary interview with the main character—or any character or object.
9. Make a newspaper which summarizes or presents elements from the book. Include as many regular departments of a newspaper (sports, comics, lovelorn, classified ads, business, and so on) as you desire.
10. Write your own book on the same theme, perhaps writing some and outlining the rest.
11. Rewrite a section of the book in either radio or stage script.
12. Select a passage or quotation which has special significance for you. Write it down and then tell why it is meaningful.
13. Rewrite the story or part of the story as a news article.
14. Rewrite part of the book in a different time period—space age future, cavemen, wild West, etc.
15. Write some trivia questions to exchange with someone else.
16. Write a chapter which tells what happened before or after the book.
17. If the book were made into a movie, choose who would play the characters. (See if you can select real people familiar to your classmates.)
18. Write a letter from some character to a real or fictitious person not in the story.
19. Write the same scene from three or four different points of view.
20. Write a simplified version of the story in picture book form.
21. Write a review of the book.

Art and Craft Activities

1. Make a diorama of an important scene in the book.
2. Construct a mobile representative of the book or some part of it.
3. Draw portraits of the main character(s).
4. Draw a mural which highlights events from the book or retells the story.
5. Draw a picture in the same style as the illustrator, or using the same medium (pen and ink, collage, watercolor, etc.).
6. Cut out words from newspapers and magazines for a word collage which gives a feeling for the book.
7. Use stitching or liquid embroidery to make a wall hanging or decorate a T-shirt with art related to the story.
8. Draw a coat of arms for a character(s) and explain the significance of each symbol.
9. Draw a silhouette of a person, scene, or object from the book.

FIGURE 14–6 Reader response activities to enhance reading.

10. Design a new dust jacket for the book.

11. Illustrate what you believe is the most important idea or scene from the book.

12. Make a poster advertising the book.

13. Make a time line of the important events in the book.

14. Make a roll movie of the book which can be shown on a t.v. set made from a box using your own illustrations, photographs, or pictures cut from magazines.

15. Retell the story using a flannel board and bits or string, yarn and felt—or create recognizable characters to use in the retelling.

16. Identify the important places in the book on a map of your own making.

17. Make paper dolls and clothes of the main character(s).

18. Make a travel poster inviting tourists to visit the setting of the book.

19. Construct a scene or character out of clay.

20. Design a costume for a character to wear.

21. Prepare and serve a food that the characters ate or which is representative of the book.

Drama, Music, and Assorted Activities

1. Make puppets—sack masks, socks, or finger—of the characters and produce a puppet show of the book.

2. Dress as a character and present some of the character's feelings, or tell about a part of the book, or summarize very briefly the story.

3. Videotape a dramatized scene from the book.

4. Write a song which tells about the book.

5. Conduct an interview between an informed moderator and character(s) . . . maybe t.v. news?

6. Research music from the time of the book, and find some songs the characters may have sung.

7. Pantomime a scene from the book.

8. Perform a scene from the book with one person taking all the parts.

9. Choosing a familiar tune, write lyrics which tell about the book.

10. For each character in the book, choose a musical selection which typifies that person.

11. Give a sales pitch to get listeners excited about the book.

12. Give a party for characters and their friends, or for characters from many books. Invite parents and have characters present themselves.

13. Research some real aspect of the book and present your newly found facts.

14. Bring something from home which reminds you of the book. Explain.

15. Choose a real life person who reminds you of a character in the book. Explain.

16. Select one passage which is the focal point of the book. Explain.

17. Collect and display a collage of quotes that you like from the book.

18. Make a board game using characters and elements from the book. Have pitfalls (lose a turn, etc.) and rewards (shake again, etc.) reflecting parts of the book.

19. Find other books on the same subject and set up a display with them.

20. Perform a choral reading from the book, or write something about the book to perform in a choral reading.

21. Emphasize the setting of the book using any or all of the following: a) objects, b) food, c) costumes, d) culture, e) music, f) art.

FIGURE 14–6 *continued*

using natural, enjoyable text proved to be the key to eventual success. Standardized achievement test scores (Metropolitan Achievement Test) after a year of treatment showed that these no-progress children were off and running. Average increase in the overall reading scores was 7.5 months (grade equivalent) and in word knowledge was 6.25 months (grade equivalent), a significant increase for children whose former test scores showed no progress.

Even older children who have had years of failure with reading and writing have been exposed to literature-based programs with notable success. Fader, Duggins, Finn, and McNeil (1976) flooded secondary classrooms in inner-city Detroit with paperbacks, finding great success in raising reading achievement and developing the reading interests of high school students who traditionally did not read often or well. But their literature-based program was best put to the test with hard-core subjects—students at the W. J. Maxey Boys' Training School in Whitmore Lake, Michigan. Fader et al. provided hundreds of paperbacks for the W. J. Maxey students, along with the time to read them and without requiring the usual book reports or summaries. Another midwestern boys' training school was used as a control group. Although no significant differences were found in control and experimental groups at the outset, by the end of the school year, the boys at W. J. Maxey showed significant gains over the control group on measures of self-esteem, literacy attitudes, anxiety, verbal proficiency, and reading comprehension. In some instances, the control group's scores actually decreased from the year before, whereas the experimental group's surged ahead, even doubling control group scores.

Stalled children also showed marked improvement in a classroom study with fifth-grade children. With the entire class, Tunnell (1986) employed a literature-based reading/writing program adapted from the program suggested by Eldredge and Butterfield (1986). Eight of the 28 students in his classroom were reading disabled, receiving Chapter I or resource instruction in a pull-out program. After 7 months of treatment, the standardized tests (SRA) were administered, and the average gain in the overall reading score was a grade equivalent of 1.1. The eight reading-disabled children, who also were virtually stalled in their reading achievement progress, posted an average gain of 1.3 with a comprehension gain of 2.0. Even more noteworthy was the swing in reading attitudes in all children. A 13-question reading attitude survey was administered to the class in August and again in April. Negative attitudes toward books and reading almost disappeared as their self-concept in relationship to literacy rose. (See also Morrison & Moser, 1998; Tunnell, Calder, Justen, & Waldrop, 1988.) Krashen and McQuillan (1998) noted success in their late intervention program that focused on "massive free voluntary reading" (p. 410). They concluded that there was no critical period for learning to read and that free reading significantly helped both home-schooled children who became successful late readers and "recovered" dyslexics (p. 409).

It is important to note that gains in reading skills using a literature-based approach are not limited to students at risk. In the studies by Eldredge and Butterfield (1986), Holdaway (1982), and Tunnell et al. (1988), the average and above-average readers made progress equal to and most often better than students in traditional programs, as measured by the typical achievement tests.

▼▼▼▼▼▼▼▼

Providing a Complete Profile of the Child

Certainly, test scores alone do not demonstrate what a child knows about reading and shed very little light on the progress he or she has made over time. The reading inventories and assessments we offered earlier in the chapter begin to paint a more comprehensive picture of the child as a reader, writer, and user of language. Still, these alone do not provide a complete profile of the child.

Our purpose, then, is to collect a variety of assessments and anecdotal records that allow us to see each child fully and to inform our instruction accordingly. This notion of using multiple indicators is known as *triangulation* to educational researchers

(Nachmias & Nachmias, 1987), and in the end it builds a *corroborative framework* (Vacca, Vacca, & Gove, 2000) that helps us to proceed with our instruction. Portfolios, like the one Jennifer presented to her parents at the beginning of the chapter, offer that bigger portrait.

Portfolios Complete the Picture

In Jennifer's portfolio were copies of her two Classroom Reading Miscue Assessments (CRMA) that Darigan had done at the beginning of the year and just before the conference period. Also included were the scores from her California Aptitude Test. But also in her 2-inch ring binder were the most important things she had done in the last 3 months. It contained:

> brainstorming ideas for writing projects and new ideas for writing projects
> rough drafts and final drafts of books she had written
> tests in all of her subjects
> reading learning logs
> reading extension activities she had done for three books she had read
> samples of her best work (and her not-so-good work for comparison)
> photographs of her various projects she had done in science and social studies
> her standardized CAT scores
> notes and anecdotal records kept by Darigan
> a table of contents for the portfolio
> an introductory note describing her reflections and what she has accomplished

These artifacts, collaboratively selected by the teacher and student, offer a clearer portrait of the child as a reader and writer and user of language (Farr & Tone, 1994; Tierney, Carter, & Desai, 1991).

The strength of a literature-based program can be demonstrated with a sound system for assessment and evaluation that combines a number of triangulated elements. Test scores, along with reading assessments and student-teacher portfolio collaborations, can offer a more comprehensive picture of each child in your class and help inform your instruction. These portraits help to inform parents and administrators as well as encourage the child to reflect on his or her progress over time.

▼▼▼▼▼▼▼▼

Summary

In this chapter, we looked at specific ways to evaluate children's reading. We first made a case for a more holistic approach to reading instruction, paying heed to the way children construct their own meaning and become more strategic and fluent. We looked at a number of ways to observe children's reading behaviors and to keep records that showed their progress. Periodically throughout the school year, we need to listen to children read aloud and use an instrument, such as the Classroom Reading Miscue Assessment or a more detailed Modified Miscue Analysis, to determine each child's progress. By knowing what children can do while reading as well as looking at the miscues they make, we can begin to build a reading profile for them. Retellings of these samples help us determine what meaning was made by the student. Further, we recommended recording what the child does while reading silently during SSR and documenting how much the child reads daily and weekly. We discussed children with reading problems and how wide, authentic reading is a vital "recovery" agent. We looked at how we can motivate children to want to read, noting the teacher's reading aloud as a best first step, encouraging favorable responses to books, holding grand conversations and literature circles, all to provide a positive reading forum. Finally, we noted that overall progress as a reader cannot be shown in a simple reading test score and that portfolios more adequately demonstrate reading capabilities and progress.

▼▼▼▼▼▼▼
Children's Literature References

Avi. (1991). *Nothing but the truth.* New York: Orchard.

Banks, Lynne Reid. (1981). *The Indian in the cupboard.* New York: Doubleday.

Banks, Lynne Reid. (1992). *The adventures of King Midas.* New York: Morrow.

Banks, Lynne Reid. (1993). *The mystery of the cupboard.* New York: Morrow.

Beatty, Patricia. (1984). *Turn homeward, Hannalee.* New York: Morrow.

Gantos, Jack. (1998). *Joey Pigza swallowed the key.* New York: Farrar, Straus & Giroux.

Lowry, Lois. (1979). *Anastasia Krupnik.* New York: Houghton Mifflin.

McKenzie, Ellen Kindt. (1990). *Stargone John.* New York: Henry Holt.

Monjo, F. N. (1970). *The drinking gourd* (Fred Brenner, Illus.). New York: Harper & Row.

Polacco, Patricia. (1998). *Thank you, Mr. Falker.* New York: Philomel.

Sachar, Louis. (1987). *There's a boy in the girls' bathroom.* New York: Knopf.

Steig, William. (1969). *Sylvester and the magic pebble.* New York: Windmill.

▼▼▼▼▼▼▼
Professional References

Anderson, R. C., Hiebert, E. H., Scott, J. A., & Wilkinson, I. A. G. (1985). *Becoming a nation of readers: The Report of the commission on reading.* Washington, DC: The National Institute of Education, U. S. Department of Education.

Baumann, J. F., & Murray, B. A. (1994). Current practices in reading assessment. In K. D. Wood & B. Algozzine (Eds.), *Teaching reading to high-risk learners* (pp. 149–195). Boston: Allyn & Bacon.

Boehnlein, M. (1987). Reading intervention for high risk first-graders. *Educational Leadership, 44,* 32–37.

Burns, P. C. (1998). *Informal reading inventory: Preprimer to twelfth grade.* Boston: Houghton Mifflin.

Cambourne, B., & Turbill, J. (1990). Assessment in whole language classrooms: Theory into practice. *Elementary School Journal, 90,* 337–349.

Chomsky, C. (1978). When you still can't read in third grade: After decoding, what? In J. Samuels (Ed.), *What research has to say about reading instruction* (pp. 13–30). Newark, DE: International Reading Association.

Clay, M. (1985). *The early detection of reading difficulties.* Portsmouth, NH: Heinemann.

Cullinan, B. (1981). *The power of reading.* Address at the annual convention of the Utah Council of the International Reading Association, Salt Lake City, UT, 5 March.

Cunningham, P. M., & Allington, R. L. (1999). *Classrooms that work: They can all read and write* (2nd ed.). New York: Longman.

Daniels, H. (1994). *Literature circles: Voice and choice in the student-centered classroom.* York, ME: Stenhouse.

Deford, D. E., Lyons, C. A., & Pinnell, G. S. (1991). *Bridges to literacy: Learning from reading recovery.* Portsmouth, NH: Heinemann.

Eeds, M., & Peterson, R. (1997). Literature studies revisited: Some thoughts on talking with children about books. *The New Advocate, 10*(1), 49–59.

Eldredge, J. L., & Butterfield, D. (1986). Alternatives to traditional reading instruction. *The Reading Teacher, 40,* 32–37.

Fader, D., Duggins, J., Finn, T., & McNeil, E. (1976). *The new hooked on books.* New York: Berkley.

Farr, R., & Tone, B. (1994). *Portfolio and performance assessment.* Fort Worth, TX: Harcourt Brace.

Gillet, J. W., & Temple, C. (2000). *Understanding reading problems: Assessment and instruction.* New York: Longman.

Goodman, K. (1967). Reading: A psycholinguistic guessing game. *Journal of the Reading Specialist, 6,* 126–135.

Goodman, K. (1985). A linguistic study of cues and miscues in reading. In H. Singer & R. Ruddell (Eds.), *Theoretical models and processes of reading* (3rd ed.). (pp. 129–134). Newark, DE: International Reading Association.

Goodman, K. (1990). Reading: The psycholinguistic guessing game. In K. Goodman, L. B. Bird, & Y. M. Goodman (Eds.), *The whole language catalog* (p. 98). Glencoe, IL: McGraw-Hill.

Holdaway, D. (1982). Shared book experience: Teaching reading using favorite books. *Theory into Practice, 21,* 293–300.

Johnston, P. H. (1984). Prior knowledge and reading comprehension test bias. *Reading Research Quarterly, 19* (2), 219–239.

Krashen, S. (1991). *The power of reading.* Englewood, CO: Libraries Unlimited.

Krashen, S., & McQuillan, J. (1998). The case for later intervention: Once a good reader, always a good reader. In C. Weaver (Ed.), *Reconsidering a balanced approach to reading* (pp. 409–424). Urbana, IL: NCTE.

Larrick, N. (1987). Illiteracy starts too soon. *Phi Delta Kappan, 69,* 184–189.

Leinhardt, G., Sigmond, N., & Cooley, W. W. (1981). Reading instruction and its effects. *American Educational Research Journal, 18,* 343–361.

L'Engle, M. (1980). *Walking on water: Reflections on faith and art.* Wheaton, IL: H. Shaw.

May, F. (1998). *Reading as communication: To help children to write and read.* Upper Saddle River, NJ: Merrill/Prentice Hall.

McCormick, S. (1987). *Remedial and clinical reading instruction.* New York: Merrill/Macmillan.

McIntyre, E., & Freppon, P. A. (1994). A comparison of children's development of alphabetic knowledge. *Research in the Teaching of English, 28* (4), 391–417.

Morrison, T. G., & Moser, G. P. (1998). Increasing students' achievement and interest in reading. *Reading Horizons, 38* (4), 233–245.

Nachmias, D., & Nachmias, C. (1987). *Research methods in the social studies.* New York: St. Martins Press.

Peterson, R., & Eeds, M. (1994). *Grand conversations: Literature groups in action.* Ontario: Scholastic.

Raphael, T. E., & McMahon, S. I. (1994). Book club: An alternative framework for reading instruction. *The Reading Teacher, 48,* 102–116.

Reutzel, D. R., Cooter, R. B., Jr. (1990). Whole language: Comparative effects on first-grade reading achievement. *The Journal of Educational Research, 5* (5), 252–257.

Rhodes, L. K., & Shanklin, N. (1993). *Windows into literacy: Assessing learners K–8.* Portsmouth, NH: Heinemann.

Root, S. L., Jr. (1975). Lecture, University of Georgia, Athens, Georgia, 21 March.

Rosenshine, B., & Stevens, R. (1984). Classroom instruction in reading. In P. D. Pearson (Ed.), *Handbook of reading research* (pp. 745–798). New York: Longman.

Tierney, R. J., Carter, M. A., & Desai, L. E. (1991). *Portfolio assessment in the reading-writing classroom.* Norwood, MA: Christopher-Gordon.

Tunnell, M. O. (1986). The natural act of reading: An affective approach. *The Advocate, 5,* 156–164.

Tunnell, M. O., Calder, J. E., Justen, J. E., III, & Waldrop, P. B. (1988). An affective approach to reading: Effectively teaching reading to mainstreamed handicapped children. *The Pointer, 32,* 38–40.

Vacca, J. L., Vacca, R. T., & Gove, M. K. (2000). *Reading and learning to read.* New York: Longman.

Wells, D. (1995). Leading grand conversations. In N. Roser & M. Martinez (Eds.), *Book talk and beyond: Children and teachers respond to literature* (pp. 132–139). Newark, DE: International Reading Association.

Wood, K. D., & Algozzine, B. (1994). *Teaching reading to high-risk students.* Boston: Allyn & Bacon.

TEACHING ACROSS THE CURRICULUM WITH CHILDREN'S LITERATURE

15
CHAPTER
▼▼▼▼▼▼▼

If you want to cover
Health Issues—Over Time

Consider as a READ ALOUD

Fever 1793,
by Laurie Halse Anderson

Consider as a TEXT SET

Time for Andrew,
by Mary Downing Hahn

Running Out of Time,
by Margaret Haddix

The Apprenticeship of Lucas Whitaker,
by Cynthia DeFelice

When Plague Strikes: The Black Death, Smallpox, AIDS,
by James Cross Giblin

An Acquaintance with Darkness,
by Ann Rinaldi

FEVER 1793
by Laurie Halse Anderson

LAURIE HALSE AN

Student Response

I found this book to be very serious and now try to see myself in one of the character's positions. It is very hard. I espeacilly liked her grandfather. He had a big heart and a good spirit. He was so kind and gentle. I was devistated to see him die. I felt so bad for Mattie. She had to make grown-up decisions, when she was so young. I was glad she finally found Eliza. I really enjoyed reading this book. Thank you for suggesting this book to me.

Drew

To visit a classroom exploring the issues of Teaching Across the Curriculum with Children's Literature, please go to Chapter 15 of our companion website at **www.prenhall.com/darigan**

When Gerald, a fifth grader in Darigan's classroom, was reading Wilson Rawls's book **Where the Red Fern Grows,** he had a number of questions about "those incredible redbone hounds of Billy's." During SQUIRT (their acronym for Super Quiet Un-Interrupted Reading Time, more often referred to as Sustained Silent Reading), he was just bursting with curiosity, wanting to know more about these adept hunting canines and their ability to track even the slyest of all of the forest animals—the raccoon. With a great deal of trepidation, he approached Darigan, knowing that any discussion—any—was strictly forbidden. "I sure would like to know more about those dogs and how they catch those ol' ring-tail coons."

Darigan replied, "Well, I don't have any books that would help you here in the room. Where do you suppose you *could* find out more?"

"The library," he blurted. "Dr. D, do you suppose I could run down to the library for just a second to get some books? I'll be right back."

Darigan gladly allowed him that "second" and he returned with a stack of five books and a verve to learn more about these hounds. What ensued was a nonfiction report on hunting with a dog that he wrote during Writer's Workshop. As he studied these animals, he found he wanted to share that learning and so wrote a book, "Redboned Hounds."

Students who begin just like Gerald and are self-motivated will continue their education as long as they breathe. In our estimation, an education is not always the same as having a diploma. Just as it is possible to obtain a sheepskin without much education having taken place, it is also possible to become educated without formal instruction. Getting an education is a personal decision, a commitment to learning. And at its best, it is prompted by the knowing teacher who nurtures that discovery process by allowing and, more important, by encouraging children to seek answers to the many questions they ask.

What distinguishes truly educated people, what identifies them and sets them apart, is that they are readers. This is true even for a school dropout who spent 70% of his life in prison. Take Wilbert Rideau, for instance. When he was 18 years old, he robbed a bank, killed the teller, and was sent to the Louisiana State Prison for life. After a few angry years of doing nothing but sitting and rebelling, Rideau picked up a book and spent a number of weeks reading it. Then he picked up another. Although he had left school in only the eighth grade, English hardly being his favorite subject, he soon found that he was reading two books a day on a wide variety of subjects, history being his favorite.

"I read about Napoleon, Muhammed, Lincoln, Washington, Bolivar, Sukarno," says Rideau. "I came to realize that a lot of people had terrible beginnings, but they lifted themselves up and gave something back to the world. I read *Profiles in Courage.* I'll never forget what it said—that a man does what he must, regardless of the cost." One day, a guard passed him a copy of Ayn Rand's *Atlas Shrugged.* Its message of self-reliance became Rideau's credo. "I started seeing that no matter how bad things looked, it was all on me whether I made something of myself or I died in some nameless grave" (quoted in Colt, 1993, p. 71).

Rideau went on to initiate and become editor of *The Angolite,* the convict magazine. It was so good that it became required reading in training classes for new correctional officers. It spawned a book containing its best articles, and also became the first prison publication ever nominated for a National Magazine Award (an honor it has since earned six times). In addition, it was first to win the Robert F. Kennedy Journalism Award, the George Polk Award, and the American Bar Association Silver Gavel Award (Colt, 1993, p. 72).

▼▼▼▼▼▼▼

The Types of Books We Teachers Use

Schools use books as tools in the trade of education. We see those books falling into three distinct categories: reference books, textbooks, and trade books. Each type of book is philosophically different from the others and serves a different purpose but, as we will see, all have a place in the elementary classroom. *Reference books* are those volumes a person consults for an immediate answer to a specific question, such as a dictionary, encyclopedia, atlas, and thesaurus. When Gerald wanted information on the redbone hound, it was to reference books that the librarian directed him first. *Textbooks,* on the other hand, are designed for use in formal instruction. They present a dispassionate view of a subject in an organized, methodical manner. In chapter 8, "Historical Fiction," we discussed some of the limitations of textbooks and elaborate on that in the next section. *Trade books* is the term given to books published for the retail market—books written for and sold in the trade. Trade books are typically available in bookstores and libraries. They are written by people who have something personal and important to say, hoping their words will appeal to readers who seek knowledge, insight, pleasure, or entertainment.

Students who read books because of a school assignment usually read textbooks. Anyone who has finished high school has only to consider how often teachers required reading from each of the three categories to determine that textbooks are used far more often than the other two types. Estimates from our classes of college students about the percentage of textbook time heaped on children coming up through the public school ranks offer no surprises. The range has been surprisingly consistent throughout the years, from a low of 60% to a high of 95%, with most responses hovering around 80 to 85%. Trade books are estimated to occupy only between 10 and 30% of school reading time, and reference books 5 to 15%.

Though textbooks are most commonly used in the classroom—far more often than the other two types of books—they are hardly found to be the most liked. The fact is, textbooks have been targeted as one reason social studies is the most universally disliked of all school subjects at all levels (Sewall, 1988). When students from grades 3 to 12 were asked how education could be improved, 40% said textbooks should be improved—a higher percentage than those who think they need better teachers (Roper Organization, 1987).

Jim Trelease (1988, p. xiv) suggests one reason why textbooks do not have student appeal: Textbooks are written by either committees or an author who has to please a committee of editors, who in turn must please a curriculum committee, which must please a school board (yet another committee). We also believe that beyond these in-house editorial constraints, further restrictions occur in attempting to court the two top adoption states in this country, Texas and California. By attempting to please these two disparate groups, textbooks become far more safe and, in the end, boring.

So textbook writing and publishing decisions are made on the basis of the lowest common denominator—the fewest number of committee members or special interest groups who will be offended by a pabulum text. The result is a book without a personality and voice, a textbook without texture. And for this reason, no one grows up having a favorite textbook. You've never heard someone say, "I'll always remember my sixth-grade science book, *Meadows and Streams.* Man, that was my favorite!"

That textbooks do not excite students is not a new trend. Over 400 years ago, in the play *Romeo and Juliet,* Shakespeare referred then to the same feelings students have now for their textbooks. The first time the two lovers meet and pledge their devotion to one another—which is so deep and consuming they are willing to forsake everything for it, including family, worldly goods, and life itself—Romeo speaks figuratively to show the intensity of their love. "Love goes toward love, as schoolboys from their books" (Shakespeare, 2.2.157–158). How powerful is their love? As powerful as the revulsion schoolboys feel for their textbooks.

A quick look at both textbooks and trade books can help us capitalize on the strengths of each in the educational process. To prepare for the points to follow, consider the following two passages about dinosaurs. The first is excerpted from a textbook, and the other comes from an informational picture book.

To find out more about Jean Craighead George and other authors and illustrators on the World Wide Web, visit Chapter 15 on the companion website at **www.prenhall.com/darigan**

BOOKMARK

INTEGRATING TECHNOLOGY: AUTHORS ON THE WORLD WIDE WEB

The official site of *Jean Craighead George,* author of fiction and nonfiction related to the wonders of nature, is beautifully constructed and includes a question-and-answer section (with illustrations by Jean Craighead George), some great multimedia excerpts, a suggested process for writing your own stories, and information about her current projects.

Millions of years ago, most land animals were reptiles. Dinosaurs of all sizes roamed the land. Flying reptiles had beaks with teeth. Their wings were covered with leathery skin, not feathers. Other reptiles swam in the seas. They had fish-shaped bodies with tails and fins. Their scientific name means "fish lizard." But they were not fish. They had lungs and breathed air. (*Holt Science* [fifth grade]. Holt, Rinehart and Winston, 1989, p. 326)

Scientists long thought that dinosaurs, like today's reptiles, were cold-blooded animals. THE NEWS IS: Some dinosaurs may have been warm-blooded. *Deinonychus*—"terrible claw"—is one of those dinosaurs.

Deinonychus was fairly small. It had the sharp teeth of a meat-eater, hands shaped for grasping prey, and powerful hind legs. It also had a huge, curved claw on one toe of each hind foot. This was a claw shaped for ripping and slashing.

To attack, *Deinonychus* must have stood on one hind foot and slashed with the other. Or it must have leaped and attacked with both hind feet. Today's reptiles are not nimble enough to do anything like that. And as cold-blooded animals, they do not have the energy to attack that way. Warm-blooded animals do. . . .

Warm-blooded animals grow much faster than cold-blooded ones. A young ostrich, for example, shoots up 5 feet in a year. A young crocodile grows only about one foot.

Bones in the nesting grounds of Montana show that duckbills were 13 inches long when they hatched. Scientists think young duckbills were 10 feet long at the end of their first year. If that is right, it is a sign of an animal that grew fast—perhaps of a warm-blooded one. (***The News About Dinosaurs**, by Patricia Lauber, p. 32)

Strengths of Trade Books

Trade books offer the following advantages in teaching the curriculum. They provide a far deeper content than textbooks. Trade books focus on a subject and bring it to life with interesting observations and details. The reader comes away with a richer, deeper understanding of the topic. Textbooks, on the other hand, can offer only a broad, and consequently shallow, view of any one subject. They do not allow for the kind of compelling presentation available in trade books. For example, the Holt science text just quoted devotes only that one paragraph to dinosaurs. It is difficult, if not impossible, to give readers any real insight in such a small space.

Trade books can provide many differing perspectives. Hundreds of books about dinosaurs are available and dozens more are produced each year, rounding out a reader's knowledge as vast as that reader is willing to continue to pursue the subject. Textbooks offer one perspective. "No one book, whatever its type, can truly answer every question about a particular subject. Trade books offer the opportunity to explore a broad range of topics as well as to examine in-depth a single topic" (Holmes & Ammon, 1985, p. 366).

Up-to-Date Resources

Because trade books are generally on a publishing schedule of two major lists per year, publishers are able to use the most recent information and research to keep their books current. Trade books are produced more quickly than textbooks, offering the latest findings even on old subjects (dinosaurs and the new warm-blooded theory). In contrast, most school districts can afford a new textbook in each subject area only every 5 to 10 years, which presents a distinct disadvantage in this information-rich age.

Language Use

The writing style found in textbooks tends to be formal and rather stiff. Trade books, on the other hand, often are written in a conversational fashion. Trade books have the space to make meaningful comparisons (a crocodile to an ostrich) and use more detail to enlarge understanding (duckbill babies in Montana). Textbooks depend on short sentences and on what Fielding, Wilson, and Anderson (1986) regard as a "basket of facts" style (p. 152).

To make a narrative "readable," textbook publishers break up complex sentences, shorten paragraphs, and excise stylistic flourishes. The conjunctions, modifiers, and clauses that help create subtle connections and advance students' understandings are routinely cut. The result is, at its best, straightforward—and, at its worst, choppy, monotonic, metallic prose (Sewall, 1988, p. 555).

Yet another advantage to trade books is the rich language they employ. The words used in trade books create images ("hands shaped for grasping prey," "leaped and attacked with both feet") and are more precise and colorful ("nimble," "slashing"). The sentences are varied and read more interestingly, both silently and aloud. Go ahead and try it: Read aloud the two preceding excerpts and see which you think is the richer. We would be very surprised if you felt it to be the former selection.

Strength in Voice

Voice is of utmost concern in the children's trade book market. Trade books allow a human being to emerge in the writing. Information has more power to influence others when it has been filtered through the human mind and heart. Textbooks, conversely, tend to remain detached and impersonal.

Trade books meet head-on the individual reading levels in any one classroom. Let's face it: In any classroom, the reading levels of students vary widely. Any fourth-grade teacher, for example, will tell you that he or she has kids as low as primer level and as high as two, three, and even more grades above fourth. Likewise, as first-grade teacher Simona Lynch states in chapter 13, she has entering students who can read at the fourth grade and up, but a good many of her charges still don't even know their letters. Because of the number and variety of trade books, even students with reading problems can locate books that they can read, enjoy, and learn from, and that allow them to contribute to class discussions.

Wide Variety in Trade Books

Trade books come in varied formats and structures, shapes, sizes, and lengths. The illustrations and diagrams in trade books tend to be larger and more appealing than those found in textbooks. As we mentioned in chapter 10, on informational books, the Dorling Kindersley "Eyewitness" format has done much to create a whole new wave of exciting books steeped in facts and dripping with the juices of learning. They tend to structure information so it is natural and clearly understood. Textbooks, on the other hand, have a predictable, industrial look. They are dense and compact, and generally have smaller illustrations and diagrams. The structure of content is not always clear.

As we said, too many social studies and science texts are simply "baskets of facts," little more than loosely connected lists of propositions about a topic. The structure of textbook chapters is likely to be murky. There are simple structures that are accepted among the canons of exposition, such as cause-effect, temporal sequence, and comparison/contrast. Yet it is seldom that one finds a content-area textbook selection that is clearly organized according to one of these structures. Students are more likely to encounter these structures and to learn to understand and appreciate them when they read good nonfiction trade books (Fielding, Wilson, & Anderson, 1986, p. 152).

Trade books are, indeed, tools perfect for lifelong learning. They are available in all libraries and bookstores. They are the books people go to most often when they want to learn something further about their world after they leave school. Trade books are the stuff of "real life" reading. Textbooks are limited to formal education and can be found only in classrooms and academic bookstores. Regular bookstores have none of them, and libraries very few. Doesn't this cause you to think, "If schools are to prepare children for lifelong learning, why do they rely so heavily on a tool that is not available for their use in the future?"

Strengths of Textbooks

Don't think we are totally against textbooks; on the contrary, we see them aptly serving three useful purposes in the classroom, two for the teacher and one for the student.

First, textbooks identify subject matter students are expected to learn. Textbooks provide the content boundaries for which the school district makes the teacher responsible, and teachers of all levels of experience and ability need to know what is required of them in each subject area. Even though the classroom teacher also can find this information in a state or district curriculum guide, the textbook is usually more easily accessible.

Second, textbooks provide a resource for subject areas where the educator might be unskilled or about which they are unsure. Particularly for new teachers, who simply haven't had the time or experience to become knowledgeable and proficient in all subject areas, the textbook provides them with a crutch while they are gaining the knowledge, experience, and insight they need before they can call a subject area their own. We have always held that the best resource in a classroom is a skilled and experienced teacher, one who knows the material and how to present it so students will become involved. The teacher should work continually to faithfully model as that resource, replacing the textbook with personalized, interesting materials and approaches as soon as possible. Some teachers will be able to do this relatively quickly; others will need longer. But the situation to avoid is becoming textbook dependent. If the goal is to have excited and interested students, the text needs to become a secondary source, or sometimes even abandoned, as soon as possible.

Third, textbooks serve students who already have an interest in a particular subject. The strength of the textbook approach is that it provides a generalized overview of a particular topic. When a reader comes to a textbook with an interest and curiosity about the subject, the textbook can serve as a worthwhile resource. As a successful way of exciting the uninitiated about a topic, however, textbooks largely fail. Yet, they are used most frequently in the educational process as an introduction to a subject, the very way in which they do not perform well.

Education and Trade Books

The purpose of both fiction and nonfiction trade books is not so much to inform, which they do very well, as it is to excite, to introduce, and to let the reader in on the irresistible secrets of life on planet Earth. Indeed, no uninteresting subjects exist on this sphere—nor are there any interesting ones. All *subjects* are neutral. What makes them appealing, or boring, is how we are introduced to them. What makes the difference between a reader's being enthusiastic or bored is the viewpoint, the perspective, the care, and the skill of the one doing the introducing. Interesting perspectives simply are easier to find in trade books than in texts. And today's informational trade books often are tantalizing (see chapter 10). They help create interest in young readers. Although subjects by their nature are neither interesting nor uninteresting, the books indeed are.

In addition to using appealing informational books to generate interest in a subject, a teacher who knows fiction has another advantage in bringing students to the curriculum. Historical fiction, for instance, sheds light on history in a way that non-fiction has difficulty duplicating. As we mentioned in chapter 8, Cynthia Stokes Brown (1994) says that by introducing historically accurate fiction, complete with its compelling plot and well-developed characters, history can come alive by allowing children more readily to "identify . . . with heroes and heroism and . . . explore their own lives and identity, character and convictions through heroic stories" (p. 5).

When children are interested in what they read, and read broadly—whether fiction, nonfiction, or both—they can learn much of value from trade books. People are able to grow and develop intellectually without the carefully monitored presentation of information typical to the schooling and textbooks we know, as these three examples show:

1. *Robert Howard Allen has never seen his father.* Divorced before he was born, Robert's mother left him at age 6 to be raised by his grandfather, three great-aunts, and great-uncle, all of whom lived in the same house in rural Tennessee. After his grandfather taught him to read, Robert regularly read the Bible to a blind great-aunt. "From age seven he read thousands of books—from Donald Duck comics to Homer, James Joyce and Shakespeare. . . . He began picking up books at yard sales, and by his early 20s he had some 2000 volumes" (Whittemore, 1991, p. 4).

Robert Howard Allen stayed home and helped, and he read. He never went to school, not even for a day. At age 30, he easily passed a high school equivalency test, and at age 32, he showed up at Bethel College in McKenzie, Tennessee. Three years later, he graduated summa cum laude with a GPA of 3.92. He continued his education by enrolling in graduate school at Vanderbilt University. Having earned his Ph.D. in English, he is currently a visiting lecturer at Murray State College in Kentucky (Whittemore, 1991).

2. *During her childhood, Lauralee Summer and her mother moved frequently from one homeless shelter to another.* She remembers sitting on her mother's lap and listening to stories. " 'She was about 20 months old when I began reading to her every single night,' says [Lauralee's mother], who recalls a well-thumbed book of nursery rhymes. 'I read the same book every night. That was the only book we had' " (Gloster, 1994, p. 1).

With money for her fourth birthday, Lauralee bought a See & Say book and taught herself to read. She soon was visiting libraries, as mother and daughter moved among shelters and welfare hotels in three states. At age 10, Lauralee tried fourth-grade classes in two Santa Barbara schools, then quit in favor of reading to herself at the shelter. Eventually, she did attend school, an alternative program for nontraditional students during her senior year, where she took the Scholastic Aptitude Test (SAT) and scored 1460, putting her in the 99.7 percentile of America's high school seniors. Lauralee applied to Harvard University and was admitted to the 1994 freshman class with a full scholarship (Gloster, 1994).

3. *Cushla Yeoman was born with multiple handicaps.* Chromosome damage caused her spleen, kidneys, and mouth cavity to be deformed and prevented her from holding anything in her hand until she was 3 years old. She could not see clearly more than a foot away. Muscle spasms kept her from sleeping more than 2 hours a night. She was diagnosed as mentally and physically retarded, and doctors recommended that she be institutionalized.

Cushla's parents had seen her respond to the picture books they read aloud, so they kept her home and increased their reading to 14 picture books a day, week after week and month after month. By age 5, Cushla was pronounced by doctors to be socially well adjusted and intellectually well above average (Butler, 1980).

Now, we are not suggesting that the best way to learn is outside of school—far from it. Yet people can and do learn beyond the walls of formal education. All of us need to recognize that books can create interest in readers, that people learn better when they are interested, and that people can learn a great deal by reading widely on their own.

To find out more about Carol Hurst's website and other sites with teaching ideas, visit Chapter 15 on the companion website at **www.prenhall. com/darigan**

INTEGRATING TECHNOLOGY: ACTIVITIES USING THE WORLD WIDE WEB

Carol Hurst has created an excellent website with numerous reviews and ideas for use in the classroom. Hurst's website includes some interesting lesson plans that are presented by *Book*, by *Curriculum Areas*, and by *Subject*, making the site extremely useful when planning the integration of literature across the curriculum.

▼▼▼▼▼▼

Teaching the Curriculum With Trade Books

As we have shown, trade books, textbooks, and reference books are different from one another and should all be used and used differently. If we ignore those differences and, say, use trade books exactly as we use texts, the trade books lose much of their power. We need to avoid using Eric Carle's *The Very Hungry Caterpillar* as the core of 32 separate language arts activities, or devising 19 mathematical procedures from Arnold Lobel's *Frog and Toad Are Friends*. The strength of trade books is their ability to create interest. Recognizing that they also can be used for instruction, we need to choose ways to preserve their ability to stimulate readers and not turn the books into reading assignments with lists of questions to be answered.

One way to show students the appeal of trade books in the instructional program is for teachers to read and use them. As we have mentioned again and again, teachers should read these books aloud, doing think alouds to model the way they fit into a unit of study or simply to answer a single question. Children won't see how books, from the library or classroom shelves, fit into daily instruction unless the teachers include them as a natural part of classroom learning.

An easy way to bring the books into lessons is to ask the librarian for titles on a subject to be taught—for instance, magnetism. Look through the books until you find enough interesting ideas, experiments, or information for a lesson or unit, and then present it to the class, showing the books that gave you the information.

Teachers' use of these books is particularly important in the lower grades, where children have more limited reading abilities. The teacher can read aloud a wide variety of books to the class, provide easier texts for those beginning to read while also having on hand more challenging books for those already reading independently.

A very popular unit in the primary grades is one on butterflies. Here are some wonderful books to support such a theme. Because many of these units culminate in hatching Lady Wing butterflies, you may want to begin by reading aloud Eve Bunting's book *The Butterfly House*, illustrated by Greg Shed. It sets the stage for your inquiry and will excite the children with the possibilities of raising their own butterflies.

Middle- and upper-grade children will be able to make more of their own discoveries, as outlined in three approaches that follow.

The Individual Reading Approach

Holmes and Ammon (1985) devised a strategy to use with an entire class, grades 3 and above, but it can be adapted for use with groups, individuals, or children in the lower grades. It is designed to be used as a series of

ALTERNATE TEXT SET

Butterflies

Read Aloud

The Butterfly House, by Eve Bunting

Text Set

Crinkleroot's Guide to Knowing Butterflies and Moths, by Jim Arnosky

The Butterfly Alphabet Book, by Brian Cassie and Jerry Pollotta

Aldita and the Forest, by Thelma Catterwell

The Big Bug Book, by Margery Facklam

Caterpillar, Caterpillar, by Vivian French

Monarch Butterfly, by Gail Gibbons

Monarchs, by Kathryn Lasky

Monarch Butterflies: Mysterious Travelers, by Bianca Lavies

The Butterfly Alphabet, by Kjell Bloch Sandved

Pets in a Jar, by Seymour Simon

---

lessons instead of one presentation, and has four steps: readiness, reading, response, and record keeping.

Readiness (not to be confused with the archaic term *reading readiness*)

First, the teacher plans something to activate prior knowledge of a subject, such as a discussion in which students share facts they already know about the topic. Another way to activate prior knowledge is to generate word associations as a class. The topic "dinosaurs," for instance, may elicit words like *huge, fighters,* and *extinct.* After this introduction, each student generates a personally interesting question about dinosaurs, writes it on a small piece of poster board, and puts it randomly on the wall or a bulletin board. Finally, the teacher asks students if any of the questions are related. Similar questions are grouped and become a subtopic. Student groups then select a subtopic, such as "birth and death of dinosaurs," and proceed to step two.

Reading

After the teacher collects dinosaur books of varied lengths and difficulty levels, he or she allows students to choose their own books and read silently, focusing on the subtopic or one of the questions within it, or reading for a general overview. After the reading, the teacher directs the class in collecting data by taking each subtopic in turn, asking for information the students have found, and writing it on an

Cover from **The Butterfly House** by Eve Bunting, illustrated by Greg Shed. Illustrations copyright © 1999 by Greg Shed. Reprinted by permission of Scholastic Inc.

overhead projector or chart. During the activity, children might present conflicting facts. This provides a chance to do what seldom happens at school—return to their sources to corroborate information. In one session, for instance, a child identified the largest dinosaur as a *Brachiosaurus* whereas another said it was a *Tyrannosaurus rex*. A rereading clarified the point and showed the *Tyrannosaurus rex* to be the largest *meat-eating* dinosaur. If rereading offers no solution, other possibilities for clarification should be explored, such as looking at the recency of publication and consulting still other sources.

Response

Now the class is ready to summarize together the information under each subtopic and perhaps enrich their learning with more reading, a field trip, or a guest lecturer. They may further make personal responses with art projects, constructing models, and writing projects.

Record Keeping

During this series of lessons, students keep their own records of the books they consulted and their proposed responses in a folder where they also place a variety of pieces of evidence: snippets of work, drafts, note cards, and the like (Holmes & Ammon, 1985). The teacher has access to their folders for evaluation.

The Large-Group Reading Approach

Brozo and Tomlinson (1986) incorporate fiction as well as nonfiction into the content curriculum. They suggest using trade books, especially reading them aloud to the class, to introduce and extend the textbook in a four-step approach.

Step 1. Identify Salient Concepts.

Textbooks only hint at many important concepts that need a closer look if students are to identify and understand them. Consider the following description of Nazis and Jews in a fifth-grade textbook:

> German soldiers rounded up and transported Jews and other minorities from all over Europe to death camps called concentration camps. The Nazis killed 11 million men, women, and children at the camps. Six million of those killed were Jews. The remaining victims included Gypsies, Russians, Poles, and others. This mass murder is known as the *Holocaust,* which means total destruction. (*Build Our Nation,* Houghton Mifflin, 1997, p. 552)

This paragraph is the entire entry for the Holocaust in that text. It hints at the drama and tragedy of the Holocaust but provides no details or insight into this terrible event. To personalize students' understanding, the teacher needs to identify the unmentioned but important concepts that underlie the Holocaust. Asking questions like the following can identify these salient concepts: What are the driving forces behind the events? What phenomena described in the textbook have affected ordinary people or may do so in the future? What universal patterns of behavior related to this event should be explained? Such questions lead us to pursue core elements of Nazi persecution of the Jews, such as prejudice, inhumanity, and the abuse of power.

Step 2. Identify Appropriate Trade Books to Help Teach Concepts.

Subject guides, such as Sharon Dreyer's *The Bookfinder* (1977–1995, vols. 1–5) and the annual publication *Subject Guide to Children's Books in Print* (1999), help teachers find books to strengthen their collections. Again, we mention the CD-ROM accompanying this text as a very helpful tool in finding the books you need. Your school and local public librarians will certainly assist with your immediate needs. Naturally, teachers should read the books before using them in class, looking for captivating nonfiction and for powerful fiction that breathe life into the important concepts to be learned. Take, for example, the following excerpt from *Friedrich*, by Hans Peter Richter. The concepts of bigotry and injustice only hinted at in the textbook entry are brought to life when an attendant at a German swimming pool in 1938 discovers that a boy retrieving his clothes is a Jew.

> "Just take a look at this!" the attendant said. . . . "This is one of the Jewish identification cards. The scoundrel lied to me . . .—a Jew that's what he is. A Jew in our swimming pool!" He looked disgusted. . . .
>
> As if he could no longer bear to touch it, the attendant threw Friedrich's identification card and its case across the counter. "Think of it! Jewish things among the clothes of respectable human beings!" he screamed, flinging the coat hanger holding Friedrich's clothes on the ground so they scattered in all directions. (pp. 76–77)

Step 3. Teach.

The teacher then reads the trade book or books to the class as a schema and interest builder before getting to the overview presented in the textbook. After providing a foundation for understanding to the whole class, then the teacher presents the main points from the text. The teacher also introduces additional trade books that are valuable to the students for elaboration and extension of content.

Step 4. Follow-up.

After the content is presented and students explore it, follow-up activities personalize and extend learning. They can be as varied as the people who create them: Imagined on-the-scene descriptions of places or events, letters to historical figures, dramatizations, interviews, and debates are a few suggestions.

The Small-Group Reading Approach

Ad Spofford teaches sixth grade and successfully uses small groups in the teaching of subject matter. He divides the students into groups of four to six members. He then gives each group children's trade books on a common topic, making sure that there is one book fewer than there are members of the group. By providing fewer books than there are people, they have to share and work together more. He then gives the group an assignment that depends on the group's reading and compiling information from the books, such as the following: "Prepare a report for the board of directors on active volcanoes within the boundaries of the United States. They have little understanding of the number and potential threat of American volcanoes, so be sure to give background and experts' opinions on how dangerous our volcanoes are. Use visuals to help present your information."

At other times, Spofford provides the books—still one fewer than than there are group members—and asks the group to generate a product using information in the titles on their table. They can decide what to present and how to present it, but each person has to make a contribution.

▼▼▼▼▼▼▼

Three Principles of Using Trade Books to Teach Subject Matter

The individual, large-group, and small-group reading approaches are not the only methods teachers can use when teaching with trade books; elements of the three techniques can be combined to form other strategies. A class can, for example, read a book together as a springboard to small-group work or individual study, bypassing the textbook completely.

As long as three principles are followed, trade books can be used to spark learning in a variety of ways:

1. *Students read trade books as they are meant to be read*—as windows to the world that do not cover a subject but, like peeling layers off the onion, uncover it.
2. *Teachers allow students to discover, or uncover, the information.* When the teacher knows *exactly* what the student should find in a given book, that book is being misused. Teachers who allow students to select their own evidence often will be pleasantly surprised at what students bring back as proof of learning even when the assignment is fairly specific (for example, "Find evidence of how animals adapt to their environment").
3. *Students share their discoveries and insights.* Teachers reinforce genuine learning by providing some means for the excited student to present new knowledge to an audience, or make a personal response to new discoveries—through an oral or written summary, poster, display, explanation to a small group, or a diary or story from the perspective of a historical figure.

▼▼▼▼▼▼▼

Looking at the Crowded Curriculum

If you look at your overburdened curriculum and the constraints it presents, we think you will want to consider a viable alternative in organizing your hectic day. Answer this: "What was added to your curriculum last year?" Was it a new twist on outcomes-based assessment, something dealing with technology, or a new spelling program your district is embracing? Think about how each year, one or two more pieces get added—or probably from your perspective, it feels like they are being "dumped" on you.

And this is not to say that what is being added is necessarily flawed or bad. We remember the groans we heard from teachers a number of years ago when the fabulously successful D.A.R.E. program was introduced into the schools. Teachers grumped as hours were carved out of their daily and weekly schedules. Yet the proof in this program has shown that dramatic changes have occurred in how children view drug use and how this is a direct result of this dynamic intervention. We know that in the case of our own children, they were given the wherewithal and vocabulary to just say "No!" to drugs. But rather than add another separate piece, such as the D.A.R.E. program, to your already bulging curriculum, we want to show you how, with a little planning, you can incorporate many of these "extras" into your ongoing curriculum.

Our alternative comes in the form of the *integrated, literature-based thematic unit.* We understand that you are responsible for teaching "the curriculum," and in some districts the expectation is that you will teach the entire curriculum, every year—as if this were humanly possible. We would like to show you how to meet many of those curricular needs while adding the various new pieces as they come down the pike.

We would agree that children do need to know a common body of knowledge that is often presented in the textbooks we discussed earlier, the basal program, or your state and district guidelines. When children have a certain base of knowledge, they are able to use those learnings in this ever-changing world so they will be able to negotiate new problems and situations with agility. But the advantage of the thematic unit is that the depth of study can be greater and learning can be tailored to each child and his or her questions, needs, and abilities.

What Should *We* Teach?

But let's also be realistic. What knowledge are we to teach? The figures on the amount of knowledge in the world and how rapidly it is growing are staggering. According to a report by the Presidents' Commission on Teacher Education for the American Association of State Colleges and Universities (1992), the total of the world's knowledge doubled during the period from 1750 to 1900. It doubled again from 1900 to 1950, again from 1950 to 1960, and yet again from 1960 to 1965. From that point, it has doubled every 5 years and at increasingly smaller intervals. In fact, by the year 2020, it is projected that world's knowledge will double every 73 days. Now, with that in mind, we would dare you to please tell us what *are* the most important bits of information to teach. With this info-boom glaring us in the face, we certainly cannot teach it all. The question becomes, where do we start?

Understand that we are not advocating you throw out your curriculum. In reality, that whole body of learning is set pretty solidly either by the state or your district, or it is given boundaries by the textbook series you have. Contained within those documents, you have a well-written and articulated curriculum. At its best, it is a distillation of all the major points in each content area and can be used as a guide for what you need to cover; what is most vital for the children of the 21st century to know.

But along with this huge body of information, this body that is growing exponentially, we must, more importantly, prepare our children to become facile learners, engaged seekers of knowledge, and the sole investigators of the answers to their own questions. As we have shown, children's trade books play a major part in these inquiries. With the wide range of topics addressed in children's literature across almost any subject imaginable, children's literature is clearly the front-running alternative. As we noted earlier in this chapter as well as in chapter 10 concerning the strengths of nonfiction and informational books, children's literature provides a much greater depth to any one subject as opposed to the superficial coverage presented in textbooks.

▼▼▼▼▼▼▼

The Integrated, Literature-Based Thematic Unit

This leads us quite naturally to the integrated thematic unit. Briefly stated, integrated, literature-based thematic units present your class with a large aggregation of books representing a wide range of readability levels all centered on an overall organizing theme or framework. These units afford the children opportunities for investigation within the curricular framework and provide them with the venue for answering personal questions that spring up during their own inquiry.

Just as important, the integrated nature of these units helps children make those all-important connections across curricular areas. Let us give you a personal example of what we mean here, one that shows the importance of one curricular area playing off of and enhancing the others.

For quite a number of years, Darigan has been a big fan of Mozart and his music—well over a decade, as a matter of fact. Half of his modest collection of CDs contains music by Mozart: He has collected all of Mozart's piano concertos, all of the piano sonatas, and most of his symphonies. He has read widely on Mozart (both in children's and adult books) and studied the man and his music. He has attended lectures on Mozart and his music and, of course, has seen most of his operas.

Oddly enough, he was introduced to a fact that he hadn't known about Mozart—a connection totally new to him—until just recently. This fact was as obvious as the nose on his face. He was doing the research for another book he was writing, one set in his home of Philadelphia. A Park Ranger at Independence Hall was relating events going on in the United States and the world while the Declaration of Independence was being written. Among those connections he made was the fact that in 1776, Mozart was alive and composing music "at the ripe old age of 20."

Darigan was shocked. Thinking back to *Amadeus,* the fictionalized film version of Mozart's life, he recalled all the actors wearing three-corner hats just like Washington and Jefferson. Somehow he had never made that connection between these great contemporaries. In his learning as a child and even growing up, that link was never made. The reason had to be because of the separation of American history and European history. And for him, the two never were linked. This is what thematic units can more ably do. But there is more.

Later, after learning that fact, he went back to his biographies with a different purpose and different questions. He wanted to learn more about Mozart and what music he composed during that important year in American history. He found that in the year 1776, Mozart had written quite a bit—two concertos for the piano, some serenades, divertimentos, as well as some serious church music. He was particularly interested in the piano concertos and dragged out his collection. Reading more closely, he learned yet another interesting fact: It seems that in Mozart's 8th Piano Concerto, K.246, the opening movement for the piano deviated in a new but logical way to all that had preceded it. It turns out that not only did the solo piano echo the opening theme the orchestra had already stated—which was common for the time—it also introduced a secondary theme that, according to Sadie (1983), was "a clear hint of the coming expansion of the [piano concerto] form's scale and range" (p. 49). In other words, Mozart was revolutionary in 1776 as well. Darigan went back and listened to that first movement, and sure enough, he could hear the secondary theme, one he also had never noticed before.

So in his investigation of his beloved Mozart, he realized how insulated his perspective was, given all that was going on in the world at that very same time. It in turn made him wonder what was also going on in China and Africa and Australia. That same excitement and expansive thinking happens with children: They can learn about the discovery of plutonium or the invention of the first automobile but have no context of the times and issues of the world with which to connect it. When connections are made, they open up an entire new world of understanding.

Note that as Darigan learned more about the times and Mozart's music, he went back to his inquiry to make more connections, to learn more. This is the portrait we would like all children to embrace and imitate. We want them to see their learning as personally important and more directed by themselves as they ultimately become masters of their own inquiries.

▼▼▼▼▼▼

Considerations in Planning a Thematic Unit

So, what are some considerations you need to keep in mind while planning these integrated, literature-based thematic units? We see topic choice as the first task and vitally important to the success of your unit of study. We address points you will need to keep in mind as you hone your topic to meet both the interests of your class and your own curricular needs. Then we look at the task of finding and collecting materials and activities that support and enhance your unit. Finally, we look at implementation in your classroom and the reflection you will necessarily have to do as you modify your unit for the next time you use it.

Topic Selection—The First BIG Step

Choosing a topic can be a tricky proposition. If you think you can drag out one of your old warhorses and simply *call* it an integrated, literature-based thematic unit, you may be in for a rude awakening. Your children will smell it out in the blink of an eye.

In general, these units we're talking about are far more open-ended than the standard day-in-and-day-out "read a section of the chapter on 'States' Rights' and answer the 'Things-To-Think-About' questions." The theme you select will add a coherent strand to the unit, while the abundance of literature and student choice available will allow individual discoveries and personal inquiries to take place.

That's not to say you can't retrieve one of the units of study you use annually and spruce it up to make it integrated, literature-based, and thematic. We're just saying that dusting off an old unit such as "Nutrition" and trying to pawn it off as a thematic unit will certainly not fly without some major modifications.

Choose a High-Interest Topic

So your first consideration is to choose a topic that will be of high interest to both *you* and *your students*. We have found that the greatest success in developing these units has come with a blend of what you need to cover in your curriculum and then taking it a step or two further by adding some metaphorical twists to your topic. For example, Pappas, Kiefer, and Levstik (1995) took a something as mundane as the nutrition unit we just mentioned, often taught in second grade, added an abundance of literature sources and meaningful activities, organized the unit in more global terms, changed the name to "Let's Eat," and ended up with a very interesting and provocative unit.

The five major subcategories they divided their unit into were "Food Math," "Food Science," "Food Art," "Fun with Food," and "Who Eats." Under the category of "Food Science," for example, Pappas et al. suggest three subheadings: "Where Does Food Come From?" "Food Changes," and "Food Chains." Listed under these subheadings is a wide array of books and activities that will guide children's learning and investigations. In the end, what the unit does is "put the concept of nutrition into a broader context than the traditional four food groups" (p. 97) and opens the children's minds to a far greater definition of nutrition, healthy eating, and food.

Later in this chapter, we share sample units we have developed to more fully describe what a true integrated, literature-based thematic unit looks like. For now, we hope you see how important the initial topic selection is.

Consider Breadth

The second consideration in topic selection for your thematic unit is to choose a topic that is broad, but not too broad. If you bite off a topic that is way too large, you will drown your students with materials and information and, losing interest, they will likely not be able to make the connections you want. Likewise, if you choose a topic that is too small, the children will hardly see it as a unit of study at all and will struggle for the lack of connections they can make. Just like the porridge in the "Three Little Bears," you need to find a topic that is "just right."

It is not unusual for teachers to overdo the units they have created; we all fall prey to this. These unwieldy studies seem to take on a life of their own and end up controlling all the time and energy in a classroom. Perhaps it is because, over the years, we have accumulated such a hefty amount of materials in a particular area that we don't want to let one shred of information go untouched or unlearned. What we often fail to recognize, in these cases, is that it took *us* years to grow into these topics of interest and, *in our own time,* we allowed the inquiry to unfold. We mistakenly expect children to have the same verve for the topic *and* study it as comprehensively over the course of the month or 6 weeks the unit runs.

Dovetail Your Thematic Unit Into Your Existing Program

Next, you need to make sure your unit fits as well as possible into your existing curriculum framework. Again, choose a topic wisely and with that in mind. For example, a conventional social studies unit on the United States Civil War can be redefined and evolve into a comprehensive unit on "Conflict." In it, you can certainly look at that era in United States history, but by further expanding the theme into conflict, you open many avenues in science, math, health, and the language arts. Just think about all the things in each area that present conflict and how broadly you can construe the

To find out more about The Children's Literature Web Guide and other sources on the World Wide Web, visit Chapter 15 on the companion website at **www.prenhall. com/darigan**

INTEGRATING TECHNOLOGY: SOURCES ON THE WORLD WIDE WEB

If you have time to go to only one site when surfing the web for children's literature, this should probably be the one. David Brown at the University of Calgary has compiled an incredible source of information at *The Children's Literature Web Guide*. The website is very comprehensive and includes award lists, conference information, links to resources for parents, teachers, storytellers, writers and illustrators, links to on-line stories . . . The list of materials goes on and on. A search engine at the site helps locate information.

theme seen as conflict. In science, there is the conflict of nature against human interference in the world's forests. In math, there is the continual dynamic of fractions needing to be reduced to lowest terms. In health, there is the ever-existent fight between germs and bacteria and the human and animal organisms. The possibilities are endless and the unit becomes all the easier to plan because of this fact.

Gather Materials

Your next step is to begin brainstorming possible books, materials, and activities that will lend themselves to your theme. We have found that doing this with your grade level colleagues is most productive. You, for instance, may know of a number of books that work with the theme of the Civil War, but one book you mention may prompt one of your team members to think of another book or activity that you would have never considered. You will see how the ideas start to flow like Niagara Falls as you plan.

Keep in mind that you want to include both fiction and nonfiction. We tend to operate with a mind-set that a unit of study must be chock full of facts and be only a nonfiction inquiry. But, as we have mentioned in our earlier chapters on historical fiction and on informational books, the human connection is far better expressed through fiction. How better for a child to come to understand something as abstract as the horrors of a civil war than to read about it in books such as Patricia Beatty's **Turn Homeward, Hannalee**, her **Charley Skedaddle**, (1987) and Douglas Rees's **Lightning Time**?

While planning your books, you will also want to be on the lookout for good read alouds. These books, as we have also echoed in previous chapters, need to be stimulating and fast-paced and must provide suitable comparisons to the other books the children are reading. Darigan found Belinda Hurmence's book **A Girl Called Boy** an excellent choice for their work on the Civil War. He combined it with a nice assortment of picture books, also something you won't want to forget. Books such as Ann Turner's **Nettie's Trip South** and Patricia Lee Gauch's **Thunder at Gettysburg** were short and provided a new perspective in the class's discussions of that conflict. More recent titles to be included are **Follow the Drinking Gourd: A Story of the Underground Railroad**, by Bernardine Connelly, **A Place Called Freedom**, by Scott Russell Sanders, **Barefoot: Escape on the Underground Railroad**, by Pamela Duncan Edwards, **Mr. Lincoln's Whiskers**, by Karen B. Winnick, and **The Blue and the Gray**, by Eve Bunting.

Organize Your Unit—Using a Web

You may find that organizing the "meandering thoughts" your collective minds go through during this brainstorming process is best done on a web. We usually use a large hunk of white butcher paper. Place your topic in the middle of the paper, then as you start to cluster and combine the books and activities you have listed, you'll see some overall categories emerge.

Take, for example, our own sample unit that we entitled "Time and Time Again." We chose the time travel novel as the core for our model integrated, literature-based thematic unit. Clearly, it addresses the study of history and social studies in a fresh, provocative way. Characters thrust back in time are able to see, firsthand, the conditions of the era. Further, they are often introduced to some of the dynamics and social conditions that prompted, say, the Great Depression, as is seen in Jackie French's ***Somewhere Around the Corner***, or 19th-century slavery, as seen in Janet Lunn's ***The Root Cellar***.

But time travel can do more readily what historical fiction and informational books cannot, and that is allow the reader the opportunity to view the conditions of the times through contemporary, 21st-century eyes. Though the texts are fictional, children are more able to integrate conditions of the past and historical concepts into their own schemas because they take the past and make it a *living and continuous process* (Yolen, 1989, p. 248). Finally, time travel offers the reader the chance to learn a valuable lesson, "not only about history and the conditions of the times and places visited, but, more importantly, about him- or herself, as well" (Darigan & Woodcock, 1999, p. 35).

In preparation for this unit, we sampled well over 100 books before settling on 45 titles that suited our needs. We then laid them out on two large tables and grouped them by their similarities. For example, we noted that there was a block of books where the time travelers interacted with their own relatives from the not too distant past—their grandparents or their parents when they were children. A number of others had to do with slavery and the American Civil War. Still others thrust the main characters back in time an even 100 years. Using these groups, we determined our tentative main headings, such as: "Time and Time Again—With Families," "Times of Slavery," and "What Difference Can 100 Years Make?" to mention only a few.

Be Ready to Adapt and Be Flexible

After working through all these obvious matches, we moved on to the curricular areas beyond reading that we wanted to accent, such as math, science, art, and health. But here is where we met our first roadblock and where we altered our initial plan, which had been to stick rigidly to time travel novels. As we were considering our subcategory "Health Issues—Over Time," we chose two books to focus on. Mary Downing Hahn's ***Time for Andrew***, which addresses diphtheria as young Drew, a boy of the present, is thrust back to 1910 where his distant relative, also named Andrew, is suffering and obviously dying from the disease. When the two boys, who look identical, switch places, the Andrew of 1910 is able to travel to the present and receive modern health care. But he enjoys the present so much that he decides he does not want to return to his own time. In the end, a game of marbles decides the fate of the boys.

Another book dealing with diphtheria is Margaret Peterson Haddix's ***Running Out of Time***. This book finds an 1840s community also suffering from the effects of the disease. The twist in the novel occurs when we find out that the main character Jessie, her family, as well as all the others in the town are actually residing in a "living history village." More important, we find out that the time is really "now." Going against the stated wishes of the museum's administration, Jessie's mother smuggles her out, where she seeks modern medical attention. Her confrontation with the contemporary world, where even a telephone is foreign to her, adds to the fast-paced plot line.

As we discussed Haddix's book, the three of us all had to agree that it was not really a time travel novel, though the effects were certainly the same. So we wondered, "If we can include this book under that health umbrella (Darigan had already published it in a *Book Links* article he did in March, 1999) why couldn't we add yet another favorite to the health list?" Why, then, could we not add Cynthia DeFelice's ***The Apprenticeship of Lucas Whitaker***? This book deals with the onset of consumption, more commonly known today as tuberculosis. Young Lucas is in conflict between his respect for the barber/surgeon he is apprenticing under and the unusually maudlin folk remedy the general populace has adopted.

But if we were to add it, we would also have to include Laurie Halse Anderson's *Fever 1793*, describing the great yellow fever epidemic in the United States. Opening up the flood gates, we weren't sure where the list would end. Should we also include James Cross Giblin's wonderful book ***When Plague Strikes: The Black Death, Small-pox, AIDS?*** Hahn's book is real, 100% time travel fantasy and Haddix's book is a crossover between contemporary and historical fiction with an added hint of time travel. The two titles by DeFelice and Anderson are both clearly historical fiction, whereas Giblin's book is informational. Because they are all so strong and compelling, we decided to add them all. So, making this adjustment, we expanded our topic to include books that were not just time travel but that also played with time or described another time.

As you can see in the final web we constructed for our unit "Time and Time Again" (see Figure 15–1), we have listed a large amount of books and activities; these make up the "materials" for the unit. We have found that a double-paged web, like we have shown here, is very helpful for students to have in their hands. We also enlarged these boxed categories and made them into a full-blown bulletin board.

▼▼▼▼▼▼▼

Getting Your Unit Started

The construction of the unit is seemingly complete—or so you think. For the purpose of "this" unit for "this" year, it *is* complete. But we warn you that down the road, years from now, you will be in a shop or bookstore and you'll see a book, a game, or some sort of curiosity and remark, "Oh, I could use that for my time travel unit (or my Changes unit, or my Nutrition unit). It would fit just perfectly with . . . " To which your significant other will shake his or her head and walk away knowing—here's yet another piece to add to the bursting collection of teacher materials you hoard. And it is true that we add to our materials every year. Prepare yourself: These units never end.

From ***Time Flies,*** by Eric Rohmann. Copyright © 1994 by Eric Rohmann. Used by permission of Crown Children's Books, a division of Random House, Inc.

Share a Book

Once you have collected all the materials you need, it is time to get the unit rolling. For the "Time and Time Again" unit, we suggest starting out by "reading" Eric Rohmann's Caldecott Honor book, *Time Flies*. This wordless picture book shows a bird flying back in time; back to the time of the dinosaurs.

As you show your class the story and tell them what is going on, at the same time, you can elicit a lot of conversation among the children. They will pick up on things you never saw before. The idea is to give the children a sense of what going back in time is all about. As you end the book, you are ready to introduce them to the web (Figure 15–1).

Introduce the Web

We suggest you hand out the copies of the web, similar to the spread we show in Figure 15–1, and display all the books that will make up the unit. You will want to discuss the various subcategories, noting the general flavor for each and mentioning which curricular area they best address. When you are finished, you will want to ask the children if they have any questions, comments, or additions for the unit. You may be surprised at all they will be able to add.

Next, spend 10 or 15 more minutes reading aloud from the ongoing novel that you will be sharing with the class throughout the course of the unit. For "Time and Time Again," we suggest Felice Holman's book *Real*. In this book, Colly, a young boy in 1932, is quite enamored with Hollywood and how, to him, the movies make everything seem so "real." His father is a Hollywood stunt man, and when he gets injured in a riding accident, the pair head out into the desert to live in an old adobe cabin of Colly's grandfather. In Colly's wanderings, the boy is thrust back in time to 1774. He meets a young Native American boy named Sparrow who is stuck in a cyclical scenario, wanting to be released from the trap known as "Forever Day."

The first thing *Real* offers the children in your classroom is a good view of the time travel novel, which gives them the basic structure of the genre. As you read, you can have them keep record of how their book compares and contrasts to the read aloud. Further, it also acts as a perfect springboard for you to address a variety of connections ripe for potential investigation. By reading the book, for instance, and showing some footage of movies of the era, you may spark a number of children's interest in old films from the 1930s. They can research them and report their findings back to class. Comparing budget and salaries from then to now might make for some interesting math problems. Other children may find the portrayal of "Indians" worth investigating. They will readily see the portrayal of Native Americans to be stereotypic in that time and in most cases reprehensible. Still others will be interested in the dynamic going on between the native population and the white intruders. By book's end, Holman, of course, helps readers to see the great wealth of knowledge and tradition present in what appeared at the book's beginning to be very monocultural.

Allow for Student Choice in the Unit

After the read aloud on the first day of the unit, you will want to provide the children with plenty of time to look carefully at the web you have prepared. As you describe time travel books you have listed and that they may want to read, you can also tell them about the corresponding activities that are available.

Finally, you will want them to spend time thinking of what books and activities they are most interested in. Once satisfied with their choices, they will need to fill out a learning contract for their study of this integrated, literature-based thematic unit (an example is shown in Figure 15–2). We have found that these student contracts significantly help set up the serious nature of the class inquiry and provide structure and focus to those who need it. One thing you may want to make clear in your own mind as well as communicate to your students is that if a child finds that a book is too difficult

Time of War

The Devil's Arithmetic, by Jane Yolen

Dark Shade, by Jane Louise Curry

The Root Cellar, by Janet Lunn

Soldier's Heart, by Gary Paulsen

Pink and Say, by Patricia Polacco

Charley Skedaddle, by Patricia Beatty

Across Five Aprils, by Irene Hunt

Turn Homeward, *Hannalee*, by Patricia Beatty

A Ballad of the Civil War, by Mary Stoltz

Research the specific war presented in your book. Find out what the issues were, and use a Venn diagram to list both perspectives. • Make clay models of the various weapons used in the war you read about. • Make a roll movie showing a news flash covering one of the major battles in your book. • Draw and label the uniforms soldiers wore during the war you read about. • Write a series of diary entries from the perspective of your main character. • As the main character, write a letter home to your family telling them your first war experiences.

Time Warp Trio Times by Jon Scieszka

2095

The Not-So-Jolly Roger
Compare your book with a friend who read Fleischman's *The 13th Floor*.

Knights of the Kitchen Table

The Good, the Bad, and the Goofy

Your Mother Was a Neanderthal

Tut Tut

Read two books from this series and compare them using a Venn diagram. • Draw portraits of the Time Warp Trio with costumes and surrounding background taken from the time of whatever book you read. • Prepare your book for the movie version. Cast parts with classmates or real stars and write the script for the first two chapters. • Pick another favorite time period and write a story about the Time Warp Trio going to that era. • Send your idea to Scieszka—he needs all the ideas he can get.

Time and Time Again

What Difference Can 100 Years Make?

Switching Well, by Peni R. Griffin

Both Sides of Time, by Caroline B. Cooney

Out of Time, by Caroline B. Cooney

Prisoner of Time, by Caroline B. Cooney

Paper Quake, by Kathryn Reiss

Create the front page of a newspaper that includes weather, news, editorial commentary, and advertisements for the day of the great San Francisco earthquake.

Jeremy Visick, by David Wiseman
Research a disaster and write a time travel tale that centers around that mishap.

The Orphan of Ellis Island, by Elvira Woodruff

Write a time travel tale using a relative of your own who immigrated from another country. Sampling old catalogs from a century ago, prepare an advertisement page for the local newspaper. • Compare and contrast your book with one from a friend in this category. Show your results with a Venn diagram. • Draw the dresses and formal wear of 100 years ago. • Write a pamphlet on the customs and manners of 100 years ago.

Story Time—Analyze This!

Pale Phoenix, by Kathryn Reiss

The Princess in the Pigpen, by Jane Resh Thomas

The Transall Saga, by Gary Paulsen

A String in the Harp, by Nancy Bond

The Children of Green Knowe, by L. M. Boston

Analyze your book according to some or all of the following criteria:
1. Was the 20th-century child facing a problem or in some kind of trouble?
2. Are the characters able to "control" the time travel?
3. What devices/methods/props are used to transport the person through time?
4. Does the child go back to the same place or time?
5. Is the child believed by the people from the past or future? Is the child even seen?
6. How does the character return to his or her own time?
7. Does the character bring back any evidence or proof of his or her travel?
8. How has the character changed as a result of his or her time travel?
9. Has any time elapsed while the character has been gone? Are the parallel times equal?

FIGURE 15–1 Web for "Time and Time Again."

Times of Slavery

A Girl Called Boy, by Belinda Hermence
Draw a picture of the special talisman, or make a clay model using descriptions from the book.

Nightjohn, by Gary Paulsen

Something Upstairs, by Avi
Write a story about an unjustly treated slave and how he or she escapes.

True North, by Kathryn Lasky

Running for our Lives, by Glennette Tilley Turner

Sweet Clara and the Freedom Quilt, by Deborah Hopkinson

Study the constellations and draw a sky map highlighting the North Star—the direction runaway slaves traveled on the Underground Railroad. • Write a biography of Harriet Tubman.

Health Issues—Over Time

Time for Andrew, by Mary Downing Hahn

Running Out of Time, by Margaret Peterson Haddix
Research diphtheria and report on the "modern" ways it is cured.

Fever 1793, by Laurie Halse Anderson
Research yellow fever and tell how it was contracted and eventually cured.

The Apprenticeship of Lucas Whitaker, by Cynthia DeFelice

Out of Time, by Caroline B. Cooney
Research consumption or tuberculosis and report on the "modern" ways it is cured.

When Plague Strikes, by James Cross Giblin
Research another sickness, such as malaria or polio. Write your report on its symptoms, its effects on humankind, and its cures.

An Acquaintance With Darkness, by Ann Rinaldi

Interview a medical doctor concerning outbreaks of other diseases around the world. Find out what is being done to reach a cure for them and report back to the class. • Make a diorama of an 18th century doctor's office. • Find various other folk remedies for diseases and make a medical manual for them.

Time to Visit Castles

Moon Window, by Jane Louse Curry

Webster's Leap, by Eileen Dunlop
Collect and record lute, mandolin, and recorder music from the 16th century, perhaps by Vivaldi, and play it as a backdrop for other Castle reports.

The Boggart, by Susan Cooper

Stephen Biesty's Cross-Sections: Castles, by Richard Platt

Castle, by David Macaulay

Write a time travel tale where a castle is the central setting. Be sure to include detailed research on what you've learned about these beautiful structures. • Make a "Cross-Section" book of your own that shows the setting of one of the above novels. • Write "castle trivia questions" to stump another friend who has read the same book as you have.

Time and Time Again With Families

Stonewords, by Pam Conrad
Write an obituary for Zoe Louise.

Mr. Was, by Pete Hautman
Write a time travel tale where the portal to another time is a door similar to the one in Boggs End.

A Dig in Time, by Peni R. Griffin

Building Blocks, by Cynthia Voigt
Research a relative either near or distant. Create your own time travel tale with you meeting the relative when he or she is at your age. Include the person as one of the main characters.

The 13th Floor, by Sid Fleischman

Research the Salem Witch Trials and write a newspaper article describing them, adding characters from *The 13th Floor*. • Talk to one of your relatives about his or her roots. Write a time travel story that takes you back to your country of origin. • Draw a family portrait for one of the above books as the family appeared back in time.

Windows Into Time

The Window, by Jeanette Ingold
Create a large shadowbox using a refrigerator-size carton. Draw a mural of Mandy's bedroom and window on one of the outer sides. Cut a window hole so you can see into the past (and the box). On the far inside side of the box, paint another mural that Mandy would have viewed from the past.

Time Windows, by Kathryn Reiss
Use a window, as author Kathryn Heiss did, to allow a main character in your own story to view the past or the future—tell his or her story.

Moon Window, by Jane Louise Curry
Use fire as a vehicle to set up the problem of your own time travel story.

Window of Time, by Karen Weinberg

Design a beautiful window and use it as your time travel portal for an original story. • Learn how stained glass is made and report on the details of your study. • Choose a place (a monument, old store, or house) that you would like to know more about. Research this as a "setting" using primary written sources and oral histories and set your own time travel tale there.

Student Contract for "Time and Time Again"

_____ 1. I will read the following two books from the web:
_____ by _____
_____ by _____

_____ 2. I will participate in all class and small-group discussions.

_____ 3. I will satisfactorily complete all assignments neatly and hand them in on time.

_____ 4. I will complete a Venn diagram or learning log comparing my first book listed above to *Real.*

_____ 5. I will complete a learning log for my second book with summaries and reactions from my reading.

_____ 6. I will complete the following **three** activities from the web. I have chosen:
a. _____
b. _____
c. _____

I agree to complete all of the above assignments by (place date here) ___ /___ /___

_____   _____
Student's Signature   Teacher's Signature

FIGURE 15–2   Individual student learning contract.

or is not to his or her liking, he or she can easily switch to something else on the web as a substitute. All that need be done is to make the new selection and to have it approved by the teacher.

▼▼▼▼▼▼▼

Assessing the Integrated, Literature-Based Thematic Unit

After completing the unit, you will need to assess two things. First, you will need to know how the children performed individually in the unit. Second, and just as important, you'll want to assess how successful the unit and your teaching were. Using this information, you can adjust for the next time you teach it.

Grading scales or rubrics can be of great use in assessing and evaluating student performance. They present a fair way to grade children's performance, and because they can be passed out before work on the unit actually begins, all the children in your class will know your clearly stated objectives and expectations. Because they are easy to create and very adaptable using your computer's cut-and-paste capabilities, you can maintain a standard format that your children will be familiar with but one you can tailor to the express requirements of each unit. Using a sliding scale of 1 to 5, you can arrive at a reasonable grade that includes effort and final products. We include in Figure 15-3 an example of a rubric we would use for our unit "Time and Time Again."

Returning to the student contract, because that lists the criteria we set up in the first place, we list in the rubric the main objectives and give the numerical value for how the child performed. By using a grading scale such as the one shown here, you can assess the children's effort and performance in a fair way—and in almost every case, the students will probably rate themselves about the same. Further, one of the beauties of these grading scales is that they are so adaptable to each unit that you teach. As we already noted, you can cut and paste the change in objectives that occurs as students learn and progress as readers, writers, and learners.

_____ The student participated in class and small-group discussions.

_____ The student read the first assigned book and completed a Venn diagram comparing it to **Real.**

_____ The student read the second assigned book and completed a learning log offering summaries and reactions to his or her reading.

_____ On the first web activity, the student chose to do _____ and completed it successfully.

_____ On the second web activity, the student chose to do _____ and completed it successfully.

_____ On the third web activity, the student chose to do _____ and completed it successfully.

_____ Total Score (30 points possible)

Score Indicators:

1 = Poor effort: student either handed in incomplete work or quality was poor

2 = Below average effort: student handed in all work that was of marginal quality

3 = Average effort: student completed all work and quality was good

4 = Good effort: student completed all work and quality was better than average

5 = Excellent effort: student completed all work and quality was superb

FIGURE 15–3 Unit assessment.

Assessing the Unit and Your Teaching

Next you need to reflect on the overall success of the unit and how you taught. You may want to contemplate and answer the following questions:

1. What books, materials, and activities did you find most effective?
2. What books, materials, and activities did you find not to work well? Would you delete them, or are they worth minor adjustment and a second chance?
3. Was your topic appropriate? Was it broad enough, yet not too expansive?
4. How did you accommodate differences in abilities? What could you do that would be even more effective?
5. What lessons were particularly effective?
6. What lessons didn't seem to work? How would you adjust them for greater success?
7. What ideas do you have for teaching this unit in the future?
8. How would you make more links to other cross-curricular areas?
9. What did students like about this unit?
10. What are student suggestions for improving this unit?

After you reflect on your children's performance and your overall assessment in regard to the success of the unit, we think it is best to make notes to yourself so the next time you teach this unit, you will have pertinent information fresh at hand.

▼▼▼▼▼▼▼

A Primary Version of an Integrated, Literature-Based Thematic Unit

We include also a unit for the primary grades. Because the teachers in our schools address dinosaurs so heavily at the second-grade level, we thought it wise to provide this web (Figure 15–4).

Digging Dinosaurs and Finding Fossils

Searching for Velociraptor, by Lowell Dingus and Mark Norell
Bring any fossils you have to school and make a class museum.

Digging Up Dinosaurs, by Aliki
Ask a dinosaur expert to come to your classroom and give a presentation.

Prehistoric Pinkerton, by Steven Kellogg

Colossal Fossil: The Dinosaur Riddle Book, by Mike Thayler
Write some dinosaur riddles yourself using Thayler's technique.

Big Old Bones, by Carol Carrick

Illustrate your favorite part of the book you read. Rewrite the text to match what you've drawn. • Using a familiar song, write lyrics telling about the book you read.

How Did Dinosaurs Become Extinct?

What Happened to the Dinosaurs?, by Franklyn M. Branley

Dinosaur Ghosts: The Mystery of Coelophysis, by Lynett J. Gillette

Killer Asteroids, by Margaret Poynter

What Happened to Patrick's Dinosaur?, by Carol Carrick

Whatever Happened to the Dinosaurs?, by Bernard Most

Make a page for a class Big Book that answers, "Why did the dinosaurs become extinct?" • Make a roll movie that presents a news report covering the extinction of dinosaurs. • Along with a friend, draw a mural depicting the way your book considers the reason for the extinction of dinosaurs. Hang your works in the hallway for all to see.

Dinosaurs Today

Prehistoric Pinkerton, by Steven Kellogg

Dinosaur Garden, by Liza Donnelly

Can I Have a Segosaurus, Mom? Can I? Please?, by Lois G. Grambling

Dinosaur Bob, by William Joyce

If the Dinosaurs Came Back, by Bernard Most
Write about a dinosaur REALLY coming to our time.

Patrick's Dinosaur, by Carol Carrick

Jacob Two-Two and the Dinosaur, by Mordecai Richler

The Dinosaur's New Clothes, by Diane Goode

Write your own retelling of a favorite folk tale using dinosaurs as main characters. • Write a letter to your teacher explaining why a dinosaur would be a great class pet. • Write a story: *The Trouble With Dinosaurs*. • Bake dinosaur cookies.

Dinosaurs

We're Caught in Dinosaur Times

Time Train, by Paul Fleischman

Time Flies, by Eric Rohmann

Dinosaur Garden, by Liza Donnelly

Dinosaur World, by Christopher Santoro

Big Book of Dinosaurs, by Angela Wilkes

Take a trip to a local museum and learn all you can about dinosaurs. Report back to class. • Make a diorama display of a dinosaur museum. Include several types of dinosaurs. • Pretend you were lost in a dinosaur museum; what would you see? Write a story.

Dinosaur Informational Books

Amazing Dinosaurs, by Dougal Dixon

Dinosaur: The Essential Guide, by Disney

Dinosaurs!: The Biggest Baddest Strangest Fastest, by Howard Zimmerman

Guide to Dinosaurs, by David Lambert

Utahraptor: The Deadliest Dinosaur, by Don Lessem

Seismosaurus: The Longest Dinosaur, by Don Lessem

Ornithomimids: The Fastest Dinosaur, by Don Lessem

Trodon: The Smartest Dinosaur, by Don Lessem

Gigantic: How Big Were the Dinosaurs?, by Patrick O'Brien

Did Triceratops Have Polka Dots? First Questions and Answers About Dinosaurs, by Time-Life

Dinosaur Valley, by Mitsuhiro Kurokawa

Compare and contrast the class lizard with the dinosaurs. • Give an oral report on your favorite dinosaur. • Make a class informational book on dinosaurs. • Research lizards of today and compare them to dinosaurs.

FIGURE 15–4 Web for dinosaurs.

Trade books can be used to learn beyond the set curriculum most of us seem to be bound by. They explore so much more of the world than is covered in traditional school subjects: child labor laws, the development of dynamite, the making of baseball bats, printing paper money, living with a terminal disease, illustrating comic books, and on and on. It is difficult to find a topic in the world that is *not* the focus of a children's book. The idea of the integrated, literature-based thematic unit is that it will spark interests in children that exist within and outside the traditional school subjects. Children are then free to find books about things that go beyond what they will learn in school, yet are still very appealing to them. After their investigations, they should have a chance to share their new knowledge. Using trade books to learn subject matter provides children freedom to discover while still keeping them accountable.

If we want children to develop intellectually, we make the greatest strides when we concentrate on helping them become curious. A curious person is observant and aware, asks questions, and tries to find the answers to them. Being curious is a mindset and is a common denominator of those who discover and who solve problems. It is the curious who continue to learn under their own power. As Rabelais reportedly advised us, "Children are not vessels to be filled but fires to be lit." Because trade books reflect the curiosity and humanity of authors who have learned to see and who wish to share that vision, they have the spark that can light that flame.

▼▼▼▼▼▼▼

Summary

In this chapter, we first discussed the attributes, strengths, and weaknesses of textbooks, reference books, and trade books. We settled on trade books as the foundation for thematic units of study based on their strength in language, voice, and variety. We discussed the "crowded curriculum" and showed how thematic study can actually enhance and diffuse the ever-growing expectations laid upon teachers. We showed how to plan a unit of study, gather necessary materials, organize for instruction, and assess and evaluate the success of the unit. Finally, we provided an intermediate unit of study, "Time and Time Again," and a primary unit, "Dinosaurs," as examples of literature-based thematic units to model the process and to get teachers thinking about how they can develop a unit such as these, given their own interests and curriculum requirements.

▼▼▼▼▼▼▼

Children's Literature References

Aliki. (1988). *Digging up dinosaurs*. New York: Harper & Row.

Anderson, Laurie Halse. (2000). *Fever 1793*. New York: Simon & Schuster.

Arnosky, Jim. (1996). *Crinkleroot's guide to knowing butterflies and moths*. New York: Simon & Schuster.

Avi. (1988). *Something upstairs: A tale of ghosts*. New York: Orchard.

Barton, Byron. (1990). *Bones, bones, dinosaur bones*. New York: Crowell.

Beatty, Patricia. (1984). *Turn homeward, Hannalee*. New York: Morrow.

Beatty, Patricia. (1987). *Charley Skedaddle*. New York: Morrow.

Bond, Nancy. (1976). *A string in the harp*. New York: Atheneum.

Boston, Lucy. (1951). *The children of Green Knowe*. San Diego: Harcourt.

Branley, Franklyn M. (1989). *What happened to the dinosaurs?* (Marc Simont, Illus.). New York: Crowell.

Bunting, Eve. (1996). *The blue and the gray* (Ned Bittinger, Illus.). New York: Scholastic.

Bunting, Eve. (1999). *Butterfly house* (Greg Shed, Illus.). New York: Scholastic.

Burgess, Melvin. (1992). *An angel for May*. New York: Simon & Schuster.

Carle, Eric. (1969). *The very hungry caterpillar*. New York: Philomel.

Carrick, Carol. (1983). *Patrick's dinosaur* (Donald Carrick, Illus.). New York: Clarion.

Carrick, Carol. (1986). *What happened to Patrick's dinosaur?* (Donald Carrick, Illus.). New York: Clarion.

Carrick, Carol. (1992). *Big old bones* (Donald Carrick, Illus.). New York: Clarion.

Cassie, Brian, & Pollotta, Jerry. (1995). *The butterfly alphabet book*. New York: Charlesbridge.

Catterwell, Thelma. (1998). *Aldita and the forest*. Boston: Houghton Mifflin.

Connelly, Bernardine. (1997). *Follow the drinking gourd: A story of the Underground Railroad* (Yvonne Buchanan, Illus.). New York: Simon & Schuster.

Conrad, Pam. (1990). *Stonewords.* New York: Harper & Row.

Cooney, Caroline B. (1995). *Both sides of time.* New York: Bantam Doubleday.

Cooney, Caroline B. (1996). *Out of time.* New York: Bantam Doubleday.

Cooney, Caroline B. (1998). *Prisoner of time.* New York: Bantam Doubleday.

Cooper, Susan. (1993). *The boggart.* New York: McElderry.

Curry, Jane Louise. (1996). *Moon window.* New York: McElderry.

Curry, Jane Louise. (1998). *Dark shade.* New York: McElderry.

DeFelice, Cynthia. (1996). *The apprenticeship of Lucas Whitaker.* New York: Farrar, Straus & Giroux.

Dingus, Lowell, & Norell, Mark. (1996). *Searching for Velociraptor.* New York: HarperCollins.

Disney. (2000). *Dinosaur: The essential guide.* New York: Dorling Kindersley.

Dixon, Dougal. (2000). *Amazing dinosaurs.* Honesdale, PA: Boyds Mills.

Donnelly, Liza. (1991). *Dinosaur garden.* New York: Scholastic.

Dunlop, Eileen. (1995). *Webster's leap.* New York: Holiday House.

Edwards, Pamela Duncan. (1997). *Barefoot: Escape on the Underground Railroad* (Henry Cole, Illus.). New York: HarperCollins.

Facklam, Margery. (1994). *The big bug book.* Boston: Little, Brown.

Fleischman, Paul. (1991). *Time train* (Claire Ewart, Illus.). New York: HarperCollins.

Fleischman, Sid. (1995). *The 13th floor.* New York: Greenwillow.

French, Jackie. (1995). *Somewhere around the corner.* New York: Henry Holt.

French, Vivian. (1993). *Caterpillar, caterpillar.* Cambridge, MA: Candlewick.

Gauch, Patricia Lee. (1975). *Thunder at Gettysburg* (Stephen Gammell, Illus.). New York: Coward.

Gibbons, Gail. (1989). *Monarch butterfly.* New York: Holiday House.

Giblin, James Cross. (1995). *When plague strikes: The black death, smallpox, AIDS.* New York: HarperCollins.

Gillette, Lynett J. (1997). *Dinosaur ghosts: The mystery of Coelophysis.* New York: Dial.

Goode, Diane. (1999). *The dinosaur's new clothes.* New York: Scholastic.

Grambling, Lois G. (1998). *Can I have a Stegosaurus, Mom? Can I? Please?* (H. B. Lewis, Illus.). New York: Troll.

Griffin, Peni. (1991). *A dig in time.* New York: McElderry.

Griffin, Peni. (1993). *Switching well.* New York: McElderry.

Gurney, James. (1992). *Dinotopia: A land apart from time.* New York: Turner.

Haddix, Margaret Peterson. (1995). *Running out of time.* New York: Simon & Schuster.

Hahn, Mary Downing. (1994). *Time for Andrew: A ghost story.* New York: Clarion.

Hautman, Pete. (1996). *Mr. Was.* New York: Simon & Schuster.

Hearn, Diane Dawson. (1999). *Dad's dinosaur day.* New York: Aladdin.

Hoff, Syd. (1958). *Danny and the dinosaur.* New York: Harper.

Hoff, Syd. (1995). *Happy birthday, Danny and the dinosaur.* New York: HarperCollins.

Holman, Felice. (1997). *Real.* New York: Atheneum.

Hopkins, Lee Bennett. (1987). *Dinosaurs* (Murray Tinkelman, Illus.). San Diego: Harcourt Brace.

Hopkinson, Deborah. (1993). *Sweet Clara and the freedom quilt* (James Ransome, Illus.). New York: Knopf.

Hunt, Irene. (1964). *Across five Aprils.* New York: Follett.

Hurmence, Belinda. (1982). *A girl called Boy.* Boston: Houghton Mifflin.

Ingold, Jeanette. (1996). *The window.* San Diego: Harcourt Brace.

Joyce, William. (1988). *Dinosaur Bob.* New York: Harper & Row.

Kellogg, Steven. (1987). *Prehistoric Pinkerton.* New York: Dial.

Kurokawa, Mitsuhiro. (1997). *Dinosaur valley.* San Francisco: Chronicle.

Lambert, David. (2000). *Guide to dinosaurs.* New York: Dorling Kindersley.

Lasky, Kathryn. (1993). *Monarchs.* San Diego: Harcourt Brace.

Lasky, Kathryn. (1996). *True north: A tale of the Underground Railroad.* New York: Scholastic.

Lauber, Patricia. (1989). *The news about dinosaurs.* New York: Bradbury Press.

Lavies, Bianca. (1992). *Monarch butterflies: Mysterious travelers.* New York: Dutton.

Lessem, Don. (1996a). *Ornithomimids: The fastest runner* (Donna Braginetz, Illus.). Minneapolis: Carolrhoda.

Lessem, Don. (1996b). *Seismosaurus: The longest dinosaur* (Donna Braginetz, Illus.). Minneapolis: Carolrhoda.

Lessem, Don. (1996c). *Trodon: The smartest dinosaur* (Donna Braginetz, Illus.). Minneapolis: Carolrhoda.

Lessem, Don. (1996d). *Utahraptor: The deadliest dinosaur* (Donna Braginetz, Illus.). Minneapolis: Carolrhoda.

Lobel, Arnold. (1970). *Frog and Toad are friends.* New York: Harper & Row.

Lunn, Janet. (1981). *The root cellar.* New York: Puffin.

Macaulay, David. (1978). *Castle.* Boston: Houghton Mifflin.

Morgan, Rowland. (1997). *In the next three seconds . . .* (Rod Josey & Kira Josey, Illus.). New York: Lodestar.

Most, Bernard. (1995). *If the dinosaurs came back.* San Diego: Harcourt Brace.

O'Brien, Patrick. (1999). *Gigantic: How big were the dinosaurs?* New York: Henry Holt.

Park, Ruth. (1982). *Playing beatie bow.* New York: Atheneum.

Paulsen, Gary. (1993). *Nightjohn.* New York: Delacorte.

Paulsen, Gary. (1998a). *Soldier's heart: A novel of the Civil War.* New York: Delacorte.

Paulsen, Gary. (1998b). *The transall saga.* New York: Delacorte.

Pearce, Philippa. (1986). *Tom's midnight garden.* New York: HarperCollins.

Peck, Richard. (1995). *Lost in cyberspace.* New York: Dial.

Platt, Richard. (1994). *Stephen Biesty's cross-sections: Castles.* New York: Dorling Kindersley.

Polacco, Patricia. (1994). *Pink and Say.* New York: Philomel.

Poynter, Margaret. (1996). *Killer asteroids.* New York: Enslow.

Rees, Douglas. (1997). *Lightning time.* New York: DK Ink/Jackson.

Reiss, Kathryn. (1991). *Time windows.* San Diego: Harcourt Brace.

Reiss, Kathryn. (1994). *Pale phoenix.* San Diego: Harcourt Brace.

Reiss, Kathryn. (1998). *Paperquake: A puzzle.* San Diego: Harcourt Brace.

Rey, Margret. (1989). *Curious George and the dinosaur.* Boston: Houghton Mifflin.

Richler, Mordecai. (1998). *Jacob Two-Two and the dinosaur* (Norman Eyolfson, Illus.). Plattsburgh, NY: Tundra.

Richter, Hans Peter. (1970). *Friedrich.* New York: Holt, Rinehart and Winston.

Rinaldi, Ann. (1997). *An acquaintance with darkness.* San Diego: Harcourt Brace.

Rohmann, Eric. (1994). *Time flies.* New York: Crown.

Sanders, Scott Russell. (1997). *A place called freedom* (Thomas B. Allen, Illus.). New York: Atheneum.

Sandved, Kjell Bloch. (1996). *The butterfly alphabet.* New York: Scholastic.

Santoro, Christopher. (1997). *Dinosaur world.* New York: Random House.

Scieszka, Jon. (1991a). *Knights of the kitchen table.* New York: Viking.

Scieszka, Jon. (1991b). *The not-so-jolly Roger.* New York: Viking.

Scieszka, Jon. (1992). *The good, the bad, and the goofy.* New York: Viking.

Scieszka, Jon. (1993). *Your mother was a Neanderthal.* New York: Viking.

Scieszka, Jon. (1996). *Tut tut.* New York: Viking.

Simon, Seymour. (1979). *Pets in a jar* (Betty Fraser, Illus.). New York: Puffin.

Simon, Seymour. (1997). *The time machine and other cases* (S. D. Schindler, Illus.). New York: Morrow.

Sirof, Harriet. (1996). *Bring back yesterday.* New York: Atheneum.

Stoltz, Mary. (1997). *A ballad of the Civil War* (Sergio Martinez, Illus.). New York: HarperCollins.

Talbott, Hudson. (1987). *We're back! A dinosaur's story.* New York: Crown.

Thomas, Jane Resh. (1989). *The princess in the pigpen.* New York: Clarion.

Time-Life. (1995). *Did Triceratops have polka dots? First questions and answers about dinosaurs.* New York: Time-Life.

Turner, Ann. (1987). *Nettie's trip south* (Ronald Himler, Illus.). New York: Macmillan.

Turner, Glennette Tilley. (1994). *Running for our lives.* New York: Holiday House.

Voigt, Cynthia. (1984). *Building blocks.* New York: Atheneum.

Weinberg, Karen. (1991). *Window of time.* New York: White Mane.

Winnick, Karen. (1996). *Mr. Lincoln's whiskers.* Honesdale, PA: Boyds Mills.

Wiseman, David. (1981). *Jeremy Visick.* Boston: Houghton Mifflin.

Woodruff, Elvira. (1997). *The orphan of Ellis Island: A time travel adventure.* New York: Scholastic.

Yolen, Jane. (1988). *Devil's arithmetic.* New York: Viking.

Zimmerman, Howard. (2000). *Dinosaurs!: The biggest, baddest, strangest, fastest.* New York: Atheneum.

▼▼▼▼▼▼▼

Professional References

Brown, C. S. (1994). *Connecting with the past: History workshop in the middle and high schools.* Portsmouth, NH: Heinemann.

Brozo, W. G., & Tomlinson, C. M. (1986). Literature: The key to lively content courses. *The Reading Teacher, 40*(3), 288–293.

Build Our Nation. (1997). Boston: Houghton Mifflin.

Butler, D. (1980). *Cushla and her books.* Boston: The Horn Book.

Colt, G. H. (1993, March). The most rehabilitated prisoner in America. *Life Magazine,* 69–76.

Darigan, D., & Woodcock, M. L. (1999). Time travel. *Booklinks, 8*(4), 35–41.

Dreyer, S. (1977–1995). *The Bookfinder* (vols. 1–5). Circle Pines, MN: American Guidance Service.

Fielding, L., Wilson, P. T., & Anderson, R. C. (1986). A new focus on free reading. In T. Raphael (Ed.), *The context of school-based literacy* (pp. 149–160). New York: Random House.

Gloster, R. (1994, 4 June). After a childhood of disarray, girl heads to Harvard. *The Daily Herald,* Provo, Utah, p. 1.

Holmes, B. C., & Ammon, R. I. (1985). Teaching content with trade books: A strategy. *Childhood Education, 61* (5) 366–370.

Holt Science. (1989). New York: Holt, Rinehart and Winston.

Pappas, C. C., Kiefer, B. Z., & Levstik, L. S. (1995). *An integrated language perspective in the elementary school: Theory into action.* White Plains, NY: Longman.

Presidents' Commission on Teacher Education. (1992). *Teacher education for the twenty-first century.* Washington, DC: American Association of State Colleges and Universities.

Roper Organization. (1987). *The American Chicle youth poll.* New York: Roper Organization.

Sadie, S. (1983). *The new grove Mozart.* New York: W. W. Norton.

Sewall, G. T. (1988). American history textbooks: Where do we go from here? *Phi Delta Kappan,* 553–558.

Shakespeare, W. (1993). *Romeo and Juliet.* New York: Dover.

Subject guide to children's books in print. (1999). New York: R. R. Bowker. (Published annually.)

Trelease, J. (1988). Introduction. In B. Kobrin, *Eyeopeners!* (p. xiv). New York: Viking.

Whittemore, H. (1991). The most precious gift. *Parade Magazine, 22,* 4–6.

Yolen, J. (1989). An experiential act. *Language Arts, 66* (3), 246–251.

A

APPENDIX
▼▼▼▼▼▼▼

BOOK SELECTION AIDS

Professional Organizations

American Library Association (ALA)

50 Huron St.
Chicago, IL 60611
Phone: (800) 545-2433; TDD for the Deaf (888) 814-7692
Website: http://www.ala.org

Founded in 1876, the ALA is the oldest and largest national library association in the world. It works to maintain the highest quality of library and informational services in institutions available to the public. Included in its membership are libraries, librarians, library trustees, and others who are concerned with literacy and informational services. The ALA publishes *Booklist*, one of the most respected book review journals.

■ *Association for Library Service to Children (ALSC).* A branch of the ALA, the ALSC focuses on library services for children. Through many committees, it evaluates and selects print and nonprint materials to use in libraries for children, beginning in preschool and extending through the junior high years. Other duties include serving as advocates for the child, assisting the professional development of librarians, and recognizing quality literature by giving out appropriate awards. Awards granted by the ALSC include the John Newbery and Randolph Caldecott Medals, the Mildred L. Batchelder Award, and the Laura Ingalls Wilder Award. The ALSC publishes, in cooperation

with the YALSA (see the next entry), the *Journal of Youth Services.*

■ *Young Adult Library Services Association (YALSA).* Also a branch of the ALA, the YALSA is similar in purpose and responsibilities to the ALSC, but its special focus is on library services for older youth beyond the elementary level. Like the ALSC, the YALSA is concerned with selecting and evaluating books, being advocates for young people, assisting the professional development of librarians, and making library services accessible. In cooperation with the ALSC, YALSA publishes the *Journal of Youth Services.*

Children's Book Council (CBC)

568 12 West 37th St.
New York, NY 10018
Phone: (212) 966-1990; (800) 999-2160 (orders only)
Website: http://www.cbcbooks.org

The CBC sponsors National Children's Book Week in November and develops children's book programs related to various disciplines through joint committees with library, bookselling, and education associations. Each year, the council cosponsors the designation of outstanding trade books through its participation in the following: Children's Choices (with the International Reading Association), Outstanding Science Trade Books for Children (with the National Science Teachers Association), and Notable Children's Trade Books in the Field of Social Studies (with the

National Council of Social Studies). The CBC also sponsors the Children's Books Mean Business Project and the Not Just for Children Anymore Program.

The Children's Literature Association (ChLA)

P.O. Box 138
Battle Creek, MI 49016-0138
Phone: (616) 965-8180
Website: http://ebbs.english.vt.edu/chla

The Children's Literature Association is an organization under the umbrella of the Modern Language Association (MLA). It encourages serious scholarship and research in the area of children's literature and provides an outlet for scholarship through conferences and publications. The ChLA sponsors the Phoenix Award for books that are at least 20 years old that have not won any major awards. This organization also grants scholarships to people doing innovative research in the field.

International Reading Association (IRA)

800 Barksdale Rd.
P.O. Box 8139
Newark, DE 19714-8139
Phone: (302) 731-1600
Website: http://www.reading.org

IRA seeks to improve the quality of reading instruction at all educational levels, to stimulate and promote the lifetime reading habit and an awareness of the impact of reading, and to encourage the development of every reader's proficiency to the highest possible level. The organization disseminates information pertaining to research on reading, including information on adult literacy, computer technology and reading, early childhood and literacy development, international education, literature for children and adolescents, and teacher education and effectiveness. IRA publishes *The Reading Teacher*, a journal for elementary-level teachers interested in reading education. IRA also promotes children's literature through its annual book awards (IRA Children's Book Awards) and through its cooperation with the Children's Book Council in administering Children's Choices, an annual booklist chosen by young readers.

National Council of Teachers of English (NCTE)

1111 Kenyon Rd.
Urbana, IL 61801
Phone: (217) 328-3870; (800) 369-6283
Website: http://www.ncte.org

NCTE works to increase the effectiveness of instruction in English language and literature. Conferences, workshops, and other presentations provide information and aids for teachers involved in formulating objectives, writing and evaluating guides, and planning in-service programs for teacher education. Children's literature is promoted through award programs for nonfiction writing (Orbis Pictus Award) and poetry (Excellence in Poetry for Children Award). NCTE publishes *Language Arts*, a journal for elementary-level teachers interested in language education.

■ ***Children's Literature Assembly (CLA).*** A branch of NCTE, CLA publishes *The Journal of Children's Literature*, previously known as *The Bulletin*, which includes book reviews and articles about children's literature and reading, thematic groupings of books, research updates, proceedings of NCTE workshops, and ideas for incorporating children's literature in the classroom. CLA also sponsors the NCTE Notable Books in the Language Arts, an annual list of the outstanding children's books with a language arts emphasis, and several yearly workshops and other programs that focus on children's literature.

▼▼▼▼▼▼

Publications About Children's Literature

Review Sources

Appraisal
Children's Science Book Review Committee
Northeastern University
403 Richards Hall
Boston, MA 02215
Phone: (617) 373-7539

This quarterly periodical publishes detailed evaluative book reviews by both practicing children's librarians and subject specialists of all new children's and young adult science trade books.

Booklist
American Library Association
P.O. Box 607
Mt. Morris, IL 61054-7564
Phone: (888) 350-0949
Website: http://www.ala.org/booklist/008.html

This review journal describes its purpose as "to provide a guide to current print and nonprint materials worthy of consideration for purchase by small and medium-sized public libraries and school library media centers." The journal includes subject and title, cumulative, and advertisers indexes and is published biweekly (except monthly in July and August). *Booklist* publishes annually a list of best books titled "Editor's Choice" as well as ALA Notable Children's Books and Best Books for Young Adults.

Bulletin of the Center for Children's Books
University of Illinois Press
1325 S. Oak St.
Champaign, IL 61820

Phone: (217) 244-0324
Website: http://edfu.lis.uiuc.edu/puboff/bccb

This periodical reviews and rates current children's books, classifying each by grade/age level, and includes information about adapting each for classroom use. The bulletin appears monthly from September to July, and the July issue includes the annual index.

Children's Book Review Index
Gale Research Inc.
27500 Drake Rd.
Farmington, MI 48331
Phone: (800) 877-4253
Website: http://www.Galegroup.com

The index includes more than 21,000 review citations that give access to reviewers' comments and opinions on more than 9,000 books written and/or recommended for children through age 10. The publication makes it easy to find a review by an author's name, book title, or illustrator, and it fully indexes over 500 periodicals.

Horn Book Magazine
Horn Book, Inc.
56 Roland St., Suite 200
Boston, MA 02129
Phone: (800) 325-1170
Website: http://www.hbook.com

Published six times per year, the magazine contains reviews of books that the editorial staff considers to be the best as well as articles about literature, interviews with authors, and other news about children's literature. *Horn Book* cosponsors the Boston Globe/Horn Book Awards for children's fiction, nonfiction, and picture books and publishes yearly a list of the reviewers' choices of best books called "Fanfare." The July/August issue presents the acceptance speeches of Newbery and Caldecott award winners. The November/December issue includes the annual index.

Kirkus Reviews
770 Broadway
New York, NY 10003
Phone: (212) 777-4554
http://www.bowker.com/lrg/home/entries/kirkus
    _review,review_journals.html

Kirkus is published on the 1st and the 15th of each month. It makes an effort to review a book 2 months before the book's official publication date, or as early as possible. The reviewers note outstanding books in each issue with a diamond symbol called a "pointer."

School Library Journal
P.O. Box 16388
North Hollywood, CA 91615-6388
Phone: (800) 595-1066
Website: http://www.cahners.com/mainmag/slj.htm

This monthly journal is one of the most comprehensive providers of news, information, and reviews for librarians and media specialists who serve children and young adults in school and public libraries. A special issue in December includes an index and a "Best Books" section. Subscribers can also request a free supplement, titled *Star Track: For Teachers and Other Adults Who Support Good Reading*. Sent twice each year, *Star Track* compiles reviews of outstanding books, organizing them according to genre and subject matter.

Bibliographies

A to Zoo: Subject Access to Children's Picture Books. 1993. By Carolyn W. and John A. Lima. 4th ed. New York: R. R. Bowker.

Most useful for teachers of preschool and the early grades, this source lists 12,000 picture books for children. A chapter at the beginning briefly chronicles the history of children's picture books. Indexed by author, illustrator, title, and subject.

Adventuring With Books: A Booklist for Pre-K–Grade 6. 2000. Edited by Kathryn Pierce. 11th ed. Urbana, IL: NCTE.

Published every 5 years by the NCTE, this bibliography provides annotated listings of fiction and nonfiction books recommended for children before and during the elementary school years. Books are grouped according to subject matter.

Best Books for Children: Preschool through Grade 6. 1994. 5th ed. Edited by John T. Gillespie and Corinne J. Naden. New Providence, NJ: R. R. Bowker.

Contains over 17,000 annotated titles listed by topic, ranging from literature to history to science to recreation. Author, illustrator, title, and subject/grade level indexes are also provided.

The Bookfinder: A Guide to Children's Literature About the Needs and Problems of Youth Aged 2–15. 1977, 1981, 1985, 1989, 1995. By Sharon Spredemann Dreyer. Circle Pines, MN: American Guidance Service.

Critical annotations of recommended books are found in subject indexes according to which needs and problems of children the books address. The third edition includes a cumulative index of the first three volumes.

Children's Books in Print. New York: R. R. Bowker (published annually).

All books in print are indexed by title, author, and illustrator. Publishers and their addresses are listed as well as detailed information relevant to purchase of books. Also available in compact disc format; monthly updates.

The Children's Catalog. 1996. Edited by Juliette Yaakov and Anne Price. 17th ed. New York: H. W. Wilson.

Published every 5 years, with annual supplements, this extensive retrospective source is arranged in two sections. The first section lists and describes professional resources, trade books, and magazines recommended for young people, from preschool to sixth grade. The second section is a comprehensive index of entries arranged by author, title, and subject. Other editions for junior high and high school readers are also available.

The Elementary School Library Collection: A Guide to Books and other Media. 1992. Edited by Linda L. Homa. 21st ed. Williamsport, PA: Brodart.

Books, magazines, and nonprint media for teachers and parents of children are described according to their quality, reading level, and interest level. Entries are indexed by subject, title, author, and illustrator. A new edition is published every 2 years.

Eyeopeners II!: Children's Books to Answer Children's Questions About the World Around Them. 1995. By Beverly Kobrin. New York: Scholastic.

Eyeopeners II, like Kobrin's first volume, *Eyeopeners*, is a terrific resource for "all adults involved with children." With over 800 nonfiction books included, this resource provides titles for topics from airplanes to words.

Horn Book Guide to Children's and Young Adult Books. Edited by Roger Sutton. Boston: Horn Book.

Published in March and September of each year since 1990, this guide lists the children's books published within each 6-month period. Fiction is organized by age; nonfiction by the Dewey Decimal System. Author, subject, and title indexes, as well as ratings, further classify books.

Your Reading: A Booklist for Junior High and Middle School Students. 1993. Edited by C. Anne Webb. 9th ed. Urbana, IL: NCTE.

Like *Adventuring With Books*, this source is published and frequently updated by the NCTE and includes topically arranged annotated listings of fiction and nonfiction books. Unlike *Adventuring With Books*, however, *Your Reading* is geared for young adults and is designed for use by the young readers themselves.

Other Journals

Book Links: Connecting Books, Libraries, and Classrooms
American Library Association
P.O. Box 615
Mt. Morris, IL 61054-7564
Phone: (888) 350-0950
Website: http://www.ala.org/booklinks/008.html

Published by the ALA every 2 months since 1991, this journal is designed for teachers, librarians, library media specialists, booksellers, parents, and other adults interested in exploring themes with children through literature.

Bookbird: World of Children's Books
International Board of Books for Young People
(IBBY)

Attn. Evelyn Holmberg
University of Toronto Press
5201 Dufferin St.
North York, ON M3H5T8
CANADA
Website: http://www.usbby.org/bookbird/bird.htm

Bookbird's articles examine the children's book authors, illustrators, titles, and publishing trends from around the world.

CBC Features
Attn: Publications Order
568 Broadway, Suite 404
New York, NY 10012
Phone: (800) 999-2160; (212) 966-1990
Website: http://www.cbcbooks.org

Formerly titled *The Calendar*, this semiannual newsletter is published by the Children's Book Council. Often themed, it includes profiles of authors written by experts in the field of children's literature and listings of free or inexpensive materials.

Children's Literature in Education: An International Quarterly
Kluwer Academics/Human Science Press
233 Spring St.
New York, NY 10013-1578
Phone: (800) 221-9369; (212) 620-8000
Website: http://www.kap.nl

This journal is published four times each year with features that include interviews with and articles by or about authors and illustrators of children's literature, best practice ideas for the classroom, critical evaluations of books, and commentaries on social issues.

Journal of Children's Literature
Children's Literature Assembly
National Council of Teachers of English
1111 W. Kenyon Rd.
Urbana, IL 61801-1096
Phone: (800) 369-6283; (217) 328-3870
Website: http://www.ncte.org

This periodical contains articles and features on all aspects of children's literature, including news and items of interest to members.

Journal of Youth Services (JOYS)
American Library Association
50 Huron St.
Chicago, IL 60611
Phone: (800) 545-2433; (312) 944-6780
Website: http://www.ala.org

Published four times a year by the ALSC and YALSA, *JOYS* provides news and information about ALSC and YALSA, information for librarians about current techniques and trends, and thorough reviews of professional resources.

Language Arts
National Council of Teachers of English
1111 W. Kenyon Rd.
Urbana, IL 61801-1096
Phone: (800) 369-6283; (217) 328-3870
Website: http://www.ncte.org

The periodical presents themed issues on topics relating to the teaching of English and the language arts as well as practical teaching ideas, annotations of children's books, and reviews of professional resources. It is published monthly from September through April.

The New Advocate
Christopher-Gordon Publishers, Inc.
480 Washington St.
Norwood, MA 02062
Phone: (508) 543-8729

This periodical contains articles on creating, teaching, and appreciating children's literature; profiles of authors and illustrators; and reviews of children's books and literature resources for teachers. *The New Advocate* is published quarterly, with an additional issue each October devoted to one theme.

The Reading Teacher
International Reading Association
800 Barksdale Rd.
P.O. Box 8139
Newark, DE 19714-8139
Phone: (302) 731-1600
Website: http://www.reading.org

This periodical focuses on the theory and practice of teaching reading skills to elementary school children. Features include children's and professional book reviews, research reports, and practical teaching ideas. Published eight times a year.

B

APPENDIX

▼▼▼▼▼▼▼

CHILDREN'S BOOK AWARDS

Children's book awards have proliferated in recent years; today there are well over 100 awards and prizes presented by a variety of organizations in the United States alone. The awards may be given for books of a specific genre or simply for the best of all children's books published within a given period. An award may honor a particular book or an author/illustrator for a lifetime contribution to the world of children's literature. Most children's book awards are chosen by adults, but now a growing number of children's choice book awards exist. The larger national awards given in most countries are the most influential and have helped considerably to raise public awareness about the fine books being published for young readers. Of course, readers are wise not to put too much faith in award-winning books. An award doesn't necessarily mean a good reading experience, but it does provide a starting place when choosing books.

▼▼▼▼▼▼▼

National Awards

United States of America

Randolph Caldecott Medal.   Sponsored and administered by the Association for Library Service to Children, an arm of the American Library Association, the Caldecott Medal is presented to the illustrator of the most distinguished picture book for children published in the United States during the preceding year. A variable number of honor books also may be named by the Caldecott Selection Committee. Eligibility for this award is limited to U.S. citizens and residents. Named for the 19th-century British illustrator, the Caldecott Medal is America's major picture book award.

1938   *Animals of the Bible, a Picture Book.* Text selected from the King James *Bible* by Helen Dean Fish. Illustrated by Dorothy P. Lathrop. Lippincott.
Honor Books:
Seven Simeons: A Russian Tale, by Boris Artzybasheff. Viking.

Four and Twenty Blackbirds, compiled by Helen Dean Fish. Illustrated by Robert Lawson. Stokes/Lippincott.

1939   *Mei Li,* by Thomas Handforth. Doubleday.
Honor Books:
The Forest Pool, by Laura Adams Armer. McKay/Longmans.
Wee Gillis, by Munro Leaf. Illustrated by Robert Lawson. Viking.
Snow White and the Seven Dwarfs. Translated and illustrated by Wanda Gág. Coward-McCann.
Barkis, by Clare Turlay Newberry. Harper.
Andy and the Lion, by James Daugherty. Viking.

1940   *Abraham Lincoln,* by Ingri d'Aulaire and Edgar Parin d'Aulaire. Doubleday.
Honor Books:
Cock-a-Doodle-Doo, by Berta and Elmer Hader. Macmillan.

Madeline, by Ludwig Bemelmans. Viking.
The Ageless Story, by Lauren Ford. Dodd.

1941 *They Were Strong and Good*, by Robert Lawson.
Viking.
Honor Book:
April's Kittens, by Clare Turlay Newberry.
Harper.

1942 *Make Way for Ducklings*, by Robert McCloskey.
Viking.
Honor Books:
An American ABC, by Maud and Miska
Petersham. Macmillan.
In My Mother's House, by Ann Nolan Clark.
Illustrated by Velino Herrera. Viking.
Paddle-to-the-Sea, by Holling Clancy Holling.
Houghton Mifflin.
Nothing at All, by Wanda Gág. Coward-McCann.

1943 *The Little House*, by Virginia Lee Burton.
Houghton Mifflin.
Honor Books:
Dash and Dart, by Mary and Conrad Buff.
Viking.
Marshmallow, by Clare Turlay Newberry. Harper.

1944 *Many Moons*, by James Thurber. Illustrated by
Louis Slobodkin. Harcourt.
Honor Books:
Small Rain: Verses from the Bible. Text arranged
from the Bible by Jessie Orton Jones. Illustrated
by Elizabeth Orton Jones. Viking.
Pierre Pigeon, by Lee Kingman. Illustrated by
Arnold Edwin Bare. Houghton Mifflin.
The Mighty Hunter, by Berta and Elmer Hader.
Macmillan.
A Child's Good Night Book, by Margaret Wise
Brown. Illustrated by Jean Charlot. Scott.
Good Luck Horse, by Chih-Yi Chan. Illustrated by
Plato Chan. Whittlesey.

1945 *Prayer for a Child*, by Rachel Field. Illustrated by
Elizabeth Orton Jones. Macmillan.
Honor Books:
Mother Goose: Seventy-Seven Verses With Pictures.
Illustrated by Tasha Tudor. Walck.
In the Forest, by Marie Hall Ets. Viking.
Yonie Wondernose, by Marguerite de Angeli.
Doubleday.
The Christmas Anna Angel, by Ruth Sawyer.
Illustrated by Kate Seredy. Viking.

1946 *The Rooster Crows*, selected and illustrated by
Maud and Miska Petersham. Macmillan.
Honor Books:
Little Lost Lamb, by Golden MacDonald.
Illustrated by Leonard Weisgard. Doubleday.
Sing Mother Goose, by Opal Wheeler. Illustrated
by Marjorie Torrey. Dutton.
*My Mother Is the Most Beautiful Woman in the
World*, retold by Becky Reyher. Illustrated by
Ruth Gannett. Lothrop.
You Can Write Chinese, by Kurt Wiese. Viking.

1947 *The Little Island*, by Golden MacDonald.
Illustrated by Leonard Weisgard. Doubleday.
Honor Books:
Rain Drop Splash, by Alvin Tresselt. Illustrated by
Leonard Weisgard. Lothrop.
Boats on the River, by Marjorie Flack. Illustrated
by Jay Hyde Barnum. Viking.
Timothy Turtle, by Al Graham. Illustrated by
Tony Palazzo. Viking.
Pedro, the Angel of Olvera Street, by Leo Politi.
Scribner's.
*Sing in Praise: A Collection of the Best Loved
Hymns*, by Opal Wheeler. Illustrated by Marjorie
Torrey. Dutton.

1948 *White Snow, Bright Snow*, by Alvin Tresselt.
Illustrated by Roger Duvoisin. Lothrop.
Honor Books:
Stone Soup: An Old Tale, by Marcia Brown.
Scribner's.
McElligot's Pool, by Dr. Seuss (pseud. for Theodor
Geisel). Random House.
Bambino the Clown, by George Schreiber. Viking.
Roger and the Fox, by Lavinia Davis. Illustrated by
Hildegard Woodward. Doubleday.
Song of Robin Hood, edited by Anne Malcolmson.
Illustrated by Virginia Lee Burton. Houghton
Mifflin.

1949 *The Big Snow*, by Berta and Elmer Hader.
Macmillan.
Honor Books:
Blueberries for Sal, by Robert McCloskey. Viking.
All Around Town, by Phyllis McGinley. Illustrated
by Helen Stone. Lippincott.
Juanita, by Leo Politi. Scribner's.
Fish in the Air, by Kurt Wiese. Viking.

1950 *Song of the Swallows*, by Leo Politi. Scribner's.
Honor Books:
America's Ethan Allen, by Stewart Holbrook.
Illustrated by Lynd Ward. Houghton Mifflin.
The Wild Birthday Cake, by Lavinia R. Davis.
Illustrated by Hildegard Woodward. Doubleday.
The Happy Day, by Ruth Krauss. Illustrated by
Marc Simont. Harper.
Henry-Fisherman, by Marcia Brown. Scribner's.
Bartholomew and the Oobleck, by Dr. Seuss
(pseud. for Theodor Geisel). Random House.

1951 *The Egg Tree*, by Katherine Milhous. Scribner's.
Honor Books:
Dick Whittington and His Cat, translated and
illustrated by Marcia Brown. Scribner's.
The Two Reds, by Will (pseud. for William
Lipkind). Illustrated by Nicolas (pseud. for
Nicolas Mordvinoff). Harcourt.
If I Ran the Zoo by Dr. Seuss (pseud. for Theodor
Geisel). Random House.
T-Bone, the Baby-Sitter, by Clare Turlay
Newberry. Harper.
The Most Wonderful Doll in the World, by Phyllis
McGinley. Illustrated by Helen Stone. Lippincott.

1952 *Finders Keepers*, by Will (pseud. for William Lipkind). Illustrated by Nicolas (pseud. for Nicolas Mordvinoff). Harcourt.
Honor Books:
Mr. T. W. Anthony Woo, by Marie Hall Ets. Viking.
Skipper John's Cook, by Marcia Brown. Scribner's.
All Falling Down, by Gene Zion. Illustrated by Margaret Bloy Graham. Harper.
Bear Party, by William Pène du Bois. Viking.
Feather Mountain, by Elizabeth Olds. Houghton Mifflin.

1953 *The Biggest Bear*, by Lynd Ward. Houghton Mifflin.
Honor Books:
Puss in Boots, Translated and illustrated by Marcia Brown. Scribner's.
One Morning in Maine, by Robert McCloskey. Viking.
Ape in a Cape: An Alphabet of Odd Animals, by Fritz Eichenberg. Harcourt.
The Storm Book, by Charlotte Zolotow. Illustrated by Margaret Bloy Graham. HarperCollins.
Five Little Monkeys, by Juliet Kepes. Houghton Mifflin.

1954 *Madeline's Rescue*, by Ludwig Bemelmans. Viking.
Honor Books:
Journey Cake, Ho! by Ruth Sawyer. Illustrated by Robert McCloskey. Viking.
When Will the World Be Mine? by Miriam Schlein. Illustrated by Jean Charlot. Scott.
The Steadfast Tin Soldier, by Hans Christian Andersen. Translated by M. R. James. Illustrated by Marcia Brown. Scribner's.
A Very Special House, by Ruth Krauss. Illustrated by Maurice Sendak. Harper.
Green Eyes, by Abe Birnbaum. Capitol.

1955 *Cinderella, or the Little Glass Slipper*, by Charles Perrault. Translated and illustrated by Marcia Brown. Scribner's.
Honor Books:
Book of Nursery and Mother Goose Rhymes, compiled and illustrated by Marguerite de Angeli. Doubleday.
Wheel on the Chimney, by Margaret Wise Brown. Illustrated by Tibor Gergely. Lippincott.
The Thanksgiving Story, by Alice Dalgliesh. Illustrated by Helen Sewell. Scribner's.

1956 *Frog Went A-Courtin'*, retold by John Langstaff. Illustrated by Feodor Rojankovsky. Harcourt.
Honor Books:
Play With Me, by Marie Hall Ets. Viking.
Crow Boy, by Taro Yashima. Viking.

1957 *A Tree Is Nice*, by Janice May Udry. Illustrated by Marc Simont. Harper.
Honor Books:
Mr. Penny's Race Horse, by Marie Hall Ets. Viking.
1 Is One, by Tasha Tudor. Walck.
Anatole, by Eve Titus. Illustrated by Paul Galdone. McGraw.

Gillespie and the Guards, by Benjamin Elkin. Illustrated by James Daugherty. Viking.
Lion, by William Pène du Bois. Viking.

1958 *Time of Wonder*, by Robert McCloskey. Viking.
Honor Books:
Fly High, Fly Low, by Don Freeman. Viking.
Anatole and the Cat, by Eve Titus. Illustrated by Paul Galdone. McGraw.

1959 *Chanticleer and the Fox*, by Chaucer. Adapted and illustrated by Barbara Cooney. Crowell.
Honor Books:
The House That Jack Built (La maison que Jacques a bâtie): A Picture Book in Two Languages, by Antonio Frasconi. Harcourt.
What Do You Say, Dear? A Book of Manners for All Occasions, by Sesyle Joslin. Illustrated by Maurice Sendak. Scott.
Umbrella, by Taro Yashima. Viking.

1960 *Nine Days to Christmas*, by Marie Hall Ets and Aurora Labastida. Illustrated by Marie Hall Ets. Viking.
Honor Books:
Houses from the Sea, by Alice E. Goudey. Illustrated by Adrienne Adams. Scribner's.
The Moon Jumpers, by Janice May Udry. Illustrated by Maurice Sendak. Harper.

1961 *Baboushka and the Three Kings*, by Ruth Robbins. Illustrated by Nicolas Sidjakov. Parnassus.
Honor Book:
Inch by Inch, by Leo Lionni. Obolensky.

1962 *Once a Mouse*, retold by Marcia Brown. Scribner's.
Honor Books:
The Fox Went Out on a Chilly Night: An Old Song, by Peter Spier. Doubleday.
Little Bear's Visit, by Else Minarik. Illustrated by Maurice Sendak. Harper.
The Day We Saw the Sun Come Up, by Alice Goudey. Illustrated by Adrienne Adams. Scribner's.

1963 *The Snowy Day*, by Ezra Jack Keats. Viking.
Honor Books:
The Sun Is a Golden Earring, by Natalia Belting. Illustrated by Bernarda Bryson. Holt.
Mr. Rabbit and the Lovely Present, by Charlotte Zolotow. Illustrated by Maurice Sendak. Harper & Row.

1964 *Where the Wild Things Are*, by Maurice Sendak. Harper & Row.
Honor Books:
Swimmy, by Leo Lionni. Pantheon.
All in the Morning Early, by Sorche Nic Leodhas (pseud. for Leclaire Alger). Illustrated by Evaline Ness. Holt.
Mother Goose and Nursery Rhymes, by Philip Reed. Atheneum.

1965 *May I Bring a Friend?* by Beatrice Schenk de Regniers. Illustrated by Beni Montresor. Atheneum.

Honor Books:
Rain Makes Applesauce, by Julian Scheer.
Illustrated by Marvin Bileck. Holiday House.
The Wave, by Margaret Hodges. Illustrated by
Blair Lent. Houghton Mifflin.
A Pocketful of Cricket, by Rebecca Caudill.
Illustrated by Evaline Ness. Holt.

1966   *Always Room for One More,* by Sorche Nic
Leodhas (pseud. for Leclaire Alger). Illustrated by
Nonny Hogrogian. Holt.
Honor Books:
Hide and Seek Fog, by Alvin Tresselt. Illustrated
by Roger Duvoisin. Lothrop.
Just Me, by Marie Hall Ets. Viking.
Tom Tit Tot, adapted by Joseph Jacobs. Illustrated
by Evaline Ness. Scribner's.

1967   *Sam, Bangs and Moonshine,* by Evaline Ness. Holt.
Honor Book:
One Wide River to Cross, adapted by Barbara
Emberley. Illustrated by Ed Emberley. Prentice Hall.

1968   *Drummer Hoff,* adapted by Barbara Emberley.
Illustrated by Ed Emberley. Prentice Hall.
Honor Books:
Frederick, by Leo Lionni. Pantheon.
Seashore Story, by Taro Yashima. Viking.
The Emperor and the Kite, by Jane Yolen.
Illustrated by Ed Young. World.

1969   *The Fool of the World and the Flying Ship: A
Russian Tale,* by Arthur Ransome. Illustrated by
Uri Shulevitz. Farrar, Straus & Giroux.
Honor Book:
*Why the Sun and the Moon Live in the Sky: An
African Folktale,* by Elphinstone Dayrell.
Illustrated by Blair Lent. Houghton Mifflin.

1970   *Sylvester and the Magic Pebble,* by William Steig.
Windmill.
Honor Books:
Goggles! by Ezra Jack Keats. Macmillan.
Alexander and the Wind-Up Mouse, by Leo
Lionni. Pantheon.
Pop Corn and Ma Goodness, by Edna Mitchell
Preston. Illustrated by Robert Andrew Parker. Viking.
Thy Friend, Obadiah, by Brinton Turkle. Viking.
The Judge: An Untrue Tale, by Harve Zemach.
Illustrated by Margot Zemach. Farrar.

1971   *A Story, a Story: An African Tale,* by Gail E.
Haley. Atheneum.
Honor Books:
The Angry Moon, retold by William Sleator.
Illustrated by Blair Lent. Atlantic/Little, Brown.
Frog and Toad Are Friends, by Arnold Lobel.
Harper & Row.
In the Night Kitchen, by Maurice Sendak. Harper
& Row.

1972   *One Fine Day,* by Nonny Hogrogian. Macmillan.
Honor Books:
If All the Seas Were One Sea, by Janina Domanska.
Macmillan.

Moja Means One: Swahili Counting Book, by
Muriel Feelings. Illustrated by Tom Feelings. Dial.
Hildilid's Night, by Cheli Duran Ryan. Illustrated
by Arnold Lobel. Macmillan.

1973   *The Funny Little Woman,* retold by Arlene Mosel.
Illustrated by Blair Lent. Dutton.
Honor Books:
Hosie's Alphabet, by Hosea Baskin, Tobias Baskin,
and Lisa Baskin. Illustrated by Leonard Baskin.
Viking.
When Clay Sings, by Byrd Baylor. Illustrated by
Tom Bahti. Scribner's.
Snow-White and the Seven Dwarfs, by the
Brothers Grimm. Translated by Randall Jarrell.
Illustrated by Nancy Ekholm Burkert. Farrar,
Straus & Giroux.
Anansi the Spider: A Tale from the Ashanti, adapted
and illustrated by Gerald McDermott. Holt.

1974   *Duffy and the Devil,* retold by Harve Zemach.
Illustrated by Margot Zemach. Farrar, Straus &
Giroux.
Honor Books:
Three Jovial Huntsmen, adapted and illustrated by
Susan Jeffers. Bradbury.
Cathedral: The Story of Its Construction, by David
Macaulay. Houghton Mifflin.

1975   *Arrow to the Sun,* adapted and illustrated by
Gerald McDermott. Viking.
Honor Book:
Jambo Means Hello: Swahili Alphabet Book, by
Muriel Feelings. Illustrated by Tom Feelings. Dial.

1976   *Why Mosquitoes Buzz in People's Ears,* retold by
Verna Aardema. Illustrated by Leo and Diane
Dillon. Dial.
Honor Books:
The Desert Is Theirs, by Byrd Baylor. Illustrated by
Peter Parnall. Scribner's.
Strega Nona, retold and illustrated by Tomie de
Paola. Prentice Hall.

1977   *Ashanti to Zulu: African Traditions,* by Margaret
Musgrove. Illustrated by Leo and Diane Dillon.
Dial.
Honor Books:
The Amazing Bone, by William Steig. Farrar,
Straus & Giroux.
The Contest, by Nonny Hogrogian. Greenwillow.
Fish for Supper, by M. B. Goffstein. Dial.
The Golem: A Jewish Legend, retold and illustrated
by Beverly Brodsky McDermott. Lippincott.
Hawk, I'm Your Brother, by Byrd Baylor.
Illustrated by Peter Parnall. Scribner's.

1978   *Noah's Ark,* by Peter Spier. Doubleday.
Honor Books:
Castle, by David Macaulay. Houghton Mifflin.
It Could Always Be Worse, retold and illustrated
by Margot Zemach. Farrar, Straus & Giroux.

1979   *The Girl Who Loved Wild Horses,* by Paul Goble.
Bradbury.

Honor Books:
Freight Train, by Donald Crews. Greenwillow.
The Way to Start a Day, by Byrd Baylor. Illustrated by Peter Parnall. Scribner's.

1980 *Ox-Cart Man*, by Donald Hall. Illustrated by Barbara Cooney. Viking.
Honor Books:
Ben's Trumpet, by Rachel Isadora. Greenwillow.
The Treasure, by Uri Schulevitz. Farrar, Straus & Giroux.
The Garden of Abdul Gasazi, by Chris Van Allsburg. Houghton Mifflin.

1981 *Fables*, by Arnold Lobel. Harper & Row.
Honor Books:
The Bremen-Town Musicians, retold and illustrated by Ilse Plume. Doubleday.
The Grey Lady and the Strawberry Snatcher, by Molly Bang. Four Winds.
Mice Twice, by Joseph Low. Atheneum.
Truck, by Donald Crews. Greenwillow.

1982 *Jumanji*, by Chris Van Allsburg. Houghton Mifflin.
Honor Books:
A Visit to William Blake's Inn: Poems for Innocent and Experienced Travelers, by Nancy Willard. Illustrated by Alice and Martin Provensen. Harcourt.
Where the Buffaloes Begin, by Olaf Baker. Illustrated by Stephen Gammell. Warne.
On Market Street, by Arnold Lobel. Illustrated by Anita Lobel. Greenwillow.
Outside Over There, by Maurice Sendak. Harper & Row.

1983 *Shadow*, by Blaise Cendrars. Translated and illustrated by Marcia Brown. Scribner's.
Honor Books:
When I Was Young in the Mountains, by Cynthia Rylant. Illustrated by Diane Goode. Dutton.
A Chair for My Mother, by Vera B. Williams. Greenwillow.

1984 *The Glorious Flight: Across the Channel with Louis Blériot*, by Alice and Martin Provensen. Viking.
Honor Books:
Ten, Nine, Eight, by Molly Bang. Greenwillow.
Little Red Riding Hood, by the Brothers Grimm. Retold and illustrated by Trina Schart Hyman. Holiday House.

1985 *Saint George and the Dragon*, adapted by Margaret Hodges. Illustrated by Trina Schart Hyman. Little, Brown.
Honor Books:
Hansel and Gretel, adapted by Rika Lesser. Illustrated by Paul O. Zelinsky. Dodd.
The Story of Jumping Mouse, retold and illustrated by John Steptoe. Lothrop.
Have You Seen My Duckling? by Nancy Tafuri. Greenwillow.

1986 *The Polar Express*, by Chris Van Allsburg. Houghton Mifflin.

Honor Books:
The Relatives Came, by Cynthia Rylant. Illustrated by Stephen Gammell. Bradbury.
King Bidgood's in the Bathtub, by Audrey Wood. Illustrated by Don Wood. Harcourt.

1987 *Hey, Al*, by Arthur Yorinks. Illustrated by Richard Egielski. Farrar, Straus & Giroux.
Honor Books:
The Village of Round and Square Houses, by Ann Grifalconi. Little, Brown.
Alphabatics, by Suse MacDonald. Bradbury.
Rumpelstiltskin, by the Brothers Grimm. Retold and illustrated by Paul O. Zelinsky. Dutton.

1988 *Owl Moon*, by Jane Yolen. Illustrated by John Schoenherr. Philomel.
Honor Book:
Mufaro's Beautiful Daughters, retold by John Steptoe. Lothrop.

1989 *Song and Dance Man*, by Karen Ackerman. Illustrated by Stephen Gammell. Knopf.
Honor Books:
Free Fall, by David Wiesner. Lothrop.
Goldilocks and the Three Bears, retold and illustrated by James Marshall. Dial.
Mirandy and Brother Wind, by Patricia McKissack. Illustrated by Jerry Pinkney. Knopf.
The Boy of the Three-Year Nap, by Dianne Snyder. Illustrated by Allen Say. Houghton Mifflin.

1990 *Lon Po Po: A Red-Riding Hood Story from China*, translated and illustrated by Ed Young. Philomel.
Honor Books:
Hershel and the Hanukkah Goblins, by Eric Kimmel. Illustrated by Trina Schart Hyman. Holiday House.
The Talking Eggs, adapted by Robert D. San Souci. Illustrated by Jerry Pinkney. Dial.
Bill Peet: An Autobiography, by Bill Peet. Houghton Mifflin.
Color Zoo, by Lois Ehlert. Lippincott.

1991 *Black and White*, by David Macaulay. Houghton Mifflin.
Honor Books:
Puss 'n Boots, by Charles Perrault. Illustrated by Fred Marcellino. Farrar, Straus & Giroux.
"More, More, More," Said the Baby: 3 Love Stories, by Vera B. Williams. Greenwillow.

1992 *Tuesday*, by David Wiesner. Clarion.
Honor Book:
Tar Beach, by Faith Ringgold. Crown.

1993 *Mirette on the High Wire*, by Emily Arnold McCully. Putnam.
Honor Books:
Seven Blind Mice, by Ed Young. Philomel.
The Stinky Cheese Man & Other Fairly Stupid Tales, by Jon Scieszka. Illustrated by Lane Smith. Viking.
Working Cotton, by Sherley Anne Williams. Illustrated by Carole Byard. Harcourt.

1994 *Grandfather's Journey*, by Allen Say. Houghton Mifflin.
Honor Books:
Peppe the Lamplighter, by Elisa Bartone. Illustrated by Ted Lewin. Lothrop.
In the Small, Small Pond, by Denise Fleming. Holt.
Owen, by Kevin Henkes. Greenwillow.
Raven: A Trickster Tale from the Pacific Northwest, by Gerald McDermott. Harcourt.
Yo! Yes? by Chris Raschka. Orchard.

1995 *Smoky Night*, by Eve Bunting. Illustrated by David Diaz. Harcourt.
Honor Books:
Swamp Angel, by Anne Isaacs. Illustrated by Paul O. Zelinsky. Dutton.
John Henry, by Julius Lester. Illustrated by Jerry Pinkney. Dial.
Time Flies, by Eric Rohmann. Crown.

1996 *Officer Buckle and Gloria*, by Peggy Rathmann. Putnam.
Honor Books:
Alphabet City, by Stephen T. Johnson. Viking.
Tops & Bottoms, by Janet Stevens. Harcourt.
The Faithful Friend, by Robert D. San Souci. Illustrated by Brian Pinkney. Simon & Schuster.
Zin! Zin! Zin! a Violin, by Lloyd Moss. Illustrated by Marjorie Priceman. Simon & Schuster.

1997 *The Golem*, by David Wisniewski. Clarion.
Honor Books:
Hush! A Thai Lullaby, by Minfong Ho. Illustrated by Holly Meade. Orchard.
The Graphic Alphabet, edited by Neal Porter. Illustrated by David Pelletier. Orchard.
The Paperboy, by Dav Pilkey. Orchard.
Starry Messenger, by Peter Sís. Farrar, Straus & Giroux.

1998 *Rapunzel*, retold and illustrated by Paul O. Zelinsky. Dutton.
Honor Books:
The Gardener, by Sarah Stewart. Illustrated by David Small. Farrar, Straus & Giroux.
Harlem, by Walter Dean Myers. Illustrated by Christopher Myers. Scholastic.
There Was an Old Lady Who Swallowed a Fly, by Simms Taback. Viking.

1999 *Snowflake Bentley*, by Jacqueline Briggs Martin. Illustrated by Mary Azarian. Houghton.
Honor Books:
Duke Ellington: The Piano Prince and His Orchestra, by Andrea Davis Pinkney. Illustrated by Brian Pinkney. Hyperion.
No, David! by David Shannon. Blue Sky/Scholastic.
Snow, by Uri Shulevitz. Farrar, Straus & Giroux.
Tibet Through the Red Box, by Peter Sís. Farrar, Straus & Giroux.

2000 *Joseph Had a Little Overcoat*, by Simms Taback. Viking.

Honor Books:
A Child's Calender, by John Updike. Illustrated by Trina Schart Hyman. Holiday House.
Sector 7, by David Wiesner. Clarion.
When Sophie Gets Angry-Really Really Angry . . ., by Molly Bang. Scholastic.
The Ugly Duckling, adapted from Hans Christian Andersen by Jerry Pinkney. Illustrated by Jerry Pinkney. Morrow.

2001 *So You Want To Be President*, by Judith St. George. Illustrated by David Small. Philomel.
Honor Books:
Casey at the Bat, by Ernest Lawrence Thayer. Illustrated by Christopher Bing. Handprint.
Click, Clack, Moo, Cows that Type, by Doreen Cronin. Illustrated by Betsy Lewin. Simon & Schuster.
Olivia, by Ian Falconer. Atheneum.

John Newbery Medal.

Sponsored and administered by the Association for Library Service to Children, an arm of the American Library Association, the Newbery Medal is presented to the author of the most distinguished contribution to children's literature published in the United States during the preceding year. A variable number of honor books also may be named by the Newbery Selection Committee. Eligibility for this award is limited to U.S. citizens and residents. Named for the 18th-century British publisher, the Newbery Medal is one of the world's oldest and most prestigious children's book prizes.

1922 *The Story of Mankind*, by Hendrik Willem Van Loon. Liveright.
Honor Books
The Great Quest, by Charles Boardman Hawes. Little, Brown.
Cedric the Forester, by Bernard G. Marshall. Appleton.
The Old Tobacco Shop, by William Bowen. Macmillan.
The Golden Fleece and the Heroes Who Lived Before Achilles, by Padraic Colum. Macmillan.
Windy Hill, by Cornelia Meigs. Macmillan.

1923 *The Voyages of Doctor Dolittle*, by Hugh Lofting. Lippincott.
(No record of the honor books.)

1924 *The Dark Frigate*, by Charles Boardman Hawes. Little, Brown.
(No record of the honor books.)

1925 *Tales from Silver Lands*, by Charles J. Finger. Illustrated by Paul Honoré. Doubleday.
Honor Books:
Nicholas, by Anne Carroll Moore. Putnam.
Dream Coach, by Anne and Dillwyn Parrish. Macmillan.

1926 *Shen of the Sea*, by Arthur Bowie Chrisman. Illustrated by Else Hasselriis. Dutton.

Honor Book:
The Voyagers, by Padraic Colum. Macmillan.

1927 *Smoky, the Cowhorse*, by Will James. Scribner's.
(No record of the honor books.)

1928 *Gay-Neck, The Story of a Pigeon*, by Dhan Gopal
Mukerji. Illustrated by Boris Artzybasheff. Dutton.
Honor Books:
The Wonder Smith and His Son, by Ella Young.
McKay/Longmans.
Downright Dencey, by Caroline Dale Snedeker.
Doubleday.

1929 *The Trumpeter of Krakow*, by Eric P. Kelly.
Illustrated by Angela Pruszynska. Macmillan.
Honor Books:
The Pigtail of Ah Lee Ben Loo, by John Bennett.
McKay/Longmans.
Millions of Cats, by Wanda Gág. Coward-
McCann.
The Boy Who Was, by Grace T. Hallock. Dutton.
Clearing Weather, by Cornelia Meigs. Little,
Brown.
The Runaway Papoose, by Grace P. Moon.
Doubleday.
Tod of the Fens, by Eleanor Whitney. Macmillan.

1930 *Hitty: Her First Hundred Years*, by Rachel Field.
Illustrated by Dorothy P. Lathrop. Macmillan.
Honor Books:
*The Tangle-Coated Horse and Other Tales: Episodes
from the Fionn Saga*, by Ella Young. Illustrated by
Vera Brock. Longmans.
Vaino: A Boy of New Finland, by Julia Davis Adams.
Illustrated by Lempi Ostman. Dutton.
Pran of Albania, by Elizabeth C. Miller. Doubleday.
The Jumping-Off Place, by Marian Hurd
McNeely. McKay/Longmans.
A Daughter of the Seine, by Jeanette Eaton. Harper.
Little Blacknose, by Hildegarde Hoyt Swift.
Illustrated by Lynd Ward. Harcourt.

1931 *The Cat Who Went to Heaven*, by Elizabeth
Coatsworth. Illustrated by Lynd Ward. Macmillan.
Honor Books:
Floating Island, by Anne Parrish. Harper.
The Dark Star of Itza, by Alida Malkus. Harcourt.
Queer Person, by Ralph Hubbard. Doubleday.
Mountains Are Free, by Julia Davis Adams. Dutton.
Spice and the Devil's Cave, by Agnes D. Hewes.
Knopf.
Meggy McIntosh, by Elizabeth Janet Gray.
Doubleday.
Garram the Hunter: A Boy of the Hill Tribes, by
Herbert Best. Illustrated by Allena Best (Erick
Berry). Doubleday.
Ood-Le-Uk, The Wanderer, by Alice Lide and
Margaret Johansen. Illustrated by Raymond
Lufkin. Little, Brown.

1932 *Waterless Mountain*, by Laura Adams Armer.
Illustrated by Sidney Armer and Laura Adams
Armer. McKay/Longmans.

Honor Books:
The Fairy Circus, by Dorothy Lathrop. Macmillan.
Calico Bush, by Rachel Field. Macmillan.
Boy of the South Seas by Eunice Tietjens. Coward-
McCann.
Out of the Flame, by Eloise Lownsbery.
McKay/Longmans.
Jane's Island, by Marjorie Hill Alee. Houghton
Mifflin.
The Truce of the Wolf and Other Tales of Old Italy,
by Mary Gould Davis. Harcourt.

1933 *Young Fu of the Upper Yangtze*, by Elizabeth
Foreman Lewis. Illustrated by Kurt Wiese. Holt.
Honor Books:
Swift Rivers, by Cornelia Meigs. Little, Brown.
The Railroad to Freedom, by Hildegarde Swift.
Harcourt.
Children of the Soil, by Nora Burglon. Doubleday.

1934 *Invincible Louisa: The Story of the Author of "Little
Women,"* by Cornelia Meigs. Little, Brown.
Honor Books:
The Forgotten Daughter, by Caroline Dale
Snedeker. Doubleday.
Swords of Steel, by Elsie Singmaster. Houghton
Mifflin.
ABC Bunny, by Wanda Gág. Coward McCann.
Winged Girl of Knossos, by Erick Berry. Appleton.
New Land, by Sarah L. Schmidt. McBride.
The Apprentice of Florence, by Anne Kyle.
Houghton Mifflin.
*The Big Tree of Bunlahy: Stories of My Own
Countryside*, by Padraic Colum. Illustrated by
Jack Yeats. Macmillan.
Glory of the Seas, by Agnes D. Hewes. Illustrated
by N. C. Wyeth. Knopf.

1935 *Dobry*, by Monica Shannon. Illustrated by Atanas
Katchamakoff. Viking.
Honor Books:
The Pageant of Chinese History, by Elizabeth
Seeger. McKay/Longmans.
Davy Crockett, by Constance Rourke. Harcourt.
A Day on Skates: The Story of a Dutch Picnic, by
Hilda Van Stockum. Harper.

1936 *Caddie Woodlawn* by Carol Ryrie Brink.
Illustrated by Kate Seredy. Macmillan.
Honor Books:
Honk: The Moose, by Phil Strong. Illustrated by
Kurt Wiese. Dodd.
The Good Master, by Kate Seredy. Viking.
Young Walter Scott, by Elizabeth Janet Gray. Viking.
All Sail Set, by Armstrong Sperry. Winston.

1937 *Roller Skates*, by Ruth Sawyer. Illustrated by
Valenti Angelo. Viking.
Honor Books:
Phoebe Fairchild: Her Book, by Lois Lenski.
Lippincott.
Whistler's Van, by Idwal Jones. Viking.
The Golden Basket, by Ludwig Bemelmans.
Viking.

Winterbound, by Margery Bianco. Viking.
Audubon, by Constance Rourke. Harcourt Brace.
The Codfish Musket, by Agnes D. Hewes.
Doubleday.

1938   *The White Stag,* by Kate Seredy. Viking.
Honor Books:
Bright Island, by Mabel L. Robinson. Random
House.
Pecos Bill, by James Cloyd Bowman. Little, Brown.
On the Banks of Plum Creek, by Laura Ingalls
Wilder. Harper.

1939   *Thimble Summer,* by Elizabeth Enright. Holt.
Honor Books:
*Leader by Destiny: George Washington, Man and
Patriot,* by Jeanette Eaton. Harcourt.
Penn, by Elizabeth Janet Gray. Viking.
Nino, by Valenti Angelo. Viking.
"Hello, the Boat!" by Phyllis Crawford. Holt.
Mr. Popper's Penguins, by Richard and Florence
Atwater. Little, Brown.

1940   *Daniel Boone,* by James H. Daugherty. Viking.
Honor Books:
The Singing Tree, by Kate Seredy. Viking.
Runner of the Mountain Tops, by Mabel L.
Robinson. Random House.
By the Shores of Silver Lake, by Laura Ingalls
Wilder. Harper.
Boy with a Pack, by Stephen W. Meader. Harcourt
Brace.

1941   *Call It Courage,* by Armstrong Sperry. Macmillan.
Honor Books:
Blue Willow, by Doris Gates. Viking.
Young Mac of Fort Vancouver, by Mary Jane Carr.
Crowell.
The Long Winter, by Laura Ingalls Wilder. Harper.
Nansen, by Anna Gertrude Hall. Viking.

1942   *The Matchlock Gun,* by Walter D. Edmonds.
Illustrated by Paul Lantz. Dodd.
Honor Books:
Little Town on the Prairie, by Laura Ingalls
Wilder. Harper.
George Washington's World, by Genevieve Foster.
Scribner's.
Indian Captive: The Story of Mary Jemison, by
Lois Lenski. Lippincott.
Down Ryton Water, by Eva Roe Gaggin.
Illustrated by Elmer Hader. Viking.

1943   *Adam of the Road,* by Elizabeth Janet Gray.
Illustrated by Robert Lawson. Viking.
Honor Books:
The Middle Moffat, by Eleanor Estes. Harcourt
Brace.
"Have You Seen Tom Thumb?" by Mabel Leigh
Hunt. Lippincott.

1944   *Johnny Tremain,* by Esther Forbes. Illustrated by
Lynd Ward. Houghton Mifflin.
Honor Books:
These Happy Golden Years, by Laura Ingalls
Wilder. Harper.

Fog Magic, by Julia L. Sauer. Viking.
Rufus M., by Eleanor Estes. Harcourt Brace.
Mountain Born, by Elizabeth Yates.
Coward-McCann.

1945   *Rabbit Hill,* by Robert Lawson. Viking.
Honor Books:
The Hundred Dresses, by Eleanor Estes. Harcourt
Brace.
The Silver Pencil, by Alice Dalgliesh. Scribner's.
Abraham Lincoln's World, by Genevieve Foster.
Scribner's.
Lone Journey: The Life of Roger Williams, by
Jeanette Eaton. Illustrated by Woodi Ishmael.
Harcourt.

1946   *Strawberry Girl,* by Lois Lenski. Lippincott.
Honor Books:
Justin Morgan Had a Horse, by Marguerite Henry.
Follett.
The Moved-Outers, by Florence Crannell Means.
Houghton Mifflin.
Bhimsa, the Dancing Bear, by Christine Weston.
Scribner's.
New Found World, by Katherine B. Shippen. Viking.

1947   *Miss Hickory,* by Carolyn Sherwin Bailey.
Illustrated by Ruth Gannett. Viking.
Honor Books:
The Wonderful Year, by Nancy Barnes. Messner.
The Big Tree, by Mary and Conrad Buff. Viking.
The Heavenly Tenants, by William Maxwell.
Harper.
The Avion My Uncle Flew, by Cyrus Fisher. Appleton.
The Hidden Treasure of Glaston, by Eleanore M.
Jewett. Viking.

1948   *The Twenty-One Balloons,* by William Pène du
Bois. Lothrop.
Honor Books:
Pancakes-Paris, by Claire Huchet Bishop. Viking.
Li Lun, Lad of Courage, by Carolyn Treffinger.
Abingdon.
*The Quaint and Curious Quest of Johnny Longfoot,
The Shoe-King's Son,* by Catherine Besterman.
Bobbs-Merrill.
*The Cow-Tail Switch, And Other West African
Stories,* by Harold Courlander and George
Herzog. Holt.
Misty of Chincoteague, by Marguerite Henry.
Illustrated by Wesley Dennis. Rand.

1949   *King of the Wind,* by Marguerite Henry.
Illustrated by Wesley Dennis. Rand.
Honor Books:
Seabird, by Holling Clancy Holling. Houghton
Mifflin.
Daughter of the Mountains, by Louise Rankin.
Viking.
My Father's Dragon, by Ruth S. Gannett. Random
House.
Story of the Negro, by Arna Bontemps. Knopf.

1950   *The Door in the Wall,* by Marguerite de Angeli.
Doubleday.

Honor Books:
Tree of Freedom, by Rebecca Caudill. Viking.
The Blue Cat of Castle Town, by Catherine Coblentz. McKay/Longmans.
Kildee House, by Rutherford Montgomery. Doubleday.
George Washington, by Genevieve Foster. Scribner's.
Song of the Pines, by Walter and Marion Havighurst. Holt.

1951   *Amos Fortune, Free Man,* by Elizabeth Yates. Illustrated by Nora Unwin. Dutton.
Honor Books:
Better Known as Johnny Appleseed, by Mabel Leigh Hunt. Lippincott.
Gandhi, Fighter Without a Sword, by Jeanette Eaton. Morrow.
Abraham Lincoln, Friend of the People, by Clara I. Judson. Follett.
The Story of Appleby Capple, by Anne Parrish. Harper.

1952   *Ginger Pye,* by Eleanor Estes. Harcourt Brace.
Honor Books:
Americans Before Columbus, by Elizabeth Chesley Baity. Viking.
Minn of the Mississippi, by Holling Clancy Holling. Houghton Mifflin.
The Defender, by Nicholas Kalashnikoff. Scribner's.
The Light at Tern Rock, by Julia L. Sauer. Viking.
The Apple and the Arrow, by Mary and Conrad Buff. Houghton Mifflin.

1953   *Secret of the Andes,* by Ann Nolan Clark. Illustrated by Jean Charlot. Viking.
Honor Books:
Charlotte's Web, by E. B. White. Harper & Row.
Moccasin Trail, by Eloise J. McGraw. Coward-McCann.
Red Sails to Capri, by Ann Weil. Viking.
The Bears on Hemlock Mountain, by Alice Dalgliesh. Scribner's.
Birthdays of Freedom, Vol. 1, by Genevieve Foster. Scribner's.

1954   *And Now Miguel,* by Joseph Krumgold. Illustrated by Jean Charlot. Crowell.
Honor Books:
All Alone, by Claire Huchet Bishop. Viking.
Shadrach, by Meindert DeJong. Harper.
Hurry Home, Candy, by Meindert DeJong. Harper.
Theodore Roosevelt, Fighting Patriot, by Clara I. Judson. Follett.
Magic Maize, by Mary and Conrad Buff. Houghton Mifflin.

1955   *The Wheel on the School,* by Meindert DeJong. Illustrated by Maurice Sendak. Harper.
Honor Books:
The Courage of Sarah Noble, by Alice Dalgliesh. Scribner's.

Banner in the Sky, by James Ramsey Ullman. Lippincott.

1956   *Carry on, Mr. Bowditch,* by Jean Lee Latham. Houghton Mifflin.
Honor Books:
The Golden Name Day, by Jennie D. Lindquist. Harper.
The Secret River, by Marjorie Kinnan Rawlings. Scribner's.
Men, Microscopes and Living Things, by Katherine B. Shippen. Viking.

1957   *Miracles on Maple Hill,* by Virginia Sorensen. Illustrated by Beth and Joe Krush. Harcourt Brace.
Honor Books:
Old Yeller, by Fred Gipson. Harper.
The House of Sixty Fathers, by Meindert DeJong. Harper.
Mr. Justice Holmes, by Clara I. Judson. Follett.
The Corn Grows Ripe, by Dorothy Rhoads. Viking.
The Black Fox of Lorne, by Marguerite de Angeli. Doubleday.

1958   *Rifles for Watie,* by Harold Keith. Illustrated by Peter Burchard. Crowell.
Honor Books:
The Horsecatcher, by Mari Sandoz. Westminster.
Gone-Away Lake, by Elizabeth Enright. Harcourt Brace.
The Great Wheel, by Robert Lawson. Viking.
Tom Paine, Freedom's Apostle, by Leo Gurko. Crowell.

1959   *The Witch of Blackbird Pond,* by Elizabeth George Speare. Houghton Mifflin.
Honor Books:
The Family Under the Bridge, by Natalie S. Carlson. Harper.
Along Came a Dog, by Meindert DeJong. Harper.
Chucaro: Wild Pony of the Pampa, by Francis Kalnay. Harcourt.
The Perilous Road, by William O. Steele. Harcourt.

1960   *Onion John,* by Joseph Krumgold. Illustrated by Symeon Shimin. Crowell.
Honor Books:
My Side of the Mountain, by Jean Craighead George. Dutton.
America Is Born by Gerald Johnson. Morrow.
The Gammage Cup, by Carol Kendall. Harcourt Brace.

1961   *Island of the Blue Dolphins,* by Scott O'Dell. Houghton Mifflin.
Honor Books:
America Moves Forward, by Gerald Johnson. Morrow.
Old Ramon, by Jack Schaefer. Houghton Mifflin.
The Cricket in Times Square, by George Selden. Farrar, Straus & Giroux.

1962   *The Bronze Bow,* by Elizabeth George Speare. Houghton Mifflin.

Honor Books:
Frontier Living, by Edwin Tunis. World.
The Golden Goblet, by Eloise J. McGraw. Coward.
Belling the Tiger, by Mary Stolz. Harper.

1963 *A Wrinkle in Time,* by Madeleine L'Engle. Farrar, Straus & Giroux.
Honor Books:
Thistle and Thyme, by Sorche Nic Leodhas (pseud. for Leclaire Alger). Holt.
Men of Athens, by Olivia Coolidge. Houghton Mifflin.

1964 *It's Like This, Cat,* by Emily Cheney Neville. Harper & Row.
Honor Books:
Rascal, by Sterling North. Dutton.
The Loner, by Esther Wier. McKay/Longmans.

1965 *Shadow of a Bull,* by Maia Wojciechowska. Atheneum.
Honor Book:
Across Five Aprils, by Irene Hunt. Follett.

1966 *I, Juan de Pareja,* by Elizabeth Borten de Treviño. Farrar, Straus & Giroux.
Honor Books:
The Black Cauldron, by Lloyd Alexander. Holt.
The Animal Family, by Randall Jarrell. Pantheon.
The Noonday Friends, by Mary Stolz. Harper & Row.

1967 *Up a Road Slowly,* by Irene Hunt. Follett.
Honor Books:
The King's Fifth, by Scott O'Dell. Houghton Mifflin.
Zlateh the Goat and Other Stories, by Isaac Bashevis Singer. Harper & Row.
The Jazz Man, by Mary H. Weik. Atheneum.

1968 *From the Mixed-Up Files of Mrs. Basil E. Frankweiler,* by E. L. Konigsburg. Atheneum.
Honor Books:
Jennifer, Hecate, Macbeth, William McKinley, and Me, Elizabeth, by E. L. Konigsburg. Atheneum.
The Black Pearl, by Scott O'Dell. Houghton Mifflin.
The Fearsome Inn, by Isaac Bashevis Singer. Scribner's.
The Egypt Game, by Zilpha Keatley Snyder. Atheneum.

1969 *The High King,* by Lloyd Alexander. Holt.
Honor Books:
To Be a Slave, by Julius Lester. Dial.
When Shlemiel Went to Warsaw and Other Stories, by Isaac Bashevis Singer. Farrar, Straus & Giroux.

1970 *Sounder,* by William H. Armstrong. Harper & Row.
Honor Books:
Our Eddie, by Sulamith Ish-Kishor. Pantheon.
The Many Ways of Seeing: An Introduction to the Pleasure of Art, by Janet Gaylord Moore. World.
Journey Outside, by Mary Q. Steele. Viking.

1971 *Summer of the Swans,* by Betsy Byars. Viking.
Honor Books:
Kneeknock Rise, by Natalie Babbitt. Farrar, Straus & Giroux.

Enchantress from the Stars, by Sylvia Louise Engdahl. Atheneum.
Sing Down the Moon, by Scott O'Dell. Houghton Mifflin.

1972 *Mrs. Frisby and the Rats of NIMH,* by Robert C. O'Brien. Atheneum.
Honor Books:
Incident at Hawk's Hill, by Allan W. Eckert. Little, Brown.
The Planet of Junior Brown, by Virginia Hamilton. Macmillan.
The Tombs of Atuan, by Ursula K. LeGuin. Atheneum.
Annie and the Old One, by Miska Miles. Little, Brown.
The Headless Cupid, by Zilpha Keatley Snyder. Atheneum.

1973 *Julie of the Wolves,* by Jean Craighead George. Harper & Row.
Honor Books:
Frog and Toad Together, by Arnold Lobel. Harper & Row.
The Upstairs Room, by Johanna Reiss. Crowell.
The Witches of Worm, by Zilpha Keatley Snyder. Atheneum.

1974 *The Slave Dancer,* by Paula Fox. Bradbury.
Honor Book:
The Dark Is Rising, by Susan Cooper. Atheneum/McElderry.

1975 *M. C. Higgins, the Great,* by Virginia Hamilton. Macmillan.
Honor Books:
Figgs & Phantoms, by Ellen Raskin. Dutton.
My Brother Sam Is Dead, by James Lincoln Collier and Christopher Collier. Four Winds.
The Perilous Gard, by Elizabeth Marie Pope. Houghton Mifflin.
Philip Hall Likes Me, I Reckon Maybe, by Bette Greene. Dial.

1976 *The Grey King,* by Susan Cooper. Atheneum/McElderry.
Honor Books:
The Hundred Penny Box, by Sharon Bell Mathis. Viking.
Dragonwings, by Laurence Yep. Harper & Row.

1977 *Roll of Thunder, Hear My Cry,* by Mildred D. Taylor. Dial.
Honor Books:
Abel's Island, by William Steig. Farrar, Straus & Giroux.
A String in the Harp, by Nancy Bond. Atheneum/McElderry.

1978 *Bridge to Terabithia,* by Katherine Paterson. Crowell.
Honor Books:
Anpao: An American Indian Odyssey, by Jamake Highwater. Lippincott.
Ramona and Her Father, by Beverly Cleary. Morrow.

1979   *The Westing Game,* by Ellen Raskin. Dutton.
Honor Book:
The Great Gilly Hopkins, by Katherine Paterson.
Crowell.

1980   *A Gathering of Days: A New England Girl's Journal, 1830–32,* by Joan Blos. Scribner's.
Honor Book:
The Road From Home: The Story of an Armenian Girl, by David Kherdian. Greenwillow.

1981   *Jacob Have I Loved,* by Katherine Paterson.
Crowell.
Honor Books:
The Fledgling, by Jane Langton. Harper & Row.
A Ring of Endless Light, by Madeleine L'Engle.
Farrar, Straus & Giroux.

1982   *A Visit to William Blake's Inn: Poems for Innocent and Experienced Travelers,* by Nancy Willard.
Illustrated by Alice and Martin Provensen.
Harcourt.
Honor Books:
Ramona Quimby, Age 8, by Beverly Cleary.
Morrow.
Upon the Head of the Goat: A Childhood in Hungary, 1939–1944, by Aranka Siegal. Farrar, Straus & Giroux.

1983   *Dicey's Song,* by Cynthia Voigt. Atheneum.
Honor Books:
The Blue Sword, by Robin McKinley. Greenwillow.
Dr. DeSoto, by William Steig. Farrar, Straus & Giroux.
Graven Images, by Paul Fleischman. Harper & Row.
Homesick: My Own Story, by Jean Fritz. Putnam.
Sweet Whispers, Brother Rush, by Virginia Hamilton. Philomel.

1984   *Dear Mr. Henshaw,* by Beverly Cleary. Morrow.
Honor Books:
The Sign of the Beaver, by Elizabeth George Speare.
Houghton Mifflin.
A Solitary Blue, by Cynthia Voigt. Atheneum.
Sugaring Time, by Kathryn Lasky. Photographs by Christopher Knight. Macmillan.
The Wish Giver, by Bill Brittain. Harper & Row.

1985   *The Hero and the Crown,* by Robin McKinley.
Greenwillow.
Honor Books:
Like Jake and Me, by Mavis Jukes. Illustrated by Lloyd Bloom. Knopf.
The Moves Make the Man, by Bruce Brooks. Harper & Row.
One-Eyed Cat, by Paula Fox. Bradbury.

1986   *Sarah, Plain and Tall,* by Patricia MacLachlan.
Harper & Row.
Honor Books:
Commodore Perry in the Land of the Shogun, by Rhoda Blumberg. Lothrop.
Dogsong, by Gary Paulsen. Bradbury.

1987   *The Whipping Boy,* by Sid Fleischman.
Greenwillow.

Honor Books:
On My Honor, by Marion Dane Bauer. Clarion.
Volcano: The Eruption and Healing of Mount St. Helens, by Patricia Lauber. Bradbury.
A Fine White Dust, by Cynthia Rylant. Bradbury.

1988   *Lincoln: A Photobiography,* by Russell Freedman.
Clarion.
Honor Books:
After the Rain, by Norma Fox Mazer. Morrow.
Hatchet, by Gary Paulsen. Bradbury.

1989   *Joyful Noise: Poems for Two Voices,* by Paul Fleischman. Harper & Row.
Honor Books:
In the Beginning: Creation Stories from Around the World, by Virginia Hamilton. Harcourt.
Scorpions, by Walter Dean Myers. Harper & Row.

1990   *Number the Stars,* by Lois Lowry. Houghton Mifflin.
Honor Books:
Afternoon of the Elves, by Janet Taylor Lisle.
Orchard.
Shabanu, Daughter of the Wind, by Suzanne Fisher Staples. Knopf.
The Winter Room, by Gary Paulsen. Orchard.

1991   *Maniac Magee,* by Jerry Spinelli. Little, Brown.
Honor Book:
The True Confessions of Charlotte Doyle, by Avi.
Orchard.

1992   *Shiloh,* by Phyllis Reynolds Naylor. Atheneum.
Honor Books:
Nothing But the Truth, by Avi. Orchard.
The Wright Brothers: How They Invented the Airplane, by Russell Freedman. Holiday House.

1993   *Missing May,* by Cynthia Rylant. Orchard.
Honor Books:
The Dark-Thirty: Southern Tales of the Supernatural, by Patricia McKissack. Illustrated by Brian Pinkney. Knopf.
Somewhere in Darkness, by Walter Dean Myers.
Scholastic.
What Hearts, by Bruce Brooks. Laura Geringer Books (Harper).

1994   *The Giver,* by Lois Lowry. Houghton Mifflin.
Honor Books:
Crazy Lady! by Jane Leslie Conly. HarperCollins.
Dragon's Gate, by Laurence Yep. HarperCollins.
Eleanor Roosevelt: A Life of Discovery, by Russell Freedman. Clarion.

1995   *Walk Two Moons,* by Sharon Creech.
HarperCollins.
Honor Books:
Catherine, Called Birdy, by Karen Cushman.
Clarion.
The Ear, the Eye and the Arm, by Nancy Farmer.
Orchard.

1996   *The Midwife's Apprentice,* by Karen Cushman.
Clarion.

Honor Books:
The Watsons Go to Birmingham—1963, by
Christopher Paul Curtis. Delacorte.
The Great Fire, by Jim Murphy. Scholastic.
What Jamie Saw, by Carolyn Coman. Front Street.
Yolanda's Genius, by Carol Fenner. McElderry.

1997   *The View from Saturday*, by E. L. Konigsburg.
Atheneum.
Honor Books:
A Girl Named Disaster, by Nancy Farmer. Orchard.
Moorchild, by Eloise McGraw. McElderry.
The Thief, by Megan Whalen Turner. Greenwillow.
Belle Prater's Boy, by Ruth White. Farrar, Straus &
Giroux.

1998   *Out of the Dust*, by Karen Hesse. Scholastic.
Honor Books:
Ella Enchanted, by Gail Carson Levine.
HarperCollins.
Lily's Crossing, by Patricia Reilly Giff. Delacorte.
Wringer, by Jerry Spinelli. HarperCollins.

1999   *Holes*, by Louis Sachar. Farrar, Straus & Giroux.
Honor Book:
A Long Way from Chicago, by Richard Peck. Dial.

2000   *Bud, Not Buddy*, by Christopher Paul Curtis.
Delacorte.
Honor Books:
Getting Near to Baby, by Audrey Couloumbis.
Putnam.
Our Only May Amelia, by Jennifer L. Holm.
HarperCollins.
26 Fairmont Avenue, by Tomie dePaola. Putnam.

2001   *A Year Down Yonder*, by Richard Peck. Dial Books
for Young Readers.
Honor Books:
Because of Winn-Dixie, by Kate DiCamillo.
Candlewick.
Hope Was Here, by Joan Bauer. Putnam.
Joey Pigza Loses Control, by Jack Gantos. Farrar,
Straus, & Giroux.
The Wanderer, by Sharon Creech. Joanna Cotler
Books, HarperCollins.

Canada

Amelia Frances Howard-Gibbon Medal. Sponsored and
administered by the Canadian Library Association since
1971, the Amelia Frances Howard-Gibbon Medal is presented to the illustrator of the most outstanding artwork in
a children's book published in Canada during the preceding
year. Eligibility for this award is limited to citizens and residents of Canada.

**Canadian Library Association Book of the Year for
Children Award.** Sponsored and administered by the
Canadian Library Association since 1947, the Canadian Library Association Book of the Year for Children Award is
presented to the authors of the outstanding children's books
published during the preceding year. Only Canadian citizens
are eligible for this award.

Great Britain

Carnegie Medal. Sponsored and administered since 1937
by the British Library Association, the Carnegie Medal is
presented to the author of a children's book of outstanding
merit, written in English and first published in the United
Kingdom in the preceding year.

Kate Greenaway Medal. Sponsored and administered
since 1956 by the British Library Association, the Kate
Greenaway Medal is presented to the illustrator of the most
distinguished picture book first published in the United
Kingdom in the preceding year.

Australia

Children's Books of the Year Awards. The Children's
Books of the Year Awards program began in 1946 under the
direction of various agencies in Australia. In 1959, the administration of the award program was taken over by the
Children's Book Council of Australia. Currently, four
awards are given annually: The Picture Book of the Year
Award, The Children's Book for Younger Readers Award,
The Children's Book of the Year for Older Readers Award,
and The Eve Pownall Award for Information Books. Eligibility for the awards is limited to authors and illustrators
who are Australian residents or citizens.

New Zealand

Russell Clark Award. Sponsored and administered by
the New Zealand Library and Information Association
since 1978, the Russell Clark Award is given "for the most
distinguished illustrations for a children's book; the illustrator must be a citizen or resident of New Zealand." The
award is given annually to a book published in the previous year.

Esther Glen Award. Sponsored and administered by the
New Zealand Library and Information Association since
1945, the Esther Glen Award is presented to the author of
the most distinguished contribution to New Zealand's literature for children published in the previous year. Eligibility
for the Esther Glen Award is limited to New Zealand residents and citizens.

▼▼▼▼▼▼

Awards for a Body of Work

Hans Christian Andersen Award

Sponsored and administered by the International Board on
Books for Young People, the Hans Christian Andersen
Awards honor biennially one author (since 1956) and one illustrator (since 1966) for his or her entire body of work. This
truly international award is chosen by a panel of judges representing several countries. The award must be given to a living author or illustrator who has made important and time-

proven contributions to international children's literature. The Americans who have won the Hans Christian Andersen Medal are Meindert DeJong (1962), Maurice Sendak (1970), Scott O'Dell (1972), Paula Fox (1978), and Virginia Hamilton (1992).

NCTE Award Excellence in Poetry for Children

Sponsored and administered by the National Council of Teachers of English, the Excellence in Poetry for Children Award was given annually from 1977 to 1982, but beginning with the 1985 award, it is now presented every 3 years. The award is presented to a living American poet whose body of work is considered an outstanding contribution to poetry for children ages 3 through 13.

Laura Ingalls Wilder Award

Sponsored and administered by the Association for Library Service to Children, an arm of the American Library Association, the Laura Ingalls Wilder Award is presented to a U.S. author or illustrator whose body of work is deemed to have made a substantial and lasting contribution to literature for children. The Wilder Award was first given in 1954. Between 1960 and 1980, it was presented every 5 years, but as of 1983, it has been awarded every 3 years. Winners include Laura Ingalls Wilder (1954), Clara Ingram Judson (1960), Ruth Sawyer (1965), E. B. White (1970), Beverly Cleary (1975), Theodor S. Geisel (Dr. Seuss) (1980), Maurice Sendak (1983), Jean Fritz (1986), Elizabeth George Speare (1989), Marcia Brown (1992), Virginia Hamilton (1995), and Russell Freedman (1998).

▼▼▼▼▼▼▼

Other Selected Awards

Boston Globe/Horn Book Award

Since 1967, *The Boston Globe* and *The Horn Book Magazine*, one of America's oldest and most prestigious children's book review sources, have sponsored awards for children's book writing and illustration. As of 1976, three Boston Globe/Horn Book Awards have been presented annually: Outstanding Fiction or Poetry, Outstanding Nonfiction, and Outstanding Illustration.

Carter G. Woodsen Award

Since 1974, the National Council for the Social Studies has sponsored awards for the most distinguished social science books for young readers that treat with sensitivity and accuracy topics related to ethnic minorities and race relations within the United States. The annual awards are given to books published in the United States in the preceding year, and since 1980, winners for both elementary and secondary school readers have been named.

Coretta Scott King Award

Since 1970, the Social Responsibilities Round Table, with the support of the American Library Association, has sponsored and administered the Coretta Scott King Award. This award commemorates the life and dreams of Dr. Martin Luther King as well as the continued work of his wife, Coretta Scott King, for peace and world brotherhood. It also recognizes the creative work of black authors. Beginning in 1974, two awards have been presented, one to a black author and one to a black illustrator whose books for young readers published in the preceding year are deemed outstanding, educational, and inspirational.

Edgar Allan Poe Award

Since 1962, The Mystery Writers of America have presented an award for the Best Juvenile Novel in the fields of mystery, suspense, crime, and intrigue. In 1989, a second category was added: Best Young Adult Novel. A ceramic bust of Edgar Allan Poe is presented to the winners in all categories, which include adult fiction and filmmaking. The Edgars are the mystery writers' equivalent of Hollywood's Oscars.

International Reading Association Children's Book Award

Since 1975, the International Reading Association has sponsored and administered an award presented to new authors of children's books. Publishers worldwide nominate books whose authors show special promise for a successful career in writing for children. As of 1987, two awards were given annually, one for novels and another for picture books. In 1995, a third award was added for informational books.

Mildred L. Batchelder Award

Since 1968, the Association for Library Service to Children, an arm of the American Library Association, has presented an award to an American publisher for the most outstanding children's book originally published in another country in a language other than English and subsequently translated and published in the United States during the previous year.

National Book Awards

A consortium of book publishing groups has presented the National Book Awards since 1950. The sponsors' goal was to enhance the public's awareness of exceptional books written by fellow Americans and to increase the popularity of reading in general. The awards are given in these categories: Fiction, Nonfiction, Poetry, and Young People's Literature.

Orbis Pictus Award for Outstanding Nonfiction for Children

The Orbis Pictus Award has been given annually since 1990 by the National Council of Teachers of English. Only nonfiction or informational children's books published in the United States during the preceding year are considered. The selection committee chooses the most outstanding contribution by examining each candidate's "accuracy, organization, design, writing style, and usefulness for classroom teaching in grades K–8." One winner and up to five honor books are selected each year. The award is named for the book *Orbis Pictus (The World in Pictures)*, which is considered to be the first book created exclusively for children. This nonfiction work was written and illustrated by Johann Amos Comenius in 1659.

Phoenix Award

Since 1985, the Children's Literature Association has sponsored an award for "a book for children published twenty years earlier which did not win a major award at the time of its publication but which, from the perspective of time, is deemed worthy of special recognition for its literary quality." Consideration is limited to titles published originally in English.

Pura Belpré Award

The Pura Belpré Award is cosponsored by the Association for Library Services to Children and the National Association to Promote Library Services to the Spanish Speaking, both part of the American Library Association. First presented in 1996, this award is given biennially to a writer and an illustrator who are Latino/ Latina and who have produced works that best portray, affirm, and celebrate the Latino cultural experience. The Pura Belpré Award is named after the first Latina librarian from the New York Public Library.

Scott O'Dell Award for Historical Fiction

The Scott O'Dell Award, first presented in 1984, is given to the author of a distinguished work of historical fiction written for children or adolescent readers. The winning books must be written in English, published by a U.S. publisher, and set in the New World (North, Central, or South America). The award was originated and donated by the celebrated children's author Scott O'Dell and is administered and selected by an Advisory Board chaired by Zena Sutherland, formerly of the *Bulletin of the Center for Children's Books*.

Robert F. Sibert Informational Book Award

This is a new award established by the Association for Library Service to Children, a division of the American Library Association. This award is to be awarded annually to the author of the most distinguished informational book published during the preceding year. The award is named after Robert F. Sibert, president of Bound to Stay Bound Books, Inc. of Jacksonville, Illinois, and is sponsored by the company. ALSC administers the award.

▼▼▼▼▼▼▼

State Children's Choice Awards

Most U.S. states now have an organization, such as a state library or children's literature association, that sponsors a chil-dren's choice book award. Typically, schoolchildren nominate books, and an adult committee narrows the list to about 20 titles. Then during the year, schools participating in the award process will make the books available to children. To vote, the children must have read or had read to them a specified number of the titles. Only children may vote. Following is a list of the state children's choice award programs for specific states and regions:

Alabama	Emphasis on Reading: Children's Choice Book Award Program, since 1980 (three categories: grades K–2, 3–5, 6–8)
Arizona	Arizona Young Readers Award, since 1977 (grades K–4)
Arkansas	Charlie May Simon Children's Book Award, since 1971 (grades 4–6)
California	California Young Reader Medals, since 1975 (four categories: primary, intermediate, junior high, and senior high)
Colorado	Colorado Children's Book Award, since 1976 (elementary grades) Blue Spruce Award, since 1985 (young adult)
Connecticut	Nutmeg Children's Book Award, since 1993 (grades 4–6)
Delaware	The Delaware Diamonds Program
Florida	Florida Reading Association Children's Book Award, since 1987 (grades K–2) Sunshine State Young Reader's Award, since 1984 (grades 3–8)
Georgia	Georgia Children's Book Award, since 1969 (grades 4–8) Georgia Children's Picture Storybook Award, since 1977 (grades K–3)
Hawaii	Nene Award, since 1964 (grades 4–6)
Illinois	Rebecca Caudill Young Readers' Book Award, since 1988 (grades 4–8)
Indiana	Young Hoosier Award, since 1975 (two awards: grades 4–6, grades 6–8) Young Hoosier Picture Book Award, since 1992 (grades K–3)
Iowa	Iowa Children's Choice Award, since 1980 (grades 3–6) Iowa Teen Award, since 1985 (grades 6–9)
Kansas	William Allen White Children's Book Award, since 1953 (grades 4–8)
Kentucky	Kentucky Bluegrass Award, since 1983 (two divisions: grades K–3 and grades 4–8)
Maine	Maine Student Book Award, since 1989 (grades 4–8)

Maryland	Maryland Children's Book Award, since 1988 (three categories: primary, intermediate, middle school)
	The Black Eyed Susan Award, since 1992 (grades 4–6 and 6–9)
Massachusetts	Massachusetts Children's Book Award, since 1976 (grades 4–6). An award for grades 7–9 was presented during the years 1978–1983.
Michigan	Michigan Young Readers' Awards, since 1980
Minnesota	Maud Hart Lovelace Award, since 1980 (grades 3–8)
Missouri	Mark Twain Award, since 1972 (grades 4–8)
	The Show Me Award, since 1998 (grades 1–3)
Montana	Treasure State Award, since 1991 (grades K–3)
	Nebraska Golden Sower Award for Fiction, since 1981 (grades 4–6)
	Golden Sower Award for Picture Book, since 1983 (grades K–3)
	Golden Sower Award for Young Adults, since 1993 (grades 6–9)
Nevada	Nevada Young Readers' Award, since 1988 (four categories: primary, grades K–3; young reader, grades 4–6; intermediate, grades 6–8; young adult, grades 9–12)
New Hampshire	Great Stone Face Award, since 1980 (grades 4–6)
New Jersey	Garden State Children's Book Awards, since 1977 (three categories: easy to read, younger fiction, younger nonfiction)
	The New Jersey Reading Association M. Jerry Weiss Award, since 1994 (three divisions: primary, intermediate, secondary; award for each division presented every third year on a revolving basis)
	Garden State Teen Book Award, since 1995 (three categories: fiction, grades 6–8; fiction, grades 9–12; nonfiction)
New Mexico	Land of Enchantment Book Award, since 1981 (grades 4–8)
North Carolina	The Children's Book Award, since 1999 (two categories: picture book and junior book)
North Dakota	Flicker Tale Children's Book Award, since 1978 (two categories: picture book and juvenile)
Ohio	Buckeye Children's Book Awards, since 1982 (three divisions: grades K–2, grades 3–5, grades 6–8)
Oklahoma	Sequoyah Children's Book Award, since 1959 (grades 3–6)
	Sequoyah Young Adult Book Award, since 1988 (grades 7–9)
	Pacific Northwest Young Reader's Choice Awards (Alaska, U.S.A.; Alberta, Canada; British Columbia, Canada; Idaho, U.S.A.; Montana, U.S.A.; Oregon, U.S.A.; Washington, U.S.A.), since 1940 (grades 4–8). Since 1991, an award for grades 9–12 has also been given.
Pennsylvania	Keystone to Reading Book Award, since 1984
	Pennsylvania Young Reader's Choice Award, since 1992 (grades K–8 with some variation in grade categories from year to year)
Rhode Island	Rhode Island Children's Book Award, since 1991 (grades 3–6)
South Carolina	South Carolina Children's Book Award, since 1976 (grades 3–6)
	South Carolina Junior Book Award, since 1993 (grades 6–9)
	South Carolina Young Adult Book Award, since 1980 (grades 9–12)
South Dakota	Prairie Pasque Children's Book Award, since 1987 (grades 4–6)
Tennessee	Volunteer State Book Award, since 1979 (three divisions: grades K–3, grades 4–6, young adult)
Texas	The Texas Bluebonnet Award, since 1981 (grades 3–6)
Utah	Utah Children's Book Award, since 1980 (grades 3–6)
	Utah Informational Book Award, since 1986 (grades 3–6)
	Utah Young Adults' Book Award, since 1991 (grades 7–12)
	Utah Picture Book Award, since 1996
Vermont	Dorothy Canfield Fisher Children's Book Award, since 1957 (grades 4–8)
Virginia	Virginia Young Readers Program, since 1982 (four divisions: primary, elementary, middle school, high school)
Washington	Washington Children's Choice Picture Book Award, since 1982 (grades K–3)
	The Sasquatch Chapter Book Reading Award, since 1999 (grades 4–6)
West Virginia	West Virginia Children's Book Award, since 1985 (grades 3–6)
Wisconsin	Golden Archer Award, since 1974 (three categories: primary, intermediate, middle/junior high)
Wyoming	Indian Paintbrush Book Award, since 1986 (grades 4–6)
	Soaring Eagle Young Adult Book Award, since 1989 (two divisions: grades 7–9, grades 10–12); since 1992, a single award (grades 7–12)

▼▼▼▼▼▼▼▼

Lists of the Best Books

The American Library Association

Notable Children's Books, an annual list of outstanding children's books chosen by a committee of the Association for Library Service to Children. Available in pamphlet form (American Library Association, 50 Huron Street, Chicago, IL 60611).

Best Books for Young Adults, an annual list of outstanding young adult books chosen by a committee of the Young Adult Library Services Association. Available in pamphlet form (American Library Association, 50 Huron Street, Chicago, IL 60611). YALSA also offers two other lists, Quick Picks for Reluctant Young Adult Readers and Popular Paperbacks for Young Adults.

School Library Journal

School Library Journal Best Books, an annual list of the best books reviewed in *School Library Journal.* Appears in the December issue.

The Horn Book Magazine

Hornbook Fanfare, an extremely selective annual list of highly recommended books chosen from among the books reviewed in *The Horn Book Magazine.* Appears in the March/April issue.

The Children's Book Council

Children's Choices. In cooperation with the International Reading Association, the Children's Book Council sponsors a project that produces an annual list of about 100 titles that 10,000 young readers from five project locations across the country have selected as their "best reads." Appears in the October issue of IRA's journal *The Reading Teacher.*

Outstanding Science Trade Books for Children. In cooperation with The National Science Teachers Association (NSTA), the CBC sponsors an annual listing of the best science books for young readers. Appears in the March issue of NSTA's journal *Science and Children.*

Notable Children's Trade Books in the Field of Social Studies. In cooperation with The National Council for the Social Studies (NCSS), the CBC sponsors an annual listing of the best social studies trade books (fiction and nonfiction) for young readers. Appears in the April/May issue of NCSS's journal *Social Studies.*

Others

There are many other "best books" lists prepared by a variety of organizations and individuals. Some others of note:

- Blue Ribbons (*The Bulletin of the Center for Children's Books*)

- Books for the Teenage Reader; 100 Titles for Reading and Sharing (New York Public Library)

- Children's Books of the Year (Children's Literature Center, Library of Congress)

- Editor's Choice (*Booklist,* American Library Association)

- *New York Times* Best Illustrated Children's Books of the Year (*New York Times Book Review Supplement*)

- Notable Books for a Global Society (International Reading Association, Children's Literature Special Interest Group)

- Notable Books in the Language Arts (National Council of Teachers of English, Children's Literature Assembly)

- Parents' Choice Awards (Parents' Choice Foundation)

- Teachers' Choices (International Reading Association)

- VOYA Nonfiction Honor List (*Voice of Youth Advocates,* Young Adult Library Services Association, American Library Association)

For complete lists of all the awards and the award-winning books, see the latest edition of *Children's Books: Awards and Prizes* published by the Children's Book Council.

C
APPENDIX

PUBLISHERS' ADDRESSES

Following is a list of selected publishers. Publishers' addresses and names may have changed since this list was compiled. Many of the changes reflect mergers and acquisitions of publishing houses. For example, Bradbury Press was subsumed by Simon & Schuster Books for Young Readers. Despite the change in the publisher's name and ownership, a student in your class who wants to write a letter to Judy Blume could write the author at the address for Bradbury Press, one of the publishing names long associated with Blume's books. That address would get the student's letter to Simon & Schuster. For up-to-date information and for a more comprehensive listing, however, consult the most current edition of *Books in Print* or *Children's Books in Print*.

Abrams
100 Fifth Ave.
New York, NY 10010

Addison-Wesley Publishing Co., Inc.
One Jacob Way
Reading, MA 01867

Aladdin Books
1230 Avenue of the Americas
New York, NY 10020

Atheneum Publishers
1230 Avenue of the Americas
New York, NY 10020

Avon Books
1350 Avenue of the Americas
New York, NY 10019

Bantam Books, Inc.
1540 Broadway
New York, NY 10036

Peter Bedrick Books, Inc.
2112 Broadway, Suite 318
New York, NY 10023

Beech Tree Books
1350 Avenue of the Americas
New York, NY 10019

Berkley Publishing Group
200 Madison Ave.
New York, NY 10010

Blue Sky Press
555 Broadway
New York, NY 10012

Boyds Mills Press
815 Church St.
Honesdale, PA 18431

Bradbury Press
1230 Avenue of the Americas
New York, NY 10020

Browndeer Press
525 B St., Suite 1900
San Diego, CA 92101

Camelot
1350 Avenue of the Americas
New York, NY 10019

Candlewick Press
2067 Massachusetts Ave.
Cambridge, MA 02140

Carolrhoda Books, Inc.
241 First Ave. N.
Minneapolis, MN 55401

Chelsea House Publishers
1974 Sproul Road, Suite 400
Broomall, PA 19008-0914

Children's Book Press
6400 Hollis St., Suite 4
Emeryville, CA 94608

Children's Press
Sherman Turnpike
Danbury, CT 06816

Chronicle Books
85 2nd St., Sixth Floor
San Francisco, CA 94105

Clarion Books
215 Park Ave. S.
New York, NY 10003

Cobblehill Books
375 Hudson St.
New York, NY 10014

Creative Education, Inc.
123 S. Broad St.
P.O. Box 227
Mankato, MN 56001

Crowell
10 E. 53rd St.
New York, NY 10022

Crown Publishers
1540 Broadway
New York, NY 10036

Crown Publishing Group
201 E. 50th St.
New York, NY 10022

Delacorte
1540 Broadway
New York, NY 10036

Dell Publishing Co., Inc.
1540 Broadway
New York, NY 10036

Dial Books for Young Readers
345 Hudson St.
New York, NY 10014

Dillon Press
1230 Avenue of the Americas
New York, NY 10020

DK Publishing, Inc. (Dorling Kindersley)
95 Madison Ave.
New York, NY 10016

Dover
180 Varick St.
New York, NY 10014

Doubleday
1540 Broadway
New York, NY 10036

Dutton
345 Hudson St.
New York, NY 10014

Farrar, Straus & Giroux, Inc.
19 Union Square W.
New York, NY 10003

Four Winds Press
1230 Avenue of the Americas
New York, NY 10020

Front Street Books
P.O. Box 280
Arden, NC 28704

David R. Godine, Publisher, Inc.
9 Lewis St.
P.O. Box 9103
Lincoln, MA 01773

Golden Books/Western
850 Third Ave.
New York, NY 10022

Green Tiger Press
1230 Avenue of the Americas
New York, NY 10020

Greenwillow Books
1350 Avenue of the Americas
New York, NY 10019

Grosset & Dunlap
345 Hudson St.
New York, NY 10014

Gulliver Books
525 B St., Suite 1900
San Diego, CA 92101

Harcourt Brace and Co.
525 B St., Suite 1900
San Diego, CA 92101

HarperCollins Children's Books
1350 Avenue of the Americas
New York, NY 10019

Harper Trophy
1350 Avenue of the Americas
New York, NY 10019

Holiday House, Inc.
425 Madison Ave.
New York, NY 10017

Henry Holt & Co.
115 W. 18th St.
New York, NY 10011

Houghton Mifflin Co.
222 Berkeley St.
Boston, MA 02116

Hyperion Books for Children
114 Fifth Ave.
New York, NY 10011

Jewish Publication Society
1930 Chestnut St.
Philadelphia, PA 19103

Joy Street Books
3 Center Plaza
Boston, MA 02108

Kane/Miller Book Publishers
P.O. Box 315229
Brooklyn, NY 11231-0529

Alfred A. Knopf, Inc.
201 E. 50th St.
New York, NY 10022

Lee and Low Books
95 Madison Ave.
New York, NY 10016

Lerner Publications Co.
241 First Ave. N.
Minneapolis, MN 55401

Lippincott
10 E. 53rd St.
New York, NY 10022

Little, Brown & Co., Inc.
3 Center Plaza
Boston, MA 02108

Lodestar Publishing
345 Hudson St.
New York, NY 10014

Lothrop, Lee & Shepard Books
1350 Avenue of the Americas
New York, NY 10019

Macmillan Publishing Co.
1230 Avenue of the Americas
New York, NY 10020

Margaret K. McElderry Books
1230 Avenue of the Americas
New York, NY 10020

McGraw-Hill Book Co.
1221 Avenue of the Americas
New York, NY 10020

William Morrow & Co., Inc.
1350 Avenue of the Americas
New York, NY 10019

Morrow Junior Books
1350 Avenue of the Americas
New York, NY 10019

John Muir Publications
P.O. Box 613
Santa Fe, NM 87504

Mulberry Books
1350 Avenue of the Americas
New York, NY 10019

National Geographic Press
1145 17th St. NW
Washington, DC 20036

North-South Books
1123 Broadway, Suite 800
New York, NY 10010

Orchard Books
95 Madison Ave.
New York, NY 10016

Oxford University Press, Inc.
198 Madison Ave.
New York, NY 10016

Parents Magazine Press
685 Third Ave.
New York, NY 10017

Pantheon Books, Inc.
201 E. 50th St.
New York, NY 10022

Penguin Putnam Books for Young Readers
345 Hudson St.
New York, NY 10014

Philomel Books
345 Hudson St.
New York, NY 10014

Picture Book Studio
1230 Avenue of the Americas
New York, NY 10020

Price Stern Sloan, Inc.
11835 W. Olympic Blvd., 5th Floor
Los Angeles, CA 90064

Puffin Books
345 Hudson St.
New York, NY 10014

G. P. Putnam Sons
345 Hudson St.
New York, NY 10014

Random House, Inc.
201 E. 50th St.
New York, NY 10022

Rizzoli International Publications, Inc.
300 Park Ave. S.
New York, NY 10010

Scholastic, Inc.
555 Broadway
New York, NY 10012

Charles Scribner's Sons
1230 Avenue of the Americas
New York, NY 10020

Sierra Club Books for Children
3 Center Plaza
Boston, MA 02108

Simon & Schuster Books for Young Readers
1230 Avenue of the Americas
New York, NY 10020

Steward, Tabori & Chang, Inc.
575 Broadway
New York, NY 10012

St. Martin's Press
175 Fifth Ave.
New York, NY 10010

Tambourine Books
1350 Avenue of the Americas
New York, NY 10019

Troll Communications
100 Corporate Dr.
Mahwah, NJ 07430

Tundra Books
P.O. Box 1030
Plattsburgh, NY 12901

Tupelo
1350 Avenue of the Americas
New York, NY 10019

Viking
345 Hudson St.
New York, NY 10014

Walker & Co.
435 Hudson St.
New York, NY 10014

Frederick Warne & Co., Inc.
345 Hudson St.
New York, NY 10014

Franklin Watts, Inc.
Sherman Turnpike
Danbury, CT 06816

Albert Whitman & Co.
6340 Oakton St.
Morton Grove, IL 60053

Wordsong
815 Church St.
Honesdale, PA 18431

INDEX

AUTHOR, ILLUSTRATOR, TITLE

INDEX

SUBJECT

CREDITS

Chapter 1

p. 3   From *The Seven Chinese Brothers* by Margaret Mahy illustrated by Jean and Mou-sien Tseng. Text copyright © 1990 by Margaret Mahy. Illustrations copyright © 1990 by Jean and Mou-sien Tseng. Reprinted by permission of Scholastic Inc.

p. 17   Text excerpt from *Joey Pigza Swallowed the Key* by Jack Gantos. Copyright © 1998 by Jack Gantos. Reprinted by permission of Farrar, Straus, & Giroux, LLC.

p. 18   From *Mick Harte Was Here* by Barbara Park, copyright © 1995 by Barbara Park. Jacket art copyright © 1995 by John Nickle. Used by permission of Alfred A. Knopf Children's Books, a division of Random House, Inc.

p. 19   Text excerpt from *Like Sisters on the Homefront* by Rita Williams-Garcia, copyright © 1995 Rita Williams-Garcia. Used by permission of Lodestar Books, an affiliate of Dutton Children's Books, a division of Penguin Putnam, Inc.

p. 17, 20   Text excerpts from *Maniac Magee* by Jerry Spinelli, copyright © 1990 by Jerry Spinelli. Published by Little, Brown & Company.

Chapter 2

p. 29   Jacket design and excerpt from *The Painter Who Loved Chickens* by Olivier Dunrea. Copyright © 1995 by Olivier Dunrea. Reprinted by permission of Farrar, Straus, & Giroux, LLC.

p. 31   Text excerpt from *The Illyrian Adventure* by Lloyd Alexander. Copyright © 1986 by Lloyd Alexander. Reprinted by permission of Dutton Children's Books, an imprint of Penguin Putnam, Inc.

p. 32   Definitions from *The Oxford English Dictionary Compact Edition*, copyright © 1971, copyright © 1984 Oxford University Press.

pp. 32–33   Reprinted by permission of Farrar, Straus and Giroux, LLC: Excerpt and jacket design from *Tuck Everlasting* by Natalie Babbitt. Copyright © 1975 by Natalie Babbitt.

p. 38   From *Why We Have Thanksgiving* (1982) by Margaret Hillert, Follett.

p. 39   *The Boston Coffee Party* by Doreen Rappaport, text copyright © 1988 by Doreen Rappaport. Used by permission of HarperCollins Publishers.

p. 46, no. 1   From *Lon Po Po: A Red Riding Hood Story From China* by Ed Young. Copyright © 1989 by Ed Young. Reprinted by permission of Philomel, an imprint of Penguin Putnam, Inc.

p. 46, no. 2   Illustration from *Frog Goes to Dinner* by Mercer Mayer, copyright © 1974 by Mercer Mayer. Used by permission of Dial Books for Young Readers, an imprint of Penguin Putnam, Inc.

p. 46, no. 3   Illustration from *Blueberries for Sal* by Robert McCloskey, copyright © 1948, renewed © 1976 by Robert McCloskey. Used by permission of Viking Penguin, a division of Penguin Putnam, Inc.

p. 46, no. 4   Cover from *Suddenly!* by Colin McNaughton, copyright © 1994 by Colin McNaughton. Published by Harcourt Brace & Co. Reprinted by permission of Harcourt.

p. 47, no. 5   Illustrations from *Anno's Journey* by Mitsumasa Anno, copyright © 1977 by Anno Mitsumasa. Translation © 1978 by Fukuinan Shoten, Publishers. Published by Philomel, an imprint of Penguin Putnam, Inc.

p. 47, no. 6   Reprinted with the permission of Simon & Schuster Books for Young Readers, an imprint of Simon & Schuster Children's Publishing Division from *The Relatives Came* by Cynthia Rylant, illustrated by Stephen Gammell. Illustrations copyright © 1985 Stephen Gammell.

p. 47, no. 7   Illustration from *The Polar Express* by Chris Van Allsburg. Jacket painting copyright © 1985 by Chris Van Allsburg. Reprinted by permission of Houghton Mifflin Company. All rights reserved.

p. 47, no. 8   Illustration from *Rapunzel* by Paul O. Zelinsky, copyright © 1997 by Paul O. Zelinsky. Published by Dutton Children's Books, an imprint of Penguin Putnam, Inc.

p. 47, no. 9   *Willy the Dreamer* copyright © 1997 by Anthony Browne. Reproduced by permission of the publisher Candlewick Press Inc., Cambridge, MA, on behalf of Walter Books Ltd., London.

p. 48, no. 10   Illustration from *A Chair for My Mother* by Vera B. Williams, copyright © 1982 by Vera B. Williams. Published by Greenwillow/William Morris. Reprinted by permission of HarperCollins Publishers.

p. 48, no. 11   Cover of *Mirette & Bellini Cross Niagara Falls* by Emily Arnold McCully, copyright © 2000 by Emily Arnold McCully. Reprinted by permission of G. P. Putnam's Sons, a division of Penguin Putnam, Inc.

p. 48, no. 12   *Grandma Moses: Joy Ride* copyright © 2000 by Grandma Moses Properties Co., New York. Reprinted by permission.

p. 48, no. 13   Cover from *Sector 7* by David Wiesner. Jacket illustration copyright © 1999 by David Wiesner. Reprinted by permission of Clarion Books/Houghton Mifflin Company. All rights reserved.

p. 49, no. 14   Cover from *The Widow's Broom* by Chris Van Allsburg. Jacket art copyright © 1992 by Chris Van Allsburg. Reprinted by permission of Houghton Mifflin Company. All rights reserved.

p. 49, no. 15   *Ben's Trumpet* by Rachel Isadora, copyright © 1979 by Rachel Isadora Maiorano. Used by permission of HarperCollins Publishers.

p. 49, no. 16   Illustration from *Miz Berlin Walks* by Jane Yolen, copyright © 1997 by Jane Yolen, illustrations copyright © 1997 by Floyd Cooper. Reprinted by permission of Philomel Books, a division of Penguin Putnam, Inc.

p. 49, no. 17 *Too Much Talk*. Text copyright © 1995 by Angela Shelf Medearis; illustrations copyright © 1995 by Stefano Vitale. Reproduced by permission of the publisher Candlewick Press Inc., Cambridge, MA.

p. 49, no. 18 Illustration from *Hilda Hen's Scary Night*, copyright © 1996 by Mary Wormwell, first published in Great Britain by Victor Gollancz, reprinted by permission of Harcourt, Inc.

p. 50, no. 19 Illustration from *Seven Blind Mice* by Ed Young, copyright © 1992 by Ed Young. Reprinted by permission of Philomel Books, a division of Penguin Putnam, Inc.

p. 50, no. 20 Illustration from *Golem* by David Wisniewski. Copyright © 1996 by David Wisniewski. Reprinted by permission of Clarion Books/Houghton Mifflin Company. All rights reserved.

p. 50, no. 21 Illustration from *Iron Horses* by Verla Kay, illustrated by Michael McCurdy, text copyright © 1999 by Verla Kay, illustrations copyright © 1999 by Michael McCurdy. Reprinted by permission of G. P. Putnam's Sons, an imprint of Penguin Putnam, Inc.

p. 50, no. 22 Illustration from *Mouse Views: What the Class Pet Saw* by Bruce McMillan, copyright © 1993 by Bruce McMillan. Published and reprinted by permission of Holiday House, Inc.

p. 50, no. 23 *The Paper Crane* by Molly Bang copyright © 1985 Molly Garrett Bang. Used by permission of HarperCollins Publishers.

p. 51, no. 24 Cover illustration by C. B. Mordan from *Lost! A Story in String* written by Paul Fleischman. Illustrations copyright © 2000 by C. B. Mordan. Reprinted by permission of Henry Holt and Company, LLC.

p. 51, no. 25 *Little Gold Star: A Spanish American Cinderella Tale* by Robert D. San Souci, copyright © 2000 by Robert D. San Souci. Used by permission of HarperCollins Publishers.

p. 51, no. 26 *Round Trip* by Ann Jonas, copyright © 1983 by Ann Jonas. Used by permission of HarperCollins Publishers.

p. 51, no. 27 Cover from *Missing Mitten Mystery* by Steven Kellogg, copyright © 2000 by Steven Kellogg. Reprinted by permission of Dial Books, an imprint of Penguin Putnam, Inc.

p. 51, no. 28 From *St. George and the Dragon* by Margaret Hodges. Copyright © 1984 by Margaret Hodges (text); copyright © 1984 by Trina Schart Hyman (illustrations). By permission of Little, Brown and Company, Inc.

p. 52, no. 29 Illustration from *Tuesday*. Text and illustrations copyright © 1991 by David Wiesner. Reprinted by permission of Houghton Mifflin Co./Clarion Books. All rights reserved.

p. 52, no. 30, and p. 53, no. 34 Illustrations from *Deep in the Forest* by Brinton Turkle, copyright © 1976 by Brinton Turkel. Reprinted by permission of Dutton Children's Books, a division of Penguin Putnam, Inc.

p. 52, no. 31 Reprinted with the permission of Atheneum Books for Young Readers, an imprint of Simon & Schuster Children's Publishing Division from *The Hunter* by Mary Casanova, illustrated by Ed Young. Illustrations copyright © 2000 Ed Young.

p. 52, no. 32 Illustration from *The Secret of the Stones* by Robert D. San Souci, illustrated by James Ransome, Phyllis Fogleman, text copyright © 2000 by Robert D. San Souci, illustrations copyright © 2000 by James Ransome. Reprinted by permission of Phyllis Fogleman Books, a division of Penguin Putman, Inc.

p. 53, no. 33 Cover from *Tops and Bottoms* by Janet Stevens, copyright © 1995 by Janet Stevens. Published by Harcourt Brace & Co. Reprinted by permission of Harcourt.

Chapter 3

p. 73 *When Jessie Came Across the Sea* Text copyright © 1997 Amy Hest. Ill copyright © 1997 P. J. Lynch. Reproduced by permission of the publisher Candlewick Press Inc., Cambridge, MA.

p. 84 "When It Rains, It Rains" from *When It Rains, It Rains* by Bill Martin, Jr. copyright © 1972 by Bill Martin. Used by permission.

p. 86 Text excerpt from *It looked Like Spilt Milk* by Charles G. Shaw copyright © 1947 by Charles G. Shaw, renewed 1975 by Ethan Allen. Used by permission of HarperCollins Publishers.

p. 87 Poem "Brown Bear, Brown Bear" from *Brown Bear, Brown Bear, What Do You See?* By Bill Martin, Jr. copyright © 1995 by Bill Martin, Jr. Published by Harcourt Brace & Co. Reprinted by permission of Harcourt.

p. 88 Text excerpt from *Each Peach Pear Plum* by Janet and Allan Ahlberg (Viking, 1978. Copyright © 1978 by Janet and Allan Ahlberg. Reprinted by permission of Penguin Books Lt., UK.

p. 88 Text excerpt from *Higgledy Piggledy Hobbledy Hoy* by Dorothy Butler copyright © 1991 by Dorothy Butler. Used by permission of HarperCollins Publishers.

p. 88 "Bathwater's Hot" from *Bathwater's Hot* by Shirley Hughes, copyright © 1985 by Shirley Hughes. Published by Lothrop, Lee and Shepard Co. Used by permission.

p. 90 From *Old Black Fly* by Jim Aylesworth. Text copyright © 1992 by Jim Aylesworth. Used by permission of Henry Holt and Company, LLC.

p. 98 Excerpt from *Kermit the Hermit* by Bill Peet. Copyright © 1965, and renewed 1993 by Bill Peet. Used by permission of Houghton Mifflin Company. All rights reserved.

p. 102 *Julius, the Baby of the World* by Kevin Henkes, copyright © 1990 by Kevin Henkes. Used by permission of HarperCollins Publishers.

Chapter 4

p. 115 Cover and Poem "Prayer" from *Brown Angels: An Album of Pictures and Verse* by Walter Dean Myers, copyright © 1993 by Walter Dean Myers. Used by permission of HarperCollins Publishers.

p. 120 "A Flamingo" from *A Hippopotamusn't* by J. Patrick Lewis. Copyright © 1990 by J. Patrick Lewis.

Used by permission of Dial Books for Young Readers, a division of Penguin Putnam, Inc.

p. 122   Used by permission of Farrar, Straus and Giroux, LLC: "Cow" from *All the Small Poems and Fourteen More* by Valerie Worth. Copyright © 1987, 1994 by Valerie Worth.

p. 123   "Pencils" by Barbara Esbensen from *A Jar of Tiny Stars: Children Select Their Favorite Poems* by Bernice E. Cullinan, ed. Copyright © 1996 by Boyds Mills Press. Used by permission.

p. 123   From *I Thought I Heard the City* by Lilian Moore. Copyright © 1969, 1997 Lilian Moore. Used by permission of Marian Reiner for the author.

p. 123   Poem "Song of the Train" from *One at a Time* by David McCord. Copyright © 1952 by David McCord. Used by permission of Little, Brown and Company (Inc.).

p. 124   Poem "My Box" from *The Way Things Are and Other Poems* by Myra Cohn Livingston. Copyright © 1974 Myra Cohn Livingston. Used by permission of Marian Reiner.

pp. 124–125   Poem "Fall" from *Runny Days, Sunny Days* by Aileen Fisher. Copyright © 1958, 1986 by Aileen Fisher. Used by permission of Marian Reiner for the author.

p. 125   Poem "My Forehead ON Cold Glass of Window" from *Touch the Poem* by Arnold Adoff. Copyright © 2000 by Arnold Adoff. Used by permission of The Blue Sky Press, an imprint of Scholastic Inc. Used by permission of Scholastic Inc.

pp. 125–126   Poem "Bobsled" from *Elympics* by X. J. Kennedy. Copyright © 1999 by X. J. Kennedy. Illustrations © 1999 by Graham Percy. Used by permission of Philomel Books, an imprint of Penguin Putnam, Inc.

p. 126   Poem "Daddy Fixed Breakfast and Mummy Slept Late" from *You Read to Me, I'll Read to You* by John Ciardi. Copyright © 1962 by John Ciardi. Used by permission of HarperCollins Publishers.

p. 127   Cover and poem from *Fresh Paint: New Poems* by Eve Merriam, copyright © 1986 by Eve Merriam. Published by Macmillan Publishing Company. Used by permission. All rights reserved.

p. 128   "Keepsake" from *Honey I Love and Other Poems*, by Eloise Greenfield. Text copyright © 1987 by Eloise Greenfield. Used by permission of Harper-Collins Publishers.

p. 128   Poem "Mary Had a Little Lamb" from *The Lore and Language of Schoolchildren* by Iona Opie and Peter Opie (1959). Used by permission of the authors.

p. 129   Haiku "Take the butterfly" from *One at a Time* by David McCord. Copyright © 1970 by David McCord. Used by permission of Little, Brown and Company Inc.

p. 131   Cover and poem from *The New Kid on the Block* by Jack Prelutsky, copyright © 1984 by Jack Prelutsky. Used by permission of HarperCollins Publishers.

p. 132   Poem "The Little Boy and the Old Man" from *A Light in the Attic* by Shel Silverstein, copyright © 1981 by Evil Eye Music. Used by permission of Harper-Collins Publishers.

pp. 138–139   Cover and poem from *Joyful Noise* by Paul Fleischman, text copyright © 1988 by Paul Fleischman, illustrations copyright © 1988 by Eric Beddows. Used by permission of HarperCollins Publishers.

p. 140   Poem "Splash" from *Coconut Kind of Day: Island Poems* by Lynn Joseph. Text copyright © 1990 by Lynn Joseph. Used by permission of HarperCollins Publishers.

p. 141   Used by permission of Atheneum Books for Young Readers, an imprint of Simon & Schuster Children's Publishing Division from *Casey at the Bat* by Ernest Lawrence Thayer, illustrated by Gerald Fitzgerald. Copyright © 1994 Gerald Fitzgerald.

p. 146   "Things" from *Honey, I Love and Other Poems* by Eloise Greenfield. Text copyright © 1978 by Eloise Greenfield. Used by permission of HarperCollins Publishers.

Chapter 5

p. 153   *The Egyptian Cinderella* by Shirley Climo, text copyright © 1989 by Shirley Climo. Illustrations copyright © 1989 by Ruth Heller. Used by permission of HarperCollins Publishers.

p. 162   Excerpt from *There Was an Old Lady Who Swallowed a Fly* by Simms Tayback, copyright © 1997 by Simms Tayback. Used by permission of Viking, a division of Penguin Putnam, Inc.

p. 178   Text excerpt from *Wishful Thinking–Or Hopeful Dreaming* by Lloyd Alexander, copyright © 1968 by Lloyd Alexander. Used by permission.

p. 181   Excerpt from *Read Aloud Handbook*, by Jim Trelease, copyright © 1979, 1982, 1985, 1995 by Jim Trelease. Used by permission of Viking Penguin, a division of Penguin Putnam, Inc.

Chapter 6

p. 193   Cover and text from *The Dragon's Boy* by Jane Yolen, copyright © 1990 by Jane Yolen. Used by permission of HarperCollins Publishers.

p. 218   Text excerpt from *The Rainbabies* by Laura Melmed, text copyright © 1992 by Laura Melmed. Used by permission of HarperCollins Publishers.

Chapter 7

p. 235   From *Crash* by Jerry Spinelli, jacket illustration by Eleanor Hoyt, jacket photograph by Stan Ries. Text copyright © 1996 by Jerry Spinelli. Jacket illustration copyright © 1996 by Eleanor Hoyt. Jacket photograph copyright © 1996 by Stan Ries. Used by permission of Alfred A. Knopf Children's Books, a division of Random House, Inc.

p. 243   Excerpt from *Mick Harte Was Here* by Barbara Park. Text copyright © 1995 by Barbara Park. Used by permission of Alfred A. Knopf Children's Books, a division of Random House, Inc.

Chapter 8

p. 268   From *Mr. Tucket* by Gary Paulsen, copyright © 1994 by Gary Paulsen. Used by permission of Dell Publishing, a division of Random House, Inc.

p. 269   Excerpt from *Dandelions* text copyright © 1995 by Eve Bunting. Used by permission of Harcourt, Inc.

p. 270   Excerpt from *Prairie Songs* by Pam Conrad. Copyright © 1984 Pam Conrad. HarperCollins Children's Books. Used by permission of HarperCollins Publishers.

p. 272 From *The Man Who Was Poe* by Avi, cover illustration by Ted Lewin. Published by Orchard Books, an imprint of Scholastic Inc. Text copyright © 1989 by Avi, illustration copyright © 1989 by Ted Lewin. Used by permission.

p. 278 Text excerpt from *Rifles for Watie* by Harold Keith. Text copyright © 1957 by Harold Keith. Used by permission of HarperCollins Publishers.

Chapter 9

p. 291 From *We Had a Picnic this Sunday Past* by Jacqueline Woodson. Text copyright © 1997 by Jacqueline Woodson. Illustrations copyright © 1997 Diane Greenseid. Used by permission of Hyperion Books for Children.

Chapter 10

p. 325 Cover and text excerpt from *Zipping, Zapping, Zooming Bats* by Ann Earle, text copyright © 1995 by Anne Earle. Illustrations copyright © 1995 by Henry Cole. Used by permission of HarperCollins Publishers.

pp. 336–337 Text excerpt from *The Black Americans: A History in Their Own Words* (1984) by Milton Meltzer, pp. 49–50, published by HarperCollins Publishers.

p. 338 Excerpt from *Kinderlager: An Oral History of Young Holocaust Survivors* copyright © 1996 by Milton J. Nieuwsma. Published by Holiday House. Used by permission of Holiday House.

p. 344 Excerpt from *How Do Astronauts Scratch an Itch?* By David Feldman, copyright © 1996 by David Feldman. Used by permission of Penguin Putnam, Inc.

pp. 348–349 Excerpt from *Growing Up in Coal Country* by Susan Campbell Bartoletti. Copyright © 1996 by Susan Campbell Bartoletti. Used by permission of Houghton Mifflin Company. All rights reserved.

Chapter 11

p. 369 Cover from *A Picture Book of Sojourner Truth* copyright © 1994 by David A. Adler (text); copyright © 1994 by Gershom Griffith (illustrations). Published by Holiday House. Used by permission of Holiday House.

pp. 372, 375, 380 Excerpt from *Lincoln: A Photobiography* by Russell Freedman. Copyright © 1987 by Russell Freedman. Used by permission of Clarion Books/Houghton Mifflin Company. All rights reserved

p. 383 Excerpt from *Will You Sign Here, John Hancock?* Copyright © 1976 by Jean Fritz. Used by permission of Coward-McCann, a division of Penguin Putman Inc.

Chapter 12

p. 403 Reprinted with the permission of Atheneum Books for Young Readers, an imprint of Simon & Schuster Children's Publishing Division from *The Graduation of Jake Moon* by Barbara Park, text copyright © 2000 Barbara Park.

p. 410 Poem from *One at a Time* by David McCord. Copyright © 1965 1966 by David McCord. Used by permission of Little, Brown and Company (Inc.).

Chapter 13

p. 433 Cover and text excerpt from *Tornado* by Betsy Byars, text copyright © 1996 by Betsy Byars. Used by permission of HarperCollins Publishers.

p. 437 Family Circus cartoon reprinted with special permission of King Features Syndicate.

p. 465 Text excerpt from *Each Peach Pear Plum* by Janet and Allan Ahlberg (Viking, 1978). Copyright © 1978 Janet and Allan Ahlberg. Used by permission of Penguin Books Lt., UK.

Chapter 14

p. 471 *Thank You, Mr. Falker* by Patricia Polacco, copyright © 1998 by Patricia Polacco. Used by permission of Philomel Books, a division of Penguin Putnam, Inc.

Chapter 15

p. 495 Reprinted with the permission of Simon & Schuster Books for Young Readers, an imprint of Simon & Schuster Children's Publishing Division from *Fever 1793* by Laurie Halse Anderson. Text copyright © 2000 by Laurie Halse Anderson.

p. 505 Excerpt copyright © 1970 by Hans Peter Richter. Used by permission of the author.